for Mummy

Happy Birthday
with very much
love from
Isabel

# THE FISCHER-DIESKAU BOOK OF LIEDER

# THE FISCHER-DIESKAU
# BOOK OF LIEDER

*The texts of over 750 songs in German
chosen and introduced*

by

## DIETRICH FISCHER-DIESKAU

with English translations by
## GEORGE BIRD
## AND
## RICHARD STOKES

LONDON
VICTOR GOLLANCZ LTD
PAN BOOKS LTD
1976

Originally published under the title *Texte Deutscher Lieder*

© 1968 Deutscher Taschenbuch Verlag GmbH & Co. KG, München

English translations © George Bird and Richard Stokes 1976

The translators were assisted by a grant from The Arts' Council of Great Britain

ISBN 0 575 01852 6

## ACKNOWLEDGEMENTS

Material by the following authors is copyright and is reprinted in each case by permission of the copyright holders mentioned:

Richard Dehmel: 'Befreit' and 'Der Arbeitsmann' from *Dichtungen—Briefe—Dokumente*, edited by Paul Johannes Schindler.
© 1963, Hoffmann und Campe Verlag, Hamburg.
Richard Dehmel: 'Stiller Gang' and 'Wiegenlied'.
Vera Tügel-Dehmel, Hamburg.
Stefan George: Fifteen poems from *Die Bücher der Hirten- und Preisgedichte, der Sagen und Sänge und der Hängenden Gärten.*
© 1950, 1958, Verlag Helmut Küpper previously Georg Bondi, Düsseldorf and Munich.
Carl Hauptmann: 'Nacht'.
Marte Pohl, Berlin.
Hermann Hesse: 'Beim Schlafengehen', 'Frühling', 'September' and 'Ravenna I' from *Gesammelte Schriften in 7 Bänden. Band 1: Gedichte.*
© 1958, Suhrkamp Verlag, Frankfurt am Main. Used with permission of Jonathan Cape, London, and Farrar, Straus & Giroux Inc., New York.
'Ravenna I' also appears in Jonathan Cape's edition of *Poems* by Hermann Hesse translated by James Wright.
Alfred Mombert: 'Nun ich der Riesen Stärksten überwand', 'Schlafend trägt man mich' and 'Warm die Lüfte' from *Dichtungen. Gesamtausgabe in drei Bänden*, edited by E. Herberg. Book 1: *Gedicht-Werke.*
© 1964, Kösel Verlag, Munich.
Rainer Maria Rilke: 'Das Marienleben' and 'Traumgekrönt' from *Sämtliche Werke*, edited by Rilke-Archiv, in association with Ruth Sieber-Rilke, and Ernst Zinn. Book 1: *Gedichte.*
© 1962, Insel Verlag, Frankfurt am Main.
Also by permission of the Hogarth Press, London and W. W. Norton & Company, Inc., New York.
Stefan Zweig: 'Ein Drängen ist in meinem Herzen' from *Silberne Saiten. Gedichte und Nachdichtungen*, edited by Richard Friedenthal.
© 1966, S. Fischer Verlag, Frankfurt am Main.

*Printed in Great Britain by*
*The Camelot Press Ltd, Southampton*

# CONTENTS

# TRANSLATORS' NOTE

In these translations we have tried to convey the full sense, and as much as possible of the tone, of the originals. To this end, we chart a middle course between, on the one hand, the extreme of literal prose translation in which all poetic semblance is stifled, and on the other, the extreme of verse translation in which sense and the order of lines are distorted for the sake of the metre and rhyme. We prefer *green grass* to *verdant sward* but do not suppress poetic diction or archaisms or even rhythm and rhyme, where we think they help convey tone. So far as possible, we observe the German line order.

We have resisted the temptation to explain, either in footnotes or in the process of translation, lines which depend for their sense on facts not explicit in the poem. For example, we have not explained Mignon's 'So laßt mich scheinen, bis ich werde', which, as the context of the poem in the novel *Wilhelm Meister* makes clear, means: 'Let me remain attired as an angel until I become one.'

Where the German is itself a translation, we translate the German as it stands. As a result, the Bible and Shakespeare, for instance, do not look quite as we know them.

We offer our work with that sense of humility and partial satisfaction which the delightful, but impossible, task of translation always imposes.

To Livia Gollancz and Clarence Paget, for their support and encouragement, we are deeply grateful.

GEORGE BIRD

RICHARD STOKES

# A NOTE ON ARRANGEMENT
## AND INDEXING

This is not an anthology in the normal sense, but a reference book for the recital-goer, record-lover and musician. To enable texts to be quickly and easily located, individual songs have been arranged by German title (or, when there is no title, under first line) alphabetically. At the same time, the practice has been adopted of determining order not by key-words but by actual title, i.e. with article and preposition used for the purpose of alphabetical arrangement (so that *Der Zwerg* is followed by *Des Antonius von Padua Fischpredigt*). In cases of identical titles, the alphabetical order is that of first lines. Song-cycles have been kept together, and appear under title of cycle within the general alphabetical arrangement. Poems within cycles may be found with the aid of the title- and first-line index at the end of the book, which includes all titles and all first lines.

With each poem and song-cycle the name of poet and composer is given. Where the same words have been set by different composers the names of most of them are given, but the list does not claim to be complete. Similarly, where, within song-cycles, individual poems have been set by other composers, their names are supplied after the text. As a rule, date of composition and opus number are given; when they are not, either the work has no opus number or the date of composition is unknown or doubtful. In cases of the same text having been set several times by the same composer, the date and opus number of only the best-known setting is indicated.

The printed text (occasionally slightly modified by the composer) is generally that of the poem as set. Where several variants exist, the version preferred is that which is best known. Textual omissions and alterations are not specially denoted, but additions (e.g. 'O Freunde, nicht diese Töne . . .' in Schiller's *An die Freude*) are shown in square brackets. Where French and Italian poems have been set by composers, German versions are not given. In a few strophic songs of great length (e.g. the nine verses of Schubert's *Litanei*), only those verses most often sung are printed.

To provide a complete collection has proved impracticable, and to ensure that this volume shall be both compact and handy, selection has been restricted to some 750 poems.

# GERMAN SONG—AN ESSAY

When one surveys the history of piano-accompanied song, as it has developed since, say, Mozart, one is led to investigate the interplay between poetic stimulus and the composer as both assimilator and interpreter. And for this reason, an anthology of the verse that has inspired musical settings may be understood not as an undertaking of literary scholarship, but rather as an illumination of reasons for the gradual decline in this genre as a form of musical expression. For the Lied has undergone no encouraging regeneration, and it would need a composer as optimistic as Hans Werner Henze, declining to share Gustav Mahler's final feelings as regards the symphony, to achieve in this sphere anything of validity for the future.

With this in mind, it must be remembered that, beyond the current repertoire, those piano-accompanied solos, duets, trios, quartets and choral songs, whose origin falls within the period of concern to us here, are, while exhibiting remarkable inner unity, temporarily a final integral part of a thousand years of song. And viewing thus the time-span of German romantic song, one sees highlighted, as the essential point of departure for any conceivable future development, the need to express human feeling, to communicate, and to renounce mere sound-play. Only if the Lied can, in this manner, inspire again major musical works will its existence be assured. The growing number of people all over the world who attend Lieder recitals testifies to the need.

The restrictions arising from national musical character, and from special appeal to very specific classes, have ceased to apply. No longer does the Lied exist for the bourgeoisie as during its seemingly final shaping in the nineteenth century. On the contrary, the Lieder-recital and Lieder-record audience embraces the whole range of society.

There was once, as Hermann Kretschmar put it, a time without Lieder, around 1700, when a sudden decrease in new works, brought about by the intrusion of the aria into home music-making, created gaps. Even where, as with Telemann, delightful ariettas entered the void, the scenic or scenically-related predominated over the specifically lyrical. There was, as there is today, a vain search to provide, in new musical styles, vocal communication for the emotions bound up with the poem. In 1736 in Leipzig, as the first outstanding attempt, appeared the *Singende Muse an der Pleiße* by Sperontes, a typical example of over-refined rococo of French import, scarcely any longer susceptible of vocal performance, being excessively complicated in the coloratura borrowed from the piano. The expressive content of the works of these minor rococo masters is pitifully ineffectual if compared to the emotional outbursts of the baroque composers. With an eye to sales, they exhaust themselves in a strange, sentimental posture compounded of Enlightenment and cynicism.

Simultaneously with the beginnings of a stylistic reform in instrumental music, on the part of Haydn, Mozart and Beethoven, attempts at stylistic change in lyric poetry made themselves apparent, and consequently in Lieder composition too. These attempts may be seen to be rooted in a turning away from ossified formalism, and in a return to simple nature and spontaneity. After Bach and Handel, who had represented the boundary stones between two epochs, filling out for the last time the vocal forms of the past with significant content, it is in the realm of song that a kind of childhood stage in musical art is to be observed. The opera of this time represented a mood of spiritual uprising: the Italians availed themselves of folk-based song for their dialect operas, as opposed to earlier practice. The French opéra comique and the English ballad opera soon followed. The Germans brought the development to its close with the Singspiel which makes its contribution to the regeneration of German lyric poetry and gives rise to a new branch, the art song. It will be sufficient to indicate here that, not until half a century after the Singspiel *Die verwandelten Weiber*, 1766 (poet—Weiße, composer—Hiller), which provided the up-beat, did the Berlin School of Reichardt and Zelter arrive at the point of allowing itself to be genuinely inspired by poetry. Of course, the musical setting did not yet presume to place itself on a level with the lyric. Goethe's two friends were observing the Master's dictum that music had to adopt a 'servant attitude' vis-à-vis the poem. Unlike Hugo Wolf, later, who, using the words in his own fashion, made himself the interpreter of Mörike's poetry.

The intensified need for expression, after the period of mere artistic skill, also compelled concentration on piano accompaniment. Melody and a few sparse basic elements of continuo were not, by themselves, able to satisfy the new requirements. Instead, accompaniment was to be an integral part of composition. But it was not until the nineteenth century that the piano song fully became a form of artistic expression, and also set an authoritative tone for the development of music.

As already suggested, the lyric poetry set to music over the period will not be viewed in its literary aspects, since it is with the history of music that we are dealing. And often the intrinsic value of the poem has not played the main rôle in its selection by composers. Nor, in our context, can literary forebears or successors be of such interest as the effect of the poetry on the music. There are thus different points of emphasis among the poets to be considered. How else to explain why Novalis, Leuthold, Fontane and George have been set so seldom, or not at all; whereas such figures as Wilhelm Müller and Hermann Allmers, who are scarcely noted by literary history, have continued to live through music? It is curious to note that Allmers took grave exception to Brahms' setting of his *Feldeinsamkeit*, through which he was to be immortalized.

The preference shown by Lieder composers for certain poets is not easy to explain; was it personal appeal or simply circumstances of life operating externally that was decisive for partnership, as with Beethoven and Jeitteles, Schubert and Mayrhofer, Wagner and Mathilde Wesendonck, Brahms and Klaus Groth? Generally, and often unconsciously, a composer's flair for harmonizing his own creativity with the personal character of the poet was predominant. If, in the process, poems of negligible worth were employed, it was not the fault of literary unpretentiousness or lack of taste. For the mystery of the creative spark's kindling defies rational explanation.

Also, various attitudes to the setting of their verse were adopted by poets. Although Goethe was indifferent towards his contemporaries Schubert and Berlioz, and rejected as impudent their extensive grant of autonomy to accompaniment, he did, with his maxim 'the poem has not been completed until set to music', lay down a fundamental prerequisite for the future creation of Lieder. Basically, however, he still adhered to the eighteenth-century recipe, that the musical shaping of the first verse must hold good for the subsequent verses, as had been illustrated, to the extent of thirty-two verses, in Kirnberger's *Lenore*, and in the undiscriminating musical treatment of Bürger's ballads by Zumsteeg. Even Schubert followed this pattern with, amongst others, a few of Goethe's poems—*Der Gott und die Bajadere*, for instance. Beethoven, in his Gellert songs, set each time only the first verse to music, merely indicating by repeat signs the possibility of a further selection of verses.

For Beethoven, moreover, the text was an aid, so to speak, in finding oratorical expression for the essential nature of his own being. Just as in his opera *Fidelio* he sought a libretto of ethical content, finding it in the glorification of marital love, so for the Lied he sought material which was of value in providing a suitable medium for the highly personal confession. He was the first to attempt to comprehend content as a complete whole, without losing himself in poetic detail. This overall view led him to be the first to conceive the form of the Lieder cycle (*An die ferne Geliebte*) as it has seldom been realized with such thematic concentration since. The autobiographical nature of his Lieder-utterance determined a choice of texts that was only apparently non-literary—Goethe, whose poems he favoured more strongly in the first decade of the nineteenth century because he felt them to be especially close to his music, was an exception. Tiedge, Matthisson and Haugwitz supplied him with the desired truths condensed into formulae, while he, by means of omissions, alterations, small additions or repetitions, freely intervened in their shaping.

In the nineteenth century, music aspired to a full measure of independence in lyrical expression, attempting to give voice to all that had not been said, and to rethink, or, if possible, think more profoundly, all that had been thought—in which process the aim was not that of illustrative sound-painting, in so far as it could be avoided, but of an essential appropriateness to the verse. The metrical and speech-melodic origins of the poem were to be made audible. Stereotyped composition was no longer sufficient. What mattered was appropriate inspiration. It was the beginning of qualitative selection.

Even of Haydn it was said that he allowed his texts to be selected by friends, such as Privy Councillor von Greiner. Certainly, the acquaintance of Mrs Anne Hunter which he had made in England, led to the composition of a book of canzonettas that prophetically anticipated Spohr and Marschner. A look at the Viennese composers around him led to encounters with Gottsched, Hagedorn, Gleim, Weiße and Jacobi—Klopstock, Claudius, Herder and Bürger were already well known. The dearth of literary interest on the part of Lieder-composers determined Reichardt, in 1796, to incorporate in his *Lieder geselliger Freunde* nothing of 'such justly honoured men as Haydn, Mozart and Dittersdorf'. Mozart, certainly, is cited unjustly here. For Constanze, in a letter to the publisher Breitkopf, reports that her husband had opened a book in which was collected a supply of poems to be set. The finest yield of this anthology, Goethe's *Das Veilchen*, may be considered a genuine art-song, since complete agreement is achieved between words and music, the piano exhibits an independent pre-, inter- and postlude, and poem and composition yield each other nothing in quality. Mozart was certainly more at home in the world of poetry than Haydn. But, after all, in Vienna they wanted 'songs any cabby could sing from memory'.

In the new century, the composer turned reader and fastidious judge. He intervened, when necessary, to effect improvements: as did Schumann— an enthusiastic botanist—who altered 'spreading its leafy leaves' in Mosen's *Der Nußbaum*, to 'spreading its leafy branches'. Schumann, Brahms and Wolf, knowing many outstanding poems from memory, were constantly occupied with those just published. Peter Cornelius acted as his own lyric poet. The practice of varying the strophic form was used by Mendelssohn and Brahms in order to revitalize the conventional. Mörike was first revealed to an extensive audience by Hugo Wolf. 'Through-composition', in the sense of a creative intervention into the poetic content, became gradually more prevalent.

New standards were set from the beginning by Schubert with his *Gretchen am Spinnrade* and *Erlkönig*. In general, his choice of text has been variously evaluated—indeed, even felt to be uncritical and unliterary. No one, however, can deny Schubert his instinct for those elements in a poem which call for music. Apart from which, friends—Anselm Hütten-brenner, for instance—reported cases of his rejecting requests for settings, because of unsuitable subject matter. A poem had, above all, to inspire him musically, and his extraordinary fecundity in Lieder composition should not mislead anyone into regarding him as one who would set anything. He was captivated by some outstanding poems for the whole of his creative period, and he set them in a number of completely different versions, as, for example, Goethe's *An den Mond*; and two versions existed of his *Schäfers Klagelied* as early as 1814; later he again set it twice to music. Thus Schubert differed essentially in his behaviour from Beethoven, who wrested his final form out of unremitting struggle.

What has been described in Schubert's Lieder as romantic does not, however, mean any dissolution of the formal structure decreed in the Lied by the text. On the contrary, with him the music illuminates the content of the poems and their poetic expressions. The Lied, as a work of art in itself, becomes a poem. By comparing Schubert's late Heine settings from *Das Buch der Lieder*, then fresh from the press, with Schumann's *Dichterliebe*, which comes in a freely adapted order from the same book, the development of keyboard composition can be clearly studied.

The prominence of the instrument was ever more emphasized, most characteristically with Schumann in the length of the postlude which, in concluding a cycle with weighty significance, struggles to express the unstated, or even an imagined continuation. Where, in the Lieder cycles, the instrumental *narrations* recall what has already been heard, a distant kinship might well be discovered with the Leitmotivs used a decade later in *Der Ring des Nibelungen*. But with Wagner their use is of course something far more tangible. Schumann withdraws in the less precisely defined atmosphere of an extension of previously stated moods. Schubert, by comparison, requires far slighter instrumental expansion, grants less scope to the piano, and in his statement keeps only to what is essential in the poem. Certainly the impression that Schumann achieves an integral fusion of voice and piano is in fact misleading, as I have found repeatedly confirmed. The Heine songs from Schubert's *Schwanengesang* exemplify how an inner unity is arrived at which is beyond description, in spite of a considerable baldness about the notes as set down on paper, and an inhibiting isolation of singer and accompanist.

Quite essentially incisive and detrimental in its effect to the youthful naïvety of *inspiration*-music-making was the rise of musicology. Romantic historicism revives at first an awareness of the poetry of preceding centuries. But vast areas of earlier music began to be opened up as well. The selection of material and the possibilities for transposition are bewildering. Schumann pursued studies in the style of Bach and carried them over into the Lied (*Im Rhein, im heiligen Strome*; *Stirb', Lieb' und Freud'*; *Auf einer Burg*). Medieval sources were opened up, ecclesiastical modes were used by Franz and Brahms.

When one looks back, the effect produced in the settings of the eighteenth century (and in those of early Beethoven) by poets like Matthisson, Hölty, Gleim and Bürger is thoroughly contemporary. But with Schubert's Klopstock, and Brahms' Hölty, the distance in time is noticeable, and then with Richard Strauss, in his setting of Klopstock's *Rosenband*, it becomes charming, but stylistically odd and questionable, since what he undertakes is, so to speak, a rococo pastiche-adaptation of Straussian inspiration. A very similar feeling is produced by Pfitzner's Lied *Sonst*. In our own day, Benjamin Britten, taking William Blake's proverbs and poems as themes for modern interpretation, has proceeded differently, but at the same time—and in this he is an exception—he has kept aloof from pretentiousness, this being particularly true of his Hölderlin cycle.

Hölderlin was not exploited for the purposes of the Lied prior to the more intellectual activity of modern composers. In Austria, the curious Joseph Matias Hauer, who conducted by correspondence a controversy with Schoenberg as to the authorship of the twelve-tone system, was virtually guided to his 'discovery' by way of Hölderlin, employing in the process the harmonium as accompaniment. Wolfgang Fortner set Hölderlin in music of terse linearity, Hermann Reutter in crisp harmony. On the other hand, Heine and Robert Reinick have disappeared almost completely from the Lieder-writers' pool, having been drawn on exhaustively by their contemporaries Schumann and Liszt. In view of this, it is certainly surprising that Heine's poetic prose, which might present itself as a basis for composition, should so far have been neglected by modern composers. The disillusionment in the tail of the poem, so typical of Heine's lyrics, was often overlooked by Schumann. Heine's romantically-tinged irony and pointed rhyming were no doubt to be judged as being in opposition to the successors of Klopstock. Occasionally this element of parody *was* translated into music by Schumann and Franz, albeit rather shamefacedly, as for instance in *Die beiden Brüder* and *Ein Jüngling liebt' ein Mädchen*.

Typical of Schumann is his receptivity to the psychological and the atmospheric, and depiction of both in a shift of significance towards harmony. Rhythm is obliged to moderate its claims. Absolute musicality ceases to be sole regulator for the course of composition. For the sake of a definite overall impression, the poem's inner laws are taken less into account, which, with Goethe, is of particular significance. Whenever, in Schubert's *Wilhelm Meister* songs, the poetic form is embodied naturally into the statement, Schumann, at the same point, conveys only that which is sentimentally romantic, deepening it musically.

With Robert Franz, as with a few other of Schumann's successors, it is love songs that predominate. Apart from Heine, he set Franz Osterwald, Geibel, Lenau and Eichendorff, and, within self-imposed limits, showed considerable capacity for transformation. In his music he bestowed on the poets named such national appeal that by 1890 he could record popularity equal to that of Schubert, Schumann and Brahms, at which the by then deaf old man was much astonished.

Herder's collection of folk songs and adaptations, *Stimmen der Völker*, provided a basis for settings of which the best known is the Scottish ballad *Edward*. Before Loewe and Tchaikovsky, it had been set by many minor composers, and finally by Brahms in the form of a piano ballad. Herder's original poem provided a particularly characteristic example of what, as a result of hyper-scholarly processes of thought, is accessible to music only with difficulty. In spite of which, Schiller, another intellectually burdened lyricist, was set comparatively often. His inspiring flights of ideas, genuine pathos and classical attitude stirred musicians to activity. It was Schubert, first and foremost, who achieved outstanding results with his Schiller settings, as is shown by *Dithyrambe, Die Götter Griechenlands*, and, courageously, in view of their scale and length, *Der Taucher* and *Die Bürgschaft*. In the process he took joyous advantage of the opportunity to colour already clearly sketched pictures. And it may have been these extended forms which helped him away from the sparse, merely charmingly suggestive props of his earliest work, and led him to think further to the point of highly personal musical statement.

Epoch-making, and dominant in all directions, was the effect of Goethe who, in his lyric poetry, allowed unequivocal intelligibility of image to retire behind the conception of divine nature. No outward exuberance, but great inner intensity predominates. Just as he himself called his poems 'songs', so music became the basic element of his poetry. It is not only in the lyric poem but also in the ballad and the verse drama that there is much of lyrical quality, calling for music and often, too, conceived for music. His rhythm is varied and variable, and allows freedom for shaping. Goethe stands at the beginning and at the end of the art of the Lied, being set effectively by Beethoven as well as by Busoni. It was he who pointed the possible ways for setting verse, either to be followed or reacted against. His *West-östlicher Divan* was set not only by Wolf and Schoeck; but Schubert in *Was bedeutet die Bewegung*, Mendelssohn in his duets, and Schumann had already been stimulated by it. Among poets, a whole succession of German orientalists were influenced by him. Goethe wrote in the spirit of Hafiz. Daumer, translated Hafiz and sounded like Goethe. Rückert and Platen, too, exploited the charm of exotic colour. Goethe, the traveller in Italy, imitated antiquity in the classical manner, and, in so doing, found his own imitators. Paul Heyse and Emanuel Geibel discovered Italian and Spanish poets of previous centuries, and thus provided the pattern for Schumann's *Spanisches Liederspiel*, and Wolf's *Italienisches Liederbuch* and *Spanisches Liederbuch*. Conrad Ferdinand Meyer, with his historian's attitude, found in Hans Pfitzner and Othmar Schoeck composers who extended the inner dimensions of a poem and bestowed the warmth of personal feeling on the often classically cool verse of this Swiss poet.

Theodor Körner, on the other hand, paid homage to the stylistic model of Schiller. Körner's poems, set to music by Carl Maria von Weber, achieved expression characteristic of the period following the Wars of Liberation. Such might have been the case with Schenkendorf, except that Brahms, his one notable setter, concentrated on him as an author of love poems—a sphere in which he was practically unknown.

By a wide detour, via the study of unaccompanied choral singing, Johannes Brahms became occupied with the German folk song which, previously, had opened itself to no other composer in similar depth.

For him it was to become a foundation on which he was able to build further in the art song. From the literary point of view, Herder and Goethe, and also the Romantics, had long since made preliminary advances into these enticing and original areas. In addition to Arnim and Brentáno's famous Romantic collection, *Des Knaben Wunderhorn*, Johann Nikolaus Böhl had collected genuine old airs as early as 1810. In 1826 Silcher commenced publication primarily of Swabian folk songs. Finally, however, in 1839, Ludwig Erk presented Germans with a series of folk-song transcriptions which spurred Brahms to respond with his own demanding arrangements. Of Brahms' Lieder-writing in general it can be said that two forces are principally at work: on the one hand, a conservative, formally emphatic attitude confirmed by his dictum that the strophic song is indeed the highest of all song forms; on the other hand, contact with all the streams of refinement of his time reveals itself in his highly sensitively harmonized expression of emotion. The occasionally robust tonality of his piano accompaniments confront the singer with the task of shaping his tone instrumentally, which is tantamount to a repression of the purely declamatory, not least when in tender songs he allows piano phrases to spin themselves out. Brahms was not so decisively influenced stylistically as Wolf by the poets' originality, but was an expert selector of text, with sympathy for rather out-of-the-way authors like Candidus, Daumer, Halm, Lemcke and Wenzig, and less regard for the often-set Rückert, Reinick, Wilhelm Müller and even Goethe. Brahms, as a long-naturalized Viennese, did not deny his North German nature, particuarly when taking up Klaus Groth's and Theodor Storm's songs of home. Childhood memories and melancholy reminiscence (rain-songs!) received through him essentially similar expression.

One of the most beautiful of Brahms' songs, *Mit vierzig Jahren*, comes from the orientalist and Wars-of-Liberation poet, Friedrich Rückert. Fortunately, in Rückert's six fat volumes of poetry, as well as a great deal of incidental verse, there is sufficient of human involvement and still generally valid subjects to attract composers. Schubert, Schumann, Brahms and—perhaps most impressively Gustav Mahler in the *Kindertotenlieder* (a selection of five out of nearly a hundred poems dealing with the same material) and in certain songs of *Aus letzter Zeit*, amongst them that peak of achievement *Ich bin der Welt abhanden gekommen*—have kept Rückert's ardent confessions of love and distressing doubts resoundingly alive.

Neither composers nor audience were able to make a great deal of the majority of their patriotic poets. Herwegh, Dahn, Wildenbruch and Hoffmann von Fallersleben did not escape literary ephemerality by being set to music. At the most, balladesque verses by Freiligrath, Alexis and Chamisso were set, as occasion arose.

But interest in the ballad seems today to have suffered severely. Only the masterpieces have managed to survive, amongst them Schubert's

*Erlkönig* from Goethe, and Schumann's *Belsazar* from Heine. The listeners' readiness repeatedly to anticipate well-known punch-lines, with curiosity and pleasure, seems diminished. Certainly it will not, in the end, depend on the structure of future audiences whether pleasure in the ballad can be re-awakened. Assuredly, one will have to fall back on the work—not so far fully exploited even by certain specialist ballad singers of the past—of Carl Loewe, of whom Wagner, during the first rehearsals of *Der Ring* in 1875, observed (as noted by Eugen Gura in his reminiscences), 'He is, really and truly, a serious master who handles the beautiful German language with significance, and who cannot be revered sufficiently highly.' Loewe's rediscovery will, perhaps, be impeded by his musical volubility and manner of writing, which, as a result of his extensive knowledge, is somewhat too diverse. But it must not be forgotten that he was one of the most prolific Goethe setters, and that amongst his merits is to have set to music at least two Fontane poems, *Tom der Reimer* and *Archibald Douglas*. At all events, the ballad ought not to be dispensed with as a training exercise in vivid portrayal.

Those features which with Goethe foreshadowed and pre-embodied Romanticism were most productively followed by Friedrich Schlegel, whose *Waldesnacht*, as well as many other poems, was set boldly and with inspiration by Schubert. On the other hand, Clemens Brentano has found amazingly little response in composers, although his *Wunderhorn*, compiled jointly with Achim von Arnim, appears at various times in the literature of the Lied, above all with Gustav Mahler, whose early work is very much in the spirit of that book, inspired equally by fancifully melancholy love poems (*Lieder eines fahrenden Gesellen* in part) as by ironic parables (*Des Antonius von Padua Fischpredigt*). Richard Strauss is unique in coming musically to terms with Brentano's original poems. Goethe's sponsorship is also betrayed in the romances from Ludwig Tieck's *Magelone* novella, which in the settings of Carl Maria von Weber and, of course, the young Brahms, are elevated to quite a different level. Without Franz Schubert, the Dessau librarian Wilhelm Müller, with his novella-like series of songs, *Die schöne Müllerin* and *Die Winterreise* (to say nothing here of the *Student Song Book*, in which Müller is represented by roguish drinking songs), would have been hard put to commend himself to posterity. In this he was crucially fortunate: for the happy combination of Müller's autobiographically endorsed misfortune in love, and vivid pathetic fallacy, led Schubert to the loftiest and most potently convincing summits of the Lied.

A poet whose language is music in itself, yet who did not repress music but rather enticed it forth through suggestive tenderness and enriched it by melody, was Joseph von Eichendorff. What is perhaps Schumann's most beautiful song opus, the *Liederkreis*, Opus 39, was prompted by this poet. Hugo Wolf, with a whole batch of gems not previously set to music, emphasized the bold, reckless or lightly ironic pieces. Hans Pfitzner, with his preference for natural sound, fastened on Eichendorff's rapt intro-spection. Mendelssohn, Brahms, Reger, Schoeck, Schwarz-Schilling and, not least, Mahler's pupil Bruno Walter, also felt themselves inspired by this poet's simplicity, free as it is of anything mythical, and inconceivable in a language other than German.

The *Schilflieder* of Nikolaus Lenau, a poet of more complex intellectual origins whose language strives to free itself from Goethe's influence, were set to music by Richard Strauss and the composer-violinist Henri Marteau. Lenau was brought as a pathological case to Justinus Kerner at his private hospital at Weinsberg. Kerner, a neurologist, necromancer and passionate poet, provided Schumann with the poems for one of his chief lyrical works, the collection of songs, Opus 35, which like *Die Winterreise* ends as a whisper in silent despair. Hugo Wolf, too, remembered this poet. Only now and then did Uhland, with his near folk-song and balladesque verses, appear: with Schubert (*Frühlingsglaube*), Kreutzer and Liszt.

The song as musical recitation owes an incomparable debt to Mörike. It was he who inspired Hugo Wolf to his declamatory style; quickly perfected, this style remained without consequence for the development of the Lied, even in Wolf's own oeuvre. Nevertheless, it opened up to the interpreter hitherto undreamt-of possibilities for penetrating the poet's language. As a generalization, it could be maintained that Mörike was the last lyric poet who could justifiably demand that he be set to music. After him lyric poetry was already leading into new areas of refinement, signifying only apparent rejuvenation for music; its restricting effect only we descendants can recognize. It may safely be said, without detriment to the poetry of succeeding generations, that it is in the period between Goethe and Mörike or Gottfried Keller that the richest living sources of German song are to be found.

The difficulties to which Wolf exposed both performer and listener were new and manifold. Technical accuracy was demanded to a degree that disconcerted his contemporaries. Until Wolf, no one had required per-formances with such a wide range of aural effects. The declamatory shape of the song seemed unsurpassable; Wolf, without demur, did away with bel canto and coloratura. Yet in spite of that and the intuitive powers of his ideas, a trace of incompleteness was never quite overcome. Many musicians, even today, have hesitated in their approval, as did Brahms, who criticized his insufficient knowledge of composition—earning him the undying resentment of Wolf, the music critic. Wolf too had something of the folie de grandeur, common to the slaves of Wagner, that sought to equal the Master—and this is why he too, unwittingly, became party to the rift between over-refined *l'art pour l'art* on the one hand, and, on the other, vacuous, pseudo folk-music—so for a time accelerating the end of the Lied. With Wolf, of course, there can be no talk of implication; rather was he victim of a historical process. And the modernist composer who finds everything in the past dead and ossified, who is prepared at all times to supply 'something new for the day' has, let us admit, had his day, or at least soon will. There are increasing signs that the idea of conforming with 'experimentation at all costs' will soon be thrown overboard by a distinguished minority. At that time, however, when Hugo Wolf's first inspired songs appeared, Hauptmann and Ibsen were with deadly earnest insisting upon an anti-Romantic portrayal of our own world in art. Their contemporaries, on the other hand, attempted to flee the wickedness of commerce, machines and big business. Wolf found salvation in his veneration for the great poets of the past. In fact he fulfilled what Schubert, in *Die Winterreise*, had shown as possible ways of shaping the soul's affairs. But he appeared as the complete Wagnerian in his utter allegiance to speech-melody, and in his faithful adherence to the principles advanced by Hans Sachs in *Die Meistersinger*. He even gave a direct music quotation of Wagner's Sachs in *Kein Meister fällt vom Himmel*. It was Wolf's good fortune as a composer to begin his career under the influence of Schumann, and, like Schumann, he shifted the essential musical emphasis to the piano part. In doing so, he countered the danger of interpreting the poem in a purely recitative fashion through harmonic daring and advanced compositional technique. Wolf was not a composer of the large-scale dramatic form. The birth of his opera *Der Corregidor* was attended by prolonged libretto labour-pains, and because of its anti-dramatic series of lyric scenes, cannot hold its own on the stage. When Hugo Wolf ventured to write a big song, as in *Prometheus* and particularly the Goethe volumes, he was only partially credible. Spiritual introspection is his most individual domain, and nowhere is this expressed more passionately and exquisitely than in the Mörike and Eichendorff songs. But in the Goethe accompaniments too, and in the incorporation of southern musical characteristics in the Spanish and Italian songs, what rivets the attention is the wonderfully transparent piano writing, at times virtually resembling the four parts of a string quartet. And finally, this young musician, who broke away from tradition and reflected every fluctuation of his time, gave shattering evidence of how to overcome anxiety neuroses and hardship. None other has been able, like him, with obsessional concentration in short bursts of creativity and with a similarly intense response to the poem, to exhaust so utterly each new poet discovered. From this passionate devotion to the task in hand, there develops in each of his Lieder volumes a particular style, born from the process of recasting great literature from a modern viewpoint into the most personal musical language.

Detlev von Liliencron, who heard Wolf give the first performance of his Mörike songs, wrote rapturously:

> *In the Mörike volume,*
> *on the first page,*
> *you, modest man, set*
> *the poet's portrait in admiration.*
> *What composer ever did that?*

He, whose poems had so often been set to music, could not but have been aware. Although Liliencron did not appreciate one of Brahms' most celebrated songs (*Auf dem Kirchhofe*), Reger and Richard Strauss gave him satisfaction, the latter with the delightfully ironic *Bruder Liederlich*. Liliencron saw in the young Arno Holz of the Berlin Group at the turn of the century the emergence of a 'new race of poets'. But with him the Lied neared its temporary end. The young Richard Strauss still felt drawn to Dehmel's social poems (*Der Arbeitsmann*; *Der Steinklopfer*) and created out of *Befreit* a much-sung pièce de résistance for those operatic voices which were then thrusting their way on to the concert platform. Dehmel talked of rhythm and rhyme as 'tyrannical'. Arno Holz and Otto Julius Bierbaum agreed with him. What then became 'tyrannical' was of a different nature: semi-nonsense, disillusionment and finally—the random.

It is noticeable that since about 1870 the best compositions have had to wait relatively long for general recognition. Some exceptions—compositions on mainly second-rate texts such as *Traum durch die Dämmerung* (Bierbaum) or *Mariae Wiegenlied* (Boelitz)—only confirmed what was gradually becoming the rule. And the most popular Lieder of that time came from pens of respected, but today rightly forgotten, minor masters, such as Curschmann, Abt, Rubinstein, Hermann, Bohm and Lassen. Similarly, the poetically mediocre (Hartleben and Bethge), in the way it inspired music, supplanted the lyrical status of a Nietzsche or a George—two enemies of that very German middle class which most responded to the Lied. Bethge adapted *Chinesische Flöte* (by Li Po and others), thus confirming contemporary taste for translated poetry, also indicated by strong response from composers, such as Mahler in his infinitely expressive orchestral song-cycle *Das Lied von der Erde*. Schumann's preoccupation with Byron, Burns; Geibel's translations from the Spanish; Brahms' settings of German translations of Serbian and Magyar poems; and Wolf's discovery of the Michelangelo sonnets are earlier examples of this trend.

Franz Liszt, too, should be considered here—three times, convincingly and in different form, he set Petrarch's sonnets to music. And yet it seems to us that the pessimists among the conservatives of that century, led by Schumann and Brahms, showed good judgment in viewing Palestrina, Bach, Mozart and Beethoven as peaks in the history of music no longer to be reached. Those who thought otherwise found their herald in Franz Liszt. And they too sensed what Nietzsche wanted to say with his 'danger of decadence' distilled from the writings of Schopenhauer. But ideas merged from all sides, and their contrary natures, it was believed, would have a salutary effect in speeding up the development of styles, though at the cost of natural growth. A new school was formed, the New German School. The Allgemeiner Deutscher Musikverein recognized that musical creativity had in many ways been arrested, but announced in its statutes that it would overcome this lifelessness 'systematically with new means of expression' by using new programmatic musical concepts. This assault with new instrumentation, new programme music and many other kinds of sensory stimulus found an echo in the new German song. The piano part became virtuoso and orchestral, music became vastly more literary, the Lied became theatrical. With its newly acquired occasional orchestral accompaniment, it resembled a scene from opera, and led via Mahler and the early Schoenberg straight into expressionistic atonality. Liszt was among the first who were prepared to welcome each innovation without reserve, as a result bringing about amazing progress—a breed which up to the present day has suffered no lack of progeny.

Peter Cornelius appeared as an outsider among the New German School, attempting to shield himself from the devouring influence of Wagner and Liszt by, amongst other things, concentrating on song-writing. It is true that his role of composer and poet reflected the ambitions of the New German School (the much earlier Karl Michael Bellman or Adam Krieger cannot be compared). Yet his cycles, *Trauer und Trost*, *Vater Unser* and *Weihnachtslieder*, deserve to be remembered.

Among the many amateur composers appearing on the scene at this time, Nietzsche presented a typically interesting case, with his settings of Lou Andreas-Salomé (*Gebet an das Leben*), Pushkin, Lord Byron, Chamisso and Petöfy. In Liszt's solo songs, the strong influence of French culture on his life can be seen from his choice of texts: Béranger, Hugo, Dumas are represented. Tennyson too, whose *Enoch Arden* was later to be used by Richard Strauss for curious melodramatic purposes. However, it is Goethe and Heine who were preferred in Liszt's great variety of songs, even though their poems were treated as extended arias (*Die Lorelei* is eight pages long) or totally dramatized. His quite forgotten *Die Glocken von Marling*, to a poem by Emil Kuh, pointed already to the beginnings of Impressionism.

In 1885, that is to say before Wolf's most important works, Richard Strauss began to write songs. One of the first poets to inspire him was Hermann Gilm, who at times verges on the sentimental, as in *Allerseelen*. Count Schack soon followed: charming, polished poems—producing charming, polished music. With such collective titles as *Schlichte Weisen* (Simple Airs), a title suggested by Strauss' friend Alexander Ritter, we imagine we are safe from art and artistic skill—yet, as in Reger's collection of the same name, there is not an inch conceded as far as difficulty and Art Nouveau refinement are concerned. Then occasionally we find Lenau, for example in the effectively pale *O wärst du mein*, until Bierbaum's *Traum durch die Dämmerung*, roughly contemporary with Reger's setting of the same poem, made Strauss famous as a Lieder composer. Here French Impressionism combined with German love of concrete art, and a new association was formed which successfully rebelled against the New German School. Brahms, who after all was the first to inspire the young Strauss, was in comparison made to look undeservedly patriarchal by the music critics at the turn of the century. Above all, it was Richard Strauss' infallible sense of possibilities for developing the human voice that stood him in good stead. Inspired by the voice and singing of his fiancée, Pauline de Ahna (later to become his wife), he poured gold into his soprano cantilenas, and his sopranos have responded with gratitude ever since. The faint pencil marks in his library's many volumes of poetry reveal the titles for which he would await the right moment for musical inspiration. Rarely did this occur immediately after the first reading. Like Mozart, his spiritual ancestor, he collected in this way a store, of which, unfortunately, only a fraction was exploited.

Richard Strauss' sometimes lightweight style of composition must be viewed against the background of Art Nouveau, the Munich Secession and Wolzogen's cabaret. Consequently he paid increasing attention to his own generation of poets—Falke, Dehmel, Mackay—and Strauss, the Prussian Music Director, in pseudo-revolutionary manner, permitted himself with Dehmel's *Arbeitsmann* (*The Labourer*) to demand an eight-hour day, more from the temptation to re-coin such things artistically. Henkell, Heine and C. F. Meyer inspired him, together with his creative experience of music-drama (by then mastered with *Salome* and *Elektra*), to write pieces which have very much their own individual style. *Blindenklage* and *Im Spätboot* should in particular be mentioned here because of their new vocal style: large-interval leaps, extended range and a forcing of meaning and gesture into the widest possible vocal intervals—characteristics that can be observed in the polemical retort, the *Krämerspiegellieder*, that, with Alfred Kerr, he wrote about pressing and rapacious publishers. The dominant role of the piano in late Romantic song scores triumphs in this work. Strauss' songs appeal to the senses as well as to one's artistic sense, thus freeing the Germans from the rather exclusive humourlessness which, till then, had kept the production of their Lied aloof from international influence.

As long as Max Reger accompanied his own songs at the piano, there was a general conviction that this side in particular of his output would endure. He once said that there would come a time when his *Schlichte Weisen* would be sung in every German home as a matter of course. Such optimism has since faded, clearly in many cases unjustly. The degree to which taste has meanwhile lagged behind may have been caused by a load of excessive polyphony and a mania for modulation. And Reger was not always over-fastidious in his choice of text. Yet if we search his numerous volumes of Lieder for substantial poets—an easy task now that the complete edition has at last been published—we see that he showed himself capable, especially in the early songs, of subtly analysing metrical problems, of sustaining, in close relation to the poem, a mood strikingly captured in both melody and harmony. Storm, Hebbel, Stefan Zweig, Hölderlin, Goethe and Dehmel are still today effective in his settings.

The ideas and musical language of Hans Pfitzner were decisively influenced by Eichendorff and Romanticism in general. The mysterious lines of affinity in the history of music are rarely so clearly manifested as when one listens to Schumann's *Auf einer Burg*, which, though emanating from Eichendorff, sounds like a premonition of a Pfitzner song. Pfitzner may thus be seen as the last heir and preserver of the spirit of Schumann the Lieder composer, uniting with astonishing appropriateness the archaic and spontaneously Romantic elements. Like Othmar Schoeck, he was consciously opposed to that 'progress' condemned as constructivist. But, though Pfitzner played the Romantic, he also showed himself determined to give a different colour to Romanticism. Consciously looking back to the past, he was at the same time the most vehement representative of the German middle-class ideal of culture. With a scholar's fervour he buried himself in the past, strove to unearth things of beauty buried in the Middle Ages and to solve scholarly problems. The singularity of this phenomenon is evident: Wagnerian out of a feeling for the still unfulfilled mission of Wagnerism, Schumannian and Brahmsian from creative gift, he might have led one to suppose in him an aptitude for reconciling such contradictions. But his rigid conviction of decline all around, born of a surfeit of character and theory, interfered with this secular task.

Since the time of Liszt, the price for all that is artificially new has been lack of direction—and not only in German-speaking countries. In France, Satie, Roussel and Les Six grappled, each in his own way, with Impressionism. The increasing isolation of man is also something the creative artist is obliged to experience. Successful German songs acquire rarity value. From Finland, thanks to the efforts of a German, the baritone Gerhard Hüsch, news of Yrjö Kilpinen reached Germany. His German songs, particularly the Morgenstern volumes, have for some time now enjoyed great popularity. Anton Webern achieved a graphic concentration of the essentials, propounded by his teacher Schoenberg, and later buried under a weight of elaboration. Alban Berg composed impressive orchestral songs to Altenberg's postcard texts, but again they are disappearing from concert programmes. Aribert Reimann, a pupil of Blacher, set to music Paul Celan's surrealistically charming words with delicate colouring and an impressive art of suggestion. Hans Werner Henze, in his *Neopolitanische Gesänge* with orchestra, has given rise to the greatest hopes for rediscovery of lost melody. But, as has been said, one has to wait a long time for the emergence of a piece, worthy of performance, that can expect at least a short life in the concert halls.

This survey, by its very nature a sketch which must leave many a late Romantic master unconsidered, has now to turn its attention to the function of the Lied, its place in cultural life. We can learn much by looking at songs for different numbers of voices. When, for example, the song is an unaccompanied quartet, as in many splendid Schubert pieces for men's voices or mixed choir, it is an expression of the conviviality of hiking and hunting. Not so the solo song: this began in the drawing-room as something private, as soliloquy, or as a most intimate declaration of feeling—

and was frequently far removed from professional music-making. In the solo or duet one simply communicated to others. If Lieder were sung, they were performed among friends in the home. The demand for ensemble led to quartet singing, as in Brahms' *Liebesliederwalzer* for four hands. The Lied was for a long time excluded from concert programmes. The first Schubert song to be sung in public in Vienna was *Schäfers Klagelied* in 1819; then from 1821, the tenor Vogl championed his friend's songs in the concert hall, albeit on a decidedly modest scale, treating him as a protégé. The era of the specialized Lieder recitalist emerged. Julius Stockhausen, on retiring from the stage, became the first interpreter of song cycles, and with Brahms or Clara Schumann as accompanist, gave the first complete performances of Schubert's *Schöne Müllerin* and Schumann's *Dichterliebe*. To him was dedicated Brahms' *Die schöne Magelone*. Julius Messchaert, Julia Culp, Elena Gerhardt, Raimund von Zurmühlen, Georg A. Walter, Ludwig Wüllner were also typical embodiments of this kind of ideal singer. Alongside Vogl and his French comrade-in-arms Lablache, it was Franz Liszt, with his much scorned transcriptions, who, through piano arrangements alone, assisted greatly in the propagation of Schubert song.

But this formed the breach, allowing one to see ahead to the end of *Hausmusik*. The composer by then had in mind the professional singer and the large public he hoped to win for himself. The amateur at home must have felt himself to be a mere shadowy imitator—completely so today, since perfection is stereophonically preserved and delivered into the drawing-room, so nipping in the bud any attempts to perform.

The technical demands were much greater on pianist than singer, and they were indeed decisively increased by the great virtuosi among composers. And so the trend was developed in the Lied for the piano to predominate, with the voice expressing itself only occasionally and in declamatory fashion. The realms of the soul were gladly abandoned. Virtuoso display, the external, thrust itself forward. At one time a change was still believed possible—after the end of the First World War, when disgust at the by then prolific compositions was expressed in Fritz Jödes' Manifesto: 'and Lieder, Lieder, or rather a flood of Lieder, and always for solo voice and piano, and as the most recent offshoot of fashion Lieder with lute accompaniment; whoever has a glimmer of musical talent and cannot write these things—well, there simply isn't anyone who doesn't these days.' But this Youth Movement reform programme was only short-lived. The impotence of the highly cultivated Lied was challenged by the vocal glories of the *Wandervogel* movement. It also proved possible, as was intended, to revive the folk song and the street-ballad, and yet these efforts did not bear fruit in furthering musical development. Others, with musicology as their starting-point, tried to revive the *Minnesang*, the late Gothic chanson, the madrigal and the figured-bass song, and got no further than the community spirit of choral societies. When, with their revolutionary clean-up long completed, these still influential phenomena are viewed in the light of the present day, an impression of archaizing remoteness from general musical development cannot be dismissed.

The present inevitable exhaustion coincides with the fatigue of lyrical expression. Goethe was not so wide of the mark to view the future with dreadful misgiving, and feel the German language's capacities for expression to have been exhausted by his own plenitude. The Golden Age of the classical-romantic Lied represented a final cultural-historical event, limited only by national boundaries. The school that people outside Germany named Romantic—a definition that included the classical period—had spread, blazing the way, towards France and Italy, and had, through its poetry, kindled the culture of all Europe. The gem-like Russian romances of Glinka, Tchaikovsky and Mussorgsky contributed decisively to the transformation, and were the basis for the looser structure of composition practised by the impressionists Debussy and Ravel. Finally, the effect of the emancipation of the great libertarian poets (Rimbaud, Trakl, Heym) from Western characteristics was to abolish the parochial significance of the Lied, which was so typically German-Austrian. Their unrestrained, relentless language was matched by the music. A general disillusionment that penetrated to the soul's depths had taken the place of Rilke's and George's attempts to make significant pronouncements about human life and the cosmos. Today's artist, it seems, has lost the inclination to feel responsible for humanity.

The singer's voice, however, will remain responsible, and symbolically so, by representing the most direct expression of the harmony of form and content, of husk and kernel. It might, given the general shift in emphasis towards the fashionably aesthetic, become the voice of conscience—especially so in an age which, being dominated by technology, the mass and universal levelling, calls for a particular effort to reveal it fully. The interpreter as a kind of builder of bridges to the new that is to come—whatever name it may go under—is left with the glorious task of preserving, by means of immaculate performance, the existing creations of the masters.

Such a recognition that the Lied, as a genre, is in danger of extinction, increases the Lieder singer's duty, which goes far beyond what used to be considered his professional task. Though we arrive at a perfect mastery of the instrument to be played, the work, its spirit, threatens to elude us. It is not easy for us to discern the principles of organization which have provided the work with its spiritual substance. We can only strive to hear the music in our own minds in the same spirit in which it presented itself to its creator. Certainly in songs of today, which are by no means easy to listen to, there occur passages of pseudo lucidity, suggested by the sound of the human voice and capable of adding new meanings which are, in fact, completely non-existent. To do justice, on the other hand, to a real and simple song, such as Schumann's setting of Eichendorff's *In der Fremde*, becomes considerably more difficult. I have in mind the hearing of a note's colour-value, the singer's ever-changing view of the song, the stamping upon the music of the composer's own personal characteristics. Perhaps this is still most readily achieved in the realm of song: the poetry assists us. Singing is, moreover, the most living and therefore most sensitive link between sounds. Our vocal organs remain responsive to give form to what comes to us from a past age.

We have attempted to reconstruct the conflicting and also, in part, degenerate tendencies of the recent decades of song-writing. But this should in no way lead to a mere state of resignation. True, people everywhere believe they sense in man a loss of wholeness, and also see, losing itself in dissonance, the 'harmony as a gift of love', which Schlegel attempted to understand as an ideal union of feeling and knowledge. But the Romantics were certainly wrong to view growing awareness of every pulsation of the heart's fever as identical with decay. Certainly the Lied as an expression of the assurance of beauty's permanence in art cannot merely have been a childish dream on the part of the Romantics. On the contrary: it is through awareness, through union of heart and mind (leaving aside the misleading concept of the intelligence), that the endurance of art may result. The struggle for such unity will be carried on by cool and fervent hearts, and also in what today can, still, be called the art of Lieder composition.

Music and poetry have a common domain, from which they draw inspiration and in which they operate: the landscape of the soul. Together, they have the power to lend intellectual form to what is sensed and felt, to transmute both into a language that no other art can express. The magic power that dwells in music and poetry has the ability ceaselessly to transform us.

DIETRICH FISCHER-DIESKAU

# THE LIEDER TEXTS

## Abbitte / Plea for Forgiveness

FRIEDRICH HÖLDERLIN

*Wolfgang Fortner, 1933; Hans Pfitzner: op. 29, no. 1, 1922*

Heilig Wesen! gestört hab ich die
  goldene
Götterruhe dir oft, und der geheimeren,
Tiefern Schmerzen des Lebens
Hast du manche gelernt von mir.

O vergiß es, vergib! gleich dem
  Gewölke dort
Vor dem friedlichen Mond, geh ich
  dahin, und du
Ruhst und glänzest in deiner
Schöne wieder, du süßes Licht!

Holy Being! Often have I spoilt your
  golden
god's repose, and of the more secret
deeper agonies of life
many have you learnt from me.

Oh forget, forgive. As those
  clouds
before the tranquil moon, I shall pass,
  and you
will rest and gleam in your
beauty once more, sweet light!


## Abenddämmerung / Dusk

ADOLF FRIEDRICH VON SCHACK

*Johannes Brahms: op. 49, no. 5, 1868*

Sei willkommen, Zwielichtstunde!
Dich vor allen lieb ich längst,
Die du, lindernd jede Wunde,
Unsre Seele mild umfängst.

Hin durch deine Dämmerhelle,
In den Lüften, abendfeucht,
Schweben Bilder, die der grelle
Schein des lauten Tags gescheucht.

Träume und Erinnerungen
Nahen aus der Kinderzeit,
Flüstern mit den Geisterzungen
Von vergangner Seligkeit.

Und zu Jugendlust-Genossen
Kehren wir ins Vaterhaus;
Arme, die uns einst umschlossen,
Breiten neu sich nach uns aus.

Nach dem Trennungsschmerz, dem
  langen,
Dürfen wir noch einmal nun
Denen, die dahingegangen,
Am geliebten Herzen ruhn.

Und indes zum Augenlide
Sanft der Schlummer niederrinnt,
Sinkt auf uns ein selger Friede
Aus dem Land, wo jene sind.

Welcome, twilight hour!
You above all have I long loved,
who, soothing every wound,
gently embrace our souls.

Through your dusky brightness,
in the breezes, evening-moist,
float images which the harsh
light of noisy day has banished.

Dreams and memories
of childhood days draw near,
whisper with ghostly tongues
of bygone ecstasy.

And to youthful joy's companions
we return to our parents' house;
arms which once embraced us,
reach out to us anew.

After long agony of
  separation
we can now, once more,
rest on the dear hearts
of those departed.

And whilst into our eyelids
slumber gently flows,
blissful peace sinks upon us
from that land in which they are.

## Abendempfindung / Evening Thoughts

JOACHIM HEINRICH CAMPE

*Wolfgang Amadeus Mozart: K 523, 1787*

Abend ist's, die Sonne ist
  verschwunden,
Und der Mond strahlt Silberglanz;
So entfliehn des Lebens schönste
  Stunden,
Fliehn vorüber wie im Tanz.

Evening. The sun has
  vanished,
and the moon sheds a silver gleam;
thus flit life's finest
  hours,
flit by as in a dance.

Bald entflieht des Lebens bunte Szene,
Und der Vorhang rollt herab;
Aus ist unser Spiel, des Freundes Träne
Fließet schon auf unser Grab.

Away soon will flit life's pageant,
and the curtain come rolling down;
our play is done, the friend's
tear falls already on our grave.

Bald vielleicht (mir weht, wie Westwind
  leise,
Eine stille Ahnung zu),
Schließ ich dieses Lebens Pilgerreise,
Fliege in das Land der Ruh.

Soon maybe (like the westwind,
  wafts
upon me a quiet presentiment),
this pilgrimage of life I shall end,
and fly to the land of rest.

Werdet ihr an meinem Grabe weinen,
Trauernd meine Asche sehn,
Dann, o Freunde, will ich euch
  erscheinen
Und will himmelauf euch wehn.

If you will then weep by my grave,
and mourning, upon my ashes gaze,
then, O friends, shall I
  appear
and waft you heavenwards.

Schenk auch du ein Tränchen mir und
  pflücke
Mir ein Veilchen auf mein Grab,
Und mit deinem seelenvollen Blicke
Sieh dann sanft auf mich herab.

And you, my love, bestow on me a
  tear,
and pluck me a violet for my grave,
and with your soulful gaze,
look down then gently on me.

Weih mir eine Träne, und ach! schäme
Dich nur nicht, sie mir zu weihn;
Oh, sie wird in meinem Diademe
Dann die schönste Perle sein!

Consecrate a tear to me, and ah, be
only not ashamed to do so;
oh, in my diadem will it
then be the fairest of the pearls.

## Abendlied / Evening Hymn

MATTHIAS CLAUDIUS

*Johann Friedrich Reichardt, ed. 1779–81; Othmar Schoeck: op. 52, no. 2 f, ed. 1937;
Franz Schubert, 1816*

Der Mond ist aufgegangen,
die goldnen Sternlein prangen
am Himmel hell und klar;
der Wald steht schwarz und schweiget,
und aus den Wiesen steiget
der weiße Nebel wunderbar.

The moon has risen,
the golden stars shine
in the sky bright and clear;
the wood stands black and silent,
and from the meadows rises,
wondrously, the white mist.

Wie ist die Welt so stille
und in der Dämmrung Hülle
so traulich und so hold
als eine stille Kammer,

How still the world,
and, veiled in faint light,
cosy and kind
as a quiet chamber,

wo ihr des Tages Jammer
verschlafen und vergessen sollt.

where the misery of the day
you shall forget in sleep.

Seht ihr den Mond dort stehen?
Er ist nur halb zu sehen
und ist doch rund und schön!
So sind wohl manche Sachen,
die wir getrost belachen,
weil unsre Augen sie nicht sehn

You see the moon up there?
Only half is to be seen,
yet round it is and fair.
Just so are many things
which happily we mock,
because our eyes cannot see.

Wir stolze Menschenkinder
sind eitel arme Sünder
und wissen gar nicht viel;
wir spinnen Luftgespinste
und suchen viele Künste
und kommen weiter von dem Ziel.

We proud human beings
are poor vain sinners,
and know so very little;
airy nothings we spin,
many arts we seek,
and move further from our goal.

Gott, laß dein Heil uns schauen,
auf nichts Vergänglichs bauen,
nicht Eitelkeit uns freun.
Laß uns einfältig werden
und vor dir hier auf Erden
wie Kinder fromm und fröhlich sein.

God, may we see Thy salvation,
build upon nothing transitory,
and rejoice not in vanity.
Make us simple,
and, before Thee, here on earth,
as meek and joyful as children.

Wollst endlich sonder Grämen
aus dieser Welt uns nehmen
durch einen sanften Tod,
und wenn du uns genommen,
laß uns in Himmel kommen,
du, unser Herr und unser Gott!

Mayest Thou, at the end, take us
without affliction hence
by an easy death,
and having taken us,
grant we may enter Heaven,
Thou, our Lord and God.

So legt euch denn, ihr Brüder,
in Gottes Namen nieder!
Kalt ist der Abendhauch.
Verschon uns, Gott, mit Strafen
und laß uns ruhig schlafen
und unsern kranken Nachbar auch!

So brothers, lay yourselves
in God's name down.
Cold is the breath of evening.
Spare us, God, Thy punishments,
and grant peaceful sleep to us
and our sick neighbour too.

## Abendlied unterm gestirnten Himmel / Evening Song beneath a Starry Sky

H. GOEBEL

*Ludwig van Beethoven, 1820*

Wenn die Sonne niedersinket,
Und der Tag zur Ruh sich neigt,
Luna freundlich leise winket,
Und die Nacht herniedersteigt;

When the sun sinks down,
and day draws to its close,
when Luna, gently, kindly, beckons,
and the night descends;

Wenn die Sterne prächtig schimmern,
Tausend Sonnenstrahlen flimmern:
Fühlt die Seele sich so groß,
Windet sich vom Staube los.

when stars in splendour shimmer,
when a thousand sunbeams glitter,
so great the soul then feels
and from the dust breaks free;

Schaut so gern nach jenen Sternen,
Wie zurück ins Vaterland,
Hin nach jenen lichten Fernen,
Und vergißt der Erde Tand;

so gladly gazes at those stars,
as if toward its native land,
gazes at those bright far ones,
and forgets earth's vanity;

Will nur ringen, will nur streben,
Ihrer Hülle zu entschweben:
Erde ist ihr eng und klein,
Auf den Sternen möcht sie sein.

wants only to struggle, strive,
of earthly covering to float free:
earth is too small, too narrow,
upon the stars it would be.

Ob der Erde Stürme toben,
Falsches Glück den Bösen lohnt:
Hoffend blicket sie nach oben,
Wo der Sternenrichter thront.

Whether earth's tempests rage,
or false fortune reward the evil,
hopefully aloft it gazes
to the Starry Judge's throne.

Keine Furcht kann sie mehr quälen,
Keine Macht kann ihr befehlen;
Mit verklärtem Angesicht,
Schwingt sie sich zum Himmelslicht.

Fear can torture it no more,
no power can command it;
with transfigured countenance
it soars to heaven's light.

Eine leise Ahnung schauert
Mich aus jenen Welten an;
Lange nicht mehr dauert
Meine Erdenpilgerbahn,

Vague presentiment instils in me
from those worlds a sense of awe;
not long now will last
my earthly pilgrimage;

Bald hab ich das Ziel errungen,
Bald zu euch mich aufgeschwungen,
Ernte bald an Gottes Thron
Meiner Leiden schönen Lohn.

soon shall I have gained the goal,
soon shall I have soared to you,
soon shall I at God's throne reap
my sorrows' beautiful reward.


## Abends / At Eventide

JOSEPH VON EICHENDORFF

*Robert Franz: op. 16, no. 4; Hans Pfitzner: op. 9, no. 5, 1888–89;
Othmar Schoeck: op. 20, no. 7, 1905–14*

Abendlich schon rauscht der Wald
Aus den tiefsten Gründen,
Droben wird der Herr nun bald,
Bald die Stern anzünden;
Wie so stille in den Gründen
Abendlich nur rauscht der Wald.

At eventide, the forest murmurs
from the deepest valleys;
God, on high, will soon now
set alight the stars;
how soft in the valleys
the forest murmurs at eventide.

Alles geht zu seiner Ruh,
Wald und Welt versausen,
Schauernd hört der Wandrer zu,
Sehnt sich wohl nach Hause,
Hier in Waldes grüner Klause,
Herz, geh endlich auch zur Ruh.

All goes to its rest,
world and forest cease to stir;
in awe, the wanderer listens,
yearning for home.
Here, in the forest's green cell,
heart, go too at last to rest.


## Abends am Strand / Beach at Evening

HEINRICH HEINE

*Robert Schumann: op. 45, no. 3, 1840*

Wir saßen am Fischerhause,
Und schauten nach der See;
Die Abendnebel kamen,
Und stiegen in die Höh'

We sat by the fisherman's cottage,
and gazed out at the sea;
the mists of evening came
and climbed aloft.

Im Leuchtturm wurden die Lichter
Allmählich angesteckt,
Und in der weiten Ferne
Ward noch ein Schiff entdeckt.

At the lighthouse the lights
were gradually kindled,
and in the far distance
was sighted one more ship.

Wir sprachen von Sturm und
    Schiffbruch,
Vom Seemann, und wie er lebt,
Und zwischen Himmel und Wasser,
Und Angst und Freude schwebt.

We talked of storm and
    shipwreck,
of the sailor and how he lives,
poised between sky and sea,
between fear and joy.

Wir sprachen von fernen Küsten,
Vom Süden und vom Nord,
Und von den seltsamen Menschen
Und seltsamen Sitten dort.

We talked of distant shores,
of South and of North,
and of the strange people
and strange customs there.

Am Ganges duftet's und leuchtet's,
Und Riesenbäume blühn,
Und schöne, stille Menschen
Vor Lotosblumen knien.

The Ganges is fragrant, sparkling,
the giant trees bloom there,
and handsome, quiet people
kneel to lotus flowers.

In Lappland sind schmutzige Leute,
Plattköpfig, breitmäulig und klein;
Sie kauern ums Feuer, und backen
Sich Fische, und quäken und schrein.

In Lapland are dirty people,
flat-headed, big-mouthed and small;
they squat over fires, fry
fish, and squeak and scream.

Die Mädchen horchten ernsthaft,
Und endlich sprach niemand mehr;
Das Schiff war nicht mehr sichtbar,
Es dunkelte gar zu sehr.

Earnestly the girls listened,
at last no one spoke any more;
the ship was no more to be sighted,
it was growing far too dark.

## *Ablösung im Sommer* / *Summer Relief*

from *Des Knaben Wunderhorn*

Kurt Hessenberg: *op. 15, no. 9, ed. 1942; Gustav Mahler, ca. 1880–83*

Kuckuck hat sich zu Tod gefallen
An einer hohlen Weiden,
Wer soll uns diesen Sommer lang
Die Zeit und Weil vertreiben?
Ei, das soll tun Frau Nachtigall,
Die sitzt auf grünem Zweige;
Sie singt und springt, ist allzeit froh,
Wenn andre Vögel schweigen.

Cuckoo's delighted himself to death
on a hollow willow tree.
Who, for this long summer,
shall beguile the time for us?
Oh, that shall Mistress Nightingale,
who sits on a green bough;
she sings, she darts, is ever glad,
when other birds are silent.

## *Abschied* / *Farewell*

EDUARD MÖRIKE

Hugo Wolf, *1888*

Unangeklopft ein Herr tritt abends bei
    mir ein:
»Ich habe die Ehr, Ihr Rezensent zu
    sein.«
Sofort nimmt er das Licht in die Hand,
Besieht lang meinen Schatten an der
    Wand,

One evening, without knocking, in
    comes a gentleman:
'I have the honour,' he says, 'to be your
    critic.'
At once he picks up the light,
looks long at my shadow on the
    wall,

Rückt nah und fern: »Nun, lieber
  junger Mann,
Sehn Sie doch gefälligst mal Ihre Nas
  so von der Seite an!
Sie geben zu, daß das ein Auswuchs
  is.«
—Das? Alle Wetter—gewiß!
Ei Hasen! ich dachte nicht,
All mein Lebtage nicht,
Daß ich so eine Weltnase führt' im
  Gesicht!!

Der Mann sprach noch Verschiednes
  hin und her,
Ich weiß, auf meine Ehre, nicht mehr;
Meinte vielleicht, ich sollt ihm
  beichten.
Zuletzt stand er auf; ich tat ihm leuchten.
Wie wir nun an der Treppe sind,
Da geb ich ihm, ganz frohgesinnt,
Einen kleinen Tritt
Nur so von hinten aufs Gesäße
  mit—
Alle Hagel! ward das ein Gerumpel,
Ein Gepurzel, ein Gehumpel!
Dergleichen hab ich nie gesehn,
All mein Lebtage nicht gesehn,
Einen Menschen so rasch die Treppe
  hinabgehn!

stepping close and standing back: 'Now
  young man,
do just kindly see how your nose looks
  from the side!
That, you will admit, is a nose and a
  half.'
Is it? Good heavens—to be sure!
Bless my soul! I never,
never in all my life, imagined
my face had such a world-sized
  nose!!

Various other things the man said, about
  this and that,
what, I truly no longer remember;
maybe he thought I should have a
  confession to make.
He rose at last. I lit him out.
At the top of the stairs,
I gave him, merrily,
a wee kick
on the backside to be getting along
  with . . .
And by thunder! The rumbling,
the tumbling, the stumbling!
I never saw the like before,
never in all my life
have I seen a man go down stairs so
  fast!

## *Ach weh mir unglückhaftem Mann | Ah, Unhappy Man That I Am*

FELIX DAHN

*Richard Strauss: op. 21, no. 4, 1887–88*

Ach weh mir unglückhaftem Mann,
Daß ich Geld und Gut nicht habe,
Sonst spannt' ich gleich vier Schimmel
  an
Und führ' zu dir im Trabe.
Ich putzte sie mit Schellen aus,
Daß du mich hört'st von weitem,
Ich steckt' ein'n großen Rosenstrauß
An meine linke Seiten.
Und käm' ich an dein kleines Haus,
Tät' ich mit der Peitsche schlagen,
Da gucktest du zum Fenster 'naus:
Was willst du? Tät'st du fragen.
Was soll der große Rosenstrauß,
Die Schimmel an dem Wagen?
Dich will ich, rief ich, komm heraus!
Da tät'st nimmer fragen.
Nun, Vater, Mutter, seht sie an
Und küßt sie rasch zum Scheiden,
Weil ich nicht lange warten kann,
Meine Schimmel woll'ns nicht leiden.
Ach weh mir unglückhaftem Mann,
Daß ich Geld und Gut nicht habe.

Ah, unhappy man that I am
to have no gold, no goods,
or four white horses I'd
  harness
and drive to you at a trot.
I'd deck them with little bells
for you to hear me from afar,
a grand rose bouquet I'd place
at my left side.
And when I came to your little house,
I'd crack my whip,
and you'd look from the window:
'What do you want?' you'd ask.
'Why the great bouquet of roses,
the white horses and the carriage?'
'It's you I want,' I'd cry, 'Come.'
And no more questions would you ask.
'Now, father, mother, look at her,
kiss her quickly goodbye,
for I cannot wait long,
my white horses won't have it.'
Ah, unhappy man that I am
to have no gold, no goods.

36

## Adelaide | Adelaide

FRIEDRICH MATTHISSON

*Ludwig van Beethoven: op. 46, 1795-96*

Einsam wandelt dein Freund im
  Frühlingsgarten,
Mild vom lieblichen Zauberlicht
  umflossen,
Das durch wankende Blütenzweige
  zittert,
Adelaide!

In der spiegelnden Flut, im Schnee der
  Alpen,
In des sinkenden Tages
  Goldgewölken,
Im Gefilde der Sterne strahlt dein
  Bildnis,
Adelaide!

Abendlüfte im zarten Laube
  flüstern,
Silberglöckchen des Mais im Grase
  säuseln,
Wellen rauschen und Nachtigallen
  flöten:
Adelaide!

Einst, o Wunder! entblüht auf meinem
  Grabe
Eine Blume der Asche meines Herzens;
Deutlich schimmert auf jedem
  Purpurblättchen:
Adelaide!

Lonely your friend wanders the spring
  garden
lapped in the magical sweet
  light
that quivers through swaying blossomed
  boughs,
Adelaide!

In the mirroring waves, in the Alpine
  snows,
in the gold cloud masses of departing
  day,
in the region of stars your image
  shines,
Adelaide!

Evening breezes whisper in the tender
  foliage,
the silvery bells of May stir in the
  grass,
waves splash and nightingales
  sing:
Adelaide!

One day, O miracle, upon my grave
  shall bloom
a flower from the ashes of my heart;
clearly shall shimmer on every purple
  leaf:
Adelaide!


## Agnes | Agnes

EDUARD MÖRIKE

*Johannes Brahms: op. 59, no. 5, 1873; Hugo Wolf, 1888*

Rosenzeit! Wie schnell vorbei,
Schnell vorbei
Bist du doch gegangen!
Wär mein Lieb nur blieben treu,
Blieben treu,
Sollte mir nicht bangen.

Um die Ernte wohlgemut,
Wohlgemut
Schnitterinnen singen.
Aber ach! mir kranken Blut,
Mir kranken Blut
Will nichts mehr gelingen.

Schleiche so durchs Wiesental
So durchs Tal,

Time of roses! How quickly by,
quickly by
have you sped!
Had my love but stayed true,
stayed true,
I should feel no fear.

Joyously at harvest time,
joyously,
sing the woman reapers.
But oh, I am sick,
I am sick,
I can do nothing any more.

So by meadow vale I steal,
by meadow vale,

Als im Traum verloren,
Nach dem Berg, da tausendmal,
Tausendmal
Er mir Treu geschworen.

as if lost in a dream,
to the hill where a thousand times,
thousand times,
he swore to be true.

Oben auf des Hügels Rand,
Abgewandt,
Wein ich bei der Linde;
An dem Hut mein Rosenband,
Von seiner Hand,
Spielet in dem Winde.

Up where the hill begins,
turning aside,
I weep by the lime tree;
on my hat the rosy ribbon,
a present from his hand,
plays in the wind.

## All mein Gedanken | All My Thoughts

FELIX DAHN

*Max Reger: op. 75, no. 9, 1903; Richard Strauss: op. 21, no. 1, 1887–88*

All mein Gedanken, mein Herz und
   mein Sinn,
Da, wo die Liebste ist, wandern sie hin.
Gehn ihres Weges trotz Mauer und
   Tor,
Da hält kein Riegel, kein Graben nicht
   vor,
Gehn wie die Vögelein hoch durch die
   Luft,
Brauchen kein Brücken über Wasser
   und Kluft,
Finden das Städtlein und finden das
   Haus,
Finden ihr Fenster aus allen heraus

All my thoughts, my heart and
   mind,
wander to where my loved one is.
They go their way despite wall and
   gate,
no bar, no ditch is proof against
   them,
go, like the birds, high through the
   air,
needing no bridge over water and
   gorge,
they find the town and find the
   house,
find her window amongst all the others

Und klopfen und rufen:
Mach auf, laß uns ein,
Wir kommen vom Liebsten
Und grüßen dich fein,
Mach auf, mach auf, laß uns ein.

and knock and shout:
Open up, let us in,
we come from your love,
and you we greet,
open up, open up, let us in.

## Alle | All

CONRAD FERDINAND MEYER

*Wilhelm Kempff: op. 52, no. 6; Othmar Schoeck: op. 60, no. 18, 1946*

Es sprach der Geist: Sieh auf! Es war
   im Traume.
Ich hob den Blick. In lichtem
   Wolkenraume
sah ich den Herrn das Brot den
   Zwölfen brechen
und ahnungsvolle Liebesworte sprechen.
Weit über ihre Häupter lud die Erde
er ein mit allumarmender
   Gebärde.

The spirit spoke: Look up! It was a
   dream.
My gaze I raised. In that bright cloudy
   chamber
I saw the Lord break bread for the
   twelve
and speak portentous words of love.
Way beyond their heads, he invited
the earth to him, with all-embracing
   gesture.

Es sprach der Geist: Sieh auf! Ein
   Linnen schweben
sah ich und vielen schon das Mahl
   gegeben,

The spirit spoke: Look up! Floating,
   linen
I saw, and many already presented with
   that feast,

da breiteten sich unter tausend
    Händen
die Tische, doch verdämmerten die
    Enden
in grauen Nebel, drin auf bleichen
    Stufen
Kummergestalten saßen ungerufen.

Es sprach der Geist: Sieh auf! Die
    Luft umblaute
ein unermeßlich Mahl, soweit ich
    schaute,
da sprangen reich die Brunnen auf des
    Lebens,
da streckte keine Schale sich vergebens,
da lag das ganze Volk auf vollen
    Garben,
kein Platz war leer und keiner durfte
    darben.

then out, under a thousand hands,
    stretched
the tables, their ends, however,
    receding
in grey mist, where, on pale
    steps,
figures of sorrow sat, unsummoned

The spirit spoke: Look up! In the
    blue,
an immeasurable feast, as far as I
    gazed,
there life's fountains gushed richly
    up,
there no bowl was held out in vain,
there all the people lay upon full
    sheaves,
no place was empty, none was allowed
    to want.

## *Allerseelen* | *All Souls*

HERMANN VON GILM

*Richard Strauss: op. 10, no. 8, 1882–83*

Stell auf den Tisch die duftenden
    Reseden,
Die letzten roten Astern trag herbei,
Und laß uns wieder von der Liebe
    reden,
Wie einst im Mai.

Gib mir die Hand, daß ich sie heimlich
    drücke
Und wenn man's sieht, mir ist es
    einerlei,
Gib mir nur einen deiner süßen Blicke,
Wie einst im Mai.

Es blüht und duftet heut auf jedem
    Grabe,
Ein Tag im Jahr ist ja den Toten frei,
Komm an mein Herz, daß ich dich
    wieder habe,
Wie einst im Mai.

Set on the table the fragrant
    mignonettes,
bring in the last red asters,
and let us speak of love
    again,
as once in May.

Give me your hand to press in
    secret,
if people see, I do not
    care;
give me but one of your sweet looks,
as once in May.

Each grave today has flowers, is
    fragrant,
for one day each year belongs to the dead,
come close to my heart, and so be mine
    again,
as once in May.

## *Als Luise die Briefe ihres ungetreuen Liebhabers verbrannte* | *On Louise's Burning Her Faithless Lover's Letters*

GABRIELE VON BAUMBERG

*Wolfgang Amadeus Mozart: K 520, 1787*

Erzeugt von heißer Phantasie,
In einer schwärmerischen Stunde
Zur Welt Gebrachte, geht zugrunde,
Ihr Kinder der Melancholie!

Begotten by ardent fantasy,
brought in a rapturous hour
into the world, perish,
children of melancholy!

Ihr danket Flammen euer Sein,
Ich geb euch nun den Flammen wieder,
Und all die schwärmerischen Lieder,
Denn ach! er sang nicht mir allein!

To flames you owe your being,
to flames I now restore you,
and all those rapturous songs,
for ah, not for me alone he sang!

Ihr brennet nun, und bald, ihr Lieben,
Ist keine Spur von euch mehr hier.
Doch ach! der Mann, der euch
  geschrieben,
Brennt lange noch vielleicht in mir.

Now you burn, and soon, my dears,
no trace of you will here remain.
But ah, the man who wrote
  you,
may yet long still burn in me.

## Alte Laute / Old Sounds

JUSTINUS KERNER

*Robert Schumann: op. 35, no. 12, 1840*

Hörst du den Vogel singen?
Siehst du den Blütenbaum?
Herz! kann dich das nicht bringen
Aus deinem bangen Traum?

Do you hear the bird singing?
Do you see the blossoming tree?
Heart, can that not bring you
out of your fearful dream?

Was hör ich? Alte Laute
Wehmütger Jünglingsbrust,
Der Zeit, als ich vertraute
Der Welt und ihrer Lust.

What do I hear? Old sounds
of a melancholy youthful breast,
from that time when I trusted
the world and its joy.

Die Tage sind vergangen,
Mich heilt kein Kraut der Flur;
Und aus dem Traum, dem bangen,
Weckt mich ein Engel nur.

Those days have gone,
no meadow herb will heal me;
and from the fearful dream,
only an angel will wake me.

## Alte Liebe / Old Love

KARL CANDIDUS

*Johannes Brahms: op. 72, no. 1, 1876*

Es kehrt die dunkle Schwalbe
aus fernem Land zurück,
die frommen Störche kehren
und bringen neues Glück.
An diesem Frühlingsmorgen,
so trüb' verhängt und warm
ist mir, als fänd' ich wieder
den alten Liebesharm.
Es ist, als ob mich leise
wer auf die Schulter schlug,
als ob ich säuseln hörte,
wie einer Taube Flug.
Es klopft an meine Türe,
und ist doch niemand draus;
ich atme Jasmindüfte
und habe keinen Strauß.
Es ruft mir aus der Ferne,
ein Auge sieht mich an,
ein alter Traum erfaßt mich
und führt mich seine Bahn.

The dark swallow returns
from a distant land,
the pious storks return
and bring new happiness.
On this spring morning,
so sadly veiled and warm,
I seem to rediscover
love's sorrow of old.
It is as if, gently,
my shoulder were tapped,
as though I heard a whispering
as of a dove in flight.
My door is knocked,
yet no one is outside;
scents of jasmine I breathe,
yet have no bouquet.
I am summoned from afar,
an eye is watching me,
I am seized by an old dream
and led along its way.

## Alte Liebe rostet nie | Old Love Lasts Forever

JOHANN MAYRHOFER

*Franz Schubert, 1816*

Alte Liebe rostet nie,
Hört ich oft die Mutter sagen—
Alte Liebe rostet nie,
Muß ich nun erfahrend klagen.

Wie die Luft umgibt sie mich,
Die ich einst die Meine nannte,
Die ich liebte ritterlich,
Die mich in die Ferne sandte.

Seit die Holde ich verlor,
Hab' ich Meer und Land gesehen—
Vor der schönsten Frauen Flor
Durft' ich unerschüttert stehen:

Denn aus mir ihr Bildnis trat
Zürnend wie zum Kampf mit ihnen,
Mit dem Zauber, den sie hat,
Mußte sie das Spiel gewinnen.

Da der Garten, dort das Haus,
Wo wir oft so traulich kosten!
Seh' ich recht? sie schwebt heraus—
Wird die alte Liebe rosten?

Old love lasts forever,
I often heard my mother say—
Old love lasts forever,
I must, experienced, now complain.

She is about me, as the air is,
she whom once I called my own,
whom I loved in courtly fashion,
who dispatched me to distant parts.

Ever since I lost my sweet one,
lands and oceans have I seen,
and the loveliest of women
have I gazed upon unmoved:

for from within me stepped her image,
angry, as if with them to battle,
and such is the magic she possesses,
never could she fail to win.

There the garden, there the house,
where so often we made love!
Do I see aright? She comes floating—
old love, will it last forever?


## Alte Weisen | Old Airs

GOTTFRIED KELLER

*Hans Pfitzner: op. 33, nos. 1–8, 1923*

I
Mir glänzen die Augen
Wie der Himmel so klar;
Heran und vorüber,
Du schlanker Husar!

Heran und vorüber
Und wieder zürück!
Vielleicht kann's geschehen,
Du findest dein Glück!

Was weidet dein Rapp mir
Den Reseda dort ab?
Soll das nun der Dank sein
Für die Lieb, so ich gab?

Was richten deine Sporen
Mein Spinngarn zugrund?
Was hängt mir am Hage
Deine Jacke so bunt?

I
My eyes sparkle
as bright as the sky;
come on and come by,
tall hussar!

Come on and come by
and come back again!
It may happen
that you will find joy!

Why does your black charger
crop my mignonette?
Shall that be the thanks
for the love that I gave?

Why are your spurs
ruining my yarn?
Why, on my hedge, hangs
your jacket so gay?

Troll nur dich von hinnen
Auf deinem groben Tier
Und laß meine freudigen
Sternaugen mir!

Just you go away
on that beast of yours,
and leave my joyful
starry eyes to me!

2
Ich fürcht nit Gespenster,
Keine Hexen und Feen,
Und lieb's, in ihre tiefen
Glühaugen zu sehn.

2
No ghost do I fear,
no fairy, no witch,
and love to gaze
into their deep glowing eyes.

Am Wald in dem grünen
Unheimlichen See,
Da wohnet ein Nachtweib,
Das ist weiß wie der Schnee.

By the wood, in the green
and eerie lake,
dwells a night-witch,
as white as the snow.

Es haßt meiner Schönheit
Unschuldige Zier;
Wenn ich spät noch vorbeigeh,
So zankt es mit mir.

She hates my beauty's
innocent adornment;
when I pass by late,
she rants at me.

Jüngst, als ich im Mondschein
Am Waldwasser stand,
Fuhr sie auf ohne Schleier,
Ohne alles Gewand.

A while ago, by moonlight,
as I stood by the wood-lake,
up she rose, with no veil,
with no garments at all.

Es schwammen ihre Glieder
In der taghellen Nacht;
Der Himmel war trunken
Von der höllischen Pracht.

Her limbs were bathed
in the day-bright night;
the heavens were drunk
with the hellish splendour.

Aber ich hab entblößet
Meine lebendige Brust;
Da hat sie mit Schande
Versinken gemußt!

But I laid bare
my living breast,
at which, for shame,
she was forced to sink.

3
Du milchjunger Knabe,
Was siehst du mich an?
Was haben deine Augen
Für eine Frage getan?

3
Young milk-sop,
why gaze at me?
What is the question your eyes
have asked?

Alle Ratsherrn der Stadt
Und alle Weisen der Welt
Bleiben stumm auf die Frage,
Die deine Augen gestellt!

All the town's councillors,
all the world's wise men,
remain dumb at the question
your eyes have put.

Ein leeres Schneckhäusel,
Schau, liegt dort im Gras:
Da halte dein Ohr dran,
Drin brümmelt dir was!

A snail shell
lies there, look, in the grass:
put that to your ear,
it will mutter you something!

(*Johannes Brahms: op. 86, no. 1, 1878; Hugo Wolf, 1890*)

4
Wandl ich in dem Morgentau
Durch die dufterfüllte Au,
Muß ich schämen mich so sehr
Vor den Blümlein ringsumher!

4
When I wander in the morning dew
through the scent-filled meadow,
so ashamed I'm forced to feel
by all the flowers around.

| | |
|---|---|
| Täublein auf dem Kirchendach,<br>Fischlein in dem Mühlenbach<br>Und das Schlänglein still im Kraut,<br>Alles fühlt und nennt sich Braut. | The dove on the church roof,<br>the fish in the mill stream,<br>the snake quiet in the weeds,<br>all are brides in name and feeling. |
| Apfelblüt im lichten Schein<br>Dünkt sich stolz ein Mütterlein;<br>Freudig stirbt so früh im Jahr<br>Schon das Papillonenpaar. | Apple blossom, shining bright,<br>feels proudly motherly;<br>joyous, so early in the year perish<br>the butterfly couple. |
| Gott, was hab ich denn getan,<br>Daß ich ohne Lenzgespan,<br>Ohne einen süßen Kuß<br>Ungeliebet sterben muß?<br>*(Hugo Wolf, 1890)* | God, what then have I done<br>that I, with no spring mate,<br>with not one sweet kiss,<br>must die unloved. |

5

| | |
|---|---|
| Singt mein Schatz wie ein Fink,<br>Sing ich Nachtigallensang;<br>Ist mein Liebster ein Luchs,<br>O so bin ich eine Schlang! | If my love sings like a finch,<br>my song is the nightingale's;<br>if my dearest is a lynx,<br>oh, then I'm a viper! |
| O ihr Jungfraun im Land,<br>Vom Gebirg und über See,<br>Überlaßt mir den Schönsten,<br>Sonst tut ihr mir weh! | O maidens of the land,<br>from mountain and over lake,<br>leave me the handsomest,<br>or you'll do me harm! |
| Er soll sich unterwerfen<br>Zum Ruhm uns und Preis!<br>Und er soll sich nicht rühren,<br>Nicht laut und nicht leis! | Submit he shall,<br>to our glory and praise!<br>And shall not stir,<br>either loudly or soft! |
| O ihr teuren Gespielen,<br>Überlaßt mir den stolzen Mann!<br>Er soll sehn, wie die Liebe<br>Ein feurig Schwert werden kann!<br>*(Hugo Wolf, 1890)* | O dear playfellows,<br>that proud man leave to me.<br>He shall see how love<br>can become a fiery sword! |

6

| | |
|---|---|
| Röschen biß den Apfel an,<br>Und zu ihrem Schrecken<br>Brach und blieb ein Perlenzahn<br>In dem Butzen stecken. | Rosie bit into the apple,<br>and to her horror<br>a pearly tooth broke<br>and stuck in the core. |
| Und das gute Kind vergaß<br>Seine Morgenlieder;<br>Tränen ohne Unterlaß<br>Perlten nun hernieder. | And the good child forgot<br>her morning songs;<br>tears unceasing<br>came pearling down. |

7

| | |
|---|---|
| Tretet ein, hoher Krieger,<br>Der sein Herz mir ergab!<br>Legt den purpurnen Mantel<br>Und die Goldsporen ab! | Come in, noble warrior<br>who has given me his heart.<br>Take off your purple cloak<br>and golden spurs. |
| Spannt das Roß in den Pflug,<br>Meinem Vater zum Gruß!<br>Die Schabrack mit dem Wappen<br>Gibt nen Teppich meinem Fuß! | Your charger put to the plough,<br>as a salute to my father.<br>The crested saddle-cloth<br>give as a carpet to my feet. |

Euer Schwertgriff muß lassen
Für mich Gold und Stein,
Und die blitzende Klinge
Wird ein Schüreisen sein.

Und die schneeweiße Feder
Auf dem blutroten Hut
Ist zu 'nem kühlenden Wedel
In der Sommerzeit gut.

Und der Marschalk muß lernen,
Wie man Weizenbrot backt,
Wie man Wurst und Gefüllsel
Um die Weihnachtszeit hackt!

Nun befehlt eure Seele
Dem heiligen Christ!
Euer Leib ist verkauft,
Wo kein Erlösen mehr ist!

    (*Hugo Wolf*, *1890*)

Your sword-hilt must abandon
to me its gold and stones,
and its glittering blade
shall serve as a poker.

And the snow-white plume
on your blood-red hat
as a cooling fan
in summertime will do.

And the Marshal must learn
how wheat bread is baked,
how sausage and stuffing
at Christmas is chopped.

Your soul now commend
to the Holy Saviour.
Your body is sold,
there's no redeeming it more.

8
Wie glänzt der helle Mond so kalt und
    fern,
Doch ferner schimmert meiner
    Schönheit Stern!

Wohl rauschet weit von mir des Meeres
    Strand,
Doch weiterhin liegt meiner Jugend
    Land!

Ohn Rad und Deichsel gibt's ein
    Wägelein,
Drin fahr ich bald zum Paradies
    hinein.

Dort sitzt die Mutter Gottes auf dem
    Thron,
Auf ihren Knien schläft ihr selger Sohn.

Dort sitzt Gott Vater, der den Heilgen
    Geist
Aus seiner Hand mit Himmelskörnern
    speist.

In einem Silberschleier sitz ich dann
Und schaue meine weißen Finger an.

Sankt Petrus aber gönnt sich keine
    Ruh,
Hockt vor der Tür und flickt die alten
    Schuh.

    (*Hugo Wolf*, *1890*)

8
How cold, how far off the bright moon
    gleams,
but further off glimmers my beauty's
    star!

Far from me is the sea-shore's
    roar,
but further away lies the land of my
    youth!

A small cart there is, with no wheels
    no shafts;
in it I shall soon travel to
    Paradise.

There, enthroned, God's Mother will
    sit,
her blessed Son asleep on her knee

God the Father will sit feeding the
    Holy Ghost
by hand with heavenly
    grains.

In a silver veil I shall sit then,
gazing at my white fingers.

But Saint Peter will grant himself no
    rest;
at the door he'll squat, mending his old
    shoes.

## Am Grabe Anselmos | At Anselmo's Grave

MATTHIAS CLAUDIUS

*Franz Schubert: op. 6, no. 3, 1816*

Daß ich dich verloren habe,
Daß du nicht mehr bist,
Ach! daß hier in diesem Grabe
Mein Anselmo ist,
Das ist mein Schmerz! das ist mein
   Schmerz!
Seht, wir liebten uns, wir beide,
Und solang' ich bin, kommt Freude
Niemals wieder in mein Herz.

That I should have lost you,
that you should be no more,
oh, that here, in this grave,
my Anselmo should be,
that is my grief, that is my
   grief!
Behold, we loved each other, we two,
and while I live, joy will come
no more into my heart.

## An Chloe | To Chloë

JOHANN GEORG JACOBI

*Wolfgang Amadeus Mozart: K 524, 1787*

Wenn die Lieb aus deinen blauen,
Hellen, offnen Augen sieht,
Und vor Lust hineinzuschauen
Mir's im Herzen klopft und glüht;
Und ich halte dich und küsse
Deine Rosenwangen warm,
Liebes Mädchen, und ich schließe
Zitternd dich in meinen Arm!

When love gazes from your blue,
bright, open eyes,
and with joy of gazing into them
my heart throbs and glows;
when I hold you and kiss
ardently your rosy cheeks,
dear maiden, and clasp
you trembling in my arms,

Mädchen, Mädchen, und ich drücke
Dich an meinen Busen fest,
Der im letzten Augenblicke
Sterbend nur dich von sich läßt;
Den berauschten Blick umschattet
Eine düstre Wolke mir,
Und ich sitze dann ermattet,
Aber selig neben dir.

maiden, maiden, and press
you firmly to my breast
which at the very last,
only at death, will let you go—
then is my enraptured gaze
overshadowed by a sombre cloud,
and I sit, then, weary,
but blissful, beside you.

## An den Mond | To the Moon

JOHANN WOLFGANG GOETHE

*Hans Pfitzner: op. 18, 1906; Franz Schubert, 1815;*
*Carl Friedrich Zelter, 1812*

Füllest wieder Busch und Tal
Still mit Nebelglanz,
Lösest endlich auch einmal
Meine Seele ganz;

Wood and vale again you fill
silently with gleam of mist,
and at last set free
my soul entirely;

Breitest über mein Gefild
Lindernd deinen Blick,
Wie des Freundes Auge mild
Über mein Geschick.

you spread over my domain
soothingly your gaze,
gently as a friend's eye
upon my fate.

Jeden Nachklang fühlt mein Herz
Froh' und trüber Zeit,
Wandle zwischen Freud und Schmerz
In der Einsamkeit.

Fließe, fließe, lieber Fluß!
Nimmer werd ich froh;
So verrauschte Scherz und Kuß,
Und die Treue so.

Ich besaß es doch einmal,
Was so köstlich ist!
Daß man doch zu seiner Qual
Nimmer es vergißt!

Rausche, Fluß, das Tal entlang,
Ohne Rast und Ruh,
Rausche, flüstre meinem Sang
Melodien zu,

Wenn du in der Winternacht
Wütend überschwillst,
Oder um die Frühlingspracht
Junger Knospen quillst.

Selig, wer sich vor der Welt
Ohne Haß verschließt,
Einen Freund am Busen hält
Und mit dem genießt,

Was, von Menschen nicht gewußt
Oder nicht bedacht,
Durch das Labyrinth der Brust
Wandelt in der Nacht.

My heart feels every echo
of glad and troubled times,
I walk between joy and pain
in loneliness.

Flow on, dear river!
Never shall I be glad,
love and laughter have rolled away
—and faithfulness—just so.

Once I did possess
that which is so precious!
That which, to one's torment,
is forgotten never.

Murmur on, river, through the vale,
on without cease,
on, whispering melodies
for my song,

when, on winter nights,
you rage and flood;
or you lap the spring-time glory
of young buds.

Happy he, who, without hate,
shuts himself from the world,
holding to his heart one friend,
and with him enjoys

that which, unknown to men,
or not pondered,
through the labyrinth of the heart
wanders in the night.

## An den Schlaf / To Sleep

EDUARD MÖRIKE

*Hugo Wolf, 1888*

Schlaf! süßer Schlaf! obwohl dem Tod
  wie du nichts gleicht,
Auf diesem Lager doch willkommen
  heiß ich dich!
Denn ohne Leben so, wie lieblich lebt
  es sich!
So weit vom Sterben, ach, wie stirbt
  es sich so leicht!

Sweet sleep, though naught so much
  resembles death as you,
upon this couch I still declare you
  welcome!
For lifeless thus to be, how sweet is
  living!
So far from dying, oh, how easy
  dying!

## An den Sonnenschein / To Sunshine

ROBERT REINICK

*Robert Schumann: op. 36, no. 4, 1840*

O Sonnenschein, o Sonnenschein!
Wie scheinst du mir ins Herz hinein,
Weckst drinnen lauter Liebeslust,
Daß mir so enge wird die Brust!

O sunshine, O sunshine,
how you shine into my heart,
rousing within such pure joy of love
as to oppress the breast.

| | |
|---|---|
| Und enge wird mir Stub und Haus, | Oppressive too grow room and house, |
| Und wenn ich lauf zum Tor hinaus, | and when out to the gate I run, |
| Da lockst du gar ins frische Grün | you lure even into the fresh country |
| Die allerschönsten Mädchen hin! | the fairest maidens! |

O Sonnenschein! Du glaubest wohl,
Daß ich wie du es machen soll,
Der jede schmucke Blume küßt,
Die eben nur sich dir erschließt?

O sunshine! Do you then believe
that I should do as you
who kiss each pretty flower
that opens just for you?

Hast doch so lang die Welt erblickt,
Und weißt, daß sich's für mich nicht
   schickt;
Was machst du mir denn solche Pein?
O Sonnenschein! o Sonnenschein!

So long have you beheld the world
and know: for me that is not
   seemly;
why then cause me such agony,
O sunshine! O sunshine!

## *An die ferne Geliebte* / *To the Distant Beloved*

ALOYS JEITTELES

*Ludwig van Beethoven: op. 98, nos. 1–6, 1816*

1
Auf dem Hügel sitz ich spähend
In das blaue Nebelland,
Nach den fernen Triften sehend,
Wo ich dich, Geliebte, fand.

1
On the hill I sit, gazing
into the blue haze,
towards the far meadows
where, beloved, I found you.

Weit bin ich von dir geschieden,
Trennend liegen Berg und Tal
Zwischen uns und unserm Frieden,
Unserm Glück und unsrer Qual.

Far am I parted from you,
mountain and valley intervene
between us and our peace,
our happiness and our pain.

Ach, den Blick kannst du nicht sehen,
Der zu dir so glühend eilt,
Und die Seufzer, sie verwehen
In dem Raume, der uns teilt.

Ah, you cannot see the look
that hastens so warm your way,
and sighs—they are lost
in the separating space.

Will denn nichts mehr zu dir dringen,
Nichts der Liebe Bote sein?
Singen will ich, Lieder singen,
Die dir klagen meine Pein!

Will then nothing reach you any more,
be messenger of love?
I shall sing, sing songs,
to pour out my pain to you!

Denn vor Liedesklang entweichet
Jeder Raum und jede Zeit,
Und ein liebend Herz erreichet,
Was ein liebend Herz geweiht!

For at sound of song,
time and space recede,
and a loving heart is reached
by what a loving heart has blessed.

2
Wo die Berge so blau
Aus dem nebligen Grau
Schauen herein,
Wo die Sonne verglüht,
Wo die Wolke umzieht,
Möchte ich sein!

2
Where the mountains so blue,
from the misty grey,
look hither,
where the sun's glow fades,
where sky clouds over,
there would I be!

Dort im ruhigen Tal
Schweigen Schmerzen und Qual.

There, in the peaceful valley,
pain and torment cease.

Wo im Gestein
Still die Primel dort sinnt,
Weht so leise der Wind,
Möchte ich sein!

Hin zum sinnigen Wald
Drängt mich Liebesgewalt,
Innere Pein.
Ach, mich zög's nicht von hier,
Könnt ich, Traute, bei dir
Ewiglich sein!

3
Leichte Segler in den Höhen
Und du Bächlein klein und schmal,
Könnt mein Liebchen ihr erspähen,
Grüßt sie mir viel tausendmal.

Seht, ihr Wolken, sie dann gehen
Sinnend in dem stillen Tal,
Laßt mein Bild vor ihr entstehen
In dem luftgen Himmelssaal.

Wird sie an den Büschen stehen,
Die nun herbstlich falb und kahl,
Klagt ihr, wie mir ist geschehen,
Klagt ihr, Vöglein, meine Qual.

Stille Weste, bringt im Wehen
Hin zu meiner Herzenswahl
Meine Seufzer, die vergehen
Wie der Sonne letzter Strahl.

Flüstr' ihr mein Liebesflehen,
Laß sie, Bächlein, klein und schmal,
Treu in deinen Wogen sehen
Meine Tränen ohne Zahl!

4
Diese Wolken in den Höhen,
Dieser Vöglein muntrer Zug
Werden dich, o Huldin, sehen.
Nehmt mich mit im leichten Flug!

Diese Weste werden spielen
Scherzend dir um Wang und Brust,
In den seidnen Locken wühlen.
Teilt ich mit euch diese Lust!

Hin zu dir von jenen Hügeln
Emsig dieses Bächlein eilt.
Wird ihr Bild sich in dir spiegeln,
Fließ zurück dann unverweilt!

5
Es kehret der Maien, es blühet die Au.
Die Lüfte, sie wehen so milde, so lau.
Geschwätzig die Bäche nun rinnen.
Die Schwalbe, die kehret zum
    wirtlichen Dach,

Where, in the rock,
the pensive primrose is,
and the wind blows so soft,
there would I be!

Away to the thoughtful wood
am I driven by force of love,
by inner pain.
Ah, I would not be drawn from here,
could I, beloved, but be with you
eternally!

3
Light sailing clouds on high,
and you, small brook,
if you can spy my love—
a thousand greetings to her.

If, clouds, you then see her walk,
thoughtful in the quiet valley,
make me appear to her
in heaven's airy hall.

If she be standing by bushes,
autumn yellow now and bare,
pour out to her my fate,
pour out, birds, my torment.

Quiet westwinds, carry
to my true-love
my sighs which fade
as the sun's last ray.

Whisper to her my entreaties,
let her, small brooklet,
truly see in your ripples,
my never-ending tears!

4
These clouds on high,
this cheerful flight of birds
will see you, O fairest.
Take me lightly winging too.

These westwinds playfully
will waft on cheek and breast,
will ruffle your silken tresses.
Would I might share that joy!

To you from those hills
this busy brook hurries.
Should she be mirrored in you,
flow forthwith back to me.

5
May returns, the meadow blooms.
The breezes blow so gentle, so mild.
The brooks run chattering.
The swallow returns to the hospitable
    roof,

Sie baut sich so emsig ihr bräutlich
  Gemach,
Die Liebe soll wohnen da drinnen.
Sie bringt sich geschäftig von kreuz
  und von quer
Manch weicheres Stück zu dem
  Brautbett hieher,
Manch wärmendes Stück für die
  Kleinen.
Nun wohnen die Gatten beisammen so
  treu,
Was Winter geschieden, verband nun
  der Mai,
Was liebet, das weiß er zu einen.
Es kehret der Maien, es blühet die Au.
Die Lüfte, sie wehen so milde, so lau.
Nur ich kann nicht ziehen von hinnen.
Wenn alles, was liebet, der Frühling
  vereint,
Nur unserer Liebe kein Frühling
  erscheint,
Und Tränen sind all ihr Gewinnen.

builds eagerly her bridal
  chamber,
wherein love shall dwell.
From here, from there busily she
  brings
many soft bits for the bridal
  bed,
many warm bits for the little
  ones.
Now the pair live together so
  true.
What winter has parted, May has
  joined.
All who love he can unite.
May returns, the meadow blooms,
the breezes blow so gentle, so mild.
I alone cannot journey from here.
When spring is uniting all who
  love,
for our love alone does no spring
  appear,
and tears are its only gain.

6
Nimm sie hin denn, diese Lieder,
Die ich dir, Geliebte, sang,
Singe sie dann abends wieder
Zu der Laute süßem Klang.

6
Accept, then, these songs
I sang for you, beloved;
sing them again at evening
to the lute's sweet sound.

Wenn das Dämmrungsrot dann ziehet
Nach dem stillen blauen See,
Und sein letzter Strahl verglühet
Hinter jener Bergeshöh;

As evening red draws
toward the calm blue lake,
and its last ray fades
behind that mountain height;

Und du singst, was ich gesungen,
Was mir aus der vollen Brust
Ohne Kunstgepräng erklungen,
Nur der Sehnsucht sich bewußt:

and you sing what I sang
from a full heart
without art or show,
aware only of longing;

Dann vor diesen Liedern weichet,
Was geschieden uns so weit,
Und ein liebend Herz erreichet,
Was ein liebend Herz geweiht.

then, at these songs, shall
what parts us so far, recede,
and a loving heart be reached
by what a loving heart has blessed.

## An die Freude | To Joy

FRIEDRICH SCHILLER

*Ludwig van Beethoven: Symphony, no. 9, 4th movement, op. 125;*
*Franz Schubert: op. 111, no. 1, 1815*

[O Freunde, nicht diese Töne!
Sondern laßt uns angenehmere
  anstimmen,
Und freudenvollere.]

(O friends, not these notes!
Let us rather strike up
  pleasanter
and more joyful.)

Freude, schöner Götterfunken,
Tochter aus Elysium,
Wir betreten feuertrunken,
Himmlische, dein Heiligtum.

Joy, beautiful divine spark,
daughter of Elysium,
we, in ardent rapture, enter
heavenly one, your sanctuary.

Deine Zauber binden wieder,
Was die Mode streng geteilt;
Alle Menschen werden Brüder,
Wo dein sanfter Flügel weilt.

Wem der große Wurf gelungen,
Eines Freundes Freund zu sein;
Wer ein holdes Weib errungen,
Mische seinen Jubel ein!
Ja—wer auch nur eine Seele
Sein nennt auf dem Erdenrund!
Und wer's nie gekonnt, der stehle
Weinend sich aus diesem Bund!

Freude trinken alle Wesen
An den Brüsten der Natur,
Alle Guten, alle Bösen
Folgen ihrer Rosenspur.
Küsse gab sie uns und Reben,
Einen Freund, geprüft im Tod.
Wollust ward dem Wurm gegeben,
Und der Cherub steht vor Gott.

Froh, wie seine Sonnen fliegen,
Durch des Himmels prächt'gen Plan,
Laufet, Brüder, eure Bahn,
Freudig wie ein Held zum Siegen.

Seid umschlungen, Millionen!
Diesen Kuß der ganzen Welt!
Brüder—überm Sternenzelt
Muß ein lieber Vater wohnen.

Ihr stürzt nieder, Millionen?
Ahnest du den Schöpfer, Welt?
Such ihn überm Sternenzelt,
Über Sternen muß er wohnen.

Your magic powers bind afresh
what fashion strictly has set apart;
all men become brothers
where your gentle wing does rest.

He who's had the great good fortune
to be the friend of a friend;
he who's won himself a fair lady,
let him join in and rejoice!
Yes—and he who only one soul
in the world can call his own!
And he who never could, let him
steal weeping from this company!

Joy is drunk by all living creatures
at mother nature's breast,
all the good and all the wicked
follow upon her rosy trail.
Kisses she gave to us and vines,
and a friend tried in death.
The worm was given earth's delight,
and the cherub stands before God.

Happy as the firmament's suns
flying over heaven's glorious space,
run, brothers, your course,
joyfully as heroes to victory.

Be embraced, you millions!
This kiss is for all the world!
Brothers, above the starry firmament
must a loving Father dwell.

Do you fall prostrate, millions?
Do you sense the Creator, world?
Seek him above the starry firmament,
above the stars he must dwell.

## An die Freunde | To My Friends

JOHANN MAYRHOFER

*Franz Schubert, 1819*

Im Wald, im Wald da grabt mich ein,
ganz stille, ohne Kreuz und Stein:
denn was ihr türmet, überschneit
und überrindet Winterszeit.

Und wenn die Erde sich verjüngt
und Blumen meinem Hügel bringt,
des freut Euch, Guten, freuet Euch,
dies alles ist dem Toten gleich.

Doch nein, denn Eure Liebe spannt
die Äste in das Geisterland,
und die Euch führt zu meinem Grab,
zieht mich gewaltiger herab.

In the forest, the forest, bury me,
all silently, with no cross, no stone:
for, whatever you raise high, winter
will cover with snow and ice.

And when earth grows young again,
and for my mound brings flowers,
be glad of it, good people, glad—
none of it matters to him who's dead.

But no, for your love stretches
into the land of spirits its branches,
and that which brings you to my grave,
draws me the more powerfully down.

## An die Geliebte / To the Beloved

J. L. STOLL

*Ludwig van Beethoven, 1811; Franz Schubert, 1815*

O daß ich dir vom stillen Auge
In seinem liebevollen Schein
Die Tränen von der Wange
    sauge,
Eh sie die Erde trinket ein!

Wohl hält sie zögernd auf der Wange
Und will sie heiß der Treue weihn.
Nun ich sie so im Kuß empfange,
Nun sind auch deine Schmerzen mein,
    ja mein!

Oh that from your calm eye
with its loving light
I might drink the tears from your
    cheek,
before earth drinks them!

Well they do to linger on your cheek,
warmly to hallow it to fidelity.
And as now I receive it in my kiss,
now are your sorrows mine, yes
    mine!


## An die Geliebte / To the Beloved

EDUARD MÖRIKE

*Hugo Wolf, 1888*

Wenn ich, von deinem Anschaun tief
    gestillt,
Mich stumm an deinem heilgen Wert
    vergnüge,
Dann hör ich recht die leisen Atemzüge
Des Engels, welcher sich in dir
    verhüllt,

Und ein erstaunt, ein fragend Lächeln
    quillt
Auf meinem Mund, ob mich kein
    Traum betrüge,
Daß nun in dir, zu ewiger
    Genüge,
Mein kühnster Wunsch, mein einziger,
    sich erfüllt?

Von Tiefe dann zu Tiefe stürzt mein
    Sinn,
Ich höre aus der Gottheit nächtger
    Ferne
Die Quellen des Geschicks melodisch
    rauschen.

Betäubt kehr ich den Blick nach oben
    hin,
Zum Himmel auf—da lächeln alle
    Sterne;
Ich kniee, ihrem Lichtgesang zu
    lauschen.

When, in the deep calm I feel at seeing
    you,
I take dumb pleasure in your blessed
    worth,
then truly do I hear gently breathing
the angel who within you
    dwells,

and an amazed, a questioning smile
    rises
to my lips: may not a dream it be,
    deceiving me,
now that, in you, to my eternal
    satisfaction,
my boldest, my only wish is being
    fulfilled?

Deeper, ever deeper then plunge my
    senses;
from the dark distances of Godhead I
    hear
the melodious splashing of the springs of
    fate.

Bewildered, my gaze I upwards
    turn
to heaven—where all the stars are
    smiling;
I kneel to hearken to their song of
    light.

## An die Hoffnung | To Hope

CHRISTOPH AUGUST TIEDGE: from *Urania*

Ludwig van Beethoven: op. 32, 1805

Die du so gern in heilgen Nächten
  feierst,
Und sanft und weich den Gram
  verschleierst,
Der eine zarte Seele quält,
O Hoffnung! laß durch dich
  emporgehoben,
Den Dulder ahnen, daß dort oben
Ein Engel seine Tränen zählt!

Wenn, längst verhallt, geliebte Stimmen
  schweigen;
Wenn unter ausgestorbnen Zweigen
Verödet die Erinnrung sitzt:
Dann nahe dich, wo dein Verlaßner
  trauert,
Und, von der Mitternacht umschauert,
Sich auf versunkne Urnen stützt.

Und blickt er auf, das Schicksal
  anzuklagen,
Wenn scheidend über seinen Tagen
Die letzten Strahlen untergehn:
Dann laß ihn um den Rand des
  Erdentraumes
Das Leuchten eines Wolkensaumes
Von einer nahen Sonne sehn!

You, who so gladly on hallowed nights
  hold sway,
and softly and gently veil the
  grief
which torments a tender soul,
O Hope, let, by you raised
  up,
the sufferer sense that, on high,
an angel numbers his tears!

When, long hushed, loved voices speak
  no more;
when, beneath dead branches,
memory, desolate, sits:
then approach where your forsaken one
  mourns,
and, enwrapped in midnight's awe,
supports himself against subsided urns.

And if he raise his eyes to accuse his
  fate,
when, departing upon his days,
the last rays set:
then, about the rim of this earthly
  dream,
the gleaming cloud-hem
of a near sun let him see

## An die Leier | To My Lyre

FRANZ VON BRUCHMANN: after Anacreon

Franz Schubert: op. 56, no. 2, 1822

Ich will von Atreus' Söhnen,
Von Kadmus will ich singen!
Doch meine Saiten tönen
Nur Liebe im Erklingen.

Ich tauschte um die Saiten,
Die Leier möcht ich tauschen!
Alcidens Siegesschreiten
Sollt ihrer Macht entrauschen!

Doch auch die Saiten tönen
Nur Liebe im Erklingen!
So lebt denn wohl, Heroen!
Denn meine Saiten tönen,
Statt Heldensang zu drohen,
Nur Liebe im Erklingen.

Of Atreus' sons,
of Cadmus will I sing!
But my strings sound
forth only love.

I have changed the strings,
I would gladly change the lyre!
Alcides' march of victory
should roar forth from its might!

But even those strings
sound forth only love!
So farewell, then, heroes!
For my strings,
instead of heroic song's menace,
sound forth only love.

## An die Mark / To the March of Brandenburg

ILSE VON STACH-LERNER

*Hans Pfitzner: op. 15, no. 3, 1904*

| | |
|---|---|
| Bereifte Kiefern, atemlose Seen, | Hoar-frosted pines, breathless lakes, |
| Die träumen einem dunklen Auge gleich | dreaming like dark eyes, |
| In ew'ger Sehnsucht von des Frühlings Reich; | in an eternal yearning for spring's realm; |
| Und drüber hin ein schwarzer Zug von Kräh'n. | and beyond, a black flight of crows. |
| | |
| Viel junges Leben will die Sonne sehn. | Young life in plenty wants to see the sun. |
| Da sitzt die Schwermut schon am Waldesrand | Melancholy sits at the forest edge, |
| Und schreibt geheime Zeichen in den Sand, | inscribing secret signs upon the sand, |
| Kein Frühlingssturm wird ihre Schrift verweh'n. | no spring storm will obliterate her script. |
| | |
| Und eines Tages kommt der junge Mai; | And one day young May arrives; |
| Und dennoch—unter glückverlor'nen Küssen | and yet—amidst happy, abandoned kisses |
| Lebt ein Bewußtsein, daß wir sterben müssen, | lives an awareness that we have to die, |
| Daß alles nur ein Traum und schmerzlich sei. | that all is but a dream and full of pain. |
| | |
| Dies Land, da Wunsch und Hoffnung selig sind, | This land, since desire and hope are blessed, |
| Und doch in ihrem rätselvollen Wesen | and yet, in their mysterious nature |
| Von stiller Trauer niemals zu erlösen, | never to be redeemed from silent sorrow, |
| Dies Land ist meine Heimat und ich bin sein Kind. | this land is my homeland and I am its child. |

## An die Musik / To Music

FRANZ SCHOBER

*Franz Schubert: op. 88, no. 4, 1817*

| | |
|---|---|
| Du holde Kunst, in wieviel grauen Stunden, | O kindly Art, in how many a grey hour |
| Wo mich des Lebens wilder Kreis umstrickt, | when I am caught in life's unruly round, |
| Hast du mein Herz zu warmer Lieb entzunden, | have you fired my heart with ardent love |
| Hast mich in eine beßre Welt entrückt! | and borne me to a better world! |
| | |
| Oft hat ein Seufzer, deiner Harf entflossen, | Often, has a sigh from your harp, |
| Ein süßer, heiliger Akkord von dir | a chord, sweet and holy, from you, |
| Den Himmel beßrer Zeiten mir erschlossen, | opened for me a heaven of better times; |
| Du holde Kunst, ich danke dir dafür! | O kindly Art, for that I thank you! |

## An die Nachtigall / To the Nightingale

LUDWIG CHRISTOPH HEINRICH HÖLTY

*Johannes Brahms: op. 46, no. 4, 1864; Franz Schubert: op. 172, no. 3, 1815*

Geuß nicht so laut der liebentflammten
  Lieder
Tonreichen Schall
Vom Blütenast des Apfelbaums
  hernieder,
O Nachtigall!

Du tönest mir mit deiner süßen
  Kehle
Die Liebe wach;
Denn schon durchbebt die Tiefen
  meiner Seele
Dein schmelzend »Ach«.

Dann flieht der Schlaf von neuem
  dieses Lager,
Ich starre dann
Mit nassem Blick und totenbleich und
  hager
Den Himmel an.

Fleuch, Nachtigall, in grüne
  Finsternisse,
Ins Haingesträuch,
Und spend im Nest der treuen Gattin
  Küsse,
Entfleuch, Entfleuch!

Pour not so loudly love-inflamed
  songs'
rich sounds
down from the apple's blossom
  bough,
O nightingale!

Your sweet throat
  calls
love awake in me;
for already my innermost soul
  thrills
to your melting 'Ah'.

Sleep again then flees this
  couch,
and I gaze,
moist-eyed, haggard, deathly
  pale
to heaven.

Fly, nightingale, to green dark
  places,
to the woodland thicket,
and in your nest kiss your faithful
  wife,
fly away, away!


## An die Parzen / To the Fates

FRIEDRICH HÖLDERLIN

*Wolfgang Fortner, 1933; Paul Hindemith, 1935;
Hermann Reutter: op. 56, no. 1, ed. 1944*

Nur einen Sommer gönnt, ihr
  Gewaltigen!
Und einen Herbst zu reifem Gesange
  mir,
Daß williger mein Herz, vom
  süßen
Spiele gesättiget, dann mir sterbe.

Die Seele, der im Leben ihr göttlich
  Recht
Nicht ward, sie ruht auch drunten im
  Orkus nicht;
Doch ist mir einst das Heilge, das
  am
Herzen mir liegt, das Gedicht gelungen,

Just one summer, Mighty Ones,
  grant,
and one autumn, for mellow song, to
  me,
so that more willingly my heart, of
  sweet
playing surfeited, may then die.

My soul, to which, in life, its divine
  right
did not fall, no rest shall find in Orcus
  either;
yet if once, that sacred thing that
  nearest
to my heart does lie, my verse, succeed,

Willkommen dann, o Stille der
    Schattenwelt!
Zufrieden bin ich, wenn auch mein
    Saitenspiel
Mich nicht hinabgeleitet;
    einmal
Lebt ich, wie Götter, und mehr bedarfs
    nicht.

welcome then, O silent world of
    shades!
Contented I shall be, even though my
    lyre
should not accompany me below to you;
    once
have I lived as gods live, and no more
    is called for.

## *An die Tauben* | *To the Pigeons*

MAX VON SCHENKENDORF

*Johannes Brahms: op. 63, no. 4, 1874*

Fliegt nur aus, geliebte Tauben!
Euch als Boten send' ich hin;
Sagt ihr, und sie wird euch glauben,
Daß ich krank vor Liebe bin.

Off you just fly, dear pigeons!
You as messengers I send;
tell her, she will believe you,
that I am sick for love.

Ihr könnt fliegen, ihr könnt eilen,
Tauben, froh bergab und an;
Ich muß in der Ferne weilen,
Ewig ein gequälter Mann.

You can fly, can speed
gaily, pigeons, up-hill and down;
I have to remain far off,
forever a tormented man.

Auch mein Brieflein soll noch gehen
Heut zu ihr, mein Liebesgruß,
Soll sie suchen auf den Höhen,
An dem schönen, grünen Fluß.

My letter, too, shall go
to her today, my loving greeting,
shall seek her in the high places,
by the beautiful green river.

Wird sie von den Bergen steigen
Endlich in das Niederland?
Wird sich mir die Sonne zeigen,
Die zu lange schon verschwand?

Will she come down from the hills
at last to the lowlands?
Will the sun show itself to me,
having vanished for too long?

Vögel, Briefe, Liebesboten,
Lied und Seufzer, sagt ihr's hell:
Suche ihn im Reich der Toten,
Liebchen, oder komme schnell.

Birds, letters, love's messengers,
songs and sighs, tell her clearly:
'Seek him in the realm of the dead,
my dear, or come at once.'

## *An eine Äolsharfe* | *To an Aeolian Harp*

EDUARD MÖRIKE

*Johannes Brahms: op. 19, no. 5, 1858–59; Hugo Wolf, 1888*

Angelehnt an die Efeuwand
Dieser alten Terrasse,
Du, einer luftgebornen Muse
Geheimnisvolles Saitenspiel,
Fang an,
Fange wieder an
Deine melodische Klage!

Reclining against the ivy wall
of this ancient terrace,
you, a zephyr-born muse's
mysterious lyre,
begin,
begin anew
your melodious plaint!

Ihr kommet, Winde, fernherüber,
Ach! von des Knaben,
Der mir so lieb war,
Frisch grünendem Hügel.

From afar, winds, you come,
ah, from the boy
who was so dear to me,
from his fresh green mound.

55

Und Frühlingsblüten unterwegs
  streifend,
Übersättigt mit Wohlgerüchen,
Wie süß bedrängt ihr das Herz!
Und säuselt her in die
  Saiten,
Angezogen von wohllautender Wehmut,
Wachsend im Zug meiner Sehnsucht,
Und hinsterbend wieder.

Aber auf einmal,
Wie der Wind heftiger herstößt,
Ein holder Schrei der Harfe
Wiederholt, mir zu süßem Erschrecken,
Meiner Seele plötzliche Regung;
Und hier—die volle Rose streut,
  geschüttelt,
All ihre Blätter vor meine Füße!

And brushing, on your way, spring's
  blossom,
perfume-surfeited,
how sweetly you afflict the heart!
And murmuring amongst the strings
  you come,
by harmonious melancholy drawn,
swelling, fanned by my desire,
and again dying.

But suddenly,
at a more violent gust,
from the harp a lovely cry
repeats, to my sweet dismay,
the sudden agitation of my soul;
and here—the full rose, shaken,
  strews
all her petals at my feet!

## An Mignon | To Mignon

JOHANN WOLFGANG GOETHE

*Franz Schubert: op. 19 no. 2, 1815; Carl Friedrich Zelter, 1797*

Über Tal und Fluß getragen,
Ziehet rein der Sonne Wagen.
Ach, sie regt in ihrem Lauf,
So wie deine, meine Schmerzen,
Tief im Herzen,
Immer morgens wieder auf.

Kaum will mir die Nacht noch
  frommen,
Denn die Träume selber kommen
Nun in trauriger Gestalt,
Und ich fühle dieser Schmerzen,
Still im Herzen
Heimlich bildende Gewalt.

Schon seit manchen schönen Jahren
Seh ich unten Schiffe fahren,
Jedes kommt an seinen Ort;
Aber ach, die steten Schmerzen,
Fest im Herzen
Schwimmen nicht im Strome fort.

Schön in Kleidern muß ich kommen,
Aus dem Schrank sind sie genommen,
Weil es heute Festtag ist;
Niemand ahnet, daß von Schmerzen
Herz im Herzen
Grimmig mir zerrissen ist.

Heimlich muß ich immer weinen,
Aber freundlich kann ich scheinen
Und sogar gesund und rot;
Wären tödlich diese Schmerzen
Meinem Herzen,
Ach, schon lange wär ich tot.

Carried over vale and river,
the sun chariot passes unsullied.
Ah, passing, it stirs
your agonies and mine,
deep in our hearts,
each morning ever anew.

Now night scarce avails
  me,
for dreams themselves come
now in sad guise,
and of these agonies I feel,
quiet in my heart,
the secretly growing power.

For many a year
have I seen ships sailing below,
each arriving where it should;
but ah, the constant agonies,
firm seated in my heart,
float not away on the stream.

In fine clothes must I appear,
from the wardrobe they are fetched,
because today's a holiday;
no one suspects with what agony
my innermost heart
is grimly rent.

In secret I must forever weep,
but cheerful I can seem,
even healthy and ruddy;
were these agonies fatal
to my heart
ah, I would be long since dead.

## An Schwager Kronos / To Coachman Chronos

JOHANN WOLFGANG GOETHE

*Franz Schubert: op. 19, no. 1, 1816*

Spute dich, Kronos!
Fort den rasselnden Trott!
Bergab gleitet der Weg;
Ekles Schwindeln zögert
Mir vor die Stirne dein Zaudern.
Frisch, holpert es gleich,
Über Stock und Steine den Trott
Rasch ins Leben hinein!

Nun schon wieder
Den eratmenden Schritt
Mühsam berghinauf,
Auf denn, nicht träge denn,
Strebend und hoffend hinan!

Weit, hoch, herrlich
Rings den Blick ins Leben hinein,
Vom Gebirg zum Gebirg
Schwebet der ewige Geist,
Ewigen Lebens ahndevoll.

Seitwärts des Überdachs Schatten
Zieht dich an
Und ein Frischung verheißender Blick
Auf der Schwelle des Mädchens da.
Labe dich!—Mir auch, Mädchen,
Diesen schäumenden Trank,
Diesen frischen Gesundheitsblick!

Ab denn, rascher hinab!
Sieh, die Sonne sinkt!
Eh sie sinkt, eh mich Greisen
Ergreift im Moore Nebelduft,
Entzahnte Kiefer schnattern
Und das schlotternde Gebein.

Trunknen vom letzten Strahl
Reiß mich, ein Feuermeer
Mir im schäumenden Aug,
Mich geblendeten Taumelnden
In der Hölle nächtliches Tor.

Töne, Schwager, ins Horn,
Raßle den schallenden Trab,
Daß der Orkus vernehme: wir kommen,
Daß gleich an der Tür
Der Wirt uns freundlich empfange.

Stir yourself, Chronos!
On at a rattling trot!
Downhill the way runs;
the head reels, revolts
at your dawdling.
On, heedless of bumps,
over stick, over stone, speed
on into life!

Now once more,
breathless, at a walk,
toiling uphill—
up, then, not sluggard—
striving, hoping, up!

High, wide, glorious
the view around into life,
from range to range
the eternal spirit floats,
presaging life eternal.

Aside from your career
a shady roof draws you,
and the refreshment-promising gaze
of the girl on the step.
Revive yourself! For me, too, girl,
that sparkling draught,
that bright, health-giving look!

Down, then, faster down!
See, the sun sinks!
Before it sinks, and I, an old man,
am trapped on the misty moor,
toothless jaws champing,
bones shaking,

snatch me, still drunk
with its last ray, a fiery sea
raging in my eyes,
blinded, staggering,
into hell's night gate.

Sound, coachman, your horn,
rattle resoundingly on.
Tell Orcus we're coming,
let mine host be waiting
at the door to welcome us.

## An Silvia | To Silvia

WILLIAM SHAKESPEARE: from *Two Gentlemen of Verona*
translated by EDUARD VON BAUERNFELD

*Franz Schubert: op. 106, no. 4, 1826*

Was ist Silvia, saget an,
Daß sie die weite Flur preist?
Schön und zart seh ich sie nahn,
Auf Himmelsgunst und Spur weist,
Daß ihr alles untertan.

Ist sie schön und gut dazu?
Reiz labt wie milde Kindheit;
Ihrem Aug eilt Amor zu,
Dort heilt er seine Blindheit,
Und verweilt in süßer Ruh.

Darum Silvia, tön, o Sang,
Der holden Silvia Ehren;
Jeden Reiz besiegt sie lang,
Den Erde kann gewähren:
Kränze ihr und Saitenklang!

Tell me, what is Silvia
that the wide meadow extols her?
Dainty and fair I see her coming,
a sign of heaven's favour is
that all are subject to her.

Is she fair and kind as well?
Refreshing her gentle child-like charm;
Cupid hastens to her eyes,
there cures his blindness
and tarries in sweet peace.

Therefore to Silvia, sound, O song,
to sweet Silvia's renown;
long has she won every grace
that earth can grant:
garlands bring her and sound of strings!

## Anakreons Grab | Anacreon's Grave

JOHANN WOLFGANG GOETHE

*Hugo Wolf, 1888*

Wo die Rose hier blüht, wo Reben um
    Lorbeer sich schlingen,
Wo das Turtelchen lockt, wo sich das
    Grillchen ergötzt,
Welch ein Grab ist hier, das alle Götter
    mit Leben
Schön bepflanzt und geziert? Es ist
    Anakreons Ruh.
Frühling, Sommer und Herbst genoß
    der glückliche Dichter;
Vor dem Winter hat ihn endlich der
    Hügel geschützt.

Here, where the rose blooms, where
    vine round laurel twines,
where the turtle dove calls, where
    cricket doth delight,
what grave is here, that it with life all
    gods
should plant and ornament with beauty?
    Here rests Anacreon.
Spring, summer, autumn that happy
    poet has enjoyed;
from winter, at the last, has this mound
    protected him.

## Andenken | Remembrance

FRIEDRICH MATTHISSON

*Ludwig van Beethoven, 1809; Hugo Wolf, 1877*

Ich denke dein,
wenn durch den Hain
der Nachtigallen
Akkorde schallen!
Wann denkst du mein?

I think of you
when, through the wood,
the nightingales'
chords sound forth!
When do you think of me?

Ich denke dein
im Dämmerschein
der Abendhelle
am Schattenquelle!
Wo denkst du mein?

Ich denke dein
mit süßer Pein
mit bangem Sehnen
und heißen Tränen!
Wie denkst du mein?

O denke mein,
bis zum Verein
auf besserm Sterne!
In jeder Ferne
denk' ich nur dein!

I think of you
in the twilight
of evening
by the shadowed spring!
Where do you think of me?

I think of you
in sweet agony,
with fearful longing
and passionate tears!
How do you think of me?

O think of me
until we are united
on a better star!
However far away,
I think only of you!


## *Archibald Douglas* | *Archibald Douglas*

THEODOR FONTANE

*Carl Loewe: op. 128, ed. 1858*

»Ich hab es getragen sieben Jahr
und kann es nicht tragen mehr,
wo immer die Welt am schönsten war,
mir war sie öd und leer.

Ich will hintreten vor sein Gesicht
in dieser Knechtsgestalt,
er kann meine Bitte versagen nicht,
ich bin ja worden alt.

Und trüg er noch den alten Groll,
frisch wie am ersten Tag,
so komme, was da kommen soll,
und komme, was da mag.«

Graf Douglas sprichts. Am Weg ein
    Stein
lud ihn zu harter Ruh,
er sah in Wald und Feld hinein,
die Augen fielen ihm zu.

Er trug einen Harnisch, rostig und
    schwer,
darüber ein Pilgerkleid,—
da horch, vom Waldrand scholl es her
wie von Hörnern und Jagdgeleit.

Und Kies und Staub aufwirbelte dicht,
her jagte Meut und Mann,
und ehe der Graf sich aufgericht't,
waren Roß und Reiter heran.

König Jakob saß auf hohem Roß,
Graf Douglas grüßte tief;

'I have borne it seven years,
and cannot bear it more;
the world, wherever most beautiful,
has been to me void and drear.

'Before him will I go,
clad in this vassal's guise,
my plea he cannot refuse,
for I am now grown old.

'If still the ancient grudge he bears
fresh as on that first day,
then happen what shall,
and happen what may.'

So spake Lord Douglas. A wayside
    rock
invited him to hard repose,
over field he looked and forest,
his eyes did close.

Mail he was wearing, heavy and
    rusted,
thereover, a pilgrim's coat—
when hark, from forest's edge sounds
as of bugles and a hunt.

Pebble and dust went whirling thick,
running came men and hounds,
and ere the lord has risen,
horses and riders were hard by.

King James sat on a lofty steed,
Lord Douglas bowed down low;

59

dem König das Blut in die Wange
  schoß,
der Douglas aber rief:

»König Jakob, schaue mich gnädig an
und höre mich in Geduld,
was meine Brüder dir angetan,
es war nicht meine Schuld.

Denk nicht an den alten Douglasneid,
der trotzig dich bekriegt,
denk lieber an deine Kinderzeit,
wo ich dich auf den Knien gewiegt.

Denk lieber zurück an Stirling-Schloß,
wo ich Spielzeug dir geschnitzt,
dich gehoben auf deines Vaters Roß
und Pfeile dir zugespitzt.

Denk lieber zurück an Linlithgow,
an den See und den Vogelherd,
wo ich dich fischen und jagen froh
und schwimmen und springen gelehrt.

O denk an alles, was einsten war,
und sänftige deinen Sinn—
ich hab es gebüßet sieben Jahr,
daß ich ein Douglas bin.«

»Ich seh dich nicht, Graf Archibald,
ich hör deine Stimme nicht,
mir ist, als ob ein Rauschen im Wald
von alten Zeiten spricht.

Mir klingt das Rauschen süß und traut,
ich lausch ihm immer noch,
dazwischen aber klingt es laut:
Er ist ein Douglas doch.

Ich seh dich nicht, ich höre dich nicht,
das ist alles, was ich kann—
ein Douglas vor meinem Angesicht
wär ein verlorener Mann.«

König Jakob gab seinem Roß den
  Sporn,
bergan ging jetzt sein Ritt,
Graf Douglas faßte den Zügel vorn
und hielt mit dem Könige Schritt.

Der Weg war steil, und die Sonne stach,
und sein Panzerhemd war schwer,
doch ob er schier zusammenbrach,
er lief doch nebenher.

»König Jakob, ich war dein Seneschall,
ich will es nicht fürder sein,
ich will nur warten dein Roß im Stall
und ihm schütten die Körner ein.

crimson rushed to the royal
  cheek,
Douglas, however, cried:

'Look mercifully upon me, Sire,
and in patience hear me out;
that which my brothers did to you,
it was no fault of mine.

'Think not of the Douglas envy old,
that defiant against you wars,
but rather of your childhood days
when I rocked you on my knee.

'Think rather of Stirling Castle,
where once I carved you toys,
lifted you on your father's horse,
and sharpened arrows for you.

'Think rather back to Linlithgow,
to the loch and the fowling floor,
to where I taught you to fish and hunt,
to jump and how to swim.

'Oh think of all that once has been,
And let your heart relent—
for I have atoned for seven years
that I am of Douglas kin.'

'I see you not, Lord Archibald,
your voice I cannot hear,
for me, it's as if the rustling wood
did speak of olden times.

'To me is that rustling sweet and dear,
I am listening to it still,
but ever throughout there echoes loud:
He is of Douglas kin.

'I see you not, I hear you not,
is all that I can say,
a Douglas who came within my sight—
he were as good as dead.'

King James put spur to his
  steed,
and uphill rode away,
Douglas hung on at the horse's head,
and with the king kept pace.

The way was steep, the sun burned,
his mail shirt weighed him down,
but though his body almost broke,
he still ran on beside.

'Sire, I was your seneschal,
I no longer ask to be, but only
to care for your horse in his stall,
and pour the oats for his feed.

Ich will ihm selber machen die Streu
und es tränken mit eigner Hand,
nur laß mich atmen wieder aufs neu
die Luft im Vaterland.

Und willst du nicht, so hab einen Mut,
und ich will es danken dir,
und zieh dein Schwert und triff mich
   gut
und laß mich sterben hier.«

König Jakob sprang herab vom Pferd,
hell leuchtete sein Gesicht,
aus der Scheide zog er sein breites
   Schwert,
aber fallen ließ er es nicht.

»Nimms hin, nimms hin und trag es
   neu
und bewache mir meine Ruh,
der ist in tiefster Seele treu,
wer die Heimat liebt wie du.

Zu Roß! Wir reiten nach Linlithgow,
und du reitest an meiner Seit,
da wollen wir fischen und jagen froh,
als wie in alter Zeit.«

'I myself his straw will strew,
and will water him, with my own hand,
only let me once more breathe again
the air of my native land.

'And if you won't, then be bold,
and thankful to you I'll be,
and draw your sword and strike me
   full,
and let me perish here.'

King James leapt down from his horse,
his face was shining bright,
his broadsword from its scabbard he
   drew,
but did not let it fall.

'Take it, take it, and wear it
   anew,
and guard my peace for me,
for he is loyal in heart and soul
who his homeland loves as you.

'To horse! We ride to Linlithgow,
and you ride by my side,
there shall we, happy, hunt and fish,
as in days gone by.'

## Auf das Trinkglas eines verstorbenen Freundes / To the Drinking Glass of a Departed Friend

JUSTINUS KERNER

*Robert Schumann: op. 35, no. 6, 1840*

Du herrlich Glas, nun stehst du leer,
Glas, das er oft mit Lust gehoben;
Die Spinne hat rings um dich her
Indes den düstren Flor gewoben.

Jetzt sollst du mir gefüllet sein
Mondhell mit Gold der deutschen
   Reben!
In deiner Tiefe heilgen Schein
Schau ich hinab mit frommem Beben.

Was ich erschau in deinem Grund
Ist nicht Gewöhnlichen zu nennen.
Doch wird mir klar zu dieser Stund,
Wie nichts den Freund vom Freund
   kann trennen.

Auf diesen Glauben, Glas so hold!
Trink ich dich aus mit hohem Mute.
Klar spiegelt sich der Sterne Gold,
Pokal, in deinem teuren Blute!

Glorious glass, now you are empty,
glass he raised often with delight;
around you the spider has spun
meanwhile his sombre crape.

Now shall you be filled for me
moonbright with the gold of German
   vines!
Into the sacred lustre of your depths
I gaze, devoutly trembling.

What I behold in those depths,
to ordinary mortals cannot be told.
Yet at this hour grows clear to me
how nothing can part friend from
   friend.

To that belief, then, glass so fair,
I drain you in exalted mood!
The stars' gold is clear mirrored,
goblet, in your precious blood!

61

Still geht der Mond das Tal
    entlang.
Ernst tönt die mitternächtge Stunde.
Leer steht das Glas! Der heilge Klang
Tönt nach in dem kristallnen Grunde.

Silent the moon moves through the
    vale.
Gravely sounds the midnight hour.
Empty is the glass! Those solemn tones
echo in its crystal depths.


## Auf dem Kirchhofe | At the Cemetery

DETLEV VON LILIENCRON

*Johannes Brahms: op. 105, no. 4, 1886*

Der Tag ging regenschwer und
    sturmbewegt,
Ich war an manch vergeßnem Grab
    gewesen,
Verwittert Stein und Kreuz, die
    Kränze alt,
Die Namen überwachsen, kaum zu
    lesen.

Rainy and storm-tossed passed the
    day;
by many a forgotten grave I'd
    stood—
worn stones and crosses, ancient
    wreaths,
names overgrown and hardly to be
    read.

Der Tag ging sturmbewegt und
    regenschwer,
Auf allen Gräbern fror das Wort:
    Gewesen.
Wie sturmestot die Särge
    schlummerten,
Auf allen Gräbern taute still:
    Genesen.

Storm-tossed and rainy passed the
    day;
on every grave the icy word:
    Deceased.
Dead to the storm the coffins
    slumbered,
on every grave thawed mutely now:
    Released.


## Auf dem See | On the Lake

KARL SIMROCK

*Johannes Brahms: op. 59, no. 2, 1873*

Blauer Himmel, blaue Wogen,
Rebenhügel um den See,
Drüber blauer Berge Bogen
Schimmernd weiß im reinen Schnee.

Blue sky, blue waves,
vineyards about the lake,
beyond, a blue arc of mountains,
shimmering white in the pure snow.

Wie der Kahn uns hebt und wieget,
Leichter Nebel steigt und fällt,
Süßer Himmelsfriede lieget
Über der beglänzten Welt.

As the small boat raises and rocks us,
light mist rises and falls,
sweet heavenly peace lies
over the gleaming world.

Stürmend Herz, tu auf die Augen,
Sieh umher und werde mild:
Glück und Frieden magst du saugen
Aus des Doppelhimmels Bild.

Raging heart, open your eyes,
look about and grow gentle:
peace and happiness can you drink in
from the image of double heaven.

Spiegelnd sieh die Flut erwidern
Turm und Hügel, Busch und Stadt,
Also spiegle du in Liedern,
Was die Erde Schönstes hat.

See how the water returns, mirrored,
tower and vineyard, bush and town;
and you—mirror thus in song
earth's most beautiful possessions.

## Auf dem Wasser zu singen | To Be Sung on the Water

FRIEDRICH LEOPOLD GRAF ZU STOLBERG

*Franz Schubert: op. 72, 1823*

Mitten im Schimmer der spiegelnden
  Wellen
Gleitet, wie Schwäne, der wankende
  Kahn;
Ach, auf der Freude sanftschimmernden
  Wellen
Gleitet die Seele dahin wie der Kahn;
Denn von dem Himmel herab auf die
  Wellen
Tanzet das Abendrot rund um den
  Kahn.

Über den Wipfeln des westlichen
  Haines
Winket uns freundlich der rötliche
  Schein,
Unter den Zweigen des östlichen
  Haines
Säuselt der Kalmus im rötlichen
  Schein;
Freude des Himmels und Ruhe des
  Haines
Atmet die Seel im errötenden Schein.

Ach, es entschwindet mit tauigem
  Flügel
Mir auf den wiegenden Wellen die
  Zeit.
Morgen entschwindet mit schimmerndem
  Flügel
Wieder wie gestern und heute die
  Zeit,
Bis ich auf höherem, strahlendem
  Flügel
Selber entschwinde der wechselnden
  Zeit.

Amidst the shimmer of mirroring
  waves
swan-like glides the wavering
  skiff;
ah, on joy's gently shimmering
  waves
the soul goes gliding on like the skiff;
for from heaven onto the
  waves
the evening glow dances around the
  skiff.

Over the tops of the westerly
  wood,
friendly beckons the reddish
  gleam,
beneath the branches of the easterly
  wood
the sweet-flag murmurs in the reddish
  gleam;
the joy of heaven, the peace of the
  wood
the soul inhales in the reddening gleam.

Alas, away on dewy
  wings
from me on the rocking waves flees
  time.
Tomorrow away on shimmering
  wings
as yesterday, as today, again will flee
  time,
until I upon loftier, radiant
  wings
myself shall flee the changing
  time.


## Auf der Bruck | On the Bruck

ERNST SCHULZE

*Franz Schubert: op. 93, no. 2, 1825*

Frisch trabe sonder Ruh und Rast,
Mein gutes Roß, durch Nacht und
  Regen!
Was scheust du dich vor Busch und
  Ast
Und strauchelst auf den wilden Wegen?
Dehnt auch der Wald sich tief und
  dicht,
Doch muß er endlich sich erschließen;
Und freundlich wird ein fernes Licht
Uns aus dem dunkeln Tale grüßen.

Briskly without halt or rest,
good horse, on through night and
  rain!
Why shy at bush and
  branch,
and on the wild paths stumble?
Though the wood stretch deep and
  dense,
it must come at last to an end;
and cheerfully will a distant light
welcome us from the dark valley.

Wohl könnt ich über Berg und Feld
Auf deinem schlanken Rücken fliegen
Und mich am bunten Spiel der Welt,
An holden Bildern mich vergnügen;
Manch Auge lacht mir traulich zu
Und beut mir Frieden, Lieb und
    Freude,
Und dennoch eil ich ohne Ruh,
Zurück zu meinem Leide.

Denn schon drei Tage war ich fern
Von ihr, die ewig mich gebunden;
Drei Tage waren Sonn und Stern
Und Erd und Himmel mir
    verschwunden.
Von Lust und Leiden, die mein Herz
Bei ihr bald heilten, bald zerrissen,
Fühlt ich drei Tage nur den Schmerz,
Und ach! die Freude mußt ich missen!

Weit sehn wir über Land und See
Zur wärmern Flur den Vogel fliegen;
Wie sollte denn die Liebe je
In ihrem Pfade sich betrügen?
Drum trabe mutig durch die Nacht!
Und schwinden auch die dunkeln
    Bahnen,
Der Sehnsucht helles Auge wacht,
Und sicher führt mich süßes Ahnen.

Over hill, over field well might I
fly on your slender back,
and in the pageant of the world,
and in sweet images take delight;
From many an eye I've a homely smile,
an offer of peace and love and
    joy,
and yet, without rest, I speed
back to my sorrow.

For I have been three days away
from her who holds me bound for ever,
and for those three days sun and stars
and earth and sky for me have
    vanished.
Of the joy and sorrow, which with her
now healed now rent my heart,
I've felt for three days only pain,
the joy, alas, I've had to forfeit!

Far over land and sea we watch
the bird fly to a warmer meadow;
how then should love ever be
deceived in her own course?
So bravely on then through the night!
And if the dark tracks vanish
    too,
the bright eye of longing is awake,
sweet presentiment will lead me sure.

## *Auf der Donau* / *On the Danube*

JOHANN MAYRHOFER

*Franz Schubert: op. 21, no. 1, 1817*

Auf der Wellen Spiegel schwimmt der
    Kahn,
alte Burgen ragen himmelan,
Tannenwälder rauschen geistergleich,
und das Herz im Busen wird uns weich.

Denn der Menschen Werke sinken all',
wo ist Turm, wo Pforte, wo der Wall,
wo sie selbst, die Starken,
    erzgeschirmt,
die in Krieg und Jagden hingestürmt?

Trauriges Gesträppe wuchert fort,
während frommer Sage Kraft verdorrt;
und im kleinen Kahne wird uns bang,
Wellen drohn wie Zeiten Untergang.

On the wave's mirror floats the
    boat,
heavenward old castles soar,
fir woods are astir like spirits,
and the heart turns faint within us.

For the works of men all founder;
where tower, where gate, where wall?
Where the strong men, bronze
    protected,
who into war and chase went storming?

Melancholy thickets thrive apace,
whilst force of pious saga withers;
and in our tiny boat we grow afraid,
waves threaten ruin, like the times.

## Auf der Treppe sitzen meine Öhrchen | On the Steps My Ears Sit . . .

CHRISTIAN MORGENSTERN

*Paul Hindemith: op. 18, no. 4, 1922*

Auf der Treppe sitzen meine Öhrchen,
wie zwei Kätzchen, die die Milch
erwarten . . .
Auf der Treppe sitzt mein Herz und
harret,
wie ein Geistchen, Kinn in Hand
gestützet.

Doch der Bote mit den Briefen kommt
nicht.
Taub und ohne Seele drin im Zimmer
lieg ich. Wünsche nichts zurück zu
haben.
Nicht die rosa Kätzchen, nicht das
Geistchen.

On the steps my ears sit,
like two kittens expecting
milk . . .
On the steps my heart sits
waiting,
like a tiny spirit, chin on
hand.

But the post comes not with
letters.
Deaf, dispirited in my room
I lie. Nothing do I wish
restored,
neither pink kittens, nor tiny
spirit.

## Auf ein altes Bild | Inspired by an Old Picture

EDUARD MÖRIKE

*Hugo Wolf, 1888*

In grüner Landschaft Sommerflor,
Bei kühlem Wasser, Schilf und Rohr,
Schau, wie das Knäblein sündelos
Frei spielet auf der Jungfrau Schoß!
Und dort in Walde wonnesam,
Ach, grünet schon des Kreuzes
Stamm!

In a green landscape's summer flowers,
by cool water, reeds and rushes,
see how the innocent little boy
plays freely on the Virgin's lap!
And there, in the wood, blissfully
green, the timber for the
cross!

## Auf einer Wanderung | On a Walk

EDUARD MÖRIKE

*Hugo Wolf, 1888*

In ein freundliches Städtchen tret ich
ein,
In den Straßen liegt roter Abendschein.
Aus einem offnen Fenster eben,
Über den reichsten
Blumenflor
Hinweg, hört man Goldglockentöne
schweben,
Und eine Stimme scheint ein
Nachtigallenchor,
Daß die Blüten beben,
Daß die Lüfte leben,
Daß in höherem Rot die Rosen
leuchten vor.
Lang hielt ich staunend,
lustbeklommen.
Wie ich hinaus vors Tor gekommen,

Into a pleasant little town I
step,
with streets bathed in evening light.
From an open window,
across the most sumptuous show of
flowers,
gold-clock chimes
float,
and *one* voice is a chorus of
nightingales,
so that the blooms tremble,
breezes stir,
and roses glow a heightened
red.
Long I halted, marvelling, oppressed
by joy.
How I made my way out of the town,

Ich weiß es wahrlich selber nicht.
Ach hier, wie liegt die Welt so licht!
Der Himmel wogt in purpurnem
  Gewühle,
Rückwärts die Stadt in goldnem
  Rauch;
Wie rauscht der Erlenbach, wie
  rauscht im Grund die Mühle!
Ich bin wie trunken, irrgeführt—
O Muse, du hast mein Herz berührt
Mit einem Liebeshauch.

I cannot, in truth, remember.
Oh, how bright the world here!
The sky—a purple, surging
  whirl,
behind, the town—a golden
  haze.
How the alder brook babbles, the
  valley mill roars!
I am as if drunk, as if led astray—
O Muse, you have touched my heart
with a breath of love!

## *Auf Flügeln des Gesanges* | *On Wings of Song*

HEINRICH HEINE

*Felix Mendelssohn-Bartholdy: op. 34, no. 2, 1833/34*

Auf Flügeln des Gesanges,
Herzliebchen, trag ich dich fort,
Fort nach den Fluren des Ganges,
Dort weiß ich den schönsten Ort;

On wings of song,
dearest, will I bear you away,
away to the Ganges meadows,
where I know of the nicest place.

Da liegt ein rotblühender Garten
Im stillen Mondenschein,
Die Lotosblumen erwarten
Ihr trautes Schwesterlein.

A red-blossoming garden lies there
in the quiet light of the moon,
the lotus flowers are waiting
for their own sister dear.

Die Veilchen kichern und kosen,
Und schaun nach den Sternen empor,
Heimlich erzählen die Rosen
Sich duftende Märchen ins Ohr.

The violets titter, talk fondly,
and gaze to the stars above,
the roses whisper their scented
stories into each other's ear.

Es hüpfen herbei und lauschen
Die frommen, klugen Gazelln,
Und in der Ferne rauschen
Des heilgen Stromes Welln.

Here come leaping to listen
alert and gentle gazelles,
and in the distance splashing,
the waves of the sacred stream.

Dort wollen wir niedersinken
Unter dem Palmenbaum,
Und Liebe und Ruhe trinken,
Und träumen seligen Traum.

There let us sink down
beneath the palm tree,
and drink in love and peace,
and dream a blissful dream.

## *Auflösung* | *Dissolution*

JOHANN MAYRHOFER

*Franz Schubert, 1824*

Verbirg dich, Sonne,
Denn die Gluten der Wonne
Versengen mein Gebein;
Verstummt, ihr Töne,
Frühlingsschöne, flüchte dich
Und laß mich allein!

Conceal yourself, sun,
for the fires of delight
are singeing my bones;
fall silent, you sounds;
spring beauty, flee
and leave me alone.

Quillen doch aus allen Falten
Meiner Seele liebliche Gewalten,
Die mich umschlingen,
Himmlisch singen.
Geh unter, Welt,
Und störe nimmer und nimmer
Die süßen, ätherischen Chöre.

There flow from every recess
of my soul loving powers
which embrace me,
celestially singing.
Founder, world,
and disturb never more
the sweet ethereal choirs.


## Aufträge / Messages

CHRISTIAN L'EGRU

*Robert Schumann: op. 77, no. 5, 1841–50*

Nicht so schnelle, nicht so schnelle!
Wart ein wenig, kleine Welle!
Will dir einen Auftrag geben
An die Liebste mein.
Wirst du ihr vorüberschweben,
Grüße sie mir fein!

Not so fast, not so fast!
Wait a little, tiny wave!
A message I'll give you
for my beloved.
As you glide past,
greet her fondly!

Sag, ich wäre mitgekommen,
Auf dir selbst herabgeschwommen:
Für den Gruß einen Kuß
Kühn mir zu erbitten,
Doch der Zeit Dringlichkeit
Hätt es nicht gelitten.

Say, I'd have come too,
sailing on you:
for my greeting a kiss
boldly to demand,
but urgent time
would not have suffered it.

Nicht so eilig! halt! erlaube,
Kleine, leichtbeschwingte Taube!
Habe dir was aufzutragen
An die Liebste mein!
Sollst ihr tausend Grüße sagen,
Hundert obendrein.

Not so swift, stay, allow me,
little light-winged dove.
I have a message to give you
for my beloved.
A thousand greetings give her,
and a hundred more.

Sag, ich wär mit dir geflogen,
Über Berg und Strom gezogen:
Für den Gruß einen Kuß
Kühn mir zu erbitten;
Doch der Zeit Dringlichkeit
Hätt es nicht gelitten.

Say, I'd have flown with you,
over hill and stream:
for my greeting a kiss
boldly to demand,
but urgent time
would not have suffered it.

Warte nicht, daß ich dich treibe,
O du träge Mondesscheibe!
Weißt's ja, was ich dir befohlen
Für die Liebste mein:
Durch das Fensterchen verstohlen
Grüße sie mir fein!

Wait not for me to drive you,
O laggard moon!
You know my command to you
for my beloved:
secretly, through the window,
greet her fondly!

Sag, ich wär auf dich gestiegen,
Selber zu ihr hinzufliegen:
Für den Gruß einen Kuß
Mir zu erbitten,
Du seist schuld, Ungeduld
Hätt mich nicht gelitten.

Say, I would have climbed on you
to fly to her in person:
for my greeting a kiss
to demand,
but you are to blame, your impatience
would not have suffered me to.

## Aus Heliopolis | From Heliopolis

JOHANN MAYRHOFER

*Franz Schubert: op. 65, no. 3, 1822*

Im kalten, rauhen Norden
ist Kunde mir geworden
von einer Stadt, der Sonnenstadt.
Wo weilt das Schiff, wo ist der
    Pfad,
die mich zu jenen Hallen tragen?
Von Menschen konnt' ich nichts
    erfragen,
im Zwiespalt waren sie verworren.
Zur Blume, die sich Helios
    erkoren,
die ewig, ewig in sein Antlitz
    blickt,
wandt' ich mich nun und ward
    entzückt:
Wende, so wie ich, zur Sonne
deine Augen! Dort ist Wonne,
dort ist Leben; treu ergeben
pilgre zu und zweifle nicht:
Ruhe findest du im Licht.
Licht erzeuget alle Gluten,
Hoffnungspflanzen, Tatenfluten.

In the cold, rough north
news I received
of a city, city of the sun.
Where tarries the ship, where is the
    path
to bear me to those halls?
From men I could learn
    nothing—
they were confused in discord.
To that flower, chosen by Helios for
    himself,
which for ever, for ever gazes at his
    face,
I now turned and was
    enchanted:
turn, like me, towards the sun
your eyes. There is bliss,
there is life; truly devoted,
pilgrim on towards it and do not doubt:
peace shall you find in light.
Light begets all fires,
plants of hope, floods of deeds.

## Aus meinen großen Schmerzen | From My Great Agonies

HEINRICH HEINE

*Robert Franz: op. 5, no. 1; Hugo Wolf, 1878*

Aus meinen großen Schmerzen
Mach' ich die kleinen Lieder;
Die heben ihr klingend Gefieder
Und flattern nach ihrem Herzen.

From my great agonies
I make small songs;
they raise their resonant plumage
and flutter to her heart.

Sie fanden den Weg zur Trauten,
Doch kommen sie wieder und klagen,
Und klagen, und wollen nicht sagen,
Was sie im Herzen schauten.

They've found the way to my dear one,
yet, again they come and complain,
and complain, and will not say
what they have seen in her heart.

## Ave Maria | Ave Maria

WALTER SCOTT: from *The Lady of the Lake*

*Franz Schubert: op. 52, no. 6, 1825*

Ave Maria! Jungfrau mild,
Erhöre einer Jungfrau Flehen,
Aus diesem Felsen starr und wild
Soll mein Gebet zu dir hin wehen.

Ave Maria! Virgin mild,
lend ear to a virgin's plea;
from this wild, unyielding rock
shall my prayer rise to you.

Wir schlafen sicher bis zum Morgen,
Ob Menschen noch so grausam sind.
O Jungfrau, sieh der Jungfrau Sorgen,
O Mutter, hör ein bittend Kind!

Safe till morning shall we sleep,
however cruel men may be.
O Virgin, behold a virgin's cares,
O Mother, hear a pleading child!

Ave Maria unbefleckt!
Wenn wir auf diesen Fels hinsinken
Zum Schlaf, und uns dein Schutz
  bedeckt,
Wird weich der harte Fels uns dünken.

Du lächelst, Rosendüfte wehen
In dieser dumpfen Felsenkluft.
O Mutter, höre Kindes Flehen,
O Jungfrau, eine Jungfrau ruft!

Ave Maria! Reine Magd!
Der Erde und der Luft Dämonen,
Von deines Auges Huld verjagt,
Sie können hier nicht bei uns wohnen.

Wir woll'n uns still dem Schicksal
  beugen,
Da uns dein heilger Trost anweht;
Der Jungfrau wolle hold dich neigen,
Dem Kind, das für den Vater fleht!
Ave Maria!

Ave Maria undefiled!
When down upon this rock we sink
to sleep, protected by your
  care,
soft shall seem to us the rock.

You smile, and rosy fragrance
wafts through this dark cave.
O Mother, hear a child's entreaty,
to you, O Virgin, a virgin cries!

Ave Maria! Maiden pure!
Devils of earth and air,
banished by your gaze's grace,
here with us they cannot dwell.

To fate will we quietly
  submit,
now your holy comfort is upon us.
Incline in favour to this virgin,
this child who for its father prays!
Ave Maria!


## *Barkarole* / *Barcarole*

ADOLF FRIEDRICH VON SCHACK

*Joseph Marx, 1910–17; Richard Strauss: op. 17, no. 6, 1885–87*

Um der fallenden Ruder Spitzen
zittert und leuchtet ein schimmernder
  Glanz,
flieht bei jedem Schlage mit Blitzen
hin von Wellen zu Wellen im Tanz.

Mir im Busen von Liebeswonnen
zittert und leuchtet das Herz wie die
  Flut,
jubelt hinauf zu den Sternen und
  Sonnen,
bebt zu vergeh'n in der wogenden
  Glut.

Schon auf dem Felsen durchs Grün der
  Platane
seh' ich das säulengetragene Dach,
und das flimmernde Licht am Altane
kündet mir, daß die Geliebte noch
  wach.

Fliege, mein Kahn, und birg uns
  verschwiegen,
birg uns, selige Nacht des August;
süß wohl ist's, auf den Wellen sich
  wiegen,
aber süßer, süßer an ihrer Brust.

About the tips of the dipping oars
trembles, sparkles a shimmering
  gleam,
that, at each stroke, flees, flashing
and dancing from wave to wave.

From delight of love within my breast
my heart, like the water, trembles,
  sparkles,
exulting to the stars and suns on
  high,
quivering to vanish in the billowing
  glow.

On the rock, through plane-trees'
  green,
already I see the pillared roof,
and the twinkling light on the balcony
proclaims to me my love's still
  awake.

Fly, my boat, and hide us
  discreetly,
hide us, blissful August night;
sweet it is to rock on the
  waves,
but sweeter, sweeter to lie on her breast.

## Befreit | Freed

RICHARD DEHMEL

*Richard Strauss: op. 39, no. 4, 1897–98*

Du wirst nicht weinen. Leise
wirst du lächeln und wie zur Reise
geb' ich dir Blick und Kuß zurück.
Unsre lieben vier Wände, du hast sie
   bereitet,
ich habe sie dir zur Welt
   geweitet;
o Glück!

Dann wirst du heiß meine Hände
   fassen
und wirst mir deine Seele lassen,
läßt unsern Kindern mich zurück.
Du schenktest mir dein ganzes Leben,
ich will es ihnen wieder geben;
o Glück!

Es wird sehr bald sein, wir wissen's
   beide,
wir haben einander befreit vom Leide,
so gab' ich dich der Welt zurück!
Dann wirst du mir nur noch im Traum
   erscheinen
und mich segnen und mit mir weinen;
o Glück.

You will not weep. Gently
you will smile, and as before a journey,
I shall return your look and kiss.
Our dear four walls, you prepared
   them,
I have widened them for you into a
   world;
O happiness!

Then passionately you will grasp
   my hands
and leave me your soul,
leave me behind for our children.
You have given me your whole life,
I will give it to them again;
O happiness!

It will be very soon, we both
   know;
we have freed each other from grief,
so I return you to the world!
Then you will appear to me only in
   dreams
and bless me and weep with me;
O happiness!


## Begegnung | Encounter

EDUARD MÖRIKE

*Max Reger: op. 62, no. 13, 1901; Hugo Wolf, 1888*

Was doch heut nacht ein Sturm
   gewesen,
Bis erst der Morgen sich geregt!
Wie hat der ungebetne Besen
Kamin und Gassen ausgefegt!

Da kommt ein Mädchen schon die
   Straßen,
Das halb verschüchtert um sich sieht;
Wie Rosen, die der Wind zerblasen,
So unstet ihr Gesichtchen glüht.

Ein schöner Bursch tritt ihr entgegen,
Er will ihr voll Entzücken nahn:
Wie sehn sich freudig und verlegen
Die ungewohnten Schelme an!

Er scheint zu fragen, ob das Liebchen
Die Zöpfe schon zurecht gemacht,
Die heute nacht im offnen Stübchen
Ein Sturm in Unordnung gebracht.

What a storm there was last
   night,
raged until this morning!
How that uninvited brush has
swept the streets and chimneys clean!

Along the street a girl
   comes,
glancing about her, half-afraid,
like roses tossed before the wind,
ever changing is her face's glow.

A handsome lad steps to meet her,
would delightedly approach her:
oh, the joy and embarrassment
in those novice rascals' looks!

He seems to ask if his beloved
has put straight her plaits
which, last night, in her open bedroom,
were tousled by a storm.

Der Bursche träumt noch von den
  Küssen,
Die ihm das süße Kind getauscht,
Er steht, von Anmut hingerissen,
Derweil sie um die Ecke rauscht.

The lad's still dreaming of the
  kisses
which that sweet child exchanged,
and stands, captive to her charm,
while she whisks around the corner.

## Beherzigung / Reflection

JOHANN WOLFGANG GOETHE

*Hugo Wolf, 1888; Winfried Zillig, ed. 1960*

Ach, was soll der Mensch verlangen?
Ist es besser, ruhig bleiben?
Klammernd fest sich anzuhangen?
Ist es besser, sich zu treiben?

Ah, what is man to desire?
Is it better to stay quiet?
To hang on, clasping tight?
Is it better to press on?

Soll er sich ein Häuschen bauen?
Soll er unter Zelten leben?
Soll er auf die Felsen trauen?
Selbst die festen Felsen beben.

Is he to build himself a house?
Is he to live in tents?
Is he to rely upon rocks?
Even firm rocks tremble.

Eines schickt sich nicht für alle!
Sehe jeder, wie er's treibe,
Sehe jeder, wo er bleibe,
Und wer steht, daß er nicht falle!

One thing will not suit for all!
Let each see how he shall do it,
let each see where he shall stay,
and he who stands, that he not fall!

## Beherzigung / Reflection

JOHANN WOLFGANG GOETHE: from *Lila*

*Johann Friedrich Reichardt; Hugo Wolf, 1887*

Feiger Gedanken
Bängliches Schwanken,
Weibisches Zagen,
Ängstliches Klagen
Wendet kein Elend,
Macht dich nicht frei.

Cowardly thoughts'
fearful wavering,
womanish hesitancy,
anxious complaining
wards off no misery,
won't make you free.

Allen Gewalten
Zum Trutz sich erhalten;
Nimmer sich beugen,
Kräftig sich zeigen,
Rufet die Arme
Der Götter herbei.

In face of all forces
maintaining defiance,
yielding never,
showing oneself strong—
summons the arms
of the gods to one's side.

## Bei einer Trauung / At a Wedding

EDUARD MÖRIKE

*Hugo Wolf, 1888*

Vor lauter hochadligen Zeugen
Kopuliert man ihrer zwei;
Die Orgel hängt voll Geigen,
Der Himmel nicht, mein Treu!

With none but aristocratic witnesses,
the two of them are being wed.
The organ proclaims all to be fine,
but nothing else does!

Seht doch! sie weint ja greulich,
Er macht ein Gesicht abscheulich!
Denn leider freilich, freilich,
Keine Lieb ist nicht dabei.

Just look: she—crying her eyes out,
he—making a dreadful face!
For, I'm very, very much afraid,
that here, love is lacking.

## Beim Winde | In Wind

JOHANN MAYRHOFER

*Franz Schubert, 1819*

Es träumen die Wolken, die Sterne, der
   Mond,
die Bäume, die Vögel, die Blumen, der
   Strom,
sie wiegen und schmiegen sich tiefer
   zurück,
zur ruhigen Stätte, zum tauigen Bette,
   zum heimlichen Glück.

They dream—the clouds, the stars, the
   moon,
the trees, the birds, the flowers, the
   stream,
stirring and nestling deeper
   down
in a peaceful place, in a dewy bed, in
   secret joy.

Doch Blättergesäusel und Wellen-
   gekräusel verkünden Erwachen;
denn ewig geschwinde, unruhige Winde,
   sie stöhnen, sie fachen
erst schmeichelnde Regung, dann wilde
   Bewegung;
und dehnende Räume verschlingen die
   Träume.
Im Busen, im reinen, bewahre die
   Deinen;
es ströme dein Blut,
vor rasenden Stürmen besonnen zu
   schirmen
die heilige Glut.

But rustling leaves and rippling waves
   announce awakening;
for eternally swift, restless winds—they
   groan, they fan
first flattering movement, then violent
   motion;
and widening spaces swallow the
   dreams.
Your own—safeguard in your pure
   heart;
let flow your blood
to protect prudently against raging
   storms
their sacred glow.

## Belsazar | Belshazzar

HEINRICH HEINE

*Robert Schumann: op. 57, 1840*

Die Mitternacht zog näher schon;
In stummer Ruh' lag Babylon.

Midnight drew near;
Babylon lay silent and at rest.

Nur oben in des Königs Schloß,
Da flackert's, da lärmt des Königs Troß.

But above, at the king's palace,
lights flare, the king's followers roister.

Dort oben in dem Königssaal
Belsazar hielt sein Königsmahl.

Above, in the king's hall,
Belshazzar holds kingly banquet.

Die Knechte saßen in schimmernden
   Reihn,
Und leerten die Becher mit funkelndem
   Wein.

In gleaming rows the lords
   sat,
draining goblets of sparkling
   wine.

Es klirrten die Becher, es jauchzten die
   Knecht';
So klang es dem störrigen Könige
   recht.

The goblets clashed, the lords made
   merry,
noise pleasing to that obdurate
   king.

Des Königs Wangen leuchten Glut;
Im Wein erwuchs ihm kecker Mut.

Und blindlings reißt der Mut ihn
    fort;
Und er lästert die Gottheit mit
    sündigem Wort.

Und er brüstet sich frech, und lästert
    wild;
Die Knechtenschar ihm Beifall brüllt.

Der König rief mit stolzem Blick;
Der Diener eilt und kehrt zurück.

Er trug viel gülden Gerät auf dem
    Haupt;
Das war aus dem Tempel Jehovas
    geraubt.

Und der König ergriff mit frevler
    Hand
Einen heiligen Becher, gefüllt bis am
    Rand.

Und er leert ihn hastig bis auf den
    Grund
Und rufet laut mit schäumendem
    Mund:

Jehova! dir künd' ich auf ewig
    Hohn—
Ich bin der König von Babylon!

Doch kaum das grause Wort
    verklang,
Dem König ward's heimlich im Busen
    bang.

Das gellende Lachen verstummte zumal;
Es wurde leichenstill im Saal.

Und sieh! und sieh! an weißer Wand
Da kam's hervor wie Menschenhand;

Und schrieb und schrieb an weißer
    Wand
Buchstaben von Feuer, und schrieb
    und schwand.

Der König stieren Blicks da saß,
Mit schlotternden Knien und totenblaß.

Die Knechtenschar saß kalt
    durchgraut,
Und saß gar still, gab keinen Laut.

Die Magier kamen, doch keiner verstand
Zu deuten die Flammenschrift an der
    Wand.

Belsazar ward aber in selbiger Nacht
Von seinen Knechten umgebracht.

The king's cheeks blazed,
his boldness, with wine, increased.

And blindly his feelings whirl him
    away,
wickedly he blasphemes
    God.

And boldly he brags and wildly
    blasphemes;
the lords roar their applause.

The king called with haughty mien;
the serving man runs and returns.

On his head many golden vessels he
    bore,
plundered from Jehovah's
    temple.

And the king with impious hand did
    seize
a sacred goblet filled to the
    brim.

And hastily he drinks it
    dry,
and with foaming mouth, loudly
    cries:

'Jehovah! To you I proclaim eternal
    scorn—
I am the king of Babylon!'

Yet scarce had those dread words died
    away,
than the king felt secret fear in his
    heart.

The ringing laughter faded at once;
the hall grew deathly still.

And behold, behold, on the white wall
appeared the likeness of a human hand;

and on the white wall wrote and
    wrote
letters of fire, and wrote, and was
    gone.

Staring the king sat there,
trembling at knee, and pale as death.

The lords in icy horror
    sat,
and did not stir, and gave no sound.

Magicians came, but none was able
to read the fiery letters on the
    wall.

But Belshazzar, that very night,
was done to death by his lords.

## Biterolf | Biterolf

JOSEF VICTOR VON SCHEFFEL

*Hugo Wolf, 1886*

Kampfmüd' und sonnverbrannt,
fern an der Heiden Strand,
waldgrünes Thüringland
denk' ich an Dich.

Mildklarer Sternenschein,
du sollst mir Bote sein,
geh, grüß' die Heimat mein,
weit über'm Meer!

Feinden von allerwärts
trotzt meiner Waffen Erz;
wider der Sehnsucht Schmerz
schirmt mich kein Schild.

Doch wie das Herz auch klagt,
ausharr' ich unverzagt:
Wer Gottes Fahrt gewagt,
trägt still sein Kreuz.

Fight-weary, burnt by sun,
far away on the heathen shore,
forest-green Thuringia,
I think of you.

Starlight, gentle, clear,
you shall be my envoy,
go and greet my homeland
far across the sea.

Enemies from all sides
my weapons' bronze defies;
against my longing's pain
no shield protects me.

Yet however my heart complain,
undismayed I endure:
who has dared God's crusade,
bears silently his cross.

## Blicke mir nicht in die Lieder | Look Not into My Songs

FRIEDRICH RÜCKERT

*Gustav Mahler, ed. 1905*

Blicke mir nicht in die Lieder!
Meine Augen schlag' ich nieder,
Wie ertappt auf böser Tat;
Selber darf ich nicht getrauen,
Ihrem Wachsen zuzuschauen:
Deine Neugier ist Verrat.

Bienen, wenn sie Zellen bauen,
Lassen auch nicht zu sich schauen,
Schauen selber auch nicht zu.
Wenn die reifen Honigwaben
Sie zu Tag gefördert haben,
Dann vor allem nasche du!

Look not into my songs!
My eyes I lower,
as if caught doing wrong;
I cannot trust myself
to watch their growth:
your curiosity is treachery.

Bees, when they build their cells,
let no one watch either,
and do not themselves.
When the full honey-combs
they bring to light of day,
then you can nibble!

## Blindenklage | Blind Man's Lament

KARL HENCKELL

*Richard Strauss: op. 56, no. 2, 1903–06*

Wenn ich dich frage, dem das Leben
  blüht:
O sage mir, sage wie das Mohnfeld
  glüht!
Das rote Mohnfeld, wie es jauchzt und
  lacht:
Tot ist mein Pfad und ewig meine
  Nacht.

When I question you, for whom life
  blooms,
O tell me how the field of poppies
  glows!
The field of red, how it exults and
  laughs:
dead is my path, everlasting is my
  night.

Wohl manch ein Unglück schlägt den
  Menschen schwer;
Wer so viel trägt, kennt keinen Jammer
  mehr.
Die sonnenhellen Fluren wankt er
  blind
Und tappt nach Spuren, die verschüttet
  sind.

Ich träume Sonnen, strecke weit die
  Hand,
Ich möchte greifen durch die dunkle
  Wand,
Ich möchte fassen durch der Schatten
  Schicht
In roten Mohn und strahlend goldnes
  Licht.

Aus alten Zeiten zuckt ein Schimmer
  nach,
In toten Augen blieb die Sehnsucht
  wach
Und wissend von der Herrlichkeit des
  Lichts.
So ganz enterbt geh ich durch Nacht
  und Nichts.

Ob Freud, ob Leid begegnet meinen
  Wegen,
Tot ist mein Fluch, und tot ist auch
  mein Segen.

Many a blow there is that strikes man
  hard;
who bears so much, no longer knows
  distress.
Through sunbright meadows he totters
  blind,
gropes after traces buried under
  earth.

I dream of suns, stretch out my
  hand,
would like to reach through the dark
  wall,
reach through the layer of
  shadows,
into red poppies and streaming golden
  light.

From times past still a flicker
  stirs,
a longing watches still in my dead
  eyes.
And knowing of the glory of the
  light,
thus disinherited, I walk in night and
  nothing.

Whether joy or sorrow befall me on my
  ways,
dead is my curse, and dead too is my
  blessing.

## Blume und Duft / Flower and Scent

FRIEDRICH HEBBEL

*Franz Liszt, ca. 1860*

In Frühlings Heiligtume,
Wenn dir ein Duft ans Tiefste rührt,
Da suche nicht die Blume,
Der ihn ein Hauch entführt.

Der Duft läßt Ewges ahnen,
Von unbegrenztem Leben voll;
Die Blume kann nur mahnen,
Wie schnell sie welken soll.

In the sanctuary of spring,
if some scent move you deeply,
search not for the flower
from which some breath has borne it.

Scent is a foretaste of the eternal,
full of unbounded life;
the flower can but remind
how quickly it shall fade.

## Blumengruß / Flower Greeting

JOHANN WOLFGANG GOETHE

*Paul Graener: op. 94, no. 1, ed. 1932; Armin Knab, 1924–46;
Johann Friedrich Reichardt, 1809; Hugo Wolf, 1888; Carl Friedrich Zelter, 1810*

Der Strauß, den ich gepflücket,
Grüße dich vieltausendmal!
Ich habe mich oft gebücket,
Ach, wohl eintausendmal,
Und ihn ans Herz gedrücket
Wie hunderttausendmal!

May the bouquet I have plucked
greet you many thousands of times!
I have bent often—
ah, at least a thousand times,
and pressed it to my heart
something like a hundred thousand!

## Botschaft | Message

GEORG FRIEDRICH DAUMER: after Hafiz

*Johannes Brahms: op. 47, no. 1, 1868*

| | |
|---|---|
| Wehe, Lüftchen, lind und lieblich | Blow, breeze, gentle and loving |
| Um die Wange der Geliebten, | about the cheek of my beloved, |
| Spiele zart in ihrer Locke, | play tenderly in her locks, |
| Eile nicht hinwegzufliehn! | be not swift to fly away. |
| | |
| Tut sie dann vielleicht die Frage, | If then she should ask |
| Wie es um mich Armen stehe; | how things are with poor me, |
| Sprich: »Unendlich war sein Wehe, | say: 'Infinite has been his woe, |
| Höchst bedenklich seine Lage; | most critical his state; |
| | |
| Aber jetzo kann er hoffen, | but now he can hope |
| Wieder herrlich aufzuleben, | gloriously to revive, |
| Denn du, Holde, | for you, sweet one, |
| Denkst an ihn.« | are thinking of him.' |

## Breit über mein Haupt | Spread over My Head

ADOLF FRIEDRICH VON SCHACK

*Richard Strauss: op. 19, no. 2, 1885-88*

| | |
|---|---|
| Breit über mein Haupt dein schwarzes Haar, | Spread over my head your black hair, |
| Neig zu mir dein Angesicht, | lower to me your face, |
| Da strömt in die Seele so hell und klar | then into my soul so clear and bright |
| Mir deiner Augen Licht. | the light of your eyes will stream. |
| | |
| Ich will nicht droben der Sonne Pracht, | I want not the glory of the sun above, |
| Noch der Sterne leuchtenden Kranz, | nor the gleaming crown of stars, |
| Ich will nur deiner Locken Nacht | only the night of your locks do I want |
| Und deiner Blicke Glanz. | and the radiance of your looks. |

## Bruder Liederlich | Brother Dissolute

DETLEV VON LILIENCRON

*Richard Strauss: op. 41, no. 4, 1899*

| | |
|---|---|
| Die Feder am Strohhut in Spiel und Gefahren, Halli. | On my straw hat, a feather, in play and in peril, |
| Nie lernt' ich im Leben fasten, noch sparen, Hallo. | Never in my life have I learnt to fast or save, hallo. |
| Der Dirne laß ich die Wege nicht frei, | I don't stand aside for girls on paths, |
| Wo Männer sich raufen, da bin ich dabei, | where men are brawling, I am there, |
| Und wo sie saufen, da sauf ich für drei. | where men are drinking, I drink for three, |
| Halli und Hallo. | halli and hallo. |

76

Verdammt, es blieb mir ein Mädchen
   hängen,
Halli.
Ich kann sie mir nicht aus dem Herzen
   zwängen,
Hallo.
Ich glaube, sie war erst sechzehn Jahr,
Trug rote Bänder im schwarzen Haar
Und plauderte wie der lustigste Star.
Halli und Hallo.

Was hatte das Mädel zwei frische
   Backen,
Halli.
Krach, konnten die Zähne die Haselnuß
   knacken,
Hallo.
Sie hat mir das Zimmer mit Blumen
   geschmückt,
Die wir auf heimlichen Wegen gepflückt;
Wie hab ich dafür ans Herz sie gedrückt!
Halli und Hallo.

Ich schenkt ihr ein Kleidchen von
   gelber Seiden,
Halli.
Sie sagte, sie möcht mich unsäglich
   gern leiden,
Hallo.
Und als ich die Taschen ihr vollgesteckt
Mit Pralinés, Feigen und feinem
   Konfekt,
Da hat sie von morgens bis abends
   geschleckt.
Halli und Hallo.

Wir haben süperb uns die Zeit
   vertrieben,
Halli.
Ich wollte, wir wären zusammen
   geblieben,
Hallo.
Doch wurde die Sache mir stark
   ennuyant,
Ich sagt' ihr, daß mich die Regierung
   ernannt,
Kamele zu kaufen in Samarkand.
Halli und Hallo.

Und als ich zum Abschied die Hand
   gab der Kleinen,
Halli.
Da fing sie bitterlich an zu weinen,
Hallo.
Was denk ich just heut ohn Unterlaß,
Daß ich ihr so rauh gab den
   Reisepaß . . .
Wein her, zum Henker, und da liegt
   Trumpf As!
Halli und Hallo.

Damn, I once got stuck with a
   girl,
halli.
My heart I cannot free of
   her,
hallo.
Only sixteen she was, I think,
wore red ribbons in her black hair
and chattered like the merriest starling.
Halli and hallo.

What fine fresh cheeks she had, that
   girl,
halli.
Crack! How her teeth broke
   hazelnuts,
hallo.
My room she decked out with
   flowers
which we picked on secret paths;
how I pressed her to my heart for it!
Halli and hallo.

I gave her a dress of yellow
   silk,
halli.
She said she cared for me most
   terribly,
hallo.
And when I stuffed her pockets full
of pralines, figs and choice
   sweets,
she kissed and crunched from morn till
   night.
Halli and hallo.

Superbly we whiled away our
   time,
halli.
I would that we had stayed
   together,
hallo.
But the thing became a dreadful
   bore,
I'd been named, I told her, by the
   government
to sell camels in Samarkand.
Halli and hallo.

And when I gave her my hand in
   farewell,
halli.
The little girl wept bitterly,
hallo.
And what I keep thinking even today
is how rudely I gave her her marching
   orders . . .
Oh, hell, bring wine, and there's the ace
   of trumps!
Halli and hallo.

## Cäcilie | Cecily

HEINRICH HART

*Richard Strauss: op. 27, no. 2, 1893-94*

Wenn du es wüßtest,
Was träumen heißt von brennenden
    Küssen,
Von Wandern und Ruhen mit der
    Geliebten,
Aug in Auge,
Und kosend und plaudernd,
Wenn du es wüßtest,
Du neigtest dein Herz!

Wenn du es wüßtest,
Was bangen heißt in einsamen Nächten,
Umschauert vom Sturm, da niemand
    tröstet
Milden Mundes die kampfmüde Seele,
Wenn du es wüßtest,
Du kämest zu mir.

Wenn du es wüßtest,
Was leben heißt, umhaucht von der
    Gottheit
Weltschaffendem Atem,
Zu schweben empor, lichtgetragen,
Zu seligen Höhn,
Wenn du es wüßtest,
Du lebtest mit mir!

If you knew
what it is to dream of burning
    kisses,
of wandering, resting with one's
    love,
gazing at each other,
and caressing and talking,
if you knew,
you would incline your heart!

If you knew
what fear is on lonely nights,
in the awesome storm, when no one
    comforts
with soft voice the struggle-weary soul,
if you knew,
you would come to me.

If you knew
what it is to live enveloped in
    God's
world-creating breath,
to float upwards, borne on light,
to blissful heights,
if you knew,
you would live with me!


## Da fahr' ich still im Wagen | Silent I Ride in the Coach

JOSEPH VON EICHENDORFF

*Hugo Wolf, 1881*

Da fahr' ich still im Wagen,
Du bist so weit von mir,
Wohin er mich mag tragen,
Ich bleibe doch bei dir.

Da fliegen Wälder, Klüfte
Und schöne Täler tief,
Und Lerchen hoch in den Lüften,
Als ob dein' Stimme rief'.

Die Sonne lustig scheinet
Weit über das Revier,
Ich bin so froh verweinet
Und singe still in mir.

Vom Berge geht's hinunter,
Das Posthorn schallt im Grund,
Mein' Seel' wird mir so munter,
Grüß' dich aus Herzensgrund.

Silent I ride in the coach,
you are so far from me,
wherever it may bear me,
I shall remain with you.

Woods, gorges fly by,
and valleys lovely and deep,
and larks high in the air,
as if your voice were calling.

The sun shines merrily
far and wide,
tear-stained and so happy,
I sing silently within.

Downhill the way goes,
the posthorn sounds below,
my soul grows so happy,
I greet you from my heart.

## Dämmrung senkte sich von oben | Dusk Has Fallen from on High

JOHANN WOLFGANG GOETHE

*Johannes Brahms: op. 59, no. 1, 1870–71; Othmar Schoeck: op. 19a, no. 2, 1909–14*

Dämmrung senkte sich von oben,
Schon ist alle Nähe fern,
Doch zuerst emporgehoben
Holden Lichts der Abendstern.
Alles schwankt ins Ungewisse,
Nebel schleichen in die Höh,
Schwarzvertiefte Finsternisse
Widerspiegelnd ruht der See.

Nun am östlichen Bereiche
Ahn ich Mondenglanz und Glut,
Schlanker Weiden Haargezweige
Scherzen auf der nächsten Flut.
Durch bewegter Schatten Spiele
Zittert Lunas Zauberschein,
Und durchs Auge schleicht die Kühle
Sänftigend ins Herz hinein.

Dusk has fallen from on high,
already all nearby is distant,
but, first raised up,
shining sweetly, the evening star.
All falters into indistinctness,
stealthily the mists ascend;
mirroring black-deepened gloom,
the lake reposes.

Now, in the easterly reaches,
gleam and glow of moon I sense,
branchy hair of slender willows
sports upon the nearest water.
Across the play of agitated shadows
trembles Luna's magic light,
and through the eye coolness steals
softeningly into the heart.


## Dans un bois | In a Dark and Lonely Wood

ANTOINE FERRAND

*Wolfgang Amadeus Mozart: K 308, 1777?*

Dans un bois solitaire et sombre
Je me promenais l'autr' jour,
Un enfant y dormait à l'ombre,
C'était le redoutable Amour.

J'approche, sa beauté me flatte,
Mais je devais m'en défier;
Il avait les traits d'une ingrate,
Que j'avais juré d'oublier.

Il avait la bouche vermeille,
Le teint aussi frais que le sien,
Un soupir m'échappe, il s'éveille;
L'Amour se réveille de rien.

Aussitôt déployant ses ailes et saisissant
Son arc vengeur,
L'une de ses flèches, cruelles en partant,
Il me blesse au cœur.

Va! va, dit-il, aux pieds de Sylvie,
De nouveau languir et brûler!
Tu l'aimeras toute la vie,
Pour avoir osé m'éveiller.

In a dark and lonely wood
I walked, a while ago,
in its shade slept a child,
the formidable Cupid.

I approach, his beauty pleases,
but I had to be wary;
his were the traits of a faithless maid
whom I'd sworn to forget.

His lips were ruby,
his complexion fresh as hers,
a sigh escapes me, he wakes;
Cupid wakes at anything.

Opening his wings and seizing,
as he goes, his vengeful bow
and one of his cruel shafts,
he wounds me to the heart.

'Go,' he said, 'at Sylvie's feet
to languish and to burn anew!
For life shall you love her,
for daring to wake me.'

79

## Das Blümchen Wunderhold | The Flower Wondrous Kind

GOTTFRIED AUGUST BÜRGER

*Ludwig van Beethoven: op. 52, no. 8, 1793*

Es blüht ein Blümchen irgendwo
In einem stillen Tal.
Das schmeichelt Aug' und Herz so froh
Wie Abendsonnenstrahl.
Das ist viel köstlicher als Gold,
Als Perl' und Diamant.
Drum wird es «Blümchen
    Wunderhold»
Mit gutem Fug genannt.

Wohl sänge sich ein langes Lied
Von meines Blümchens Kraft;
Wie es am Leib' und am Gemüt
So hohe Wunder schafft.
Was kein geheimes Elixier
Dir sonst gewähren kann,
Das leistet traun! mein Blümchen dir.
Man säh' es ihm nicht an.

Wer Wunderhold im Busen
    hegt,
Wird wie ein Engel schön.
Das hab' ich, inniglich bewegt,
An Mann und Weib gesehn.
An Mann und Weib, alt oder jung,
Zieht's, wie ein Talisman,
Der schönsten Seelen Huldigung
Unwiderstehlich an.

Auf steifem Hals ein Strotzerhaupt,
Dess' Wangen hoch sich bläh'n,
Dess' Nase nur nach Äther schnaubt,
Läßt doch gewiß nicht schön.
Wenn irgend nun ein Rang, wenn Gold
Zu steif den Hals dir gab,
So schmeidigt ihn mein Wunderhold
Und biegt dein Haupt herab.

Es webet über dein Gesicht
Der Anmut Rosenflor;
Und zieht des Auges grellem Licht
Die Wimper mildernd vor.
Es teilt der Flöte weichen Klang
Des Schreiers Kehle mit,
Und wandelt in Zephyrengang
Des Stürmers Poltertritt.

Der Laute gleicht des Menschen Herz,
Zu Sang und Klang gebaut,
Doch spielen sie oft Lust und Schmerz
Zu stürmisch und zu laut:
Der Schmerz, wann Ehre, Macht und
    Gold
Vor deinen Wünschen fliehn,
Und Lust, wann sie in deinen Sold
Mit Siegeskränzen ziehn.

Somewhere a flower blooms
in a quiet valley.
Eye and heart it flatters so gaily,
as evening sunshine.
More precious it is than gold,
than pearl or diamond.
For which, it's justly
    called
'Flower Wondrous Kind'.

A long song could I sing
of my dear flower's virtue;
of how, on body and mind,
such great wonders it performs.
What no secret elixir
can grant you,
my flower will, forsooth.
One wouldn't believe it of it.

Who nurses Wondrous Kind to his
    breast,
grows fair as an angel.
As I, deeply moved, have seen
with man and woman.
In man and woman, young and old,
it attracts, like a talisman,
from the loveliest of souls, homage
irresistibly.

A rigid neck topped by a swollen head,
whose cheeks puff out,
whose nose sniffs only for the upper air,
is certainly unbecoming.
But if rank or gold, it is,
have made your neck too stiff,
my Wondrous Kind will make it supple,
and bow down your head.

Over your face it will waft
grace in rose abundance;
and on the eye's harsh light
lower moderating lashes.
The flute's soft tone it will impart
to the ranter's throat,
and into zephyr steps transform
the hothead's thundering feet.

The heart of man is like the lute,
made for sound and song,
but often it's played by joy and pain
too stormily and loud:
by pain, when honour, power and
    gold
take flight from your desires;
by joy, when they into your pay
in victory's crowns come marching.

O wie dann Wunderhold das
   Herz
So mild und lieblich stimmt!
Wie allgefällig Ernst und Scherz
In seinem Zauber schwimmt!
Wie man alsdann nichts tut und spricht,
Drob jemand zürnen kann!
Das macht, man trotzt und strotzet
   nicht
Und drängt sich nicht voran.

Oh, how then does Wondrous Kind
   the heart
so mild and loving make!
How pleasantly earnestness and jest
upon its magic ride!
How then one nothing says and does
at which anyone could rage!
Wherefore one does not sulk or
   strut
or force oneself in front.

O wie man dann so wohlgemut,
So friedlich lebt und webt!
Wie um das Lager, wo man ruht,
Der Schlaf so segnend schwebt!
Denn Wunderhold hält alles fern,
Was giftig beißt und sticht;
Und stäch' ein Molch auch noch so
   gern,
So kann und kann er nicht.

Oh, how joyously, how peacefully
does one then live and move!
How by the couch, whereon one rests,
does sleep, with such blessing, hover!
For Wondrous Kind keeps distant
all that with venom bites and stings;
and a monster, hard as it may
   try,
cannot, cannot hurt.

Ich sing', o Lieber, glaub' es mir,
Nichts aus der Fabelwelt,
Wenn gleich ein solches Wunder dir
Fast hart zu glauben fällt.
Mein Lied ist nur ein Widerschein
Der Himmelslieblichkeit,
Die Wunderhold auf Groß und Klein
In Tun und Wesen streut.

What I sing, believe, dear man,
is nothing from the world of fable,
even though such a wonder
is almost hard for you to believe.
My song's a mere reflection
of heaven's loveliness,
that Wondrous Kind on great and small
strews in their doing and being.

Ach! hättest du nur die gekannt,
Die einst mein Kleinod war—
Der Tod entriß sie meiner Hand
Hart hinterm Traualtar—
Dann würdest du es ganz verstehn,
Was Wunderhold vermag,
Und in das Licht der Wahrheit sehn,
Wie in den hellen Tag.

Ah, had you but known her
who was once my jewel—
whom death snatched from my hand
a step beyond the altar—
then would you wholly understand
what Wondrous Kind can achieve,
and gaze into the light of truth
as into the light of day.

Wohl hundertmal verdankt' ich ihr
Des Blümchens Segensflor.
Sanft schob sie's in den Busen mir
Zurück, wann ich's verlor.
Jetzt rafft ein Geist der Ungeduld
Es oft mir aus der Brust.
Erst, wann ich büße meine Schuld,
Bereu' ich den Verlust.

A hundred times I owed to her
the blessed flowering of that bloom.
Gently she replaced it in my breast
as often as I lost it.
A spirit of impatience now wrests
it often from within me.
And only when atoning for my guilt,
do I rue its loss.

O was des Blümchens
   Wunderkraft
Am Leib' und am Gemüt
Ihr, meiner Holdin, einst verschafft,
Faßt nicht das längste Lied!—
Weil's mehr, als Seide, Perl' und Gold
Der Schönheit Zier verleiht,
So nenn' ich's »Blümchen Wunderhold«,
Sonst heißt's—Bescheidenheit.

Oh, what the wondrous virtue of that
   flower
on the mind and body
of my sweet once wrought,
the longest song will not contain.
And because it lends more than silk,
pearl or gold, to beauty's adornment,
I name it 'Flower Wondrous Kind',
elsewhere called Modesty.

## Das Ende des Festes | The End of the Feast

CONRAD FERDINAND MEYER

*Othmar Schoeck: op. 60, no. 15, 1946*

Da mit Sokrates die Freunde
   tranken
und die Häupter auf die Polster sanken,
kam ein Jüngling, kann ich mich
   entsinnen,
mit zwei schlanken Flötenbläserinnen.

Aus den Kelchen schütten wir die
   Neigen.
Die gesprächesmüden Lippen
   schweigen.
Um die welken Kränze zieht ein
   Singen . . .
Still, des Todes Schlummerflöten
   klingen.

When friends with Socrates were
   drinking,
and heads were sinking on to cushions,
a young man came,
   I remember,
with two slender female flautists.

From our cups we shake the
   dregs,
silent fall our talk-tired
   lips.
About the faded garlands floats a
   singing . . .
Silently, death's flutes of slumber
   play.


## Das Kind | The Child

ANNETTE VON DROSTE-HÜLSHOFF

*Peter Cornelius, 1862*

Wär' ich ein Kind, ein Knäblein klein,
Ein armes, schwaches, geliebtes,
Daß die Mutter mich wiegte ein
Und süße Lieder mir sänge!
Blumen brächten die Sklavinnen auch,
Mit dem Wedel wehrten die Fliegen;
Aber Zillah, mich küssend, spräch:
»Gesegnet, mein süßes Knäbchen!«

Would I were a child, a little boy,
a poor, delicate, darling one,
so mother would rock me to sleep,
singing me sweet songs.
Slave women would bring flowers too,
ward the flies off with a fan;
but Zillah, kissing me, would say:
'Bless you, my sweet boy!'


## Das Köhlerweib ist trunken | The Charcoal Woman's Drunk

GOTTFRIED KELLER: from *Alte Weisen*

*Hugo Wolf, 1890*

Das Köhlerweib ist trunken
Und singt im Wald;
Hört, wie die Stimme gellend
Im Grünen hallt!

Sie war die schönste Blume,
Berühmt im Land;
Es warben Reich' und Arme
Um ihre Hand.

Sie trat in Gürtelketten
So stolz einher;
Den Bräutigam zu wählen,
Fiel ihr zu schwer.

The charcoal woman's drunk
and singing in the wood;
hark how her voice shrills,
making the country echo!

The sweetest flower was she,
famed in the land;
rich and poor came wooing
for her hand.

With keys at her belt
so proudly did she stride;
to choose her bridegroom
proved too hard a task.

| | |
|---|---|
| Da hat sie überlistet | Then she was outwitted |
| Der rote Wein— | by red wine— |
| Wie müssen alle Dinge | all things— |
| Vergänglich sein! | how fleeting must they be! |
| | |
| Das Köhlerweib ist trunken | The charcoal woman's drunk |
| Und singt im Wald; | and singing in the wood; |
| Wie durch die Dämmrung gellend | in the gathering dusk |
| Ihr Lied erschallt! | how shrill her song resounds! |

## Das Leben ist ein Traum | Life Is a Dream

JOHANN WILHELM LUDWIG GLEIM

*Joseph Haydn, 1784*

| | |
|---|---|
| Das Leben ist ein Traum! | Life is a dream! |
| Wir schlüpfen in die Welt und streben | We slip into the world and strive |
| Mit trunknem Sinn, erwacht kaum, | with drunken senses, scarce awake, |
| Nach ihrem Wahn und ihrem Schaum, | after its delusion and its foam, |
| Bis wir nicht mehr an Erde kleben. | until no longer to the earth we cleave. |
| Und dann, was ist's? Was ist das Leben? | And then, what is it? What is life? |
| Das Leben ist ein Traum. | Life is a dream. |
| | |
| Wir lieben, unsre Herzen schlagen, | We love, our hearts beat, |
| Und Herz mit Herz vereinet kaum, | and no sooner is heart joined to heart, |
| Wird Lieb und Scherz ein leerer | than love and jest become mere |
| Schaum, | foam, |
| Ist hingeschwunden, unter Klagen. | that vanishes to lamentation. |
| Was ist das Leben? hör ich fragen. | What, I hear asked, is life? |
| Das Leben ist ein Traum. | Life is a dream. |

## Das Lied im Grünen | Song in the Open

FRIEDRICH REIL

*Franz Schubert: op. 115, no. 1, 1827*

| | |
|---|---|
| Ins Grüne, ins Grüne, da lockt uns der Frühling, | To the open, the open, where Spring, |
| Der liebliche Knabe, | that delightful lad, beckons, |
| Und führt uns am blumenumwundenen Stabe | and, on flower-twined staff, leads us |
| Hinaus, wo die Lerchen und Amseln so wach, | to where lark and blackbird are so awake, |
| In Wälder, auf Felder, auf Hügel zum Bach, | to woods, to fields, to hill, to brook, |
| Ins Grüne, ins Grüne. | to the open, the open. |
| | |
| Im Grünen, im Grünen, da lebt es sich wonnig, | In the open, the open, life is blissful, |
| Da wandeln wir gerne | gladly we wander, |
| Und heften die Augen dahin schon von ferne, | and while yet from afar we fix our eyes there, |
| Und wie wir so wandeln mit heiterer Brust, | and as we thus wander with joyful heart, |
| Umwallet uns immer die kindliche Lust, | the child's delight flows ever about us, |
| Im Grünen, im Grünen. | in the open, the open. |

Im Grünen, im Grünen, da ruht man
   so wohl,
Empfindet so Schönes,
Und denket behaglich an dieses und
   jenes,
Und zaubert von hinnen, ach, was uns
   bedrückt,
Und alles herbei, was den Busen
   entzückt
Im Grünen, im Grünen.

In the open, the open, so sweetly
   one rests,
has such beautiful feelings,
contentedly thinks upon this,
   upon that,
conjures away, ah, things that
   oppress,
conjures up every delight for the
   heart
in the open, the open.

Im Grünen, im Grünen, da werden die
   Sterne
So klar, die die Weisen
Der Vorwelt zur Leitung des Lebens
   uns preisen,
Da streichen die Wölkchen so zart uns
   dahin,
Da heitern die Herzen, da klärt sich der
   Sinn
Im Grünen, im Grünen

In the open, the open, the stars
   grow
so clear, which the wise men
of old commend for life's
   guidance,
the clouds so tenderly touch us in
   passing,
hearts become lighter, the senses
   clear,
in the open, the open.

Im Grünen, im Grünen, da wurde
   manch Plänchen
Auf Flügeln getragen,
Die Zukunft der grämlichen Ansicht
   entschlagen,
Da stärkt sich das Auge, da labt sich
   der Blick,
Sanft wiegen die Wünsche sich hin und
   zurück
Im Grünen, im Grünen.

In the open, the open, many a
   plan
has been borne on wings,
the future—divested of its fearful
   aspect,
the eye is strengthened, the gaze
   refreshed,
the desires sway gently thither and
   back,
in the open, the open.

Im Grünen, im Grünen am Morgen,
   am Abend
In traulicher Stille
Entkeimet manch Liedchen und
   manche Idylle
Und Hymen oft kränzt den poetischen
   Scherz,
Denn leicht ist die Lockung, empfäng-
   lich das Herz
Im Grünen, im Grünen.

In the open, the open, morning and
   evening,
in the cosy stillness,
many a song germinates, and many an
   idyll,
and Hymen crowns often the poetic
   jest,
for easy the enticement, receptive the
   heart,
in the open, the open.

O gerne im Grünen bin ich schon als
   Knabe
Und Jüngling gewesen
Und habe gelernt und geschrieben,
   gelesen
Im Horaz und Plato, dann Wieland
   und Kant,
Und glühenden Herzens mich selig
   genannt,
Im Grünen, im Grünen.

Oh, gladly in the open I was as
   a boy
and a youth,
and learnt and wrote and
   read
some Horace and Plato, then
   Wieland and Kant,
and with glowing heart called myself
   happy,
in the open, the open.

Ins Grüne, ins Grüne laßt heiter uns
   folgen
Dem freundlichen Knaben.
Grünt einst uns das Leben nicht
   fürder,

To the open, the open, let us merrily
   follow
the friendly lad.
If, one day, life is no longer green for
   us,

So haben wir klüglich die grünende
Zeit nicht versäumt,
Und wenn es gegolten, doch glücklich
geträumt,
Im Grünen, im Grünen.

then we have wisely not missed the
green time,
and have, when appropriate, happily
dreamed,
in the open, the open.

## Das Lied von der Erde | The Song of the Earth

(A Symphony for tenor, contralto and orchestra)
Based on *The Chinese Flute*, by LI PO AND OTHERS, translated by HANS BETHGE
nos. 1, 3, 4, 5: LI PO
no. 2: TCHANG TSI
no. 6: MONG KOO YEN and WANG WEI

*Gustav Mahler, 1907–8*

1 *Das Trinklied vom Jammer der Erde*
Schon winkt der Wein im goldnen
Pokale.
Doch trinkt noch nicht, erst sing ich
euch ein Lied!
Das Lied vom Kummer soll auflachend
In die Seele euch klingen. Wenn der
Kummer naht,
Liegen wüst die Gärten der Seele,
Welkt hin und stirbt die Freude, der
Gesang.
Dunkel ist das Leben, ist der Tod.

Herr dieses Hauses!
Dein Keller birgt die Fülle des goldenen
Weins!
Hier diese Laute nenn ich mein!
Die Laute schlagen und die Gläser
leeren,
Das sind die Dinge, die
zusammenpassen.
Ein voller Becher Weins zur rechten
Zeit
Ist mehr wert als alle Reiche dieser
Erde.
Dunkel ist das Leben, ist der Tod.

Das Firmament blaut ewig, und die
Erde
Wird lange feststehn und aufblühn im
Lenz.
Du aber, Mensch, wie lange lebst denn
du?
Nicht hundert Jahre darfst du dich
ergötzen
An all dem morschen Tande dieser
Erde!

Seht dort hinab!
Im Mondschein auf den Gräbern hockt
Eine wild-gespenstische Gestalt. Ein
Aff ist's!
Hört ihr, wie sein Heulen hinausgellt
In den süßen Duft des Lebens!

1 *Drinking Song of the Misery of Earth*
The wine in its golden goblet
beckons.
But drink not yet. I'll sing you a song
first.
The song of sorrow shall laughingly
enter your soul. When sorrow draws
near,
desolate lie the gardens of the soul,
joy, song, fade and
perish.
Dark is life, is death.

Lord of this house!
Your cellar holds golden wine in
abundance!
Mine I call this lute here!
Striking the lute and draining
glasses,
those are the things which match
together.
A full beaker of wine at the proper
time
is worth more than all the kingdoms of
this earth.
Dark is life, is death.

The firmament is forever blue, and the
earth
will long stand firm, and blossom in
spring.
But you, man, how long will you
live?
Not a hundred years are you permitted
to delight
in all the brittle vanity of this
earth!

Look down there!
On the graves, in the moonlight, squats
a wild spectral figure. An ape it
is!
Hear how its howls screech out
into the sweet fragrance of life!

Jetzt nehmt den Wein! Jetzt ist es Zeit,
Genossen!
Leert eure goldnen Becher zu Grund!
Dunkel ist das Leben, ist der Tod.

Take now the wine. Now is the time,
friends!
Drain your golden beakers to the last!
Dark is life, is death.


2 *Der Einsame im Herbst*
Herbstnebel wallen bläulich überm
See;
Vom Reif bezogen stehen alle Gräser.
Man meint, ein Künstler habe Staub
von Jade
Über die feinen Blüten ausgestreut.

2 *The Solitary in Autumn*
Bluish above the lake seethe autumn
mists;
hoar-frost-clad is all the grass.
One would think that with jade dust an
artist
had sprinkled the fine blossoms.

Der süße Duft der Blumen ist verflogen,
Ein kalter Wind beugt ihre Stengel
nieder.
Bald werden die verwelkten goldnen
Blätter
Der Lotosblüten auf dem Wasser ziehn.

Flown is the sweet fragrance of flowers,
a cold wind bends low their
stems.
Soon the faded golden
leaves
of the lotus will drift upon the water.

Mein Herz ist müde. Meine kleine
Lampe
Erlosch mit Knistern, es gemahnt mich
an den Schlaf.
Ich komm zu dir, traute
Ruhestätte!
Ja gib mir Ruh! Ich hab Erquickung
not!

My heart is weary. My tiny
lamp
has spluttered out, reminding me of
sleep.
I am coming to you, homely place of
rest.
Yes, give me rest! I need to be
refreshed.

Ich weine viel in meinen Einsamkeiten,
Der Herbst in meinem Herzen währt
zu lange;
Sonne der Liebe, willst du nie mehr
scheinen,
Um meine bittern Tränen mild
aufzutrocknen?

I weep much in my solitude,
the autumn in my heart endures too
long;
Sun of Love, will you never more
shine
gently to dry my bitter
tears?


3 *Von der Jugend*
Mitten in dem kleinen Teiche
Steht ein Pavillon aus grünem
Und aus weißem Porzellan.

3 *Of Youth*
In the middle of the tiny pool
stands a pavilion of green
and white porcelain.

Wie der Rücken eines Tigers
Wölbt die Brücke sich aus Jade
Zu dem Pavillon hinüber.

Like a tiger's back
the bridge of jade arches
over to the pavilion.

In dem Häuschen sitzen Freunde,
Schön gekleidet, trinken, plaudern,—
Manche schreiben Verse nieder.

In this little house sit friends,
beautifully attired, drink, chat—
many write down verses.

Ihre seidnen Ärmel gleiten
Rückwärts, ihre seidnen Mützen
Hocken lustig tief im Nacken.

Their silk sleeves slide
up, their silk caps
perch merrily back on their heads.

Auf des kleinen Teiches stiller
Wasserfläche zeigt sich alles
Wunderlich im Spiegelbilde:

On the tiny pool's placid
surface all things are revealed
strangely as mirror images:

Alles auf dem Kopfe stehend,
In dem Pavillon aus grünem
Und aus weißem Porzellan.

Wie ein Halbmond steht die Brücke
Umgekehrt der Bogen. Freunde,
Schön gekleidet, trinken, plaudern.

4 *Von der Schönheit*
Junge Mädchen pflücken Blumen,
pflücken Lotosblumen
An dem Uferrande. Zwischen Büschen
Und Blättern sitzen sie, sammeln
Blüten, sammeln Blüten in den Schoß
und rufen
Sich einander Neckereien zu.

Goldne Sonne webt um die Gestalten,
Spiegelt sich im blanken Wasser wider,
Sonne spiegelt ihre schlanken Glieder,
Ihre süßen Augen wider, und der
Zephir
Hebt mit Schmeichelkosen das Gewebe
Ihrer Ärmel auf, führt den Zauber
Ihrer Wohlgerüche durch die Luft.

O sieh, was tummeln sich für schöne
Knaben
Dort an dem Uferrand auf mutgen
Rossen,
Weithin glänzend, wie die Sonnen-
strahlen;
Schon zwischen dem Geäst der grünen
Weiden
Trabt das jungfrische Volk einher!
Das Roß des einen wiehert fröhlich auf
Und scheut und saust dahin, über
Blumen, Gräser
Wanken hin die Hufe, sie zerstampfen
jäh im Sturm
Die hingesunknen Blüten,
Hei! wie flattern im Taumel seine
Mähnen,
Dampfen heiß die Nüstern,
Goldne Sonne webt um die Gestalten,
Spiegelt sie im blanken Wasser wider.

Und die schönste von den Jungfraun
sendet
Lange Blicke ihm der Sehnsucht nach.
Ihre stolze Haltung ist nur Verstellung:
In dem Funkeln ihrer großen Augen,
In dem Dunkel ihres heißen Blicks
Schwingt klagend noch die Erregung
ihres Herzens nach.

5 *Der Trunkene im Frühling*
Wenn nur ein Traum das Leben ist,
Warum dann Müh und Plag?

all standing on their heads
in the pavilion of green
and white porcelain.

Like a half-moon stands the bridge,
arch reversed. Friends,
beautifully attired, drink, chat.

4 *Of Beauty*
Young maidens pluck flowers, lotus
flowers
at the shore's edge. Amidst shrubs
and foliage they sit, gather
blossoms into their laps and
call
teasingly to each other.

Golden sun plays about the figures,
mirrors itself in the shining water,
mirrors their slender limbs,
their sweet eyes, and the
zephyr
with its caresses lifts the fabric
of their sleeves, and bears the magic
of their fragrance through the air.

Oh see the handsome young
men
at the shore's edge on lively
horses,
shining out like the sun's
rays;
amongst the green willows'
branches
the blithe young men come trotting!
The steed of one whinnies joyously,
shies, races off; over flowers,
grasses
the hooves fly trampling in their
career
the fallen blossoms,
ah, how its mane streams in the
frenzy,
its nostrils steam hotly,
golden sun plays about the figures,
mirrors them in the shining water.

And the fairest of the maidens
sends
after him long longing glances.
Her proud bearing is but a pose:
in the flash of her wide eyes,
in the darkness of her ardent gaze
her heart's agitation leaps still lamenting
after him.

5 *The Drunkard in Spring*
If life is but a dream,
why, then, toil and torment?

Ich trinke, bis ich nicht mehr kann,
Den ganzen lieben Tag.

Und wenn ich nicht mehr trinken kann,
Weil Kehl und Seele voll,
So tauml' ich bis zu meiner Tür
Und schlafe wundervoll!

Was hör ich beim Erwachen? Horch,
Ein Vogel singt im Baum.
Ich frag ihn, ob schon Frühling sei,—
Mir ist als wie im Traum.

Der Vogel zwitschert: ja! der Lenz ist
   da,
Sei kommen über Nacht,—
Aus tiefstem Schauen lauscht ich auf,
Der Vogel singt und lacht!

Ich fülle mir den Becher neu
Und leer ihn bis zum Grund
Und singe, bis der Mond erglänzt
Am schwarzen Firmament.

Und wenn ich nicht mehr singen kann,
So schlaf ich wieder ein.
Was geht mich denn der Frühling an!?
Laßt mich betrunken sein!

6 *Der Abschied*
Die Sonne scheidet hinter dem Gebirge,
In alle Täler steigt der Abend nieder
Mit seinen Schatten, die voll Kühlung
   sind.

O sieh! Wie eine Silberbarke schwebt
Der Mond am blauen Himmelssee
   herauf.
Ich spüre eines feinen Windes Wehn
Hinter den dunklen Fichten!

Der Bach singt voller Wohllaut durch
   das Dunkel:
Die Blumen blassen im Dämmerschein.
Die Erde atmet voll von Ruh und
   Schlaf.

Alle Sehnsucht will nun träumen,
Die müden Menschen gehn heimwärts,
   um im Schlaf
Vergeßnes Glück und Jugend neu zu
   lernen!

Die Vögel hocken still in ihren
   Zweigen,
Die Welt schläft ein . . . Es wehet
   kühl im Schatten meiner Fichten,
Ich stehe hier und harre meines
   Freundes;
Ich harre sein zum letzten Lebewohl.

I drink, until I can no more,
the livelong day.

And when I can drink no more,
because my gorge and soul are full,
reeling I go to my door
and I sleep wonderfully!

And, waking, what do I hear? Hark,
a bird sings in the tree.
I ask him whether spring has come—
I am as if in a dream.

The bird twitters. Yes, spring is
   here!
Overnight it has come—
from deepest contemplation I listened,
the bird sings and laughs!

Afresh I fill my beaker
and drain it to the dregs
and sing until the moon gleams
in the black firmament.

And when I can sing no more,
again I fall asleep.
What has spring to do with me!?
Let me be drunk!

6 *Farewell*
The sun departs behind the hills,
into all valleys descends the evening
with its shadows full of
   freshness.

Oh see, like a silver bark,
the moon slips over the sky's blue
   lake.
I feel the wafting of a gentle breeze
beyond the sombre spruces!

Full of melody, the stream sings in the
   dark,
the flowers, in the twilight, pale.
Earth's breathing is full of peace and
   sleep.

All desire wants now to dream,
weary men walk home to learn in
   sleep
forgotten happiness and youth
   anew!

The birds crouch silently among their
   twigs,
the world falls asleep . . . Cool it blows
   in the shadow of my spruces,
here I stand, awaiting my
   friend,
waiting to bid him a last farewell.

Ich sehne mich, o Freund, an deiner
    Seite
Die Schönheit dieses Abends zu
    genießen,—
Wo bleibst du? Du läßt mich lang
    allein!

Ich wandle auf und nieder mit meiner
    Laute
Auf Wegen, die von weichem Grase
    schwellen,—
O Schönheit! O ewigen Liebens—
    Lebens—trunkne Welt!

Er stieg vom Pferd und reichte ihm
    den Trunk
Des Abschieds dar. Er fragte ihn,
    wohin
Er führe und auch warum es müßte
    sein.
Er sprach, seine Stimme war umflort:
Du mein Freund, mir war auf dieser
    Welt das Glück nicht hold!

Wohin ich geh? Ich geh, ich wandre in
    die Berge.
Ich suche Ruhe für mein einsam Herz.
Ich wandle nach der Heimat, meiner
    Stätte!
Ich werde niemals in die Fremde
    schweifen.
Still ist mein Herz und harrt seiner
    Stunde:
Die liebe Erde allüberall blüht auf im
    Lenz und grünt
Aufs neu! Allüberall und ewig blauen
    licht die Fernen!
Ewig . . . Ewig . . .

I long, O friend, at your
    side
to enjoy the beauty of this
    evening,—
where are you? You leave me long
    alone!

Up and down I wander with my
    lute
on paths swelling with soft
    grass,—
O beauty! O eternal love—, eternal
    life-drunk world!

Dismounting, he handed
    him
the stirrup cup. Asked him
    whither
he fared, also why that must
    be.
He said, his voice muffled:
My friend, fortune has not smiled on
    me!

Whither I go? I go, I wander to the
    mountains.
I seek peace for my lonely heart.
I wander to my homeland, to my
    abode!
Never shall I roam to foreign
    parts.
Calm is my heart and waiting for its
    hour:
the dear earth everywhere blooms forth
    in spring, grows green
anew! Everywhere and eternally blue
    are the distant places!
Eternally . . . Eternally . . .

## Das Mädchen aus der Fremde / The Maiden from Another World

FRIEDRICH SCHILLER

*Johann Friedrich Reichardt, ed. 1778; Franz Schubert, 1815*

In einem Tal bei armen Hirten
Erschien mit jedem jungen Jahr,
Sobald die ersten Lerchen schwirrten,
Ein Mädchen, schön und wunderbar.

Sie war nicht in dem Tal geboren,
Man wußte nicht, woher sie kam,
Und schnell war ihre Spur verloren,
Sobald das Mädchen Abschied nahm.

Beseligend war ihre Nähe,
Und alle Herzen wurden weit,
Doch eine Würde, eine Höhe
Entfernte die Vertraulichkeit.

To poor shepherds in a valley
appeared, each young year,
with the first flitting larks,
a maiden wonderful and fair.

She was not native to the valley,
no one knew from where she came,
and trace of her was quickly lost,
as soon as the maiden went.

Enrapturing her presence was,
every heart was opened wide,
but a dignity, a grandeur,
banished familiarity.

Sie brachte Blumen mit und
  Früchte,
Gereift auf einer andern Flur,
In einem andern Sonnenlichte,
In einer glücklichern Natur.

Und teilte jedem eine Gabe,
Dem Früchte, jenem Blumen aus,
Der Jüngling und der Greis am Stabe,
Ein jeder ging beschenkt nach Haus.

Willkommen waren alle Gäste,
Doch nahte sich ein liebend Paar,
Dem reichte sie der Gaben beste,
Der Blumen allerschönste dar.

Flowers she brought with her, and
  fruits
ripened in another field,
beneath the light of another sun,
amidst a happier clime.

She bestowed on everyone a gift,
fruit to one, to another flowers;
the youth, the old man with his stick,
each one went home rewarded.

All who came to her were welcome,
but when a loving pair drew near,
them she gave her finest gifts,
the very fairest of her flowers.

## Das Mädchen spricht | The Maiden Speaks

OTTO FRIEDRICH GRUPPE

*Johannes Brahms: op. 107, no. 3, 1886*

Schwalbe, sag' mir an,
ist's dein alter Mann,
mit dem du's Nest gebaut,
oder hast du jüngst
erst dich ihm vertraut?

Sag', was zwitschert ihr,
sag', was flüstert ihr
des morgens so vertraut?
Gelt, du bist wohl auch
noch nicht lange Braut?

Swallow, tell me,
is that your old husband
you've set up nest with,
or have you only recently
entrusted yourself to him?

Tell me, what do you twitter,
what do you whisper about,
so intimately in the morning?
And you haven't, have you,
been all that long a bride?

## Das Marienleben | The Life of Mary*

RAINER MARIA RILKE

*Paul Hindemith: op. 27, nos. 1–15, 1922–23; revised setting 1948*

1 *Geburt Mariae*
O was muß es die Engel gekostet
  haben,
nicht aufzusingen plötzlich, wie man
  aufweint,
da sie doch wußten: in dieser Nacht
  wird dem Knaben
die Mutter geboren, dem Einen, der
  bald erscheint.

Schwingend verschwiegen sie sich und
  zeigten die Richtung,
wo, allein, das Gehöft lag des
  Joachim,
ach, sie fühlten in sich und im Raum
  die reine Verdichtung,
aber es durfte keiner nieder zu
  ihm.

1 *Birth of Mary*
Oh, what must it have cost the
  angels
not suddenly to burst out in song, as
  into tears,
knowing that: this night, for the
  boy,
for Him, soon to appear, the mother
  would be born.

Whirling, they said nothing of the
  way,
yet showed where, solitary, lay
  Joachim's farm,
ah, they felt, within them and in space,
  that pure
consolation, but to that farm might
  none descend.

* The German copyright holder has requested the English-language publishers to point out that these translations have been made specifically as reference for singers.

Denn die beiden waren schon so außer
    sich vor Getue.
Eine Nachbarin kam und klugte und
    wußte nicht wie,
und der Alte, vorsichtig, ging und
    verhielt das Gemuhe
einer dunkelen Kuh. Denn so war es
    noch nie.

2 *Die Darstellung Mariae im Tempel*
Um zu begreifen, wie sie damals
    war,
mußt du dich erst an eine Stelle
    rufen,
wo Säulen in dir wirken; wo du
    Stufen
nachfühlen kannst; wo Bogen voll
    Gefahr
den Abgrund eines Raumes
    überbrücken,
der in dir blieb, weil er aus solchen
    Stücken
getürmt war, daß du sie nicht mehr aus
    dir
ausheben kannst: du rissest dich denn
    ein.
Bist du so weit, ist alles in dir Stein,
Wand, Aufgang, Durchblick, Wöl-
    bung—, so probier
den großen Vorhang, den du vor dir
    hast,
ein wenig wegzuzerrn mit beiden
    Händen:
da glänzt es von ganz hohen
    Gegenständen
und übertrifft dir Atem und
    Getast.
Hinauf, hinab, Palast steht auf
    Palast,
Geländer strömen breiter aus
    Geländern
und tauchen oben auf an solchen
    Rändern,
daß dich, wie du sie siehst, der
    Schwindel faßt.
Dabei macht ein Gewölk aus
    Räucherständern
die Nähe trüb; aber das Fernste zielt
in dich hinein mit seinen graden
    Strahlen—,
und wenn jetzt Schein aus klaren
    Flammenschalen
auf langsam nahenden Gewändern
    spielt:
wie hältst du's aus?

Sie aber kam und hob
den Blick, um diese alles anzuschauen.

For distracted were those two with
    what to do.
A neighbour came, feigned wise, and
    knew not what.
Cautiously the old man went and
    stopped the mooing
of an obscure cow. For never ever yet
    had it been thus.

2 *Presentation of Mary at the Temple*
To comprehend how she was at that
    time,
yourself you must first summon to a
    place
where pillars work within you; where
    you can
feel steps; where arches full of
    danger
bridge over the abysses of a
    chamber
that has remained in you, being of such
    pieces
raised, that from within no longer can
    you
lift them; save that you tear your own
    self down.
That far advanced, if all in you is stone,
wall, stairs, vista, vaulting—, then
    assay
the great curtain that you have before
    you,
a little with both hands to tug
    away:
a gleam there is of objects wholly
    lofty
that goes beyond your power of breath
    and touch.
Upwards, downwards, palace stands on
    palace,
balustrade streams broader out from
    balustrade
and plunges at the top at such a
    brink
that to behold it, you are seized with
    vertigo.
Clouds from incense-stands make all
    the while
the nearby, dim; but what is farthest
directs into you its level
    beams—,
and if light of bright flaming
    bowls
play on vestments slowly
    nearing:
how will you endure?

She, however, came and raised
her gaze to look upon all this.

(Ein Kind, ein kleines Mädchen
  zwischen Frauen.)
Dann stieg sie ruhig, voller
  Selbstvertrauen,
dem Aufwand zu, der sich verwöhnt
  verschob:
So sehr war alles, was die Menschen
  bauen,
schon überwogen von dem Lob

in ihrem Herzen. Von der Lust
sich hinzugeben an die innern Zeichen:
Die Eltern meinten, sie hinauf-
  zureichen,
der Drohende mit der Juwelenbrust
empfing sie scheinbar: Doch sie ging
  durch alle,
klein wie sie war, aus jeder Hand
  hinaus
und in ihr Los, das, höher als die
  Halle,
schon fertig war, und schwerer als das
  Haus.


3  *Mariae Verkündigung*
Nicht daß ein Engel eintrat (das
  erkenn),
erschreckte sie. Sowenig andre, wenn
ein Sonnenstrahl oder der Mond bei
  Nacht
in ihrem Zimmer sich zu schaffen
  macht,
auffahren—, pflegte sie an der Gestalt,
in der ein Engel ging, sich zu entrüsten;
sie ahnte kaum, daß dieser Aufenthalt
mühsam für Engel ist. (O wenn wir
  wüßten,
wie rein sie war. Hat eine Hirschkuh
  nicht,
die, liegend, einmal sie im Wald
  eräugte,
sich so in sie versehn, daß sich in ihr,
ganz ohne Paarigen, das Einhorn
  zeugte,
das Tier aus Licht, das reine Tier—.)
Nicht, daß er eintrat, aber daß er dicht,
der Engel, eines Jünglings Angesicht
so zu ihr neigte; daß sein Blick und der,
mit dem sie aufsah, so zusammen-
  schlugen
als wäre draußen plötzlich alles leer
und, was Millionen schauten, trieben,
  trugen,
hineingedrängt in sie: nur sie und
  er;
Schaun und Geschautes, Aug und
  Augenweide

(A child, a small child amongst
  women.)
Then she ascended, calmly, fully
  confident,
toward the extravagance that
  moved, indulged, aside:
so very much was all that which men
  build,
outweighed already by the praise

within her heart. By the desire
to yield herself up to the inner signs:
Her parents thought that they presented
  her,
the menacing one with jewelled breast
apparently received her: yet through all
  she walked,
small as she was, away from every
  hand
and to her destiny, that, loftier than that
  hall,
already was prepared, and weightier
  than that house.


3  *The Annunciation*
That an angel entered, not that
  (understand),
alarmed her. No more than others start
if beam of sun or moon by
  night
about their chamber
  flit,
was she wont to be shocked at the shape
in which an angel went;
little did she suspect that this abode
is difficult for angels. (Oh if we were
  aware
how pure she was. Was not a hind she
  once
spied couchant in the
  forest
so affected, seeing her, that she
quite without mate, begot the
  unicorn,
the beast of light, the beast of purity—.)
Not that he entered, but that he,
the angel, a young man's countenance
inclined so close; that his gaze and hers,
looking up, so struck
  together
as if all outside were, of a sudden, void
and that which millions saw, did and
  bore
was crowded into them: just she and
  he;
seeing and things seen, eye and eye's
  delight

sonst nirgends als an dieser Stelle—: sieh,
dieses erschreckt. Und sie erschraken beide.

Dann sang der Engel seine Melodie.

nowhere but in this place—: behold,
that alarms. And they were both alarmed.

Then the angel sang his melody.


4 *Mariae Heimsuchung*
Noch erging sie's leicht im Anbeginne,
doch im Steigen manchmal ward sie schon
ihres wunderbaren Leibes inne,—
und dann stand sie, atmend, auf den hohn

Judenbergen, Aber nicht das Land,
ihre Fülle war um sie gebreitet;
gehend fühlte sie: man überschreitet
nie die Größe, die sie jetzt empfand.

Und es drängte sie, die Hand zu legen
auf den andern Leib, der weiter war.
Und die Frauen schwankten sich entgegen
und berührten sich Gewand und Haar.

Jede, voll von ihrem Heiligtume,
schützte sich mit der Gevatterin.
Ach der Heiland in ihr war noch Blume,
doch den Täufer in dem Schooß der Muhme
riß die Freude schon zum Hüpfen hin.


4 *Mary's Visitation*
She still walked easily at first,
yet sometimes, climbing, she became
conscious of her wondrous body,—
and then stood, took breath on the high

hills of Judea. But not the land
was about her, but her fullness;
walking, she felt: never surpassed
would be the greatness she now knew.

And she was urged to lay her hand
upon the other body that was further.
And toward each other the women swayed,
touching the hair and garments of the other.

Each, full of what was sacred to her,
herself protected with her kinswoman.
Ah, the Saviour in her was still a flower,
but the Baptist in her cousin's womb
by joy was so transported as to leap.


5 *Argwohn Josephs*
Und der Engel sprach und gab sich Müh
an dem Mann, der seine Fäuste ballte:
Aber siehst du nicht an jeder Falte,
daß sie kühl ist wie die Gottesfrüh.

Doch der andre sah ihn finster an,
murmelnd nur: Was hat sie so verwandelt?
Doch da schrie der Engel: Zimmermann,
merkst du's noch nicht, daß der Herrgott handelt?

Weil du Bretter machst, in deinem Stolze,
willst du wirklich *den* zu Rede stelln,
der bescheiden aus dem gleichen Holze
Blätter treiben macht und Knospen schwelln?


5 *Joseph's Mistrust*
And the angel spoke and took pains
with the man who clenched his fists:
But can you not tell by every fold
she is as fresh as is God's early morn.

But the other loured at him,
murmuring only: What transformed her so?
But then the angel cried: Carpenter,
mark you not yet the work of the Lord God?

Because you fashion planks, in your pride
will you indeed take *him* to task
who modestly from that same wood
makes leaf to shoot and bud to swell?

93

Er begriff. Und wie er jetzt die Blicke,
recht erschrocken, zu dem Engel
    hob,
war der fort. Da schob er seine
    dicke
Mütze langsam ab. Dann sang er lob.

He understood. And as now his gaze
he raised to the angel in veritable
    terror,
he was gone. Then he shoved his
    thick
cap slowly off. Then sang praise.

## 6 Verkündigung über den Hirten

Seht auf, ihr Männer. Männer dort am
    Feuer,
die ihr den grenzenlosen Himmel kennt,
Sterndeuter, hierher! Seht, ich bin ein
    neuer
steigender Stern. Mein ganzes Wesen
    brennt
und strahlt so stark und ist so ungeheuer
voll Licht, daß mir das tiefe Firmament
nicht mehr genügt. Laßt meinen Glanz
    hinein
in euer Dasein: Oh, die dunklen
    Blicke,
die dunklen Herzen, nächtige Geschicke
die euch erfüllen. Hirten, wie allein
bin ich in euch. Auf einmal wird mir
    Raum.
Stauntet ihr nicht: der große Brot-
    fruchtbaum
warf einen Schatten. Ja, das kam von
    mir.
Ihr Unerschrockenen, o wüßtet ihr,
wie jetzt auf eurem schauenden
    Gesichte
die Zukunft scheint. In diesem starken
    Lichte
wird viel geschehen. Euch vertrau ichs,
    denn
ihr seid verschwiegen; euch Grad-
    gläubigen
redet hier alles. Glut und Regen
    spricht,
der Vögel Zug, der Wind und was ihr
    seid,
keins überwiegt und wächst zur
    Eitelkeit
sich mästend an. Ihr haltet nicht
die Dinge auf im Zwischenraum der
    Brust
um sie zu quälen. So wie seine Lust
durch einen Engel strömt, so treibt
    durch euch
das Irdische. Und wenn ein Dorn-
    gesträuch
aufflammte plötzlich, dürfte noch aus
    ihm
der Ewige euch rufen,
    Cherubim,
wenn sie geruhten neben eurer Herde

## 6 Annunciation to the Shepherds from on High

Gaze up, you men. Men, there by the
    fire,
who are familiar with the boundless sky,
astrologers, look this way. See, a
    new
ascending star am I. My whole being
    burns,
shines forth, and so enormously is
full of light that the deep firmament
suffices me no longer. Let my
    radiance
enter your existence: Oh, the dark
    gazes,
dark hearts, nocturnal fates
that fill you. Shepherds, how solitary
I am in you. There is, of a sudden,
    room for me.
You did not marvel: the great bread-
    fruit tree
cast a shadow. Yes, that came from
    me.
Oh if you knew, you undismayed ones,
how now upon your gazing
    countenances
the future shines. In that powerful
    light
will much occur. To you I entrust it,
    for
you are silent men; to you upright
    believers
all that is here speaks. Rain and heat
    speak,
birds in flight, the wind and what you
    are,
none prevails and into vainness
    thrives,
growing fat. You do not,
in the breast's interstice, halt
    things
in order to torment them. Just as his joy
is poured out through an angel, so,
    through you
the earthly is impelled. And were a
    thorn bush
suddenly to flame, then from it,
    still,
might the Eternal summon you;
    cherubim,
if beside your flock they deigned

einherzuschreiten, wunderten euch
   nicht:
ihr stürztet euch auf euer Angesicht,
betetet an und nenntet dies die Erde.

Doch dieses war. Nun soll ein Neues
   sein,
von dem der Erdkreis ringender sich
   weitet.
Was ist ein Dörnicht uns: Gott fühlt
   sich ein
in einer Jungfrau Schooß. Ich bin der
   Schein
von ihrer Innigkeit, der euch geleitet.


7 *Geburt Christi*
Hättest du der Einfalt nicht, wie
   sollte
dir geschehn, was jetzt die Nacht
   erhellt?
Sieh, der Gott, der über Völkern
   grollte,
macht sich mild und kommt in dir zur
   Welt.

Hast du dir ihn größer
   vorgestellt?

Was ist Größe? Quer durch alle
   Maße,
die er durchstreicht, geht sein grades
   Los.
Selbst ein Stern hat keine solche Straße.
Siehst du, diese Könige sind groß,

und sie schleppen dir vor deinen Schooß

Schätze, die sie für die größten halten,
und du staunst vielleicht bei dieser
   Gift—:
aber schau in deines Tuches Falten,
wie er jetzt schon alles übertrifft.

Aller Amber, den man weit verschifft,

jeder Goldschmuck und das Luft-
   gewürze,
das sich trübend in die Sinne
   streut:
alles dieses war von rascher Kürze,
und am Ende hat man es bereut.

Aber (du wirst sehen): Er erfreut.


8 *Rast auf der Flucht in Aegypten*
Diese, die noch eben atemlos
flohen mitten aus dem Kindermorden:

to stride, would not marvel at
   you:
upon your faces you would fall,
venerate and call this the earth.

But these things were. Now shall new
   things be,
whereof the world will, struggling
   harder, widen.
What is a bush of thorn to us: God
   feels his way
into a virgin's womb. I am the
   gleam
of her tenderness that goes with you.


7 *Birth of Christ*
If you had not that simplicity, how
   should
have befallen you what brightens now
   the night?
Behold, the God who on nations vented
   wrath,
relents, comes into this world, in
   you.

Did you imagine that he would be
   greater?

What is greatness? Across all
   measurements
he strikes through, runs his plain
   destiny.
A star, even, has no such way as that.
Can you see, these kings are great,

yet they bear to you and to your lap

those treasures they consider greatest,
and, it may be, you marvel at these
   gifts—:
but, in the creases of your shawl,
see how already he surpasses all.

All the amber which is shipped afar,

each gold adornment and the spice of
   air
that cloudingly descends upon the
   senses:
that was all of very brief duration,
and, in the end, a matter of regret.

But He (as you will see) makes glad.


8 *Rest on the Flight into Egypt*
These who still breathless even,
fled from amidst child murder:

o wie waren sie unmerklich groß
über ihrer Wanderschaft geworden.

Kaum noch daß im scheuen Rückwärts-
    schauen
ihres Schreckens Not zergangen war,
und schon brachten sie auf ihrem
    grauen
Maultier ganze Städte in Gefahr:

denn so wie sie, klein im großen Land,
—fast ein Nichts—den starken
    Tempeln nahten,
platzten alle Götzen wie verraten
und verloren völlig den Verstand.

Ist es denkbar, daß von ihrem Gange
alles so verzweifelt sich erbost?
und sie wurden vor sich selber bange,
nur das Kind war namenlos getrost.

Immerhin, sie mußten sich darüber
eine Weile setzen. Doch da ging—
sieh: der Baum, der still sie
    überhing,
wie ein Dienender zu ihnen über:

er verneigte sich. Derselbe Baum,
dessen Kränze toten Pharaonen
für das Ewige die Stirnen schonen,
neigte sich. Er fühlte neue Kronen
blühen. Und sie saßen wie im Traum.


9 *Von der Hochzeit zu Kana*
Konnte sie denn anders, als auf
    ihn
stolz sein, der ihr Schlichtestes
    verschönte?
War nicht selbst die hohe,
    großgewöhnte
Nacht wie außer sich, da er
    erschien?

Ging nicht auch, daß er sich einst
    verloren,
unerhört zu seiner Glorie aus?
Hatten nicht die Weisesten die Ohren
mit dem Mund vertauscht? Und war
    das Haus

nicht wie neu von seiner Stimme? Ach
sicher hatte sie zu hundert Malen
ihre Freude an ihm
    auszustrahlen
sich verwehrt. Sie ging ihm staunend
    nach.

Aber da bei jenem Hochzeitsfeste,
als es unversehns an Wein gebrach,—

Oh, how imperceptibly great
they had grown in their travelling.

Scarce before, in timid looking
    back,
their terror's misery had faded,
already they were putting, on their
    grey
mule, whole towns in peril;

for, as they, small in the great land,
—nothing almost—neared gloomy
    temples,
all the idols burst, as if betrayed,
and wholly lost their meaning.

Is it conceivable that by their progress
all were so desperately enraged?
and of themselves they grew afraid,
the child alone was ineffably at ease.

Still, they had, in the course of it,
to sit down for a while. But then—
see: the tree that overhung them
    quietly,
went over to them like a serving man:

bowed low. That same tree
whose wreaths protect dead pharaohs'
brows for time everlasting,
bowed low. Felt new branches, leaves,
flourish. And they sat, as in a dream.


9 *Of the Marriage at Cana*
Could she then other than be proud of
    him
who beautified what was simplest in
    her?
Was not the lofty,
    vast-accustomed
night as if beside itself, when he
    appeared?

That once he strayed—did not that
    redound
unprecedentedly to his glory?
Had not the wisest ones, with ears
replaced their mouths? And the
    house

was it not as if new, for his voice? Ah,
certainly a hundred times she had
to keep her joy in him from shining
    forth.
Behind she followed,
    marvelling.

But then, at that marriage celebration,
when unexpectedly the wine ran out—

96

sah sie hin und bat um eine Geste
und begriff nicht, daß er widersprach.

Und dann tat er's. Sie verstand es
    später,
wie sie ihn in seinen Weg
    gedrängt:
denn jetzt war er wirklich
    Wundertäter,
und das ganze Opfer war verhängt,

unaufhaltsam. Ja, es stand geschrieben.
Aber war es damals schon
    bereit?
Sie: sie hatte es herbeigetrieben
in der Blindheit ihrer Eitelkeit.

An dem Tisch voll Früchten und
    Gemüsen
freute sie sich mit und sah nicht ein,
daß das Wasser ihrer Tränendrüsen
Blut geworden war mit diesem Wein.


10 *Vor der Passion*
O hast du dies gewollt, du hättest nicht
durch eines Weibes Leib entspringen
    dürfen:
Heilande muß man in den Bergen
    schürfen,
wo man das Harte aus dem Harten
    bricht.

Tut dirs nicht selber leid, dein liebes
    Tal
so zu verwüsten? Siehe meine Schwäche;
ich habe nichts als Milch- und Tränen-
    bäche,
und du warst immer in der Überzahl.

Mit solchem Aufwand wardst du mir
    verheißen.
Was tratst du nicht gleich wild aus mir
    hinaus?
Wenn du nur Tiger brauchst, dich zu
    zerreißen,
warum erzog man mich im
    Frauenhaus,

ein weiches reines Kleid für dich zu
    weben,
darin nicht einmal die geringste Spur
von Naht dich drückt—: so war mein
    ganzes Leben,
und jetzt verkehrst du plötzlich die
    Natur.


11 *Pietà*
Jetzt wird mein Elend voll, und namenlos
erfüllt es mich. Ich starre wie des Steins
Inneres starrt.

---

she looked, besought a sign,
and did not understand his saying no.

Then he performed it. Later she
    saw
how she had hurried him to take his
    path:
for now he was indeed one who worked
    miracles,
and the whole sacrifice was ordained,

and irresistible. Yes, written it was.
But was it, at that time, as yet
    prepared?
She—she it was had urged its coming,
in the blindness of her vanity.

At the fruit- and vegetable-piled
    table
she, with the rest, made merry, unaware
that the water of her tear glands
was, with that wine, turned into blood.


10 *Before the Passion*
If this was your will, oh you should not
have sprung from womb of
    woman:
saviours must be dug for in the
    hills,
where hard is quarried out of
    hard.

Are you yourself not sad so to
    ravage
your dear valley? Behold my weakness;
nothing I have but brooks of milk and
    tears,
and you always were in most of them.

With such pomp you were promised to
    me.
Why stepped you not fiercely straight
    from me?
If all you want is to be rent by
    tigers,
why was I reared in the house of
    women,

to weave for you a garment pure and
    soft,
with not so much as a trace of seam
to touch you—: such was my whole
    life,
and now you change your nature
    suddenly.


11 *Pietà*
Now is my misery full, unspeakably
it fills me. I gaze, as the stone's
interior gazes.

Hart wie ich bin, weiß ich nur Eins:
Du wurdest groß—
...... und wurdest groß,
um als zu großer Schmerz
ganz über meines Herzens Fassung
hinauszustehn.
Jetzt liegst du quer durch meinen
　　Schooß,
jetzt kann ich dich nicht mehr
gebären.

Hard as I am, one thing I only know:
You grew—
...... grew
to stand
as agony too great
wholly beyond my heart's grasp.
Now across my womb you
　　lie,
now I can no longer give you
birth.

## 12 Stillung Mariae mit dem Auferstandenen

Was sie damals empfanden: ist es nicht
vor allen Geheimnissen süß
und immer noch irdisch:
da er, ein wenig blaß noch vom
　　Grab,
erleichtert zu ihr trat:
an allen Stellen erstanden.
O zu ihr zuerst. Wie waren sie da
unaussprechlich in Heilung.
Ja sie heilten, das war's. Sie hatten nicht
　　nötig,
sich stark zu berühren.
Er legte ihr eine Sekunde
kaum seine nächsten
ewige Hand an die frauliche
　　Schulter.
Und sie begannen
still wie die Bäume im Frühling,
unendlich zugleich,
diese Jahreszeit
ihres äußersten Umgangs.

## 12 Consoling of Mary by the Risen Christ

What they felt at that time: is it not
sweet above all mysteries
and yet still of earth:
when he, a little pale still from the
　　tomb,
came, eased of suffering, to her:
risen in all places.
Oh first to her. How ineffable
they were in healing. Yes, they healed
and were healed, that was it. They had
　　no need
to touch each other greatly.
He laid, for a second
barely, his soon-to-be
eternal hand upon the woman's
　　shoulder.
And they began,
still as the trees in spring,
infinitely together,
this season
of their most extreme communing.

## 13 Vom Tode Mariae

I

Derselbe große Engel, welcher einst
ihr der Gebärung Botschaft nieder-
　　brachte,
stand da, abwartend daß sie ihn beachte,
und sprach: Jetzt wird es Zeit, daß du
　　erscheinst.
Und sie erschrak wie damals und erwies
sich wieder als die Magd, ihn tief
　　bejahend.
Er aber strahlte und, unendlich
　　nahend,
schwand er wie in ihr Angesicht—und
　　hieß
die weithin ausgegangenen Bekehrer
zusammenkommen in das Haus am
　　Hang,
das Haus des Abendmahls. Sie kamen
　　schwerer
und traten bange ein: Da lag,
　　entlang
die schmale Bettstatt, die in Untergang

## 13 Of the Death of Mary

I

That same important angel who once
brought down to her tidings of the
　　birth,
stood, waiting for her to notice him,
and said: It is now nearly time that you
　　appeared.
And she was, as then, alarmed, and was
again the maid, giving profound
　　assent.
But he shone out, and coming infinitely
　　near,
vanished, as if into her countenance—
　　and told
the evangelists, gone forth afar,
to gather at the house upon the
　　slope,
the House of The Supper. With
　　heavier step
they came, and, fearful, entered. There,
　　on
the narrow bed she lay, mysteriously

und Auserwählung rätselhaft
    Getauchte,
ganz unversehrt, wie eine Ungebrauchte,
und achtete auf englischen Gesang.
Nun da sie alle hinter ihren
    Kerzen
abwarten sah, riß sie vom Über-
    maß
der Stimmen sich und schenkte noch
    von Herzen
die beiden Kleider fort, die sie besaß,
und hob ihr Antlitz auf zu dem und
    dem . . .
(O Ursprung namenloser Tränen-
    Bäche).

Sie aber legte sich in ihre Schwäche
und zog die Himmel an
    Jerusalem
so nah heran, daß ihre Seele nur,
austretend, sich ein wenig strecken
    mußte:
schon hob er sie, der alles von ihr
    wußte,
hinein in ihre göttliche Natur.


14 *Vom Tode Mariae*
II
Wer hat bedacht, daß bis zu ihrem
    Kommen
der viele Himmel unvollständig war?
Der Auferstandne hatte Platz
    genommen,
doch neben ihm, durch vierundzwanzig
    Jahr,
war leer der Sitz. Und sie begannen
    schon
sich an die reine Lücke zu gewöhnen,
die wie verheilt war, denn mit seinem
    schönen
Hinüberscheinen füllte sie der Sohn.

So ging auch sie, die in die Himmel trat,
nicht auf ihn zu, so sehr es sie
    verlangte;
dort war kein Platz, nur *Er* war dort
    und prangte
mit einer Strahlung, die ihr wehe tat.
Doch da sie jetzt, die rührende Gestalt,
sich zu den neuen Seligen gesellte
und unauffällig, licht zu licht, sich
    stellte,
da brach aus ihrem Sein ein Hinterhalt
von solchem Glanz, daß der von ihr
    erhellte
Engel geblendet aufschrie: Wer ist
    die?
Ein Staunen war. Dann sahn sie alle,
    wie

immersed in her decline and her
    election,
wholly inviolate, like one quite new,
and was attentive to the angel song.
Now, seeing all of them, behind their
    candles,
waiting, she tore herself from the
    plenitude
of voices and, from her heart, made
    presents
of the two dresses she possessed,
raising her face to this one and
    that . . .
(O first source of nameless brooks of
    tears).

But she laid herself down in her frailty
and drew, here to Jerusalem, the
    heavens
so close, her soul had,
issuing, to reach up but a
    little:
already he, who knew all things about
    her,
was lifting her into her Godly nature.


14 *Of the Death of Mary*
II
Who considered that, before her
    coming,
great heaven was incomplete?
The Risen One had taken his
    place,
but for all of four and twenty
    years
the next seat had been vacant. And they
    began
to grow used to that gaping place
which was as though healed, for with
    his fair
irradiance the Son had filled it.

So, entering heaven, even she,
great though her longing was, went not
    to him;
no place was there, only *He*,
    shining
with a radiance that pained her.
But as she, that moving figure, now
went and joined the new Departed,
and, radiance against radiance, stood,
    inconspicuous,
from her burst such a reserve
of splendour that, lit by
    her,
the angel, dazzled, cried out: Who is
    she?
They marvelled. Then they all saw
    how,

Gott-Vater oben unsern Herrn
    verhielt,
so daß, von milder Dämmerung
    umspielt,
die leere Stelle wie ein wenig Leid
sich zeigte, eine Spur von Einsamkeit,
wie etwas, was er noch ertrug, ein
    Rest
irdischer Zeit, ein trockenes Gebrest—.
Man sah nach ihr; sie schaute ängstlich
    hin,
weit vorgeneigt, als fühlte sie: *ich* bin
sein längster Schmerz—: und stürzte
    plötzlich vor.
Die Engel aber nahmen sie zu sich
und stützten sie und sangen seliglich
und trugen sie das letzte Stück
    empor.

on high, God the Father restrained our
    Lord
so that, in a play of gentle
    twilight,
like a small grief, the vacant place
was revealed, a trace of solitude,
like a thing still suffered by him, a
    residue
of earthly time, a sere affliction—.
They looked at her; she gazed
    anxiously,
bent far forward, as if she felt: *I* am
his longest agony—: and darted
    ahead.
But the angels took her to themselves,
supported her, sang blissfully
and for the remaining distance bore her
    up.

15 *Vom Tode Mariae*
III
Doch vor dem Apostel Thomas, der
kam, da es zu spät war, trat der schnelle
längst darauf gefaßte Engel her
und befahl an der
    Begräbnisstelle:

15 *Of the Death of Mary*
III
But ahead of the Apostle Thomas,
come too late, stepped the swift
angel who for this had long been ready,
and at the place of burial,
    commanded:

Dräng den Stein beseite. Willst du
    wissen,
wo die ist, die dir das Herz bewegt:
Sieh: sie ward wie ein Lavendelkissen
eine Weile da
    hineingelegt,

Push aside the stone. If you would
    know
where she is who stirs your heart:
See: like a pillow of lavender she was
for a time laid there
    within

daß die Erde künftig nach ihr
    rieche
in den Falten wie ein feines Tuch.
Alles Tote (fühlst du), alles
    Sieche
ist betäubt von ihrem Wohl-Geruch.

that the earth might in future bear her
    scent,
as does a fine cloth, in its folds.
All that are dead (you feel), all that are
    sick,
are assuaged by her sweet fragrance.

Schau den Leinwand: wo ist eine
    Bleiche,
wo er blendend wird und geht nicht
    ein?
Dieses Licht aus dieser reinen
    Leiche
war ihm klärender als
    Sonnenschein.

See the linen: where is a
    bleachery
where it shall become dazzling, yet not
    shrink?
This light from the purity of this dead
    body
was more clarifying to it than the
    sunshine.

Staunst du nicht, wie sanft sie ihm
    entging?
Fast als wär sie's noch, nichts ist
    verschoben.
Doch die Himmel sind erschüttert
    oben:
Mann, knie hin und sieh mir nach und
    sing.

Are you not amazed how softly she
    went from it?
Almost as if it were still she, all is in
    place.
Yet the heavens above have been made
    to tremble:
Man, kneel down, gaze after me and
    sing.

## Das Rosenband | The Rosy Ribbon

FRIEDRICH GOTTLIEB KLOPSTOCK

*Franz Schubert, 1815; Richard Strauss: op. 36, no. 1, 1897–98*

Im Frühlingsschatten fand ich sie,
da band ich sie mit Rosenbändern:
sie fühlt es nicht und schlummerte.

In spring shade I found her,
and with rosy ribbons bound her:
she felt it not and slumbered.

Ich sah sie an; mein Leben hing
mit diesem Blick an ihrem Leben:
ich fühlt' es wohl und wußt' es nicht.

At her I gazed; my life hung,
in that gaze, on hers:
that I sensed and did not know.

Doch lispelt ich ihr sprachlos zu
und rauschte mit den Rosenbändern:
da wachte sie vom Schlummer auf.

But to her wordlessly I murmured
and stirred the rosy ribbons:
then from her slumber she awoke.

Sie sah mich an; ihr Leben hing
mit diesem Blick an meinem Leben:
und um uns ward's Elysium.

She gazed at me; her life hung,
in that gaze, on mine:
and about us was at once Elysium.

## Das Ständchen | The Serenade

JOSEPH VON EICHENDORFF

*Hugo Wolf, 1888*

Auf die Dächer zwischen blassen
Wolken schaut der Mond herfür,
Ein Student dort auf den Gassen
Singt vor seiner Liebsten Tür.

From pallid cloud the moon
looks across roofs,
in the street, a student
sings at his love's door.

Und die Brunnen rauschen wieder
Durch die stille Einsamkeit,
Und der Wald vom Berge nieder,
wie in alter, schöner Zeit.

And again, fountains murmur
in the still and loneliness,
and the woods on the mountain
murmur, as in good old times.

So in meinen jungen Tagen
Hab ich manche Sommernacht
Auch die Laute hier geschlagen
Und manch lust'ges Lied erdacht.

So, in my young days,
often on a summer's night,
I too plucked my lute here
and invented merry songs.

Aber von der stillen Schwelle
Trugen sie mein Lieb zur Ruh,
Und du, fröhlicher Geselle,
Singe, sing nur immer zu!

But from that silent door
my love has been taken to rest.
As for you, happy man,
just sing on, sing on!

## Das Veilchen | The Violet

JOHANN WOLFGANG GOETHE

*Wolfgang Amadeus Mozart: K 476, 1785*

Ein Veilchen auf der Wiese stand
Gebückt in sich und unbekannt;
Es war ein herzigs Veilchen!
Da kam ein' junge Schäferin

A violet in the meadow stood,
bowed into itself and known to none;
it was a dear sweet violet!
Then came a young shepherdess,

| Mit leichtem Schritt und munterm Sinn | light of step and gay of heart, |
|---|---|

Mit leichtem Schritt und munterm
  Sinn
Daher, daher,
Die Wiese her, und sang.

light of step and gay of
  heart,
that way, that way,
across the meadow singing.

Ach! denkt das Veilchen, wär ich nur
Die schönste Blume der Natur,
Ach! nur ein kleines Weilchen,
Bis mich das Liebchen abgepflückt
Und an dem Busen matt gedrückt,
Ach nur, ach nur
Ein Viertelstündchen lang!

Ah, thinks the violet, could I but be
the fairest flower of nature—
for just, oh just a tiny while,
till I were by my loved-one plucked,
and pressed, limp, to her bosom—
for just, oh just
one tiny quarter hour!

Ach, aber ach! das Mädchen kam
Und nicht in acht das Veilchen nahm,
Ertrat das arme Veilchen.
Es sank und starb und freut sich noch:
Und sterb ich denn, so sterb ich doch
Durch sie, durch sie,
Zu ihren Füßen doch!
[Das arme Veilchen! es war ein herzigs
  Veilchen!]

Oh, but oh, the girl drew near,
heeded the violet not at all,
crushed the poor violet underfoot,
which dying fell, yet still rejoiced:
For though I die, yet still I die
through her, through her,
and at her feet!
(Poor thing! It was a dear sweet
  violet!)

## Das verlassene Mägdlein / Forsaken Servant-girl

EDUARD MÖRIKE

*Hans Pfitzner: Jugendlieder no. 5, 1884–87; op. 30, no. 2, 1922;
Robert Schumann: op. 64, no. 2, 1841–47; Hugo Wolf, 1888*

Früh, wann die Hähne krähn,
Eh die Sternlein verschwinden,
Muß ich am Herde stehn,
Muß Feuer zünden.

At cock-crow, early,
before the tiny stars are gone,
I must be at the hearth,
must light the fire.

Schön ist der Flammen Schein,
Es springen die Funken;
Ich schaue so drein,
In Leid versunken.

Pretty the flames' glow,
the sparks leap;
I stare into them,
lost in grief.

Plötzlich, da kommt es mir,
Treuloser Knabe,
Daß ich die Nacht von dir
Geträumet habe.

Suddenly it comes to me,
unfaithful boy,
that last night
I dreamt of you.

Träne auf Träne dann
Stürzet hernieder;
So kommt der Tag heran—
O ging er wieder!

Tear upon tear
then falls;
so the day starts—
would it were gone again!

## Das Zügenglöcklein / The Passing-bell

JOHANN GABRIEL SEIDL

*Franz Schubert: op. 80, no. 2, 1826*

Kling die Nacht durch, klinge,
süßen Frieden bringe
dem, für den du tönst!
Kling in weiter Ferne,

Sound, sound the night through,
bringing sweet peace
to him you toll for,
sound out afar,

so du Pilger gerne
mit der Welt versöhnst.

Aber wer will wandern
zu den lieben andern,
die vorausgewallt?
Zog er gern die Schelle
bebt er an der Schwelle,
wenn »Herein« erschallt.

Gilt's dem bösen Sohne,
der noch flucht dem Tone,
weil er heilig ist?
Nein, es klingt so lauter
wie ein Gottvertrauter
seine Laufbahn schließt.

Aber ist's ein Müder,
den verwaist die Brüder,
dem ein treues Tier
einzig ließ den Glauben
an die Welt nicht rauben,
ruf ihn, Gott, zu Dir!

Ist's der Frohen einer,
der die Freuden reiner
Lieb' und Freundschaft teilt,
gönn' ihm noch die Wonnen
unter dieser Sonnen,
wo er gerne weilt!

you who reconcile
the pilgrim with the world.

Who is it would journey
after the other dear pilgrims
gone before?
Gladly as he may have rung,
he trembles on the threshold
at the cry of 'Enter'.

Is it for the wicked son,
still cursing the tolling,
because it is holy?
No, its ringing is as pure
as a God-fearing man's,
departing this life.

But should it be one who is weary,
abandoned by his brothers,
one whom only some loyal animal
has saved from losing
faith in the world,
him, O God, call to Thee!

Should it be one of that happy band
who share the joys
of pure love and friendship,
him still grant delight
under this sun
where he fondly tarries!


## Daß sie hier gewesen | That She Was Here

FRIEDRICH RÜCKERT

*Franz Schubert: op. 59, no. 2, 1823*

Daß der Ostwind Düfte
Hauchet in die Lüfte,
Dadurch tut er kund,
Daß du hier gewesen!

Daß hier Tränen rinnen,
Dadurch wirst du innen,
Wär's dir sonst nicht kund,
Daß ich hier gewesen!

Schönheit oder Liebe,
Ob versteckt sie bliebe,
Düfte tun es und Tränen kund,
Daß sie hier gewesen!

The easterly wind,
scenting the air,
thereby makes known
that you were here!

The tears that here flow,
through them will you know—
if not yet aware—
that I was here!

Beauty or love,
though hidden remaining,
scents make known, and tears,
that she was here!

## Dein Angesicht / Your Face

HEINRICH HEINE

*Robert Schumann: op. 127, no. 2, 1840–51*

Dein Angesicht, so lieb und schön,
Das hab ich jüngst im Traum gesehn,
Es ist so mild und engelgleich,
Und doch so bleich, so schmerzensreich.

Und nur die Lippen, die sind rot;
Bald aber küßt sie bleich der Tod.
Erlöschen wird das Himmelslicht,
Das aus den frommen Augen bricht.

Your face so sweet and fair
lately in a dream I saw,
so mild and angel-like,
yet so pale, so full of pain.

And your lips, they alone are red;
but soon will death kiss them pale.
Out will go the heavenly light
that shines from your gentle eyes.

## Dein blaues Auge / Your Eyes of Blue

KLAUS GROTH

*Johannes Brahms: op. 59, no. 8, 1873*

Dein blaues Auge hält so still,
Ich blicke bis zum Grund.
Du fragst mich, was ich sehen will?
Ich sehe mich gesund.

Es brannte mich ein glühend Paar,
Noch schmerzt das Nachgefühl:
Das deine ist wie See so klar,
Und wie ein See so kühl.

Your eyes of blue remain so still,
into their depths I gaze.
You ask me what I wish to see?
I'm gazing to be healed.

I have been burnt by two ardent eyes,
the hurt of it pains still:
your eyes are limpid as a lake,
and as a lake as cool.

## Dem Unendlichen / To the Infinite One

FRIEDRICH GOTTLIEB KLOPSTOCK

*Franz Schubert, 1815*

Wie erhebt sich das Herz, wenn es dich,
Unendlicher, denkt! Wie sinkt
  es,
Wenn's auf sich herunterschaut!
Elend schaut's wehklagend dann und
  Nacht und Tod!

Allein du rufst mich aus meiner Nacht,
  der im Elend, der im Tod hilft!
Dann denk' ich es ganz, daß du ewig
  mich schufst,
Herrlicher, den kein Preis, unten am
  Grab, oben am Thron,
Herr Herr Gott, den, dankend
  entflammt, kein Jubel genug besingt!

Weht, Bäume des Lebens, ins
  Harfengetön!
Rausche mit ihnen ins Harfengetön,
  kristallner Strom!

How soars the heart whenever,
Infinite One, it considers you! How it
  sinks
when it looks down upon itself!
Lamenting, it then sees grief, and night
  and death!

You alone, who aid in death and grief,
  call me from my night!
Then am I fully mindful that you
  made me eternal,
Majesty, whom, by grave below, at
  throne above, no praise—
Lord God, whom no gratitude-kindled
  joy—sufficiently extols!

Blow, trees of life, to the harps'
  sound!
Babble with them to the harps' sound,
  crystal stream!

Ihr lispelt und rauscht, und, Harfen,
  ihr tönt
Nie es ganz! Gott ist es, den ihr preist!

You, harps, will babble, rustle and
  sound
it never fully! God it is you laud!

Donnert, Welten, in feierlichem Gang,
  in der Posaunen Chor!
Tönt, all' ihr Sonnen auf der Straße voll
  Glanz,
In der Posaunen Chor!

Thunder, worlds, in solemn motion, in
  the host of trumpets!
Sound, all you suns, upon the glory-
  filled way,
in the host of trumpets!

Ihr Welten, donnert,
Und du, der Posaunen Chor, hallest
Nie es ganz: Gott—nie es ganz: Gott,
Gott, Gott ist es, den ihr preist!

You, worlds, will thunder,
and you, host of trumpets, echo
it never fully: never fully—God: God,
God, God, it is you laud!


## Denk es, o Seele! / Consider, Soul!

EDUARD MÖRIKE

*Hans Pfitzner: op. 30, no. 3, 1922; Hugo Wolf, 1888*

Ein Tännlein grünet wo,
Wer weiß, im Walde,
Ein Rosenstrauch, wer sagt,
In welchem Garten?
Sie sind erlesen schon,
Denk es, o Seele!
Auf deinem Grab zu wurzeln
Und zu wachsen.

A fir grows green—where
in the wood, who knows?
A rosebush—who can say
in what garden?
Already marked they are,
consider, soul,
to root upon your grave
and grow.

Zwei schwarze Rößlein weiden
Auf der Wiese,
Sie kehren heim zur Stadt
In muntern Sprüngen.
Sie werden schrittweis gehn
Mit deiner Leiche;
Vielleicht, vielleicht noch eh
An ihren Hufen
Das Eisen los wird,
Das ich blitzen sehe!

Two black horses graze
on the meadow,
home they go to town
at a merry pace.
At a walk they will go
with your corpse;
maybe . . . even before
their hooves
shed the shoes
I see flashing!


## Der Alpenjäger / The Alpine Hunter

JOHANN MAYRHOFER

*Franz Schubert: op. 13, no. 3, 1817*

Auf hohem Bergesrücken,
Wo frischer alles grünt,
Ins Land hinabzublicken,
Das nebelleicht zerrinnt,
Erfreut den Alpenjäger.

On a lofty mountain ridge,
where all is a fresher green,
to gaze down on the land,
vanishing light as mist,
is the Alpine hunter's delight.

Je steiler und je schräger
Die Pfade sich verwinden,
Je mehr Gefahr aus Schlünden,

The steeper, more slanting
the tracks wind,
the greater the gorges' danger,

So freier schlägt die Brust.
Er ist der fernen Lieben,
Die ihm daheimgeblieben,
Sich seliger bewußt.

Und ist er nun am Ziele,
So drängt sich in der Stille
Ein süßes Bild ihm vor;
Der Sonne goldne Strahlen,
Sie weben und sie malen,
Die er im Tal erkor.

the freer beats his heart.
Of his distant love
who remains at home,
he thinks more blissfully.

His goal no sooner he reaches,
than, before him in the silence,
an image obtrudes that is sweet;
the sun's golden rays,
they form and picture
his chosen one in the valley.

## Der Alpenjäger | The Alpine Hunter

FRIEDRICH SCHILLER: from *Wilhelm Tell*

*Franz Liszt, 1845*

Es donnern die Höh'n, es zittert der
    Steg,
Nicht grauet dem Schützen auf
    schwindlichem Weg.
Er schreitet verwegen auf Feldern von
    Eis,
Da pranget kein Frühling, da grünet
    kein Reis;
Tief unter den Füßen ein nebliches
    Meer,
Erkennt er die Städte der Menschen
    nicht mehr;
Durch den Riß nur der Wolken erblickt
    er die Welt,
Tief unter den Wassern das grünende
    Feld.

The high places thunder, the frail
    bridge rocks,
the hunter on his dizzy path knows no
    fear.
Boldly the ice-fields he
    strides,
where no spring is resplendent, no twig
    green;
far below his feet, a sea of
    mist,
the towns of men he knows no
    more;
through the cloud-gap only does he
    glimpse the world,
far below the torrents, the field turning
    green.

## Der Alpenjäger | The Alpine Hunter

FRIEDRICH SCHILLER

*Franz Schubert: op. 37, no. 2, 1817 (second setting)*

Willst du nicht das Lämmlein hüten?
Lämmlein ist so fromm und sanft,
Nährt sich von des Grases Blüten,
Spielend an des Baches Ranft.
»Mutter, Mutter, laß mich gehen,
Jagen nach des Berges Höhen!«

Willst du nicht die Herde locken
Mit des Hornes munterm Klang?
Lieblich tönt der Schall der Glocken
In des Waldes Lustgesang.
»Mutter, Mutter, laß mich gehen,
Schweifen auf den wilden Höhen!«

Will you not tend the little lamb?
The little lamb, so meek and mild,
feeding off the flowering grasses,
gambolling beside the brook?
'Mother, mother, let me go
hunting, to the mountain heights.'

Will you not call in the herd
with cheery sound of horn?
Sweet is the note of the bells
amid the woodland's merry song.
'Mother, mother, let me go
roving on the wild heights.'

| | |
|---|---|
| Willst du nicht die Blümlein warten, | Will you not tend the little flowers |
| Die im Beete freundlich stehn? | that stand welcoming in their bed? |
| Draußen ladet dich kein Garten, | Out there, is no inviting garden, |
| Wild ists auf den wilden Höhn! | wild it is on the wild heights! |
| »Laß die Blümlein, laß sie blühen! | 'Leave the flowers, let them bloom! |
| Mutter, Mutter, laß mich ziehen!« | Mother, mother, let me away!' |
| | |
| Und der Knabe ging zu jagen, | And to hunt the boy did go, |
| Und es treibt und reißt ihn fort, | urged on, swept away, |
| Rastlos fort mit blindem Wagen | without rest and blind with daring, |
| An des Berges finstern Ort, | to the dark place of the mountain, |
| Vor ihm her mit Windesschnelle | ahead of him, fleet as the wind, |
| Flieht die zitternde Gazelle. | flees the trembling gazelle. |
| | |
| Auf der Felsen nackte Rippen | On to the bare ribs of the crags |
| Klettert sie mit leichtem Schwung, | with an easy bound she clambers, |
| Durch den Riß geborstner Klippen | over the gaps of broken cliffs |
| Trägt sie der gewagte Sprung, | her bold spring bears her, |
| Aber hinter ihr verwogen | but close behind, audacious, |
| Folgt er mit dem Todesbogen. | he pursues with deadly bow. |
| | |
| Jetzo auf den schroffen Zinken | Now, to the jagged teeth, |
| Hängt sie, auf dem höchsten Grat, | on the highest ridge she clings, |
| Wo die Felsen jäh versinken | where the rocks drop sheer |
| Und verschwunden ist der Pfad. | and the path has vanished. |
| Unter sich die steile Höhe, | Beneath—the dizzy drop, |
| Hinter sich des Feindes Nähe. | behind her nears the foe. |
| | |
| Mit des Jammers stummen Blicken | With looks of dumb distress |
| Fleht sie zu dem harten Mann, | that cruel man she entreats, |
| Fleht umsonst, denn loszudrücken | entreats in vain, for, about to fire, |
| Legt er schon den Bogen an. | he already aims his bow. |
| Plötzlich aus der Felsenspalte | Suddenly, from the rocky cleft, |
| Tritt der Geist, der Bergesalte. | steps the Spirit of the Mountain. |
| | |
| Und mit seinen Götterhänden | And, with his godly hands, |
| Schützt er das gequälte Tier. | he protects the tomented beast. |
| »Mußt du Tod und Jammer senden«, | 'Must you send death and distress,' |
| Ruft er, »bis herauf zu mir? | he calls, 'up here to me? |
| Raum für alle hat die Erde, | Room enough for all has earth, |
| Was verfolgst du meine Herde?« | why do you persecute my herd?' |

## Der Arbeitsmann | The Labourer

RICHARD DEHMEL

*Hans Pfitzner: op. 30, no. 4, 1922; Richard Strauss: op. 39, no. 3, 1897–98*

| | |
|---|---|
| Wir haben ein Bett, wir haben ein Kind, | We have a bed, we have a child, |
| mein Weib! | my wife! |
| Wir haben auch Arbeit, und gar zu | We also have work, and work for |
| zweit, | two, |
| und haben die Sonne und Regen und | and have the sun and rain and |
| Wind, | wind, |
| und uns fehlt nur eine Kleinigkeit, | and just one small thing we lack |
| um so frei zu sein, wie die Vögel sind: | to be as free as are the birds, |
| Nur Zeit. | just time. |

Wenn wir sonntags durch die Felder
  gehn,
mein Kind,
und über den Ähren weit und breit
das blaue Schwalbenvolk blitzen sehn,
oh, dann fehlt uns nicht das bißchen
  Kleid,
um so schön zu sein, wie die Vögel
  sind:
Nur Zeit.

Nur Zeit! wir wittern Gewitterwind,
wir Volk.
Nur eine kleine Ewigkeit;
uns fehlt ja nichts, mein Weib, mein
  Kind,
als all das, was durch uns gedeiht,
um so kühn zu sein, wie die Vögel sind:
Nur Zeit.

When Sundays we go through the
  fields,
my child,
and far and wide above the corn
watch flights of blue swallows flit,
ah, then, not scraps of clothes we
  lack
to be as fine as are the
  birds:
just time.

Just time! We scent a wind of storm,
we People.
Just one brief eternity;
naught do we lack, my wife, my
  child,
save all that flourishes through us,
to be as bold as are the birds:
just time.


## Der arme Peter | Poor Peter

HEINRICH HEINE

*Robert Schumann: op. 53, no. 3, 1840*

1
Der Hans und die Grete tanzen herum,
Und jauchzen vor lauter Freude.
Der Peter steht so still und stumm,
Und ist so blaß wie Kreide.

Der Hans und die Grete sind
  Bräut'gam und Braut,
Und blitzen im Hochzeitsgeschmeide.
Der arme Peter die Nägel kaut
Und geht im Werkeltagskleide.

Der Peter spricht leise vor sich her,
Und schaut betrübet auf beide:
Ach! wenn ich nicht gar zu vernünftig
  wär',
Ich täte mir was zuleide.

2
»In meiner Brust, da sitzt ein Weh,
Das will die Brust zersprengen;
Und wo ich steh' und wo ich geh',
Will's mich von hinnen drängen.

»Es treibt mich nach der Liebsten Näh',
Als könnt's die Grete heilen;
Doch wenn ich der ins Auge seh',
Muß ich von hinnen eilen.

»Ich steig' hinauf des Berges Höh',
Dort ist man doch alleine;
Und wenn ich still dort oben steh',
Dann steh' ich still und weine.«

1
Hans and Greta dance about,
crying aloud for joy.
Peter stands so silent and dumb,
looks as white as a sheet.

Hans and Greta are groom and
  bride,
glittering with wedding jewels.
Poor Peter's gnawing at his nails
and wearing his working clothes.

Says Peter quietly to himself,
gloomily eyeing the couple:
'Had I not the sense that I
  have,
I'd do myself some harm.

2
'In my breast a pain there is
will burst my breast asunder;
wherever I stay, wherever I go,
It drives me somewhere else.

'It drives me to be near my love,
as if Greta could heal my pain;
yet whenever I look her in the eye,
I'm forced to haste away.

'To the mountain's heights I climb,
for there one is alone;
and when I'm standing quiet there,
then quiet I stand and weep.'

3
Der arme Peter wankt vorbei,
Gar langsam, leichenblaß und scheu.
Es bleiben fast, wenn sie ihn sehn,
Die Leute auf der Straße stehn.

Die Mädchen flüstern sich ins Ohr:
»Der stieg wohl aus dem Grab hervor.«
Ach nein, ihr lieben Jungfräulein,
Der legt sich erst ins Grab hinein.

Er hat verloren seinen Schatz,
Drum ist das Grab der beste Platz,
Wo er am besten liegen mag,
Und schlafen bis zum Jüngsten Tag.

3
Poor Peter, he goes tottering by,
slowly, deathly pale and shy;
they almost stop, at the sight of him,
the people in the street.

Girls whisper in each other's ear,
'He must be risen from the grave.'
Which is not so, you maidens sweet,
in his grave he's about to lie.

He has lost his own true love,
and so the grave is the best place,
where it is best for him to lie
and sleep until Judgment Day.


## Der Einsame / The Solitary

CARL LAPPE

*Franz Schubert: op. 41, 1824?*

Wenn meine Grillen schwirren,
Bei Nacht, am spät erwärmten Herd,
Dann sitz ich mit vergnügtem Sinn
Vertraulich zu der Flamme hin,
So leicht, so unbeschwert.

Ein trautes, stilles Stündchen
Bleibt man noch gern am Feuer wach,
Man schürt, wenn sich die Lohe senkt,
Die Funken auf und sinnt und denkt:
Nun abermal ein Tag!

Was Liebes oder Leides
Sein Lauf für uns dahergebracht,
Es geht noch einmal durch den Sinn;
Allein das Böse wirft man hin,
Es störe nicht die Nacht.

Zu einem frohen Traume
Bereitet man gemach sich zu,
Wann sorgenlos ein holdes Bild
Mit sanfter Lust die Seele füllt,
Ergibt man sich der Ruh.

Oh, wie ich mir gefalle
In meiner stillen Ländlichkeit!
Was in dem Schwarm der lauten Welt
Das irre Herz gefesselt hält,
Gibt nicht Zufriedenheit.

Zirpt immer, liebe Heimchen,
In meiner Klause eng und klein.
Ich duld euch gern: ihr stört mich
  nicht,
Wenn euer Lied das Schweigen bricht,
Bin ich nicht ganz allein.

When my crickets chirrup
at night by my late-burning hearth,
happily I sit,
communing with the flame,
light-hearted and at ease.

For one sweet quiet hour
it's good to linger by the fire,
stirring the sparks when the blaze
goes down, musing and thinking:
'Well, that's another day!'

Whatever joy or sorrow
the course of it has brought,
runs once more through the mind;
the bad, however, gets cast aside,
so as not to spoil the night.

For pleasant dreams
we gently compose ourselves,
and when lightly, some sweet image
fills our soul with tender joy,
we yield to rest.

Oh, how I love
my peaceful rustic life!
What, in the loud teeming world,
holds captive the unruly heart,
brings no content.

Chirp away, dear crickets,
in my own small room.
I'm glad you're there: you're no
  trouble,
and when your song breaks the silence,
I'm no longer all alone.

## Der Einsiedler / The Hermit

JOSEPH VON EICHENDORFF

*Robert Schumann: op. 83, no. 3, 1850*

Komm, Trost der Welt, du stille Nacht!
Wie steigst du von den Bergen sacht,
Die Lüfte alle schlafen,
Ein Schiffer nur noch, wandermüd',
Singt übers Meer sein Abendlied
Zu Gottes Lob im Hafen.

Come, comfort of the world, still night!
How softly from the hills you climb,
the breezes all are sleeping,
one sailor still, travel-weary,
sends over the sea his evening hymn
to God's praise from the harbour.

Die Jahre wie die Wolken gehn
Und lassen mich hier einsam stehn,
Die Welt hat mich vergessen,
Da trat'st du wunderbar zu mir,
Wenn ich beim Waldesrauschen hier
Gedankenvoll gesessen.

The years, like clouds, go by
and leave me lonely here,
forgotten by the world,
then wondrously you came to me,
as, to the wood's rustling, I sat here
deeply sunk in thought.

O Trost der Welt, du stille Nacht!
Der Tag hat mich so müd' gemacht,
Das weite Meer schon dunkelt,
Laß ausruhn mich von Lust und Not,
Bis daß das ew'ge Morgenrot
Den stillen Wald durchfunkelt.

O comfort of the world, still night!
The day has tired me so,
the wide sea darkens now,
let me rest from joy and pain,
until the eternal dawn
lights the silent wood.

## Der Feuerreiter / Fire-rider

EDUARD MÖRIKE

*Hugo Wolf, 1888*

Sehet ihr am Fensterlein
dort die rote Mütze wieder?
Nicht geheuer muß es sein,
denn er geht schon auf und nieder.
Und auf einmal welch Gewühle
bei der Brücke, nach dem Feld!
Horch, das Feuerglöcklein gellt:
    hinterm Berg,
    hinterm Berg
brennt es in der Mühle!

See, at the window
there, his red cap again?
Something must be wrong,
for he's pacing to and fro.
And all of a sudden, what a throng,
at the bridge, heading for the fields!
Hark, the fire-bell:
    over the hill,
    over the hill,
a blaze at the mill!

Schaut! da sprengt er wütend schier
durch das Tor, der Feuerreiter,
auf dem rippendürren Tier,
als auf einer Feuerleiter!
Querfeldein! Durch Qualm und
    Schwüle
rennt er schon, und ist am Ort!
Drüben schallt es fort und fort:
    hinterm Berg,
    hinterm Berg
brennt es in der Mühle.

Look, there he gallops, madly almost,
through the gate, the fire-rider,
his ribby mount
like a fireman's ladder!
Cross-country, through smoke and
    heat,
he races, and is there.
On and on the bell peals:
    over the hill,
    over the hill,
a blaze at the mill!

Der so oft den roten Hahn
meilenweit von fern gerochen,
mit des heilgen Kreuzes Span
freventlich die Glut besprochen—

You who have so often smelt
fire from many leagues away,
with the splinter of the True Cross
have sacrilegiously subdued the flames,

weh! dir grinst vom Dachgestühle
dort der Feind im Höllenschein,
Gnade Gott der Seele dein!
  Hinterm Berg,
  hinterm Berg
rast er in der Mühle!

Keine Stunde hielt es an,
bis die Mühle borst in Trümmer;
doch den kecken Reitersmann
sah man von der Stunde nimmer.
Volk und Wagen im Gewühle
kehren heim von all dem Graus;
auch das Glöcklein klinget aus:
  Hinterm Berg,
  hinterm Berg
brennts!—

Nach der Zeit ein Müller fand
ein Gerippe samt der Mützen
aufrecht an der Kellerwand
auf der beinern Mähre sitzen:
Feuerreiter, wie so kühle
reitest du in deinem Grab!
Husch! da fällts in Asche ab.
  Ruhe wohl,
  ruhe wohl
drunten in der Mühle!

ah, grinning at you from the rafters,
there, in the hellish light, the Foe.
God have mercy on your soul!
  Over the hill,
  over the hill,
he's raging through the mill!

Not an hour it was
before the mill collapsed in rubble;
but the daring horseman was
from that hour not seen again.
People, carts go thronging
homewards from the horror;
and the bell, too, ceases:
  over the hill,
  over the hill,
a blaze!—

Afterwards a miller found
a skeleton, complete with cap,
upright against the cellar wall,
mounted on the bony mare:
so cool, fire-rider,
are you riding in your grave!
Instantly into ash it falls.
  Rest in peace,
  rest in peace,
down here in the mill!

## Der Fischer / The Fisher

JOHANN WOLFGANG GOETHE

*Johann Friedrich Reichardt, 1809; Franz Schubert: op. 5, no. 3, 1815;*
*Richard Strauss: no opus number*

Das Wasser rauscht', das Wasser
  schwoll,
Ein Fischer saß daran,
Sah nach dem Angel ruhevoll,
Kühl bis ans Herz hinan.
Und wie er sitzt und wie er lauscht,
Teilt sich die Flut empor;
Aus dem bewegten Wasser rauscht
Ein feuchtes Weib hervor.

Sie sang zu ihm, sie sprach zu ihm:
Was lockst du meine Brut
Mit Menschenwitz und Menschenlist
Hinauf in Todesglut?
Ach wüßtest du, wie's Fischlein ist
So wohlig auf dem Grund,
Du stiegst herunter, wie du bist,
Und würdest erst gesund.

Labt sich die liebe Sonne nicht,
Der Mond sich nicht im Meer?
Kehrt wellenatmend ihr Gesicht
Nicht doppelt schöner her?

The waters rushed, the waters
  swelled,
a fisher sat beside,
gazing calmly at his line,
cool to the very heart.
And as he sits and as he harks,
the waves surge and divide;
and splashing from their turbulence
a watery woman bursts.

She sang to him, she spoke to him:
Why do you lure my brood
by human wit and human guile
aloft to the deadly glow?
Ah, if you knew the tiny fish,
how content they are below,
you'd clamber down here, as you are,
and be, for the first time, whole.

Does not the dear sun refresh itself,
the moon, too, in the sea?
Do not their faces, breathing waves,
return here doubly fair?

Lockt dich der tiefe Himmel nicht,
Das feuchtverklärte Blau?
Lockt dich dein eigen Angesicht
Nicht her in ewgen Tau?

Das Wasser rauscht', das Wasser schwoll,
Netzt' ihm den nackten Fuß;
Sein Herz wuchs ihm so sehnsuchtsvoll,
Wie bei der Liebsten Gruß.
Sie sprach zu ihm, sie sang zu ihm;
Da wars um ihn geschehn:
Halb zog sie ihn, halb sank er hin,
Und ward nicht mehr gesehn.

Are you not drawn by deep-blue sky,
by moisture-radiant blue?
Are you not drawn by your own face,
here, to eternal dew?

The waters rushed, the waters swelled,
made wet his naked foot;
great with longing waxed his heart
as at the greeting of his love.
She spoke to him, she sang to him;
for him the end was nigh:
half pulled, half sinking, down he went,
and never was seen more.

## Der Freund | The Friend

JOSEPH VON EICHENDORFF

*Hugo Wolf, 1888*

Wer auf den Wogen schliefe,
Ein sanft gewiegtes Kind,
Kennt nicht des Lebens Tiefe,
Vor süßem Träumen blind.

Doch wen die Stürme fassen
Zu wildem Tanz und Fest,
Wen hoch auf dunklen Straßen
Die falsche Welt verläßt:

Der lernt sich wacker rühren,
Durch Nacht und Klippen hin
Lernt der das Steuer führen
Mit sichrem, ernstem Sinn.

Der ist vom echten Kerne,
Erprobt zu Lust und Pein,
Der glaubt an Gott und Sterne,
Der soll mein Schiffmann sein!

Whoever on the waves would sleep,
a gently cradled child,
knows not the depths of life,
is with sweet dreaming blind.

But he whom the storms seize
for wild dance and feast,
whom, high upon dark paths,
the false world abandons:

learns bravely to bestir himself
through night and cliffs,
learns to steer a course
with sure and serious mind.

He is of sound heart,
proven in joy and pain,
believes in God and the stars,
my helmsman shall he be!

## Der Gang zum Liebchen | The Way to the Beloved

BOHEMIAN FOLK SONG attributed to JOSEF WENZIG

*Johannes Brahms: op. 48, no. 1, 1857*

Es glänzt der Mond nieder,
ich sollte doch wieder
zu meinem Liebchen,
wie mag es ihr gehn?

Ach weh, sie verzaget
und klaget und klaget,
daß sie mich nimmer
im Leben wird sehn!

The moon shines down,
and I ought again
to my love—
how is she faring?

Alas, she's despairing,
complaining, complaining
that me nevermore
will she see in this life.

| | |
|---|---|
| Es ging der Mond unter, | The moon went down |
| ich eilte doch munter, | and briskly I hastened |
| und eilte, daß keiner | and hastened so that none |
| mein Liebchen entführt. | should carry off my love. |
| | |
| Ihr Täubchen, o girret, | Oh coo, you doves, |
| ihr Lüftchen, o schwirret, | Oh blow, you breezes, |
| daß keiner mein Liebchen, | so that my love, |
| mein Liebchen entführt! | my love none carry off! |

## Der Gärtner / The Gardener

EDUARD MÖRIKE

*Robert Schumann: op. 107, no. 3, 1851; Hugo Wolf, 1888*

| | |
|---|---|
| Auf ihrem Leibrößlein, | On her favourite mount |
| So weiß wie der Schnee, | as white as snow, |
| Die schönste Prinzessin | the fairest princess |
| Reit't durch die Allee. | rides through the avenue. |
| | |
| Der Weg, den das Rößlein | The path where her steed |
| Hintanzet so hold, | so delightfully prances, |
| Der Sand, den ich streute, | the sand that I strewed, |
| Er blinket wie Gold. | they sparkle like gold. |
| | |
| Du rosenfarbs Hütlein, | Little pink hat, |
| Wohl auf und wohl ab, | bobbing up, bobbing down, |
| O wirf eine Feder | Oh, throw a feather |
| Verstohlen herab! | secretly down! |
| | |
| Und willst du dagegen | If you, in return, want |
| Eine Blüte von mir, | a flower from me, |
| Nimm tausend für eine, | for one, take a thousand, |
| Nimm alle dafür! | for one, take all! |

## Der Gärtner / The Gardener

JOSEPH VON EICHENDORFF

*Robert Franz: op. 10, no. 4; Armin Knab, 1918–22;*
*Hans Pfitzner: op. 9, no. 1, 1888–89; Othmar Schoeck: op. 20, no. 11, 1905–14*

| | |
|---|---|
| Wohin ich geh' und schaue, | Wherever I walk and gaze, |
| In Feld und Wald und Tal, | in field and wood and vale, |
| Vom Berg hinab in die Aue: | from mountain down to meadow: |
| Vielschöne, hohe Fraue, | most noble, beauteous lady, |
| Grüß' ich dich tausendmal. | you I greet a thousand times. |
| | |
| In meinem Garten find' ich | I find in my garden |
| Viel' Blumen, schön und fein, | many fine and beautiful flowers, |
| Viel' Kränze wohl draus wind' ich | fashion from them many garlands, |
| Und tausend Gedanken bind' ich | binding a thousand thoughts |
| Und Grüße mit darein. | and greetings with them. |

*Ihr* darf ich keinen reichen,
Sie ist zu hoch und schön,
Die müssen alle verbleichen,
Die Liebe nur ohnegleichen
Bleibt ewig im Herzen stehn.

Ich schein' wohl froher Dinge
Und schaffe auf und ab,
Und, ob das Herz zerspringe,
Ich grabe fort und singe
Und grab' mir bald mein Grab.

To her may I give none,
too noble is she and fair.
All will have to fade,
but love beyond compare
remains ever in my heart.

Cheerful I may seem,
at my work here and there,
and though my heart break,
I shall dig away and sing,
and dig soon my own grave.

## Der Genesene an die Hoffnung | He Who Has Recovered Addresses Hope

EDUARD MÖRIKE

*Hugo Wolf, 1888*

Tödlich graute mir der Morgen:
Doch schon lag mein Haupt, wie süß!
Hoffnung, dir im Schoß verborgen,
Bis der Sieg gewonnen hieß.
Opfer bracht ich allen Göttern,
Doch vergessen warest du;
Seitwärts von den ewgen Rettern
Sahest du dem Feste zu.

O vergib, du Vielgetreue!
Tritt aus deinem Dämmerlicht,
Daß ich dir ins ewig neue,
Mondenhelle Angesicht
Einmal schaue, recht von Herzen,
Wie ein Kind und sonder Harm;
Ach, nur einmal ohne Schmerzen
Schließe mich in deinen Arm!

Fatal dawned the day for me:
yet my head lay, how sweetly
hidden, hope, in your lap,
till victory was reckoned won.
Sacrifice I made to all the gods,
but you were overlooked;
from the eternal saviours set apart,
upon the feast you gazed.

O forgive, most true one,
from your twilight step forth,
that I at your eternally new
moon-bright face may
for once, from my very heart, gaze
like a child and without sorrow;
ah, just once, without agony,
enfold me in your arms!

## Der Hidalgo | The Hidalgo

EMANUEL GEIBEL

*Robert Schumann: op. 30, no. 3, 1840*

Es ist so süß zu scherzen
Mit Liedern und mit Herzen
Und mit dem ernsten Streit!
Erglänzt des Mondes Schimmer,
Da treibt's mich fort vom Zimmer,
Durch Platz und Gassen weit;
Da bin zur Lieb ich immer
Wie zum Gefecht bereit.

Die Schönen von Sevilla
Mit Fächern und Mantilla
Blicken den Strom entlang;
Sie lauschen mit Gefallen,

So sweet it is to sport
with songs and hearts
and serious quarrel!
When the moon gleams,
from my room I'm drawn,
through square and streets;
as ready for love
as for fight.

The beauties of Seville
with fan and mantilla
gaze up the river;
with favour they listen

Wenn meine Lieder schallen
Zum Mandolinenklang,
Und dunkle Rosen fallen
Mir vom Balkon zum Dank.

when my songs sound
to the mandolin,
and dark roses drop
from the balcony as thanks.

Ich trage, wenn ich singe,
Die Zither und die Klinge
Vom Toledan'schen Stahl.
Ich sing an manchem Gitter
Und höhne manchen Ritter
Mit keckem Lied zumal,
Den Damen gilt die Zither,
Die Klinge dem Rival.

Singing, I carry
my zither and my blade
of Toledo steel.
At many a lattice I sing
and mock many a knight
in bold song as well,
the zither for the ladies,
the blade for the rival.

Auf denn zum Abenteuer,
Schon losch der Sonne Feuer
Jenseits der Berge aus.
Der Mondnacht Dämmrungsstunden,
Sie bringen Liebeskunden,
Sie bringen blutgen Strauß,
Und Blumen oder Wunden
Trag morgen ich nach Haus.

Off, then, to adventure,
the sun's fire has gone out
beyond the hills.
The moon hours of night
will bring tidings of love,
will bring bloody combat,
and flowers or wounds
I'll bear home tomorrow.

### Der Himmel hat eine Träne geweint | Heaven Shed a Tear

FRIEDRICH RÜCKERT

*Max Reger: op. 35, no. 2, 1899; Robert Schumann: op. 37, no. 1, 1840*

Der Himmel hat eine Träne geweint,
Die hat sich ins Meer zu verlieren
  gemeint;
Die Muschel kam und schloß sie ein,
Du sollst nun meine Perle sein,
Du sollst nicht vor den Wogen zagen,
Ich will hindurch dich ruhig tragen.
O du, mein Schmerz, o du, meine Lust,
Du Himmelsträn' in meiner Brust!
Gib, Himmel, daß ich in reinem
  Gemüte
Den reinsten deiner Tropfen hüte.

Heaven shed a tear that thought
to lose itself in the
  sea;
the mussel came and shut it in:
My pearl shall you now be,
the waves you shall not fear,
I will bear you calmly through.
Oh you, my pain, oh you, my joy,
tear of heaven in my breast!
Grant, heaven, that I in
  purity
preserve the purest of your drops.

### Der Hirt auf dem Felsen | The Shepherd on the Rock

WILHELM MÜLLER: after *The Shepherd*

*Franz Schubert: op. 129, 1828*

Wenn auf dem höchsten Fels ich steh',
Ins tiefe Tal herniederseh',
Und singe:
Fern aus dem tiefen dunklen Tal
Schwingt sich empor der Widerhall
Der Klüfte.

When on the highest rock I stand,
gaze down into the deep valley
and sing:
from afar in the deep dark valley
floats up the echo
of the ravines.

Je weiter meine Stimme dringt,
Je heller sie mir widerklingt
Von unten.
Mein Liebchen wohnt so weit von mir,
Drum sehn ich mich so heiß nach ihr
Hinüber.

In tiefem Gram verzehr ich mich,
Mir ist die Freude hin,
Auf Erden mir die Hoffnung wich,
Ich hier so einsam bin.

So sehnend klang im Wald das
   Lied,
So sehnend klang es durch die Nacht,
Die Herzen es zum Himmel zieht
Mit wunderbarer Macht.
Der Frühling will kommen,
Der Frühling, mein Freund,
Nun mach ich mich fertig,
Zum Wandern bereit.

Je weiter meine Stimme dringt,
Je heller sie mir widerklingt
Von unten.

The further my voice reaches,
the clearer its echo
from below.
So far away my loved one lives,
wherefore I yearn so ardently to be
where she is.

With deep grief I am consumed,
my joy has gone,
abandoned am I by earthly hope,
and so lonely here.

So longingly sounded my song in the
   wood,
so longingly through the night,
drawing hearts to heaven
with wondrous power.
Spring is coming,
spring, who is my friend,
and now I make ready,
make ready to journey.

The further my voice reaches,
the clearer its echo
from below.

## Der Jäger / The Huntsman

EDUARD MÖRIKE

*Hugo Wolf, 1888*

Drei Tage Regen fort und fort,
Kein Sonnenschein zur Stunde;
Drei Tage lang kein gutes Wort
Aus meiner Liebsten Munde!

Sie trutzt mit mir und ich mit ihr,
So hat sie's haben wollen;
Mir aber nagt's am Herzen hier,
Das Schmollen und das Grollen.

Willkommen denn, des Jägers Lust,
Gewittersturm und Regen!
Fest zugeknöpft die heiße Brust,
Und jauchzend euch entgegen!

Nun sitzt sie wohl daheim und lacht
Und scherzt mit den Geschwistern;
Ich höre in des Waldes Nacht
Die alten Blätter flüstern.

Nun sitzt sie wohl und weinet laut
Im Kämmerlein, in Sorgen;
Mir ist es wie dem Wilde traut,
In Finsternis geborgen.

Three days of endless rain,
no sunshine is there now;
no kindly word for three days
from my beloved's lips.

She is sulking, so am I,
thus would she have it be;
but here at my heart it gnaws,
this sulking and this bitterness.

Welcome, then, to the hunter's joy,
to thunderstorm and rain!
Button tight the ardent breast,
and, exulting, off to meet you!

She now sits at home and laughs,
and with her sisters jests;
I harken in the forest night
to the whispering of old leaves.

Now will she sit and loudly weep
in her tiny room in sorrow;
I feel as snugly as my prey,
in darkness, safe from danger.

Kein Hirsch und Rehlein überall!
Ein Schuß zum Zeitvertreibe!
Gesunder Knall und Widerhall
Erfrischt das Mark im Leibe.—

Doch wie der Donner nun verhallt
In Tälern, durch die Runde,
Ein plötzlich Weh mich überwallt,
Mir sinkt das Herz zu Grunde.

Sie trutzt mit mir und ich mit ihr,
So hat sie's haben wollen;
Mir aber frißt's am Herzen hier,
Das Schmollen und das Grollen.

Und auf! und nach der Liebsten Haus!
Und sie gefaßt ums Mieder!
»Drück mir die nassen Locken aus,
Und küß und hab mich wieder!«

No stag, no deer, anywhere!
To pass the time—a shot!
The healthy crack and echo
restore my heart to life.

But as the thundering dies away
in the valleys all around,
I am assailed by sudden woe,
my heart sinks like a stone.

She is sulking, so am I,
thus would she have it be;
but at my heart it eats away,
this sulking and this bitterness.

Away, and to my dearest's house!
Arms round her bodice twine!
Wring out these sopping locks of mine,
kiss me and take me back!

## Der Jäger / The Huntsman

FRIEDRICH HALM

*Johannes Brahms: op. 95, no. 4, 1884*

Mein Lieb ist ein Jäger,
Und grün ist sein Kleid,
Und blau ist sein Auge,
Nur sein Herz ist zu weit.

Mein Lieb ist ein Jäger,
Trifft immer ins Ziel,
Und Mädchen berückt er,
So viel er nur will.

Mein Lieb ist ein Jäger,
Kennt Wege und Spur,
Zu mir aber kommt er
Durch die Kirchtüre nur.

My love is a huntsman,
and green is his dress,
and blue are his eyes
but his heart is too free.

My love is a huntsman,
never misses his mark,
and girls he ensnares
as many as he will.

My love is a huntsman,
he knows ways and tracks,
but to me shall he come
by the church-door alone.

## Der Jüngling am Bache / The Youth by the Brook

FRIEDRICH SCHILLER

*Franz Schubert: first setting, 1815; second setting: op. 87, no. 3, 1819*

An der Quelle saß der Knabe,
Blumen wand er sich zum Kranz,
Und er sah sie fortgerissen,
Treiben in der Wellen Tanz.
»Und so fliehen meine Tage
Wie die Quelle rastlos hin!
Und so bleichet meine Jugend,
Wie die Kränze schnell verblühn!

By the spring the youth sat,
twined a garland of flowers,
saw them snatched away,
drifting on the dancing waves.
'And so do my days speed hence
like the restless brook!
And so does my youth grow pale
like the fast-fading garlands!

| Fraget nicht, warum ich traure | 'Ask not why I mourn |
| In des Lebens Blütenzeit! | in life's bloom-time. |
| Alles freuet sich und hoffet, | All things rejoice and hope |
| Wenn der Frühling sich erneut. | with spring's renewal. |
| Aber diese tausend Stimmen | But these thousand voices |
| Der erwachenden Natur | of awakening nature, |
| Wecken in dem tiefen Busen | deep in the breast rouse, |
| Mir den schweren Kummer nur. | for me, but grievous sorrow. |

| Was soll mir die Freude frommen, | 'What shall the joy avail |
| Die der schöne Lenz mir beut? | which fair spring offers me? |
| Eine nur ists, die ich suche, | Only one there is I seek. |
| Sie ist nah und ewig weit. | She is near and eternally far. |
| Sehnend breit ich meine Arme | Longingly, I open my arms |
| Nach dem teuren Schattenbild, | to her dear shadowy form; |
| Ach, ich kann es nicht erreichen, | but cannot, alas, reach her, |
| Und das Herz bleibt ungestillt! | and my heart remains unquieted! |

| Komm herab, du schöne Holde, | 'Come down, fair sweet one, |
| Und verlaß dein stolzes Schloß! | and leave your proud castle. |
| Blumen, die der Lenz geboren, | Flowers born of spring |
| Streu ich dir in deinen Schoß. | will I strew into your lap. |
| Horch, der Hain erschallt von Liedern, | Hark, the wood resounds with song, |
| Und die Quelle rieselt klar! | and the spring ripples bright! |
| Raum ist in der kleinsten Hütte | Room there is in the tiniest hut |
| Für ein glücklich liebend Paar.« | for a couple happy in love.' |

## Der Jüngling an der Quelle | The Young Man at the Brook

JOHANN GAUDENZ VON SALIS

*Franz Schubert, 1815?*

| Leise rieselnder Quell! | Softly murmuring brook, |
| Ihr wallenden, flispernden Pappeln! | waving, whispering poplars, |
| Euer Schlummergeräusch | your slumber-sounds |
| Wecket die Liebe nur auf. | do but awaken love. |
| Linderung sucht ich bei euch, | At your side I sought relief, |
| Und sie zu vergessen, die Spröde, | and to forget her, the coy one, |
| Ach, und Blätter und Bach | and ah, leaves and brook |
| Seufzen, Geliebte, dir nach, | sigh, beloved, for you, |
| Ach, und Blätter und Bach | and ah, leaves and brook |
| Seufzen, Geliebte, dir nach. | sigh, beloved, for you. |

## Der Jüngling und der Tod | The Young Man and Death

JOSEF VON SPAUN

*Franz Schubert, 1817*

| *Der Jüngling:* | *Young man:* |
| Die Sonne sinkt, | The sun sinks, |
| Ach könnt ich mit ihr scheiden, | ah, that I might depart with it, |
| Mit ihrem letzten Strahl entfliehn! | might flee with its last ray, |
| Ach diese namenlosen Qualen meiden | escape, ah, these nameless torments |
| Und weit in schönre Welten ziehn! | and travel far to finer worlds! |

O komme, Tod!
Und löse diese Bande!
Ich lächle dir, o Knochenmann,
Entführe mich leicht in geträumte
    Lande!
O komm und rühre mich doch an,
O komm!

*Der Tod:*
Es ruht sich kühl und sanft in meinen
    Armen,
Du rufst, ich will mich deiner Qual
    erbarmen.

O Death, come
and loose these bonds.
Upon you, skeleton, I smile,
bear me to dream lands easily
    away.
O come, touch me,
come!

*Death:*
Cool and gentle it is to rest in my
    arms.
You call. I will take pity on your
    torment.


## Der Kampf / The Fight

FRIEDRICH SCHILLER

*Franz Schubert: op. 110, 1817*

Nein—länger, länger werd' ich diesen
    Kampf nicht kämpfen,
Den Riesenkampf der Pflicht.
Kannst du des Herzens Flammentrieb
    nicht dämpfen,
So fordre, Tugend, dieses Opfer
    nicht.

No, no longer will I fight this
    fight,
the monster-fight of duty.
If you cannot quench my heart's
    flames,
then, Virtue, ask not this sacrifice of
    me.

Geschworen hab ich's, ja, ich hab's
    geschworen,
Mich selbst zu bändigen.
Hier ist dein Kranz. Er sei auf ewig mir
    verloren,
Nimm ihn zurück, und laß mich
    sündigen.

Sworn have I—yes,
    sworn
my own self to subdue.
Here is your crown. To me be it lost
    forever.
Accept it back, and let me
    sin.

Zerrissen sei, was du und ich bedungen
    haben,
Sie liebt mich—deine Krone sei
    verscherzt.
Glückselig, wer, in Wonnetrunkenheit
    begraben,
So leicht wie ich den tiefen Fall
    verschmerzt.

Torn up be that which you and I
    agreed,
she loves me—forfeit be your
    crown.
Happy, who in drunkenness of bliss
    interred,
banishes, with my ease, the long fall's
    agony.

Sie sieht den Wurm an meiner Jugend
    Blume nagen
Und meinen Lenz entfloh'n;
Bewundert still mein heldenmütiges
    Entsagen,
Und großmutsvoll beschließt sie meinen
    Lohn.

The worm she sees that gnaws at my
    youth's bloom,
my spring-time she sees flown;
silent she marvels at my heroic
    denial,
and, generous, determines my
    reward.

Mißtraue, schöne Seele, dieser
    Engelgüte!
Dein Mitleid waffnet zum Verbrecher
    mich,

Mistrust, fair soul, this angel-
    kindness!
Your compassion arms and makes me
    criminal.

Gibt's in des Lebens unermeßlichem
    Gebiete,
Gibt's einen andern schönern Lohn—
    als dich?

Als das Verbrechen, das ich ewig
    fliehen wollte?
Entsetzliches Geschick!
Der einz'ge Lohn, der meine Tugend
    krönen sollte,
Ist meiner Tugend letzter Augenblick.

Is there, in the immeasurable realm of
    life,
another, finer, reward than
    you?

Than that crime I sought eternally to
    flee?
O fearful fate!
The one reward that should my virtue
    crown,
will be the moment of my virtue's end.


## Der König bei der Krönung / The King at His Coronation

EDUARD MÖRIKE

*Max Reger: op. 70, no. 2, 1902–03; Hugo Wolf, 1886*

Dir angetrauet am Altare,
O Vaterland, wie bin ich dein!
Laß für das Rechte mich und Wahre
Nun Priester oder Opfer sein!
Geuß auf mein Haupt, Herr! deine
    Schale,
Ein köstlich Öl des Friedens, aus,
Daß ich wie eine Sonne strahle
Dem Vaterland und meinem Haus!

Wedded to you at the altar,
O Fatherland, I am yours!
Let me for the right and true
now priest or offering be!
Pour out upon my head, O
    Lord,
your cup with precious oil of peace,
that I, like a sun, may shine
upon Fatherland and my home!


## Der König in Thule / The King in Thule

JOHANN WOLFGANG GOETHE: from *Faust, Part 1*

*Franz Liszt, ed. 1843; Johann Friedrich Reichardt, ed. 1809;*
*Franz Schubert: op. 5, no. 5, 1816; Carl Friedrich Zelter, ed. 1812*

Es war ein König in Thule
Gar treu bis an das Grab,
Dem sterbend seine Buhle
Einen goldnen Becher gab.

A king there was in Thule,
was faithful unto death,
to whom his lady, dying,
a golden goblet gave.

Es ging ihm nichts darüber,
Er leert' ihn jeden Schmaus;
Die Augen gingen ihm über,
So oft er trank daraus.

No thing did he love dearer,
he drained it at each feast;
and in his eyes welled tears,
whenever he drank from it.

Und als er kam zu sterben,
Zählt' er seine Städt' im Reich,
Gönnt' alles seinen Erben,
Den Becher nicht zugleich.

And when he came to die,
he totalled his kingdom's towns,
granted everything to his heirs,
the goblet, though, excepted.

Er saß beim Königsmahle,
Die Ritter um ihn her,
Auf hohem Vätersaale
Dort auf dem Schloß am Meer.

He sat at the royal banquet,
amongst his noble knights,
in the lofty hall of his fathers
in that castle by the sea.

Dort stand der alte Zecher,
Trank letzte Lebensglut,
Und warf den heilgen Becher
Hinunter in die Flut.

Er sah ihn stürzen, trinken
Und sinken tief ins Meer.
Die Augen täten ihm sinken;
Trank nie einen Tropfen mehr.

There stood that agèd drinker,
and drank his life's last glow;
and hurled the sacred goblet
into the waves below.

He watched it plunge and drink
and sink deep in the sea.
His eyes sank shut forever;
not one drop more drank he.

## Der Kreuzzug | The Crusade

KARL GOTTFRIED VON LEITNER

*Franz Schubert, 1827*

Ein Münich steht in seiner Zell
am Fenstergitter grau,
viel Rittersleut in Waffen hell,
die reiten durch die Au.

Sie singen Lieder frommer Art
in schönem, ernsten Chor,
inmitten fliegt, von Seide zart,
die Kreuzesfahn' empor.

Sie steigen an dem Seegestad
das hohe Schiff hinan.
Es läuft hinweg auf grünem Pfad,
ist bald nur wie ein Schwan.

Der Münich steht am Fenster noch,
schaut ihnen nach hinaus:
»Ich bin, wie ihr, ein Pilger doch,
und bleib ich gleich zu Haus.

Des Lebens Fahrt durch Wellentrug
und heißen Wüstensand,
es ist ja auch ein Kreuzeszug
in das gelobte Land.«

In his cell a monk stands
at the window lattice grey.
Many knights with weapons bright
ride through the meadow.

Hymns of a pious kind they sing
in chorus fine and grave,
in their midst, of dainty silk,
the cross's banner streams.

On the shore of the sea they go
aboard the lofty ship
which on its green path scuds away,
and soon is but like a swan.

Still at the window stands the monk,
gazes out after them:
'I am, like you, a pilgrim,
though I remain at home.

'Life's voyage over deceiving waves
and burning desert sand—
that also is a crusade
to the Promised Land.'

## Der Kuß | The Kiss

CHRISTIAN FELIX WEISSE

*Ludwig van Beethoven: op. 128, 1822*

Ich war bei Chloen ganz allein,
Und küssen wollt ich sie:
Jedoch sie sprach,
Sie würde schrein,
Es sei vergebne Müh.

Ich wagt es doch und küßte sie,
Trotz ihrer Gegenwehr.
Und schrie sie nicht?
Jawohl, sie schrie,
Doch lange hinterher.

I was with Chloe all alone,
and I wished to kiss her:
but she said
she would scream,
vain effort would it be.

But I dared and kissed her,
although she did resist.
And did she not scream?
Oh yes, she screamed,
but not until long after.

## Der Mohrenfürst | The Moorish Prince

FERDINAND FREILIGRATH

*Carl Loewe: op. 97, no. 1, ed. 1844*

Sein Heer durchwogte das
  Palmental.
Er wand um die Locken den
  Purpurschal;
Er hing um die Schultern die
  Löwenhaut;
Kriegerisch klirrte der Becken Laut.

Through the palmy vale his army
  surged.
His locks with purple scarf he
  wound;
his shoulders draped with lion
  skin;
the cymbals clashed for war.

Wie Termiten wogte der wilde
  Schwarm.
Den goldumreiften, den schwarzen Arm
Schlang er um die Geliebte fest:
»Schmücke dich, Mädchen, zum
  Siegesfest!

Like ants the fierce host
  swarmed.
His black, gold-banded arm
firmly he clasped about his love:
'Adorn yourself for the victory
  feast!

Sieh', glänzende Perlen bring' ich dir
  dar!
Sie flicht durch dein krauses, schwarzes
  Haar!
Wo Persias Meerflut Korallen umzischt,
Da haben sie triefende Taucher gefischt.

'See, I bring you gleaming
  pearls.
Bind them in your curly black
  hair.
Where Persia's seas over coral hiss,
by dripping divers they were fished.

Sieh', Federn vom Strauße! laß sie dich
  schmücken!
Weiß auf dein Antlitz, das dunkle,
  nicken!
Schmücke das Zelt! bereite das Mahl!
Fülle, bekränze den Siegespokal!«

'Plume of the ostrich, see, to deck
  you,
to flutter white on your dark
  face.
Deck the tent, make ready the banquet!
Fill and garland the victory cup!'

Aus dem schimmernden, weißen Zelte
  hervor
Tritt der schlachtgerüstete, fürstliche
  Mohr;
So tritt aus schimmernder Wolken Tor
Der Mond, der verfinsterte, dunkle,
  hervor.

From his shimmering white
  tent,
the Princely Moor comes
  battle-armed;
as, from shimmering portal of cloud,
the moon, eclipsed and
  dark.

Da grüßt ihn jubelnd der Seinen Ruf,
Da grüßt ihn stampfend der Rosse Huf.
Ihm rollte der Neger treues Blut,
Um des Nigers rätselhafte Flut.

He's greeted by huzzas from his men,
by the stamping of horses' hooves.
Faster runs his true negro blood
at the Niger's mysterious flood.

»So führ' uns zum Siege! so führ' uns
  zur Schlacht!«
Sie stritten vom Morgen bis tief in die
  Nacht.
Des Elefanten gehöhlter Zahn
Feuerte schmetternd die Kämpfer an.

'So lead us to victory, to
  battle!'
From dawn into the night they
  fought,
the hollow tusk of elephant
firing them with its blare.

Es fleucht der Leu, es fliehn die
  Schlangen
Vor dem Rasseln der Trommel, mit
  Schädeln behangen.

The lion takes flight, the serpents
  flee
before the rattling skull-hung
  drum.

Hoch weht die Fahne, verkündend
   Tod;
Das Gelb der Wüste färbt sich rot.—

So tobt der Kampf im Palmental!
Sie aber bereitet daheim das
   Mahl;
Sie füllt den Becher mit Palmensaft,
Umwindet mit Blumen der Zeltstäbe
   Schaft.

Mit Perlen, die Persias Flut gebar,
Durchflicht sie das krause, schwarze
   Haar,
Schmückt die Stirne mit wallenden
   Federn, und
Den Hals und die Arme mit Muscheln
   bunt.

Sie setzt sich vor des Geliebten Zelt;
Sie lauscht, wie ferne das Kriegshorn
   gellt.
Der Mittag brennt und die Sonne
   sticht;
Die Kränze welken, sie achtet's nicht.

Die Sonne sinkt, und der Abend siegt;
Der Nachttau rauscht, und der
   Glühwurm fliegt.
Aus dem lauen Strom blickt das
   Krokodil,
Als ob es der Kühle genießen will.

Es regt sich der Leu und brüllt nach
   Raub,
Elefantenrudel durchrauschen das
   Laub.
Die Giraffe sucht des Lagers Ruh',
Augen und Blumen schließen sich zu.

Ihr Busen schwillt vor Angst empor;
Da naht ein flüchtiger, blutender Mohr.
»Verloren die Hoffnung! verloren die
   Schlacht!
Dein Buhle gefangen, gen Westen
   gebracht!

Ans Meer! den blanken Menschen
   verkauft!«
Da stürzt sie zur Erde, das Haar
   zerrauft,
Die Perlen zerdrückt sie mit zitternder
   Hand,
Birgt die glühende Wange im glühenden
   Sand.

Auf der Messe, da zieht es, da stürmt
   es hinan
Zum Zirkus, zum glatten, geebneten
   Plan.

The death-heralding banner floats
   aloft;
the desert yellow is dyed with red.

So rages the fight in the palmy vale,
but at home she makes ready the
   banquet,
filling the cup with juice of palm,
twining the tent-poles with
   flowers.

With pearls born of Persia's flood
she decks her curly black
   hair,
adorns her brow with waving
   plumes,
neck and arms with bright
   seashells.

Before her beloved's tent she sits,
harks to the war-horns' distant
   bray.
Noon is ablaze, the sun beats
   down,
the garlands wilt, but she heeds not.

The sun sinks, evening triumphs;
night dew patters, fire-flies
   flit.
The crocodile gazes from the tepid
   stream,
as if to enjoy the cool.

The lion stirs and roars for
   prey,
elephant herds through the foliage
   crash,
the giraffe looks for a place to rest,
eyes and flowers are closed.

Her bosom heaves with fear—
fleeing, bleeding, comes a Moor.
'Hope is gone! The battle's
   lost!
Your love is captive, taken
   west!

'To the sea. To the white man
   sold!'
Down she hurls herself, tears her
   hair,
crushes the pearls with trembling
   hand,
hides burning cheek in burning
   sand.

At the fair all come crowding,
   rushing
to the smoothly-levelled
   hippodrome.

Es schmettern Trompeten, das Becken
klingt,
Dumpf wirbelt die Trommel, Bajazzo
springt.

Herbei, herbei!—das tobt und drängt;
Die Reiter fliegen; die Bahn
durchsprengt
Der Türkenrapp' und der Brittenfuchs;
Die Weiber zeigen den üppigen Wuchs.

Und an der Reitbahn verschleiertem
Tor
Steht ernst ein krausgelockter Mohr;
Die türkische Trommel schlägt er laut,
Auf der Trommel liegt eine
Löwenhaut.

Er sieht nicht der Reiter zierlichen
Schwung,
Er sieht nicht der Rosse gewagten
Sprung.
Mit starrem, trocknem Auge schaut
Der Mohr auf die zottige Löwenhaut.

Er denkt an den fernen, fernen Niger,
Und daß er gejagt den Löwen, den
Tiger;
Und daß er geschwungen im Kampfe
das Schwert,
Und daß er nimmer zum Lager gekehrt;

Und daß *sie* Blumen für ihn gepflückt,
Und daß *sie* das Haar mit Perlen
geschmückt—
Sein Auge ward naß; mit dumpfem
Klang
Schlug er das Fell, daß es rasselnd
zersprang.

Trumpets bray, cymbals
clash,
drums thud, clowns
caper.

This way! People roar and throng.
Riders speed by. Galloping
go
black Turkish steed and British sorrel.
Women display their shapeliness.

At the veiled gate of the
hippodrome
gravely stands a curly-haired Moor,
loudly banging a Turkish drum;
the drum is draped in lion
skin.

He sees not the riders' graceful
turns,
nor the horses' daring
leaps.
Dry-eyed, fixedly, he stares,
this Moor, at the matted lion skin.

Remembers the far-distant Niger,
remembers that he hunted lion and
tiger,
that in battle he wielded the
sword,
and to his camp returned no more;

remembers *she* plucked flowers for him,
and decked her hair with
pearls—
his eye grew moist; with hollow
thud
he hit the drum, and
shattered it.

## Der Musensohn | Son of the Muses

JOHANN WOLFGANG GOETHE

*Franz Schubert: op. 92, no. 1, 1822*

Durch Feld und Wald zu schweifen,
Mein Liedchen weg zu pfeifen,
So geht's von Ort zu Ort!
Und nach dem Takte reget
Und nach dem Maß beweget
Sich alles an mir fort.

Ich kann sie kaum erwarten,
Die erste Blum' im Garten,
Die erste Blüt' am Baum.
Sie grüßen meine Lieder,
Und kommt der Winter wieder,
Sing ich noch jenen Traum.

Through field and through forest,
piping my song,
is how I roam from place to place!
And the whole world keeps time,
and moves in rhythm
with me.

Impatiently I await
the first bloom in the garden,
the first blossom on the tree.
I greet them in my songs,
and when winter returns,
I still sing of them as a dream.

Ich sing ihn in der Weite,
Auf Eises Läng' und Breite,
Da blüht der Winter schön!
Auch diese Blüte schwindet,
Und neue Freude findet
Sich auf bebauten Höhn.

Denn wie ich bei der Linde
Das junge Völkchen finde,
Sogleich erreg ich sie.
Der stumpfe Bursche bläht sich,
Das steife Mädchen dreht sich
Nach meiner Melodie.

Ihr gebt den Sohlen Flügel
Und treibt durch Tal und Hügel
Den Liebling weit vom Haus.
Ihr lieben, holden Musen,
Wann ruh ich ihr am Busen
Auch endlich wieder aus?

Far and wide I sing them,
throughout the icy realm,
then winter blossoms fair!
That flowering, too, passes,
and new delight is found
in the villages of the hills.

For when, by the lime tree,
on young folk I chance,
I rouse them in a trice.
The bumpkin puffs his chest out,
the prim maiden twirls
in time to my melody.

You wing your favourite's feet,
and over hill and dale
drive him far from home.
Dear, kindly Muses,
when, on *her* bosom,
shall I at last again find rest?

## Der Musikant / The Musician

JOSEPH VON EICHENDORFF

*Reinhard Schwarz-Schilling, 1944; Hugo Wolf, 1888*

Wandern lieb' ich für mein Leben,
Lebe eben wie ich kann,
Wollt' ich mir auch Mühe geben,
Paßt es mir doch gar nicht an.

Schöne alte Lieder weiß ich,
In der Kälte, ohne Schuh',
Draußen in die Saiten reiß' ich,
Weiß nicht, wo ich abends ruh'.

Manche Schöne macht wohl Augen,
Meinet, ich gefiel' ihr sehr,
Wenn ich nur was wollte taugen,
So ein armer Lump nicht wär'.—

Mag dir Gott ein'n Mann bescheren,
Wohl mit Haus und Hof versehn!
Wenn wir zwei zusammen wären,
Möcht' mein Singen mir vergehn.

Journeying is my life's love,
and I live as I may,
and were I to exert myself,
it would not suit at all.

Beautiful old songs I know,
and shoeless, in the cold,
I pluck my strings in the open,
know not where at eve I'll rest.

Many a beauty gives me looks,
says she would fancy me
if I'd make something of myself,
were not such a beggar wretch.

May God give you a husband,
provide a house and home.
If we two were together,
my singing might then end.

## Der neue Amadis / The New Amadis

JOHANN WOLFGANG GOETHE

*Armin Knab, 1924–46; Ernst Krenek: op. 56, no. 2, 1927;
Hugo Wolf, 1889*

Als ich noch ein Knabe war,
Sperrte man mich ein,
Und so saß ich manches Jahr
Über mir allein
Wie in Mutterleib.

When I was still a boy,
they used to shut me in,
and so, many a year I sat
solitary,
as in the womb.

Doch du warst mein Zeitvertreib,
Goldne Phantasie,
Und ich ward ein warmer Held,
Wie der Prinz Pipi,
Und durchzog die Welt.

But you passed the time for me,
golden fantasy,
and an ardent hero I became,
like Prince Pipi,
and wandered the world.

Baute manch kristallen Schloß
Und zerstört' es auch,
Warf mein blinkendes Geschoß
Drachen durch den Bauch,
Ja, ich war ein Mann!

Built many a crystal castle
and destroyed as well,
hurled my flashing dart
into bellies of dragons,
yes, I was a man!

Ritterlich befreit' ich dann
Die Prinzessin Fisch;
Sie war gar zu obligeant,
Führte mich zu Tisch,
Und ich war galant.

Valiantly I then set free
Princess Fish;
she was too obliging,
led me in to dine,
and I was gallant.

Und ihr Kuß war Götterbrot,
Glühend wie der Wein.
Ach! ich liebte fast mich tot!
Rings mit Sonnenschein
War sie emailliert.

And ambrosia was her kiss,
glowing as the wine.
Ah, to the point of death I loved!
All in sunshine
she was bathed.

Ach! wer hat sie mir entführt?
Hielt kein Zauberband
Sie zurück vom schnellen Fliehn?
Sagt, wo ist ihr Land?
Wo der Weg dahin?

Ah, who has abducted her?
Did no magic bond
detain her from hasty flight?
Say, where is her land?
And the way to it?

## Der Nöck / The Nix

AUGUST KOPISCH

*Carl Loewe: op. 129, no. 2, 1860–61*

Es tönt des Nöcken Harfenschall:
da steht der wilde Wasserfall,
umschwebt mit Schaum und Wogen
den Nöck im Regenbogen.
Die Bäume neigen
sich tief und schweigen,
und atmend horcht die Nachtigall.—

The nix's harp gives forth its sound,
the unruly waterfall stands still,
its foam, its waves are poised
as a rainbow about the nix.
The trees bow
low and are silent,
the nightingale draws breath and listens

»O Nöck, was hilft das Singen dein?
Du kannst ja doch nicht selig sein!
Wie kann dein Singen taugen?«—
Der Nöck erhebt die Augen,
sieht an die Kleinen,
beginnt zu weinen . . .
und senkt sich in die Flut hinein.

'O nix, to what end your singing?
Blissful can you never be.
How can your singing serve?'
The nix raises his eyes,
looks at the little ones,
begins to weep . . .
and plunges into the flood.

Da rauscht und braust der Wasserfall,
hoch fliegt hinweg die Nachtigall,
die Bäume heben mächtig
die Häupter grün und prächtig.
O weh, es haben
die wilden Knaben
den Nöck betrübt im Wasserfall!

The waterfall roars and rushes,
high and away the nightingale flies,
the trees raise mightily
their green magnificent tops.
Oh dear, they have,
those noisy boys,
disturbed the nix in the waterfall!

»Komm wieder, Nöck, du singst so
   schön!
Wer singt, kann in den Himmel gehn!
Du wirst mit deinem Klingen
zum Paradiese dringen!
O komm, es haben
gescherzt die Knaben:
Komm wieder, Nöck, und singe
   schön!«

'Come back, nix, you sing so
   sweet.
Any who do, may enter heaven.
You, with those notes of yours,
will win through to paradise!
Oh come, they were
jesting, those boys.
Come back, nix. and sweetly
   sing.'

Da tönt des Nöcken Harfenschall,
und wieder steht der Wasserfall,
umschwebt mit Schaum und Wogen
den Nöck im Regenbogen.
Die Bäume neigen
sich tief und schweigen,
und atmend horcht die Nachtigall.

The nix's harp gives forth its sound
and again the waterfall stands still,
its foam. its waves are poised
as a rainbow about the nix.
The trees bow
low and are silent,
the nightingale draws breath and listens.

Es spielt der Nöck und singt mit Macht
von Meer und Erd und Himmelspracht.
Mit Singen kann er lachen
und selig weinen machen!—
Der Wald erbebet,
die Sonn entschwebet...
Er singt bis in die Sternennacht!

Powerfully the nix plays and sings
of sea, earth, heavenly splendour.
By his singing, laughter can he
cause, and blissful tears!—
The wood trembles,
the sun fades ...
He sings into the starry night!

## *Der Nußbaum* / *The Walnut Tree*

JULIUS MOSEN

*Robert Schumann: op. 25 (Myrten), no. 3, 1840*

Es grünet ein Nußbaum vor dem Haus,
Duftig, luftig breitet er blättrig die
   Äste aus.

Green before the house a walnut stands.
spreading, fragrant, airy. its leafy
   branches.

Viel liebliche Blüten stehen dran;
Linde Winde kommen, sie herzlich zu
   umfahn.

Many lovely blossoms it bears;
gentle winds visit them with loving
   embrace.

Es flüstern je zwei zu zwei gepaart,
Neigend, beugend zierlich zum Kusse
die Häuptchen zart.

Paired together, they whisper,
gracefully inclining delicate heads to
   kiss.

Sie flüstern von einem Mägdlein, das
Dächte die Nächte und Tage lang,
   wußte, ach, selber nicht was.

Whisper of a maiden who
night and day pondered, ah, and knew
   not what.

Sie flüstern, wer mag verstehn so gar
Leise Weise? flüstern von Bräut'gam
und nächstem Jahr.

Whisper—who can understand so
soft a song?—of a husband-to-be, of
   next year.

Das Mägdlein horchet, es rauscht im
   Baum;
Sehnend, wähnend sinkt es lächelnd in
   Schlaf und Traum.

The maiden listens, the tree
   rustles;
yearning, hoping, she sinks, smiling,
   into sleep and dreams.

## Der Rattenfänger | The Rat-catcher

JOHANN WOLFGANG GOETHE

*Franz Schubert, 1815; Hugo Wolf, 1888*

| | |
|---|---|
| Ich bin der wohlbekannte Sänger, | I am the celebrated singer, |
| Der vielgereiste Rattenfänger, | the widely-travelled catcher of rats, |
| Den diese altberühmte Stadt | of whom this fine old city |
| Gewiß besonders nötig hat. | assuredly has special need. |
| Und wärens Ratten noch so viele, | And be the rats however many, |
| Und wären Wiesel mit im Spiele, | and be there weasels included too, |
| Von allen säubr ich diesen Ort, | of every one I'll clear the place, |
| Sie müssen miteinander fort. | one and all, they must away. |
| | |
| Dann ist der gut gelaunte Sänger | Then is this well-disposed singer |
| Mitunter auch ein Kinderfänger, | occasionally, too, a children-catcher, |
| Der selbst die wildesten bezwingt, | who even the unruliest will subdue |
| Wenn er die goldnen Märchen singt. | by singing his golden fairy tales. |
| Und wären Knaben noch so trutzig, | And be the boys however defiant, |
| Und wären Mädchen noch so stutzig, | and be the girls however amazed, |
| In meine Saiten greif ich ein, | at my strings I pluck, |
| Sie müssen alle hinterdrein. | and one and all must follow after. |
| | |
| Dann ist der vielgewandte Sänger | Then is this many-sided singer |
| Gelegentlich ein Mädchenfänger; | occasionally a maiden-catcher; |
| In keinem Städtchen langt er an, | in never a town does he arrive, |
| Wo ers nicht mancher angetan. | where he does not enamour many. |
| Und wären Mädchen noch so blöde, | And be the girls however bashful, |
| Und wären Weiber noch so spröde, | and the ladies however demure, |
| Doch allen wird so liebebang | one and all become lovelorn |
| Bei Zaubersaiten und Gesang. | at sound of magic lute and song. |

## Der Rock | The Coat

CHRISTIAN MORGENSTERN: from *Palmström*

*Paul Graener: op. 79, no. 3, ed. 1927*

| | |
|---|---|
| Der Rock, am Tage angehabt, | The coat, worn by me by day, |
| er ruht zur Nacht sich schweigend aus; | reposeth silent for the night; |
| durch seine hohlen Ärmel trabt | through its empty sleeves doth trot |
| die Maus. | the mouse. |
| | |
| Durch seine hohlen Ärmel trabt | Through its empty sleeves doth trot |
| gespenstisch auf und ab die Maus ... | ghostlily up and down, the mouse ... |
| Der Rock, am Tage angehabt, | The coat worn by me by day, |
| er ruht zur Nacht sich aus. | reposeth silent for the night. |
| | |
| Er ruht, am Tage angehabt, | Reposeth, worn by me by day, |
| im Schoß der Nacht sich schweigend | silent in the womb of |
| aus, | night, |
| er ruht, von seiner Maus durchtrabt, | reposeth, being trotted through |
| sich aus. | by its mouse. |

## Der Sänger | The Minstrel

JOHANN WOLFGANG GOETHE: from *Wilhelm Meister*

*Franz Schubert: op. 117, 1815; Robert Schumann: op. 98a, no. 2, 1841;
Hugo Wolf, 1888*

Was hör ich draußen vor dem Tor,
Was auf der Brücke schallen?
Laß den Gesang vor unserm Ohr
Im Saale widerhallen!
Der König sprachs, der Page lief;
Der Knabe kam, der König rief:
Laßt mir herein den Alten!

Gegrüßet seid mir, edle Herrn,
Gegrüßt ihr, schöne Damen!
Welch reicher Himmel! Stern bei Stern!
Wer kennet ihre Namen?
Im Saal voll Pracht und Herrlichkeit
Schließt, Augen, euch; hier ist nicht
    Zeit,
Sich staunend zu ergetzen.

Der Sänger drückt' die Augen ein
Und schlug in vollen Tönen;
Die Ritter schauten mutig drein,
Und in den Schoß die Schönen.
Der König, dem das Lied gefiel,
Ließ, ihn zu ehren für sein Spiel,
Eine goldne Kette holen.

Die goldne Kette gib mir nicht,
Die Kette gib den Rittern,
Vor deren kühnem Angesicht
Der Feinde Lanzen splittern;
Gib sie dem Kanzler, den du hast,
Und laß ihn noch die goldne Last
Zu andern Lasten tragen.

Ich singe, wie der Vogel singt,
Der in den Zweigen wohnet;
Das Lied, das aus der Kehle dringt,
Ist Lohn, der reichlich lohnet.
Doch darf ich bitten, bitt ich eins:
Laß mir den besten Becher Weins
In purem Golde reichen.

Er setzt' ihn an, er trank ihn aus:
O Trank voll süßer Labe!
O wohl dem hochbeglückten Haus,
Wo das ist kleine Gabe!
Ergehts euch wohl, so denkt an mich,
Und danket Gott so warm, als ich
Für diesen Trunk euch danke.

'What do I hear at the gate,
what sounds on the bridge?
Let that song for our ears
echo in this hall!'
So said the king, the page ran;
the page returned, the king cried:
'Let the old man be admitted!'

'Hail to you, noble lords,
hail to you, fair ladies!
How rich a heaven! Star upon star!
Who shall tell their names?
In this hall of glory, of splendour,
close, eyes; now is no
    time
to feast yourselves and marvel.'

The minstrel shut tight his eyes
and with full-blooded tone did play;
manfully the knights gazed on,
the beautiful ladies into their laps.
The king, pleased by the song,
to honour him for his music,
sent for a chain of gold.

'The chain of gold give not to me,
the chain give to your knights,
before whose bold countenance
the enemy lances splinter;
give it to your chancellor,
and let him bear that golden burden
together with his others.

'I sing as sings the bird
that lives amongst the branches;
the song that bursts from the throat
is its own rich reward.
But if I may, one thing will I ask:
let me be served your best wine
in a goblet of pure gold.'

To his lips he put it, drank it off:
'O draught of sweet refreshment!
Happy the highly-favoured house
where that is but a small gift.
Should you fare well, then think of me,
and thank God as warmly as I
thank you for this draught.'

## Der Schäfer | The Shepherd

JOHANN WOLFGANG GOETHE: from *Jery und Bätely*

*Armin Knab, 1924-46; Hugo Wolf, 1888*

Es war ein fauler Schäfer,
Ein rechter Siebenschläfer,
Ihn kümmerte kein Schaf.

There was a lazy shepherd,
a veritable dormouse,
no sheep worried him.

Ein Mädchen konnt ihn fassen,
Da war der Tropf verlassen,
Fort Appetit und Schlaf!

A girl contrived to catch him,
then was the fool forlorn,
gone appetite and sleep!

Es trieb ihn in die Ferne,
Des Nachts zählt er die Sterne,
Er klagt und härmt sich brav.

To distant parts he's driven,
at night he counts the stars,
complaining, grieving hard.

Nun da sie ihn genommen,
Ist alles wieder kommen,
Durst, Appetit und Schlaf.

Now that she's accepted him,
everything's restored:
thirst, appetite and sleep.

## Der Schatzgräber | The Treasure-seeker

JOHANN WOLFGANG GOETHE

*Carl Loewe: op. 59, no. 3, 1836; Franz Schubert, 1815*

Arm am Beutel, krank am Herzen,
Schleppt ich meine langen Tage.
Armut ist die größte Plage,
Reichtum ist das höchste Gut!
Und, zu enden meine Schmerzen,
Ging ich, einen Schatz zu graben.
Meine Seele sollst du haben!
Schrieb ich hin mit eignem Blut.

Light of purse and sick at heart,
I have spun out my long days.
Poverty is the greatest torment,
riches are the highest good.
And to end my agony,
I went to dig for a treasure.
You shall have my soul!
I wrote with my own blood.

Und so zog ich Kreis um Kreise,
Stellte wunderbare Flammen,
Kraut und Knochenwerk zusammen:
Die Beschwörung war vollbracht.
Und auf die gelernte Weise
Grub ich nach dem alten Schatze
Auf dem angezeigten Platze;
Schwarz und stürmisch war die Nacht.

And I drew circle after circle,
magic flames I combined
with herbs and bones:
the conjuration was complete.
And, in the manner taught,
I dug for the ancient treasure
at the indicated spot.
Dark and stormy was the night.

Und ich sah ein Licht von weiten,
Und es kam gleich einem Sterne
Hinten aus der fernsten Ferne,
Eben als es Zwölfe schlug.
Und da galt kein Vorbereiten:
Heller wards mit einem Male
Von dem Glanz der vollen Schale,
Die ein schöner Knabe trug.

And far off I saw a light,
and, like a star it came,
out of the remotest distance
on the very stroke of twelve.
And, with no preliminary,
all at once there was more light
from the gleam of the full cup,
carried by a handsome boy.

Holde Augen sah ich blinken
Unter dichtem Blumenkranze;

Gentle eyes could I see sparkling
from under a close crown of flowers;

In des Trankes Himmelsglanze
Trat er in den Kreis herein.
Und er hieß mich freundlich trinken;
Und ich dacht: es kann der Knabe
Mit der schönen lichten Gabe
Wahrlich nicht der Böse sein.

in the draught's celestial glow,
he stepped into my circle.
And he kindly bade me drink,
and I thought he could, that boy,
with his bright and beautiful gift,
surely not be the Evil One.

Trinke Mut des reinen Lebens!
Dann verstehst du die Belehrung,
Kommst, mit ängstlicher Beschwörung,
Nicht zurück an diesen Ort.
Grabe hier nicht mehr vergebens:
Tages Arbeit! Abends Gäste!
Saure Wochen! Frohe Feste!
Sei dein künftig Zauberwort.

Drink the courage of pure life!
Then you will understand my teaching,
never, with anxious conjuration,
will you to this place return.
Dig no longer vainly here:
work by day and guests at eve!
Hard weeks and merry feasts!
be henceforth your magic spell.

## Der Schatzgräber / The Treasure-seeker

JOSEPH VON EICHENDORFF

*Robert Schumann: op. 45, no. 1, 1840*

Wenn alle Wälder schliefen,
Er an zu graben hub,
Rastlos in Berges Tiefen
Nach einem Schatz er grub.

When forests all slept,
he began to dig,
ceaselessly in the mountain gorge
for treasure.

Die Engel Gottes sangen
Dieweil in stiller Nacht,
Wie rote Augen drangen
Metalle aus dem Schacht.

God's angels sang,
as, in the quiet of the night,
forth came, like red eyes,
metals from the pit.

»Und wirst doch mein!« und grimmer
Wühlt er und wühlt hinab,
Da stürzen Steine und Trümmer
Über den Narren herab.

'You shall be mine!' More grimly
he burrows and burrows down,
then stones and rubble
fall in on the fool.

Hohnlachen wild erschallte
Aus der verfallnen Kluft,
Der Engelgesang verhallte
Wehmütig in der Luft.

Wild mocking laughter echoed
from the caved-in gorge,
the song of the angels died away
sadly in the air.

## Der Schmied / The Smith

LUDWIG UHLAND

*Johannes Brahms: op. 19, no. 4, 1858–59*

Ich hör meinen Schatz,
Den Hammer er schwinget,
Das rauschet, das klinget,
Das dringt in die Weite,
Wie Glockengeläute,
Durch Gassen und Platz.

I hear my loved one
swinging his hammer,
the dinning and ringing
reach out far and wide,
like pealing of bells,
through alley and square.

Am schwarzen Kamin,
Da sitzet mein Lieber,
Doch geh ich vorüber,
Die Bälge dann sausen,
Die Flammen aufbrausen
Und lodern um ihn.

By the black forge
my loved one is sitting,
but should I pass by,
the bellows start blowing,
the flames roar up
and blaze about him.


## Der Soldat | The Soldier

HANS CHRISTIAN ANDERSEN: translated by ADALBERT VON CHAMISSO

*Robert Schumann: op. 40, no. 3, 1840*

Er geht bei gedämpfter Trommel
Klang;
Wie weit noch die Stätte! der Weg wie
lang!
O wär er zur Ruh und alles vorbei!
Ich glaub', es bricht mir das Herz
entzwei!

He walks to the sound of the muffled
drum;
how far the place, the way how
long!
Oh, were he at rest, and all this done!
I think my heart must break in
two.

Ich hab' in der Welt nur ihn
geliebt,
Nur ihn, dem jetzt man den Tod doch
gibt!
Bei klingendem Spiele wird paradiert;
Dazu bin auch ich kommandiert.

None but him in the world have I
loved,
him, who now they are putting to
death.
A full parade it is, with band;
I too am detailed for the task.

Nun schaut er auf zum letzten Mal
In Gottes Sonne freudigen Strahl;
Nun binden sie ihm die Augen zu—
Dir schenke Gott die ewige Ruh!

Now he takes his last look
at the joyous ray of God's sun;
now they bandage his eyes—
God grant you peace eternal!

Es haben die Neun wohl angelegt;
Acht Kugeln haben vorbeigefegt.
Sie zitterten alle vor Jammer und
Schmerz—
Ich aber, ich traf ihn mitten ins
Herz.

The nine took aim,
eight bullets went wide.
Every man shook for pity and
pain—
but I, I shot him clean through the
heart.


## Der Spielmann | The Fiddler

HANS CHRISTIAN ANDERSEN

*Robert Schumann: op. 40, no. 4, 1840*

Im Städtchen gibt es des Jubels viel,
Da halten sie Hochzeit mit Tanz und
mit Spiel.
Dem Fröhlichen blinket der Wein so
rot,
Die Braut nur gleicht dem getünchten
Tod.

In the little town is much rejoicing,
a wedding with revel and
dance.
For the happy man the wine sparkles
red,
the bride looks like whitewashed
death.

Ja tot für den, den nicht sie vergißt,
Der doch beim Fest nicht Bräutigam
ist:

She *is* dead for him she cannot forget,
who is at the feast not as
groom;

Da steht er inmitten der Gäste im
  Krug,
Und streichelt die Geige lustig genug.

Er streichelt die Geige, sein Haar
  ergraut,
Es schwingen die Saiten gellend und
  laut,
Er drückt sie ans Herz und achtet es
  nicht,
Ob auch sie in tausend Stücken
  zerbricht.

Es ist gar grausig, wenn einer so stirbt,
Wenn jung sein Herz um Freude noch
  wirbt.
Ich mag und will nicht länger es sehn!
Das möchte den Kopf mir schwindelnd
  verdrehn!

Wer heißt euch mit Fingern zeigen auf
  mich?
O Gott—bewahr uns gnädiglich,
Daß keinen der Wahnsinn übermannt.
Bin selber ein armer Musikant.

among the guests at the inn he
  stands,
caressing his fiddle merrily enough.

Caressing his fiddle, hair turning
  grey,
the strings shrilling and
  loud,
squeezing it to his heart,
  heedless
if it smash in a thousand
  pieces.

Hideous it is for one to die thus,
heart young and still wooing
  joy.
I cannot, will not, watch any more!
My head might be set in a fatal
  whirl!

Who said to point a finger at
  me?
O God, graciously preserve us
from being overcome with madness!
I myself am a poor musician.

## Der Strom, der neben mir verrauschte / The Stream Whose Roar beside Me Faded

AUGUST VON PLATEN

*Johannes Brahms: op. 32, no. 4, 1864*

Der Strom, der neben mir verrauschte,
Wo ist er nun?
Der Vogel, dessen Lied ich lauschte,
Wo ist er nun?
Wo ist die Rose, die die Freundin
Am Herzen trug,
Und jener Kuß, der mich berauschte,
Wo ist er nun?
Und jener Mensch, der ich gewesen,
Und den ich längst
Mit einem andern Ich vertauschte,
Wo ist er nun?

The stream whose roar beside me faded,
where is it now?
The bird, to whose song I hearkened,
where is it now?
Where is the rose my friend
wore on her heart,
and that kiss which enchanted me,
where is it now?
And that man who I have been,
and whom long since
I have exchanged for another self,
where is he now?

## Der Tambour / The Drummer-boy

EDUARD MÖRIKE

*Hugo Wolf, 1888*

Wenn meine Mutter hexen könnt,
Da müßt sie mit dem Regiment
Nach Frankreich, überall mit hin,
Und wär die Marketenderin.

If my mother could work magic,
she'd have to go with the regiment
to France, and everywhere,
and be the camp follower.

Im Lager, wohl um Mitternacht,
Wenn niemand auf ist als die Wacht,
Und alles schnarchet, Roß und Mann,
Vor meiner Trommel säß ich dann:
Die Trommel müßt eine Schüssel sein,
Ein warmes Sauerkraut darein,
Die Schlegel Messer und Gabel,
Ein lange Wurst mein Sabel;
Mein Tschako wär ein Humpen gut,
Den füll ich mit Burgunderblut.
Und weil es mir an Lichte fehlt,
Da scheint der Mond in mein Gezelt;
Scheint er auch auf franzö'sch herein,
Mir fällt doch meine Liebste ein:
Ach weh! Jetzt hat der Spaß ein End!
—Wenn nur meine Mutter hexen
  könnt!

In camp, at midnight,
when no one's up, save the guard,
and everyone, man and horse, snoring,
then by my drum I'd sit:
my drum would have to be a bowl
of hot sauerkraut,
the sticks would be knife and fork,
my sabre—a long sausage;
my shako would be a good tankard
which I fill with Burgundy Blood.
And because I lack light,
the moon shines into my tent;
and it's a French-speaking moon;
suddenly I think of my beloved:
oh dear, now there's an end to my fun!
—If only my mother could work
  magic!

## Der Tambourgesell | The Drummer-boy
from *Des Knaben Wunderhorn*
*Gustav Mahler, ed. 1905*

Ich armer Tambourgesell,
Man führt mich aus dem Gewölb.
Wär ich ein Tambour blieben,
Dürft ich nicht gefangen liegen.

Poor drummer that I am,
being led from the vault.
Had I stayed a drummer,
a prisoner I'd not be.

O Galgen, du hohes Haus,
Du siehst so furchtbar aus.
Ich schau dich nicht mehr an,
Weil i weiß, i gehör daran.

O gallows, tall house,
so fearful you look,
on you I'll gaze no more,
for I know that's where I go.

Wenn Soldaten vorbeimarschieren,
Bei mir nit einquartieren.
Wann sie fragen, wer i gwesen bin:
Tambour von der Leibkompanie.

When soldiers marching by
aren't billeted with me,
and ask who I was:
Drummer, No. 1 Company.

Gute Nacht, ihr Marmelstein,
Ihr Berg und Hügelein.
Gute Nacht, ihr Offizier,
Korporal und Musketier.

Good night, marble stone,
you mountain and hills.
Good night, officers,
corporals and musketeers.

Gute Nacht, ihr Offizier,
Korporal und Grenadier.
Ich schrei mit heller Stimm,
Von euch ich Urlaub nimm.

Good night, you officers,
corporals and grenadiers.
Loud and clear I cry,
From you I'm off on leave.

## Der Tod, das ist die kühle Nacht | Death is Cool Night
HEINRICH HEINE
*Johannes Brahms: op. 96, no. 1, 1884*

Der Tod, das ist die kühle Nacht,
Das Leben ist der schwüle Tag.
Es dunkelt schon, mich schläfert,
Der Tag hat mich müd gemacht.

Death is cool night,
living is sultry day.
Dusk falls. I am drowsy,
the day has made me tired.

Über mein Bett erhebt sich ein Baum,
Drin singt die junge Nachtigall;
Sie singt von lauter Liebe,
Ich hör es, ich hör es sogar im Traum.

Above my bed rises a tree,
where the young nightingale sings;
of nothing does she sing but love,
I hear it, hear it even in dreams.


## Der Tod und das Mädchen | Death and the Maiden

MATTHIAS CLAUDIUS

*Franz Schubert: op. 7, no. 3, 1817*

*Das Mädchen:*
Vorüber, ach, vorüber!
Geh, wilder Knochenmann!
Ich bin noch jung, geh, Lieber!
Und rühre mich nicht an.

*Maiden:*
Go by, oh, go by,
harsh bony Death!
I am still young. Go, my dear,
and do not touch me.

*Der Tod:*
Gib deine Hand, du schön und zart
  Gebild!
Bin Freund und komme nicht zu
  strafen.
Sei guten Muts! Ich bin nicht wild,
Sollst sanft in meinen Armen
  schlafen!

*Death:*
Give me your hand, you fair gentle
  thing.
A friend I am and do not come to
  punish.
Be of good cheer. I am not harsh.
In my arms shall you sleep
  soft!


## Der Wanderer | The Wanderer

GEORG PHILIPP SCHMIDT VON LÜBECK

*Franz Schubert: op. 4, no. 1, 1816*

Ich komme vom Gebirge her,
Es dampft das Tal, es braust das Meer.
Ich wandle still, bin wenig froh,
Und immer fragt der Seufzer: wo?
Immer wo?

Down from the mountains I come,
the valley steams, the ocean roars.
I wander silent, little glad,
my sighs demanding ever: where?
Ever where?

Die Sonne dünkt mich hier so kalt,
Die Blüte welk, das Leben alt,
Und was sie reden, leerer Schall,
Ich bin ein Fremdling überall.

The sun seems here so cold,
blossom faded, life old,
and what they talk is empty sound,
I am a stranger everywhere.

Wo bist du, mein geliebtes Land?
Gesucht, geahnt und nie gekannt!
Das Land, das Land, so hoffnungsgrün,
Das Land, wo meine Rosen blühn,

Where are you, my beloved land?
Sought for, sensed, yet never known!
That land so green with hope,
where my roses bloom,

Wo meine Freunde wandeln gehn,
Wo meine Toten auferstehn,
Das Land, das meine Sprache spricht,
O Land, wo bist du?

where my friends walk,
where my dead are resurrected,
that land which speaks my tongue,
—O land, where are you?

Ich wandle still, bin wenig froh,
Und immer fragt der Seufzer: wo?
Immer wo?
Im Geisterhauch tönt's mir zurück:
»Dort, wo du nicht bist, dort ist das
  Glück!«

I wander silent, little glad,
my sighs demanding ever: where?
Ever where?
A ghostly whisper makes reply:
'There, where you are not, there
  is happiness.'

## Der Wanderer an den Mond / The Wanderer Addresses the Moon

JOHANN GABRIEL SEIDL

*Franz Schubert: op. 80, no. 1, 1826*

Ich auf der Erd', am Himmel du,
wir wandern beide rüstig zu:
Ich ernst und trüb, du mild und rein,
was mag der Unterschied wohl sein?
Ich wandre fremd von Land zu Land,
so heimatlos, so unbekannt;
Berg auf, Berg ab, Wald ein, Wald aus,
doch bin ich nirgend, ach! zu Haus.
Du aber wanderst auf und ab
Aus Westens Wieg' in Ostens Grab,
wallst Länder ein und Länder aus,
und bist doch, wo du bist, zu Haus.
Der Himmel, endlos ausgespannt,
ist dein geliebtes Heimatland:
O glücklich, wer, wohin er geht,
doch auf der Heimat Boden steht!

I on earth, you in the sky,
we wander, we two, briskly on:
I stern and dark, you mild and clear,
I wonder what our difference is?
I wander, a stranger, from land to land,
so homeless, so unknown;
up hill, down dale, into forest and out,
yet nowhere, alas, am I at home.
But you—you wander up and down,
from western cradle to eastern grave,
journey, a pilgrim, from land to land,
yet are, wherever you be, at home.
The heavens, infinitely spread,
are your beloved native land:
Oh happy he, who wherever he goes,
still stands upon his native soil!

## Der Zauberer / The Magician

CHRISTIAN FELIX WEISSE

*Wolfgang Amadeus Mozart: K 472, 1785*

Ihr Mädchen flieht Damöten ja!
Als ich zum erstenmal ihn sah,
da fühlt ich, sowas fühlt ich nie,
mir ward, mir ward, ich weiß nicht wie,
ich seufzte, zitterte, und schien mich
    doch zu freun;
glaubt mir, er muß ein Zaubrer sein.

Sah ich ihn an, so ward mir heiß,
bald ward ich rot, bald ward ich weiß,
zuletzt nahm er mich bei der Hand;
wer sagte mir, was ich da empfand?
Ich sah, ich hörte nichts, sprach nichts
    als ja und nein;
glaubt mir, er muß ein Zaubrer sein.

Er führte mich in dies Gesträuch,
ich wollt ihn fliehn und folgt ihm gleich;
er setzte sich, ich setzte mich;
er sprach, nur Silben stammelt ich;
die Augen starrten ihm, die meinen
    wurden klein;
glaubt mir, er muß ein Zaubrer sein.

Entbrannt drückt er mich an sein Herz,
was fühlt ich! welch ein süßer Schmerz!
Ich schluchzt, ich atmete sehr schwer,
da kam zum Glück die Mutter her;
was würd, o Götter, sonst nach so viel
    Zauberei'n
aus mir zuletzt geworden sein!

Girls, keep away from Damoeten!
When I first saw him,
I felt as I never felt before,
what became of me I don't know,
I sighed, trembled, yet seemed
    happy;
believe me, he must be a magician.

If I looked at him, I became hot,
went first red, then white.
At last he took my hand,
who could say what I felt then!
I saw, heard nothing, said just yes and
    no.
Believe me, he must be a magician.

He led me into these bushes,
I, wanting to run away, followed.
He sat down, I sat down.
He spoke, I stammered syllables.
His eyes stared, mine almost
    closed.
Believe me, he must be a magician.

Inflamed, he pressed me to his heart—
and my feelings! What sweet agony!
I sobbed, could hardly breathe,
then, fortunately, my mother came.
Ye gods, after so much
    magic,
what else would have become of me?

## Der Zufriedene | The Contented Man

C. L. REISSIG

*Ludwig van Beethoven: op. 75, no. 6, 1809*

Zwar schuf das Glück hienieden
mich weder reich noch groß,
allein ich bin zufrieden
wie mit dem schönsten Los.

Though fate on earth has made
me neither rich nor great,
yet am I content,
as if with the best of lots.

So ganz nach meinem Herzen
ward mir ein Freund vergönnt,
denn küssen, trinken, scherzen
ist auch sein Element.

A friend after my own heart
I've been vouchsafed,
for kissing, drinking, jesting
are his element as well.

Mit ihm wird froh und weise
manch Fläschchen ausgeleert!
Denn auf der Lebensreise
ist Wein das beste Pferd.

With him, gaily and wisely,
is many a bottle drained!
For, upon life's journey,
wine is the best of mounts.

Wenn mir bei diesem Lose
nun auch ein trüb'res fällt,
so denk' ich, keine Rose
blüht dornlos in der Welt.

If, for all my present lot,
a gloomier should befall,
I will think there is no rose
blooms thornless in the world.


## Der Zwerg | The Dwarf

MATTHÄUS VON COLLIN

*Franz Schubert: op. 22, no. 1, 1823?*

Im trüben Licht verschwinden schon
    die Berge,
Es schwebt das Schiff auf glatten
    Meereswogen,
Worauf die Königin mit ihrem Zwerge.

Already the mountains fade in the
    gloom,
the vessel drifts on the sea's flat
    waves,
with the queen and her dwarf on board.

Sie schaut empor zum hoch gewölbten
    Bogen,
Hinauf zur lichtdurchwirkten blauen
    Ferne,
Die mit der Milch des Himmels blau
    durchzogen.

She gazes up at the lofty
    vault,
at the distant, light-embroidered
    blue,
streaked bluely by the heavens' Milky
    Way.

Nie, habt ihr mir gelogen noch, ihr
    Sterne,
So ruft sie aus, bald werd ich nun
    entschwinden,
Ihr sagt es mir; doch sterb ich wahrlich
    gerne.

'Stars, never yet have you lied to
    me,'
she cries. 'Soon now shall I
    depart,
you tell me. Yet in truth I'll be not
    loath to die.'

Da tritt der Zwerg zur Königin, mag
    binden
Um ihren Hals die Schnur von roter
    Seide,
Und weint, als wollt er schnell vor
    Gram erblinden.

Then to the queen the dwarf comes,
    would bind
about her neck the red silk
    cord,
weeps as if to be swiftly blind with
    grief.

Er spricht: »Du selbst bist schuld an
    diesem Leide,
Weil um den König du mich hast
    verlassen;
Jetzt weckt dein Sterben einzig mir
    noch Freude.

Zwar werd ich ewiglich mich selber
    hassen,
Der dir mit dieser Hand den Tod
    gegeben,
Doch mußt zum frühen Grab du nun
    erblassen.«

Sie legt die Hand aufs Herz voll
    jungem Leben,
Und aus dem Aug die schweren
    Tränen rinnen,
Das sie zum Himmel betend will
    erheben.

»Mögst du nicht Schmerz durch meinen
    Tod gewinnen!«
Sie sagt's; da küßt der Zwerg die
    bleichen Wangen,
Drauf alsobald vergehen ihr die
    Sinnen.

Der Zwerg schaut an die Frau vom Tod
    befangen,
Er senkt sie tief ins Meer mit eignen
    Händen,
Ihm brennt nach ihr das Herz so voll
    Verlangen.
An keiner Küste wird er je mehr
    landen.

He speaks: 'For this suffering are you
    to blame,
because you have forsaken me for the
    king;
naught now will stir joy in me but your
    death.

'Forever I shall hate myself, I
    grant,
for having by this hand brought death
    to you,
but now you must pale, go early to your
    grave.'

A hand she puts to her youthful
    heart,
and heavy tears course down from the
    eyes
which she would lift to heaven in
    prayer.

'May you suffer no torment through
    my death,'
she says. The dwarf then kisses her
    pallid cheeks,
whereupon her senses
    depart.

At his lifeless lady the dwarf looks
    down,
with his own hands sinks her deep in
    the sea.
So full of desire his heart burns for
    her,
on no coast more will he ever
    land.

## Des Antonius von Padua Fischpredigt | Anthony of Padua's Fish Sermon
### from Des Knaben Wunderhorn
### Gustav Mahler, 1888–89

Antonius zur Predigt
Die Kirche find't ledig.
Er geht zu den Flüssen
Und predigt den Fischen;
Sie schlag'n mit den Schwänzen,
Im Sonnenschein glänzen.

Die Karpfen mit Rogen
Sind all' hierher zogen,
Hab'n die Mäuler aufrissen,
Sich Zuhörns beflissen:
Kein Predigt niemalen
Den Fischen so g'fallen.

Anthony, for his sermon,
finds the church empty.
To the rivers he goes
and addresses the fish
who whisk their tails
and gleam in the sun.

The spawning carp,
who have all of them come,
have mouths gaping open,
attentive and rapt.
Never was sermon
so pleasing to fish.

| | |
|---|---|
| Spitzgoschete Hechte, | Sharp-of-mouth pike, |
| Die immerzu fechten, | continually fighting, |
| Sind eilends herschwommen, | come hastily swimming |
| Zu hören den Frommen. | this devout man to hear. |
| | |
| Auch jene Phantasten, | Those oddities even, |
| Die immerzu fasten: | perpetually fasting, |
| Die Stockfisch' ich meine, | the stockfish, I mean, |
| Zur Predigt erscheinen: | for the sermon appear. |
| Kein Predigt niemalen | Never was sermon |
| Den Stockfisch' so gefallen. | so pleasing to stockfish! |
| | |
| Gut Aale und Hausen, | The good eels and sturgeon |
| Die Vornehme schmausen, | who banquet like lords, |
| Die selbst sich bequemen, | even they condescend |
| Die Predigt vernehmen. | to lend this sermon ear. |
| | |
| Auch Krebse, Schildkröten, | Crabs even, and turtles, |
| Sonst langsame Boten, | slow coaches at most times, |
| Steigen eilig vom Grund, | shoot up from below |
| Zu hören diesen Mund: | to hark to this voice. |
| Kein Predigt niemalen | Never was sermon |
| Den Krebsen so g'fallen. | so pleasing to crabs. |
| | |
| Fisch' grosse, Fisch' kleine, | Fish great and fish small, |
| Vornehm' und gemeine, | distinguished and vulgar, |
| Erheben die Köpfe | cock their heads back |
| Wie verständ'ge Geschöpfe: | like intelligent creatures, |
| Auf Gottes Begehren | at God's behest |
| Die Predigt anhören. | to give this sermon ear. |
| | |
| Die Predigt geendet, | The sermon concluded, |
| Ein jeder sich wendet, | away they each turn, |
| Die Hechte bleiben Diebe, | the pike remain thievish, |
| Die Aale viel lieben: | the eels very loving. |
| Die Predigt hat g'fallen, | The sermon was pleasing, |
| Sie bleiben wie allen. | they all stay as they were. |
| | |
| Die Krebs' geh'n zurücke, | The crabs proceed backwards, |
| Die Stockfisch' bleiben dicke, | the stockfish stay fat, |
| Die Karpfen viel fressen, | the carp, they feed amply, |
| Die Predigt vergessen. | the sermon forgotten. |
| Die Predigt hat g'fallen, | The sermon was pleasing, |
| Sie bleiben wie allen. | they all stay as they were. |

*Des Buben Schützenlied* | *The Boy's Song of the Archer*

FRIEDRICH SCHILLER: from *Wilhelm Tell*

*Robert Schumann: op. 79, no. 26, 1849*

| | |
|---|---|
| Mit dem Pfeil, dem Bogen | With bow and arrow |
| Durch Gebirg und Tal | over hill and dale, |
| Kommt der Schütz gezogen | the archer comes marching |
| Früh am Morgenstrahl. | at first light of morn. |

Wie im Reich der Lüfte
König ist der Weih,—
Durch Gebirg und Klüfte
Herrscht der Schütze frei.

Ihm gehört das Weite,
Was sein Pfeil erreicht,
Das ist seine Beute,
Was da kreucht und fleugt.

As in the breezes' realm
the kite is king,
so, over peak and gorge,
the archer reigns free.

His the wide spaces;
what his shaft will reach,
that is his prey,
whether it fly or creep.

## Des Fischers Liebesglück / Love-fortunate Fisherman

KARL GOTTFRIED VON LEITNER

*Franz Schubert, 1827*

Dort blinket
Durch Weiden und winket
Ein Schimmer
Blaßstrahlig vom Zimmer
Der Holden mir zu.

There winks
through willows and beckons
a gleam,
a pale ray from the room
of my loved one, to me.

Es gaukelt
Wie Irrlicht und schaukelt
Sich leise
Sein Abglanz im Kreise
Des schwankenden Sees.

Flitting
like Jack o' lantern, rocking
gently,
it is reflected in the circle
of the unsteady lake.

Ich schaue
Mit Sehnen ins Blaue
Der Wellen
Und grüße den hellen
Gespiegelten Strahl.

Gazing
longingly into the blue
of the waves,
I greet the bright
mirrored beam.

Und springe
Zum Ruder und schwinge
Den Nachen
Dahin auf dem flachen,
Kristallenen Weg.

And spring
to the oar and swing
the boat
that way on its flat
crystal path.

Fein Liebchen
Schleicht traulich vom Stübchen
Herunter
Und sputet sich munter
Zu mir in das Boot.

My beloved
slips trustingly down
from her room,
and happily hastens
to me in my boat.

Gelinde
Treiben die Winde
Uns wieder
See-einwärts zum Flieder
Des Ufers hin dann.

Softly
the breezes drift
us again
lake-wards to the elder
of the shore.

Die blassen
Nachtnebel umfassen
Mit Hüllen
Vor Spähern den stillen,
Unschuldigen Scherz.

The pale
night mists envelop
and veil
from watchers our quiet
innocent sport.

Und tauschen
Wir Küsse, so rauschen
Die Wellen,
Im Sinken und Schwellen
Den Horchern zum Trotz.

Nur Sterne
Belauschen uns ferne
Und baden
Tief unter den Pfaden
Des gleitenden Kahns.

So schweben
Wir selig, umgeben
Vom Dunkel,
Hoch überm Gefunkel
Der Sterne einher.

Und weinen
Und lächeln und meinen,
Enthoben
Der Erde, schon oben,
Schon drüben zu sein.

And when we give
kiss for kiss,
the waves,
swelling, sinking, lap
to vex any listeners.

The stars alone
eavesdrop in the distance
and bathe
deep under the track
of the gliding boat.

So we float on,
blissful, enclosed
by the dark,
high above
the twinkling stars.

And weeping
and smiling, we think ourselves
withdrawn
from earth, and already
up there, on the other shore.


## *Des Mädchens Klage* | *The Maiden's Lament*

FRIEDRICH SCHILLER

*Franz Schubert: op. 58, no. 3, 1816*

Der Eichwald brauset, die Wolken
ziehn,
Das Mägdlein sitzet an Ufers
Grün,
Es bricht sich die Welle mit Macht, mit
Macht,
Und sie seufzt hinaus in die finstre
Nacht,
Das Auge vom Weinen getrübet.

»Das Herz ist gestorben, die Welt ist
leer,
Und weiter gibt sie dem Wunsche
nichts mehr.
Du Heilige, rufe dein Kind zurück,
Ich habe genossen das irdische Glück,
Ich habe gelebt und geliebet!«

Es rinnet der Tränen vergeblicher Lauf,
Die Klage, sie wecket die Toten nicht
auf,
Doch nenne, was tröstet und heilet die
Brust
Nach der süßen Liebe verschwundener
Lust,
Ich, die Himmlische, wills nicht
versagen.

The oak wood roars, the clouds race
by,
on the green of the shore the maiden
sits;
the billow mightily, mightily
breaks,
and into the gloomy night she
sighs,
eyes dimmed with weeping.

'My heart is dead, the world is
void,
to no wish of mine does it yield any
more.
Holy Mother, call back your child,
I have tasted earthly joy,
have lived and loved!'

Tears vainly run their course,
the lament wakes not the dead from
sleep,
but say what will solace and heal a
breast,
when the joy of sweet love is
gone,
I, the Heavenly Maid, will deny it
not.

»Laß rinnen der Tränen vergeblichen
  Lauf,
Es wecke die Klage den Toten nicht
  auf,
Das süßeste Glück für die traurende
  Brust,
Nach der schönen Liebe verschwundener
  Lust,
Sind der Liebe Schmerzen und
  Klagen.«

'Let tears vainly run their
  course,
and lament not wake the dead from
  sleep!
The sweetest joys for the sorrowing
  breast,
when the joy of sweet love is
  gone,
are love's agony and
  lamentation.'


## Des Sennen Abschied | The Cowherd's Farewell

FRIEDRICH SCHILLER: from *Wilhelm Tell*

*Franz Liszt, 1845; Robert Schumann: op. 79, no. 23, 1849*

Ihr Matten lebt wohl!
Ihr sonnigen Weiden!
Der Senne muß scheiden,
Der Sommer ist hin.

Adieu, you meadows,
you sunny pastures!
Away must the cowherd,
the summer is gone.

Wir fahren zu Berg, wir kommen
  wieder,
Wenn der Kuckuck ruft, wenn erwachen
  die Lieder,
Wenn mit Blumen die Erde sich kleidet
  neu,
Wenn die Brünnlein fließen im
  lieblichen Mai.

We move up the mountain, we come
  again
when the cuckoo calls, when songs
  awake,
when earth is clothed anew with
  flowers,
when the springs gush in delightful
  May.

Ihr Matten lebt wohl,
Ihr sonnigen Weiden!
Der Senne muß scheiden,
Der Sommer ist hin.

Adieu, you meadows,
you sunny pastures!
Away must the cowherd,
the summer is gone.


## Dichterliebe | A Poet's Love

HEINRICH HEINE

*Robert Schumann: op. 48, nos. 1-16, 1840*

I

Im wunderschönen Monat Mai,
Als alle Knospen sprangen,
Da ist in meinem Herzen
Die Liebe aufgegangen.

I

In the wondrous month of May,
when buds were bursting open,
then it was that my heart
filled with love.

Im wunderschönen Monat Mai,
Als alle Vögel sangen,
Da hab' ich ihr gestanden
Mein Sehnen und Verlangen.

  (*Robert Franz: op. 25, no. 5*)

In the wondrous month of May,
when the birds were singing,
then it was I confessed to her
my longing and desire.

**2**

Aus meinen Tränen sprießen
Viel blühende Blumen hervor,
Und meine Seufzer werden
Ein Nachtigallenchor.

Und wenn du mich lieb hast, Kindchen,
Schenk' ich dir die Blumen all',
Und vor deinem Fenster soll klingen
Das Lied der Nachtigall.

**3**

Die Rose, die Lilie, die Taube, die
    Sonne,
Die liebt' ich einst alle in Liebeswonne.
Ich lieb' sie nicht mehr, ich liebe alleine
Die Kleine, die Feine, die Reine, die
    Eine;
Sie selber, aller Liebe Wonne,
Ist Rose und Lilie und Taube und
    Sonne.
Ich liebe alleine
Die Kleine, die Feine, die Reine, die
    Eine.

(*Robert Franz: op. 34, no. 5; Giacomo Meyerbeer, 1838*)

**4**

Wenn ich in deine Augen seh',
So schwindet all' mein Leid und Weh;
Doch wenn ich küsse deinen Mund,
So werd' ich ganz und gar gesund.

Wenn ich mich lehn' an deine Brust,
Kommt's über mich wie Himmelslust;
Doch wenn du sprichst: ich liebe dich!
So muß ich weinen bitterlich.

(*Robert Franz: op. 44, no. 5; Hugo Wolf: 1876; posth.*)

**5**

Ich will meine Seele tauchen
In den Kelch der Lilie hinein;
Die Lilie soll klingend hauchen
Ein Lied von der Liebsten mein.

Das Lied soll schauern und beben
Wie der Kuß von ihrem Mund,
Den sie mir einst gegeben
In wunderbar süßer Stund'.

(*Robert Franz: op. 43, no. 4*)

**6**

Im Rhein, im heiligen Strome,
Da spiegelt sich in den Well'n
Mit seinem großen Dome,
Das große, heilige Köln.

Im Dom da steht ein Bildnis,
Auf goldenem Leder gemalt;
In meines Lebens Wildnis
Hat's freundlich hineingestrahlt.

---

**2**

From my tears burst
many full-blown flowers,
and my sighs become
a nightingale chorus.

And if you love me, child,
I'll give you all the flowers,
and at your window shall sound
the song of the nightingale.

**3**

Rose, lily, dove,
    sun—
all once I blissfully loved.
I love them no more, alone I love
one who is small, fine, pure,
    rare;
she, most blissful of all loves,
is rose and lily and dove and
    sun.
Alone I love
one who is small, fine, pure,
    rare.

**4**

When into your eyes I look,
all my sorrow flies;
but when I kiss your lips,
then I am wholly healed.

When I recline upon your breast,
over me steals heavenly bliss;
but when you say: it's you I love!
Then bitter tears must I shed.

**5**

My soul will I bathe
in the lily's chalice;
the lily shall breathe
a song of my beloved.

The song shall tremble and quiver
like the kiss her lips
bestowed on me once,
in a sweet and lovely hour.

**6**

In the Rhine, the holy river,
mirrored in the waves,
with its great cathedral
is great and holy Cologne.

The cathedral has a picture,
painted on gilded leather;
into my life's wilderness
friendly rays it has cast.

Es schweben Blumen und Eng'lein
Um unsre liebe Frau;
Die Augen, die Lippen, die Wänglein,
Die gleichen der Liebsten genau.

Flowers and angels float
about Our Lady dear;
eyes, lips, cheeks
are the image of my love's.

(*Robert Franz: op. 18, no. 2; Franz Liszt: ed. 1843*)

7

Ich grolle nicht, und wenn das Herz
auch bricht,
Ewig verlor'nes Lieb! Ich grolle nicht.
Wie du auch strahlst in Diamanten-
pracht,
Es fällt kein Strahl in deines Herzens
Nacht.
Das weiß ich längst.

7

I bear no grudge, though my heart
breaks,
loved one forever lost! I bear no grudge.
However you may gleam in diamond
splendour,
no ray falls into the night of your
heart.
I've known that long.

Ich grolle nicht, und wenn das Herz
auch bricht.
Ich sah dich ja im Traume,
Und sah die Nacht in deines Herzens
Raume,
Und sah die Schlang', die dir am Herzen
frißt,
Ich sah, mein Lieb, wie sehr du elend
bist.
Ich grolle nicht.

I bear no grudge, though my heart
breaks.
For I saw you in my dream,
saw the night within your
heart,
and saw the serpent gnawing at your
heart,
saw, my love, how pitiful you
are.
I bear no grudge.

8

Und wüßten's die Blumen, die kleinen,
Wie tief verwundet mein Herz,
Sie würden mit mir weinen,
Zu heilen meinen Schmerz.

8

If the little flowers knew
how deep my heart is hurt,
with me they would weep
to heal my pain.

Und wüßten's die Nachtigallen,
Wie ich so traurig und krank,
Sie ließen fröhlich erschallen
Erquickenden Gesang.

If the nightingales knew
how sad I am and sick,
joyously they'd let sound
refreshing song.

Und wüßten sie mein Wehe,
Die goldenen Sternelein,
Sie kämen aus ihrer Höhe,
Und sprächen Trost mir ein.

And if *they* knew my grief,
the little golden stars,
from the sky they'd come
and console me.

Sie alle können's nicht wissen,
Nur Eine kennt meinen Schmerz;
Sie hat ja selbst zerrissen,
Zerrissen mir das Herz.

But none of them can know,
one only knows my pain;
for she it was who broke
my heart, broke my heart in two.

(*Felix Mendelssohn-Bartholdy: op. 9, no. 10, 1825–28; set by Fanny Mendelssohn-Bartholdy*)

9

Das ist ein Flöten und Geigen,
Trompeten schmettern darein;
Da tanzt wohl den Hochzeitsreigen
Die Herzallerliebste mein.

9

What a fluting and fiddling
and a blaring of trumpets!
There, dancing her wedding dance
will be my dearest love.

Das ist ein Klingen und Dröhnen,
Ein Pauken und ein Schalmei'n;
Dazwischen schluchzen und stöhnen
Die lieblichen Engelein.

What a clashing and clanging,
drumming and piping;
and sobbing and groaning
of delightful angels.

10
Hör' ich das Liedchen klingen,
Das einst die Liebste sang,
So will mir die Brust zerspringen
Von wildem Schmerzendrang.

Es treibt mich ein dunkles Sehnen
Hinauf zur Waldeshöh',
Dort löst sich auf in Tränen
Mein übergroßes Weh'.

(*Robert Franz: op. 5, no. 11*)

10
When I hear the song
my love once sang,
my heart almost breaks
from the wild rush of pain.

Vague longing drives me
up to the high forest,
where my immense grief
dissolves in tears.


11
Ein Jüngling liebt ein Mädchen,
Die hat einen andern erwählt;
Der andre liebt eine andre,
Und hat sich mit dieser vermählt.

Das Mädchen nimmt aus Ärger
Den ersten besten Mann,
Der ihr in den Weg gelaufen;
Der Jüngling ist übel dran.

Es ist eine alte Geschichte,
Doch bleibt sie immer neu;
Und wem sie just passieret,
Dem bricht das Herz entzwei.

11
A boy loves a girl,
she chooses another;
the other loves another
and her he weds.

The girl, out of spite,
takes the first man
to come her way;
the boy's badly hurt.

It is an old, old story,
remains though ever new,
and he to whom it's happened,
his heart is broken in half.

12
Am leuchtenden Sommermorgen
Geh' ich im Garten herum.
Es flüstern und sprechen die Blumen,
Ich aber wandle stumm.

Es flüstern und sprechen die Blumen,
Und schaun mitleidig mich an:
Sei unsrer Schwester nicht böse,
Du trauriger blasser Mann.

(*Robert Franz: op. 11, no. 2*)

12
One bright summer morning
I walk in the garden.
Flowers whisper and speak,
but I walk silently.

Flowers whisper and speak,
and gaze at me in pity:
'Be not angry with our sister,
sad, pale man!'


13
Ich hab' im Traum geweinet,
Mir träumt', du lägest im Grab.
Ich wachte auf, und die Träne
Floß noch von der Wange herab.

Ich hab' im Traum geweinet,
Mir träumt', du verließest mich.
Ich wachte auf, und ich weinte
Noch lange bitterlich.

Ich hab' im Traum geweinet,
Mir träumte, du wär'st mir noch gut.
Ich wachte auf, und noch immer
Strömt meine Tränenflut.

(*Robert Franz: op. 25, no. 3*)

13
I wept in my dream,
I dreamt you lay in your grave.
I woke, and tears
still flowed upon my cheek.

I wept in my dream,
I dreamt you were leaving me.
I woke, and wept on
long and bitterly.

I wept in my dream,
I dreamt you loved me still.
I woke, and still
my tears stream.

14
Allnächtlich im Traume seh' ich dich,
Und sehe dich freundlich grüßen,
Und laut aufweinend stürz ich mich
Zu deinen süßen Füßen.

Du siehest mich an wehmütiglich
Und schüttelst das blonde Köpfchen;
Aus deinen Augen schleichen sich
Die Perlentränentröpfchen.

Du sagst mir heimlich ein leises Wort
Und gibst mir den Strauß von
    Cypressen.
Ich wache auf, und der Strauß ist fort,
Und's Wort hab' ich vergessen.

14
Nightly in my dreams I see you,
see your friendly greeting,
and weeping loudly, hurl myself
at your sweet feet.

You look at me wistfully,
shaking your little fair head;
from your eyes steal
tear-drops of pearl.

A soft word you whisper me,
and give me a bouquet of
    cypress.
I wake, the cypress is gone,
and the word forgotten.

(*Robert Franz: op. 9, no. 4; Felix Mendelssohn-Bartholdy: op. 86, no. 4*)


15
Aus alten Märchen winkt es
Hervor mit weißer Hand,
Da singt es und da klingt es
Von einem Zauberland;

Wo bunte Blumen blühen
Im gold'nen Abendlicht,
Und lieblich duftend glühen,
Mit bräutlichem Gesicht;

[Und grüne Bäume singen
Uralte Melodei'n,
Die Lüfte heimlich klingen,
Und Vögel schmettern drein;

Und Nebelbilder steigen
Wohl aus der Erd' hervor,
Und tanzen luft'gen Reigen
Im wunderlichen Chor;

Und blaue Funken brennen
An jedem Blatt und Reis,
Und rote Lichter rennen
Im irren, wirren Kreis;

Und laute Quellen brechen
Aus wildem Marmorstein.
Und seltsam in den Bächen
Strahlt fort der Widerschein.]

Ach, könnt' ich dorthin kommen,
Und dort mein Herz erfreu'n,
Und aller Qual entnommen,
Und frei und selig sein!

Ach! jenes Land der Wonne,
Das seh' ich oft im Traum,
Doch kommt die Morgensonne,
Zerfließt's wie eitel Schaum.

15
A white hand beckons
from fairy tales of old,
song there is, and sounds
of a magic land,

where gay flowers bloom
in golden evening light,
and, sweet scented, glow
with bride-like faces.

(And green trees sing
old, old melodies,
stealthy breezes murmur,
and birds warble;

and misty shapes rear
from the earth,
and dance airy dances
in strange throng;

and blue sparks blaze
on every leaf and twig,
and red fires race
in mad wild circles;

and loud springs burst
from living marble, and
strange in the brooks
the reflection shines.)

Oh, could I but go there,
there gladden my heart,
from all pain removed,
blissful and free.

Oh, that land of joy,
in dreams I see it often,
but, come morning sun,
it's gone like foam.

16
Die alten bösen Lieder,
Die Träume bös' und arg,
Die laßt uns jetzt begraben,
Holt einen großen Sarg.

Hinein leg' ich gar manches,
Doch sag' ich noch nicht, was;
Der Sarg muß sein noch größer
Wie's Heidelberger Faß.

Und holt eine Totenbahre
Und Bretter fest und dick;
Auch muß sie sein noch länger,
Als wie zu Mainz die Brück'.

Und holt mir auch zwölf Riesen,
Die müssen noch stärker sein
Als wie der starke Christoph
Im Dom zu Köln am Rhein.

Die sollen den Sarg forttragen,
Und senken ins Meer hinab;
Denn solchem großen Sarge
Gebührt ein großes Grab.

Wißt ihr, warum der Sarg wohl
So groß und schwer mag sein?
Ich senkt auch meine Liebe
Und meinen Schmerz hinein.

16
The bad old songs,
the dreams wicked and bad,
let us now bury them—
fetch a big coffin.

Much will I lay in it,
though what, I won't yet say;
a bigger coffin must it be
than the Vat of Heidelberg.

And fetch a bier
and planks firm and thick;
the bier must be longer
than the bridge at Mainz.

And twelve giants fetch me,
who shall be even stronger
than St Christopher the Strong
in Cologne Cathedral on the Rhine.

They shall bear off the coffin,
and sink it in the sea;
for such a big coffin
belongs in a big grave.

Do you know why the coffin
should be so heavy and big?
I would put my love in
and my sorrow too.

## Die Allmacht | Omnipotence

JOHANN LADISLAV PYRKER

*Franz Schubert: op. 79, no. 2, 1825*

Groß ist Jehova, der Herr! Denn
    Himmel
und Erde verkünden seine Macht.
Du hörst sie im brausenden Sturm,
in des Waldstroms laut aufrauschendem
    Ruf;
du hörst sie in des grünen Waldes
    Gesäusel,
siehst sie in wogender Saaten Gold,
in lieblicher Blumen glühendem
    Schmelz,
im Glanz des sternebesäten Himmels,
furchtbar tönt sie im Donnergeroll
und flammt in des Blitzes schnell
    hinzuckendem Flug.
Doch kündet das pochende Herz dir
    fühlbarer noch
Jehovas Macht, des ewigen Gottes,
blickst du flehend empor und hoffst auf
    Huld und Erbarmen.

Great is Jehovah. the Lord! For
    heaven
and earth proclaim his might.
You hear it in the roaring storm,
in the loud rushing call of the forest
    stream;
you hear it in the greenwood's
    murmur,
behold it in the gold of waving corn,
in the glow of delightful
    flowers,
in the star-strewn heavens' gleam;
awful its sound in the roll of thunder
and its flame in the lightning's swift
    jagged flight.
But more palpably to you will the
    beating heart proclaim
the might of Jehovah, God Eternal,
if, beseeching, up you gaze, hoping for
    grace and pity.

## Die beiden Grenadiere | The Two Grenadiers

HEINRICH HEINE

*Robert Schumann: op. 49, no. 1, 1840; Richard Wagner*

Nach Frankreich zogen zwei
 Grenadier',
Die waren in Rußland gefangen.
Und als sie kamen ins deutsche
 Quartier,
Sie ließen die Köpfe hangen.

To France were marching two
 grenadiers
who had been captured in Russia.
And when they came into German
 quarters,
they hung their heads in shame.

Da hörten sie beide die traurige Mär:
Daß Frankreich verloren gegangen,
Besiegt und geschlagen das tapfere
 Heer—
Und der Kaiser, der Kaiser
 gefangen!

And here they learnt the sorry tale
that France was lost forever,
her valiant army beaten and
 smashed,
and the Emperor, the Emperor
 captured!

Da weinten zusammen die Grenadier'
Wohl ob der kläglichen Kunde.
Der eine sprach: Wie weh wird mir,
Wie brennt meine alte Wunde!

The grenadiers then wept together,
hearing these pitiful tidings.
One said, 'Ah, the agony,
my wound is a blaze of fire!'

Der andere sprach: Das Lied ist aus,
Auch ich möcht mit dir sterben,
Doch hab ich Weib und Kind zu Haus,
Die ohne mich verderben.

The other said, 'This is the end,
and gladly I'd die with you,
but I've a wife and child at home,
who without me will perish.'

Was schert mich Weib, was schert mich
 Kind,
Ich trage weit bessres Verlangen;
Laß sie betteln gehn, wenn sie hungrig
 sind—
Mein Kaiser, mein Kaiser gefangen!

'To hell with wife, to hell with
 child,
my thoughts are for things far higher;
let them beg, if they've nothing to
 eat—
my Emperor, my Emperor captured!

Gewähr mir, Bruder, eine Bitt':
Wenn ich jetzt sterben werde,
So nimm meine Leiche nach Frankreich
 mit,
Bergrab mich in Frankreichs Erde.

'Grant me, brother, one request:
if I am now to die,
take my body to France with
 you,
bury me in French soil.

Das Ehrenkreuz am roten Band
Sollst du aufs Herz mir legen;
Die Flinte gib mir in die Hand,
Und gürt' mir um den Degen.

'The cross of honour on its red ribbon
you shall lay upon my heart;
my musket give me in my hand,
and buckle my sabre on me.

So will ich liegen und horchen still,
Wie eine Schildwach', im Grabe,
Bis einst ich höre Kanonengebrüll
Und wiehernder Rosse Getrabe.

'And so will I, quiet, lie and listen,
like a sentinel in my grave,
until I hear the cannons' roar,
the whinny and thunder of horses.

Dann reitet mein Kaiser wohl über
 mein Grab,
Viel Schwerter klirren und blitzen;
Dann steig ich gewaffnet hervor aus
 dem Grab—
Den Kaiser, den Kaiser zu schützen!

'Then will my Emperor ride over my
 grave,
swords will be clashing and flashing;
and armed, I'll rise up from the
 grave—
to guard my Emperor, my Emperor!'

## Die Bekehrte / The Convert

JOHANN WOLFGANG GOETHE

*Armin Knab, 1924–46; Hugo Wolf, 1889*

Bei dem Glanz der Abendröte
Ging ich still den Weg entlang,
Damon saß und blies die Flöte,
Daß es von den Felsen klang,
So la la!

In the sunset gleam
quietly I walked the path,
Damon sat playing his flute,
making the cliffs resound,
so la la!

Und er zog mich zu sich nieder,
Küßte mich so hold, so süß.
Und ich sagte: Blase wieder!
Und der gute Junge blies,
So la la!

And he drew me down to him,
kissed me so gently, so sweetly.
And I said. 'Play again.'
And the good lad played,
so la la!

Meine Ruh ist nun verloren,
Meine Freude floh davon,
Und ich hör vor meinen Ohren
Immer nur den alten Ton,
So la la, le ralla!

My peace is now lost,
my joy is flown,
and in my ears I hear
still only that old
so la la, le ralla!

## Die drei Zigeuner / The Three Gipsies

NIKOLAUS LENAU

*Franz Liszt, 1860; Othmar Schoeck: op. 24a, no. 4, 1909–14*

Drei Zigeuner fand ich einmal
Liegen an einer Weide,
Als mein Fuhrwerk mit müder Qual
Schlich durch sandige Heide.

Three gipsies once I found
lying against a willow,
as, wearily, painfully, my cart
crawled over the sandy heath.

Hielt der eine für sich allein
In den Händen die Fiedel,
Spielt, umglüht vom Abendschein,
Sich ein feuriges Liedel.

One, on his own,
was holding his fiddle,
playing in the sunset glow
a fiery little tune.

Hielt der zweite die Pfeif' im Mund,
Blickte nach seinem Rauche,
Froh, als ob er vom Erdenrund
Nichts zum Glücke mehr brauche.

The second, pipe in mouth,
was watching the smoke,
cheerful, as if from the world
he needed no more for happiness.

Und der dritte behaglich schlief,
Und sein Cimbal am Baum hing,
Über die Saiten der Windhauch lief,
Über sein Herz ein Traum ging.

The third was comfortably asleep,
his cymbalon hanging from the tree,
the breeze playing over the strings,
a dream passing through his heart.

An den Kleidern trugen die drei
Löcher und bunte Flicken,
Aber sie boten trotzig frei
Spott den Erdengeschicken.

Their clothes the three wore
in holes and gaily patched,
but, defiantly free, they
mocked the destinies of earth.

Dreifach haben sie mir gezeigt,
Wenn das Leben uns nachtet,
Wie man's verraucht, verschläft, vergeigt,
Und es dreimal verachtet.

They showed me, this trio,
how, when life for us grows dark,
to smoke, sleep and fiddle it away,
and so to trebly scorn it.

Nach den Zigeunern lang noch schaun
Mußt' ich im Weiterfahren,
Nach den Gesichtern dunkelbraun,
Den schwarzlockigen Haaren.

Longer yet at the gipsies
had I to gaze, travelling on,
at their tanned faces,
their curly black hair.

## Die Einsame / The Solitary Woman

JOSEPH VON EICHENDORFF

*Hans Pfitzner: op. 9, no. 2, 1888–89*

Wär's dunkel, ich läg im Walde,
Im Walde rauscht's so sacht,
Mit ihrem Sternenmantel
Bedeckt mich da die Nacht,

Were it dark, in the forest I'd lie,
the forest murmurs so soft,
with her starry mantle,
night will cover me there;

Da kommen die Bächlein gegangen,
Ob ich schon schlafen tu?
Ich schlaf nicht, ich hör noch lang
Den Nachtigallen zu,

the brooklets then come asking
if I'm already asleep?
I'm not, long yet I'll listen
to the nightingales;

Wenn die Wipfel über mir schwanken,
Das klingt die ganze Nacht.
Das sind im Herzen die Gedanken,
Die singen, wenn niemand wacht.

when, above me, the tree-tops sway,
they sound the whole night through.
The heart's thoughts are they
that sing when no one is awake.

## Die Einsamkeit / Solitude

JOHANN MAYRHOFER

*Franz Schubert, 1818*

»Gib mir die Fülle der Einsamkeit.«
Im Tal, von Blüten überschneit,
da ragt ein Dom, und nebenbei
in hohem Stile die Abtei:
wie ihr Begründer, fromm und still,
der Müden Hafen und Asyl,
hier kühlt mit heiliger Betauung,
die nie versiegende Beschauung.
Doch den frischen Jüngling quälen
selbst in gottgeweihten Zellen
Bilder, feuriger verjüngt;
und ein wilder Strom entspringt
aus der Brust, die er umdämmt,
und in einem Augenblick
ist der Ruhe zartes Glück
von den Wellen weggeschwemmt.

'Solitude grant me in full measure.'
In the valley oversnowed with blossom
a cathedral soars, and, close by,
in noble style, the abbey:
like its founder, pious, quiet—
the haven and sanctuary of the weary—
assuages here the holy dew
of never-ceasing contemplation.
Yet the raw young man is tormented,
even in God-dedicated cells,
by images more fierily rejuvenated;
and a violent stream bursts forth
from the breast he dams around,
and in one instant
the tender happiness of peace
is swept away by the waves.

»Gib mir die Fülle der Tätigkeit.«
Menschen wimmeln weit und breit,
Wagen kreuzen sich und stäuben,
Käufer sich um Läden treiben,
rotes Gold und heller Stein
lockt die Zögernden hinein,
und Ersatz für Landesgrüne
bieten Maskenball und Bühne.

'Activity grant me in full measure.'
People teem far and wide,
coaches pass and raise the dust,
buyers cluster round the shops,
red gold and bright stones
lure the hesitating in,
and a substitute for green country
is offered by masked ball and stage.

Doch in prangenden Palästen,
bei der Freude lauten Festen,
sprießt empor der Schwermut Blume,
senkt ihr Haupt zum Heiligtume
seiner Jugend Unschuldlust,
zu dem blauen Hirtenland
und der lichten Quelle Rand.
Ach, daß er hinweg gemußt!

»Gib mir das Glück der
    Geselligkeit.«
Genossen, freundlich angereiht
der Tafel, stimmen Chorus an
und ebenen die Felsenbahn!
So geht's zum schönen Hügelkranz
und abwärts zu des Stromes Tanz,
und immer mehr befestiget sich
    Neigung
mit treuer, kräftiger Verzweigung.
Doch, wenn die Freunde all geschieden,
ist's getan um seinen Frieden.
Ihn bewegt der Sehnsucht Schmerz,
und er schauet himmelwärts:
das Gestirn der Liebe strahlt.
Liebe, Liebe ruft die laue Luft,
Liebe, Liebe atmet Blumenduft,
und sein Inn'res Liebe hallt.

»Gib mir die Fülle der Seligkeit.«
Nun wandelt er in Trunkenheit
an ihrer Hand in schwelgenden
    Gesprächen,
im Buchengang, an weißen Bächen,
und muß er auch durch Wüstenein,
ihm leuchtet süßer Augen Schein;
und in der feindlichsten Verwirrung
vertrauet er der holden Führung.
Doch die Särge großer Ahnen,
Siegerkronen, Sturmesfahnen
lassen ihn nicht fürder ruh'n:
und er muß ein Gleiches tun,
und wie sie unsterblich sein.
Sieh, er steigt aufs hohe Pferd,
schwingt und prüft das blanke Schwert,
reitet in die Schlacht hinein.

»Gib mir die Fülle der Düsterkeit.«
Da liegen sie im Blute
    hingestreut,
die Lippe starr, das Auge wild gebrochen,
die erst dem Schrecken Trotz
    gesprochen.
Kein Vater kehrt den Seinen mehr,
und heimwärts kehrt ein ander
    Heer,
und denen Krieg das Teuerste
    genommen,
begrüßen nun mit schmerzlichem
    Willkommen!

But in resplendent palaces,
at clamorous joyous feasts,
up shoots the flower of sadness,
bowing its head to the sanctuary
of his youth's innocent joy,
to that pastoral country blue
and the edge of the lucid spring.
Alas, that he had to leave!

'Good company grant me in full
    measure.'
Companions, amicably grouped
round the table, strike up in chorus
and make smooth the rocky way.
So on they go to the fair hill's crest
and downward to the dancing stream,
and affection is further
    strengthened
by true and powerful ramification.
Yet when the friends are all departed,
all is over with his peace.
He is stirred by an agony of yearning,
and gazes heavenwards:
love's constellation shines.
Love, calls the mild breeze, love,
love, breathes the flowers' fragrance,
and his innermost being echoes love.

'Bliss grant me in full measure.'
Now, intoxicated, he wanders,
holding her hand, revelling in
    talk,
in the beech avenue, by white brooks,
and though he traverse desert places,
the light of sweet eyes shines on him;
and in the most inimical confusion,
he trusts to that sweet leadership.
Yet the tombs of great ancestors,
victors' crowns, battle standards,
allow him no further rest:
and likewise he must act,
and like them, be immortal.
See, he mounts a lofty steed,
tests and brandishes his shining sword,
and into battle rides.

'Melancholy grant me in full measure.'
There, strewn in their own blood, they
    lie,
motionless the lips, dim the wild eye
that to horror first bid
    defiance.
No father will return more to his own,
and homeward goes a different
    army,
and those robbed by war of what is
    dearest,
now bid them a painful
    'Welcome!'

So däucht ihm des Vaterlandes
 Wächter
ein ergrimmter Brüderschlächter,
der der Freiheit edel Gut
düngt mit rotem Menschenblut.
Und er flucht dem tollen
 Ruhm
und tauschet lärmendes Gewühl
mit dem Forste, grün und kühl,
mit dem Waldesleben um.

»Gib mir die Weihe der Einsamkeit.«
Durch dichte Tannendunkelheit
dringt Sonnenblick nur halb und halb,
und färbet Nadelschichten falb.
Der Kuckuck ruft aus
 Zweiggeflecht,
an grauer Rinde pickt der Specht,
und donnernd über Klippen-
 hemmung
ergeht des Gießbachs kühne Strömung.
Was er wünschte, was er liebte,
ihn erfreute, ihn betrübte,
schwebt mit sanfter Schwärmerei
wie im Abendrot vorbei.
Jünglings Sehnsucht,
 Einsamkeit,
wird dem Greisen nun zuteil,
und sein Leben rauh und steil
führte doch zur Seligkeit.

Thus did the Fatherland's guardian
 seem to him
a grim slaughterer of his brothers,
a manurer of freedom's noble estate
with crimson human blood.
And on insane glory he calls curses
 down
and exchanges the noisy throng
for the forest green and cool,
and forest life.

'Grant me the solemnity of solitude.'
Through dense darkness of firs
the sun's gaze penetrates but partially,
colouring the needle layers pale yellow.
From the plaited branches calls the
 cuckoo,
on the grey bark drums the woodpecker
and thundering over the obstructing
 cliff,
bursts the torrent's dashing stream.
What he wished for, what he loved,
what rejoiced, what saddened him,
floats past in gentle rapture
as in the evening glow.
The yearning, solitude of the young
 man
now becomes the old man's lot,
and, by rough, steep ways his life
has led nonetheless to bliss.

## Die feindlichen Brüder | The Hostile Brothers

HEINRICH HEINE

*Robert Schumann: op. 49, no. 2, 1840*

Oben auf des Berges Spitze
Liegt das Schloß in Nacht gehüllt;
Doch im Tale leuchten Blitze,
Helle Schwerter klirren wild.

High on the mountain summit
stands the castle, veiled in night;
but in the valley lightning flashes,
shining broadswords fiercely clash.

Das sind Brüder, die dort fechten
Grimmen Zweikampf, wutentbrannt.
Sprich, warum die Brüder rechten
Mit dem Schwerte in der Hand?

Brothers it is, who are fighting,
rage-inflamed, a dreadful duel.
Pray, what are they fighting over,
each of them with sword in hand?

Gräfin Lauras Augenfunken
Zündeten den Brüderstreit;
Beide glühen liebestrunken
Für die adlig holde Maid.

Countess Laura's sparkling eyes
set alight the brothers' quarrel;
both are burning drunk with love
for that sweet and noble maid.

Welchem aber von den beiden
Wendet sich ihr Herze zu?
Kein Ergrübeln kann's entscheiden,—
Schwert heraus, enscheide du!

But to which of them, to which,
does her heart incline?
No pondering will resolve it,
out, then, sword, let you decide!

Und sie fechten kühn verwegen,
Hieb auf Hiebe niederkracht's.
Hütet euch, ihr wilden Degen,
Böses Blendwerk schleicht des Nachts.

Wehe! Wehe! blut'ge Brüder!
Wehe! Wehe! blut'ges Tal!
Beide Kämpfer stürzen nieder,
Einer in des andern Stahl.—

Viel Jahrhunderte verwehen,
Viel Geschlechter deckt das Grab;
Traurig von des Berges Höhen
Schaut das öde Schloß herab.

Aber nachts, im Talesgrunde,
Wandelt's heimlich, wunderbar;
Wenn da kommt die zwölfte Stunde,
Kämpfet dort das Brüderpaar.

And boldly determined they battle,
blow upon blow crashes down.
Fierce warriors, beware,
evil deception stalks by night.

Alack, alack now, bloody brothers!
Alack, alack now, bloody vale!
Both of the contestants fall,
each upon the other's steel,—

Many the centuries that pass,
the generations laid in the grave;
sadly, from the mountain heights,
the castle, desolate, looks down.

But at night, deep in the valley,
a secret wonder comes about;
when the midnight hour arrives
still the brothers fight it out.

*Die Forelle | The Trout*

CHRISTIAN FRIEDRICH DANIEL SCHUBART

*Franz Schubert: op. 32, 1817*

In einem Bächlein helle,
Da schoß in froher Eil
Die launische Forelle
Vorüber wie ein Pfeil.
Ich stand an dem Gestade
Und sah in süßer Ruh
Des muntern Fischleins Bade
Im klaren Bächlein zu.

Ein Fischer mit der Rute
Wohl an dem Ufer stand,
Und sah's mit kaltem Blute,
Wie sich das Fischlein wand.
Solang dem Wasser Helle,
So dacht ich, nicht gebricht,
So fängt er die Forelle
Mit seiner Angel nicht.

Doch endlich ward dem Diebe
Die Zeit zu lang. Er macht
Das Bächlein tückisch trübe,
Und eh ich es gedacht,
So zuckte seine Rute,
Das Fischlein zappelt dran,
Und ich mit regem Blute
Sah die Betrog'ne an.

In a clear brooklet,
in lively haste,
the wayward trout
flashed arrow-like by.
Standing on the bank,
contentedly I watched
the jolly little fish
swimming the clear brook.

An angler, with rod,
stood on the bank,
cold-bloodedly noting
the fish's twists and turns.
As long as the water
remains so clear, I thought,
he'll never take the trout
with his rod.

But at last the thief
tired of waiting. Artfully
he muddied the brooklet,
and the next moment,
a flick of the rod,
and there writhed the fish;
and I, with blood boiling,
looked at the deceived one.

## Die frühen Gräber | Early Graves

FRIEDRICH GOTTLIEB KLOPSTOCK

Christoph Willibald Gluck, 1775; Ernst Krenek: op. 19, no. 5, 1923;
Franz Schubert, 1815

Willkommen, o silberner Mond,
Schöner, stiller Gefährt' der Nacht!
Du entfliehst? Eile nicht, bleib',
Gedankenfreund!
Sehet, er bleibt, das Gewölk wallte nur
hin.

Des Maies Erwachen ist nur
Schöner noch, wie die Sommernacht,
Wenn ihm Tau, hell wie Licht, aus
der Locke träuft,
Und zu dem Hügel herauf rötlich er
kömmt.

Ihr Edleren, ach, es bewächst
Eure Male schon ernstes Moos!
O, wie war glücklich ich, als ich noch
mit euch
Sahe sich röten den Tag, schimmern
die Nacht!

Welcome, O silver moon,
fair, silent companion of the night!
You fly? Haste not, stay, friend of
thought!
See, it stays—it was but the clouds
that moved.

Only May's awakening
is fairer still than the summer night,
when dew, light-bright, dripping from
his locks
and reddish, up over the hill he
comes.

Ah, you who are nobler, overgrown
with solemn moss are your monuments!
Oh, how happy was I when, still with
you,
I watched day redden, night
gleam!

## Die Götter Griechenlands | The Gods of Greece

FRIEDRICH SCHILLER: fragment from the poem

Franz Schubert: 1819

Schöne Welt, wo bist du? Kehre
wieder,
Holdes Blütenalter der Natur!
Ach, nur in dem Feenland der Lieder
Lebt noch deine fabelhafte Spur.
Ausgestorben trauert das Gefilde,
Keine Gottheit zeigt sich meinem Blick.
Ach, von jenem lebenwarmen Bilde
Blieb der Schatten nur zurück.

Beautiful world, where are you? Come
again,
sweet blossom-time of nature!
Ah, only in the magic land of song
lives still your richly-fabled trace.
The fields, deserted, mourn,
no deity reveals himself to me.
Ah, of that life-warmth
only the shadow has remained.

## Die ihr des unermeßlichen Weltalls Schöpfer ehrt | You who Honour the Creator of the Infinite Universe

(Cantata)

FRANZ HEINRICH ZIEGENHAGEN

Wolfgang Amadeus Mozart: K 619, 1791

Die ihr des unermeßlichen Weltalls
Schöpfer ehrt,
Jehova nennt ihn, oder Gott  nennt Fu
ihn, oder Brahma, hört!

You who honour the Creator of the
Infinite Universe,
calling him Jehovah or God, Fu or
Brahma, give ear!

Hört Worte aus der Posaune des
Allherrschers!
Laut tönt durch Erden, Monde, Sonnen
ihr ewger Schall,
hört Menschen, hört, Menschen, sie
auch ihr!
Liebt mich in meinen Werken,
Liebt Ordnung, Ebenmaß und
Einklang!
Liebt euch, liebt euch, euch selbst und
eure Brüder,
Liebt euch selbst und eure Brüder!
Körperkraft und Schönheit sei eure
Zier,
Verstandeshelle euer
Adel!
Reicht euch der ewgen Freundschaft
Bruderhand,
die nur ein Wahn, nie Wahrheit euch
so lang entzog!
Zerbrechet dieses Wahnes Bande,
zerreißet dieses Vorurteiles Schleier,
enthüllt euch vom Gewand,
das Menschheit in Sektiererei verkleidet!
Zu Sicheln schmiedet um das Eisen,
das Menschen-, das Bruderblut bisher
vergoß!
Zersprenget Felsen mit dem schwarzen
Staube,
der mordend Blei ins Bruderherz oft
schnellte!
Wähnt nicht, daß wahres Unglück sei
auf meiner Erde!
Belehrung ist es nur, die wohltut,
wenn sie euch zu bessern Taten spornt,
die Menschen, ihr in Unglück
wandelt,
wenn töricht blind ihr rückwärts in den
Stachel schlagt,
der vorwärts, vorwärts euch antreiben
sollte.
Seid weise nur, seid kraftvoll und seid
Brüder!
Dann ruht auf euch mein ganzes
Wohlgefallen,
dann netzen Freudenzähren nur die
Wangen,
dann werden eure Klagen
Jubeltöne,
dann schaffet ihr zu Edens Tälern
Wüsten,
dann lachet alles euch in der Natur,
dann ist's erreicht, des Lebens wahres
Glück!

Harken to words from the trumpet of
the Lord of All.
Its eternal sound rings loud through
earth, moon, suns;
give ear, Man, give ear to it
also!
Love me in my works,
love order, symmetry and
harmony!
Love, love one another, yourselves and
your brother,
love yourselves and your brothers!
May you be adorned with bodily
strength and beauty,
be enobled by the clearness of your
mind!
Offer the brotherly hand of eternal
friendship,
withheld so long by delusion merely,
never truth!
Break the bonds of this error,
tear aside this veil of prejudice,
shed from yourselves the garment
that disguises humanity as sectarianism!
Into sickles beat the weapon
that till now spilt blood of man, of
brother!
Blast rocks with that black
powder
which oft into heart of brother hurled
murderous lead!
Think not that on my earth any true ill
fortune is!
Teaching alone it is which does good,
spurring you to better deeds;
you, mankind, who wander in
unhappiness,
when, foolishly blind, you kick against
the pricks
which should drive you on, forwards,
forwards.
Be but wise, be vigorous and be
brothers!
Then shall my whole favour rest upon
you,
then shall your cheeks be wetted only
by tears of joy,
then shall your laments turn into
rejoicing,
then shall you make of deserts vales of
Eden,
then shall all in nature smile upon you,
then shall be attained life's true good
fortune!

## Die junge Nonne / The Young Nun

J. N. CRAIGHER DE JACHELUTTA

*Franz Schubert: op. 43, no. 1, 1825?*

Wie braust durch die Wipfel der
heulende Sturm!
Es klirren die Balken, es zittert das
Haus!
Es rollet der Donner, es leuchtet der
Blitz,
Und finster die Nacht, wie das Grab!

Immerhin, immerhin, so tobt' es auch
jüngst noch in mir!
Es brauste das Leben, wie jetzo der
Sturm,
Es bebten die Glieder, wie jetzo das
Haus,
Es flammte die Liebe, wie jetzo der
Blitz,
Und finster die Brust, wie das
Grab.

Nun tobe, du wilder gewalt'ger Sturm,
Im Herzen ist Friede, im Herzen ist
Ruh,
Des Bräutigams harret die liebende
Braut,
Gereinigt in prüfender Glut,
Der ewigen Liebe getraut.

Ich harre, mein Heiland! mit sehnendem
Blick!
Komm, himmlischer Bräutigam, hole
die Braut,
Erlöse die Seele von irdischer Haft.
Horch, friedlich ertönet das Glöcklein
vom Turm!
Es lockt mich das süße Getön
Allmächtig zu ewigen Höhn.
Alleluja!

How the gale howls and rages in the
trees!
The rafters rattle, the house
shivers!
The thunder rolls, the lightning
flashes,
the night is black as the tomb!

Not long ago, such a storm still raged
in me!
My life raged as now the
gale,
my limbs trembled as now the
house,
my love flamed as now the
lightning,
my breast, within, was black as the
tomb!

Now rage, wild and mighty storm!
In my heart is peace, in my heart is
repose,
for her groom there waits a loving
bride,
purified by testing fire,
wedded to eternal love.

I wait, my Saviour, with longing
gaze!
Come, Heavenly Bridegroom, claim
Your bride,
deliver her soul from earthly prison.
Hark, the peaceful bell from the
tower.
That sweet sound calls me
all-powerfully to eternal heights.
Hallelujah!

## Die Kartenlegerin / The Card-reader

PIERRE JEAN DE BÉRANGER: translated by ADALBERT VON CHAMISSO

*Robert Schumann: op. 31, no. 2, 1840*

Schlief die Mutter endlich ein
Über ihrer Hauspostille?
Nadel, liege du nun stille,
Nähen, immer Nähen, nein,
Legen will ich mir die Karten,
Ei, was hab ich zu erwarten,
Ei, was wird das Ende sein?

Is mother at last asleep
over her book of sermons?
You, my needle, now lie still.
Keep sewing on? Oh no.
I shall read the cards.
Oh, what things can I expect?
Oh, what will the outcome be?

| | |
|---|---|
| Trüget mich die Ahnung nicht, | If presentiment does not deceive, |
| Zeigt sich einer, den ich meine, | one I think of will appear— |
| Schön, da kommt er ja, der eine, | good, here that one comes, |
| Cœur-Bub kannte seine Pflicht. | knave of hearts has known his duty. |
| Eine reiche Witwe? Wehe. | Rich widow? Woe is me! |
| Ja, er freit sie, ich vergehe, | Yes, he woos her, I am undone, |
| O verruchter Bösewicht. | Oh! the wicked scoundrel. |
| | |
| Herzeleid und viel Verdruß, | Heart's sorrow, much vexation, |
| Eine Schul' und enge Mauern, | a school and restricting walls, |
| Karo-König, der bedauern | king of diamonds who must pity |
| Und zuletzt mich trösten muß. | and, at last, must comfort me. |
| Ein Geschenk auf artge Weise, | A prettily delivered present, |
| Er entführt mich, eine Reise, | he elopes with me, a journey, |
| Geld und Lust im Überfluß. | money, happiness in abundance. |
| | |
| Dieser Karo-König da | That king of diamonds there |
| Muß ein Fürst sein oder König | must be a prince or king, |
| Und es fehlt daran nur wenig, | from which but a short step, |
| Bin ich selber Fürstin ja. | and I am a princess. |
| Hier ein Feind, der mir zu schaden | Here a foe who, to my hurt, |
| Sich bemüht bei seiner Gnaden, | works hard with his majesty, |
| Und ein Blonder steht mir nah. | and close to me—a fair-haired man. |
| | |
| Ein Geheimnis kommt zu Tage, | A secret comes to light of day, |
| Und ich flüchte noch beizeiten, | and, just in time, I flee— |
| Fahret wohl, ihr Herrlichkeiten, | farewell to splendour, |
| O, das war ein harter Schlag. | ah, that was a cruel blow. |
| Hin ist einer, eine Menge | The one is gone, a crowd |
| Bilden um mich ein Gedränge, | surges so about me |
| Daß ich sie kaum zählen mag. | that I can scarcely count them. |
| | |
| Kommt das dumme Fraungesicht, | That stupid female apparition, |
| Kommt die Alte da mit Keuchen, | old puffing woman, does she come |
| Lieb und Lust mir zu verscheuchen, | to scare love and happiness away |
| Eh die Jugend mir gebricht? | before my days of youth are gone? |
| Ach, die Mutter ist's, die aufwacht, | Ah, it's my mother waking up, |
| Und den Mund zu schelten aufmacht. | opening her mouth to scold. |
| Nein, die Karten lügen nicht. | No, the cards never lie. |

## Die Liebe hat gelogen | Love Has Proved False

AUGUST VON PLATEN

*Franz Schubert: op. 23, no. 1, 1822*

| | |
|---|---|
| Die Liebe hat gelogen, | Love has proved false, |
| Die Sorge lastet schwer, | sorrow presses sore, |
| Betrogen, ach! betrogen | betrayed, ah, betrayed |
| Hat alles mich umher! | am I by all around! |
| | |
| Es fließen heiße Tropfen | Warm drops course |
| Die Wange stets herab, | ever down my cheek; |
| Laß ab, mein Herz, zu klopfen, | cease, heart, to beat, |
| Du armes Herz, laß ab! | cease, wretched heart. |
| | |
| Die Liebe hat gelogen, | Love has proved false, |
| Die Sorge lastet schwer, | sorrow presses sore, |
| Betrogen, ach! betrogen | betrayed, ah, betrayed |
| Hat alles mich umher! | am I by all around! |

## Die Liebende schreibt / The Beloved Writes

JOHANN WOLFGANG GOETHE

*Johannes Brahms: op. 47, no. 5, 1868; Felix Mendelssohn-Bartholdy: op. 86, no. 3;
Franz Schubert: op. 165, no. 1, 1819*

Ein Blick von deinen Augen in die
    meinen,
Ein Kuß von deinem Mund auf
    meinem Munde,
Wer davon hat, wie ich, gewisse Kunde,
Mag dem was anders wohl erfreulich
    scheinen?

Entfernt von dir, entfremdet von den
    Meinen,
Führ ich stets die Gedanken in die
    Runde,
Und immer treffen sie auf jene Stunde,
Die einzige; da fang ich an zu weinen.

Die Träne trocknet wieder unversehens:
Er liebt ja, denk ich, her in diese
    Stille,
Und solltest du nicht in die Ferne
    reichen?

Vernimm das Lispeln dieses
    Liebewehens;
Mein einzig Glück auf Erden ist dein
    Wille,
Dein freundlicher, zu mir; gib mir ein
    Zeichen!

A look from your eyes into
    mine,
a kiss from your mouth upon my
    mouth,
who, like me, is assured of these,
can aught else delight
    her?

Far from you, a stranger to my
    own,
constantly I let my thoughts range
    round,
and always to that hour do they return,
that only hour; then I begin to weep.

Abruptly those tears dry up again:
his love, I think, he sends into this
    silence.
should you not reach into the
    distance?

Hark to the whisper of this wafting
    love;
your will is my sole happiness on
    earth,
your loving will towards me; give me a
    sign!

## Die Lorelei / The Lorelei

HEINRICH HEINE

*Franz Liszt, 1841*

Ich weiß nicht, was soll es bedeuten,
Daß ich so traurig bin;
Ein Märchen aus alten Zeiten,
Das kommt mir nicht aus dem Sinn.

Die Luft ist kühl und es dunkelt,
Und ruhig fließt der Rhein;
Der Gipfel des Berges funkelt
Im Abendsonnenschein.

Die schönste Jungfrau sitzet
Dort oben wunderbar,
Ihr goldnes Geschmeide blitzet,
Sie kämmt ihr goldenes Haar.

Sie kämmt es mit goldenem Kamme,
Und singt ein Lied dabei;
Das hat eine wundersame,
Gewaltige Melodei.

I know not what it means
that I should feel so sad;
a tale there is from old times,
that lingers in my mind.

The air is cool, day is fading,
and quietly flows the Rhine;
the mountain summit sparkles
in the evening sunshine.

The most beautiful of maidens
sits up there, wonderful,
her golden jewelry flashes,
she combs her golden hair.

With golden comb she combs it,
and sings a song the while,
a song that has a wondrous
compelling melody.

Den Schiffer im kleinen Schiffe
Ergreift es mit wildem Weh;
Er schaut nicht die Felsenriffe,
Er schaut nur hinauf in die Höh'.

The boatman in his little boat
it seizes with violent woe;
he sees not the rocky reefs,
he gazes only up.

Ich glaube, die Wellen verschlingen
Am Ende Schiffer und Kahn;
Und das hat mit ihrem Singen
Die Lorelei getan.

The waves, I believe, swallow
boat and boatman in the end;
and that, by her singing,
the Lorelei has done.

## Die Lotosblume | The Lotus-flower

HEINRICH HEINE

*Robert Franz: op. 25, no. 1; Robert Schumann: op. 25 (Myrten), no. 7, 1840*

Die Lotosblume ängstigt
Sich vor der Sonne Pracht,
Und mit gesenktem Haupte
Erwartet sie träumend die Nacht.

The lotus-flower fears
the splendour of the sun,
and with bowed head,
dreaming, awaits the night.

Der Mond, der ist ihr Buhle,
Er weckt sie mit seinem Licht,
Und ihm entschleiert sie freundlich
Ihr frommes Blumengesicht.

The moon is her lover,
and wakes her with his light,
and to him she gladly unveils
her innocent flower-like face.

Sie blüht und glüht und leuchtet,
Und starret stumm in die Höh';
Sie duftet und weinet und zittert
Vor Liebe und Liebesweh.

She blooms and glows and gleams,
gazing dumbly toward the sky;
she is fragrant and weeps and trembles
with love and the pain of love.

## Die Mainacht | May Night

LUDWIG CHRISTOPH HEINRICH HÖLTY

*Johannes Brahms: op. 43, no. 2, 1864; Franz Schubert, 1815*

Wann der silberne Mond durch die
    Gesträuche blinkt,
Und sein schlummerndes Licht über
    den Rasen streut,
Und die Nachtigall flötet,
Wandl' ich traurig von Busch zu Busch.

When the silver moon shines through
    the shrubs,
scattering its slumbering light on the
    grass,
and the nightingale flutes,
sadly, from bush to bush, I wander.

Überhüllet von Laub girret ein
    Taubenpaar
Sein Entzücken mir vor; aber ich
    wende mich,
Suche dunklere Schatten,
Und die einsame Träne rinnt.

By foliage concealed, a pair of doves
    coo
out to me their ecstasy; but I turn
    away,
seek deeper shade,
and a solitary tear flows.

Wann, o lächelndes Bild, welches wie
    Morgenrot
Durch die Seele mir strahlt, find ich
    auf Erden dich?
Und die einsame Träne
Bebt mir heißer die Wang herab!

When, O smiling image, that like
    dawn
irradiates my soul, shall I find you on
    earth?
And that solitary tear
trembles the hotter down my cheek!

159

## Die Nacht / Night

HERMANN VON GILM

*Richard Strauss: op. 10, no. 3, 1882–83*

Aus dem Walde tritt die Nacht,
Aus den Bäumen schleicht sie leise,
Schaut sich um in weitem Kreise,
Nun gib acht.

Alle Lichter dieser Welt,
Alle Blumen, alle Farben
Löscht sie aus und stiehlt die Garben
Weg vom Feld.

Alles nimmt sie, was nur hold,
Nimmt das Silber weg des Stroms,
Nimmt vom Kupferdach des Doms
Weg das Gold.

Ausgeplündert steht der Strauch,
Rücke näher, Seel an Seele;
O die Nacht, mir bangt, sie stehle
Dich mir auch.

Night steps from the wood,
slips softly from the trees,
gazes about her in a wide arc,
now beware.

All this world's lights,
all flowers, all colours
she extinguishes, and steals the sheaves
from the field.

All that is fair she takes,
the silver from the stream,
from the cathedral's copper roof
the gold.

Plundered stands the bush,
draw closer, soul to soul;
oh, the night, I fear, will steal
you, too, from me.


## Die Schale der Vergessenheit / Cup of Oblivion

LUDWIG CHRISTOPH HEINRICH HÖLTY

*Johannes Brahms: op. 46, no. 3, 1864*

Eine Schale des Stroms, welcher
    Vergessenheit
Durch Elysiums Blumen rollt,
Eine Schale des Stroms spende mir,
    Genius!
Dort, wo Phaons die
    Sängerin,
Dort, wo Orpheus vergaß seiner
    Eurydice,
Schöpf die goldene Urne voll!
Dann versenk ich dein Bild, spröde
    Gebieterin,
In den silbernen Schlummerquell!
Den allsiegenden Blick, der mir im
    Marke zuckt,
Und das Beben der weißen Brust
Und die süße Musik, welche der Lipp
    entfloß,
Tauch ich tief in den
    Schlummerquell!

A cup of that stream which as
    oblivion
rolls through Elysium's flowers,
a cup of that stream bestow on me,
    genius!
There, where the songstress forgot
    Phaon,
there, where Orpheus forgot his
    Eurydice,
there fill the golden urn!
Then, coy mistress, will I sink your
    image
in the silver source of slumber!
The all-conquering look that thrills my
    heart,
and the heaving of your white breast
and the sweet music that flowed from
    your lips,
I shall plunge deep into the source of
    slumber!

## Die schöne Magelone | The Fair Magelone

LUDWIG TIECK

*Johannes Brahms: op. 33, nos. 1–15, 1861*

1

Keinen hat es noch gereut,
Der das Roß bestiegen,
Um in frischer Jugendzeit
Durch die Welt zu fliegen.

Berge und Auen,
Einsamer Wald,
Mädchen und Frauen,
Prächtig im Kleide,
Golden Geschmeide,
Alles erfreut ihn mit schöner Gestalt.

Wunderlich fliehen
Gestalten dahin,
Schwärmerisch glühen
Wünsche in jugendlich trunkenem
    Sinn.

Ruhm streut ihm Rosen
Schnell in die Bahn,
Lieben und Kosen,
Lorbeer und Rosen
Führen ihn höher und höher hinan.

Rund um ihn Freuden,
Feinde beneiden,
Erliegend, den Held,—
Dann wählt er bescheiden
Das Fräulein, das ihm nur vor allen
    gefällt.

Und Berge und Felder
Und einsame Wälder
Mißt er zurück.
Die Eltern in Tränen,
Ach, alle ihr Sehnen—
Sie alle vereinigt das lieblichste Glück.

Sind Jahre verschwunden,
Erzählt er dem Sohn
In traulichen Stunden,
Und zeigt seine Wunden,
Der Tapferkeit Lohn.
So bleibt das Alter selbst noch jung,
Ein Lichtstrahl in der Dämmerung.

2

Traun, Bogen und Pfeil
Sind gut für den Feind,
Hilflos alleweil
Der Elende weint.
Dem Edlen blüht Heil,

1

None has yet rued
mounting his steed,
in first flush of youth,
to fly through the world.

Mountains and meadows,
lonely forest,
maidens and ladies
sumptuously arrayed,
golden jewelry,
all delights him with beauty.

Strangely
figures flit past,
rapturously glow
desires in the youthfully drunk
senses.

Fame strews roses
swiftly in his path,
love and caresses,
laurel and roses
lead him on higher and higher.

Delights surround him,
his foes, as they succumb,
envy the hero—
then modestly he chooses
the maid who pleases him
    most.

And over mountains and fields
and lonely forests
he looks back.
His parents in tears,
ah, their longing is ended—
sweetest joy now unites them all.

When years have faded,
he recounts all to his son
in quiet hours,
and shows his wounds,
the reward of valour.
Thus does age itself stay young,
a bright ray in the twilight.

2

In faith, bow and arrow
are meet for the foe,
helpless the whole while
the wretched man weeps.
For the noble happiness blooms

| | |
|---|---|
| Wo Sonne nur scheint, | wherever sun shines; |
| Die Felsen sind steil, | the rocks are steep, |
| Doch Glück ist sein Freund. | but fortune is his friend. |

**3**

| | |
|---|---|
| Sind es Schmerzen, sind es Freuden, | Are they agonies, are they joys |
| Die durch meinen Busen ziehn? | that pass through my breast? |
| Alle alten Wünsche scheiden, | All the old desires depart, |
| Tausend neue Blumen blühn. | a thousand new flowers bloom. |

| | |
|---|---|
| Durch die Dämmerung der Tränen | Through a twilight of tears |
| Seh' ich ferne Sonnen stehn,— | I see distant suns— |
| Welches Schmachten, welches Sehnen! | what yearning, what longing! |
| Wag ich's, soll ich näher gehn? | Shall I, dare I go nearer? |

| | |
|---|---|
| Ach, und fällt die Träne nieder, | Ah, and when tears fall, |
| Ist es dunkel um mich her, | dark it is about me, |
| Dennoch kömmt kein Wunsch mir | yet no desire |
| wieder, | returns, |
| Zukunft ist von Hoffnung leer. | the future is void of hope. |

| | |
|---|---|
| So schlage denn, strebendes Herz, | So beat then, striving heart, |
| So fließet denn, Tränen, herab! | so flow then tears! |
| Ach, Lust ist nur tieferer Schmerz, | Ah, joy is but deeper anguish, |
| Leben ist dunkeles Grab,— | life is a gloomy grave— |
| Ohne Verschulden | without fault |
| Soll ich erdulden? | shall I endure? |
| Wie ist's, daß mir im Traum | How is it that in my dreams |
| Alle Gedanken | my thoughts all |
| Auf und nieder schwanken, | struggle up, and flag! |
| Ich kenne mich noch kaum. | I scarce know myself. |

| | |
|---|---|
| O hört mich, ihr gütigen Sterne, | O hear me, kind stars, |
| O höre mich, grünende Flur, | O hear me, green meadow, |
| Du Liebe, den heiligen Schwur: | and you, Love, hear my sacred oath: |
| Bleib' ich ihr ferne, | if far from her I stay, |
| Sterb' ich gerne, | gladly shall I die. |
| Ach! nur in ihrem Blick | Ah, only in the light of her gaze |
| Wohnt Leben und Hoffnung und | dwell life and hope and |
| Glück! | joy! |

*(Carl Maria von Weber: op. 30, no. 6, 1813)*

**4**

| | |
|---|---|
| Liebe kam aus fernen Landen, | Love came from distant lands |
| Und kein Wesen folgte ihr, | and no one followed her, |
| Und die Göttin winkte mir, | and to me the goddess beckoned, |
| Schlang mich ein mit süßen Banden. | and enmeshed me in sweet bonds. |

| | |
|---|---|
| Da begann ich Schmerz zu fühlen, | Pain I then began to feel, |
| Tränen dämmerten den Blick, | tears bedimmed my eyes, |
| Ach! was ist der Liebe Glück, | ah, what is love's happiness, |
| Klagt' ich, wozu dieses Spielen? | I lamented, why this dallying? |

| | |
|---|---|
| Keinen hab' ich weit gefunden, | Far and wide no man I've found, |
| Sagte lieblich die Gestalt, | said the figure sweetly; |
| Fühle du nun die Gewalt, | but you: feel now that power |
| Die die Herzen sonst gebunden. | which formerly bound hearts. |

| | |
|---|---|
| Alle meine Wünsche flogen | My desires all flew |
| In der Lüfte blauen Raum, | into the blue realm of breezes, |

Ruhm schien mir ein Morgentraum,
Nur ein Klang der Meereswogen.

Ach! Wer löst nun meine Ketten?
Denn gefesselt ist der Arm,
Mich umfleugt der Sorgen Schwarm,
Keiner, keiner will mich retten?

Darf ich in den Spiegel schauen,
Den die Hoffnung vor mir hält?
Ach, wie trügend ist die Welt!
Nein, ich kann ihr nicht vertrauen.

O, und dennoch laß nicht wanken,
Was dir nur noch Stärke gibt;
Wenn die einz'ge dich nicht liebt,
Bleibt nur bittrer Tod dem Kranken.

5
So willst du des Armen
Dich gnädig erbarmen?
So ist es kein Traum?
Wie rieseln die Quellen,
Wie tönen die Wellen,
Wie rauschet der Baum!

Tief lag ich in bangen
Gemäuern gefangen,
Nun grüßt mich das Licht;
Wie spielen die Strahlen!
Sie blenden und malen
Mein schüchtern Gesicht.

Und soll ich es glauben?
Wird keiner mir rauben
Den köstlichen Wahn?
Doch Träume entschweben,
Nur lieben heißt leben,
Willkommene Bahn!

Wie frei und wie heiter!
Nicht eile nun weiter,
Den Pilgerstab fort!
Du hast überwunden,
Du hast ihn gefunden,
Den seligsten Ort!

6
Wie soll ich die Freude,
Die Wonne denn tragen?
Daß unter dem Schlagen
Des Herzens die Seele nicht scheide?

Und wenn nun die Stunden
Der Liebe verschwunden,
Wozu das Gelüste,
In trauriger Wüste
Noch weiter ein lustleeres Leben zu
    ziehn,
Wenn nirgends dem Ufer mehr
    Blumen erblühn?

fame seemed to me a dream,
but a sound of the sea waves.

Ah, who will now loose my chains?
For my arms are fettered,
a swarm of sorrows flies about me,
will no one, no one deliver me?

Dare I gaze into the glass
that hope holds before me?
Ah, how deceptive is the world!
No, I cannot trust it.

Oh, but do not let falter
what alone still gives you strength;
if the only one does not love you,
to the sufferer remains but bitter death.

5
Do you mean thus, on the poor man,
to take gracious pity?
Is this then not a dream?
How the streams ripple,
how the waves sound,
how the tree rustles!

Deep I lay, within fearful
walls, captive;
now I am greeted by light;
how the beams play!
They dazzle and reflect
my timid face.

And shall I believe it?
Will no one rob me
of this precious illusion?
But dreams vanish,
only loving is living,
O welcome path!

How clear, how cheerful!
Hasten now no further,
away with your staff!
You have overcome,
you have found it,
that most blissful place!

6
How shall I then bear
the joy and bliss?
That, at the beating
of my heart, my soul not flee?

And if now the hours
of love are vanished,
to what end the craving
in dreary waste
to drag a joyless life still
    further,
when flowers no longer bloom from the
    shore?

Wie geht mit bleibehangenen Füßen
Die Zeit bedächtig Schritt vor Schritt!
Und wenn ich werde scheiden müssen,
Wie federleicht fliegt dann ihr Tritt!

Schlage, sehnsüchtige Gewalt
In tiefer, treuer Brust!
Wie Lautenton vorüberhallt,
Entflieht des Lebens schönste Lust:
Ach, wie bald,
Bin ich der Wonne mir kaum noch
    bewußt.

Rausche, rausche weiter fort,
Tiefer Strom der Zeit,
Wandelst bald aus morgen
    heut,
Gehst von Ort zu Ort.
Hast du mich bis her getragen,
Lustig bald, dann still,
Will es nun auch weiter wagen,
Wie es werden will.

Darf mich doch nicht elend achten,
Da die einz'ge winkt,
Liebe läßt mich nicht verschmachten,
Bis dies Leben sinkt.
Nein, der Strom wird immer breiter,
Himmel bleibt mir immer heiter,
Fröhlichen Ruderschlags fahr' ich hinab,
Bring' Liebe und Leben zugleich an das
    Grab.

7
War es dir, dem diese Lippen bebten,
Dir der dargebotne süße Kuß?
Gibt ein irdisch Leben so Genuß?
Ha! Wie Licht und Glanz vor meinen
    Augen schwebten,
Alle Sinne nach den Lippen
    strebten!

In den klaren Augen blinkte
Sehnsucht, die mir zärtlich winkte,
Alles klang im Herzen wider,
Meine Blicke sanken nieder,
Und die Lüfte tönten Liebeslieder.

Wie ein Sternenpaar
Glänzten die Augen, die Wangen
Wiegten das goldene Haar,
Blick und Lächeln schwangen
Flügel und die süßen Worte gar
Weckten das tiefste Verlangen.
O Kuß! wie war dein Mund so brennend
    rot,
Da starb ich, fand ein Leben
Erst im schönsten Tod.

On what leaden feet goes time,
deliberately step by step!
And yet, if I have ever to depart,
how featherlight its tread then flits!

Beat, power of longing,
in deep true breast!
Like dying lute strains
fades life's finest joy:
ah, how soon
shall I be scarce aware of
    bliss.

Rush, rush ever on,
deep stream of time,
soon, today, tomorrow you will wander
    off,
go from place to place.
As thus far you have borne me,
now merry, now quiet,
I now will venture on further,
come what may.

I cannot now think myself wretched,
since my only one beckons,
love will not let me languish
until this life is done.
No, the stream grows ever broader,
the sky for me stays ever clear,
with cheerful strokes I'll row on down,
bring love and life together to the
    grave.

7
Was it for you that these lips trembled,
for you that sweet offered kiss?
Can life on earth give such joy?
Ah, how light and radiance danced
    before my eyes,
how all my senses strove towards those
    lips!

In those clear eyes flashed
longing, tenderly beckoning.
Everything echoed in my heart,
my gaze was lowered,
and the breezes gave forth songs of love

Like twin stars
gleamed your eyes, your cheeks
were cradled by golden hair,
gaze and smile took
wing, and sweet words
awakened deepest longing.
O kiss! How burning red your
    mouth!
I died, and found life
only in sweetest death.

8
Wir müssen uns trennen,
Geliebtes Saitenspiel,
Zeit ist es, zu rennen
Nach dem fernen erwünschten Ziel.

Ich ziehe zum Streite,
Zum Raube hinaus,
Und hab' ich die Beute,
Dann flieg ich nach Haus.

Im rötlichen Glanze
Entflieh' ich mit ihr,
Es schützt uns die Lanze,
Der Stahlharnisch hier.

Kommt, liebe Waffenstücke,
Zum Scherz oft angetan,
Beschirmet jetzt mein Glücke
Auf dieser neuen Bahn.

Ich werfe mich rasch in die Wogen,
Ich grüße den herrlichen Lauf,
Schon mancher ward niedergezogen,
Der tapfere Schwimmer bleibt obenauf.

Ha, Lust! Zu vergeuden
Das edele Blut,
Zu schützen die Freuden,
Mein köstliches Gut;
Nicht Hohn zu erleiden,
Wem fehlt es an Mut?

Senke die Zügel,
Glückliche Nacht!
Spanne die Flügel,
Daß über ferne Hügel
Uns schon der Morgen lacht.

9
Ruhe, Süßliebchen, im Schatten
Der grünen dämmernden Nacht,
Es säuselt das Gras auf den Matten,
Es fächelt und kühlt dich der Schatten,
Und treue Liebe wacht.
Schlafe, schlaf ein,
Leiser rauscht der Hain,
Ewig bin ich dein.

Schweigt, ihr versteckten Gesänge,
Und stört nicht die süßeste Ruh'!
Es lauscht der Vögel Gedränge,
Es ruhen die lauten Gesänge,
Schließ, Liebchen, dein Auge zu.
Schlafe, schlaf ein,
Im dämmernden Schein,
Ich will dein Wächter sein.

Murmelt fort, ihr Melodien,
Rausche nur, du stiller Bach!

8
We must part,
beloved lute,
time it is to race
for the desired distant goal.

I am off to the battle,
off for the spoils,
and when I've my booty,
home I shall fly.

In the reddish gleam
with her shall I flee,
my lance shall protect us,
my steel armour here.

Come, dear weapons
donned often in jest,
defend now my happiness
on this new path.

Into the billows I'll hurl myself,
their glorious course I'll greet,
many a man's been dragged under,
the bold swimmer keeps on top.

Ah, joy! To spill
noble blood,
to protect my joys,
my precious possession;
not bow to scorn,
who lacks courage for that?

Slacken the reins,
happy night!
Spread your wings,
that over the far hills
morning may smile upon us!

9
Rest, my dearest, in the shade
of green darkening night,
the grass on the meadows rustles,
the shade fans and cools you,
and true love keeps watch.
Sleep, sleep,
softer rustles the wood,
I am yours forever.

Hush, you hidden songs,
do not disturb her sweetest sleep.
The bird throng is hearkening,
their loud songs are at rest,
close your eyes, my love.
Sleep, sleep,
in the fading light
I will watch over you.

Murmur on, melodies,
babble on, quiet brook.

Schöne Liebesphantasien
Sprechen in den Melodien,
Zarte Träume schwimmen nach.
Durch den flüsternden Hain
Schwärmen goldene Bienelein
Und summen zum Schlummer dich ein.
(*Robert Franz: op. 1, no. 10*)

Fair fantasies of love
speak in these melodies,
tender dreams float after them.
Through the whispering wood
swarm golden bees
and hum you to sleep.

10

So tönet denn, schäumende Wellen,
Und windet euch rund um mich her!
Mag Unglück doch laut um mich bellen,
Erbost sein das grausame Meer!

Roar, then, foaming waves,
and writhe about me!
Around me let misfortune loudly bay,
the cruel sea let rage.

Ich lache den stürmenden Wettern,
Verachte den Zorngrimm der Flut;
O, mögen mich Felsen zerschmettern!
Denn nimmer wird es gut.

I laugh at stormy weather,
scorn the fury of the flood;
Oh, may the rocks crush me!
For never will it come right.

Nicht klag' ich und mag ich nun
   scheitern,
In wäßriger Tiefe vergehn!
Mein Blick wird sich nie mehr erheitern,
Den Stern meiner Liebe zu sehn.

I do not complain, though I now
   founder,
perish in watery depths!
Nevermore will my gaze be cheered
at the sight of my loved one's star.

So wälzt euch bergab mit Gewittern,
Und raset, ihr Stürme, mich an,
Daß Felsen an Felsen zersplittern!
Ich bin ein verlorener Mann!

So send rolling down your thunder,
and rage at me, you storms,
that rock shatter upon rock!
A lost man am I!

11

Wie schnell verschwindet
So Licht als Glanz,
Der Morgen findet
Verwelkt den Kranz,

How swiftly vanish
splendour and light,
the morrow finds
the garland withered,

Der gestern glühte
Mit aller Pracht,
Denn er verblühte
In dunkler Nacht.

that yesterday glowed
in all its splendour,
for its blossom faded
in the dark of night.

Es schwimmt die Welle
Des Lebens hin,
Und färbt sich helle,
Hat's nicht Gewinn.

On it floats, the wave
of life,
and bright as it paints itself,
it gains nothing;

Die Sonne neiget,
Die Röte flieht,
Der Schatten steiget,
Und Dunkel zieht.

the sun goes down,
the redness flees,
the shadows climb,
and dark comes on.

So schwimmt die Liebe
Zu Wüsten ab,
Ach! Daß sie bliebe
Bis an das Grab!

So does love drift
to wildernesses,
ah, that it might remain
until the grave!

Doch wir erwachen
Zu tiefer Qual:
Es bricht der Nachen,
Es löscht der Strahl,

But we awake
to deep agony:
the vessel breaks,
extinguished is the beam,

Vom schönen Lande
Weit weg gebracht
Zum öden Strande,
Wo um uns Nacht.

12
Muß es eine Trennung geben,
Die das treue Herz zerbricht?
Nein, dies nenne ich nicht Leben,
Sterben ist so bitter nicht.

Hör ich eines Schäfers Flöte,
Härme ich mich inniglich,
Seh' ich in die Abendröte,
Denk' ich brünstiglich an dich.

Gibt es denn kein wahres Lieben?
Muß denn Schmerz und Trennung sein?
Wär' ich ungeliebt geblieben,
Hätt' ich doch noch Hoffnungsschein.

Aber so muß ich nun klagen:
Wo ist Hoffnung als das Grab?
Fern muß ich mein Elend tragen,
Heimlich bricht das Herz mir ab.

13
Geliebter, wo zaudert
Dein irrender Fuß?
Die Nachtigall plaudert
Von Sehnsucht und Kuß.

Es flüstern die Bäume
Im goldenen Schein.
Es schlüpfen mir Träume
Zum Fenster herein.

Ach! kennst du das Schmachten
Der klopfenden Brust?
Dies Sinnen und Trachten
Voll Qual und voll Lust?

Beflügle die Eile
Und rette mich dir,
Bei nächtlicher Weile
Entfliehn wir von hier.

Die Segel, sie schwellen,
Die Furcht ist nur Tand:
Dort, jenseits der Wellen
Ist väterlich Land.

Die Heimat entfliehet,
So fahre sie hin!
Die Liebe, sie ziehet
Gewaltig den Sinn.

Horch! Wollüstig klingen
Die Wellen im Meer,
Sie hüpfen und springen
Mutwillig einher.

from the beautiful land
we are borne far away
to the desolate beach
where night surrounds us.

12
Must there be a parting
that breaks the faithful heart?
No, that I call not living,
dying is not so bitter.

When I hear a shepherd's flute,
inwardly I burn with grief,
when I see the sunset,
I think ardently of you.

Is there then no true love?
Must there be pain and parting?
Had I remained unloved,
I'd still have a gleam of hope.

But this must now be my complaint:
where is hope but in the grave?
Far away must I bear my grief,
secretly my heart is breaking.

13
Beloved, where tarries
your errant step?
The nightingale tells
of longing and kisses.

The trees whisper
in the golden gleam.
Dreams steal in
at my window.

Ah, do you know the yearning
of a throbbing breast?
These thoughts and strivings
full of torment and joy?

Lend your haste wings,
and rescue me,
while it is night
from here will we fly.

The sails, they are filling,
fear is but vain:
there, beyond the waves,
is a fatherly land.

Your homeland's receding,
let it then go!
Love draws
the senses powerfully.

Hark! Blissful the sound
of the waves in the sea,
leaping and jumping
playfully.

Und sollten sie klagen?
Sie rufen nach dir,
Sie wissen, sie tragen
Die Liebe von hier.

14
Wie froh und frisch mein Sinn sich
    hebt,
Zurück bleibt alles Bangen,
Die Brust mit neuem Mute strebt,
Erwacht ein neu Verlangen.

Die Sterne spiegeln sich im Meer,
Und golden glänzt die Flut.
Ich rannte taumelnd hin und her
Und war nicht schlimm, nicht gut.

Doch niedergezogen
Sind Zweifel und wankender Sinn,
O tragt mich, ihr schaukelnden Wogen
Zur längst ersehnten Heimat hin.

In lieber, dämmernder Ferne,
Dort rufen heimische Lieder,
Aus jeglichem Sterne
Blickt sie mit sanftem Auge nieder.

Ebne dich, du treue Welle,
Führe mich auf fernen Wegen
Zu der vielgeliebten Schwelle
Endlich meinem Glück entgegen!

15
Treue Liebe dauert lange,
Überlebet manche Stund',
Und kein Zweifel macht sie bange,
Immer bleibt ihr Mut gesund.

Dräuen gleich in dichten Scharen,
Fordern gleich zum Wankelmut
Sturm und Tod: setzt den Gefahren
Lieb' entgegen treues Blut.

Und wie Nebel stürzt zurücke,
Was den Sinn gefangen hält,
Und dem heitern Frühlingsblicke
Öffnet sich die weite Welt.

Errungen,
Bezwungen
Von Lieb ist das Glück,
Verschwunden
Die Stunden,
Sie fliehen zurück.
Und selige Lust
Sie stillet,
Erfüllet die trunkene, wonneklopfende
    Brust.
Sie scheide

---

And should they lament?
They are calling for you,
they know that they carry
love from here.

14
How joyfully my spirits
    soar,
all fear is left behind,
my heart strives with new courage,
new longing awakes.

The stars are mirrored in the sea,
and golden the waters gleam.
I have run reeling, this way and that,
been neither bad nor good.

But laid low
are doubt and hesitant mood,
oh bear me, rocking waves
to my long-yearned-for homeland.

In the dear, darkening distance
the songs of home are calling,
from every star
it gazes down with gentle eye.

Grow smooth, true wave,
on distant ways lead me
to that much-loved threshold,
to my love at last!

15
True love abides,
outlives many an hour,
is not frightened by doubt,
its courage remains ever sound.

Though they threaten in dense hordes,
though they provoke inconstancy—
assault and death—to these perils
love opposes true blood.

And, like mist, recoils
that which holds captive the senses,
and to the cheerful gaze of spring
the whole world opens itself.

Won,
mastered
by love is happiness,
vanished
those hours,
back they flee;
and blissful joy,
it stills,
fills the elated, delight-throbbing
    breast.
May it part

| | |
|---|---|
| Von Leide, | from sorrow |
| Auf immer | for ever, |
| Und nimmer | and never |
| Entschwinde | disappear, |
| Die liebliche, selige, himmlische Lust. | this lovely, blissful, heavenly joy. |
| Treue Liebe dauert lange, | True love abides, |
| Sie scheide | may it part |
| Von Leide, | from sorrow, |
| Und nimmer | and never |
| Entschwinde | disappear, |
| Die liebliche, selige, himmlische Lust. | this lovely, blissful, heavenly joy! |

*Die schöne Müllerin | The Miller's Beautiful Daughter*

WILHELM MÜLLER

*Franz Schubert: op. 25, nos. 1–20, 1823*

1 *Das Wandern*
Das Wandern ist des Müllers Lust,
das Wandern!
Das muß ein schlechter Müller sein,
dem niemals fiel das Wandern ein,
das Wandern.

Vom Wasser haben wir's gelernt,
vom Wasser!
Das hat nicht Rast bei Tag und Nacht,
ist stets auf Wanderschaft bedacht,
das Wasser.

Das sehen wir auch den Rädern ab,
den Rädern!
Die gar nicht gerne stille stehn,
die sich mein Tag nicht müde drehn,
die Räder.

Die Steine selbst so schwer sie sind,
die Steine!
Die tanzen mit den muntern Reihn
und wollen gar noch schneller sein,
die Steine.

O Wandern, Wandern, meine Lust,
o Wandern!
Herr Meister und Frau Meisterin,
laßt mich in Frieden weiterziehn
und wandern.

2 *Wohin?*
Ich hört' ein Bächlein rauschen
wohl aus dem Felsenquell,
hinab zum Tale rauschen
so frisch und wunderhell.

1 *Journeying*
To journey is the miller's joy,
to journey!
A wretched miller must he be
who never thought of journeying,
of journeying.

From the water we've learnt it,
from the water!
That knows no rest by day or night,
is forever bent on journeying,
the water.

We learn it from the wheels too,
the mill-wheels!
Which never willingly are still,
which never tire of turning,
the mill-wheels.

The mill-stones, heavy as they are,
the mill-stones,
they join in the merry dance,
and wish it even faster,
the mill-stones.

O journeying, journeying, my joy,
O journeying!
Master, Mistress,
let me in peace go on my way,
and journey.

2 *Whither?*
A brook I heard babbling
from its rocky source,
and heading for the valley,
so live and wondrous clear.

Ich weiß nicht, wie mir wurde,
nicht, wer den Rat mir gab,
ich mußte auch hinunter
mit meinem Wanderstab.

Hinunter und immer weiter,
und immer dem Bache nach,
und immer frischer rauschte
und immer heller der Bach.

Ist das denn meine Straße?
O Bächlein, sprich, wohin?
Du hast mit deinem Rauschen
mir ganz berauscht den Sinn.

Was sag ich denn vom Rauschen?
Das kann kein Rauschen sein:
Es singen wohl die Nixen
tief unten ihren Reihn.

Laß singen, Gesell, laß rauschen,
und wandre fröhlich nach!
Es gehn ja Mühlenräder
in jedem klaren Bach!

3 *Halt!*
Eine Mühle seh ich blinken
aus den Erlen heraus,
durch Rauschen und Singen
bricht Rädergebraus.

Ei willkommen, ei willkommen,
Süßer Mühlengesang!
Und das Haus, wie so traulich!
Und die Fenster, wie blank!

Und die Sonne, wie helle
vom Himmel sie scheint.
Ei, Bächlein, liebes Bächlein,
war es also gemeint?

4 *Danksagung an den Bach*
War es also gemeint,
mein rauschender Freund?
Dein Singen, dein Klingen,
war es also gemeint?

Zur Müllerin hin!
So lautet der Sinn.
Gelt, hab ich's verstanden?
Zur Müllerin hin.

Hat sie dich geschickt?
Oder hast mich berückt?
Das möcht ich noch wissen,
ob sie dich geschickt.

Nun wie's auch mag sein,
ich gebe mich drein:
Was ich such, hab ich funden,
wie's immer mag sein.

What seized me, I know not,
nor who put it in my mind:
I, too, made for the valley,
with my wanderer's staff.

Downward, ever downward,
keeping always to the brook,
and ever livelier babbled,
and ever clearer, the brook.

Is this, then, my path?
O brooklet, say to where.
You have, with your babbling,
quite bemused my mind.

Why do I speak of babbling?
No babbling can that be:
the water nymphs it is,
who sing and dance below.

Let nymphs sing, brook babble,
and follow cheerfully.
For mill-wheels there are
in every crystal stream!

3 *Halt!*
A mill I see bright
among the alders;
through babbling and singing
breaks the roar of wheels.

Welcome, welcome,
sweet mill-song!
And the house, how cosy!
And the windows, how they gleam!

And the sun, how brightly
it shines from the sky.
O brooklet, dear brooklet,
is this what was meant?

4 *Thanksgiving to the Brook*
Is this what was meant,
my babbling friend?
By your song, your noise,
is this what was meant?

To the miller's daughter!
That's the sense.
I've understood, haven't I?
To the miller's daughter.

Was it she who sent you?
Or have you entranced me?
That, too, I'd like to know:
if she it was who sent you.

Well, be that as it may,
I am content:
what I've sought, I've found,
be it as it may.

Nach Arbeit ich frug,
nun hab ich genug,
für die Hände, fürs Herze
voll auf genug.

5 *Am Feierabend*
Hätt ich tausend
Arme zu rühren!
Könnt ich brausend
die Räder führen!
Könnt ich wehen
durch alle Haine!
Könnt ich drehen
alle Steine!
Daß die schöne Müllerin
merkte meinen treuen Sinn!

Ach, wie ist mein Arm so schwach!
Was ich hebe, was ich trage,
was ich schneide, was ich schlage,
jeder Knappe tut mir's nach.
Und da sitz ich in der großen Runde,
in der stillen kühlen Feierstunde,
und der Meister spricht zu allen:
Euer Werk hat mir gefallen;
und das liebe Mädchen sagt
allen eine gute Nacht.

6 *Der Neugierige*
Ich frage keine Blume,
ich frage keinen Stern;
sie können mir alle nicht sagen,
was ich erführ so gern.

Ich bin ja auch kein Gärtner,
die Sterne stehn zu hoch;
mein Bächlein will ich fragen,
ob mich mein Herz belog.

O Bächlein meiner Liebe,
wie bist du heut so stumm!
Will ja nur eines wissen,
ein Wörtchen um und um,

Ja! heißt das eine Wörtchen,
das andre heißet nein,
die beiden Wörtchen schließen
die ganze Welt mir ein.

O Bächlein meiner Liebe,
was bist du wunderlich!
Will's ja nicht weitersagen,
sag, Bächlein, liebt sie mich?

7 *Ungeduld*
Ich schnitt' es gern in alle Rinden ein,
ich grüb es gern in jeden Kieselstein,
ich möcht es sän auf jedes frische Beet
mit Kressensamen, der es schnell verrät,

For work I asked,
now I have enough,
for hands, for heart,
more than enough.

5 *When Work Is Over*
Would I'd a thousand
arms to keep busy!
Would I could drive
the wheels with a roar,
could blow
through every wood,
could turn
every mill-stone,
so the fair miller's daughter
might see my true worth!

Ah, so feeble is my arm!
What I heave, what I carry,
what I cut, what I hammer—
any lad can do as much.
And then I sit with the others,
when work is over, in cool and quiet,
and the master says to all:
'I am pleased with what you've done.'
And that sweet maiden says:
'A good night to everyone.'

6 *The Inquisitive One*
I ask no flower,
I ask no star;
they cannot tell me
what I'd so like to hear.

For I am no gardener,
the stars are far too high;
I will ask my brooklet
if my heart has lied.

O brooklet of my love,
how silent you are today!
Just one thing I want to hear,
all around, one tiny word.

Yes, is one such word,
the other is No,
and by these two tiny words
my whole world is bounded.

O brooklet of my love,
how strange you are!
I'll let it go no further—
brooklet, does she love me?

7 *Impatience*
On every tree I would like to cut,
into every pebble-stone dig deep,
in every bed of fresh soil sow
cress seed that very soon would show,

auf jeden weißen Zettel möcht ich's
schreiben:
Dein ist mein Herz und soll es ewig
bleiben!

Ich möcht mir ziehen einen jungen Star,
bis daß er spräch die Worte rein und klar,
bis er sie spräch mit meines Mundes
Klang,
mit meines Herzens vollem, heißem
Drang;
dann säng er hell durch ihre
Fensterscheiben:
Dein ist mein Herz und soll es ewig
bleiben!

Den Morgenwinden möcht ich's
hauchen ein,
ich möcht es säuseln durch den regen
Hain;
oh, leuchtet' es aus jedem Blumen-
stern!
Trüg es der Duft zu ihr von nah und
fern!
Ihr Wogen, könnt ihr nichts als Räder
treiben?
Dein ist mein Herz, und soll es ewig
bleiben.

Ich meint, es müßt in meinen Augen
stehn,
auf meinen Wangen müßt man's
brennen sehn,
zu lesen wär's auf meinem stummen
Mund,
ein jeder Atemzug gäb's laut ihr
kund;
und sie merkt nichts von all dem bangen
Treiben:
Dein ist mein Herz und soll es ewig
bleiben!

8 *Morgengruß*
Guten Morgen, schöne Müllerin!
Wo steckst du gleich das Köpfchen hin,
als wär dir was geschehen?
Verdrießt dich denn mein Gruß so
schwer?
Verstört dich denn mein Blick so sehr?
So muß ich wieder gehen.

O laß mich nur von ferne stehn,
nach deinem lieben Fenster sehn,
von ferne, ganz von ferne!
Du blondes Köpfchen, komm hervor!
Hervor aus eurem runden Tor,
ihr blauen Morgensterne.

Ihr schlummertrunknen Äugelein,
ihr taubetrübten Blümelein,
was scheuet ihr die Sonne?

on every white scrap of paper
write:
Yours is my heart and shall be
ever!

A young starling I would like to train,
until he said it pure and plain,
until he said it with my voice's
sound
and with my heart's full urgent
passion;
then, in at her windows, loud he'd
sing:
Yours is my heart and shall be
ever!

To the morning winds I'd like to
breathe it,
through the stirring wood murmur
it;
oh, that it shone from every flowery
star,
were borne to her by scent from near
and far!
Waves, are wheels all you can
compel?
Yours is my heart and shall be
ever!

I would have thought it must show in
my eyes,
one ought to see it burning on my
cheeks,
it were plain to read from my mute
lips,
my every breath proclaimed it to her
loud;
and she sees naught of all this anxious
pleading:
Yours is my heart and shall be
ever!

8 *Morning Greeting*
Good morning, fair milleress!
Why do you dart your head back in,
as if something were amiss?
Does my greeting vex
you,
my gaze upset you so?
Then I must be going.

Oh, just let me stand far away,
and watch your dear window
from far, far away!
Little blond head, come out!
Gaze out from your round gates,
blue morning stars.

Little sleep-drunk eyes,
dew-afflicted little flowers,
why do you fear the sun?

Hat es die Nacht so gut gemeint,
daß ihr euch schließt und bückt und
    weint
nach ihrer stillen Wonne?

Nun schüttelt ab der Träume Flor,
und hebt euch frisch und frei empor
in Gottes hellen Morgen!
Die Lerche wirbelt in der Luft;
und aus dem tiefen Herzen ruft
die Liebe Leid und Sorgen.

### 9 Des Müllers Blumen

Am Bach viel kleine Blumen stehn,
aus hellen, blauen Augen sehn;
der Bach, der ist des Müllers Freund
und hellblau Liebchens Auge scheint,
drum sind es meine Blumen.

Dicht unter ihrem Fensterlein,
da will ich pflanzen die Blumen ein;
da ruft ihr zu, wenn alles schweigt,
wenn sich ihr Haupt zum Schlummer
    neigt,
ihr wißt ja, was ich meine.

Und wenn sie tät die Äuglein zu
und schläft in süßer, süßer Ruh,
dann lispelt als ein Traumgesicht
ihr zu: Vergiß, vergiß mein nicht!
Das ist es, was ich meine.

Und schließt sie früh die Laden auf,
dann schaut mit Liebesblick hinauf;
der Tau in euren Äugelein,
das sollen meine Tränen sein,
die will ich auf euch weinen.

### 10 Tränenregen

Wir saßen so traulich beisammen
im kühlen Erlendach,
wir schauten so traulich zusammen
hinab in den rieselnden Bach.

Der Mond war auch gekommen,
die Sternlein hinterdrein,
und schauten so traulich zusammen
in den silbernen Spiegel hinein.

Ich sah nach keinem Monde,
nach keinem Sternenschein,
ich schaute nach ihrem Bilde,
nach ihren Augen allein.

Und sahe sie nicken und blicken
herauf aus dem seligen Bach,
die Blümlein am Ufer, die blauen
sie nickten und blickten ihr nach.

---

Has night been so kind
that you close and bow and
    weep
for her quiet bliss?

Shake off the veil of dreams,
and fresh and free, arise
to God's bright morning!
The lark is warbling in the sky;
and from the heart's depths
love calls away pain and sorrow.

### 9 The Miller's Flowers

By the brook many small flowers stand,
out of bright blue eyes they gaze;
the brook—that is the miller's friend,
and bright blue shine my beloved's eyes,
therefore, my flowers are they.

Right beneath her window,
there will I plant my flowers.
There call out to her when all is silent,
when her head is laid low for
    slumber,
for you know what I mean to say.

And when she shuts her eyes,
and sleeps in sweet, sweet repose,
then, as a vision in her dreams, whisper
'Forget me not, forget me not,' to her.
That is what I mean to say.

And when, early, she opens the shutters,
then gaze up with a loving look;
the dew in your tiny eyes—
that shall be my tears,
the tears I shall weep upon you.

### 10 Rain of Tears

So close we sat together
under the cool alder roof,
gazing, so close together,
down at the rippling brook.

The moon had also come,
and after it, the stars;
so close they gazed together,
into the silver glass.

I looked at no moon,
at no gleam of stars,
at her image I looked,
at her eyes alone.

I saw them nod and gaze
up from the blissful brook,
the small blue brookside flowers
gazed and nodded back.

Und in den Bach versunken
der ganze Himmel schien,
und wollte mich mit hinunter
in seine Tiefe ziehn.

Und über den Wolken und Sternen
da rieselte munter der Bach
und rief mit Singen und Klingen:
Geselle, Geselle, mir nach!

Da gingen die Augen mir über,
da ward es im Spiegel so kraus;
sie sprach: es kommt ein Regen,
ade! ich geh nach Haus.

11 *Mein*
Bächlein, laß dein Rauschen sein!
Räder, stellt eur Brausen ein!
All ihr muntern Waldvögelein,
groß und klein,
endet eure Melodein!
Durch den Hain
aus und ein
schalle heut *ein* Reim allein:
Die geliebte Müllerin ist
    mein!
*Mein!*
Frühling, sind das alle deine Blümelein?
Sonne, hast du keinen hellern Schein?
Ach, so muß ich ganz allein,
mit dem seligen Worte mein,
unverstanden in der weiten Schöpfung
    sein.

12 *Pause*
Meine Laute hab ich gehängt an die
    Wand,
hab sie umschlungen mit einem grünen
    Band—
ich kann nicht mehr singen, mein Herz
    ist zu voll,
weiß nicht, wie ich's in Reime zwingen
    soll.
Meiner Sehnsucht allerheißesten
    Schmerz
durft ich aushauchen in Liederscherz,
und wie ich klagte so süß und
    fein,
glaubt ich doch, mein Leiden wär nicht
    klein.
Ei, wie groß ist wohl meines Glückes
    Last,
daß kein Klang auf Erden es in sich
    faßt?

Nun liebe Laute, ruh an dem Nagel hier!
Und weht ein Lüftchen über die Saiten
    dir,
und streift eine Biene mit ihren Flügeln
    dich,

And sunken in the brook
shone all the sky,
and wanted to drag me down
into its depths.

And over the clouds and stars
merrily rippled the brook,
calling, in song and sound:
'Friend, friend, follow me!'

At that my eyes brimmed over,
the glass became disturbed;
said she: 'There's rain coming.
Goodbye. I'm going home.'

11 *Mine!*
Brook, let your babbling cease;
mill-wheels, stop your roar;
blithe wood-birds all,
large and small,
end your carolling!
Throughout the wood,
in and out,
*one* rhyme today let sound about:
The miller's daughter whom I love is
    mine!
*Mine!*
Are those, spring, all your flowers?
Have you, sun, no brighter shine?
Ah, then must I be all alone,
with that blissful word Mine,
and not understood in all the
    universe.

12 *Pause*
My lute I have hung on the
    wall,
with a green ribbon I have twined
    it—
No more can I sing, my heart is too
    full,
how to force it to rhyme, I do not
    know.
The most ardent pangs of my
    yearning
I expressed in jesting song,
and, thus sweetly and tenderly
    lamenting,
I believed my agony no small
    one.
Oh, is the burden of my joy so
    great,
that no sound on earth can contain
    it?

Rest now, dear lute, here on your nail.
And if a breeze waft across your
    strings,
or a bee brush you with its
    wings,

da wird mir so bange, und es durch-
schauert mich!
Warum ließ ich das Band auch hängen
so lang?
Oft fliegt's um die Saiten mit seufzendem
Klang.
Ist es der Nachklang meiner Liebespein?
Soll es das Vorspiel neuer Lieder sein?

**13 Mit dem grünen Lautenbande**
Schad um das schöne grüne Band,
daß es verbleicht hier an der Wand,
ich hab das Grün so gern!
So sprachst du, Liebchen, heut zu mir;
gleich knüpf ich's ab und send es dir:
Nun hab das Grüne gern!

Ist auch dein ganzer Liebster weiß,
soll Grün doch haben seinen Preis,
und ich auch hab es gern.
Weil unsere Lieb ist immer grün,
weil grün der Hoffnung Fernen blühn,
drum haben wir es gern!

Nun schlinge in die Locken dein
das grüne Band gefällig ein,
du hast ja's Grün so gern.
Dann weiß ich, wo die Hoffnung wohnt,
dann weiß ich, wo die Liebe thront,
dann hab ich's Grün erst gern!

**14 Der Jäger**
Was sucht denn der Jäger am Mühlbach
hier?
Bleib, trotziger Jäger, in deinem
Revier!
Hier gibt es kein Wild zu jagen für
dich,
hier wohnt nur ein Rehlein, ein
zahmes, für mich.
Und willst du das zärtliche Rehlein sehn,
so laß deine Büchsen im Walde
stehn,
und laß deine kläffenden Hunde zu Haus,
und laß auf dem Horne den Saus und
Braus,
und schere vom Kinne das struppige
Haar,
sonst scheut sich im Garten das
Rehlein fürwahr.

Doch besser, du bliebest im Walde
dazu
und ließest die Mühlen und Müller in
Ruh.
Was taugen die Fischlein im grünen
Gezweig?
Was will denn das Eichhorn im
bläulichen Teich?

I shall feel dread and
awe.
Why have I let so long a ribbon
hang?
Often, sighing, about the strings it
flies.
Is it the echo of my love's torment,
or shall it be the prelude to new songs?

**13 To Accompany the Green Lute-ribbon**
'A pity this fine green ribbon
should fade here on the wall—
I do like green so much!'
So, my love, you said to me today;
at once I untie it and send it to you:
now enjoy the green!

Though he you love be wholly white,
green too shall have its price,
and I too am fond of it.
Because our love is evergreen,
because hope far off blossoms green,
that is why we like it!

Now in your hair nicely wind
the green ribbon,
since you are so fond of green.
Then shall I know where hope lives,
then shall I know where love reigns,
then shall I like green even more!

**14 The Hunter**
What does the hunter seek here by the
stream?
Keep, haughty hunter, to your own
preserve!
There's no game here for you to
hunt,
only one fawn, a tame one, lives here
for me.
And if you would see that tender fawn,
then leave your guns behind in the
wood,
and leave at home your yelping hounds,
and leave off hooting and tooting your
horn,
and shave that shaggy beard from your
chin,
or the fawn in her garden will be
afraid.

But better, were you to stay in the
wood,
and leave the mills and millers in
peace.
Of what use are fish among the green
twigs?
What would the squirrel seek in the
bluish pond?

Drum bleibe, du trotziger Jäger, im
  Hain,
und laß mich mit meinen drei Rädern
  allein;
und willst meinem Schätzchen dich
  machen beliebt,
so wisse, mein Freund, was ihr
  Herzchen betrübt:
Die Eber, die kommen zu Nacht aus
  dem Hain
und brechen in ihren Kohlgarten ein,
und treten und wühlen herum in dem
  Feld;
die Eber, die schieße, du
  Jägerheld!

### 15 Eifersucht und Stolz

Wohin so schnell, so kraus und wild,
  mein lieber Bach?
Eilst du voll Zorn dem frechen Bruder
  Jäger nach?
Kehr um, und schilt erst deine
  Müllerin
für ihren leichten, losen, kleinen
  Flattersinn,
kehr um!

Sahst du sie gestern Abend nicht am
  Tore stehn,
mit langem Halse nach der großen
  Straße sehn?
Wenn von dem Fang der Jäger lustig
  zieht nach Haus,
da steckt kein sittsam Kind den Kopf
  zum Fenster 'naus.

Geh, Bächlein, hin und sag ihr das;
  doch sag ihr nicht,
hörst du, kein Wort, von meinem
  traurigen Gesicht;
sag ihr: Er schnitzt bei mir sich eine
  Pfeif aus Rohr
und bläst den Kindern schöne Tänz
  und Lieder vor!

### 16 Die liebe Farbe

In Grün will ich mich kleiden,
in grünen Tränen weiden:
mein Schatz hat's Grün so gern.
Will suchen einen Zypressenhain,
eine Heide von grünen Rosmarein:
Mein Schatz hat's Grün so gern.

Wohl auf zum fröhlichen Jagen!
Wohl auf durch Heid und Hagen!
Mein Schatz hat's Jagen so gern,
Das Wild, das ich jage, das ist der Tod,
die Heide, die heiß ich die Liebesnot:
Mein Schatz hat's Jagen so gern.

So, haughty hunter, keep to the
  wood,
and leave me alone with my three
  wheels;
and if you'd be popular with my
  love,
then know, my friend, what troubles
  her heart:
the wild boar that come by night from
  the wood,
and break in amongst her cabbages,
and trample and rootle about in the
  field;
the boar, big bold hunter, are what to
  shoot!

### 15 Jealousy and Pride

Where, so fast, furrowed and wild, dear
  brook,
do you dash? After bold brother hunter,
  in anger?
Turn back, turn back, first scold your
  milleress
for fast, wanton, petty
  fickleness—
turn back!

Did you see her last night by the
  gate,
craning her neck towards the
  road?
When a hunter comes back merry from
  the kill,
no nice girl pokes head over window-
  sill.

Go, brook, tell her that, but say
  not
one word, do you hear, about me
  looking sad;
say, he's with me, he's cutting reed
  pipes,
and piping to children pretty dances
  and songs!

### 16 The Beloved Colour

I'll clothe myself in green,
in green weeping willow:
my love does so like green.
A grove of cypress I'll seek,
a heath of green rosemary:
my love does so like green.

Up, away to the merry hunt!
Up, away over heath and hedge!
My love so loves the hunt.
The game I hunt is death;
the heath I call Love's Plight;
my love so loves the hunt.

Grabt mir ein Grab im Wasen,
deckt mich mit grünem Rasen!
Mein Schatz hat's Grün so gern.
Kein Kreuzlein schwarz, kein Blümlein
  bunt,
grün, alles grün so rings und rund:
Mein Schatz hat's Grün so gern.

17 *Die böse Farbe*
Ich möchte ziehn in die Welt hinaus,
hinaus in die weite Welt;
wenn's nur so grün, so grün nicht wär
da draußen in Wald und Feld!

Ich möchte die grünen Blätter all
pflücken von jedem Zweig,
ich möchte die grünen Gräser all
weinen ganz totenbleich.

Ach Grün, du böse Farbe du,
was siehst mich immer an
so stolz, so keck, so schadenfroh,
mich armen, weißen Mann?

Ich möchte liegen vor ihrer Tür,
im Sturm und Regen und Schnee,
und singen ganz leise bei Tag und
  Nacht
das eine Wörtchen ade.

Horch, wenn im Wald ein Jagdhorn
  schallt,
so klingt ihr Fensterlein,
und schaut sie auch nach mir nicht aus,
darf ich doch schauen hinein.

O binde von der Stirn dir ab
das grüne, grüne Band;
Ade, ade! und reiche mir
zum Abschied deine Hand!

18 *Trockne Blumen*
Ihr Blümlein alle,
die sie mir gab,
euch soll man legen
mit mir ins Grab.

Wie seht ihr alle
mich an so weh,
als ob ihr wüßtet,
wie mir gescheh?

Ihr Blümlein alle,
wie welk, wie blaß?
Ihr Blümlein alle,
wovon so naß?

Ach, Tränen machen
nicht maiengrün,
machen tote Liebe
nicht wieder blühn.

Dig me a grave in the grass,
cover me with green turf:
my love does so like green.
No black cross, no bright
  flowers,
green, all green, all round!
My love does so like green.

17 *The Evil Colour*
Into the world I'd gladly go,
into the wide world;
if only it were not so green
out there in wood and field!

All green leaves I would like
to pluck from every twig,
all green grass I would like
to weep a deathly white.

Ah, green, you evil colour,
why always do you stare
so proud, so bold, so gloating
at me, poor white miller?

At her door I'd like to lie
in storm and rain and snow,
and day and night softly
  sing
the single word Farewell.

When a horn sounds in the
  wood,
hark—her window clicks,
and though not for me she looks out,
yet I can still look in.

O from your brow unbind
that green, green ribbon;
farewell, farewell! And give me,
as we part, your hand!

18 *Dry Flowers*
You tiny flowers all,
that to me she gave,
you shall be laid
with me in my grave.

Why do you all
look so sadly at me,
as if you knew
what would befall me?

You tiny flowers all,
so faded, so wan?
You tiny flowers all,
why so moist?

Ah, tears will not bring
the green of May,
nor make dead love
once more to bloom.

Und Lenz wird kommen,
und Winter wird gehn,
und Blümlein werden
im Grase stehn.

Und Blümlein liegen
in meinem Grab,
die Blümlein alle,
die sie mir gab.

Und wenn sie wandelt
am Hügel vorbei
und denkt im Herzen:
der meint' es treu!

Dann, Blümlein alle,
heraus, heraus!
Der Mai ist kommen,
der Winter ist aus.

And spring will come,
and winter depart,
and tiny flowers
appear in the grass.

And tiny flowers
will lie in my grave,
the tiny flowers all
that to me she gave.

And when she wanders
by the mound
and in her heart thinks:
His feelings were true!

Then, tiny flowers all,
appear, appear!
May is come,
the winter is past.

## 19 Der Müller und der Bach

*Der Müller:*
Wo ein treues Herze
in Liebe vergeht,
da welken die Lilien
auf jedem Beet;

da muß in die Wolken
der Vollmond gehen,
damit seine Tränen
die Menschen nicht sehen;

da halten die Englein
die Augen sich zu
und schluchzen und singen
die Seele zur Ruh.

*Der Bach:*
Und wenn sich die Liebe
dem Schmerz entringt,
ein Sternlein, ein neues,
am Himmel erblinkt;

da springen drei Rosen,
halb rot und halb weiß,
die welken nicht wieder,
aus Dornenreis.

Und die Englein schneiden
die Flügel sich ab
und gehn alle Morgen
zur Erde hinab.

*Der Müller:*
Ach, Bächlein, liebes Bächlein,
du meinst es so gut;
ach, Bächlein, aber weißt du
wie Liebe tut?

## 19 The Miller and the Brook

*Miller:*
Where a true heart
wastes away in love,
there lilies wilt
in every bed;

there behind clouds
the full moon must slip,
so that its tears
be not seen by men;

there the angels keep
closed their eyes,
and sob and sing
the soul to rest.

*Brook:*
And whenever love
breaks free from sorrow,
then a tiny new star
shines out in the sky;

then three roses,
half red and half white,
which never will fade,
from thorn sprigs spring.

And then the angels clip
the wings from their backs,
and every morning
descend here to earth.

*Miller:*
Ah, brook, dear brook,
you mean so well;
but ah, do you know
what love can do?

Ach, unten, da unten
die kühle Ruh!
Ach, Bächlein, liebes Bächlein,
so singe nur zu.

20 *Des Baches Wiegenlied*
Gute Ruh, gute Ruh!
Tu die Augen zu!
Wandrer, du müder, du bist zu Haus.
Die Treu ist hier,
sollst liegen bei mir,
bis das Meer will trinken die Bächlein
aus.

Will betten dich kühl
auf weichem Pfühl
in dem blauen kristallenen
Kämmerlein,
heran, heran
was wiegen kann,
woget und wieget den Knaben mir ein!

Wenn ein Jagdhorn schallt
aus dem grünen Wald,
will ich sausen und brausen wohl um
dich her.
Blickt nicht herein,
blaue Blümelein!
Ihr macht meinem Schläfer die Träume
so schwer.

Hinweg, hinweg
von dem Mühlensteg,
böses Mägdlein, daß ihn dein Schatten
nicht weckt!
Wirf mir herein
dein Tüchlein fein,
daß ich die Augen ihm halte bedeckt!

Gute Nacht, gute Nacht!
Bis alles wacht,
schlaf aus deine Freude, schlaf aus
dein Leid!
Der Vollmond steigt,
der Nebel weicht,
und der Himmel da oben, wie ist er so
weit!

Ah, there, down there,
is cool peace!
Ah, brook, dear brook,
just sing on.

20 *The Brook's Lullaby*
Sleep well, sleep well,
close your eyes,
weary wanderer, you are home.
There is constancy here,
with me you shall lie,
until the sea drinks all brooks
dry.

I will bed you cool
on a soft pillow
in my blue crystal
chamber.
Draw near, draw near,
all who can rock to sleep,
make waves and rock this young man.

When a hunting horn brays
from the forest green,
about you I will rush and
roar.
Look not in,
tiny blue flowers!
You'll give my sleeper such oppressive
dreams!

Away, away
from the mill-path,
wicked maid, lest your shadow wake
him.
Throw in to me
your fine handkerchief
that I may keep his eyes covered!

Good night, good night,
till all shall wake,
sleep out your joy, sleep out your
sorrow!
The full moon is rising,
the mist is yielding,
and heaven up there, how
far!

## *Die Uhr | The Time-piece*

JOHANN GABRIEL SEIDL

*Carl Loewe: op. 123, no. 3, ed. 1830*

Ich trage, wo ich gehe, stets eine Uhr
bei mir;
Wieviel es geschlagen habe, genau seh
ich an ihr.

I carry, wherever I go, a time-piece
with me;
how much time it has told, is plain for
me to see.

Es ist ein großer Meister, der künstlich
  ihr Werk gefügt,
Wenngleich ihr Gang nicht immer dem
  törichten Wunsche genügt.

Great was the master who skilfully
  fashioned it,
though its working's not always to my
  foolish wish.

Ich wollte, sie wäre rascher gegangen an
  manchem Tag;
Ich wollte, sie hätte manchmal verzögert
  den raschen Schlag.
In meinen Leiden und Freuden, in
  Sturm und in der Ruh,
Was immer geschah im Leben, sie
  pochte den Takt dazu.

Many's the day I've wished it
  faster,
I've wished sometimes to slow its rapid
  tick.
In sorrow and joy, in storm and
  tranquillity,
whatever occurred in life, it has beaten
  time.

Sie schlug am Sarge des Vaters, sie
  schlug an des Freundes Bahr,
Sie schlug am Morgen der Liebe, sie
  schlug am Traualtar.
Sie schlug an der Wiege des Kindes, sie
  schlägt, will's Gott, noch oft,
Wenn bessere Tage kommen, wie
  meine Seele es hofft.

It beat by my father's coffin, by my
  friend's bier,
beat at my love's dawning, at the altar
  when I wed.
It beat by baby's cradle, and God
  willing, shall still,
if better days are coming, as is my
  soul's hope.

Und ward sie auch einmal träger, und
  drohte zu stocken ihr Lauf,
So zog der Meister immer großmütig
  sie wieder auf.
Doch stände sie einmal stille, dann
  wär's um sie geschehn,
Kein andrer, als der sie fügte, bringt
  die Zerstörte zum Gehn.

If ever it went slower, and made as if
  to stop,
generously the master would always
  wind it more.
But were it to stop going, that would
  be the end.
None, save he who made it, can make it
  go again.

Dann müßt ich zum Meister wandern,
  der wohnt am Ende wohl weit,
Wohl draußen, jenseits der Erde, wohl
  dort in der Ewigkeit!
Dann gäb ich sie ihm zurücke mit
  dankbar kindlichem Flehn:
Sieh, Herr, ich hab nichts verdorben,
  sie blieb von selber stehn.

Then far I'd have to journey to where
  the master lives,
way beyond the earth, way out in
  eternity.
Then I would return it, and, grateful,
  child-like, say:
Lord, I did not harm it, it stopped of
  its own accord.

## Die Verschweigung / Reticence

CHRISTIAN FELIX WEISSE

*Wolfgang Amadeus Mozart: K 518, 1787*

Sobald Dämotas Chloen sieht,
So sucht er mit beredten Blicken
Ihr seine Klagen auszudrücken,
Und ihre Wange glüht.
Sie scheinet seine stillen Klagen
Mehr als zur Hälfte zu verstehn,
Und er ist jung, und sie ist schön;
Ich will nichts weiter sagen.

When Daemotas beholds his Chloe,
with eloquent glances he seeks
to tell her his complaints,
and her cheeks both glow.
His silent complaints she seems
more than half to understand,
and he is young, and she is fair;
more I will not say.

Vermißt er Chloen auf der Flur,
Betrübt wird er von dannen scheiden;
Dann aber hüpft er voller Freuden,
Entdeckt er Chloen nur.

Should he miss Chloe in the meadow,
troubled, he departs;
but then joyfully will he leap,
if he but Chloe find.

Er küßt ihr unter tausend Fragen
Die Hand, und Chloe läßt's geschehn,
Und er ist jung, und sie ist schön;
Ich will nichts weiter sagen.

Sie hat an Blumen ihre Lust,
Er stillet täglich ihr Verlangen;
Sie klopfet schmeichelnd ihm die
Wangen,
Und steckt sie an die Brust.
Der Busen bläht sich, sie zu tragen.
Er triumphiert, sie hier zu sehn,
Und er ist jung, und sie ist schön;
Ich will nichts weiter sagen.

Wenn sie ein kühler, heitrer Bach,
Beschützt von Büschen, eingeladen,
In seinen Wellen sich zu baden,
So schleicht er listig nach.
In diesen schwülen Sommertagen
Hat er ihr oftmals zugesehn,
Und er ist jung, und sie ist schön;
Ich will nichts weiter sagen.

Asking a thousand questions, he kisses
her hand, and Chloe does not resist,
and he is young, and she is fair;
more I will not say.

She for flowers has a mind,
this yearning he allays each day;
a flattering pat she gives his
cheeks,
and at her breast puts flowers.
Bearing them, her bosom swells.
Triumphant is he to see them there,
and he is young, and she is fair;
more I will not say.

If a cool and merry brook,
bush-protected, has invited
her to bathe in its waves,
he, cunningly, steals after her.
On these sultry summer days
he has often gazed at her,
and he is young, and she is fair;
more I will not say.

## Die Winterreise / Winter Journey

WILHELM MÜLLER

*Franz Schubert: op. 89, nos. 1–24, 1827*

1 *Gute Nacht*
Fremd bin ich eingezogen,
Fremd zieh' ich wieder aus.
Der Mai war mir gewogen
Mit manchem Blumenstrauß.
Das Mädchen sprach von Liebe,
Die Mutter gar von Eh',—
Nun ist die Welt so trübe,
Der Weg gehüllt in Schnee.

Ich kann zu meiner Reisen
Nicht wählen mit der Zeit,
Muß selbst den Weg mir weisen
In dieser Dunkelheit.
Es zieht ein Mondenschatten
Als mein Gefährte mit,
Und auf den weißen Matten
Such' ich des Wildes Tritt.

Was soll ich länger weilen,
Daß man mich trieb hinaus?
Laß irre Hunde heulen
Vor ihres Herren Haus;
Die Liebe liebt das Wandern—
Gott hat sie so gemacht—
Von einem zu dem andern.
Fein Liebchen, gute Nacht!

1 *Good Night*
I came here as a stranger,
and as a stranger go.
May was kind towards me,
with many bouquets of flowers.
The daughter spoke of love,
the mother—of marriage even;
and now the world is bleak,
the road deep in snow.

I cannot, for my journey,
choose the time,
but must find my own way
in this darkness.
A shadow in the moonlight
will keep me company,
and on white meadows
I'll watch for animal tracks.

Why linger any longer?
Why wait to be driven out?
Leave errant dogs to howl
at their master's door.
Love loves to wander—
God has made it so—
wander from one to another.
My dearest love, good night!

Will dich im Traum nicht stören,  
Wär schad' um deine Ruh',  
Sollst meinen Tritt nicht hören—  
Sacht, sacht die Türe zu!  
Schreib' im Vorübergehen  
Ans Tor dir: Gute Nacht,  
Damit du mögest sehen,  
An dich hab' ich gedacht.

2 *Die Wetterfahne*  
Der Wind spielt mit der Wetterfahne  
Auf meines schönen Liebchens Haus.  
Da dacht ich schon in meinem Wahne,  
Sie pfiff den armen Flüchtling aus.

Er hätt' es eher bemerken sollen,  
Des Hauses aufgestecktes Schild,  
So hätt' er nimmer suchen wollen  
Im Haus ein treues Frauenbild.

Der Wind spielt drinnen mit dem  
  Herzen  
Wie auf dem Dach, nur nicht so laut.  
Was fragen sie nach meinen Schmerzen?  
Ihr Kind ist eine reiche Braut.

3 *Gefrorene Tränen*  
Gefrorne Tropfen fallen  
Von meinen Wangen ab:  
Ob es mir denn entgangen,  
Daß ich geweinet hab'?

Ei Tränen, meine Tränen,  
Und seid ihr gar so lau,  
Daß ihr erstarrt zu Eise  
Wie kühler Morgentau?

Und dringt doch aus der Quelle  
Der Brust so glühend heiß,  
Als wolltet ihr zerschmelzen  
Des ganzen Winters Eis!

4 *Erstarrung*  
Ich such' im Schnee vergebens  
Nach ihrer Tritte Spur,  
Wo sie an meinem Arme  
Durchstrich die grüne Flur.

Ich will den Boden küssen,  
Durchdringen Eis und Schnee  
Mit meinen heißen Tränen,  
Bis ich die Erde seh'.

Wo find' ich eine Blüte,  
Wo find' ich grünes Gras?  
Die Blumen sind erstorben,  
Der Rasen sieht so blaß.

Soll denn kein Angedenken  
Ich nehmen mit von hier?

---

I'll not disturb your dreams,  
a shame to spoil your sleep,  
you shall not hear my step—  
soft, softly with the door!  
I'll write, as I go by,  
Good night upon the gate,  
so that you may see  
that I have thought of you.

2 *The Weather-vane*  
The wind plays with the vane  
on my fair beloved's house.  
I thought in my delusion  
it mocked the wretched fugitive.

Had he but seen it sooner,  
that emblem of the house,  
never would he then have looked  
to find a true-love there.

The wind plays inside with the  
  heart,  
as on the roof, but not so loud.  
What is my agony to them?  
Their child is a rich match.

3 *Frozen Tears*  
Frozen drops fall  
from my cheeks;  
have I, then, not noticed  
that I have wept

Ah, tears, my tears,  
are you so lukewarm  
that you freeze to ice  
like chill morning dew?

And yet you well  
so scalding from my breast  
as if to melt  
the ice of the whole winter!

4 *Numbness*  
Vainly I scan the snow  
for traces of her steps,  
where, on my arm, she  
walked the green meadow.

I want to kiss the ground,  
pierce ice and snow  
with my hot tears,  
until I see the earth.

Where to find a flower?  
Where to find green grass?  
The flowers are dead,  
the grass pale.

Am I to take no remembrance  
from here, then, as I go?

Wenn meine Schmerzen schweigen,
Wer sagt mir dann von ihr?

Mein Herz ist wie erstorben,
Kalt starrt ihr Bild darin;
Schmilzt je das Herz mir wieder,
Fließt auch ihr Bild dahin!

5 *Der Lindenbaum*
Am Brunnen vor dem Tore
Da steht ein Lindenbaum;
Ich träumt' in seinem Schatten
So manchen süßen Traum.

Ich schnitt in seine Rinde
So manches liebe Wort;
Es zog in Freud' und Leide
Zu ihm mich immer fort.

Ich mußt' auch heute wandern
Vorbei in tiefer Nacht,
Da hab' ich noch im Dunkeln
Die Augen zugemacht.

Und seine Zweige rauschten,
Als riefen sie mir zu:
Komm her zu mir, Geselle,
Hier find'st du deine Ruh'!

Die kalten Winde bliesen
Mir grad ins Angesicht;
Der Hut flog mir vom Kopfe,
Ich wendete mich nicht.

Nun bin ich manche Stunde
Entfernt von jenem Ort,
Und immer hör' ich's rauschen:
Du fändest Ruhe dort!

6 *Wasserflut*
Manche Trän' aus meinen Augen
Ist gefallen in den Schnee;
Seine kalten Flocken saugen
Durstig ein das heiße Weh.

Wenn die Gräser sprossen wollen
Weht daher ein lauer Wind,
Und das Eis zerspringt in Schollen
Und der weiche Schnee zerrinnt.

Schnee, du weißt von meinem Sehnen,
Sag', wohin doch geht dein Lauf?
Folge nach nur meinen Tränen,
Nimmt dich bald das Bächlein auf.

Wirst mit ihm die Stadt durchziehen,
Muntʼre Straßen ein und aus;
Fühlst du meine Tränen glühen,
Da ist meiner Liebsten Haus.

Who, when my pain is stilled,
shall speak to me of her?

My heart is as dead,
her image—numb within;
if ever again my heart melts,
even her image will go!

5 *The Linden Tree*
At the gate, by the fountain,
stands a linden tree,
in whose shade I dreamt
so many a sweet dream.

In whose bark I carved
so many a word of love;
in joy and sorrow I was drawn
to it again and again.

Today, too, I had to pass it,
at dead of night,
and though it was dark
I closed my eyes.

And its boughs rustled,
as if calling:
Come, friend, here to me,
here you shall find peace.

Chill blasts blew
full into my face,
my hat flew from my head,
I did not turn.

Now, many an hour
from that place,
still I hear it rustling:
There would you find peace!

6 *Flood Waters*
Many a tear my eyes
have shed into the snow;
its cold flakes drink
thirstily my burning grief.

When grass is ready to grow,
a mild wind comes,
the ice breaks up,
the snow melts.

You know, snow, of my longing,
where do you run to, say?
If you but follow my tears,
the brook will soon gather you in.

With it, through the town you'll go
and its lively streets;
when you feel my tears glowing,
that will be my dearest's house.

7 *Auf dem Flusse*
Der du so lustig rauschtest,
Du heller, wilder Fluß,
Wie still bist du geworden,
Gibst keinen Scheidegruß.

Mit harter, starrer Rinde
Hast du dich überdeckt,
Liegst kalt und unbeweglich
Im Sande ausgestreckt.

In deine Decke grab' ich
Mit einem spitzen Stein
Den Namen meiner Liebsten
Und Stund' und Tag hinein:

Den Tag des ersten Grußes,
Den Tag, an dem ich ging;
Um Nam' und Zahlen windet
Sich ein zerbroch'ner Ring.

Mein Herz, in diesem Bache
Erkennst du nun dein Bild?
Ob's unter seiner Rinde
Wohl auch so reißend schwillt?

8 *Rückblick*
Es brennt mir unter beiden Sohlen,
Tret' ich auch schon auf Eis und
    Schnee,
Ich möcht' nicht wieder Atem holen,
Bis ich nicht mehr die Türme seh'.

Hab' mich an jedem Stein gestoßen,
So eilt' ich zu der Stadt hinaus;
Die Krähen warfen Bäll' und Schloßen
Auf meinen Hut von jedem Haus.

Wie anders hast du mich empfangen,
Du Stadt der Unbeständigkeit!
An deinen blanken Fenstern sangen
Die Lerch' und Nachtigall im Streit.

Die runden Lindenbäume blühten,
Die klaren Rinnen rauschten hell,
Und ach, zwei Mädchenaugen glühten.—
Da war's gescheh'n um dich, Gesell!

Kommt mir der Tag in die Gedanken,
Möcht' ich noch einmal rückwärts seh'n,
Möcht' ich zurücke wieder wanken,
Vor ihrem Hause stille steh'n.

9 *Irrlicht*
In die tiefsten Felsengründe
Lockte mich ein Irrlicht hin:
Wie ich einen Ausgang finde,
Liegt nicht schwer mir in dem Sinn.

7 *On the Stream*
You who chattered so merry,
bright, wild stream,
how silent you are now;
you bid me no farewell.

A stark, hard crust
you have spread over you;
still and cold you lie
stretched in the sand.

Into your surface
with a sharp stone
I carve my dearest's name,
and the day and the hour:

the day we first met,
the day I went away;
name and numbers entwining
with a broken ring.

My heart, in this brook,
do you see your own image?
Is, I wonder, under *its* crust
just such a swelling torrent?

8 *Backward Glance*
The ground blazes beneath my feet
though I walk on ice and
    snow;
but I'll not pause for breath
till I see the spires no more.

Over every stone I stumbled,
in my haste to leave the town;
crows shied hailstones, snowballs
at my hat from every roof.

How different your greeting,
town of inconstancy!
At your gleaming windows sang
now lark, now nightingale.

Round lime-trees were in blossom,
gutters—loud with clear water,
and oh, two warm fair eyes—
and your fate, friend, was sealed!

Remembering that day,
I'd like once more to look back,
like once more to stumble back,
and stand quietly outside her house.

9 *Jack o'lantern*
Into the deepest chasms
Jack o'lantern has lured me:
how to escape, does not
greatly concern me.

Bin gewohnt das Irregehen,
's fuhrt ja jeder Weg zum Ziel;
Uns're Freuden, uns're Wehen,
Alles eines Irrlichts Spiel!

Durch des Bergstroms trock'ne Rinnen
Wind' ich ruhig mich hinab,
Jeder Strom wird's Meer gewinnen,
Jedes Leiden auch sein Grab.

10 *Rast*
Nun merk' ich erst, wie müd' ich bin,
Da ich zur Ruh' mich lege;
Das Wandern hielt mich munter hin
Auf unwirtbarem Wege.

Die Füße frugen nicht nach Rast,
Es war zu kalt zum Stehen;
Der Rücken fühlte keine Last,
Der Sturm half fort mich wehen.

In eines Köhlers engem Haus
Hab' Obdach ich gefunden;
Doch meine Glieder ruh'n nicht aus:
So brennen ihre Wunden.

Auch du, mein Herz, in Kampf und
    Sturm
So wild und so verwegen,
Fühlst in der Still' erst deinen Wurm
Mit heißem Stich sich regen!

11 *Frühlingstraum*
Ich träumte von bunten Blumen,
So wie sie wohl blühen im Mai;
Ich träumte von grünen Wiesen
Von lustigem Vogelgeschrei.

Und als die Hähne krähten,
Da ward mein Auge wach;
Da war es kalt und finster,
Es schrien die Raben vom Dach.

Doch an den Fensterscheiben,
Wer malte die Blätter da?
Ihr lacht wohl über den Träumer,
Der Blumen im Winter sah?

Ich träumte von Lieb' um Liebe,
Von einer schönen Maid,
Von Herzen und von Küssen,
Von Wonne und Seligkeit.

Und als die Hähne krähten,
Da ward mein Herze wach;
Nun sitz ich hier alleine
Und denke dem Traume nach.

Die Augen schließ' ich wieder,
Noch schlägt das Herz so warm.

Well used I am to straying,
—any road leads to the goal:
our joys, our woes,
are all a Jack o' Lantern game!

Down the mountain stream's
dry gullies I wind my way—
every stream will find the sea,
every sorrow—its grave.

10 *Rest*
My weariness I notice only
as I lie down to rest.
Walking, I kept going
on the desolate road.

My feet asked no halt—
too cold for standing still;
my back felt no burden,
the storm helped blow me along.

In a charcoal-burner's hovel
I have found lodging
but no repose for my limbs:
such their burning wounds.

And you, heart, in storm
    and strife,
so fierce, so bold,
only now in the lull feel
the fierce pangs stir!

11 *Dream of Spring*
I dreamt of gay flowers
such as bloom in May;
I dreamt of green meadows,
merry calling of birds.

And at cock-crow,
my eyes awoke;
cold it was, and dark,
ravens croaked from the roof.

But there, on the windows,
who painted those leaves?
Are you mocking the dreamer
who saw flowers in winter?

I dreamt of love requited,
of a beautiful girl,
of caressing and kissing,
joy and rapture.

And at cock-crow,
my heart awoke;
now I sit here alone,
recalling my dream.

Again I close my eyes,
my heart still beats so warm.

Wann grünt ihr Blätter am Fenster?
Wann halt' ich mein Liebchen im Arm?

When, leaves, will you turn green?
When shall I hold my love in my arms?

12 *Einsamkeit*
Wie eine trübe Wolke
Durch heit're Lüfte geht,
Wenn in der Tanne Wipfel
Ein mattes Lüftchen weht:

12 *Loneliness*
Like a dark cloud
across clear skies,
when in the fir top
a feeble breeze stirs,

So zieh ich meine Straße
Dahin mit trägem Fuß,
Durch helles, frohes Leben
Einsam und ohne Gruß.

I go my way,
slow-footed, through
bright, joyous life,
lonely, ungreeted.

Ach, daß die Luft so ruhig!
Ach, daß die Welt so licht!
Als noch die Stürme tobten,
War ich so elend nicht.

Oh, the still air . . .
Oh, the bright world
While storms raged,
I was not so wretched.

13 *Die Post*
Von der Straße her ein Posthorn klingt.
Was hat es, daß es so hoch aufspringt,
Mein Herz?

13 *The Post*
From the road a posthorn sounds.
What causes you to leap so,
my heart?

Die Post bringt keinen Brief für dich.
Was drängst du denn so wunderlich,
Mein Herz?

No post will there be for you.
Why, then, surge so strangely,
my heart?

Nun ja, die Post kommt aus der Stadt,
Wo ich ein liebes Liebchen hatt',
Mein Herz!

But oh, the post's from that town
where I had a true love once,
my heart!

Willst wohl einmal hinüberseh'n
Und fragen, wie es dort mag geh'n,
Mein Herz?

Do you want to look out
and ask how things are there,
my heart?

14 *Der greise Kopf*
Der Reif hatt' einen weißen Schein
Mir übers Haar gestreuet;
Da glaubt' ich schon ein Greis zu sein
Und hab' mich sehr gefreuet.

14 *Grey Head*
With white sheen the frost
had sprinkled my hair;
I thought myself an old man,
and rejoiced.

Doch bald ist er hinweggetaut,
Hab' wieder schwarze Haare,
Daß mir's vor meiner Jugend graut—
Wie weit noch bis zur Bahre!

But quickly it's melted and gone,
my hair is black again,
so that I shudder at my youth—
how far still to the grave!

Vom Abendrot zum Morgenlicht
Ward mancher Kopf zum Greise.
Wer glaubt's? und meiner ward es nicht
Auf dieser ganzen Reise!

From sunset red to morning light,
many a head has grown grey,
yet mine, would you believe,
has not, in all this journey!

15 *Die Krähe*
Eine Krähe war mit mir
Aus der Stadt gezogen,
Ist bis heute für und für
Um mein Haupt geflogen.

15 *The Crow*
One crow has come
from the town with me,
forever, to this day,
circling my head.

Krähe, wunderliches Tier,
Willst mich nicht verlassen?

O crow, strange creature,
do you refuse to leave me?

Meinst wohl, bald als Beute hier
Meinen Leib zu fassen?

Nun, es wird nicht weit mehr geh'n
An dem Wanderstabe.
Krähe, laß mich endlich seh'n
Treue bis zum Grabe!

16 *Letzte Hoffnung*
Hie und da ist an den Bäumen
Manches bunte Blatt zu seh'n,
Und ich bleibe vor den Bäumen
Oftmals in Gedanken steh'n.

Schaue nach dem einen Blatte,
Hänge meine Hoffnung dran;
Spielt der Wind mit meinem Blatte,
Zitt'r' ich, was ich zittern kann.

Ach, und fällt das Blatt zu Boden,
Fällt mit ihm die Hoffnung ab;
Fall' ich selber mit zu Boden,
Wein' auf meiner Hoffnung Grab.

17 *Im Dorfe*
Es bellen die Hunde, es rasseln die
    Ketten;
Es schlafen die Menschen in ihren
    Betten,
Träumen sich manches, was sie nicht
    haben,
Tun sich im Guten und Argen erlaben;

Und morgen früh ist alles zerflossen.
Je nun, sie haben ihr Teil genossen
Und hoffen, was sie noch übrig ließen,
Doch wieder zu finden auf ihren Kissen.

Bellt mich nur fort, ihr wachen Hunde,
Laßt mich nicht ruh'n in der
    Schlummerstunde!
Ich bin zu Ende mit allen Träumen.
Was will ich unter den Schläfern
    säumen?

18 *Der stürmische Morgen*
Wie hat der Sturm zerrissen
Des Himmels graues Kleid!
Die Wolkenfetzen flattern
Umher im matten Streit.

Und rote Feuerflammen
Zieh'n zwischen ihnen hin;
Das nenn' ich einen Morgen
So recht nach meinem Sinn!

Mein Herz sieht an dem Himmel
Gemalt sein eig'nes Bild—
Es ist nichts als der Winter
Der Winter, kalt und wild!

Do you hope, as prey,
soon to seize my body?

Not far, then, left to tramp,
staff in hand;
O crow, let me at last see
faithfulness unto death!

16 *Last Hope*
Here and there on trees
bright leaves may be seen,
and by those trees
I often stop in thought.

For one leaf I look
to attach my hope to;
if the wind toys with it,
I tremble in every limb.

Ah, and if it falls to earth,
my hope falls with it;
I, too, fall to the ground,
and weep on my hope's grave.

17 *In the Village*
Dogs bark, chains
    rattle;
folk are abed and
    asleep,
dreaming of much they do not
    possess,
refreshing themselves, in good and bad;

by morn, all will have vanished.
Still, they have enjoyed their share,
and what they have left, they hope,
on their pillows, to rediscover.

Bark, send me away, watchful dogs,
let me not rest at slumber's
    hour!
I am finished with all dreaming.
Why linger among
    sleepers?

18 *Stormy Morning*
How the storm has rent
the grey garment of the sky!
Cloud tatters flit about
in weary strife.

And red flames of fire
flash among them;
that's what I call a morning
after my own mind.

In that sky my heart sees
painted its own image—
nothing it is but winter,
winter cold and wild!

## 19 Täuschung

Ein Licht tanzt freundlich vor mir her,
Ich folg' ihm nach die Kreuz und Quer;
Ich folg' ihm gern und seh's ihm an,
Daß es verlockt den Wandersmann.
Ach! wer wie ich so elend ist,
Gibt gern sich hin der bunten List,
Die hinter Eis und Nacht und Graus
Ihm weist ein helles, warmes Haus.
Und eine liebe Seele drin.—
Nur Täuschung ist für mich Gewinn!

## 20 Der Wegweiser

Was vermeid' ich denn die Wege,
Wo die ander'n Wand'rer gehn,
Suche mir versteckte Stege
Durch verschneite Felsenhöh'n?

Habe ja doch nichts begangen,
Daß ich Menschen sollte scheu'n,—
Welch ein törichtes Verlangen
Treibt mich in die Wüstenei'n?

Weiser stehen auf den Straßen,
Weisen auf die Städte zu,
Und ich wand're sonder Maßen
Ohne Ruh' und suche Ruh'.

Einen Weiser seh' ich stehen
Unverrückt vor meinem Blick;
Eine Straße muß ich gehen,
Die noch keiner ging zurück.

## 21 Das Wirtshaus

Auf einen Totenacker
Hat mich mein Weg gebracht;
Allhier will ich einkehren,
Hab' ich bei mir gedacht.

Ihr grünen Totenkränze
Könnt wohl die Zeichen sein,
Die müde Wand'rer laden
Ins kühle Wirtshaus ein.

Sind denn in diesem Hause
Die Kammern all besetzt?
Bin matt zum Niedersinken,
Bin tödlich schwer verletzt.

O unbarmherz'ge Schenke,
Doch weisest du mich ab?
Nun weiter denn, nur weiter,
Mein treuer Wanderstab!

## 22 Mut

Fliegt der Schnee mir ins Gesicht,
Schüttl' ich ihn herunter.
Wenn mein Herz im Busen spricht,
Sing' ich hell und munter.

## 19 Delusion

A kindly light dances ahead;
I follow this way and that—
follow gladly, and see
it misleads the wanderer.
Oh, any man as wretched as I,
readily falls for the trickery
that shows, beyond ice, night
and horror, a bright warm house.
And within it, one sweet soul . . .
Delusion only is what I gain!

## 20 The Sign-post

Why do I avoid the ways
that other wanderers tread,
and seek out hidden paths
over snowy rocky heights?

For I have done no wrong
that I should shun men—
what foolish craving
drives me into desolate places?

On roads stand sign-posts
pointing to towns,
and I wander on and on
restlessly in search of rest.

One sign-post I see standing,
immovable, before my gaze;
one road I must tread, by which
no one has yet returned.

## 21 The Inn

To a graveyard
my way has brought me;
here will I lodge,
I thought.

You green wreaths
must be the signs
inviting weary travellers
into the cool inn.

Are, then, at this house
the rooms all taken?
I am tired enough to drop,
wounded unto death.

Pitiless inn,
do you turn me away?
Well, on, then, on,
my trusty staff!

## 22 Courage

If snow drives into my face,
I shake it off.
When my heart speaks within,
loudly I sing, and gaily.

| | |
|---|---|
| Höre nicht, was es mir sagt,<br>Habe keine Ohren;<br>Fühle nicht, was es mir klagt,<br>Klagen ist für Toren. | I don't hear what it says,<br>I have no ears;<br>nor feel what it laments—<br>lamenting is for fools. |
| Lustig in die Welt hinein<br>Gegen Wind und Wetter!<br>Will kein Gott auf Erden sein,<br>Sind wir selber Götter! | Merrily into the world,<br>in teeth of wind and weather!<br>If there is no God on earth,<br>gods we are ourselves! |

### 23 Die Nebensonnen / 23 Mock Suns

| | |
|---|---|
| Drei Sonnen sah ich am Himmel steh'n,<br>Hab' lang und fest sie angeseh'n;<br>Und sie auch standen da so stier,<br>Als wollten sie nicht weg von mir.<br>Ach, *meine* Sonnen seid ihr nicht!<br>Schaut ander'n doch ins Angesicht!<br>Ja, neulich hatt' ich auch wohl drei;<br>Nun sind hinab die besten zwei.<br>Ging nur die dritt' erst hinterdrein!<br>Im Dunkel wird mir wohler sein. | Three suns in the sky I saw,<br>long and hard I looked;<br>they also stopped and stared,<br>as if unwilling to go away.<br>You are not, alas, *my* suns!<br>You look other people in the face!<br>Lately, yes, I did have three;<br>but the best two now are down.<br>Would but the third go too!<br>In the dark I'd fare better. |

### 24 Der Leiermann / 24 The Organ-grinder

| | |
|---|---|
| Drüben hinterm Dorfe<br>Steht ein Leiermann,<br>Und mit starren Fingern<br>Dreht er, was er kann. | There, beyond the village<br>an organ-grinder stands,<br>and with numb fingers<br>plays as best he can. |
| Barfuß auf dem Eise<br>Wankt er hin und her,<br>Und sein kleiner Teller<br>Bleibt ihm immer leer. | Barefoot on the ice<br>he staggers to and fro,<br>and his little plate<br>stays forever empty. |
| Keiner mag ihn hören,<br>Keiner sieht ihn an,<br>Und die Hunde knurren<br>Um den alten Mann. | No one cares to listen,<br>no one looks at him,<br>and dogs snarl<br>around the old man. |
| Und er läßt es gehen,<br>alles wie es will,<br>Dreht, und seine Leier<br>Steht ihm nimmer still. | And he lets it happen,<br>everything as it will,<br>and plays on,<br>his hurdy-gurdy never still. |
| Wunderlicher Alter!<br>Soll ich mit dir gehn?<br>Willst zu meinen Liedern<br>Deine Leier drehn? | Strange old man,<br>shall I go with you?<br>Will you, to my songs,<br>play your hurdy-gurdy? |

## Die Zigeunerin / The Gipsy Woman

JOSEPH VON EICHENDORFF

*Hugo Wolf, 1887*

| | |
|---|---|
| Am Kreuzweg, da lausche ich, wenn<br>   die Stern'<br>Und die Feuer im Walde verglommen,<br>Und wo der erste Hund bellt von fern,<br>Da wird mein Bräut'gam herkommen. | At the cross-road I listen when<br>   stars<br>have died out, and the fires in the wood,<br>and where, afar, the first dog barks,<br>from there my intended will come. |

»Und als der Tag graut', durch das Gehölz
Sah ich eine Katze sich schlingen,
Ich schoß ihr auf den nußbraunen Pelz,
Wie tat die weitüber springen!«—

's ist schad' nur ums Pelzlein, du kriegst mich nit!
Mein Schatz muß sein wie die andern!
Braun und ein Stutzbart auf ung'rischen Schnitt
Und ein fröhliches Herze zum Wandern.

'And at dawn, through the copse,
I saw a cat slinking,
and at her nut-brown coat I fired,
and how she went leaping!'—

The coat's a pity, you shan't have me!
My loved one must be like the others!
Brown, with beard of Hungarian trim,
and a happy heart for wandering.


## Die zu späte Ankunft der Mutter | The Mother's Over-tardy Arrival

CHRISTIAN FELIX WEISSE

*Joseph Haydn, 1781*

Beschattet von blühenden Ästen,
gekühlet von spielenden Westen,
lag Rosilis am Bache hier
und Hylas neben ihr.

By blossoming branches shaded,
by sportive west winds cooled,
Rosalis lay here by the brook
and Hylas at her side.

Von Lenz und Liebe gerühret,
ward Hylas zum Küssen verführet.
Er küßte sie, er drückte sie,
daß sie um Hilfe schrie.

Moved by love and spring,
Hylas was seduced to kiss.
He kissed her, he squeezed her,
so that she cried for help.

Die Mutter kam eilend und fragte,
was Hylas für Frevel hier wagte?
Die Tochter rief: es ist geschehn,
ihr könnt nun wieder gehn.

Hastening came mother, asking
what iniquity Hylas was daring.
The daughter cried: it is over,
you can now be off again.


## Dithyrambe | Dithyramb

FRIEDRICH SCHILLER

*Franz Schubert: op. 60, no. 2, 1824*

Nimmer, das glaubt mir, erscheinen die Götter,
Nimmer allein.
Kaum daß ich Bacchus, den lustigen, habe,
Kommt auch schon Amor, der lächelnde Knabe,
Phöbus der Herrliche findet sich ein.
Sie nahen, sie kommen, die Himmlischen alle,
Mit Göttern erfüllt sich die irdische Halle.

Sagt, wie bewirt ich, der Erdegeborne,
Himmlischen Chor?
Schenket mir euer unsterbliches Leben,

Never, believe me, do the gods appear
singly, never.
Scarce do I receive Bacchus, the merry,
than also comes Amor, the smiling boy,
and Phoebus, the glorious.
Hither they come, the Heavenly Ones all,
the earthly hall fills with gods.

Say how shall I, earth-born, entertain the heavenly throng?
Bestow on me your eternal life.

Götter! Was kann euch der Sterbliche geben?
Hebet zu eurem Olymp mich empor!
Die Freude, sie wohnt nur in Jupiters Saale,
O füllet mit Nektar, o reicht mir die Schale!

Reich ihm die Schale! Schenke dem Dichter,
Hebe, nur ein.
Netz ihm die Augen mit himmlischem Taue,
Daß er den Styx, den verhaßten, nicht schaue,
Einer der Unsern sich dünke zu sein.
Sie rauschet, sie perlet, die himmlische Quelle,
Der Busen wird ruhig, das Auge wird helle.

gods! What can a mortal give you?
Raise me up to your Olympus.
Joy dwells only in Jupiter's hall.
Oh fill with nectar the cup, Oh pass it to me!

Pass the cup to him. Pour for the poet,
Hebe, pour.
Moisten his eyes with celestial dew,
so that Styx, the hated, he shall not behold,
thinking himself of our number.
The celestial source—it murmurs, it sparkles;
the breast grows calm, the eye grows bright.

## Drei Gedichte von Michelangelo / Three Poems by Michelangelo

Translated by WALTER ROBERT-TORNOW

*Hugo Wolf, 1897*

I

Wohl denk ich oft an mein vergangnes Leben,
Wie es vor meiner Liebe für dich war;
Kein Mensch hat damals acht auf mich gegeben,
Ein jeder Tag verloren für mich war;

Ich dachte wohl, ganz dem Gesang zu leben,
Auch mich zu flüchten aus der Menschen Schar.
Genannt in Lob und Tadel bin ich heute,
Und, daß ich da bin, wissen alle Leute!

I

Often of my past life I think,
how it was before my love for you;
no one at that time heeded me,
and each day was for me a loss;

wholly to live for song I thought,
even to flee the host of men.
Today in praise and censure I am named,
and all people know that I exist!

2

Alles endet, was entstehet.
Alles, alles rings vergehet,
Denn die Zeit flieht,
Und die Sonne sieht,
Daß alles rings vergehet,
Denken, Reden, Schmerz und Wonne;
Und die wir zu Enkeln hatten
Schwanken wie bei Tag die Schatten,
Wie ein Dunst im Windeshauch.
Menschen waren wir ja auch,
Froh und traurig, so wie ihr,
Und nun sind wir leblos hier,
Sind nur Erde, wie ihr sehet.
Alles endet, was entstehet.
Alles, alles rings vergehet.

2

All ends that has beginning,
all, all around us dies,
for time is fleeting,
and the sun sees
that all around us dies,
thought, speech, pain and bliss;
and those who were our grandchildren
waver, as the shadows by day,
as haze in a breath of wind.
We, too, once were flesh and blood,
sad and happy, just as you,
and now we are lifeless here,
are but earth, as you can see.
All ends that has beginning,
all, all around us dies.

3
Fühlt meine Seele das ersehnte Licht
  von Gott,
Der sie erschuf? ist es der Strahl
Von andrer Schönheit aus dem
  Jammertal,
Der in mein Herz Erinnrung weckend
  bricht?

Ist es ein Klang, ein Traumgesicht,
Das Aug und Herz mir füllt mit
  einemmal
In unbegreiflich glühnder Qual,
Die mich zu Tränen bringt? ich weiß
  es nicht.

Was ich ersehne, fühle, was mich
  lenkt,
Ist nicht in mir: sag mir, wie ich's
  erwerbe?
Mir zeigt es wohl nur eines andren
  Huld;

Darein bin ich, seit ich dich sah,
  versenkt.
Mich treibt ein Ja und Nein, ein Süß
  und Herbe—
Daran sind, Herrin, deine Augen
  schuld.

3
Does my soul feel the longed-for light of
  God,
who made it? Is it a ray
of other beauty from the vale of
  tears
that breaks into my heart awakening
  memory?

Is it a sound, a dream vision
that all at once fills heart and
  eye
in inexplicably growing agony
that reduces me to tears? I know
  not.

What I long for, what I feel, what
  guides me
is not in me: how, tell me, shall I win
  it?
Only another's grace is like to show
  me;

In that am I, since seeing you,
  absorbed.
Yes and no is my impulse, sweetness,
  bitterness—
for that, mistress, your eyes are to
  blame.

*Drei Lieder der Ophelia | Ophelia's Three Songs*

WILLIAM SHAKESPEARE: from *Hamlet*

*Richard Strauss: op. 67, nos. 1–3, 1918–19*

1
Wie erkenn ich mein Treulieb
Vor andern nun?
An dem Muschelhut und Stab
Und den Sandalschuhn.

Er ist tot und lange hin,
Tot und hin, Fräulein!
Ihm zu Häupten grünes Gras,
Ihm zu Fuß ein Stein.
Oho!

Auf seinem Bahrtuch, weiß wie Schnee,
Viel liebe Blumen trauern.
Sie gehn zu Grabe naß, o weh!
Vor Liebesschauern.

2
Guten Morgen, 's ist Sankt Valentinstag,
So früh vor Sonnenschein.
Ich junge Maid am Fensterschlag
Will Euer Valentin sein.

1
How shall I know my true love
from others now?
By his cockle hat and staff
and his sandal shoes.

He is dead and long gone,
dead and gone, lady!
At his head green grass,
at his feet a stone.
O, ho!

On his pall-cloth white as snow,
many sweet flowers mourn.
Alas, to the grave they'll go wet,
with love's showers.

2
Good morning, it's St Valentine's Day,
so early before sunshine.
I, young maid at the window,
will be your Valentine.

Der junge Mann tut Hosen an,
Tät auf die Kammertür,
Ließ ein die Maid, die als Maid
Ging nimmermehr herfür.

Bei Sankt Niklas und Charitas!
Ein unverschämt Geschlecht!
Ein junger Mann tut's, wenn er kann,
Fürwahr, das ist nicht recht.
Sie sprach: Eh Ihr gescherzt mit mir,
Verspracht Ihr mich zu frein.
Ich bräch's auch nicht beim Sonnenlicht,
Wärst du nicht kommen herein.

3
Sie trugen ihn auf der Bahre bloß,
Leider, ach leider, den Liebsten!
Manche Träne fiel in des Grabes
    Schoß—
Fahr wohl, fahr wohl, meine Taube!

Mein junger frischer Hansel ist's,
Der mir gefällt—Und kommt er
    nimmermehr?
Er ist tot, o weh!
In dein Totbett geh,
Er kommt dir nimmermehr.

Sein Bart war weiß wie Schnee,
Sein Haupt wie Flachs dazu.
Er ist hin, er ist hin,
Kein Trauern bringt Gewinn:
Mit seiner Seele Ruh
Und mit allen Christenseelen!
Darum bet ich! Gott sei mit euch!

The young man put trousers on,
opened the chamber door,
let in the maid who as a maid
departed nevermore.

By St Nicholas and Charity,
a shameless breed!
A young man does it when he can,
for truth, that is not right.
She said: Before you trifled with me,
you promised me to wed.
I'd not by sunlight break my word
if you had not come in.

3
They carried him naked on his bier,
alas, alas, the dear one!
Many a tear in the grave's lap
    dropped,
farewell, farewell, my dove!

My young fresh Johnnie it is
I love—and will he come never
    more?
He is dead, oh woe!
To your deathbed go,
he will come to you never more.

His beard was white as snow,
and his head like flax.
He is gone, he is gone,
of mourning nothing comes;
to his soul peace,
and to all Christian souls!
For that I pray! God be with you!

*Drei Psalmen / Three Psalms*

Translated by MARTIN LUTHER

*Boris Blacher, 1943*

*Psalm 142*
Ich schreie zum Herrn mit meiner
    Stimme;
ich flehe zum Herrn mit meiner
    Stimme;
ich schütte meine Rede vor ihm aus
und zeige an vor ihm meine Not.
Wenn mein Geist in Ängsten ist,
so nimmst du dich meiner an.
Sie legen mir Stricke auf dem Wege,
    darauf ich gehe.
Schaue zur Rechten und siehe!
da will mich niemand kennen.
Ich kann nicht entfliehen;
niemand nimmt sich meiner Seele an.
Herr, zu dir schreie ich und sage:

*Psalm 142*
I cry with my voice to the
    Lord;
with my voice I beseech the
    Lord;
I pour out my speech before Him
and tell Him of my need.
When my spirit is in anguish,
You take my part.
They lay a snare for me on the path I
    walk.
Look to the right hand and behold:
there no one will acknowledge me.
I cannot fly;
no one cares for my soul.
Lord, to You do I cry and say:

Du bist meine Zuversicht, mein Teil
 im Lande der Lebendigen.
Merke auf meine Klage,
denn ich werde sehr geplagt;
errette mich von meinen Verfolgern,
denn sie sind mir zu mächtig.
Führe meine Seele aus dem Kerker,
daß ich danke deinem Namen.
Die Gerechten werden sich zu mir
 sammeln,
wenn du mir wohltust.

*Psalm 141*
Herr, ich rufe zu dir, eile zu mir;
vernimm meine Stimme, wenn ich dich
 anrufe.
Mein Gebet müsse vor dir taugen wie
 ein Rauchopfer,
mein Händeaufheben wie ein
 Abendopfer.
Herr, behüte meinen Mund und
 bewahre meine Lippen.
Neige mein Herz nicht auf etwas Böses,
ein gottlos Wesen zu führen mit den
 Übeltätern,
daß ich nicht esse von dem, was ihnen
 geliebt.
Der Gerechte schlage mich freundlich
 und strafe mich;
das wird mir so wohl tun wie Balsam auf
 meinem Haupt;
denn ich bete stets, daß sie mir nicht
 Schaden tun.
Ihre Führer müssen gestürzt werden
 über einen Fels;
so wird man dann meine Rede hören,
 daß sie lieblich sei.
Unsre Gebeine sind zerstreut bis zur
 Hölle,
wie wenn einer das Land pflügt und
 zerwühlt.
Denn auf dich, Herr, Herr, sehen
 meine Augen;
ich traue auf dich, verstoße meine Seele
 nicht.
Bewahre mich vor dem Stricke, den sie
 mir gelegt haben,
und vor der Falle der Übeltäter.
Die Gottlosen müssen in ihr eigen Netz
 fallen miteinander,
ich aber immer vorübergehen.

*Psalm 121*
Ich hebe meine Augen auf zu den
 Bergen,
von welchen mir Hilfe kommt.
Meine Hilfe kommt von dem Herrn,
der Himmel und Erde gemacht hat.
Er wird deinen Fuß nicht gleiten lassen,
und der dich behütet, schläft nicht.

You are my refuge, my portion in the
 land of the living.
Pay heed to my complaint,
for I am much tormented;
deliver me from my persecutors,
for they are too powerful for me.
Lead my soul forth from prison
that I may thank Your name.
The righteous will gather around
 me
if You do good to me.

*Psalm 141*
Lord, I call upon You, hasten to me;
give ear to my voice when I
 call.
My prayer let serve as an incense
 offering before You,
the raising of my hands—as an evening
 sacrifice.
Lord, guard my mouth and watch over
 my lips.
Incline not my heart to any evil,
to lead a godless life with the
 evil-doers,
that I should not eat of that which is
 pleasing to them.
Let the just man strike me in kindness
 and punish me;
that shall be as good to me as balsam
 upon my head;
for I pray continually that they should
 not harm me.
Their leaders must be hurled from a
 crag;
so shall people hear my speech that it
 be pleasing.
Our bones are scattered as far as
 hell,
as when land is ploughed and rooted
 up.
For my eyes look to You, Lord,
 Lord;
in You I trust, repulse not my
 soul.
Preserve me from the snare they have
 laid for me,
and from the trap of the evil-doers.
The godless must together fall into
 their own net,
but I always walk by.

*Psalm 121*
I lift up my eyes to the
 hills
from which help comes to me.
My help comes from the Lord
who made heaven and earth.
He will not let your foot slide
and he that keeps you, does not sleep.

Siehe, der Hüter Israels schläft noch
  schlummert nicht.
Der Herr behütet dich,
der Herr ist dein Schatten über deiner
  rechten Hand,
daß dich des Tages die Sonne nicht
  steche
noch der Mond des Nachts.
Der Herr behüte dich vor allem Übel,
er behüte deine Seele.
Der Herr behüte deinen Ausgang und
  Eingang
von nun an bis in Ewigkeit.

Behold, the keeper of Israel neither
  sleeps nor slumbers.
The Lord keeps you,
The Lord is your shadow upon your
  right hand,
that the sun not burn you by
  day
nor the moon by night.
May the Lord keep you from all evil,
may He keep your soul.
May the Lord keep your going out and
  coming in
from now until eternity.


## Du bist die Ruh | Repose You Are

FRIEDRICH RÜCKERT

*Franz Schubert: op. 59, no. 3, 1823*

Du bist die Ruh,
Der Friede mild,
Die Sehnsucht du,
Und was sie stillt.

You are repose,
and gentle peace,
longing you are,
and what quiets it.

Ich weihe dir
Voll Lust und Schmerz
Zur Wohnung hier
Mein Aug und Herz.

To you I dedicate,
full of joy and pain,
as a dwelling here,
my eye and heart.

Kehr ein bei mir
Und schließe du
Still hinter dir
Die Pforte zu.

Come, enter in
and close
softly behind you
the gate.

Treib andern Schmerz
Aus dieser Brust!
Voll sei dies Herz
Von deiner Lust.

Drive other pain
from this breast.
Full be this heart
of your joy.

Dies Augenzelt,
Von deinem Glanz
Allein erhellt,
O füll es ganz!

The temple of these eyes,
by your gleam
alone is lit,
oh fill it wholly!


## Du bist wie eine Blume | You Are Like a Flower

HEINRICH HEINE

*Franz Liszt, ca. 1840; Robert Schumann: op. 25 (Myrten), no. 24, 1840;*
*Hugo Wolf, 1876*

Du bist wie eine Blume
So hold und schön und rein;
Ich schau dich an, und Wehmut
Schleicht mir ins Herz hinein.

You are like a flower,
so sweet and fair and pure;
at you I gaze, and melancholy
steals into my heart.

Mir ist, als ob ich die Hände
Aufs Haupt dir legen sollt,
Betend, daß Gott dich erhalte
So rein und schön und hold.

I feel as if my hands
I ought to lay upon your head,
praying that God preserve you
so pure and fair and sweet.

## Du liebst mich nicht / You Love Me Not

AUGUST VON PLATEN

*Franz Schubert: op. 59, no. 1, 1822*

Mein Herz ist zerrissen, du liebst mich
   nicht!
Wiewohl ich dir flehend und werbend
   erschien,
Und liebebeflissen, du liebst mich
   nicht!
Du hast es gesprochen, mit Worten
   gesagt,
Mit allzu gewissen, du liebst mich
   nicht!
So soll ich die Sterne, so soll ich den
   Mond,
Die Sonne vermissen, du liebst mich
   nicht!
Was blüht mir die Rose, was blüht der
   Jasmin,
Was blühn die Narzissen, du liebst
   mich nicht!

My heart is broken, you love me
   not!
Though I have come beseeching and
   wooing,
and ardently zealous, you love me
   not!
You have said it, put it into
   words,
words all too clear, you love me
   not!
So the stars, so the
   moon,
So the sun shall I miss, you love me
   not!
What to me the blooming of rose, of
   jasmine,
of narcissus, you love me
   not!

## Du meines Herzens Krönelein / You the Coronet of My Heart

FELIX DAHN

*Max Reger: op. 76, no. 1, 1903–04; Richard Strauss: op. 21, no. 2, 1887–88*

Du meines Herzens Krönelein,
Du bist von lautrem Golde,
Wenn andere daneben sein,
Dann bist du noch viel holde.

You the coronet of my heart,
of pure gold you are,
and when others stand beside you,
then you are more charming still.

Die andern tun so gern gescheit,
Du bist gar sanft und stille,
Daß jedes Herz sich dein erfreut,
Dein Glück ist's, nicht dein Wille.

The others like to seem clever,
gentle and quiet you are,
that in you every heart rejoices,
is your happiness, not your will.

Die andern suchen Lieb und Gunst
Mit tausend falschen Worten,
Du ohne Mund und Augenkunst
Bist wert an allen Orten.

The others seek love and favour
with a thousand false words;
you, with no art of tongue, of eyes,
are esteemed in every place.

Du bist als wie die Ros im Wald,
Sie weiß nichts von ihrer Blüte,
Doch jedem, der vorüberwallt,
Erfreut sie das Gemüte.

You are like the rose in the forest,
knowing nothing of its bloom,
but of everyone who pasees,
gladdening the mind.

## Du sprichst, daß ich mich täuschte | You Say I Was in Error

AUGUST VON PLATEN

*Johannes Brahms: op. 32, no. 6, 1864*

Du sprichst, daß ich mich täuschte,
Beschworst es hoch und hehr,
Ich weiß ja doch, du liebtest,
Allein du liebst nicht mehr!

Dein schönes Auge brannte,
Die Küsse brannten sehr,
Du liebtest mich, bekenn es,
Allein du liebst nicht mehr!

Ich zähle nicht auf neue,
Getreue Wiederkehr.
Gesteh nur, daß du liebtest,
Und liebe mich nicht mehr!

You say I was in error,
by all that is holy you swore,
but I know that you did love,
but do not any more.

Your beautiful eyes smouldered,
your kisses were as fire,
you did love me, admit it,
but you do not any more.

I do not count on any fresh
and faithful return to me.
Just own, that you did love,
and do not any more.

## Edward | Edward

Scottish ballad, translated by JOHANN GOTTFRIED HERDER

*Johannes Brahms: op. 75, no 1 (duet); Carl Loewe: op. 1, no. 1, 1818;
Franz Schubert, 1827; Peter Ilych Tchaikovsky: op. 46 (6 Duets), 1880;*

Dein Schwert, wie ist's von Blut so
    rot?
Edward, Edward!
Dein Schwert, wie ist's von Blut so rot?
    —Oh!
O ich hab geschlagen meinen Geier tot,
Mutter, Mutter!
O ich hab geschlagen meinen Geier tot,
Und keinen hab ich wie er—Oh!

Deins Geiers Blut ist nicht so rot,
Edward, Edward!
Deins Geiers Blut ist nicht so rot,
Mein Sohn, bekenn mir frei—Oh!
O ich hab geschlagen mein Rotroß tot,
Mutter, Mutter!
O ich hab geschlagen mein Rotroß tot,
Und's war so stolz und treu—Oh!

Dein Roß war alt und hast's nicht
    not,
Edward, Edward!
Dein Roß war alt und hast's nicht
    not,
Dich drückt ein andrer Schmerz—Oh!
O ich hab geschlagen mein' Vater tot,
Mutter, Mutter!
O ich hab geschlagen meinen Vater tot,
Und weh, weh ist mein Herz—Oh!

Your sword, why is it with blood so
    red?
Edward, Edward!
Your sword, why is it with blood so
    red?—Oh!
O I have struck my falcon dead,
mother, mother!
O I have struck my falcon dead,
and none have I like him—Oh!

Your falcon's blood is not so red,
Edward, Edward!
Your falcon's blood is not so red,
my son, confess to me freely—Oh!
O I have struck my chestnut dead,
mother, mother!
O I have struck my chestnut dead,
and he was so proud and true—Oh!

Your horse was old and you need him
    not,
Edward, Edward!
Your horse was old and you need him
    not,
a different sorrow afflicts you—Oh!
O I have struck my father dead,
mother, mother!
O I have struck my father dead,
and sore, sore is my heart—Oh!

|  |  |
|---|---|
| Und was für Buße willt du nun tun? | And what penance will you now do? |
| Edward, Edward! | Edward, Edward! |
| Und was für Buße willt du nun tun? | And what penance will you now do? |
| Mein Sohn, bekenn mir mehr—Oh! | My son, confess to me more—Oh! |
| Auf Erden soll mein Fuß nicht ruhn, | On earth my foot shall never rest, |
| Mutter, Mutter! | mother, mother! |
| Auf Erden soll mein Fuß nicht ruhn, | On earth my foot shall never rest, |
| Will gehn fern übers Meer—Oh! | I shall go far over the sea—Oh! |

Und was soll werden dein Hof und Hall?
Edward, Edward!
Und was soll werden dein Hof und Hall?
So herrlich sonst und schön—Oh!
Ich laß es stehn, bis es sink und fall,
Mutter, Mutter!
Ich laß es stehn, bis es sink und fall,
Mag nie es wiedersehn—Oh!

And what shall become of house and home?
Edward, Edward!
And what shall become of house and home?
So lordly and fair till now—Oh!
I'll let it stand till it sink and fall,
mother, mother!
I'll let it stand till it sink and fall,
I want never to see it again—Oh!

Und was soll werden dein Weib und Kind?
Edward, Edward!
Und was soll werden dein Weib und Kind,
Wenn du gehst übers Meer?—Oh!
Die Welt ist groß, laß sie betteln drin,
Mutter, Mutter!
Die Welt ist groß, laß sie betteln drin,
Ich seh sie nimmermehr—Oh!

And what shall become of wife and child?
Edward, Edward!
And what shall become of wife and child
when you go over the sea?—Oh!
The world is wide, let them beg there,
mother, mother!
The world is wide, let them beg there,
I shall see them nevermore—Oh!

Und was willt du lassen deiner Mutter teur?
Edward, Edward!
Und was willt du lassen deiner Mutter teur?
Mein Sohn, sag mir—Oh!
Fluch will ich euch lassen und höllisch Feuer,
Mutter, Mutter!
Fluch will ich euch lassen und höllisch Feuer,
Denn Ihr, Ihr rietet's mir!—Oh!

And what will you leave your mother dear?
Edward, Edward!
And what will you leave your mother dear?
Tell me that, my son—Oh!
To curses I'll leave you and hell fire,
mother, mother!
To curses I'll leave you and hell fire,
for you, you counselled me to it—Oh!

## Ein Drängen | An Urgency

STEFAN ZWEIG

*Joseph Marx: Lieder, second series, no. 24; Max Reger: op. 97, no. 3, 1906*

Ein Drängen ist in meinem Herzen.
  Ein Beben
Nach einem großen, segnenden Erleben,
Nach einer Liebe, die die Seele weitet
Und jede fremde Regung niederstreitet!

In my heart—an urgency. A
  trembling
to be blessed by some great experience,
for a love to open wide the soul
and fight down any alien stirring!

Ich harre Tage, Stunden, lange
 Wochen,
Mein Herz bleibt stumm, die Worte
 ungesprochen,
In müde Lieder flüchtet sich mein
 Sehnen,
Und heiße Nächte trinken meine
 Tränen.

Days, hours, long weeks I
 wait,
my heart stays dumb, the words
 unspoken,
into weary songs my longing
 flees,
and ardent nights drink in my
 tears.


## Ein Fichtenbaum steht einsam | Lonely Stands a Spruce Tree

HEINRICH HEINE

*Robert Franz: op. 16, no. 3; Franz Liszt, 1855; Joseph Marx, 1908*

Ein Fichtenbaum steht einsam
Im Norden auf kahler Höh'.
Ihn schläfert; mit weißer Decke
Umhüllen ihn Eis und Schnee.

Lonely stands a spruce tree
on a naked northern height,
and drowses. In a white blanket
it is wrapped by ice and snow.

Er träumt von einer Palme,
Die, fern im Morgenland,
Einsam und schweigend trauert
Auf brennender Felsenwand.

Of a palm tree it is dreaming,
which, in the distant orient,
grieves, silent and lonely,
on a blazing rocky wall.


## Ein Sonett | A Sonnet

A French sonnet of the 13th century, translated by JOHANN GOTTFRIED HERDER

*Johannes Brahms: op. 14, no. 4, 1858; Carl Friedrich Zelter, 1802*

Ach, könnt' ich, könnte vergessen sie,
Ihr schönes, liebes, liebliches Wesen,
Den Blick, die freundliche Lippe, die!
Vielleicht ich möchte genesen!
Doch ach, mein Herz, mein Herz kann
 es nie!
Und doch ist's Wahnsinn, zu hoffen sie!
Und um sie schweben
Gibt Mut und Leben,
Zu weichen nie!—
Und dann, wie kann ich vergessen sie,
Ihr schönes, liebes liebliches Wesen,
Den Blick, die freundliche Lippe, die!
Viel lieber nimmer genesen!

Ah, would I could forget her,
her fine, loving, lovely nature,
her look, her friendly lips, ah, them!
I might perhaps be healed!
Yet ah, my heart, my heart can
 never!
And yet to hope for her is madness!
And to hover around her
gives zest and courage
to waver never!—
And then, how can I forget her,
her fine, loving, lovely nature,
her look, her friendly lips, ah, them!
Much better never to be healed!


## Ein Stündlein wohl vor Tag | An Hour before Day

EDUARD MÖRIKE

*Robert Franz: op. 28, no. 2; Hugo Wolf, 1888*

Derweil ich schlafend lag,
Ein Stündlein wohl vor Tag,
Sang vor dem Fenster auf dem Baum
Ein Schwälblein mir, ich hört es kaum,
Ein Stündlein wohl vor Tag.

As I lay sleeping,
an hour before day,
by the window, on the tree, sang
for me a swallow, I could scarcely hear,
an hour before day.

»Hör an, was ich dir sag,
Dein Schätzlein ich verklag:
Derweil ich dieses singen tu,
Herzt er ein Lieb in guter Ruh,
Ein Stündlein wohl vor Tag.«

'Hark well to what I say,
of your sweetheart I complain:
while I sing this,
he clasps a love in sweet repose,
an hour before day.'

O weh! nicht weiter sag!
O still! nichts hören mag!
Flieg ab! flieg ab von meinem Baum!
Ach, Lieb und Treu ist wie ein Traum

Oh, woe! Say no more.
Oh, quiet! Nothing do I wish to hear.
Fly away, away from my tree.
Ah, love and faithfulness are like a
  dream,

Ein Stündlein wohl vor Tag!

an hour before day!

## Ein Tagewerk / One Day's Work

GOTTFRIED KELLER

*Othmar Schoeck: op. 55, no. 23, 1941-43*

I

Vom Lager stand ich mit dem Frühlicht
  auf
Und nahm hinaus ins Freie meinen
  Lauf,
Wo duftiggrau die Morgendämmrung
  lag,
Umflorend noch den rosenroten Tag;
Mich einmal satt zu gehn in Busch und
  Feldern
Vom Morgen früh bis in die späte
  Nacht,
Und auch ein Lied zu holen in den
  Wäldern,
Hatt ich zum festen Vorsatz mir
  gemacht.

I

At first light from my couch I
  rose,
into the open made my
  way,
where the dawn lay, grey and
  fragrant,
still veiling the rose-red day;
to walk my fill in wood and
  field
from early morning until late at
  night,
and from the woods to draw a
  song—
that had become my firm
  intent.

Rein war der Himmel, bald zum Tag
  erhellt,
Der volle Lebenspuls schlug durch die
  Welt;
Die Lüfte wehten und der Vogel sang,
Die Eichen wuchsen und die Quelle
  sprang.
Die Blumen blühten und die Früchte
  reiften,
Ein jeglich Gras tat seinen Atemzug;
Die Berge standen und die Wolken
  schweiften
In gleicher Luft, die meinen Odem trug.

Pure the sky, soon brightening into
  day,
life's full pulse was beating through the
  world,
breezes blew, the birds sang,
oak trees grew and springs were
  gushing,
flowers were blossoming, fruits
  ripening,
every grassy blade was drawing breath;
the mountains stood, and clouds
  drifted
in that same air which bore my breath.

Ich schlenderte den lieben Tag entlang,
Im Herzen regte sich der Hochgesang;
Es brach sich Bahn der Wachtel heller
  Schlag,
Jedoch mein Lied—es rang sich nicht
  zu Tag.
Der Mittag kam, ich lag an Silberflüssen,
Die Sonne sucht ich in der klaren
  Flut

The livelong day I tramped my way,
high exultation stirring in my heart;
the quail's loud song was breaking
  forth,
my song, however, broke not
  through.
Midday came, by silver streams I lay,
and in the crystal floods I sought the
  sun

Und durfte nicht von Angesicht sie
  grüßen,
Der ich allein in all dem Drang
  geruht.

Die Sonne sank und ließ die Welt der
  Ruh,
Die Abendnebel gingen ab und zu;
Ich lag auf Bergeshöhen matt und
  müd,
Tief in der Brust das ungesungne Lied.
Da nickten, spottend mein, die
  schwanken Tannen,
Auch höhnend sah das niedre Moos
  empor
Mit seinen Würmern, die geschäftig
  spannen,
Und lachend brach das Firmament
  hervor.

Vom Osten wehte frisch und voll der
  Wind:
»Was suchst du hier, du müßig
  Menschenkind,
Du stumme Pfeife in dem Orgelchor,
Schlemihl, der träumend Raum und
  Zeit verlor?
Dir ward das Leichteste, das Lied,
  gegeben,
Das, selbst sich bauend, aus der Kehle
  bricht;
Du aber legst dein unbeholfen Leben
Wie einen Stein ihm auf den Weg zum
  Licht!«

Sprach so der Wind? O nein, so sprach
  der Schmerz,
Der mir wie Ketten hing ums dunkle
  Herz!
Ein fremder Körper ohne Form und
  Schall,
So, deuchte mir, lag ich im regen
  All.
Und Luft und Tannen, Berge, Moos
  und Sterne,
Sie schlangen lächelnd ihren weiten
  Kranz;
Wie an der Insel sich das Meer, das
  ferne,
Brach sich an mir ihr friedlich milder
  Glanz.

2
Aber ein kleiner goldener Stern
Sang und klang mir in die Ohren:
»Tröste dich nur, dein Lied ist fern,
Fern bei uns und nicht verloren!

Findest du nicht oft einen Klang,
Wie zu früh herüber geklungen?

and did not dare to greet her to her
  face,
I who in all that urgency, alone took
  rest.

The sun set and left the world to
  peace,
the mists of evening came and went;
weary and tired, on a mountain top I
  lay,
my unsung song deep in my breast.
The pliant firs then nodded, mocking
  me,
and scornfully the nether moss gazed
  up
with its worms who busily did
  spin,
and laughingly the firmament burst
  forth.

From the east the wind blew, full and
  fresh:
'What, idle son of man, do you seek
  here,
you, the organ's one unsounding pipe,
a Schlemihl dreaming time and space
  away?
To you the easiest was given,
  song
that, self-forming, breaks forth
  from the throat;
but you have set your ungainly life
like a stone upon its path to
  light!'

Spoke so the wind? No, so spoke the
  pain
hanging like chains about my gloomy
  heart!
A different body, lacking shape and
  sound,
in the industrious universe I seemed to
  lie.
And breeze and firs, mountains, moss
  and stars
wove smilingly their extensive
  garland;
and as the distant sea upon the
  isle,
so broke upon me their peacefully mild
  gleam.

2
But one tiny golden star
sang and rang in my ears:
'Be consoled, your song is far,
far away, with us, not lost!

'Do you not often find one note
reaches you as if too soon?

| | |
|---|---|
| Also hat sich heut dein Sang<br>Heimlich zu uns hinüber geschwungen! | So, today, has your song<br>risen secretly to us. |
| Dort, im donnernden<br>  Weltgesang,<br>Wirst du ein leises Lied erkennen,<br>Das dir, wie fernster Glockenklang,<br>Diesen Sommertag wird nennen. | 'There, in the world's thunderous<br>  melody,<br>you will recognize one gentle song<br>that, like most distant bells,<br>shall name for you this summer day. |
| Denn die Ewigkeit ist nur<br>Hin und her ein tönendes Weben;<br>Vorwärts, rückwärts wird die Spur<br>Deiner Schritte klingend erbeben, | 'For eternity is but<br>a resonant stirring here and there;<br>forwards, backwards will the traces<br>of your steps reverberate, |
| Deiner Schritte durch das All,<br>Bis, wie eine singende Schlange,<br>Einst dein Leben den vollen Schall<br>Findet im Zusammenhange.« | 'of your steps through the universe,<br>until, like a singing serpent,<br>one day, your life its full sound<br>in context shall discover.' |

## Eine gute, gute Nacht | A Good, Good, Night

GEORG FRIEDRICH DAUMER

*Johannes Brahms: op. 59, no. 6, 1873*

| | |
|---|---|
| Eine gute, gute Nacht<br>Pflegst du mir zu sagen,<br>Über dieses eitle Wort,<br>O wie muß ich klagen! | A good, good night<br>you were wont to bid me;<br>at those vain words,<br>oh, how I must protest! |
| Daß du meiner Seele Glut<br>Nicht so grausam nährtest,<br>Eine gute, gute Nacht,<br>Daß du sie gewährtest. | Oh that you my soul's fire<br>did not so cruelly nourish!<br>A good, good night—<br>oh that you should grant it! |

## Eine sehr gewöhnliche Geschichte | An Old, Old Story

CHRISTIAN FELIX WEISSE

*Joseph Haydn, 1781*

| | |
|---|---|
| Philint stand jüngst vor Babets Tür<br>und klopft' und rief: Ist niemand hier?<br>Ich bin Philint, laß mich hinein!<br>Sie kam und sprach: Nein, nein! | Lately was Philint at Babet's door,<br>knocking, calling: Is no one here?<br>It's me, Philint, let me in!<br>She came and said: No, no! |
| Er seufzt' und bat recht jämmerlich.<br>Nein, sagte sie, ich fürchte dich!<br>Es ist schon Nacht, ich bin allein:<br>Philint, es kann nicht sein! | Sighing, most wretchedly he pleaded.<br>No, she said, you alarm me!<br>It is night, I am alone:<br>Philint, this cannot be! |
| Bekümmert will er wieder gehn,<br>da hört er schnell den Schlüssel drehn.<br>Er hört: Auf einen Augenblick,<br>doch geh auch gleich zurück! | Grieved, he is about to go,<br>but hears the key turned quickly.<br>He hears: For one brief instant come,<br>then back you go again! |

| | |
|---|---|
| Die Nachbarn plagt die Neugier sehr; | Curiosity plagued the neighbours sore; |
| sie warteten der Wiederkehr. | they waited for him to reappear. |
| Er kam auch, doch erst morgens früh. | And come he did, but at early morn. |
| Ei, ei, wie lachten sie! | Oh, oh, and how they did laugh! |


### Einerlei | One and the Same

ACHIM VON ARNIM

*Richard Strauss: op. 69, no. 3, 1918–19*

| | |
|---|---|
| Ihr Mund ist stets derselbe, | Her mouth is the same always, |
| sein Kuß mir immer neu | its kiss is ever new, |
| ihr Auge noch dasselbe, | still the same her eyes are, |
| sein freier Blick mir treu; | their frank gaze true to me; |
| | |
| O du liebes Einerlei, | O you sweet one-and-the-same, |
| wie wird aus dir so mancherlei! | the diversity that comes of you! |


### Eingelegte Ruder | Shipped Oars

CONRAD FERDINAND MEYER

*Hans Pfitzner: op. 32, no. 3, 1923*

| | |
|---|---|
| Meine eingelegten Ruder triefen, | My shipped oars drip, |
| Tropfen fallen langsam in die Tiefen. | slowly the drops drip into the depths. |
| | |
| Nichts, das mich verdroß! Nichts, das mich freute! | Nothing there was to grieve me! Or to gladden! |
| Niederrinnt ein schmerzenloses Heute! | A today devoid of pain is trickling down! |
| | |
| Unter mir—ach, aus dem Licht verschwunden— | Beneath me—ah, vanished from the light— |
| träumen schon die schönern meiner Stunden. | the finer of my hours already dream. |
| | |
| Aus der blauen Tiefe ruft das Gestern: | Out of the blue deep cries yesterday: |
| Sind im Licht noch manche meiner Schwestern? | Are in the light still many of my sisters? |


### Einsamkeit | Solitude

JOHANN WOLFGANG GOETHE

*Max Reger: op. 75, no. 18, 1903; Winfried Zillig, ed. 1960*

| | |
|---|---|
| Die ihr Felsen und Bäume bewohnt, o heilsame Nymphen, | O wholesome nymphs who inhabit rocks and trees, |
| Gebet jeglichem gern, was er im stillen begehrt! | to each give gladly what he silently desires! |
| | |
| Schaffet dem Traurigen Trost, dem Zweifelhaften Belehrung | Solace bring to the sad, to the uncertain—counsel, |
| Und dem Liebenden gönnt, daß ihm begegne sein Glück. | and to the lover grant that happiness be his. |

Denn euch gaben die Götter, was sie
den Menschen versagten,
Jeglichem, der euch vertraut, tröstlich
und hilfreich zu sein.

For the gods gave you what to men
they denied:
to be, to each who trusts you, aid and
comfort.


## Elfenlied | Elf-song

EDUARD MÖRIKE

*Hugo Wolf, 1888*

Bei Nacht im Dorf der Wächter rief:
»Elfe!«
Ein ganz kleines Elfchen im Walde
schlief—wohl um die Elfe!—
Und meint, es rief ihm aus dem Tal
Bei seinem Namen die
Nachtigall,
Oder Silpelit hätt ihm gerufen.
Reibt sich der Elf die Augen aus,
Begibt sich vor sein Schneckenhaus
Und ist als wie ein trunken Mann,
Sein Schläflein war nicht voll getan,
Und humpelt also tippe tapp
Durchs Haselholz ins Tal hinab,
Schlupft an der Mauer hin so dicht,
Da sitzt der Glühwurm, Licht an
Licht.
»Was sind das helle Fensterlein?
Da drin wird eine Hochzeit sein:
Die Kleinen sitzen beim Mahle
Und treiben's in dem Saale;
Da guck ich wohl ein wenig 'nein!«
—Pfui, stößt den Kopf an harten Stein!
Elfe, gelt, du hast genug?
Guckuck! Guckuck!

The village watch cried out at night
'Eleven!'
An elfin elf asleep in the wood, at
eleven,
thinks that, from the valley,
the nightingale is calling him by
name,
or Silpelit summoning him.
The elf rubs his eyes,
ventures from his snail-shell home,
and is like a drunken man—
not having slept his fill—
and hobbles hobble-hobble
down through the hazels to the valley,
keeping ever so close to the wall
where the glow-worms sit, light by
light.
'What bright windows are those?
Must be a wedding going on there,
with the little ones sitting at the table
and having fun in the ballroom—
I'll just take a peep!'
—Shame, he bangs his head on stone!
Elf, don't you think you've had enough?
Cuckoo! Cuckoo!


## Elvershöh | Elves' Hill

Translated from the Danish by JOHANN GOTTFRIED HERDER

*Carl Loewe: op. 3, no. 2, ed. 1825*

Ich legte mein Haupt auf Elvershöh,
Mein' Augen begannen zu sinken,
Da kamen gegangen zwei Jungfrau'n
schön,
Die täten mir lieblich winken.

On Elves' Hill my head I laid,
my eyes began to close,
two lovely maids came walking
by,
and prettily did wave.

Die eine, die strich mein weißes Kinn,
Die zweite lispelt' ins Ohr mir:
»Steh auf, du muntrer Jüngling, auf!
Erheb', erhebe den Tanz hier!

One fondled my white chin,
one whispered in my ear:
'Merry young man, arise, arise,
let there be dancing here!

Steh auf, du muntrer Jüngling, auf!
Erheb', erhebe den Tanz hier!
Meine Jungfrau'n soll'n dir Lieder
singen,
Die schönsten Lieder zu hören.«

'Merry young man, arise, arise!
Let there be dancing here!
My maidens shall sing songs to
you,
the fairest there are to hear.'

Die eine begann zu singen ein Lied,
Die schönste aller Schönen;
Der brausende Strom, er floß nicht
    mehr
Und horcht' den süßen Tönen.

Der brausende Strom, er floß nicht
    mehr,
Stand still und horchte fühlend,
Die Fischlein schwammen in heller Flut,
Mit ihren Feinden spielend.

Die Fischlein all' in heller Flut,
Sie scherzten auf und nieder;
Die Vöglein all' im grünen Wald,
Sie hüpften, zirpten Lieder.

»Hör' an, du muntrer Jüngling, hör' an!
Willst du hier bei uns bleiben?
Wir wollen dich lehren das Runenbuch
Und Zaubereien schreiben.

Ich will dich lehren, den wilden Bär
Zu binden mit Wort und Zeichen;
Der Drache, der ruht auf rotem Gold,
Soll schnell dir fliehn und weichen.«

Sie tanzten hin, sie tanzten
    her;
Zu buhlen ihr Herz begehrt'.
Der muntre Jüngling, er saß da,
Gestützet auf sein Schwert.

»Hör' an, du muntrer Jüngling, hör' an!
Willst du nicht mit uns sprechen,
So reißen wir dir mit Messer und
    Schwert
Das Herz aus, uns zu rächen.«

Und da, mein gutes, gutes Glück!
Der Hahn fing an zu kräh'n.
Ich wär' sonst blieben auf Elvershöh,
Bei Elvers Jungfrau'n schön.

Drum rat' ich jedem Jüngling,
Der zieht nach Hofe fein,
Er setze sich nicht auf Elvershöh,
Allda zu schlummern ein!

One began to sing a song,
fairest of fair was she;
the noisy torrent ceased to
    flow
and harked to the melody.

The noisy torrent ceased to
    flow,
stood still and listened, moved,
tiny fish swam in the bright flood
and sported with their foes.

The tiny fish in their bright flood
went jesting up and down;
the tiny birds in their green wood,
chirruped songs and hopped around.

'Give ear, give ear, merry young man,
will you not with us stay?
The Book of Runes we'll teach you,
the art of writing spells.

'The wild bear will I teach you
to bind with word and sign;
the dragon that rests upon red gold,
shall before you turn and flee.'

Here they danced and there they
    danced,
their hearts for dalliance yearned.
The merry young man stayed sitting,
supported on his sword.

'Give ear, give ear, merry young man,
for if to us no word you'll say,
we, with knife and sword, will
    rip
your heart out as revenge.'

At which, to my good fortune,
the cock began to crow!
Or I had remained on Elves' Hill,
with the elf maidens fair.

For which I advise all young men,
who make their way to court,
not to sit upon Elves' Hill,
nor there to fall asleep!

## Epiphanias / Epiphany

JOHANN WOLFGANG GOETHE

*Ernst Pepping, 1946; Hugo Wolf, 1888*

Die heilgen drei König' mit ihrem
    Stern,
Sie essen, sie trinken, und bezahlen
    nicht gern;
Sie essen gern, sie trinken gern,
Sie essen, trinken, und bezahlen nicht
    gern.

The Three Wise Men complete with
    star,
they eat, drink and are loath to
    pay;
gladly they eat, gladly they drink,
they eat, drink and are loath to
    pay.

| | |
|---|---|
| Die heilgen drei König' sind kommen allhier, | The Three Wise Men here are come, |
| Es sind ihrer drei und sind nicht ihrer vier; | three in number, and not four, |
| Und wenn zu dreien der vierte wär, | and if to three a fourth there were, |
| So wär ein heilger drei König mehr. | the Three Wise Men would be one more. |
| | |
| Ich erster bin der weiß' und auch der schön', | I, the first, am the white, the handsome, |
| Bei Tage solltet ihr erst mich sehn! | and by day you should behold me! |
| Doch ach, mit allen Spezerein | But alas, for all these spices, I |
| Werd ich sein Tag kein Mädchen mir erfrein. | will woo no maid till the day I die. |
| | |
| Ich aber bin der braun' und bin der lang', | But I am the brown and I am the tall, |
| Bekannt bei Weibern wohl und bei Gesang. | well known to women, and to song. |
| Ich bringe Gold statt Spezerein, | Gold I bring instead of spice, |
| Da werd ich überall willkommen sein. | and so shall be welcomed everywhere. |
| | |
| Ich endlich bin der schwarz' und bin der klein' | Last, I am the black and I am the small, |
| Und mag auch wohl einmal recht lustig sein. | and I have a mind to be right merry. |
| Ich esse gern, ich trinke gern, | Gladly I eat, gladly I drink, |
| Ich esse, trinke und bedanke mich gern. | gladly I eat, drink and say thank you. |
| | |
| Die heilgen drei König' sind wohlgesinnt, | The Three Wise Men are kindly inclined, |
| Sie suchen die Mutter und das Kind; | they seek the mother and the child; |
| Der Joseph fromm sitzt auch dabei, | Joseph too sits devoutly by, |
| Der Ochs und Esel liegen auf der Streu. | the ox and the ass lie on the straw. |
| | |
| Wir bringen Myrrhen, wir bringen Gold, | We bring myrrh, we bring gold, |
| Dem Weihrauch sind die Damen hold; | the frankincense the ladies like; |
| Und haben wir Wein von gutem Gewächs, | and when we have wine of goodly growth, |
| So trinken wir drei so gut als ihrer sechs. | we drink enough, we three, for six. |
| | |
| Da wir nun hier schöne Herrn und Fraun, | And seeing here fine ladies and men, |
| Aber keine Ochsen und Esel schaun, | but oxen and asses seeing none, |
| So sind wir nicht am rechten Ort | so we've reached the wrong place, |
| Und ziehen unseres Weges weiter fort. | and shall go futher on our way. |

## Er ist's | Spring it is . . .

EDUARD MÖRIKE

*Robert Schumann: op. 79, no. 24, 1849; Hugo Wolf, 1888*

| | |
|---|---|
| Frühling läßt sein blaues Band | Spring lets its blue ribbon |
| Wieder flattern durch die Lüfte; | flutter once more in the breeze; |
| Süße, wohlbekannte Düfte | sweet, familiar fragrance |
| Streifen ahnungsvoll das Land. | drifts portentous through the land. |

Veilchen träumen schon,
Wollen balde kommen.
Horch, von fern ein leiser Harfenton!
Frühling, ja du bists!
Dich hab ich vernommen!

Violets are dreaming,
soon will be here.
Hark, softly, from afar, a harp!
Yes, Spring, it is you!
I have caught your sound!

## Erlafsee | Erlaf Lake

JOHANN MAYRHOFER

*Franz Schubert: op. 8, no. 3, 1817*

Mir ist so wohl, so weh'
Am stillen Erlafsee:
Heilig Schweigen in Fichtenzweigen,
Regungslos der blaue Schoß,
Nur der Wolken Schatten flieh'n
Überm dunklen Spiegel hin,
Frische Winde kräuseln linde
Das Gewässer
Und der Sonne güld'ne Krone flimmert
  blässer.
Mir ist so wohl, so weh'
Am stillen Erlafsee.

So glad I feel, so sad,
by quiet Erlaf lake:
holy the spruce boughs' silence,
motionless the blue lap,
only cloud shadows flit
over the dark mirror,
fresh winds crinkle
the water
and paler glitters the sun's gold
  crown.
So glad I feel, so sad,
by quiet Erlaf lake.

## Erlkönig | Erl-king

JOHANN WOLFGANG GOETHE

*Carl Loewe: op. 1, no. 3, 1818; Franz Schubert: op. 1, 1815*

Wer reitet so spät durch Nacht und
  Wind?
Es ist der Vater mit seinem Kind;
Er hat den Knaben wohl in dem Arm,
Er faßt ihn sicher, er hält ihn warm.

Who rides so late through night and
  wind?
It is the father with his child;
he has his arm about the boy,
he holds him safe, he keeps him warm.

»Mein Sohn, was birgst du so bang dein
  Gesicht?«—
»Siehst, Vater, du den Erlkönig nicht?
Den Erlenkönig mit Kron und
  Schweif?«—
»Mein Sohn, es ist ein
  Nebelstreif.«—

'My son—why hide your face in such
  fear?'—
'Father—the Erl-king, don't you see?
The Erl-king in crown and
  robes?'—
'My son, it is a streak of
  mist.'—

›Du liebes Kind, komm, geh mit mir!
Gar schöne Spiele spiel ich mit dir;
Manch bunte Blumen sind an dem
  Strand,
Meine Mutter hat manch gülden
  Gewand.‹

'Dear child, come, come go with me,
wonderful games will I play with you;
many fair flowers are on the
  shore,
my mother has many a garment of
  gold.'

»Mein Vater, mein Vater, und hörest
  du nicht,
Was Erlenkönig mir leise
  verspricht?«—

'My father, my father, don't·you
  hear
what the Erl-king softly promises
  me?'—

»Sei ruhig, bleibe ruhig, mein Kind:
In dürren Blättern säuselt der
    Wind.«—

›Willst, feiner Knabe, du mit mir gehn?
Meine Töchter sollen dich warten
    schön;
Meine Töchter führen den nächtlichen
    Reihn
Und wiegen und tanzen und singen
    dich ein.‹

»Mein Vater, mein Vater, und siehst du
    nicht dort
Erlkönigs Töchter am düstern
    Ort?«—
»Mein Sohn, mein Sohn, ich seh es
    genau:
Es scheinen die alten Weiden so
    grau.«—

›Ich liebe dich, mich reizt deine
    schöne Gestalt;
Und bist du nicht willig, so brauch ich
    Gewalt.‹
»Mein Vater, mein Vater, jetzt faßt er
    mich an!
Erlkönig hat mir ein Leids getan!«—

Dem Vater grausets, er reitet geschwind,
Er hält in Armen das ächzende Kind,
Erreicht den Hof mit Mühe und Not:
In seinen Armen das Kind war tot.

'Be quiet, stay quiet, my child:
the rustle it is of dry leaves in the
    wind.'—

'Will you, fine boy, come with me?
My daughters shall take good care of
    you;
my daughters lead our nightly
    dance,
they'll rock and dance and sing you to
    sleep.'

'My father, my father, don't you
    see
the Erl-king's daughters there in the
    gloom?'—
'My son, my son, I see very
    well:
it is the old willows gleaming so
    grey.'—

'I love you. Your beauty excites
    me;
if you're not willing, I'll take you by
    force.'
'My father, my father, he seizes
    me!
The Erl-king has hurt me . . .'—

The father shudders, swiftly he rides,
the moaning child he holds in his arms;
he gains the manor in great distress;
in his arms the child was dead.

## Erschaffen und Beleben / Creation and Animation

JOHANN WOLFGANG GOETHE: from *West-östlicher Divan*, 'Book of the Minstrel'

*Richard Strauss: op. 87, no. 2, 1922–35; Hugo Wolf, 1889*

Hans Adam war ein Erdenkloß,
Den Gott zum Menschen machte;
Doch bracht er aus der Mutter
    Schoß
Noch vieles Ungeschlachte.

Die Elohim zur Nas hinein
Den besten Geist ihm bliesen;
Nun schien er schon was mehr zu sein,
Dann fing er an zu niesen.

Doch mit Gebein und Glied und
    Kopf
Blieb er ein halber Klumpen,
Bis endlich Noah für den Tropf
Das Wahre fand, den Humpen.

Hans Adam was a lump of clay
that God made into man;
yet he produced from his mother's
    womb
much more that was uncouth.

Via his nose, the Deity
blew the very best spiri in;
and this seemed an improvement,
for he began to sneeze.

Yet with head and limbs and
    members,
half a lump he still remained,
till Noah for the dolt at last
found the right thing, a glass.

Der Klumpe fühlt sogleich den
   Schwung,
Sobald er sich benetzet,
So wie der Teig durch Säuerung
Sich in Bewegung setzet.

So, Hafis, mag dein holder Sang,
Dein heiliges Exempel
Uns führen, bei der Gläser Klang,
Zu unsres Schöpfers Tempel.

The lump feels
   animation
the moment that he drinks,
just as dough, through leavening,
sets itself astir.

So may, Hafiz, your sweet song,
and your blessed example,
conduct us at the glasses' clink
to our Creator's temple.


## Erster Verlust | First Loss

JOHANN WOLFGANG GOETHE

*Armin Knab, 1924–46; Felix Mendelssohn-Bartholdy: op. 99, 1, 1841–45,
Franz Schubert: op. 5, no. 4, 1815; Carl Friedrich Zelter, 1807*

Ach, wer bringt die schönen Tage,
Jene Tage der ersten Liebe,
Ach, wer bringt nur eine Stunde
Jener holden Zeit zurück!

Einsam nähr ich meine Wunde,
Und mit stets erneuter Klage
Traur ich ums verlorne Glück.

Ach, wer bringt die schönen Tage,
Jene holde Zeit zurück.

Oh, who will bring the fair days back,
those days of first love,
oh, who will bring but one hour
of that sweet time back!

Lonely, I feed my wound,
and with ever-renewed lament
mourn the happiness I lost.

Oh, who will bring the fair days,
that sweet time back!


## Erstes Grün | First Green

JUSTINUS KERNER

*Robert Schumann: op. 35, no. 4, 1840*

Du junges Grün, du frisches Gras!
Wie manches Herz durch dich genas,
das von des Winters Schnee erkrankt,
oh wie mein Herz nach dir verlangt!

Schon wächst du aus der Erde Nacht,
wie dir mein Aug entgegen lacht!
Hier in des Waldes stillem Grund
drück ich dich, Grün, an Herz und
   Mund.

Wie treibts mich von den Menschen
   fort!
Mein Leid das hebt kein Menschenwort,
Nur junges Grün ans Herz gelegt,
macht, daß mein Herze stiller schlägt.

Young green, fresh grass,
how many a heart you have healed
that fell ill from winter's snow,
how great my heart's desire for you!

Already from earth's night you grow,
how my eye laughs to greet you!
Here, in the forest's silent depths,
you, green, I press to heart, to
   lips.

How great my urge to quit human-
   kind!
No human word will lift my grief,
only green grass, put to my heart,
will make my heart beat calmer.

## Es leuchtet meine Liebe / The Gleam of My Love

HEINRICH HEINE

*Robert Schumann: op. 127, no. 3, 1840–51*

Es leuchtet meine Liebe
In ihrer dunkeln Pracht,
Wie'n Märchen, traurig und trübe,
Erzählt in der Sommernacht.

»Im Zaubergarten wallen
Zwei Buhlen, stumm und allein;
Es singen die Nachtigallen,
Es flimmert der Mondenschein.

Die Jungfrau steht still wie ein Bildnis,
Der Ritter vor ihr kniet.
Da kommt der Riese der Wildnis,
Die bange Jungfrau flieht.

Der Ritter sinkt blutend zur Erde,
Es stolpert der Riese nach Haus—«
Wenn ich begraben werde,
Dann ist das Märchen aus.

The gleam of my love
in its dark splendour
is like a tale, sad and gloomy,
told on a summer night.

'In the magic garden wander
two lovers, silent, alone;
the nightingales are singing,
the moon is glittering.

'The maiden stands, a portrait,
the knight before her kneels.
Then comes the wild-place ogre,
the terrified maiden flees.

'Down the knight sinks, bleeding,
the ogre stumbles home—'
and when I'm dead and buried,
this story will be done.


## Es liebt sich so lieblich im Lenze / So Lovely Is Love in Spring

HEINRICH HEINE

*Johannes Brahms: op. 71, no. 1, 1877*

Die Wellen blinken und fließen dahin,
Es liebt sich so lieblich im Lenze!
Am Flusse sitzet die Schäferin
Und windet die zärtlichsten Kränze.

Das knospet und quillt und duftet und
    blüht,
Es liebt sich so lieblich in Lenze!
Die Schäferin seufzt aus tiefer Brust:
»Wem geb ich meine Kränze?«

Ein Reiter reitet den Fluß entlang,
Er grüßet so blühenden Mutes,
Die Schäferin schaut ihm nach so bang,
Fern flattert die Feder des Hutes.

The waves go glittering by,
so lovely is love in spring!
The shepherdess sits by the river,
weaving most delicate garlands.

A budding, scenting, gushing,
    blooming,
so lovely is love in spring!
The shepherdess deeply sighs:
'To whom shall I give my garlands?'

A horseman beside the river rides,
and so gallantly salutes,
alarmed, the shepherdess stares after,
his hat plume floats afar.


## Es muß ein Wunderbares sein / Something Wonderful There Must Be

OSKAR VON REDWITZ

*Franz Liszt, 1857*

Es muß ein Wunderbares sein
Ums Lieben zweier Seelen,
Sich schließen ganz einander ein,
Sich nie ein Wort verhehlen,

Something wonderful there must be
about the loving of two souls,
locking each other wholly in,
never hiding any word,

Und Freud und Leid
Und Glück und Not
So miteinander tragen,
Vom ersten Kuß bis in den Tod
Sich nur von Liebe sagen.

and joy and sorrow,
happiness and misery
thus bearing with each other,
from the first kiss unto death,
speaking but of love together.

## *Es träumte mir | I Dreamt*

GEORG FRIEDRICH DAUMER

*Johannes Brahms: op. 57, no. 3, 1871*

Es träumte mir,
Ich sei dir teuer;
Doch zu erwachen
Bedurft' es kaum.
Denn schon im Traume
Bereits empfand ich,
Es sei ein Traum.

I dreamt
I was dear to you;
but to awake
there scarce was need.
For in my dream
I already knew
it was a dream.

## *Fahrt zum Hades | Journey to Hades*

JOHANN MAYRHOFER

*Franz Schubert, 1817*

Der Nachen dröhnt, Cypressen flüstern,
Horch, Geister reden schaurig
    drein;
Bald werd' ich am Gestad', dem düstern,
Weit von der schönen Erde sein.

The bark groans, cypresses whisper,
hark—spirit discourse breaks in
    awesomely;
soon shall I be on that gloomy shore,
remote from the fair earth.

Da leuchten Sonne nicht, noch Sterne,
Da tönt kein Lied, da ist kein
    Freund.
Empfang die letzte Träne, Ferne,
Die dieses müde Auge weint.

There, gleam neither stars nor sun,
there, sounds no song, no friend is
    there.
Accept, distant one, the final tear
shed by this weary eye.

Schon schau' ich die blassen Danaiden,
Den fluchbeladnen Tantalus;
Es murmelt todesschwangern Frieden,
Vergessenheit, dein alter Fluß.

Already the pallid Danaides I see,
curse-burdened Tantalus;
and deathful peace is murmured,
O oblivion, by your ancient river.

Vergessen nenn' ich zwiefach Sterben,
Was ich mit höchster Kraft
    gewann,
Verlieren, wieder es erwerben—
Wann enden diese Qualen? Wann?

To forget I call a two-fold dying,
what I, with my best strength, have
    won,
that to lose, that to win again—
when will these torments end? When?

## Feldeinsamkeit | Field Solitude

HERMANN ALLMERS

*Johannes Brahms: op. 86, no. 2, 1877*

Ich ruhe still im hohen grünen Gras
Und sende lange meinen Blick nach
  oben,
Von Grillen rings umschwirrt ohn
  Unterlaß,
Von Himmelsbläue wundersam
  umwoben.

Die schönen weißen Wolken ziehn dahin
Durchs tiefe Blau, wie schöne stille
  Träume;
Mir ist, als ob ich längst gestorben bin
Und ziehe selig mit durch ewge Räume.

Quiet I rest in tall green grass
and upward long direct my
  gaze,
by unremittant crickets
  ringed,
enfolded wondrously by blue
  sky.

The fine white clouds go drifting by
through the deep blue like fine silent
  dreams;
I feel as if I have long been dead,
and happy, drift in eternal regions too.

## Fischerweise | Fisherman's Song

FRANZ XAVER VON SCHLECHTA

*Franz Schubert: op. 96, no. 4, 1826*

Den Fischer fechten Sorgen
Und Gram und Leid nicht an;
Er löst am frühen Morgen
Mit leichtem Sinn den Kahn.

The fisherman no sorrow,
no pain, no grief assails;
at break of day he casts off
his boat with easy mind.

Da lagert rings noch Friede
Auf Wald und Flur und Bach,
Er ruft mit seinem Liede
Die gold'ne Sonne wach.

Peace still lies all around
in wood and field and stream,
but he, with his singing,
awakes the golden sun.

Er singt zu seinem Werke
Aus voller frischer Brust,
Die Arbeit gibt ihm Stärke,
Die Stärke Lebenslust.

He sings, while he is working,
from full and lively breast,
his labours give him vigour,
his vigour—zest for life.

Bald wird ein bunt Gewimmel
In allen Tiefen laut
Und plätschert durch den Himmel,
Der sich im Wasser baut.

And soon in motley fashion,
the depths will teem and sound,
and, splashing, break the heavens
that on the waters rest.

Doch wer ein Netz will stellen,
Braucht Augen klar und gut,
Muß heiter gleich den Wellen
Und frei sein wie die Flut.

But whoever wants to set nets,
needs eyes both good and clear,
must be cheerful as the waves,
and free as is the tide.

Dort angelt auf der Brücke
Die Hirtin. Schlauer Wicht,
Entsage deiner Tücke,
Den Fisch betrügst du nicht.

There on the bridge is fishing
the shepherdess. Sly thing,
give up your trickery,
this fish you'll not take in.

## Flohlied des Mephisto | Mephistopheles' Song of the Flea

JOHANN WOLFGANG GOETHE: from *Faust, Part i*

*Ludwig van Beethoven: op. 75, no. 3, 1809; Ferruccio Busoni: ed., 1964;
Modest Mussorgsky*

Es war einmal ein König,
Der hatt einen großen Floh,
Den liebt er gar nicht wenig:
Als wie seinen eignen Sohn.
Da rief er seinen Schneider,
Der Schneider kam heran:
»Da, miß dem Junker Kleider
Und miß ihm Hosen an!«

In Sammet und in Seide
War er nun angetan,
Hatte Bänder auf dem Kleide,
Hatt auch ein Kreuz daran,
Und war sogleich Minister
Und hatt einen großen Stern.
Da wurden seine Geschwister
Bei Hof auch große Herrn.

Und Herrn und Fraun am Hofe,
Die waren sehr geplagt,
Die Königin und die Zofe
Gestochen und genagt,
Und durften sie nicht knicken
Und weg sie jucken nicht.—
Wir knicken und erstichen
Doch gleich, wenn einer sticht!

A king there was once,
who had a great flea,
whom he loved not a little:
as he might his own son.
He called to him his tailor,
the tailor running came:
'Measure garments for this noble,
and for breeches do the same.'

In silk and in velvet
he was now attired,
sashes he had about his coat,
and wore a cross there too,
became forthwith a minister
and had a mighty star.
His brothers and his sisters
were also grand at court.

And courtly lords and ladies
were tormented very sore,
the queen, her maid-in-waiting
were bitten and were gnawed,
but they could not nip them,
nor scratch and make them go.—
Yet we nip and choke them
as soon as any bite!

## Frage | Question

JUSTINUS KERNER

*Robert Schumann: op. 35, no. 9, 1840*

Wärst du nicht, heilger Abendschein!
Wärst du nicht, sternerhellte Nacht!
Du Blütenschmuck! Du üppger Hain!
Und du, Gebirg, voll ernster
    Pracht!
Du Vogelsang aus Himmeln hoch!
Du Lied aus voller Menschenbrust!
Wärst du nicht, ach, was füllte noch
In arger Zeit ein Herz mit Lust?

If you, holy evening star, were not,
and you, star-illumined night,
adorning blossoms, luxuriant wood,
you, mountains, filled with solemn
    glory,
you, song of birds from heaven on high,
you, song from a full human heart,
if you were not, ah, what still would fill
a heart with joy in adversity?

## Fragment aus dem Aischylos | Fragment from Aeschylus

JOHANN MAYRHOFER

*Franz Schubert, 1816*

So wird der Mann, der sonder Zwang
    gerecht ist,
Nicht unglücklich sein, versinken ganz
    in Elend kann er nimmer;

So shall the man who is by nature
    just
be not unhappy, wholly into misery can
    he never sink;

| | |
|---|---|
| Indes der frevelnde Verbrecher im Strome der Zeit Gewaltsam untergeht, wenn am zerschmetterten Maste Das Wetter die Segel ergreift. Er ruft, von keinem Ohr vernommen, Kämpft in des Strudels Mitte, hoffnungslos. Des Frevlers lacht die Gottheit nun, Sieht ihn, nun nicht mehr stolz, In Banden der Not verstrickt, Umsonst die Felsbank fliehn; An der Vergeltung Fels scheitert sein Glück, Und unbeweint versinkt er. | whilst in the stream of time the impious wrongdoer perishes violently when, on the shattered mast, the weather grips the sails. Unheard by any ear, he cries, struggles hopelessly in the whirlpool's eye. At the impious one the gods now laugh, see him, now no longer proud, enmeshed in bonds of distress, vainly fleeing the rocky reef; on the rock of retribution founders his fortune, and unlamented, he sinks. |

## Frauenliebe und -leben | Woman's Love and Life

ADALBERT VON CHAMISSO

Robert Schumann: op. 42, nos. 1–8, 1840

| | |
|---|---|
| I Seit ich ihn gesehen, Glaub ich blind zu sein; Wo ich hin nur blicke, Seh ich ihn allein; Wie im wachen Traume Schwebt sein Bild mir vor, Taucht aus tiefstem Dunkel Heller nur empor. | I Since seeing him, I think I am blind; wherever I look, him only I see; as in a waking dream he floats before me, rising out of darkest depths only more brightly. |
| Sonst ist licht- und farblos Alles um mich her, Nach der Schwestern Spiele Nicht begehr ich mehr, Möchte lieber weinen Still im Kämmerlein; Seit ich ihn gesehen, Glaub ich blind zu sein. | For the rest, dark and pale is all around, for my sisters' games I am no longer eager, I would rather weep quietly in my room; since seeing him, I think I am blind. |
| 2 Er, der Herrlichste von allen, Wie so milde, wie so gut. Holde Lippen, klares Auge, Heller Sinn und fester Mut. | 2 He, the most wonderful of all, so gentle, so good. Sweet lips, bright eyes, clear mind and firm resolve. |
| So wie dort in blauer Tiefe Hell und herrlich jener Stern, Also er an meinem Himmel Hell und herrlich, hehr und fern. | As there in the blue depths that star, clear and wonderful, so is he in my heaven, clear and wonderful, majestic, remote. |
| Wandle, wandle deine Bahnen; Nur betrachten deinen Schein, Nur in Demut ihn betrachten, Selig nur und traurig sein. | Wander, wander your ways; just to watch your radiance, just to watch it in humility, just to be blissful and sad! |
| Höre nicht mein stilles Beten, Deinem Glücke nur geweiht; | Hear not my silent prayer for your happiness alone; |

Darfst mich niedre Magd nicht kennen,
Hoher Stern der Herrlichkeit.

Nur die Würdigste von allen
Darf beglücken deine Wahl
Und ich will die Hohe segnen
Viele tausend Mal.

Will mich freuen dann und weinen,
Selig, selig bin ich dann,
Sollte mir das Herz auch brechen,
Brich, o Herz, was liegt daran?

3
Ich kann's nicht fassen, nicht glauben,
Es hat ein Traum mich berückt;
Wie hätt' er doch unter allen
Mich Arme erhöht und beglückt?

Mir war's, er habe gesprochen:
»Ich bin auf ewig Dein«,
Mir war's, ich träume noch immer,
Es kann ja nimmer so sein.

O laß im Traume mich sterben,
Gewieget an seiner Brust,
Den seligen Tod mich schlürfen
In Tränen unendlicher Lust.

4
Du Ring an meinem Finger,
Mein goldenes Ringelein,
Ich drücke dich fromm an die Lippen,
An das Herze mein.

Ich hatt' ihn ausgeträumet,
Der Kindheit friedlich schönen Traum,
Ich fand allein mich, verloren
Im öden unendlichen Raum.

Du Ring an meinem Finger,
Da hast du mich erst belehrt,
Hast meinem Blick erschlossen
Des Lebens unendlichen, tiefen Wert.

Ich will ihm dienen, ihm leben,
Ihm angehören ganz,
Hin selber mich geben und finden
Verklärt mich in seinem Glanz.

5
Helft mir, ihr Schwestern,
Freundlich mich schmücken,
Dient der Glücklichen heute, mir,
Windet geschäftig
Mir um die Stirne
Noch der blühenden Myrte Zier.

Als ich befriedigt,
Freudigen Herzens,

me, lowly maid, you must not know,
lofty, wonderful star.

Only the most worthy woman of all
may your choice favour
and that exalted one will I bless
many thousands of times.

Then shall I rejoice and weep,
be blissful, blissful then;
even if my heart should break,
then break, O heart, what matter?

3
I cannot grasp it, believe it,
I am in the spell of a dream;
how, from amongst all, has he
raised and favoured poor me?

He said, I thought,
'I am forever yours,'
I was, I thought, still dreaming,
for it can never be so.

O let me, dreaming, die,
cradled on his breast;
blissful death let me savour,
in tears of endless joy.

4
Ring on my finger,
my little golden ring,
devoutly I press you to my lips,
to my heart.

I had finished dreaming
childhood's tranquil pleasant dream,
alone I found myself, forlorn
in boundless desolation.

Ring on my finger,
you have first taught me,
unlocked my eyes
to life's deep, boundless worth.

I will serve him, live for him,
belong wholly to him,
yield to him and find
myself transfigured in his light.

5
Help me, sisters,
in kindness to adorn myself,
serve me, the happy one, today,
eagerly twine
about my brow
the flowering myrtle.

When I, content,
with joyous heart,

Sonst dem Geliebten im Arme lag,
Immer noch rief er,
Sehnsucht im Herzen,
Ungeduldig den heutigen Tag.

Helft mir, ihr Schwestern,
Helft mir verscheuchen
Eine törichte Bangigkeit;
Daß ich mit klarem
Aug ihn empfange,
Ihn, die Quelle der Freudigkeit.

Bist, mein Geliebter,
Du mir erschienen,
Gibst du mir, Sonne, deinen Schein?
Laß mich in Andacht,
Laß mich in Demut,
Laß mich verneigen dem Herren mein.

Streuet ihm, Schwestern,
Streuet ihm Blumen,
Bringt ihm knospende Rosen dar.
Aber euch, Schwestern,
Grüß ich mit Wehmut,
Freudig scheidend aus eurer Schar.

6
Süßer Freund, du blickest
Mich verwundert an,
Kannst es nicht begreifen,
Wie ich weinen kann;
Laß der feuchten Perlen
Ungewohnte Zier
Freudig hell erzittern
In dem Auge mir.

Wie so bang mein Busen,
Wie so wonnevoll!
Wüßt ich nur mit Worten,
Wie ich's sagen soll;
Komm und birg dein Antlitz
Hier an meiner Brust,
Will ins Ohr dir flüstern
Alle meine Lust.

Weißt du nun die Tränen,
Die ich weinen kann,
Sollst du nicht sie sehen,
Du geliebter Mann?
Bleib an meinem Herzen,
Fühle dessen Schlag,
Daß ich fest und fester
Nur dich drücken mag.

Hier an meinem Bette
Hat die Wiege Raum,
Wo sie still verberge
Meinen holden Traum;
Kommen wird der Morgen,
Wo der Traum erwacht;

lay in my beloved's arms,
still would he call
with yearning heart,
impatiently for today.

Help me, sisters,
help me banish
foolish fear;
so that I, clear-
eyed, may receive him,
the source of joy.

You, my beloved,
have appeared before me,
will you, sun, give me your radiance?
Let me in reverence,
let me in humility,
let me bow to my lord.

Sisters,
strew flowers for him,
offer budding roses.
But you, sisters,
I salute sadly,
departing, joyous, from your throng.

6
Sweet friend, you look
at me in wonder,
cannot understand
how I can weep;
these moist pearls let,
as a strange adornment,
tremble joyous bright
in my eyes.

How anxious my heart,
how full of bliss!
If only I knew words
to say it;
come, hide your face,
here, against my breast,
for me to whisper you
my full joy.

Now you know the tears
that I can weep,
are you not to see them,
beloved man?
Stay against my heart,
feel its beat,
so that I may press you
ever closer.

Here by my bed
is the cradle's place,
where, silent, it shall hide
my sweet dream.
The morning will come
when that dream will awake,

Und daraus dein Bildnis
Mir entgegen lacht.

7
An meinem Herzen, an meiner Brust,
Du meine Wonne, du meine Lust.
Das Glück ist die Liebe,
Die Lieb ist das Glück,
Ich hab's gesagt und nehm's nicht
    zurück.
Hab überschwenglich mich geschätzt,
Bin überglücklich aber jetzt.
Nur die da säugt, nur die da
    liebt
Das Kind, dem sie die Nahrung gibt;
Nur eine Mutter weiß allein,
Was lieben heißt und glücklich sein.
O wie bedauer' ich doch den Mann,
Der Mutterglück nicht fühlen kann.
Du lieber, lieber Engel du,
Du schaust mich an und lächelst dazu.
An meinem Herzen, an meiner Brust,
Du meine Wonne, du meine Lust.

8
Nun hast du mir den ersten Schmerz
    getan,
Der aber traf,
Du schläfst, du harter, unbarmherz'ger
    Mann,
Den Todesschlaf.

Es blicket die Verlassne vor sich hin,
Die Welt ist leer.
Geliebet hab ich und gelebt,
Ich bin nicht lebend mehr.

Ich zieh mich in mein Innres still
    zurück,
Der Schleier fällt;
Da hab ich dich und mein verlornes
    Glück,
Du meine Welt.

and your image
laugh up at me.

7
At my heart, at my breast,
you my delight, you my joy!
Happiness is love,
love is happiness,
I have said and will not take
    back.
I thought myself rapturous,
but now I am delirious with joy.
Only she who suckles, only she who
    loves
the child she nourishes;
only a mother knows
what it means to love and be happy.
Oh, how I pity the man
who cannot feel a mother's bliss.
You dear, dear angel,
you look at me and smile.
At my heart, at my breast,
you my delight, you my joy!

8
Now you have caused me my first
    pain,
but it has struck me hard.
You, harsh, pitiless man are
    sleeping
the sleep of death.

The deserted one stares ahead,
the world is void.
Loved have I and lived,
I am living no longer.

Quietly I withdraw into
    myself,
the veil falls;
there I have you and my lost
    happiness,
my world.

## Freisinn | Liberalism

JOHANN WOLFGANG GOETHE: from *West-östlicher Divan*, 'Book of the Minstrel'

Robert Schumann: op. 25 (*Myrten*), no. 2, 1840

Laßt mich nur auf meinem Sattel gelten!
Bleibt in euren Hütten, euren Zelten!
Und ich reite froh in alle Ferne,
Über meiner Mütze nur die Sterne.

Er hat euch die Gestirne gesetzt
Als Leiter zu Land und See;
Damit ihr euch daran ergötzt,
Stets blickend in die Höh.

Be my life's worth only in the saddle!
You in your huts, your tents can stay!
And joyful I'll ride into the distance,
with naught but the stars above my cap.

He has set for you the constellations
to guide you over land and sea;
that you should take delight in them,
gazing ever up.

## Freiwilliges Versinken / Voluntary Sinking

JOHANN MAYRHOFER

*Franz Schubert, 1820*

Wohin, o Helios? Wohin? In kühlen
  Fluten
Will ich den Flammenleib versenken,
Gewiß im Innern, neue Gluten
Der Erde Feuerreich zu schenken.

Ich nehme nicht, ich pflege nur zu
  geben;
Und wie verschwenderisch mein Leben,
Umhüllt mein Scheiden gold'ne
  Pracht,
Ich scheide herrlich, naht die Nacht.

Wie blaß der Mond, wie matt die
  Sterne!
Solang ich kräftig mich bewege;
Erst wenn ich auf die Berge meine
  Krone lege,
Gewinnen sie an Mut und Kraft in
  weiter Ferne.

Whither away, O Helios? In cool
  waters
will I sink my fiery body,
certain within, of bestowing
fresh glows to earth's realm of fire.

I do not take, am wont only to
  give;
and profligate as my life is,
golden splendour envelops my
  departure,
in glory I depart, come the night.

How pale the moon, how faint the
  stars,
so long as I am powerfully in motion;
not till I set down my crown upon the
  hills,
do they, far off, gain in heart and
  strength.

## Freundliche Vision / Kind Vision

OTTO JULIUS BIERBAUM

*Richard Strauss: op. 48, no. 1, 1900*

Nicht im Schlafe hab' ich das geträumt,
hell am Tage sah ich's schön vor mir.
Eine Wiese voller Margeriten;
tief ein weißes Haus in grünen Büschen;
Götterbilder leuchten aus dem Laube.
Und ich geh' mit einer, die mich lieb hat,
ruhigen Gemütes in die Kühle
dieses weißen Hauses, in den Frieden,
der voll Schönheit wartet, daß wir
  kommen.
Und ich geh' mit einer, die mich lieb
  hat,
in den Frieden voll Schönheit.

I did not dream it in my sleep,
clear by day I saw it fair before me.
A meadow full of marguerites;
a white house deep in verdant shrubs;
from the foliage gleam statues of gods.
And I, with one who loves me, walk,
with heart at peace, into the cool
of this white house, into the peace
that, full of beauty, waits our
  coming.
And I walk, with one who loves
  me,
into the beauty-filled peace.

## Frühling übers Jahr / Perennial Spring

JOHANN WOLFGANG GOETHE

*Hugo Wolf, 1888*

Das Beet, schon lockert
Sichs in die Höh,
Da wanken Glöckchen
So weiß wie Schnee;

Already the flower-bed
breaks loose to the sky,
tiny bells waver,
white as snow;

Safran entfaltet
Gewaltge Glut,
Smaragden keimt es
Und keimt wie Blut.
Primeln stolzieren
So naseweis,
Schalkhafte Veilchen,
Versteckt mit Fleiß;
Was auch noch alles
Da regt und webt,
Genug, der Frühling,
Er wirkt und lebt.

saffron sends forth
a vehement glow;
an emeraldine budding,
a budding blood-red,
primroses parading
so impudent,
the wily violet
hidden with care;
and as for all else
that is astir,
no more . . . Spring
is alive, and at work.

Doch was im Garten
Am reichsten blüht,
Das ist des Liebchens
Lieblich Gemüt.
Da glühen Blicke
Mir immerfort,
Erregend Liedchen,
Erheiternd Wort;
Ein immer offen,
Ein Blütenherz,
Im Ernste freundlich
Und rein im Scherz.
Wenn Ros und Lilie
Der Sommer bringt,
Er doch vergebens
Mit Liebchen ringt.

But what in the garden
most richly blooms,
that is my loved one's
feelings so dear.
Here burn her glances
for me without cease,
stirring to song,
enlivening speech;
an ever-open
blossoming heart,
in grave matters kindly,
innocent in jest.
Though summer brings,
rose and lily,
vainly shall summer
compete with my love.

## Frühlingsfahrt / Spring Voyage

JOSEPH VON EICHENDORFF

*Robert Schumann: op. 45, no. 2, 1840*

Es zogen zwei rüst'ge Gesellen
Zum erstenmal von Haus,
So jubelnd recht in die hellen,
In die klingenden, singenden Wellen
Des vollen Frühlings hinaus.

Forth two lusty fellows went
from home for the first time,
out so exultant into the bright
sounding singing waves
of springtime at its height.

Die strebten nach hohen Dingen,
Die wollten, trotz Lust und Schmerz,
Was Recht's in der Welt vollbringen,
Und wem sie vorüber gingen,
Dem lachten Sinnen und Herz.—

For lofty things they strove,
desired, despite joy and pain,
to accomplish something in the world,
and those they passed on the way,
were merry in heart and mind.

Der erste, der fand ein Liebchen,
Die Schwieger kauft' Hof und Haus;
Der wiegte gar bald ein Bübchen,
Und sah aus heimlichem Stübchen
Behaglich ins Feld hinaus.

The first, he found a loved one,
her family bought them house and home;
soon he was rocking a baby boy
and gazing from a homely parlour
at ease out at his field.

Dem zweiten sangen und logen
Die tausend Stimmen im Grund,
Verlockend' Sirenen, und zogen
Ihn in der buhlenden Wogen
Farbig klingenden Schlund.

The second was sung and lied to
by the thousand voices from the deep,
enticing sirens, who drew him
into the amorous billows'
gaily resounding gulf.

| | |
|---|---|
| Und wie er auftaucht' vom Schlunde, | And when from the gulf he surfaced, |
| Da war er müde und alt, | he was weary and old, |
| Sein Schifflein das lag im Grunde, | his vessel lay at the bottom, |
| So still war's rings in der Runde, | around him was such stillness, |
| Und über die Wasser weht's kalt. | over the water it blew so cold. |
| | |
| Es singen und klingen die Wellen | Singing and sounding, the waves |
| Des Frühlings wohl über mir; | of spring float over me; |
| Und seh' ich so kecke Gesellen, | and when I see such bold fellows, |
| Die Tränen im Auge mir schwellen— | the tears come welling to my eyes— |
| Ach, Gott, führ' uns liebreich zu Dir! | ah, guide us, God, lovingly to Thee! |

## *Frühlingsglaube | Spring Faith*

LUDWIG UHLAND

*Felix Mendelssohn-Bartholdy: op. 9, no. 8, 1825–28; Franz Schubert: op. 20, no. 2, 1820*

| | |
|---|---|
| Die linden Lüfte sind erwacht, | Gentle breezes are awake, |
| Sie säuseln und weben Tag und Nacht, | murmuring, stirring night and day, |
| Sie schaffen an allen Enden. | everywhere active, creative. |
| O frischer Duft, o neuer Klang! | Oh fresh fragrance, oh new sounds! |
| Nun, armes Herze, sei nicht bang! | Now, poor heart, be not afraid. |
| Nun muß sich alles, alles wenden. | Now must all things, all things change. |
| | |
| Die Welt wird schöner mit jedem Tag, | Daily the world grows fairer, |
| Man weiß nicht, was noch werden mag, | what may yet come, we do not know, |
| Das Blühen will nicht enden; | to blooming there is no end; |
| Es blüht das fernste, tiefste Tal: | the farthest, deepest valley blooms: |
| Nun, armes Herz, vergiß der Qual! | now, poor heart, forget your torment. |
| Nun muß sich alles, alles wenden. | Now must all things, all things change. |

## *Fünf Gedichte für eine Frauenstimme | Five Poems for Woman's Voice*

MATHILDE WESENDONK

*Richard Wagner, 1857–58*

| | |
|---|---|
| 1 *Der Engel* | 1 *The Angel* |
| In der Kindheit frühen Tagen | In early days of childhood, |
| Hört ich oft von Engeln sagen, | often I heard talk of angels |
| Die des Himmels hehre Wonne | who heaven's glorious bliss |
| Tauschen mit der Erdensonne, | exchange for the sun of earth, |
| | |
| Daß, wo bang ein Herz in Sorgen | so that when, in dread sorrow, a heart |
| Schmachtet vor der Welt verborgen, | yearns, hidden from the world; |
| Daß, wo still es will verbluten, | when it wishes silently to bleed |
| Und vergehn in Tränenfluten, | and perish in streams of tears; |
| | |
| Daß, wo brünstig sein Gebet | when its fervent prayer |
| Einzig um Erlösung fleht, | begs only for deliverance— |
| Da der Engel niederschwebt, | then down that angel floats |
| Und es sanft gen Himmel hebt. | and raises it gently to heaven. |
| | |
| Ja, es stieg auch mir ein Engel nieder, | And to me an angel has come down, |
| Und auf leuchtendem Gefieder | and upon gleaming wings, |
| Führt er, ferne jedem Schmerz, | it bears far from every pain |
| Meinen Geist nun himmelwärts! | my spirit now heavenwards! |

2 *Stehe still!*
Sausendes, brausendes Rad der Zeit,
Messer du der Ewigkeit;
Leuchtende Sphären im weiten All,
Die ihr umringt den Weltenball;
Urewige Schöpfung, halte doch ein,
Genug des Werdens, laß mich sein!

Halte an dich, zeugende Kraft,
Urgedanke, der ewig schafft!
Hemmet den Atem, stillet den Drang,
Schweigend nur eine Sekunde lang!
Schwellende Pulse, fesselt den Schlag;
Ende, des Wollens ewger Tag!

Daß in selig süßem Vergessen
Ich mög alle Wonne ermessen!
Wenn Auge in Auge wonnig trinken,
Seele ganz in Seele versinken;
Wesen in Wesen sich wiederfindet,
Und alles Hoffens Ende sich kündet,
Die Lippe verstummt in staunendem
    Schweigen,
Keinen Wunsch mehr will das Innre
    zeugen:
Erkennt der Mensch des Ewgen Spur,
Und löst dein Rätsel, heilge Natur!

3 *Im Treibhaus* (Studie zu *Tristan und
    Isolde*)
Hochgewölbte Blätterkronen,
Baldachine von Smaragd,
Kinder ihr aus fernen Zonen,
Saget mir, warum ihr klagt?

Schweigend neiget ihr die Zweige,
Malet Zeichen in die Luft,
Und der Leiden stummer Zeuge
Steiget aufwärts, süßer Duft.

Weit in sehnendem Verlangen
Breitet ihr die Arme aus,
Und umschlinget wahnbefangen
Öder Leere nichtgen Graus.

Wohl, ich weiß es, arme Pflanze;
Ein Geschicke teilen wir,
Ob umstrahlt von Licht und Glanze,
Unsre Heimat ist nicht hier!

Und wie froh die Sonne scheidet
Von des Tages leerem Schein,
Hüllet der, der wahrhaft leidet,
Sich in Schweigens Dunkel ein.

Stille wird's, ein säuselnd Weben
Füllet bang den dunklen Raum:
Schwere Tropfen seh ich schweben
An der Blätter grünem Saum.

2 *Stand Still!*
Whirring, rushing wheel of time,
measure of eternity;
gleaming spheres in the wide universe,
you who surround the globe of earth;
eternal creation, cease,
enough of becoming, let me be!

Cease, generative powers,
primal, ever-creating thought!
Stop your breath, still your urge
in silence for just one second!
Surging pulses, fetter your beating;
end, eternal day of willing!

That in blessed, sweet oblivion
I might measure all my bliss!
When eye drinks eye in bliss,
soul drowns utterly in soul;
being rediscovers itself in being,
and the goal of every hope is near;
when lips are mute in silent
    wonder,
and the heart no further wish
    desires—
then man perceives eternity's sign,
and solves your riddle, holy Nature!

3 *In the Greenhouse* (study for *Tristan
    and Isolde*)
High-vaulted leafy crowns,
canopies of emerald,
children of distant zones,
tell me why you grieve?

Silent, you bend your branches,
draw signs upon the air,
and, as mute witness to your sorrows,
a sweet fragrance rises.

With longing and desire, wide
you open your arms,
and, victim of delusion, embrace
desolation's awful void.

Well I know, poor plant;
one fate we share,
though bathed in light and glory,
our homeland is not here!

And as, gladly, the sun parts
from the empty gleam of day,
so he truly suffers, veils
himself in the dark of silence.

Quiet it grows, a whisper, a stir
fills the dark room uneasily:
heavy drops I see hanging
on the leaves' green edge.

4 *Schmerzen*
Sonne, weinest jeden Abend
Dir die schönen Augen rot,
Wenn im Meeresspiegel badend
Dich erreicht der frühe Tod!

Doch erstehst in alter Pracht,
Glorie der düstren Welt,
Du am Morgen neu erwacht,
Wie ein stolzer Siegesheld!

Ach, wie sollte ich da klagen,
Wie, mein Herz, so schwer dich sehn,
Muß die Sonne selbst verzagen,
Muß die Sonne untergehn?

Und gebieret Tod nur Leben,
Geben Schmerzen Wonne nur:
O wie dank ich, daß gegeben
Solche Schmerzen mir Natur!

5 *Träume* (Studie zu *Tristan und
    Isolde*)
Sag, welch wunderbare Träume
Halten meinen Sinn umfangen,
Daß sie nicht wie leere Schäume
Sind in ödes Nichts vergangen?

Träume, die in jeder Stunde,
Jedem Tage schöner blühn,
Und mit ihrer Himmelskunde
Selig durchs Gemüte ziehn!

Träume, die wie hehre Strahlen
In die Seele sich versenken,
Dort ein ewig Bild zu malen:
Allvergessen, Eingedenken!

Träume, wie wenn Frühlingssonne
Aus dem Schnee die Blüten küßt,
Daß zu nie geahnter Wonne
Sie der neue Tag begrüßt,

Daß sie wachsen, daß sie blühen,
Träumend spenden ihren Duft,
Sanft an deiner Brust verglühen,
Und dann sinken in die Gruft.

4 *Anguish*
Sun, each evening you weep
your fair eyes red,
when, bathing in the sea's mirror,
you are overtaken by early death.

Yet, in your old splendour, you rise,
glory of the sombre world,
newly awakened in the morning,
a proud, heroic conqueror!

Ah, why should I lament,
and see you, my heart, so oppressed,
if the sun itself must despair,
if the sun must sink?

And if death beget only life,
and anguish bring only delight:
oh, how I give thanks that
nature gave me such anguish!

5 *Dreams* (study for *Tristan and
    Isolde*)
Say, what wondrous dreams
embrace my senses,
that they have not, like bubbles,
vanished to a desolate void?

Dreams, that with each hour,
each day bloom fairer,
and with their heavenly tidings
pass blissfully through the mind!

Dreams, which like sacred rays
plunge into the soul,
there to paint an eternal picture:
forgetting all, remembering one!

Dreams, as when spring sun
kisses the buds from the snow,
so that into never-suspected bliss
the new day welcomes them,

so that they grow and bloom,
dreaming bestow their scent,
gently glow and die upon your breast,
then sink into the grave.

*Fünfzehn Gedichte aus ›Das Buch der
hängenden Gärten‹*

STEFAN GEORGE

*Arnold Schönberg: op. 15, 1908–09*

I
Unterm schutz von dichten blätter-
    gründen
Wo von sternen feine flocken schneien ·

*Fifteen poems from 'The Book of the
Hanging Gardens'*

I
Sheltered by dense leafy
    depths
where from stars fine flakes snow ·

Sachte stimmen ihre leiden künden ·
Fabeltiere aus den braunen schlünden
Strahlen in die marmorbecken speien ·
Draus die kleinen bäche klagend
  eilen:
Kamen kerzen das gesträuch entzünden ·
Weisse formen das gewässer teilen.

2
Hain in diesen paradiesen
Wechselt ab mit blütenwiesen
Hallen · buntbemalten fliesen.
Schlanker störche schnäbel kräuseln
Teiche die von fischen schillern ·
Vögel-reihen matten scheines
Auf den schiefen firsten trillern
Und die goldnen binsen säuseln—
Doch mein traum verfolgt nur eines.

3
Als neuling trat ich ein in dein gehege
Kein staunen war vorher in meinen
  mienen ·
Kein wunsch in mir eh ich dich blickte
  rege.
Der jungen hände faltung sieh mit
  huld ·
Erwähle mich zu denen die dir dienen
Und schone mit erbarmender geduld
Den der noch strauchelt auf so fremdem
  stege.

4
Da meine lippen reglos sind und brennen
Beacht ich erst wohin mein fuss
  geriet:
In andrer herren prächtiges gebiet.
Noch war vielleicht mir möglich mich
  zu trennen ·
Da schien es dass durch hohe gitterstäbe
Der blick vor dem ich ohne lass
  gekniet
Mich fragend suchte oder zeichen gäbe.

5
Saget mir auf welchem pfade
Heute sie vorüberschreite—
Dass ich aus der reichsten lade
Zarte seidenweben hole ·
Rose pflücke und viole ·
Dass ich meine wange breite ·
Schemel unter ihrer sohle.

6
Jedem werke bin ich fürder tot.
Dich mir nahzurufen mit den sinnen ·
Neue reden mit dir auszuspinnen ·
Dienst und lohn gewährung und verbot ·
Von allen dingen ist nur dieses not
Und weinen dass die bilder immer
  fliehen

voices soft proclaim their agonies ·
fable creatures from brown gorges
spew jets into marble basins ·
from them small brooks rush
  complaining:
come are candles to ignite the bushes ·
white forms part the waters.

2
Woodland in these paradises
alternates with flowery meadows ·
halls · gaily painted floorstones.
Beaks of slender storks ruffle
pools that opalesce with fish ·
rows of birds dull gleaming
warble on the jutting roofs
and the golden rushes murmur—
yet my dream pursues one thing alone.

3
A novice I entered your preserve
before no awe was in my
  mien ·
no desire in me before I saw
  you.
See with favour the clasping of young
  hands ·
elect me to those who wait upon you
and with merciful patience spare
him who stumbles yet on so strange a
  path.

4
As my lips move not and are afire
I first pay heed to where my foot is
  come:
the sumptuous domain of other lords.
Still possible it was for me to break
  away ·
then it seemed that through high bars
the gaze to which I have unceasing
  knelt
questioning sought me or gave signs.

5
Tell me upon which path
she should today pass by—
that I from the richest chest
dainty woven silk may fetch ·
pluck rose and violet ·
that I may spread my cheek ·
a stool beneath her sole.

6
To any labour I am henceforth dead.
To call you by the senses to my side ·
new discourses devise with you ·
wage and service warrant and ban ·
of all things only this is needful
and to weep that images ever
  flee

Die in schöner finsternis gediehen—
Wann der kalte klare morgen droht.

which flourished in fair darkness—
when cold clear morning threatens.

7

Angst und hoffen wechselnd mich
    beklemmen ·
Meine worte sich in seufzer dehnen ·
Mich bedrängt so ungestümes sehnen
Dass ich mich an rast und schlaf nicht
    kehre
Dass mein lager tränen schwemmen
Dass ich jede freude von mir wehre
Dass ich keines freundes trost begehre.

7

Fear and hope alternately oppress
    me ·
my words lengthen into sighs ·
so assailed am I by violent longing
that I turn no more to rest and
    sleep
that my couch by tears is watered
that every pleasure I repel
that I no friend's comfort crave.

8

Wenn ich heut nicht deinen leib berühre
Wird der faden meiner seele reissen
Wie zu sehr gespannte sehne.
Liebe zeichen seien trauerflöre
Mir der leidet seit ich dir gehöre.
Richte ob mir solche qual
    gebühre ·
Kühlung sprenge mir dem
    fieberheissen
Der ich wankend draussen lehne.

8

If today your body I do not touch
the fibre of my soul will rend
as though a sinew overwrought.
Sweet tokens let be mourning bands
to me who suffer since becoming yours.
Judge if for me such torment be
    proper ·
coolness dispense upon me fever
    hot
wavering hesitant without.

9

Streng ist uns das glück und spröde ·
Was vermocht ein kurzer kuss?
Eines regentropfens guss
Auf gesengter bleicher öde
Die ihn ungenossen schlingt ·
Neue labung missen muss
Und vor neuen gluten springt.

9

Hard on us is fortune and unyielding ·
what has one brief kiss power to do?
The shedding of one rain-drop
on parched bleached desert
which gulps it unenjoyed ·
which must lack new refreshment
and crack beneath new heat.

10

Das schöne beet betracht ich mir im
    harren ·
Es ist umzäunt mit purpurn-schwarzem
    dorne
Drin ragen kelche mit geflecktem sporne
Und sammtgefiederte geneigte farren
Und flockenbüschel wassergrün und
    rund
Und in der mitte glocken weiss und
    mild—
Von einem odem ist ihr feuchter mund
Wie süsse frucht vom himmlischen
    gefild.

10

That fair flower bed I study
    waiting ·
hedged it is with black purple
    thorn
in it rear calyxes with speckled spur
and velvet feathered inclined ferns
and cotton tufts watery green and
    round
and in the centre globes white and
    mild—
of one breath are their moist mouths
like sweet fruit of heavenly
    fields.

11

Als wir hinter dem beblümten tore
Endlich nur das eigne hauchen spürten
Warden uns erdachte seligkeiten?
Ich erinnere dass wie schwache rohre
Beide stumm zu beben wir begannen
Wenn wir leis nur an uns rührten
Und dass unsre augen rannen—
So verbliebest du mir lang zu seiten.

11

When we beyond the flowery gate
at last felt only our own breathing
knew we imagined kinds of bliss?
I recall that like feeble reeds
we both began silently to tremble
as we but gently touched
and that our eyes ran with tears—
long thus at my side did you remain.

12
Wenn sich bei heilger ruh in tiefen
   matten
Um unsre schläfen unsre hände
   schmiegen ·
Verehrung lindert unsrer glieder brand:
So denke nicht der ungestalten schatten
Die an der wand sich auf und unter
   wiegen ·
Der wächter nicht die rasch uns scheiden
   dürfen
Und nicht dass vor der stadt der weisse
   sand
Bereit ist unser warmes blut zu
   schlürfen.

13
Du lehnest wider eine silberweide
Am ufer · mit des fächers starren spitzen
Umschirmest du das haupt dir wie mit
   blitzen
Und rollst als ob du spieltest dein
   geschmeide.
Ich bin im boot das laubgewölbe
   wahren
In das ich dich vergeblich lud zu
   steigen . .
Die weiden seh ich die sich tiefer neigen
Und blumen die verstreut im wasser
   fahren.

14
Sprich nicht immer
Von dem laub ·
Windes raub ·
Vom zerschellen
Reifer quitten ·
Von den tritten
Der vernichter
Spät im jahr.
Von dem zittern
Der libellen
In gewittern
Und der lichter
Deren flimmer
Wandelbar.

15
Wir bevölkerten die abend-düstern
Lauben · lichten tempel · pfad und
   beet
Freudig—sie mit lächeln ich mit
   flüstern—
Nun ist wahr dass sie für immer geht.
Hohe blumen blassen oder brechen ·
Es erblasst und bricht der weiher glas
Und ich trete fehl im morschen
   gras ·
Palmen mit den spitzen fingern stechen.

12
When in blessed peace in deep
   meadows
about our temples our hands
   twine themselves ·
adoration soothes our members' fire :
consider not the shadows without shape
that upon the wall move up and
   down ·
nor the guards who may swiftly part
   us
nor that the white sand beyond the
   town
is ready to gulp down our ardent
   blood.

13
You lean against a willow
by the water · with the fan's stiff lace
you shield your head as if with
   lightning
and as if playing roll your
   jewelry.
I am in the boat leafy vaults watch
   over
into which I vainly bade you
   step . .
the willows I see bowing lower
and flowers sailing scattered in the
   water.

14
Speak not always
of the leaves ·
wind's plunder ·
of the dashing
of ripe quinces ·
of the tread
of the destroyers
late in the year.
Of the trembling
of dragon-flies
in thunder-storms
and of lights
whose glimmer
is inconstant.

15
We peopled the evening-gloomy
arbours · bright temples · path and
   border
joyfully—she with smiling I with
   whispers—
now it is true that she goes forever.
Tall flowers pale or break ·
the glass of pools pales and breaks
and I stumble in decomposing
   grass ·
holly with its pointed fingers pricks.

| | |
|---|---|
| Mürber blätter zischendes gewühl | The hissing throng of brittle leaves |
| Jagen ruckweis unsichtbare hände | unseen hands urge fitfully away |
| Draussen um des edens fahle wände. | outside about eden's fallow walls. |
| Die nacht ist überwölkt und schwül. | Sultry the night and clouded over. |

## Fußreise | Journey on Foot

EDUARD MÖRIKE

*Hugo Wolf, 1888*

| | |
|---|---|
| Am frischgeschnittnen Wanderstab, | When, with fresh-cut stick, |
| Wenn ich in der Frühe | at early morn, |
| So durch die Wälder ziehe, | I walk in the woods, |
| Hügel auf und ab: | up hill and down: |
| Dann, wie's Vöglein im Laube | then, like the small bird in the trees, |
| Singet und sich rührt, | singing and stirring, |
| Oder wie die goldne Traube | or the golden grape |
| Wonnegeister spürt | sensing spirits of delight |
| In der ersten Morgensonne: | in the first morning sun, |
| So fühlt auch mein alter, lieber | my dear old Adam feels |
| Adam Herbst- und Frühlingsfieber, | autumn- and spring-fever too, |
| Gottbeherzte, | God-heartened, |
| Nie verscherzte | never-foolishly wasted |
| Erstlings-Paradieseswonne. | first-delight-of-paradise. |
| | |
| Also bist du nicht so schlimm, o alter | So you are not so bad, old |
| Adam, wie die strengen Lehrer sagen; | Adam, as hard preceptors say: |
| Liebst und lobst du immer doch, | but keep on loving and lauding, |
| Singst und preisest immer noch, | singing and extolling, |
| Wie an ewig neuen Schöpfungstagen, | as if each were a new day of Creation, |
| Deinen lieben Schöpfer und Erhalter. | your dear Creator and Keeper. |
| | |
| Möcht es dieser geben, | Would he grant it be so, |
| Und mein ganzes Leben | and my whole life |
| Wär im leichten Wanderschweiße | were the gentle sweat |
| Eine solche Morgenreise! | of just such a morning journey! |

## Ganymed | Ganymede

JOHANN WOLFGANG GOETHE

*Franz Schubert: op. 19, no. 3, 1817; Hugo Wolf, 1889*

| | |
|---|---|
| Wie im Morgenglanze | How in the morning radiance |
| Du rings mich anglühst, | you glow upon me from all sides, |
| Frühling, Geliebter! | Spring, beloved! |
| Mit tausendfacher Liebeswonne | With love's thousandfold bliss |
| Sich an mein Herz drängt | to my heart thrusts itself |
| Deiner ewigen Wärme | your eternal ardour's |
| Heilig Gefühl, | sacred feeling, |
| Unendliche Schöne! | beauty unending! |

Daß ich dich fassen möcht
In diesen Arm!

Ach, an deinem Busen
Lieg ich, schmachte,
Und deine Blumen, dein Gras
Drängen sich an mein Herz.
Du kühlst den brennenden
Durst meines Busens,
Lieblicher Morgenwind!
Ruft drein die Nachtigall
Liebend nach mir aus dem Nebeltal.

Ich komm, ich komme!
Wohin? Ach, wohin?

Hinauf! Hinauf strebt's.
Es schweben die Wolken
Abwärts, die Wolken
Neigen sich der sehnenden Liebe.
Mir! Mir!
In euerm Schoße
Aufwärts!
Umfangend umfangen!
Aufwärts an deinen Busen,
Alliebender Vater!

Might I clasp you
in these arms!

Ah, at your breast
I lie, languish,
and your flowers, your grass
thrust themselves to my heart.
You cool the burning
thirst of my bosom,
sweet morning wind!
The nightingale calls me
lovingly from the misty vale.

I come, I come!
Whither? Ah, whither?

Upwards! Upwards the striving.
The clouds float
down, the clouds
bow down to yearning love.
To me! To me!
In your lap
upwards!
Embracing embraced!
Upwards to your bosom,
All-loving Father!

## Gebet / Prayer

FRIEDRICH HEBBEL

*Hans Pfitzner: op. 26, no. 1, 1916; Max Reger: op. 4, no. 1, 1890–91*

Die du über die Sterne weg
Mit der geleerten Schale
Aufschwebst, um sie am ewgen Born
Eilig wieder zu füllen:
Einmal schwenke sie noch, o Glück,
Einmal, lächelnde Göttin!
Sieh, ein einziger Tropfen hängt
Noch verloren am Rande,
Und der einzige Tropfen genügt,
Eine himmlische Seele,
Die hier unten im Schmerz erstarrt,
Wieder in Wonne zu lösen.
Ach! sie weint dir süßren Dank
Als die anderen alle,
Die du glücklich und reich gemacht.
Laß ihn fallen, den Tropfen!

You, who beyond the stars,
with emptied cup
soar, in order at the eternal spring
swiftly to replenish it:
give one more shake, O Fortune,
one more, Smiling Goddess!
See, one single drop hangs
still on the rim, forlorn,
and that single drop will suffice,
one heavenly soul,
rigid with agony here below,
to release again in delight.
Ah, sweeter thanks will she weep you
than all the others
you have made happy and rich.
Let it fall, that drop!

## Gebet / Prayer

EDUARD MÖRIKE

*Othmar Schoeck: op. 62, no. 33, 1947–49; Hugo Wolf, 1888*

Herr! schicke was du willt,
Ein Liebes oder Leides;
Ich bin vergnügt, daß beides
Aus deinen Händen quillt.

Lord! Send what Thou wilt,
delight or pain;
I am content that both
flow from Thy hands.

| | |
|---|---|
| Wollest mit Freuden | May it be Thy will neither with joys |
| und wollest mit Leiden | nor with sorrows |
| Mich nicht überschütten! | to overwhelm me! |
| Doch in der Mitten | For midway between |
| Liegt holdes Bescheiden. | lies blessed moderation. |

## Geh unter, schöne Sonne | Set, Fair Sun

FRIEDRICH HÖLDERLIN

*Wolfgang Fortner, 1933*

| | |
|---|---|
| Geh unter, schöne Sonne, sie achteten | Set, fair sun, they heeded you |
| Nur wenig dein, sie kannten dich, | but little, knew you, Holy One, |
| Heilge, nicht, | not, |
| Denn mühelos und stille bist du | for silently and without effort |
| Über den Mühsamen aufgegangen. | have you risen above those in toil. |
| | |
| Mir gehst du freundlich unter und auf, | For me, O light, kindly you rise and |
| o Licht, | set, |
| Und wohl erkennt mein Auge dich, | and well, glorious one, my eyes know |
| herrliches! | you! |
| Denn göttlich stille ehren lernt | For I learnt how to pay silent divine |
| ich, | honour |
| Da Diotima den Sinn mir heilte. | when Diotima healed my senses. |
| | |
| O du, des Himmels Botin, wie lauscht | O heaven's heraldess, how to you I |
| ich dir, | hearkened, |
| Dir, Diotima! Liebe! wie sah von | Diotima! My love! How, looking from |
| dir | you, |
| Zum goldnen Tage dieses Auge | up at the golden day, these eyes gazed, |
| Glänzend und dankend empor. Da | sparkling and grateful. The |
| rauschten | brooks |
| | |
| Lebendiger die Quellen, es | then babbled more lively, dark earth's |
| atmeten | blossoms |
| Der dunkeln Erde Blüten mich liebend | breathed lovingly upon |
| an, | me, |
| Und lächelnd über Silberwolken | and above silver clouds, smiling, |
| Neigte sich segnend herab der Äther. | the sky bent low to me in blessing. |

## Geheimes | Secret

JOHANN WOLFGANG GOETHE: from *West-östlicher Divan*, 'Book of Love'

*Franz Schubert: op. 14, no. 2, 1821*

| | |
|---|---|
| Über meines Liebchens Äugeln | My love has a look |
| Stehn verwundert alle Leute; | that makes men wonder; |
| Ich, der Wissende, dagegen, | but I alone |
| Weiß recht gut, was das bedeute. | well know its meaning. |
| | |
| Denn es heißt: ich liebe diesen, | It is: *him* I love, |
| Und nicht etwa den und jenen. | not him or him. |
| Lasset nur, ihr guten Leute, | So quit, good men, |
| Euer Wundern, euer Sehnen! | admiring and desiring! |

Ja, mit ungeheuren Mächten
Blicket sie wohl in die Runde;
Doch sie sucht nur zu verkünden
Ihm die nächste süße Stunde.

Great, yes, the power
of her glances;
but meant only to tell
him of their next sweet hour.

## Geheimnis | Secret

KARL CANDIDUS

*Johannes Brahms: op. 71, no. 3, 1877*

O Frühlings-Abenddämmerung!
O laues, lindes Wehn!
Ihr Blütenbäume, sprecht,
Was tut ihr so zusammenstehn?

O springtime dusk!
O mild and gentle breeze!
You trees in blossom, speak,
why stand you so together?

Vertraut ihr das Geheimnis euch
Von unsrer Liebe süß?
Was flüstert ihr einander zu
Von unsrer Liebe süß?

Do you tell the secret
of our sweet love?
What do you whisper together
of our sweet love?

## Genialisch Treiben | Activity of Genius

JOHANN WOLFGANG GOETHE

*Hugo Wolf, 1889*

So wälz ich ohne Unterlaß,
Wie Sankt Diogenes, mein Faß.
Bald ist es Ernst, bald ist es Spaß;
Bald ist es Lieb, bald ist es Haß;
Bald ist es dies, bald ist es das;
Es ist ein Nichts und ist ein Was.
So wälz ich ohne Unterlaß,
Wie Sankt Diogenes, mein Faß.

So do I roll, without respite,
like Saint Diogenes, my barrel.
Now it's in earnest, now it's in jest;
now it is love, now it is hate;
now it is this, now it is that;
it is a nothing and it is a something.
So do I roll, without respite,
like Saint Diogenes, my barrel.

## Gesang Weylas | Weyla's Song

EDUARD MÖRIKE

*Hugo Wolf, 1888*

Du bist Orplid, mein Land!
Das ferne leuchtet;
Vom Meere dampfet dein besonnter
    Strand
Den Nebel, so der Götter Wange
    feuchtet.

Orplid you are, my land
that distant gleams!
From off the sea your sunny shore lets
    steam
the mist, which bedews the gods'
    cheeks.

Uralte Wasser steigen
Verjüngt um deine Hüften, Kind!
Vor deiner Gottheit beugen
Sich Könige, die deine Wärter sind.

Ancient waters rise,
rejuvenated, child, about your waist!
To your divinity bow low
the kings who your attendants are.

## Gesänge des Harfners / The Harper's Songs

JOHANN WOLFGANG GOETHE: from *Wilhelm Meister*

*Franz Schubert: op. 12, no. 1–3, 1816; Robert Schumann: op. 98a, nos. 6, 3, 8, 1841;*
*Hugo Wolf, 1888; Carl Friedrich Zelter: 1795 (nos. 1 and 2), 1816 (no. 2, 2nd setting);*
*1818 (no. 3)*

1

Wer sich der Einsamkeit ergibt,
Ach! der ist bald allein;
Ein jeder lebt, ein jeder liebt
Und läßt ihn seiner Pein.

Ja! laßt mich meiner Qual!
Und kann ich nur einmal
Recht einsam sein,
Dann bin ich nicht allein.

Es schleicht ein Liebender lauschend
  sacht,
Ob seine Freundin allein?
So überschleicht bei Tag und Nacht
Mich Einsamen die Pein,
Mich Einsamen die Qual.
Ach, werd ich erst einmal
Einsam im Grabe sein,
Da läßt sie mich allein!


2

Wer nie sein Brot mit Tränen aß,
Wer nie die kummervollen Nächte
Auf seinem Bette weinend saß,
Der kennt euch nicht, ihr himmlischen
  Mächte.

Ihr führt ins Leben uns hinein,
Ihr laßt den Armen schuldig werden,
Dann überlaßt ihr ihn der Pein:
Denn alle Schuld rächt sich auf Erden.
  *(Franz Liszt, ca. 1860)*


3

An die Türen will ich schleichen,
Still und sittsam will ich stehn,
Fromme Hand wird Nahrung reichen,
Und ich werde weitergehn.
Jeder wird sich glücklich scheinen,
Wenn mein Bild vor ihm erscheint,
Eine Träne wird er weinen,
Und ich weiß nicht, was er weint.


1

Who gives himself to loneliness,
ah, he is soon alone;
others—they live, they love
and leave him to his pain.

Yes! To my torment leave me!
And can I but once
truly lonely be,
then I'll not be alone.

A lover softly spying
  steals
—his loved one, is she alone?
So, by day and night, steals
upon me who am lonely, the pain,
upon me who am lonely, the torment.
Ah, when I shall be at last
lonely in my grave,
then will it leave me alone!


2

Who never ate his bread in tears,
who never throughout sorrowful nights,
sat weeping on his bed,
he knows not you, Heavenly
  Powers.

You bring us into life,
the poor man you let fall into guilt,
then leave him to his pain:
for all guilt is suffered for on earth.


3

From door to door will I steal,
quiet and humble will I stand,
a pious hand will pass food,
and I shall go on my way.
Each will think himself happy,
seeing me before him,
a tear will he weep,
and I shall not know why.

230

## Gesellenlied / Apprentice Song

ROBERT REINICK

*Hugo Wolf, 1888*

Kein Meister fällt vom Himmel!
Und das ist auch ein großes Glück!
Der Meister sind schon viel zu viel':
Wenn noch ein Schock vom Himmel
    fiel',
wie würden uns Gesellen
die vielen Meister prellen,
trotz unserm Meisterstück.

Kein Meister fällt vom Himmel!
Gottlob, auch keine Meisterin!
Ach, lieber Himmel, sei so gut,
wenn droben eine brummen tut,
behalte sie in Gnaden,
daß sie zu unserm Schaden
nicht fall' zur Erde hin!

Kein Meister fällt vom Himmel!
Auch keines Meisters Töchterlein!
Zwar hab' ich das schon lang gewußt,
und doch—was wär' das eine Lust,
wenn jung und hübsch und munter
solch' Mädel fiel herunter
und wollt' mein Herzlieb sein.

Kein Meister fällt vom Himmel!
Das ist mein Trost auf dieser Welt;
drum mach' ich, daß ich Meister werd':
und wird mir dann ein Weib beschert,
dann soll aus dieser Erden
mir schon ein Himmel werden,
aus dem kein Meister fällt.

A master falls not from the sky,
and that's a good thing too!
Far too many already there are,
and were another batch to
    fall,
how would we apprentices
by all of them get diddled
despite our masterpieces.

A master falls not from the sky!
Praise God, nor master's wife!
Ah, dear heaven, be so kind,
if one up there is grumbling,
in mercy keep her where she is,
that she, to our discomfort,
should not drop down to earth!

A master falls not from the sky!
Nor master's daughter either!
Full long that's been known to me,
and yet, what pleasure that would be,
if, young and fair and merry,
such a maiden were to fall,
and my true love be.

A master falls not from the sky!
Which in this world's my comfort;
so I'm intent on being one,
and if then I'm given a wife,
then shall this earth
be a heaven for me
from which no master falls.

## Gewalt der Minne / Power of Love

WALTHER VON DER VOGELWEIDE

*Hans Pfitzner: op. 24, no. 2, 1909*

Wer gab dir, Minne, die Gewalt,
Daß du so allgewaltig bist?
Du zwingest beide, jung und alt,
Dagegen gibt es keine List.

Ich lobe Gott, seit deine Band
Mich sollen fesseln, seit so recht ich hab
    erkannt
Wo treuer Dienst sei an der Zeit,
Da weich ich niemals ab:
O Gnade, Königinne,
Laß sein mein Leben dir geweiht!

Who gave you, Love, the power
to be so all-powerful?
Young and old, both you compel,
no cunning is proof against it.

God I praise, since your bonds
shall bind me, and I so truly
    see
when for true service it is time,
never therefrom shall I depart:
O mercy, Queen,
let my life be dedicated to you!

## Glückes genug | Abundant Happiness

DETLEV VON LILIENCRON

*Max Reger: op. 37, no. 3, 1899; Richard Strauss: op. 37, no. 1, 1896–98*

Wenn sanft du mir im Arme schliefst,
Ich deinen Atem hören konnte,
Im Traum du meinen Namen riefst,
Um deinen Mund ein Lächeln
   sonnte—
Glückes genug.

Und wenn nach heißem, ernstem Tag
Du mir verscheuchtest schwere Sorgen,
Wenn ich an deinem Herzen lag
Und nicht mehr dachte an ein Morgen—
Glückes genug.

When softly in my arms you slept,
and I could hear you breathe,
you, in your dream, did call my name,
about your mouth there beamed a
   smile—
abundant happiness that was.

And when, after a hot, hard day
you banished weighty care from me,
when against your heart I lay
and of a tomorrow thought no more—
abundant happiness that was.


## Gottes Segen | God's Blessing

JOSEPH VON EICHENDORFF

*Kurt Hessenberg: op. 30, no. 4, ed. 1950; Max Reger: op. 76, no. 31, 1907*

Das Kind ruht aus vom Spielen,
Am Fenster rauscht die Nacht,
Die Engel Gottes im Kühlen
Getreulich halten Wacht.

Am Bettlein still sie stehen,
Der Morgen graut noch kaum,
Sie küssen's, eh sie gehen,
Das Kindlein lacht im Traum.

The child from play is resting,
at the window rustles night,
in the cold, God's angels
keep their faithful guard.

By the bed they stand silent,
the dawn is still scarce grey,
before they go, they kiss him,
the child laughs in his dream.


## Graf Eberstein | Count Eberstein

LUDWIG UHLAND

*Carl Loewe: op. 9, Vol. VI, no. 5, 1834*

Zu Speyer im Saale, da hebt sich ein
   Klingen,
mit Fackeln und Kerzen ein Tanzen
   und Singen.
Graf Eberstein
führet den Reihn
mit des Kaisers holdseligem Töchterlein.

Und als er sie schwingt nun im
   luftigen Reigen,
da flüstert sie leise (sie kann's nicht
   verschweigen):
»Graf Eberstein,
hüte dich fein!
Heut nacht wird dein Schlößlein
   gefährdet sein.«

In the hall at Speyer a clinking of
   glasses,
by candle- and torch-light a skipping
   and dancing.
Count Eberstein
leads the dance
with the Emperor's charming daughter.

And while he whirls her in airy
   dance,
softly she whispers—she cannot stay
   silent—
'Count Eberstein,
look to your self!
This night is your castle in
   peril.'

«Ei«, denket der Graf, »Euer kaiserlich
   Gnaden,
so habt Ihr mich darum zum Tanze
   geladen!«
Er sucht sein Roß,
läßt seinen Troß
und jagt nach seinem gefährdeten
   Schloß.

Um Ebersteins Feste, da wimmelts von
   Streitern,
sie schleichen im Nebel mit Haken und
   Leitern.
Graf Eberstein
grüßet sie fein,
er wirft sie vom Wall in die Gräben
   hinein.

Als nun der Herr Kaiser am Morgen
   gekommen,
da meint er, es seie die Burg schon
   genommen.
Doch auf dem Wall
tanzen mit Schall
der Graf und seine Gewappneten all:

»Herr Kaiser, beschleicht Ihr ein
   andermal Schlösser,
tut's not, Ihr versteht aufs Tanzen
   Euch besser.
Euer Töchterlein
tanzet so fein,
dem soll meine Feste geöffnet sein.«

Im Schlosse des Grafen, da hebt sich
   ein Klingen,
mit Fackeln und Kerzen ein Tanzen
   und Springen.
Graf Eberstein
führet den Reihn
mit des Kaisers holdseligem Töchterlein.

Und als er sie schwingt nun im
   bräutlichen Reigen,
da flüstert er leise, nicht kann er's
   verschweigen:
»Schön Jungfräulein,
hüte dich fein!
Heute nacht wird ein Schlößlein
   gefährdet sein.«

'Ah,' thinks the count, 'your Imperial
   Majesty,
so that's why you've bidden me here to
   the ball!'
He seeks out his horse,
leaves his companions,
and races to his imperilled
   home.

About Eberstein's castle warriors are
   swarming,
creeping through mist with grapnel and
   ladder.
Count Eberstein
provides a warm welcome,
hurling them down from the wall to the
   moat.

And when the next morning the
   Emperor came riding,
he expected to find the castle was
   taken.
But on the walls
dance with great din
the count and all his men-at-arms.

'If, Sire, again you would steal up on
   castles,
you will need to know more about
   dancing.
Your daughter
dances so excellently,
to her shall my castle be open.'

In the castle of the count a clinking of
   glasses,
by candle- and torch-light a skipping
   and dancing.
Count Eberstein
leads the dance
with the Emperor's charming daughter.

And while he whirls her in bridal
   dance,
softly he whispers—he cannot stay
   silent,
'Beautiful maiden,
look to yourself!
This night one small castle's in
   peril.'

## Greisengesang / Old Man's Song

FRIEDRICH RÜCKERT

*Franz Schubert: op. 60, no. 1, 1823*

Der Frost hat mir bereifet des Hauses
   Dach;
doch warm ist mir's geblieben im
   Wohngemach.

The frost has berimed the roof of my
   house;
yet warm I've remained in the
   parlour.

Der Winter hat die Scheitel mir weiß
gedeckt;
doch fließt das Blut, das rote, durchs
Herzgemach.
Der Jugendflor der Wangen, die Rosen
sind
gegangen, all gegangen einander nach,—
wo sind sie hingegangen? ins Herz
hinab:
Da blühn sie nach Verlangen, wie vor
so nach.
Sind alle Freudenströme der Welt
versiegt?
Noch fließt mir durch den Busen ein
stiller Bach.
Sind alle Nachtigallen der Flur
verstummt?
Noch ist bei mir im Stillen hier eine
wach.
Sie singet: Herr des Hauses! verschleuß
dein Tor,
daß nicht die Welt, die kalte, dring ins
Gemach.
Schleuß aus den rauhen Odem der
Wirklichkeit,
und nur dem Duft der Träume gib
Dach und Fach!

Winter has whitened the crown of my
head;
yet through my heart's chamber red
blood flows.
My cheeks' youthful flora, the roses
are
gone, gone one after the other—
gone where? Down into the
heart,
there, now as before, to blossom as
desired.
Has the world's every joyous stream
run dry?
Still, in my breast, there flows a quiet
brook.
Are all the meadow's nightingales
hushed?
Here, with me, in the silence, one still
wakes.
Lord of the house, it sings, lock up
your gate,
that the chill world not penetrate to the
parlour.
Shut out the cold breath of
reality,
and house and home give only to
dreams' fragrance!

## Grenzen der Menschheit | Limits of Man

JOHANN WOLFGANG GOETHE

*Franz Schubert, 1821; Hugo Wolf, 1889*

Wenn der uralte
Heilige Vater
Mit gelassener Hand
Aus rollenden Wolken
Segnende Blitze
Über die Erde sät,
Küss' ich den letzten
Saum seines Kleides,
Kindliche Schauer
Treu in der Brust.

When the age-old
holy Father
with calm hand
from rumbling cloud
sows flashes of blessing
over the earth,
I kiss the uttermost
hem of his garment,
child-like awe
loyal in my breast.

Denn mit Göttern
Soll sich nicht messen
Irgendein Mensch.
Hebt er sich aufwärts
Und berührt
Mit dem Scheitel die Sterne,
Nirgends haften dann
Die unsichern Sohlen,
Und mit ihm spielen
Wolken und Winde.

For against the gods
shall measure himself
no mortal.
If he upraise himself
and brush
with his head the stars,
no hold then
have his precarious soles,
and with him sport
cloud and wind.

| | |
|---|---|
| Steht er mit festen | If he stand, firm- |
| Markigen Knochen | marrowy-boned |
| Auf der wohlgegründeten | on the well-founded |
| Dauernden Erde, | enduring earth, |
| Reicht er nicht auf, | he does not reach up |
| Nur mit der Eiche | even with oak |
| Oder der Rebe | or vine |
| Sich zu vergleichen. | to compare. |
| | |
| Was unterscheidet | What distinguishes |
| Götter von Menschen? | gods from mortals? |
| Daß viele Wellen | That many waves |
| Vor jenen wandeln, | in their sight roll, |
| Ein ewiger Strom: | an eternal stream: |
| Uns hebt die Welle, | us the wave lifts, |
| Verschlingt die Welle, | the wave swallows, |
| Und wir versinken. | and we sink. |
| | |
| Ein kleiner Ring | Narrow is the ring |
| Begrenzt unser Leben, | that limits our life, |
| Und viele Geschlechter | and many the generations |
| Reihen sich dauernd | forever joining |
| An ihres Daseins | their existence's |
| Unendliche Kette. | infinite chain. |

## *Gretchen am Spinnrade* | *Gretchen at the Spinning-wheel*

JOHANN WOLFGANG GOETHE: from *Faust, Part 1*

*Franz Schubert: op. 2, 1814; Louis Spohr: op. 25, no. 3, 1809*

| | |
|---|---|
| Meine Ruh ist hin, | My peace is gone, |
| Mein Herz ist schwer, | my heart is sore, |
| Ich finde sie nimmer | never shall I find |
| und nimmermehr. | peace ever more. |
| | |
| Wo ich ihn nicht hab, | Where he is not, |
| Ist mir das Grab, | there is my grave, |
| Die ganze Welt | all the world |
| Ist mir vergällt. | to me is gall. |
| | |
| Mein armer Kopf | My poor head |
| Ist mir verrückt, | is crazed, |
| Mein armer Sinn | my poor wits |
| Ist mir zerstückt. | destroyed. |
| | |
| Nach ihm nur schau ich | Only for him I gaze |
| Zum Fenster hinaus, | from the window, |
| Nach ihm nur geh ich | only for him I go |
| Aus dem Haus. | from the house. |
| | |
| Sein hoher Gang, | His superior walk, |
| Sein' edle Gestalt, | his noble air, |
| Seines Mundes Lächeln, | his smiling mouth, |
| Seiner Augen Gewalt. | his compelling eyes. |
| | |
| Und seiner Rede | And his words— |
| Zauberfluß, | their magic flow, |

Sein Händedruck,
Und ach, sein Kuß!

the press of his hand,
and ah, his kiss!

Mein Busen drängt
Sich nach ihm hin.
Ach dürft ich fassen
Und halten ihn,

My heart craves
for him,
oh, to clasp
and to hold,

Und küssen ihn,
So wie ich wollt,
An seinen Küssen
Vergehen sollt!

and kiss him,
just as I liked,
and in his kisses
pass away!

## Gruppe aus dem Tartarus / Group from Tartarus

FRIEDRICH SCHILLER

*Franz Schubert: op. 24, no. 1, 1817*

Horch—wie Murmeln des empörten
  Meeres,
Wie durch hohler Felsen Becken weint
  ein Bach,
Stöhnt dort dumpfigtief ein schweres—
  leeres,
Qualerpreßtes Ach!

Hark—like the angered ocean's
  murmuring,
like a brook weeping through rocky
  hollows,
groans yonder, dankly deep, a grievous,
  vain,
torment-extracted moan.

Schmerz verzerret
Ihr Gesicht—Verzweiflung sperret
Ihren Rachen fluchend auf.
Hohl sind ihre Augen—ihre Blicke
Spähen bang nach des Cocytus Brücke,
Folgen tränend seinem Trauer-
  lauf.

Agony contorts
their faces—despair opens
wide their jaws in imprecation.
Hollow their eyes—their gaze
fixes fearfully on Cocytus' Bridge,
or, weeping, follows Cocytus' drear
  course.

Fragen sich einander ängstlich leise,
Ob noch nicht Vollendung sei?
Ewigkeit schwingt über ihnen Kreise,
Bricht die Sense des Saturns entzwei.

Softly and in fear, each of the other asks
whether it be not yet the end.
Eternity above them whirls in circles,
and shatters Saturn's sickle asunder.

## Hat gesagt—bleibt's nicht dabei / At What's Said It Never Stops

from *Des Knaben Wunderhorn*

*Max Reger: op. 75, no. 12, 1903; Richard Strauss: op. 36, no. 3, 1897–98*

Mein Vater hat gesagt,
Ich soll das Kindlein wiegen,
Er will mir auf den Abend
Drei Gaggeleier sieden;
Siedt er mir drei,
Ißt er mir zwei,
Und ich mag nicht wiegen
Um ein einziges Ei.

My father's said
I'm to rock the child,
and in the evening he'll
coddle three eggs for me;
if he coddles me three,
he'll eat two for me,
and I don't care to rock
for one single egg.

| | |
|---|---|
| Mein Mutter hat gesagt,<br>Ich soll die Mägdlein verraten,<br>Sie wollt mir auf den Abend<br>Drei Vögelein braten;<br>Brät sie mir drei,<br>Ißt sie mir zwei,<br>Um ein einziges Vöglein<br>Treib ich kein Verräterei. | My Mother's said<br>I'm to tell on the maids,<br>and in the evening she'll<br>roast three fowls for me;<br>if she roasts me three,<br>she'll eat two for me,<br>for one single fowl<br>I'll no traitress be. |
| Mein Schätzlein hat gesagt,<br>Ich soll sein gedenken,<br>Er wöllt mir auf den Abend<br>Drei Küßlein auch schenken;<br>Schenkt er mir drei,<br>Bleibt's nicht dabei,<br>Was kümmert michs Vöglein,<br>Was schiert mich das Ei. | My sweetheart's said<br>I'm to think of him,<br>and in the evening he<br>will give me three kisses;<br>if he gives me three,<br>it'll not stop at that,<br>what'll I care for the fowl,<br>what'll I care for the egg. |

## Heidenröslein / Wild Rose

JOHANN WOLFGANG GOETHE

*Johann Friedrich Reichardt, 1809; Franz Schubert: op. 3, no. 3, 1815*

| | |
|---|---|
| Sah ein Knab ein Röslein stehn,<br>Röslein auf der Heiden,<br>War so jung und morgenschön,<br>Lief er schnell, es nah zu sehn,<br>Sahs mit vielen Freuden.<br>Röslein, Röslein, Röslein rot,<br>Röslein auf der Heiden. | A boy saw a wild rose growing,<br>wild rose on the heath,<br>was so young and morning-fair,<br>fast he ran to see it near,<br>saw it with great joy.<br>Wild rose, wild rose, wild rose red,<br>wild rose on the heath. |
| Knabe sprach: Ich breche dich,<br>Röslein auf der Heiden!<br>Röslein sprach: Ich steche dich,<br>Daß du ewig denkst an mich,<br>Und ich wills nicht leiden.<br>Röslein, Röslein, Röslein rot,<br>Röslein auf der Heiden. | Said the boy: You will I pick,<br>wild rose on the heath!<br>Said the wild rose: You I'll prick,<br>that you'll forever think of me,<br>and suffer it I will not.<br>Wild rose, wild rose, wild rose red,<br>wild rose on the heath. |
| Und der wilde Knabe brach<br>'s Röslein auf der Heiden;<br>Röslein wehrte sich und stach,<br>Half ihm doch kein Weh und Ach,<br>Mußt es eben leiden.<br>Röslein, Röslein, Röslein rot,<br>Röslein auf der Heiden. | And that unruly boy did pick<br>the wild rose on the heath;<br>the rose fought back and pricked,<br>oh-ing and ah-ing helped not at all,<br>he had just to suffer.<br>Wild rose, wild rose, wild rose red,<br>wild rose on the heath. |

## Heimat / Homeland

GUSTAV FALKE

*Max Reger: op. 76, no. 37, 1909*

| | |
|---|---|
| Ich habe lieb die helle<br>Sonne und ihren Schein;<br>Der Tag ist mein Geselle,<br>Und treu will ich ihm sein. | I love the bright<br>sun and its shine;<br>the day is my companion,<br>and to him I'll be true. |

Doch steigt aus Sternengründen
Die stille Nacht herauf,
Ist es mir, als stünden
Der Heimat Türen auf.

But when from starry vales
the silent night ascends,
it seems as if opened
were my homeland's doors.


## Heimkehr / Homecoming

ADOLF FRIEDRICH VON SCHACK

*Richard Strauss: op. 15, no. 5, 1884–86*

Leiser schwanken die Äste,
der Kahn fliegt uferwärts,
heim kehrt die Taube zum Neste,
zu dir kehrt heim mein Herz.

The branches wave more gently,
shorewards flies the boat,
home to its nest the dove goes,
home to you comes my heart.

Genug am schimmernden Tage,
wenn rings das Leben lärmt,
mit irrem Flügelschlage
ist es in's Weite geschwärmt.

Enough, by shimmering day,
amidst the clamour of life,
on errant wing-beats
has it ranged afar.

Doch nun die Sonne geschieden
und Stille sich senkt auf den Hain,
fühlt es: bei dir ist der Frieden,
die Ruh' bei dir allein.

But now the sun has departed
and silence descends on the wood,
my heart feels: with you is peace,
with you alone is rest.


## Heimliche Aufforderung / Secret Invitation

JOHN HENRY MACKAY

*Richard Strauss: op. 27, no. 3, 1893–94*

Auf, hebe die funkelnde Schale empor
zum Mund,
Und trinke beim Freudenmahle dein
Herz gesund.
Und wenn du sie hebst, so winke mir
heimlich zu,
Dann lächle ich und dann trinke ich
still wie du . . .

Raise to your lips the sparkling
cup,
drink, at this feast, your heart to
health.
And raising it, sign to me in
secret,
I'll then smile, and quiet as you, will
drink.

Und still gleich mir betrachte um uns
das Heer
Der trunknen Schwätzer—verachte sie
nicht zu sehr.
Nein, hebe die blinkende Schale, gefüllt
mit Wein,
Und laß beim lärmenden Mahle sie
glücklich sein.

And quiet as I, about us regard the
host
of drunken talkers—scorn them not too
much.
No, raise the twinkling wine-filled
cup,
let them be happy at their noisy
feast.

Doch hast du das Mahl genossen, den
Durst gestillt,
Dann verlasse der lauten Genossen
festfreudiges Bild,
Und wandle hinaus in den Garten zum
Rosenstrauch,
Dort will ich dich dann erwarten nach
altem Brauch,

But having eaten, satisfied your
thirst,
quit the loud company's gay festive
scene,
and to the garden wander, to the
rosebush—
there I'll wait, as long our custom's
been,

Und will an die Brust dir sinken, eh
 du's gehofft,
Und deine Küsse trinken, wie ehmals
 oft,
Und flechten in deine Haare der Rosen
 Pracht.
O komm, du wunderbare, ersehnte
 Nacht!

and, ere you know, I'll sink upon your
 breast,
drinking your kisses, as many times
 before,
and in your hair I'll twine the roses'
 splendour.
Wonderful and longed-for night, O
 come!


## Heimweh / Homesickness

JOSEPH VON EICHENDORFF

*Hugo Wolf, 1888*

Wer in die Fremde will wandern,
Der muß mit der Liebsten gehn,
Es jubeln und lassen die andern
Den Fremden alleine stehn.

He who would journey abroad
must go with his beloved,
others, in their joy, leave
the stranger standing alone.

Was wisset ihr, dunkele Gipfel,
Von der alten, schönen Zeit?
Ach, die Heimat hinter den Gipfeln,
Wie liegt sie von hier so weit.

What do you know, dark summits,
of the happy days now past?
Oh, homeland beyond the mountains,
how far it lies from here.

Am liebsten betracht ich die Sterne,
Die schienen, wie ich ging zu ihr,
Die Nachtigall hör ich so gerne,
Sie sang vor der Liebsten Tür.

I love best to watch the stars
that shone as to her I went,
I love to hear the nightingale
that sang at my loved one's door.

Der Morgen, das ist meine Freude!
Da steig ich in stiller Stund
Auf den höchsten Berg in die Weite,
Grüß dich, Deutschland, aus
 Herzensgrund!

But dawn, that's my delight!
At that peaceful hour I climb
the highest mountain,
and from my heart I greet you,
 German land!


## Heinrich der Vogler / Henry the Fowler

JOHANN NEPOMUK VOGL

*Carl Loewe: op. 56, no. 1, 1836*

Herr Heinrich saß am Vogelherd,
Recht froh und wohlgemut;
Aus tausend Perlen blinkt und blitzt
Der Morgenröte Glut.

Lord Henry sat by his fowling floor,
right merry and well disposed;
from a thousand pearls gleam and flash
the red fires of the dawn.

In Wies und Feld, in Wald und Au,
Horch, welch ein süßer Schall!
Der Lerche Sang, der Wachtel Schlag,
Die süße Nachtigall!

In field and pasture, wood and mead,
hark how sweet the sound!
The song of lark, the call of quail,
the lovely nightingale!

Herr Heinrich schaut so fröhlich drein:
Wie schön ist heut die Welt!
Was gilt's, heut gibt's 'nen guten Fang!
Er schaut zum Himmelszelt.

Lord Henry looks about with joy:
how fair the world today!
The catch, he wagers, will be good.
He stares towards the sky.

Er lauscht und streicht sich von der
  Stirn
Das blondgelockte Haar . . .
Ei doch! was sprengt denn dort heran
Für eine Reiterschar?

He listens, stroking from his
  brow
his fair and curling hair . . .
But ah, who comes here galloping—
what mounted band is this?

Der Staub wallt auf, der Hufschlag
  dröhnt,
Es naht der Waffen Klang;
Daß Gott! die Herrn verderben mir
Den ganzen Vogelfang!

Dust billows up, hoof-beats
  drum,
the clank of arms draws near;
Great God! The ruin they will be
of all my fowling sport!

Ei nun! was gibt's? Es hält der Troß
Vorm Herzog plötzlich an,
Herr Heinrich tritt hervor und spricht:
Wen sucht ihr Herrn? Sagt an!

But now what's this? The cavalcade
reins up before the Duke.
Lord Henry, he steps out and says,
'Whom seek you, good sirs? Speak.'

Da schwenken sie die Fähnlein bunt
Und jauchzen: Unsern Herrn!
Hoch lebe Kaiser Heinrich, hoch!
Des Sachsenlandes Stern!

Their pennants gay they flourish then,
and, exulting, cry, 'Our Lord!
Henry our Emperor, long live he,
of Saxony the Star!'

Sich neigend knien sie vor ihm hin
Und huldigen ihm still,
Und rufen, als er staunend fragt:
's ist deutschen Reiches Will!

To him they kneel, with heads inclined,
and silent homage pay,
and to his astonished question, roar,
'By the German Empire's will!'

Da blickt Herr Heinrich tief bewegt
Hinauf zum Himmelszelt:
Du gabst mir einen guten Fang!
Herr Gott, wie dir's gefällt!

Lord Henry then, affected deep, gazes
up towards the sky:
'A goodly catch Thou hast given me!
Be it, Lord, as Thou dost please!'

## *Heiß' mich nicht reden | Bid Me not Speak*

### (Mignon's song)

JOHANN WOLFGANG GOETHE: from *Wilhelm Meister*

*Franz Schubert: op. 62, no. 2, 1826; Robert Schumann: op. 98a, no. 5, 1841;
Hugo Wolf, 1888; Carl Friedrich Zelter, 1796*

Heiß' mich nicht reden, heiß' mich
  schweigen,
Denn mein Geheimnis ist mir Pflicht;
Ich möchte dir mein ganzes Innre
  zeigen,
Allein das Schicksal will es nicht.

Bid me not speak, bid me be
  silent,
for I am bound to secrecy;
you would I show all that is
  within,
but fate will not have it so.

Zur rechten Zeit vertreibt der Sonne
  Lauf
Die finstre Nacht, und sie muß sich
  erhellen;
Der harte Fels schließt seinen Busen auf,
Mißgönnt der Erde nicht die
  tiefverborgnen Quellen.

At the due time the sun's career
  banishes
dark night, and it must grow
  light;
the unyielding rock unlocks its bosom,
grudges not the earth her deep-hid
  springs.

Ein jeder sucht im Arm des Freundes
  Ruh,
Dort kann die Brust in Klagen sich
  ergießen;

Everyone, in a friend's arms, seeks
  peace,
there the heart can pour forth its
  complaint;

Allein ein Schwur drückt mir die
    Lippen zu,
Und nur ein Gott vermag sie
aufzuschließen.

but an oath seals tight my
    lips,
a god alone can open
them.

## Heliopolis | Heliopolis

JOHANN MAYRHOFER

*Franz Schubert, 1822*

Fels auf Felsen hingewälzet,
fester Grund und treuer Halt;
Wasserfälle, Windesschauer,
unbegriffene Gewalt.

Rock rolled upon rock,
firm ground, firm footing;
cascades, windy blasts,
uncomprehended power.

Einsam auf Gebirges Zinne,
Kloster wie auch Burgruine,
grab' sie Erinn'rung ein,
denn der Dichter lebt vom Sein.

On the mountain pinnacle, alone,
monastery and castle ruin,
engrave them in memory,
for the poet lives by being.

Atme du den heil'gen Äther,
schling die Arme um die Welt,
nur dem Würdigen, dem Großen
bleibe mutig zugesellt.

Breathe the sacred ether,
fling arms about the world,
with the great, the worthy only
boldly stay in company.

Laß die Leidenschaften sausen
im metallenen Akkord,
wenn die starken Stürme brausen,
findest du das rechte Wort.

Let the passions bluster
in brazen harmony,
when strong storms rage,
the right word you will find.

## Herbstgefühl | Autumn Feeling

ADOLF FRIEDRICH VON SCHACK

*Johannes Brahms: op. 48, no. 7, 1867*

Wie wenn im frost'gen Windhauch
    tödlich
Des Sommers letzte Blüte krankt,
Und hier und da nur, gelb und rötlich
Ein einzeln Blatt im Windhauch
    schwankt,
So schauert über mein Leben
Ein nächtig trüber kalter Tag,
Warum noch vor dem Tode beben,
O Herz, o Herz, mit deinem ewgen
    Schlag!
Sieh rings entblättert das
    Gestäude!
Was spielst du, wie der Wind am Strauch,
Noch mit der letzten welken Freude?
Gib dich zur Ruh, bald stirbt sie auch.

As when, mortally, in wind's frosty
    breath,
summer's last bloom is afflicted,
and but here and there, yellow, reddish,
one solitary leaf waves in that
    breath,
so over my life shivers
a cold, nocturnally sombre day—
why before death still tremble,
heart, O heart, with your eternal
    beat!
Around see the shrubberies, stripped
    of leaves!
Why play, as the wind at the shrub,
still with that last faded joy?
Go to your rest, it too, soon will die.

## Herr Lenz | Master Spring

EMANUEL VON BODMAN

*Richard Strauss: op. 37, no. 5, 1896–98*

Herr Lenz springt heute durch die
    Stadt
in einer blauen Hose.
Und wer zwei junge Beine hat,
Springt säftefroh, springt sonnensatt
und kauft sich bei ihm Lose.

Dort biegt er um das Giebelhaus,
die Taschen voller Gaben,
da strecken sich die Hände aus,
ein jeder möchte einen Strauß
hei! für sein Mädel haben.

Ich hole mir auch einen Schatz
hinweg von Glas und Schüssel.
Hut auf! Wir rennen übern Platz!
Herr Lenz, für ihren Busenlatz
ein'n gelben Himmelsschlüssel!

Master Spring leaps through town
    today,
clad in breeches blue,
and anyone with two young legs,
sap-joyous, leaps; sun-sated, leaps,
to buy of his lottery.

There, round the gable house he turns,
his pockets full of gifts,
there the hands go stretching out,
every man would have a nosegay
for his sweetheart, ho!

And I will fetch myself a love
away from her glasses and dishes.
Your hat! Let's run across the square!
To unlock her bosom, Master Spring,
a yellow cowslip give me!

## Herr Oluf | Lord Oluf

JOHANN GOTTFRIED HERDER

*Carl Loewe: op. 2, no. 2, 1824*

Herr Oluf reitet spät und weit,
zu bieten auf seine Hochzeitleut.

Da tanzen die Elfen auf grünem Strand,
Erlkönigs Tochter reicht ihm die Hand:

»Willkommen, Herr Oluf, komm tanze
    mit mir,
zwei goldene Sporen schenke ich dir.«

»Ich darf nicht tanzen, nicht tanzen ich
    mag,
denn morgen ist mein Hochzeitstag.«

»Tritt näher, Herr Oluf, komm tanze
    mit mir,
ein Hemd von Seide schenke ich dir,

ein Hemd von Seide, so weiß und fein,
meine Mutter bleicht's mit Monden-
    schein.«

»Ich darf nicht tanzen, nicht tanzen ich
    mag,
denn morgen ist mein Hochzeitstag.«

»Tritt näher, Herr Oluf, komm tanze
    mit mir,
einen Haufen Goldes schenke ich dir.«

Lord Oluf rides late and far
to summon his wedding guests.

Elves are dancing upon a green shore,
the Erl-king's daughter offers her hand.

'Welcome, Lord Oluf, come, dance with
    me,
two golden spurs will I give to thee.'

'I cannot dance, to dance I've no
    mind,
for tomorrow is my wedding-day.'

'Step nearer, Lord Oluf, come, dance
    with me,
a shirt of silk will I give to thee,

a shirt of silk so white and fine,
bleached by my mother with
    moonbeam's shine.'

'I cannot dance, to dance I've no
    mind,
for tomorrow is my wedding-day.'

'Step nearer, Lord Oluf, come dance with
    me,
a heap of gold will I give to thee.'

»Einen Haufen Goldes nähme ich wohl;
doch tanzen ich nicht darf noch soll.«

'A heap of gold would I gladly take;
but dance I neither can nor may.'

»Und willst du, Herr Oluf, nicht tanzen
mit mir,
soll Seuch und Krankheit folgen
dir.«

'And if, Lord Oluf, thou'll not dance
with me,
then plague and sickness shall follow
thee.'

Sie tät ihm geben einen Schlag auf's
Herz,
sein Lebtag fühlt er nicht solchen
Schmerz.

A buffet she deals him to the
heart,
never in his life such pain did he
feel.

Drauf tät sie ihn heben auf sein Pferd:
»Reit hin zu deinem Fräulein wert!«

Then on to his horse she heaves him up:
'Ride away to thy lady so dear!'

Und als er kam vor Hauses Tür,
seine Mutter zitternd stand dafür.

And when he came to his house's door,
his mother, trembling, stood before.

»Sag an, mein Sohn, sag an mir gleich,
Wovon du bist so blaß und bleich?«

'Tell me, my son, tell me straightway,
from what thou art so pallid and pale.'

»Und sollt ich nicht sein blaß und
bleich,
ich kam in Erlenkönigs Reich.«

'And should I not be pallid and
pale,
I have been in the Erl-king's realm.

»Sag an, mein Sohn, so lieb und traut,
was soll ich sagen deiner Braut?«

'Tell me, my son, so beloved and dear,
what shall I say to your bride-to-be?'

»Sagt ihr, ich ritt in den Wald zur Stund
zu proben allda mein Ross und Hund.«

'Say to her I rode just now to the wood,
there to try my horse and hound.'

Frühmorgens, als der Tag kaum
war,
da kam die Braut mit der
Hochzeitschar.

At early morn, when day had scarce
dawned,
arrived his bride with the wedding
throng.

Sie schenkten Met, sie schenkten
Wein;
»Wo ist Herr Oluf, der Bräutgam
mein?«

They poured out mead, they poured out
wine;
'Where is Lord Oluf, my husband-
to-be?'

»Herr Oluf ritt in den Wald zur Stund,
zu proben allda sein Ross und Hund.«

'Lord Oluf rode just now to the wood,
there to try his horse and hound.'

Die Braut hob auf den Scharlach
rot:
da lag Herr Oluf und war tot.

The bride raised up the cloth scarlet
red;
there lay Lord Oluf, and was dead.

## Hoffnung | Hope

FRIEDRICH SCHILLER

*Johann Friedrich Reichardt, 1809; Franz Schubert, 1819*

Es reden und träumen die Menschen
viel
Von bessern künftigen Tagen,
Nach einem glücklichen goldenen Ziel

Much men talk and
dream
of better days to come,
towards a happy, golden goal

Sieht man sie rennen und jagen.
Die Welt wird alt und wird wieder jung,
Doch der Mensch hofft immer
    Verbesserung.

Die Hoffnung führt ihn ins Leben ein,
Sie umflattert den fröhlichen Knaben,
Den Jüngling locket ihr Zauberschein,
Sie wird mit dem Greis nicht begraben,
Denn beschließt er im Grabe den
    müden Lauf,
Noch am Grabe pflanzt er—die
    Hoffnung auf.

Es ist kein leerer schmeichelnder Wahn,
Erzeugt im Gehirne des Toren,
Im Herzen kündet es laut sich an:
Zu was Besserm sind wir geboren!
Und was die innere Stimme spricht,
Das täuscht die hoffende Seele nicht.

we see them chasing and running.
The world grows old, and young again,
but man hopes ever for
    better.

Hope brings man into the world,
flutters round the merry boy,
youth is drawn by its magic gleam,
with the greybeard it's not buried—
though he end in the grave his
    weary run,
yet still at the graveside he plants
    hope.

No empty, flattering delusion is it,
engendered in the brain of a fool;
loudly it is proclaimed in the heart:
'We have been born for better!'
And what is said by the inner voice
does not deceive the hoping soul.


## Hussens Kerker | Hus's Dungeon

CONRAD FERDINAND MEYER

*Hans Pfitzner: op. 32, no. 1, 1923*

Es geht mit mir zu Ende,
Mein' Sach' und Spruch ist schon
Hoch über Menschenhände
Gerückt vor Gottes Thron,
Schon schwebt auf einer Wolke,
Umringt von seinem Volke
Entgegen mir des Menschen Sohn.

Den Kerker will ich preisen,
Der Kerker, der ist gut!
Das Fensterkreuz von Eisen
Blickt auf die frische Flut,
Und zwischen seinen Stäben
Seh' ich ein Segel schweben.
Darob im Blau die Firne ruht.

Wie nah die Flut ich fühle,
Als läg' ich drein versenkt,
Mit wundersamer Kühle
Wird mir der Leib getränkt—
Auch seh' ich eine Traube
Mit einem roten Laube,
Die tief herab ins Fenster hängt.

Es ist die Zeit zu feiern!
Es kommt die große Ruh'!
Dort lenkt ein Zug von Reihern
Dem ew'gen Lenze zu,
Sie wissen Pfad und Stege,
Sie kennen ihre Wege—
Was, meine Seele, fürchtest du?

My end draws near,
my case, my sentence have
passed, out of human hands,
to the lofty throne of God;
already, cloud-borne,
ringed by His host,
toward me comes the Son of Man.

I will extol my dungeon,
my dungeon, it is good.
The window cross of iron
looks over the cool tide,
and between its bars,
poised, I see a sail,
above, in the blue, rests snow.

How close I feel the waters,
as if I lay sunk within,
in wondrous coolness
is my body steeped—
a grape bunch, too, I see,
with red foliage,
at the window hanging in.

Time it is to celebrate!
Great peace is now at hand!
There a flight of herons
leads to eternal spring,
they know of paths, of tracks,
they know their ways—
what, my soul, do you **fear**?

## Hyazinthen | Hyacinths

THEODOR STORM

*Hermann Reutter: op. 58, no. 2, ed. 1948*

Fern hallt Musik; doch hier ist stille
Nacht,
Mit Schlummerduft anhauchen mich
die Pflanzen:
Ich habe immer, immer dein gedacht;
Ich möchte schlafen, aber du mußt
tanzen.

Es hört nicht auf, es rast ohn
Unterlaß;
Die Kerzen brennen und die Geigen
schreien,
Es teilen und es schließen sich die
Reihen,
Und alle glühen; aber du bist blaß.

Und du mußt tanzen; fremde Arme
schmiegen
Sich an dein Herz; o leide nicht
Gewalt!
Ich seh dein weißes Kleid vorüberfliegen
Und deine leichte, zärtliche Gestalt.—

Und süßer strömend quillt der Duft der
Nacht
Und träumerischer aus dem Kelch der
Pflanzen.
Ich habe immer, immer dein gedacht;
Icb möchte schlafen, aber du mußt
tanzen.

Distant music; but here, silent
night,
the flowers waft at me their slumber-
scent:
always, always I have thought of you;
I would sleep, but you must
dance.

No end there is, a whirling without
cease,
the candles blaze, the fiddles
scream,
the rows of dancers open out and
close,
all are flushed, but you are pale.

And you must dance; other arms are
twined
about your heart; oh, endure no
violence!
I see your white dress go flying past,
your graceful, delicate shape.

And the scent of night more sweetly
wells,
and dreamier, from the chalice of the
flowers:
always, always I have thought of you;
I would sleep, but you must
dance.


## Hyperions Schicksalslied | Hyperion's Song of Fate

FRIEDRICH HÖLDERLIN

*Johannes Brahms: op. 54; Wolfgang Fortner, 1933*

Ihr wandelt droben im Licht
Auf weichem Boden, selige Genien!
Glänzende Götterlüfte
Rühren euch leicht,
Wie die Finger der Künstlerin
Heilige Saiten.

Schicksallos, wie der schlafende
Säugling, atmen die Himmlischen;
Keusch bewahrt
In bescheidener Knospe,
Blühet ewig
Ihnen der Geist,
Und die seligen Augen
Blicken in stiller
Ewiger Klarheit.

You wander on high, in light,
on ground that is soft, blessed genii!
Shining, godly zephyrs
brush you as lightly
as the player's fingers
holy strings.

Fateless, like sleeping
infants, the Celestial breathe;
chastely preserved
in modest bud,
in eternal blossom
their spirit lives,
and their blissful eyes
gaze in calm
everlasting clarity.

Doch uns ist gegeben,
Auf keiner Stätte zu ruhn,
Es schwinden, es fallen
Die leidenden Menschen
Blindlings von einer
Stunde zur andern,
Wie Wasser von Klippe
Zu Klippe geworfen,
Jahrlang ins Ungewisse hinab.

Yet to us is given
in no place to rest—
they vanish, they fall,
suffering mortals,
blindly from one
hour to the next,
like water flung
from cliff to cliff
for years into the unknown down.

## Ich atmet' einen linden Duft | I Breathed a Gentle Fragrance

FRIEDRICH RÜCKERT

*Gustav Mahler, ed. 1905*

Ich atmet' einen linden Duft.
Im Zimmer stand
Ein Zweig der Linde,
Ein Angebinde
Von lieber Hand.
Wie lieblich war der Lindenduft!

I breathed a gentle fragrance.
In the room stood
a sprig of lime,
the gift
of a dear hand:
how lovely the fragrance was!

Wie lieblich ist der Lindenduft!
Das Lindenreis
Brachst du gelinde;
Ich atme leis
Im Duft der Linde
Der Liebe linden Duft.

How lovely the fragrance is!
That sprig of lime,
tenderly you broke;
softly I breathe
in the fragrant lime
love's gentle fragrance.

## Ich bin der Welt abhanden gekommen | Lost Am I to the World

FRIEDRICH RÜCKERT

*Gustav Mahler, ed. 1905*

Ich bin der Welt abhanden gekommen,
mit der ich sonst viele Zeit verdorben;
sie hat so lange nichts von mir
    vernommen,
sie mag wohl glauben, ich sei gestorben!

Lost am I to the world,
with which I used to waste much time;
so long has it heard naught of
    me,
well may it think me dead!

Es ist mir auch gar nichts daran gelegen,
ob sie mich für gestorben hält.
Ich kann auch gar nichts sagen dagegen,
denn wirklich bin ich gestorben der
    Welt.

Nor is it to me of consequence
if it should so consider me.
Nor can I say aught against it,
for truly I am dead to the
    world.

Ich bin gestorben dem Weltgetümmel
und ruh' in einem stillen Gebiet!
Ich leb' allein in meinem Himmel,
in meinem Lieben, in meinem Lied.

Dead am I to the world's tumult
and rest in a quiet realm!
I live alone in my heaven,
in my love and in my song.

## Ich ging mit Lust durch einen grünen Wald | I Walked with Joy in Woodland Green

from *Des Knaben Wunderhorn*

*Gustav Mahler, ca. 1880–83*

Ich ging mit Lust durch einen grünen
   Wald,
ich hört' die Vöglein singen;
sie sangen so jung, sie sangen so alt,
die kleinen Waldvöglein im grünen
   Wald!
Wie gern hört' ich sie singen!

Nun sing, nun sing, Frau Nachtigall!
Sing du's bei meinem Feinsliebchen:
Komm schier, wenn's finster ist,
wenn niemand auf der Gasse ist,
dann komm zu mir!
Herein will ich dich lassen!

Der Tag verging, die Nacht brach an,
er kam zu Feinsliebchen, Feinsliebchen
   gegangen.
Er klopft so leis' wohl an den Ring:
»Ei schläfst du oder wachst mein Kind!
Ich hab so lang gestanden!«

[Es schaut der Mond durchs Fensterlein
zum holden, süßen Lieben,
die Nachtigall sang die ganze Nacht.
Du schlafselig Mägdelein, nimm dich in
   Acht!
Wo ist dein Herzliebster geblieben?]

I walked with joy in woodland
   green,
I heard the small birds singing;
so young they sang, so old they sang,
the tiny birds in woodland
   green!
How gladly I heard them sing!

Now sing, Mistress Nightingale,
sing at my beloved's house:
come soon when it is dark,
when nobody is in the street,
then come to me.
I will let you in!

The day passed, night fell,
he came to his
   beloved.
He taps so softly on the ring:
'Ah, are you asleep or awake, my dear?
So long have I been standing!'

(The moon looks through the window,
at the dear sweet love,
the nightingale sang all the night.
Sleepy little maid, take
   care!
Where is your dearest love?)

## Ich liebe dich | I Love You

K. F. HEROSSEE

*Ludwig van Beethoven, 1797?*

Ich liebe dich, so wie du mich,
Am Abend und am Morgen,
Noch war kein Tag, wo du und ich
Nicht teilten unsre Sorgen.

Auch waren sie für dich und mich
Geteilt leicht zu ertragen;
Du tröstetest im Kummer mich,
Ich weint in deine Klagen.

Drum Gottes Segen über dir,
Du, meines Lebens Freude.
Gott schütze dich, erhalt dich mir,
Schütz und erhalt uns beide.

I love you as you love me,
at evening and at morning,
no day there was when you and I
did not share our sorrows.

And for me and you they were,
when shared, an easy burden;
you comforted me in my distress,
I wept when you lamented.

So on you God's blessing be,
you, my life's delight.
God protect you, keep you for me,
protect and keep us both.

## Ich liebe dich | I Love You

DETLEV VON LILIENCRON

*Richard Strauss: op. 37, no. 2, 1896–98*

Vier adlige Rosse
Voran unserm Wagen,
Wir wohnen im Schlosse
In stolzem Behagen.

Die Frühlichterwellen
Und nächtens der Blitz,
Was all sie erhellen,
Ist unser Besitz.

Und irrst du verlassen,
Verbannt durch die Lande;
Mit dir durch die Gassen
In Armut und Schande!

Es bluten die Hände,
Die Füße sind wund,
Vier trostlose Wände,
Es kennt uns kein Hund.

Steht silberbeschlagen
Dein Sarg am Altar,
Sie sollen mich tragen
Zu dir auf die Bahr,

Und fern auf der Heide
Und stirbst du in Not,
Den Dolch aus der Scheide,
Dir nach in den Tod!

Four noble steeds
we have to our carriage,
we live in the castle
in comfortable pride.

First surging brightness
and lightning at night,
all they illumine,
all that is ours.

Though forlorn you wander,
an exile, through the world,
I'll walk the alleys with you
in poverty and shame.

Our hands will bleed,
our feet be sore,
the four walls cheerless,
not a dog will know us.

If, silver-fitted,
your coffin's at the altar,
they shall bear me
on the bier to join you.

If away on the heath
or in distress you die,
then dagger I'll draw
and follow you in death!

## Ich trage meine Minne | I Bear My Love

KARL HENCKELL

*Richard Strauss: op. 32, no. 1, 1896*

Ich trage meine Minne vor Wonne
stumm
Im Herzen und im Sinne mit mir herum.
Ja, daß ich dich gefunden, du liebes
Kind,
Das freut mich alle Tage, die mir
beschieden sind.

Und ob auch der Himmel trübe,
kohlschwarz die Nacht,
Hell leuchtet meiner Liebe goldsonnige
Pracht.
Und lügt auch die Welt in Sünden, so
tut mir's weh,
Die arge muß erblinden vor deiner
Unschuld Schnee.

I bear my love, with rapture
mute,
about with me in heart and thought.
Yes, that I have found you, sweet
child,
will cheer me all my allotted
days.

And though skies be dim, the night
coal-black,
bright shines the gold sun's splendour
of my love.
And though the world may sinfully lie,
I'm sorry—
the bad world must be blinded by your
purity's snow.

## Ich Wollt ein Sträußlein binden / I Would Have Bound a Nosegay

CLEMENS BRENTANO

*Richard Strauss: op. 68, no. 2, 1918/19*

Ich wollt ein Sträußlein binden,
Da kam die dunkle Nacht,
Kein Blümlein war zu finden,
Sonst hätt ich dir's gebracht.

Da flossen von den Wangen
Mir Tränen in den Klee,
Ein Blümlein aufgegangen
Ich nun im Garten seh.

Das wollte ich dir brechen
Wohl in dem dunklen Klee,
Doch fing es an zu sprechen:
»Ach, tue mir nicht weh!

Sei freundlich im Herzen,
Betracht dein eigen Leid,
Und lasse mich in Schmerzen
Nicht sterben vor der Zeit!«

Und hätt's nicht so gesprochen,
Im Garten ganz allein,
So hätt ich dir's gebrochen,
Nun aber darf's nicht sein.

Mein Schatz ist ausgeblieben,
Ich bin so ganz allein.
Im Lieben wohnt Betrüben,
Und kann nicht anders sein.

I would have bound a nosegay,
but dark night came,
no flower could I find,
or I'd have brought it.

Then from my cheeks
tears flowed on the clover,
one flower has come up
in the garden, I see.

For you I tried to pluck it
in the dark clover,
but it spoke up and said
'Ah, do me no harm!

'Be kind in your heart,
behold your own grief,
and let me not in agony
die before my time.'

And had it not spoken so,
in the garden all alone,
for you I would have plucked it,
but that now cannot be.

My love has not come,
I am so very alone.
In love dwells affliction,
no different can it be.


## Ihr Glocken von Marling / Bells of Marling

EMIL KUH

*Franz Liszt, 1874*

Ihr Glocken von Marling, wie brauset
  ihr so hell!
Ein wohliges Lauten, als sänge der
  Quell.
Ihr Glocken von Marling, ein heil'ger
  Gesang
Umwallet wie schützend den weltlichen
  Klang.
Nehmt mich in die Mitte der tönenden
  Flut;
Ihr Glocken von Marling, behütet
  mich gut.

Bells of Marling, how clear you
  peal,
a cheerful sound, like a brook's
  singing!
Bells of Marling, a sacred
  hymn
protectively walls the sounds of this
  world.
Bear me to the middle of the resonant
  flood;
bells of Marling, watch over me
  well.

## Ihr, ihr Herrlichen! | Majestic Ones!

FRIEDRICH HÖLDERLIN: from the poem *Die Eichbäume*

*Max Reger: op. 75, no. 6, 1903*

Ihr, ihr Herrlichen! Steht, wie ein Volk
von Titanen
In der zahmeren Welt und gehört nur
euch und dem Himmel,
Der euch nährt' und erzog und der
Erde, die euch geboren.
Keiner von euch ist noch in der
Menschen Schule gegangen,
Und ihr drängt euch fröhlich und frei,
aus kräftiger Wurzel,
Untereinander herauf und ergreift, wie
der Adler die Beute,
Mit gewaltigen Armen den Raum, und
gegen die Wolken
Ist euch heiter und groß die sonnige
Krone gerichtet.
Eine Welt ist jeder von euch, wie die
Sterne des Himmels
Lebt ihr, jeder ein Gott, in freiem
Bunde zusammen.

Majestic ones! You stand like a race of
Titans
in a tamer world; yours you are alone,
and Heaven's
who nourished, reared you, and Earth's,
who bore you.
None of you has walked yet in the
school of men,
and happy and free, you thrust from
powerful root
up together, seizing, as the eagle its
prey,
space in your mighty arms; and to the
clouds
point your sunny crowns, serenely and
grandly.
Each of you is a world; like the stars of
heaven
you live, each a god, in free union
together.

## Im Abendrot | In the Evening Glow

CARL LAPPE

*Franz Schubert, 1824*

O wie schön ist deine Welt,
Vater, wenn sie golden strahlet!
Wenn dein Glanz herniederfällt,
Und den Staub mit Schimmer malet,
Wenn das Rot, das in der Wolke blinkt,
In mein stilles Fenster sinkt!

Könnt ich klagen, könnt ich zagen?
Irre sein an dir und mir?
Nein, ich will im Busen tragen
Deinen Himmel schon allhier.
Und dies Herz, eh es zusammenbricht,
Trinkt noch Glut und schlürft noch
Licht.

Oh, how beautiful your world,
Father, when it shines golden!
When your radiance descends,
making lustrous the dust,
and the red, gleaming in the cloud,
sinks into my quiet window!

Could I complain, lose heart,
doubt you, and myself?
No, your Heaven will I carry
here, in my bosom.
And this heart, ere it fail,
shall still drink glow and
light.

## Im April | In April

EMANUEL GEIBEL

*Max Reger: op, 4, no. 4, 1890–91*

Du feuchter Frühlingsabend,
Wie hab' ich dich so gern!
Der Himmel ist wolkenverhangen,
Nur hier und da ein Stern.

Dewy spring evening,
so fond of you am I!
The sky is hung with cloud,
a star but here and there.

Wie leiser Liebesodem  
Hauchet so lau die Luft,  
Es steigt aus allen Talen  
Ein warmer Veilchenduft.  

Ich möcht' ein Lied ersinnen,  
Das diesem Abend gleich,  
Und kann den Klang nicht finden  
So dunkel, mild und weich.  

Mild as love's gentle breath  
the breeze blows,  
from every valley rises  
a warm violet fragrance.  

A song would I make  
to match this evening,  
and cannot find that chord  
so dark, mild and gentle.  

## Im Frühling | In Spring

EDUARD MÖRIKE

*Hugo Wolf, 1888*

Hier lieg ich auf dem Frühlingshügel:  
Die Wolke wird mein Flügel,  
Ein Vogel fliegt mir voraus.  
Ach, sag mir, alleinzige Liebe,  
Wo du bleibst, daß ich bei dir bliebe!  
Doch du und die Lüfte, ihr habt kein  
    Haus.  

Der Sonnenblume gleich steht mein  
    Gemüte offen,  
Sehnend,  
Sich dehnend  
In Lieben und Hoffen.  
Frühling, was bist du gewillt?  
Wann werd ich gestillt?  

Die Wolke seh ich wandeln und den  
    Fluß,  
Es dringt der Sonne goldner Kuß  
Mir tief bis ins Geblüt hinein;  
Die Augen, wunderbar berauschet,  
Tun, als schliefen sie ein,  
Nur noch das Ohr dem Ton der Biene  
    lauschet.  
Ich denke dies und denke das,  
Ich sehne mich und weiß nicht recht  
    nach was:  
Halb ist es Lust, halb ist es Klage;  
Mein Herz, o sage,  
Was webst du für Erinnerung  
In golden grüner Zweige Dämmerung?  
—Alte unnennbare Tage!  

Here I lie on the spring hill:  
the cloud becomes my wings,  
a bird flies before me.  
Oh, tell me, one-and-only love,  
where you are, that I may be with you!  
But you and the breezes have no  
    home.  

Sunflower-like my heart lies  
    open,  
yearning,  
reaching up  
in loving and hoping.  
Spring, what is your will?  
When shall I be stilled?  

The cloud I see go its way, and the  
    river;  
the sun kisses its gold  
deep into my veins;  
my eyes, marvellously enthralled,  
close, as if in sleep,  
yet my ear harks still to the humming  
    bee.  
I think this and think that,  
yearn, and know not quite for  
    what:  
half joy it is, and half complaint;  
oh say, my heart,  
what memories you weave  
in golden-green bough twilight?  
—Past, unutterable days!  

## Im Frühling | In Spring

ERNST SCHULZE

*Franz Schubert, 1826*

Still sitz ich an des Hügels Hang,  
Der Himmel ist so klar,  

Silent, I sit on the hillside,  
the heavens are so clear,

Das Lüftchen spielt im grünen Tal,
Wo ich beim ersten Frühlingsstrahl
Einst, ach so glücklich war.

the breeze plays in the green valley,
where, in spring's first gleam,
I was once, ah, so happy.

Wo ich an ihrer Seite ging
So traulich und so nah,
Und tief im dunklen Felsenquell
Den schönen Himmel blau und hell
Und sie im Himmel sah.

Where at her side I walked,
so fondly and so close,
and, deep in the dark rocky stream,
saw the fair heavens blue and bright,
and in the heavens her too.

Sieh, wie der bunte Frühling schon
Aus Knosp und Blüte blickt!
Nicht alle Blüten sind mir gleich,
Am liebsten pflückt ich von dem Zweig,
Von welchem sie gepflückt!

See, how gaily-coloured spring
peeps from bud and blossom!
All blossom is not alike to me,
most gladly from that branch I'd pick
from which she once picked.

Denn alles ist wie damals noch,
Die Blumen, das Gefild;
Die Sonne scheint nicht minder hell,
Nicht minder freundlich schwimmt im
     Quell
Das blaue Himmelsbild.

For all is still as once it was,
the flowers and the field;
no less brightly shines the sun,
and no less kindly in the
     stream
heaven's blue image floats.

Es wandeln nur sich Will und Wahn,
Es wechseln Lust und Streit,
Vorüber flieht der Liebe Glück,
Und nur die Liebe bleibt zurück,
Die Lieb und ach, das Leid.

Will and delusion, they only change,
joy alternates with quarrel,
happiness of love flies by,
and love alone remains,
love, and ah, the pain.

O wär ich doch ein Vöglein nur
Dort an dem Wiesenhang,
Dann blieb ich auf den Zweigen hier,
Und säng ein süßes Lied von ihr,
Den ganzen Sommer lang.

Oh, if only I were a tiny bird,
there on the meadow's bank,
then on these branches here I'd stay,
and sing a sweet song of her,
all the summer through.

## Im Spätboot | Last Boat

CONRAD FERDINAND MEYER

*Richard Strauss: op. 56, no. 3, 1903–06*

Aus der Schiffsbank mach ich meinen
     Pfühl.
Endlich wird die heiße Stirne kühl!
O wie süß erkaltet mir das
     Herz!
O wie weich verstummen Lust und
     Schmerz!
Über mir des Rohres schwarzer Rauch
Wiegt und biegt sich in des Windes
     Hauch.
Hüben hier und wieder drüben dort
Hält das Boot an manchem kleinen Port:
Bei der Schiffslaterne kargem Schein
Steigt ein Schatten aus und niemand
     ein.
Nur der Steurer noch, der wacht und
     steht!

Of the boat's bench I make my
     couch.
My burning brow at last is cooled!
Oh, how sweetly cold my heart
     becomes!
Oh, how gently pain and joy are
     stilled!
Over me the black smoke of the funnel
curves and wavers in the
     breeze.
First at this bank, then at that,
the boat puts in at many a little port:
by the ship's lantern's meagre glow,
a shadow lands and no one comes
     aboard.
Only the helmsman, still standing,
     watching!

Nur der Wind, der mir im Haare weht!
Schmerz und Lust erleiden sanften Tod.
Einen Schlummrer trägt das dunkle
   Boot.

Only the wind, blowing in my hair!
Pain and joy die a gentle death.
A slumberer is borne by the dark
   boat.


## Immer leiser wird mein Schlummer | Ever Lighter Grows My Slumber

HERMANN LINGG

*Johannes Brahms: op. 105, no. 2, 1886; Hans Pfitzner: op. 2, no. 6, 1888–89*

Immer leiser wird mein Schlummer,
Nur wie Schleier liegt mein Kummer
Zitternd über mir.
Oft im Traume hör ich dich
Rufen drauß vor meiner Tür,
Niemand wacht und öffnet dir,
Ich erwach und weine bitterlich.

Ever lighter grows my slumber,
but my sorrows lie like a haze,
trembling over me.
Often in my dreams I hear you
calling outside my door,
no one is awake to let you in,
I wake and weep bitterly.

Ja, ich werde sterben müssen,
Eine andre wirst du küssen,
Wenn ich bleich und kalt.
Eh die Maienlüfte wehn,
Eh die Drossel singt im Wald:
Willst du mich noch einmal sehn,
Komm, o komme bald!

Yes, I shall have to die,
another will you kiss
when I am pale and cold.
Ere May breezes blow,
ere the thrush sings in the wood—
if you once more would see me,
come, oh come soon!


## In Danzig | In Danzig

JOSEPH VON EICHENDORFF

*Hans Pfitzner: op. 22, no. 1, 1907*

Dunkle Giebel, hohe Fenster,
Türme tief aus Nebeln sehn,
Bleiche Statuen wie Gespenster
Lautlos an den Türen stehn.

Dark gables, tall windows,
spires gaze deep in mist,
pale statues like spectres
stand soundless at doors.

Träumerisch der Mond drauf scheinet,
Dem die Stadt gar wohl gefällt,
Als läg' zauberhaft versteinet
Drunten eine Märchenwelt.

Dreaming the moon lights
the town it so favours,
as if magically turned to stone
below it lay a fairy world.

Ringsher durch das tiefe Lauschen,
Über alle Häuser weit,
Nur des Meeres fernes Rauschen—
Wunderbare Einsamkeit!

Around, through deep somnolence,
over all houses,
only the distant roar of the sea
—wondrous solitude!

Und der Türmer wie vor Jahren
Singet ein uraltes Lied:
Wolle Gott den Schiffer wahren,
Der bei Nacht vorüberzieht!

And the watchman, as for years,
sings an old, old song:
may God protect the sailor
who sails by in the night.

## In der Frühe | At Daybreak

EDUARD MÖRIKE

*Hugo Wolf, 1888*

Kein Schlaf noch kühlt das Auge mir,
Dort gehet schon der Tag herfür
An meinem Kammerfenster.
Es wühlet mein verstörter Sinn
Noch zwischen Zweifeln her und hin
Und schaffet Nachtgespenster.
Ängste, quäle
Dich nicht länger, meine Seele!
Freu dich! schon sind da und dorten
Morgenglocken wach geworden.

No sleep yet cools my eyes,
already day begins to rise
at the window of my room.
My troubled mind still casts
about among my doubts,
creating nightmares.
Alarm, torment
yourself no more, my soul!
Be glad! Here and there
morning bells have woken.

## In questa tomba oscura | In this Dark Tomb

GIUSEPPE CARPANI

*Ludwig van Beethoven, 1808*

In questa tomba oscura lasciami riposar;
Quando vivevo, ingrata, dovevi a me
  pensar.
Lascia che l'ombre ignude godansi pace
  almen
E non bagnar mie ceneri d'inutile
  velen.

In this dark tomb let me rest;
you ought, thankless one, to have
  thought of me, when I lived.
Leave at least naked shades to enjoy
  their peace,
and bathe not my ashes with ineffectual
  venom.

## In Waldeseinsamkeit | In Forest Solitude

KARL VON LEMCKE

*Johannes Brahms: op. 85, no. 6, 1879*

Ich saß zu deinen Füßen
in Waldeseinsamkeit;
Windesatmen, Sehnen
ging durch die Wipfel breit.

At your feet I sat
in forest solitude;
the breeze and longing
stir the spreading trees.

In stummem Ringen senkt' ich
das Haupt in deinen Schoß,
und meine bebenden Hände
um deine Knie ich schloß.

I sank in silent struggle
my head upon your lap,
and my trembling hands
I clasped about your knees.

Die Sonne ging hinunter,
der Tag verglühte all.
Ferne, ferne, ferne
sang eine Nachtigall.

The sun went down,
the day glowed all away.
And far, far, far off
sang a nightingale.

# Italienisches Liederbuch / Italian Songbook

PAUL HEYSE: after LEOPARDI, GIUSTI, CARDUCCI and ADA NEGRI

Hugo Wolf: nos. 1–7, 1890; nos. 8–22, 1891; nos. 23–46, 1896

**1**

Auch kleine Dinge können uns entzücken,
Auch kleine Dinge können teuer sein.
Bedenkt, wie gern wir uns mit Perlen
    schmücken;
Sie werden schwer bezahlt und sind
    nur klein.
Bedenkt, wie klein ist die Olivenfrucht,
Und wird um ihre Güte doch gesucht.
Denkt an die Rose nur, wie klein sie ist,
Und duftet doch so lieblich, wie ihr wißt.

**1**

Even small things may delight us,
even small things may be precious.
Think how gladly we deck ourselves in
    pearls;
for much they are sold, and are only
    small.
Think how small the olive is,
and yet it is sought for its virtue.
Think only of the rose, how small it is,
yet smells so sweet, as you know.

**2**

Mir ward gesagt, du reisest in die Ferne.
Ach, wohin gehst du, mein geliebtes
    Leben?
Den Tag, an dem du scheidest, wüßt
    ich gerne;
Mit Tränen will ich das Geleit dir
    geben.
Mit Tränen will ich deinen Weg
    befeuchten—
Gedenk an mich, und Hoffnung wird
    mir leuchten!
Mit Tränen bin ich bei dir
    allerwärts—
Gedenk an mich, vergiß es nicht, mein
    Herz!

**2**

I was told you were going far away.
Oh, where are you going, my dearest
    love?
The day you leave, I would gladly
    know;
my tears will be your
    escort.
With tears will I bedew your
    path—
Think of me, and hope will shine on
    me!
Through tears will I be with you
    everywhere—
Think of me, do not forget, my
    love!

**3**

Ihr seid die Allerschönste weit und breit,
Viel schöner als im Mai der Blumenflor.
Orvietos Dom steigt so voll
    Herrlichkeit,
Viterbos größter Brunnen nicht empor.
So hoher Reiz und Zauber ist dein
    eigen,
Der Dom von Siena muß sich vor dir
    neigen.
Ach, du bist so an Reiz und Anmut reich,
Der Dom von Siena selbst ist dir nicht
    gleich.

**3**

You are the fairest far and wide,
fairer by far than flowers in May.
Orvieto Cathedral does not rise so
    glorious,
nor Viterbo's grandest fountain.
Such lofty charm and magic are your
    own,
Siena Cathedral must bow before
    you.
Oh, so rich you are in grace and charm,
even Siena Cathedral is not your
    peer.

**4**

Gesegnet sei, durch den die Welt
    entstund;
Wie trefflich schuf er sie nach allen
    Seiten!
Er schuf das Meer mit endlos tiefem
    Grund,
Er schuf die Schiffe, die hinübergleiten,
Er schuf das Paradies mit ewgem Licht,
Er schuf die Schönheit und dein
    Angesicht.

**4**

Blessed be he, through whom the world
    began;
how excellent on every side he made
    it!
He made the sea of unfathomable
    depth,
he made the ships that glide across,
he made paradise with its eternal light,
he made beauty and your
    face.

5

Selig ihr Blinden, die ihr nicht zu
schauen
Vermögt die Reize, die uns Glut
entfachen;
Selig ihr Tauben, die ihr ohne Grauen
Die Klagen der Verliebten könnt
verlachen;
Selig ihr Stummen, die ihr nicht den
Frauen
Könnt eure Herzensnot verständlich
machen;
Selig ihr Toten, die man hat begraben!
Ihr sollt vor Liebesqualen Ruhe
haben.


6

Wer rief dich denn? Wer hat dich
herbestellt?
Wer hieß dich kommen, wenn es dir zur
Last?
Geh zu dem Liebchen, das dir mehr
gefällt,
Geh dahin, wo du die Gedanken hast.
Geh nur, wohin dein Sinnen steht und
Denken!
Daß du zu mir kommst, will ich gern
dir schenken.
Geh zu dem Liebchen, das dir mehr
gefällt!
Wer rief dich denn? Wer hat dich
herbestellt?


7

Der Mond hat eine schwere Klag
erhoben
Und vor dem Herrn die Sache kund
gemacht;
Er wolle nicht mehr stehn am Himmel
droben,
Du habest ihn um seinen Glanz
gebracht.
Als er zuletzt das Sternenheer
gezählt,
Da hab es an der vollen Zahl gefehlt;
Zwei von den schönsten habest du
entwendet,
Die beiden Augen dort, die mich
verblendet.


8

Nun laß uns Frieden schließen, liebstes
Leben,
Zu lang ist's schon, daß wir in Fehde
liegen.
Wenn du nicht willst, will ich mich dir
ergeben;
Wie könnten wir uns auf den Tod
bekriegen?


5

Blessed you blind who cannot
see
those charms that fan our
ardour;
blessed you deaf who, unappalled,
the laments of lovers can laugh
away;
blessed you dumb who to
women
your distress of heart cannot
convey;
blessed you dead and buried!
You shall have peace from love's
torments.


6

Who called you then? Who sent for
you?
Who bade you come, if burdensome it
is?
Go to that love who pleases you the
more,
go there, where you have your thoughts.
Go where your intention is, your
mind!
From coming to me I gladly will
excuse you.
Go to that love who pleases you the
more!
Who called you then? Who sent for
you?


7

The moon has raised a grave
complaint
and made the matter known unto the
Lord:
no longer will he stay in the sky
above,
for you have robbed him of his
radiance.
When last he made a count of all the
stars,
their number was not full;
two of the fairest you have
stolen,
those eyes, which have dazzled
me.


8

Let us now make peace, my dearest
love,
too long already have we
feuded.
If you'll not yield, then will I to
you;
how could we war to the
death?

Es schließen Frieden Könige und
Fürsten,
Und sollten Liebende nicht darnach
dürsten?
Es schließen Frieden Fürsten und
Soldaten,
Und sollt es zwei Verliebten wohl
mißraten?
Meinst du, daß, was so großen Herrn
gelingt,
Ein Paar zufriedner Herzen nicht
vollbringt?

9
Daß doch gemalt all deine Reize
wären,
Und dann der Heidenfürst das Bildnis
fände.
Er würde dir ein groß Geschenk
verehren,
Und legte seine Kron in deine
Hände.
Zum rechten Glauben müßte sich
bekehren
Sein ganzes Reich, bis an sein fernstes
Ende.
Im ganzen Lande würd es
ausgeschrieben,
Christ soll ein jeder werden und dich
lieben.
Ein jeder Heide flugs bekehrte
sich
Und würd ein guter Christ und liebte
dich.

10
Du denkst mit einem Fädchen mich zu
fangen,
Mit einem Blick schon mich verliebt
zu machen?
Ich fing schon andre, die sich höher
schwangen;
Du darfst mir ja nicht traun, siehst du
mich lachen.
Schon andre fing ich, glaub es sicherlich.
Ich bin verliebt, doch eben nicht in dich.

11
Wie lange schon war immer mein
Verlangen:
Ach, wäre doch ein Musikus mir gut!
Nun ließ der Herr mich meinen Wunsch
erlangen
Und schickt mir einen, ganz wie Milch
und Blut.
Da kommt er eben her mit sanfter
Miene,
Und senkt den Kopf und spielt die
Violine.

Peace is made by princes and by
kings,
and should not they who love crave it
too?
Peace is made by princes and by
soldiers,
and should not two who are in love
succeed?
Do you think that what great lords can
manage,
two happy hearts shall not
accomplish?

9
Would that all your charms had been
painted,
and the canvas then by the heathen prince
were found.
With a great gift he would honour
you,
and would place his crown in your
hands.
All to the true faith would have to
turn,
all, to the furthest corner of his
realm.
Throughout the land would be made
known
that each must become Christian, and
love you.
At once all the heathen would change
their faith,
become good Christians, and love
you.

10
You think to snare me with a
thread,
make me, with one glance, fall in
love?
I've caught others who've flown
higher;
you musn't trust me if you see me
laugh.
Others I've caught, believe you me.
I am in love, but not with you.

11
How long and constantly have I
wished:
oh, if only a musician loved me!
Now the Lord has granted me my
wish
and sends me one all pink and
white.
And here he comes with gentle
mien,
and bows his head, and plays the
violin.

**12**

Nein, junger Herr, so treibt man's nicht,
  fürwahr;
Man sorgt dafür, sich schicklich zu
  betragen.
Für alltags bin ich gut genug, nicht
  wahr?
Doch beßre suchst du dir an Feiertagen.
Nein, junger Herr, wirst du so weiter
  sündgen,
Wird dir den Dienst dein
  Alltagsliebchen kündgen.

**13**

Hoffärtig seid Ihr, schönes Kind, und
  geht
Mit Euren Freiern um auf stolzem Fuß.
Spricht man Euch an, kaum daß Ihr
  Rede steht,
Als kostet Euch zuviel ein holder Gruß.
Bist keines Alexanders Töchterlein,
Kein Königreich wird deine Mitgift
  sein,
Und willst du nicht das Gold, so nimm
  das Zinn;
Willst du nicht Liebe, nimm
  Verachtung hin.

**14**

Geselle, wolln wir uns in Kutten
  hüllen,
Die Welt dem lassen, den sie mag
  ergötzen?
Dann pochen wir an Tür um Tür im
  stillen:
»Gebt einem armen Mönch um Jesu
  willen.«
—O lieber Pater, du mußt später
  kommen,
Wenn aus dem Ofen wir das Brot
  genommen.
O lieber Pater, komm nur später wieder,
Ein Töchterlein von mir liegt krank
  darnieder.
—Und ist sie krank, so laßt mich zu ihr
  gehen,
Daß sie nicht etwa sterbe unversehen.
Und ist sie krank, so laßt mich nach ihr
  schauen,
Daß sie mir ihre Beichte mag vertrauen.
Schließt Tür und Fenster, daß uns
  keiner störe,
Wenn ich des armen Kindes Beichte
  höre!

**15**

Mein Liebster ist so klein, daß ohne
  Bücken
Er mir das Zimmer fegt mit seinen
  Locken.

**12**

No, young man, that's not how one
  carries on;
one takes care to behave in a decent
  manner.
For everyday I'm good enough, you
  think?
But on holidays you look for better.
No, young man, go on doing wrong like
  this,
and your everyday love gives you her
  notice.

**13**

Haughty you are, lovely child, and
  deal
arrogantly with your suitors.
When spoken to, you hardly deign
  reply,
as if a friendly greeting cost too much.
You are no Alexander's daughter,
your dowry won't be a
  kingdom;
if you don't want gold, take
  tin;
if you don't want love, take
  scorn.

**14**

Friend, shall we conceal ourselves in
  cowls,
and leave the world to him it may
  delight?
Then, secretly, we'll knock at every
  door:
'Give to a poor monk for Jesus'
  sake.'
—O dear father, later you must
  come,
when we have taken the bread from the
  oven.
O dear father, just come back later,
one of my daughters is ill in
  bed.
—And if she is, then let me to
  her,
lest she die without last ministration.
And if she is, then let me tend
  her,
that she may confess her sins to me.
Close door and window, that none
  disturb
while I hear the poor child's
  confession!

**15**

My sweetheart's so small, that without
  bending
he sweeps my room with his
  hair.

Als er ins Gärtlein ging, Jasmin zu
    pflücken,
Ist er vor einer Schnecke sehr
    erschrocken.
Dann setzt er sich ins Haus um zu
    verschnaufen,
Da warf ihn eine Fliege übern Haufen;
Und als er hintrat an mein Fensterlein,
Stieß eine Bremse ihm den Schädel ein.
Verwünscht sei'n alle Fliegen, Schnaken,
    Bremsen
Und wer ein Schätzchen hat aus den
    Maremmen!
Verwünscht sei'n alle Fliegen, Schnaken,
    Mücken
Und wer sich, wenn er küßt, so tief
    muß bücken!

16
Ihr jungen Leute, die ihr zieht ins
    Feld,
Auf meinen Liebsten sollt ihr Achtung
    geben.
Sorgt, daß er tapfer sich im Feuer hält;
Er war noch nie im Kriege all sein
    Leben.
Laßt nie ihn unter freiem Himmel
    schlafen;
Er ist so zart, es möchte sich bestrafen.
Laßt mir ihn ja nicht schlafen unterm
    Mond;
Er ginge drauf, er ist's ja nicht gewohnt.

17
Und willst du deinen Liebsten sterben
    sehen,
So trage nicht dein Haar gelockt, du
    Holde.
Laß von den Schultern frei sie
    niederwehen;
Wie Fäden sehn sie aus von purem
    Golde.
Wie goldne Fäden, die der Wind
    bewegt—
Schön sind die Haare, schön ist, die sie
    trägt!
Goldfäden, Seidenfäden
    ungezählt—
Schön sind die Haare, schön ist, die
    sie strählt!

18
Heb auf dein blondes Haupt und
    schlafe nicht,
Und laß dich ja vom Schlummer nicht
    betören.
Ich sage dir vier Worte von Gewicht,
Von denen darfst du keines überhören.
Das erste: daß um dich mein Herze
    bricht,

---

When he went to the garden to pick
    jasmine,
a snail scared him out of his
    wits.
Then when he came in to
    recover,
a fly knocked him all of a heap;
and when he came to my window,
a horse-fly stove in his head.
A curse on all flies—crane- and
    horse-
and whoever has a sweetheart from
    Maremma!
A curse on all flies, craneflies and
    midges
and whoever, for his kiss, has so to
    stoop!

16
You young men who are marching to
    war,
you are to take care of my
    beloved.
See that he keeps brave under fire;
he's never been to war in his
    life.
Never let him sleep in the
    open;
he's so delicate, he'd suffer for it.
And don't let him sleep out under the
    moon;
he'd die, he's not used to it, you see.

17
If you would see your sweetheart die
    for love,
then wear your hair not curled, my
    fairest.
Let it from your shoulders tumble
    free;
like threads it looks of pure
    gold.
Like golden threads stirred by the
    wind—
lovely her hair, lovely she who owns
    it!
Gold threads, silk threads
    unnumbered—
lovely her hair, lovely she who combs
    it!

18
Raise your blond head, and do not
    sleep,
and be not bemused by
    slumber.
Four things of moment I have to say,
none of which must you miss.
The first: for you my heart is
    breaking,

Das zweite: dir nur will ich angehören,
Das dritte: daß ich dir mein Heil
    befehle,
Das letzte: dich allein liebt meine Seele.

19
Wir haben beide lange Zeit geschwiegen,
Auf einmal kam uns nun die Sprache
    wieder.
Die Engel Gottes sind herabgeflogen,
Sie brachten nach dem Krieg den
    Frieden wieder.
Die Engel Gottes sind herabgeflogen,
Mit ihnen ist der Frieden eingezogen.
Die Liebesengel kamen über Nacht
Und haben Frieden meiner Brust
    gebracht.

20
Mein Liebster singt am Haus im
    Mondenscheine,
Und ich muß lauschend hier im Bette
    liegen.
Weg von der Mutter wend ich mich
    und weine,
Blut sind die Tränen, die mir nicht
    versiegen.
Den breiten Strom am Bett hab ich
    geweint,
Weiß nicht vor Tränen, ob der Morgen
    scheint.
Den breiten Strom am Bett weint ich
    vor Sehnen;
Blind haben mich gemacht die blutgen
    Tränen.

21
Man sagt mir, deine Mutter wolle es
    nicht;
So bleibe weg, mein Schatz, tu ihr den
    Willen.
Ach Liebster, nein! tu ihr den Willen
    nicht,
Besuch mich doch, tu's ihr zum Trotz,
    im stillen!
Nein, mein Geliebter, folg ihr
    nimmermehr,
Tu's ihr zum Trotz, komm öfter als
    bisher!
Nein, höre nicht auf sie, was sie auch
    sage;
Tu's ihr zum Trotz, mein Lieb, komm
    alle Tage!

22
Ein Ständchen Euch zu bringen kam
    ich her,
Wenn es dem Herrn vom Haus nicht
    ungelegen.

the second: yours alone do I want to be,
the third: to you my salvation I
    commend,
the last: my soul loves you alone.

19
Long have we both not spoken,
now, all at once, speech has
    returned.
The angels of God have descended,
bringing peace again after
    war.
The angels of god have descended,
with them peace has entered in.
The angels of love came overnight
and they have brought peace to my
    breast.

20
My dearest's below singing in the
    moonlight,
and I must lie listening here in
    bed.
Away from my mother I turn, and
    weep,
my tears are blood which will not
    dry.
That broad stream by the bed I've
    wept,
for my tears I cannot tell if day is
    dawning.
That bedside stream I've wept from
    yearning;
blinded I am by my tears of
    blood.

21
They tell me your mother is against
    it;
then stay away, beloved, do as she
    wants.
Oh, dearest, no! Don't do as she
    wants,
defy her, come to me in
    secret.
No, darling boy, don't ever obey her
    again,
defy her, come more often than
    before.
No, don't listen to her, whatever she
    says;
defy her, my love, come every
    day.

22
To serenade you I have
    come,
should not the master of the house
    object.

Ihr habt ein schönes Töchterlein. Es
wär
Wohl gut, sie nicht zu streng im Haus
zu hegen.
Und liegt sie schon im Bett, so bitt ich
sehr,
Tut es zu wissen ihr von meinetwegen,
Daß ihr Getreuer hier vorbeigekommen,
Der Tag und Nacht sie in den Sinn
genommen,
Und daß am Tag, der vierundzwanzig
zählt,
Sie fünfundzwanzig Stunden lang mir
fehlt.

23
Was für ein Lied soll dir gesungen
werden,
Das deiner würdig sei? Wo find ich's
nur?
Am liebsten grüb ich es tief aus der
Erden,
Gesungen noch von keiner Kreatur.
Ein Lied, das weder Mann noch Weib
bis heute
Hört oder sang, selbst nicht die ältsten
Leute.

24
Ich esse nun mein Brot nicht trocken
mehr,
Ein Dorn ist mir im Fuße stecken
blieben.
Umsonst nach rechts und links blick ich
umher,
Und keinen find ich, der mich möchte
lieben.
Wenn's doch auch nur ein altes
Männlein wäre,
Das mir erzeigt' ein wenig Lieb und
Ehre.
Ich meine nämlich so ein wohlgestalter,
Ehrbarer Greis, etwa von meinem Alter.
Ich meine, um mich ganz zu offenbaren,
Ein altes Männlein so von vierzehn
Jahren.

25
Mein Liebster hat zu Tische mich
geladen
Und hatte doch kein Haus mich zu
empfangen,
Nicht Holz noch Herd zum Kochen
und zum Braten,
Der Hafen auch war längst entzwei
gegangen.
An einem Fäßchen Wein gebrach es
auch,
Und Gläser hat er gar nicht im
Gebrauch;

A beautiful daughter you have. It
were
better not to keep her too strictly
indoors.
And if she's already in bed, then
please
let her know on my behalf
that her true love came this way,
who day and night has had her in his
mind,
and that in a day of four and twenty
hours,
I miss her
twenty-five.

23
What song shall be sung to
you
that would be worthy? Where to find
it?
I'd like best to dig it from deep in the
earth,
as yet unsung by any creature.
A song that till today no man, no
woman
has heard or sung, not even the
oldest.

24
Dry bread satisfies me no
more,
I have a thorn stuck in my
foot.
In vain I look around to left and
right,
and no one do I find to love
me.
If only there were a little old
man
to show me a little love and
respect.
I mean of course a handsome,
honourable old man of about my age.
I mean, to be quite frank,
a little old man of about
fourteen.

25
My sweetheart invited me to
dinner,
yet had no house to receive
me.
No wood, nor stove for cooking and
roasting,
and the pot had long since broken in
two.
No wine-cask was there
either,
and no glasses did he have in
use;

Der Tisch war schmal, das Tafeltuch
  nicht besser,
Das Brot steinhart und völlig stumpf
  das Messer.

26
Ich ließ mir sagen und mir ward
  erzählt,
Der schöne Toni hungre sich zu
  Tode;
Seit ihn so überaus die Liebe quält,
Nimmt er auf einen Backzahn sieben
  Brote.
Nach Tisch, damit er die Verdauung
  stählt,
Verspeist er eine Wurst und sieben
  Brote,
Und lindert nicht Tonina seine Pein,
Bricht nächstens Hungersnot und
  Teurung ein.

27
Schon streckt ich aus im Bett die
  müden Glieder,
Da tritt dein Bildnis vor mich ihn, du
  Traute.
Gleich spring ich auf, fahr in die
  Schuhe wieder
Und wandre durch die Stadt mit
  meiner Laute.
Ich sing und spiele, daß die Straße
  schallt;
So manche lauscht—vorüber bin ich
  bald.
So manches Mädchen hat mein Lied
  gerührt,
Indes der Wind schon Sang und Klang
  entführt.

28
Du sagst mir, daß ich keine Fürstin
  sei;
Auch du bist nicht auf Spaniens
  Thron entsprossen.
Nein, Bester, stehst du auf bei
  Hahnenschrei,
Fährst du aufs Feld und nicht in
  Staatskarossen.
Du spottest mein um meine Niedrigkeit,
Doch Armut tut dem Adel nichts zuleid.
Du spottest, daß mir Krone fehlt und
  Wappen,
Und fährst doch selber nur mit
  Schusters Rappen.

29
Wohl kenn ich Euern Stand, der nicht
  gering.
Ihr brauchtet nicht so tief herab-
  zusteigen,

the table was narrow, the cloth no
  better,
the bread rock hard and the knife—
  quite blunt.

26
I inquired and I was
  told:
handsome Tony's starving himself to
  death;
since love's tormented him so badly
he eats seven loaves to a
  tooth.
After meals, to steel his
  digestion,
he consumes seven and a
  sausage,
and if Tonina won't ease his agony,
there'll soon be famine and
  starvation.

27
I stretched out in bed my weary
  limbs,
when you appeared to me, my
  love.
Straight up I jump, slip on my shoes
  again
and wander through the town with my
  lute.
I sing and play and make the street
  resound;
so many women listen—I'm quickly
  by.
So many girls are moved by what I
  sing,
while song and sound are borne off on
  the wind.

28
You say to me that I am no
  princess;
but you are no descendant of the
  Spanish throne.
No, my dear, at cock-crow you get
  up,
and to the fields you go in no
  state-coach.
You mock me for my lowliness,
but poverty doesn't hurt the noble soul.
You mock me for my lack of crown and
  crest,
but Shanks' mare is all you ride
  yourself.

29
Your station is no mean one, well I
  know.
You did not need to condescend so
  far

Zu lieben solch ein arm und niedrig
Ding,
Da sich vor Euch die Allerschönsten
neigen.
Die schönsten Männer leicht besiegtet
Ihr,
Drum weiß ich wohl, Ihr treibt nur
Spiel mit mir.
Ihr spottet mein, man hat mich warnen
wollen,
Doch ach, Ihr seid so schön! Wer kann
Euch grollen?

30
Laß sie nur gehn, die so die Stolze
spielt,
Das Wunderkräutlein aus dem
Blumenfeld.
Man sieht, wohin ihr blankes Auge zielt,
Da Tag um Tag ein andrer ihr
gefällt.
Sie treibt es grade wie Toscanas Fluß,
Dem jedes Berggewässer folgen muß.
Sie treibt es wie der Arno, will mir
scheinen:
Bald hat sie viel Bewerber, bald nicht
einen.

31
Wie soll ich fröhlich sein und lachen gar,
Da du mir immer zürnest unverhohlen?
Du kommst nur einmal alle hundert
Jahr,
Und dann, als hätte man dir's
anbefohlen.
Was kommst du, wenn's die Deinen
ungern sehn?
Gib frei mein Herz, dann magst du
weitergehn.
Daheim mit deinen Leuten leb in
Frieden,
Denn was der Himmel will, geschieht
hienieden.
Halt Frieden mit den Deinigen zu
Haus,
Denn was der Himmel will, das bleibt
nicht aus.

32
Was soll der Zorn, mein Schatz, der
dich erhitzt,
Ich bin mir keiner Sünde ja bewußt.
Ach, lieber nimm ein Messer
wohlgespitzt
Und tritt zu mir, durchbohre mir die
Brust.
Und taugt ein Messer nicht, so nimm
ein Schwert,
Daß meines Blutes Quell gen Himmel
fährt.

to love a girl so humble and so
poor,
since the fairest ladies bow before
you.
The handsomest men you could easily
outdo,
from which I know you do but trifle
with me.
You're mocking me, as people tried to
warn,
but oh, you are so handsome! Who
could mind?

30
She who plays the haughty one, let her
go,
the magic herb of the flowery
field.
It's clear what her bright eyes are after,
as day after day she likes a different
man.
She carries on just like Tuscany's river,
which all mountain streams must follow.
And like the Arno, I'm inclined to
think:
now wooed by many, now by
none.

31
How should I be happy and laugh
when you are always openly so angry?
You visit me but once a hundred
years,
and then as if you had been ordered
to.
Why come here, if your family
object?
Set free my heart, and then go on your
way.
Live at home with your family in
peace;
what heaven wills, that happens here
below.
Abide in peace with your family at
home,
for what heaven wills, shall never fail
to be.

32
Why this rage, my love, that fires you
so?
For I am aware of no offence.
Oh, rather take a keenly sharpened
knife,
come to me and plunge it in my
breast.
And if a knife won't do, then take a
sword,
and let my blood spring
heavenwards.

Und taugt ein Schwert nicht, nimm des
  Dolches Stahl
Und wasch in meinem Blut all meine
  Qual.

33
Sterb ich, so hüllt in Blumen meine
  Glieder;
Ich wünsche nicht, daß ihr ein Grab
  mir grabt.
Genüber jenen Mauern legt mich
  nieder,
Wo ihr so manchmal mich gesehen habt.
Dort legt mich hin, in Regen oder
  Wind;
Gern sterb ich, ist's um dich, geliebtes
  Kind.
Dort legt mich hin in Sonnenschein und
  Regen;
Ich sterbe lieblich, sterb ich deinetwegen.

34
Und steht Ihr früh am Morgen auf
  vom Bette,
Scheucht Ihr vom Himmel alle
  Wolken fort,
Die Sonne lockt Ihr auf die Berge dort,
Und Engelein erscheinen um die Wette
Und bringen Schuh und Kleider Euch
  sofort.
Dann, wenn Ihr ausgeht in die heilge
  Mette,
So zieht Ihr alle Menschen mit Euch
  fort,
Und wenn Ihr naht der benedeiten
  Stätte,
So zündet Euer Blick die Lampen an.
Weihwasser nehmt Ihr, macht des
  Kreuzes Zeichen
Und netzet Eure weiße Stirn sodann
Und neiget Euch und beugt die Knie
  ingleichen—
O wie holdselig steht Euch alles an!
Wie hold und selig hat Euch Gott
  begabt,
Die Ihr der Schönheit Kron empfangen
  habt!
Wie hold und selig wandelt Ihr im
  Leben;
Der Schönheit Palme ward an Euch
  gegeben.

35
Benedeit die selge Mutter,
Die so lieblich dich geboren,
So an Schönheit auserkoren,
Meine Sehnsucht fliegt dir zu!
Du so lieblich von Gebärden,
Du die Holdeste der Erden,
Du mein Kleinod, meine Wonne,
Süße, benedeit bist du!

And if a sword won't do, take dagger's
  steel,
and wash my torment in my
  blood.

33
If I should die, then shroud my limbs
  in flowers;
I do not wish that you should dig a
  grave.
Lay me down by yonder
  walls,
where so often you have seen me.
There lay me down, in rain or
  wind;
Gladly I die, if it is for you, dear
  child.
There lay me down in sunshine and in
  rain;
sweetly I die, if for the sake of you.

34
And when you rise early from your
  bed,
you banish every cloud from the
  sky,
you lure the sun on to those hills,
and cherubs compete to come
and bring at once your shoes and
  clothes.
Then, when you go out to Holy
  Mass,
you draw everyone along with
  you,
and when you near the blessed
  place,
your gaze lights up the lamps.
Holy water you take, cross
  yourself,
moistening your white brow,
and bow and
  genuflect—
oh, how beautifully it all becomes you!
How sweetly, blessedly has God
  endowed you,
who have received the crown of
  beauty.
How sweetly, blessedly you walk
  through life;
the palm of beauty was bestowed on
  you.

35
Blessed your mother, now with God,
who bore you to be so sweet,
so chosen for beauty,
to you my longing flies!
You so sweet of gesture,
you the fairest on earth,
you my jewel, my bliss,
my sweet, blessed are you!

Wenn ich aus der Ferne schmachte
Und betrachte deine Schöne,
Siehe wie ich beb und stöhne,
Daß ich kaum es bergen kann!
Und in meiner Brust gewaltsam
Fühl ich Flammen sich empören,
Die den Frieden mir zerstören,
Ach, der Wahnsinn faßt mich an!

When from afar I languish
considering your beauty,
see how I groan and quiver
more than I can conceal!
And powerfully within my breast
I feel flames leap,
which destroy my peace,
ah, madness seizes me!

36
Wenn du, mein Liebster, steigst
    zum Himmel auf,
Trag ich mein Herz dir in der Hand
    entgegen.
So liebevoll umarmst du mich darauf,
Dann wolln wir uns dem Herrn zu
    Füßen legen.
Und sieht der Herrgott unsre
    Liebesschmerzen,
Macht er ein Herz aus zwei verliebten
    Herzen,
Zu einem Herzen fügt er zwei
    zusammen,
Im Paradies, umglänzt von
    Himmelsflammen.

36
When you, my love, ascend to
    Heaven,
I'll come to you my heart in
    hand.
And lovingly you will embrace me then,
then let us fall at the Lord's
    feet.
And when the Lord God beholds our
    love's torment,
one heart he'll make of two enamoured
    hearts,
two hearts he'll fashion into
    one,
lighted in Paradise by heavenly
    fire.

37
Wie viele Zeit verlor ich, dich zu lieben!
Hätt ich doch Gott geliebt in all der
    Zeit,
Ein Platz im Paradies wär mir
    verschrieben,
Ein Heilger säße dann an meiner Seit.
Und weil ich dich geliebt, schön frisch
    Gesicht,
Verscherzt ich mir des Paradieses Licht,
Und weil ich dich geliebt, schön
    Veigelein,
Komm ich nun nicht ins Paradies hinein.

37
How much time I lost in loving you!
Had I but adored God in all that
    time,
a place in Paradise would now be
    mine,
a saint would then be seated at my side.
And because I loved you, face fresh
    and fair,
I forfeited the light of Paradise,
and because I loved you, fair
    violet,
I never now shall enter Paradise.

38
Wenn du mich mit den Augen streifst
    und lachst,
Sie senkst und neigst das Kinn zum
    Busen dann,
Bitt ich, daß du mir erst ein Zeichen
    machst,
Damit ich doch mein Herz auch
    bändgen kann,
Daß ich mein Herz mag bändgen,
    zahm und still,
Wenn es vor großer Liebe springen will,
Daß ich mein Herz mag halten in der
    Brust,
Wenn es ausbrechen will vor großer
    Lust.

38
When you turn your eyes to me and
    laugh,
then lower them and bow your chin to
    breast,
I beg you first to give me
    sign,
that I may then subdue my
    heart,
that I may tame and quiet
    my heart
when it for its great love would leap;
that I may keep my heart within my
    breast,
when it would break forth for its great
    joy.

39
Gesegnet sei das Grün und wer es
    trägt!

39
Blessed be green and all that green do
    wear!

Ein grünes Kleid will ich mir machen
lassen.
Ein grünes Kleid trägt auch die
Frühlingsaue,
Grün kleidet sich der Liebling meiner
Augen.
In Grün sich kleiden ist der Jäger
Brauch,
Ein grünes Kleid trägt mein Geliebter
auch;
Das Grün steht allen Dingen lieblich an,
Aus Grün wächst jede schöne Frucht
heran.

40
O wär dein Haus durchsichtig wie ein
Glas,
Mein Holder, wenn ich mich
vorüberstehle!
Dann säh ich drinnen dich ohn
Unterlaß,
Wie blickt ich dann nach dir mit
ganzer Seele!
Wie viele Blicke schickte mir dein
Herz,
Mehr als da Tropfen hat der Fluß im
März!
Wie viele Blicke schick ich dir entgegen,
Mehr als da Tropfen niedersprühn im
Regen!

41
Heut nacht erhob ich mich um
Mitternacht,
Da war mein Herz mir heimlich
fortgeschlichen.
Ich frug: Herz, wohin stürmst du so mit
Macht?
Es sprach: Nur Euch zu sehn, sei es
entwichen.
Nun sieh, wie muß es um mein Lieben
stehn:
Mein Herz entweicht der Brust, um
dich zu sehn!

42
Nicht länger kann ich singen, denn der
Wind
Weht stark und macht dem Atem was
zu schaffen.
Auch fürcht ich, daß die Zeit umsonst
verrinnt.
Ja wär ich sicher, ging ich jetzt nicht
schlafen.
Ja wüßt ich was, würd ich nicht
heimspazieren
Und einsam diese schöne Zeit verlieren.

43
Schweig einmal still, du garstger
Schwätzer dort!

A green dress will I have
made.
A green dress too the spring-time
meadow wears,
in green dresses the darling of my
eyes.
In green is the hunters' way to
dress,
a green suit too my lover
wears;
green all things sweetly favours,
out of green grows every lovely
fruit.

40
Oh, were your house transparent as a
glass,
my love, whenever I steal
past!
Then, without cease, I could see you
within,
and how I'd gaze at you with all my
soul!
How many looks your heart would send
me,
more than the river in March has
drops!
How many the looks I would return,
more than the drops that shower down
in rain!

41
Last night I rose at
midnight,
my heart had slipped
away.
I asked: heart, where do you hasten
so?
Only to see you had it escaped, it
said.
See now how my love must
be:
my heart slips from my body to see
you!

42
No longer can I sing, for the
wind
blows hard and keeps me short of
breath.
Also I fear the time does fly in
vain,
Were I but sure, I'd go not now to
bed.
Did I but know, I'd not go walking
home
and lose this lovely time in loneliness.

43
O you beastly ranter, do be
quiet!

Zum Ekel ist mir dein verwünschtes
   Singen.
Und triebst du es bis morgen früh so
   fort,
Doch würde dir kein schmuckes Lied
   gelingen.
Schweig einmal still und lege dich
   aufs Ohr!
Das Ständchen eines Esels zög ich vor.

I find your cursed singing
   revolting.
Even if you kept it up till
   morning,
you'd still not manage a decent
   song.
Do be quiet and get to
   bed!
I'd rather hear a donkey's serenade.

44
O wüßtest du, wie viel ich deinetwegen,
Du falsche Renegatin, litt zur
   Nacht,
Indes du im verschloßnen Haus gelegen
Und ich die Zeit im Freien zugebracht.
Als Rosenwasser diente mir der Regen,
Der Blitz hat Liebesbotschaft mir
   gebracht;
Ich habe Würfel mit dem Sturm
   gespielt,
Als unter deinem Dach ich Wache
   hielt.
Mein Bett war unter deinem Dach
   bereitet,
Der Himmel lag als Decke drauf
   gebreitet,
Die Schwelle deiner Tür, das war mein
   Kissen—
Ich Ärmster, ach, was hab ich ausstehn
   müssen!

44
Oh, if you knew how much for you,
   false renegade, I've suffered in the
   night,
while you have lain locked up indoors,
and I have spent the time outside.
My rose-water has been the rain,
the lightning has brought me messages
   of love;
dice with the storm I've
   played
while keeping watch beneath your
   eaves.
Beneath your eaves was laid my
   bed,
spread with the sky as
   blanket,
my pillow the step outside your
   door—
poor wretch that I am, how I've
   suffered!

45
Verschling der Abgrund meines
   Liebsten Hütte,
An ihrer Stelle schäum ein See zur
   Stunde.
Bleikugeln soll der Himmel drüber
   schütten,
Und eine Schlange hause dort im
   Grunde.
Drin hause eine Schlange giftger Art,
Die ihn vergifte, der mir untreu ward.
Drin hause ein Schlange,
   giftgeschwollen,
Und bring ihm Tod, der mich verraten
   wollen!

45
Let the abyss engulf my lover's
   house,
and let a lake foam there this very
   hour.
Lead balls shall heaven rain upon
   it,
and a serpent dwell there at the
   bottom.
A poisonous serpent there let dwell,
to poison him who was untrue to me;
a venom-swollen serpent there let
   dwell,
and kill him who tried to betray
   me!

46
Ich hab in Penna einen Liebsten
   wohnen,
In der Maremmenebne einen andern,
Einen im schönen Hafen von Ancona,
Zum vierten muß ich nach Viterbo
   wandern;
Ein andrer wohnt in Casentino dort,
Der nächste lebt mit mir am selben Ort,
Und wieder einen hab ich in Magione,
Vier in La Fratta, zehn in Castiglione.

46
I have one lover living in
   Penna,
another in the plain of Maremma,
one in the lovely port of Ancona,
for the fourth I've to go to
   Viterbo;
another lives there, in Casentino,
the next—where I live,
and I've yet another in Magione,
four in La Fratta, ten in Castiglione.

## Jägerlied | Hunter's Song

EDUARD MÖRIKE

Karl Marx: op. 42, no. 3, 1941; Hugo Wolf, 1888

| | |
|---|---|
| Zierlich ist des Vogels Tritt im Schnee, | Dainty is the bird's step on the snow |
| Wenn er wandelt auf des Berges | when wandering on the mountain |
| Höh: | height: |
| Zierlicher schreibt Liebchens liebe Hand, | daintier my love's dear hand |
| Schreibt ein Brieflein mir in ferne Land'. | in her letter to me in a far-off land. |
| | |
| In die Lüfte hoch ein Reiher steigt, | High into the sky a heron soars |
| Dahin weder Pfeil noch Kugel fleugt: | whither no shaft or ball can fly: |
| Tausendmal so hoch und so geschwind | higher and swifter a thousandfold |
| Die Gedanken treuer Liebe sind. | are the thoughts of faithful love. |

## Jägers Abendlied | Huntsman's Evensong

JOHANN WOLFGANG GOETHE

Johann Friedrich Reichardt, ed. 1809; Franz Schubert: op. 3, no. 4, 1816

| | |
|---|---|
| Im Felde schleich ich still und wild, | Silent and fierce I creep in the fields, |
| Gespannt mein Feuerrohr. | my fowling piece cocked ready. |
| Da schwebt so licht dein liebes Bild, | And so clearly floats your dear, |
| Dein süßes Bild mir vor. | dear image before me. |
| | |
| Du wandelst jetzt wohl still und mild | Silent and gentle now you wander |
| Durch Feld und liebes Tal, | field and delightful valley, |
| Und ach, mein schnell verrauschend | and ah, does a fleeting image of |
| Bild, | me |
| Stellt sich dirs nicht einmal? | never present itself to you? |
| | |
| Des Menschen, der die Welt durchstreift | The image of a man roving the world |
| Voll Unmut und Verdruß, | in ill-humour and in anger, |
| Nach Osten und nach Westen schweift, | roving to eastward and to westward. |
| Weil er dich lassen muß. | since from you he must part. |
| | |
| Mir ist es, denk ich nur an dich, | If I but think of you, I seem |
| Als in den Mond zu sehn; | to gaze into the moon; |
| Ein stiller Friede kommt auf mich, | a quiet peace descends on me, |
| Weiß nicht, wie mir geschehn. | but how, I do not know. |

## Jetzt rede du! | Now You Speak!

CONRAD FERDINAND MEYER

Othmar Schoeck: op. 60, no. 28, 1946

| | |
|---|---|
| Du warest mir ein täglich Wanderziel, | Goal of my daily walks you were, |
| Viellieber Wald, in dumpfen | dear wood, in gloomy times of |
| Jugendtagen, | youth, |
| Ich hatte dir geträumten Glücks so viel | of so much dreamt delight I had to tell, |
| Anzuvertraun, so wahren Schmerz zu | of so much real sorrow to |
| klagen. | complain. |

Und wieder such' ich dich, du dunkler
  Hort,
Und deines Wipfelmeers gewaltig
  Rauschen—
Jetzt rede du! Ich lasse dir das Wort!
Verstummt ist Klag' und Jubel. Ich
  will lauschen.

You again I seek, sombre
  refuge,
and your mighty roaring sea of
  foliage—
now you speak! I give way to you!
Stilled are lament and joy. I'll
  listen.

## Juchhe! | Hurrah!

ROBERT REINICK

*Johannes Brahms: op. 6, no. 4, 1852*

Wie ist doch die Erde so schön, so
  schön!
Das wissen die Vögelein;
sie heben ihr leicht Gefieder,
und singen so fröhliche Lieder
in den blauen Himmel hinein.

How fair is earth how
  fair!
The tiny birds know this;
they lift their light wings,
and sing such joyous songs
into the blue sky.

Wie ist doch die Erde so schön, so
  schön!
Das wissen die Flüss' und See'n;
sie malen im klaren Spiegel
die Gärten und Städt' und Hügel,
und die Wolken, die drüber geh'n!

How fair is earth, how
  fair!
The rivers and lakes know this;
in their clear glass they paint
the gardens, towns and hills,
and clouds that scud above!

Und Sänger und Maler wissen es,
und es wissen's viel andre Leut',
und wer's nicht malt, der singt es,
und wer's nicht singt, dem klingt es
im Herzen vor lauter Freud'!

And minstrels, painters know it,
and many others too,
who paints it not, he sings it,
who sings it not, has it sounding
for sheer joy in his heart.

## Jugendgedenken | Memories of Youth

GOTTFRIED KELLER

*Hermann Reutter: op. 59, no. 1, ed. 1948; Othmar Schoeck: op. 24b, no. 10, 1906–15*

Ich will spiegeln mich in jenen Tagen,
Die wie Lindewipfelwehn entflohn,
Wo die Silbersaite, angeschlagen,
Klar, doch bebend gab den ersten Ton,
Der mein Leben lang,
Erst heut noch, widerklang,
Ob die Saite längst zerrissen
  schon;

Myself will I mirror in those days,
now, like the lime-tops' waving, passed,
when, once struck, the silver string,
clear yet tremulous, gave the first note
that throughout my life
until this day has echoed,
though the string has long since
  snapped;

Wo ich ohne Tugend, ohne Sünde,
Blank wie Schnee vor dieser Sonne lag,
Wo dem Kindesauge noch die
  Binde
Lind verbarg den blendend hellen Tag:
Du entschwundene Welt
Klingst über Wald und Feld
Hinter mir wie ferner Wachtelschlag.

when I, with no virtue, with no sin,
lay bright as snow under this sun,
when my childish eyes were still gently
  closed
to blindingly bright day:
O vanished world,
over wood and field you sound
at my back like the call of distant quail.

Wie so fabelhaft ist hingegangen
Jener Zeit bescheidne Frühlingspracht,
Wo, von Mutterliebe noch umfangen,
Schon die Jugendliebe leis erwacht
Wie, von Sonnenschein
Durchspielt, ein Edelstein,
Den ein Glücklicher ans Licht gebracht.

How fabulously has departed
the shy spring glory of that time,
when, still embraced by mother love,
gently youthful love awakes,
like a sunshine-
iridescent precious stone
brought by a happy man to light of day.

Wenn ich scheidend einst muß
  überspringen
Jene Kluft, die keine Brücke trägt,
Wird mir nicht ein Lied entgegenklingen,
Das bekannt und ahnend mich
  erregt?
O die Welt ist weit!
Ob nicht die Jugendzeit
Irgendwo noch an das Herz mir
  schlägt?

When, departing one day, I have to
  leap
the gulf that bears no bridge,
will not, in greeting, a song sound
that, known and portentous, will stir
  me?
Oh the world is wide!
Will not that time of youth
still somewhere hammer at my
  heart?

Träumerei! was sollten jene hoffen,
Die nie sahn der Jugend Lieblichkeit,
Die ein unnatürlich Los getroffen,
Frucht zu bringen ohne Blütenzeit!
Ach, was man nicht kennt,
Danach das Herz nicht brennt
Und bleibt kalt dafür in Ewigkeit!

Dreams! For what shall they hope
who never saw youth's charm,
who were afflicted by unnatural fate
to bear fruit without a time of blossom!
Ah, for that which one does not know,
the heart will never burn
and instead stay cold for eternity.

In den Waldeskronen meines Lebens
Atme fort, du kühles Morgenwehn!
Heiter leuchte, Frühstern guten
  Strebens,
Laß mich treu in deinem Scheine gehn!
Rankend Immergrün
Soll meinen Stab umblühn,
Nur noch einmal will ich rückwärts
  sehn!

Among the forest tree-tops of my life
breathe on, cool morning breeze!
Shine merry, early star of good
  endeavour,
let me walk loyally in your gleam!
Climbing evergreen
shall blossom about my staff,
just once more will I look
  back.

## Kennst du das Land | Do You Know the Land . . .

(Mignon's Song)

JOHANN WOLFGANG GOETHE: from *Wilhelm Meister*

*Ludwig van Beethoven: op. 75, no. 1, 1809; Franz Liszt, 1842;
Johann Friedrich Reichardt, ed. 1809; Franz Schubert, 1815;
Robert Schumann: op. 79 no. 29, 1849; Hugo Wolf, 1888;
Carl Friedrich Zelter, 1795*

Kennst du das Land, wo die Zitronen
  blühn,
im dunklen Laub die Goldorangen
  glühn,
ein sanfter Wind vom blauen Himmel
  weht,
die Myrte still und hoch der Lorbeer
  steht?
Kennst du es wohl?
          Dahin, dahin
möcht' ich mit dir, o mein Geliebter,
  ziehn!

Do you know the land, where the
  lemons blossom,
the oranges glow golden amongst dark
  leaves,
a gentle wind blows from the blue
  sky,
the myrtle stands silent, the laurel
  tall,
do you know it?
          There, there
would I go with you, my
  love!

Kennst du das Haus, auf Säulen ruht
sein Dach,
es glänzt der Saal, es schimmert das
Gemach,
Und Marmorbilder stehn und sehn
mich an:
was hat man dir, du armes Kind,
getan?
Kennst du es wohl?
          Dahin, dahin
möcht' ich mit dir, o mein Beschützer,
ziehn!

Kennst du den Berg und seinen
Wolkensteg?
Das Maultier sucht im Nebel seinen
Weg,
In Höhlen wohnt der Drachen alte
Brut,
es stürzt der Fels und über ihn die
Flut:
kennst du ihn wohl?
          Dahin! dahin
geht unser Weg; o Vater,
laß uns ziehn!

Do you know the house? On pillars rests
its roof,
its hall gleams, its apartment
shimmers,
and marble statues stand and gaze at
me:
What have they done to you, poor
child?
Do you know it?
          There, there
would I go with you, my
protector!

Do you know the mountain and its
cloudy path?
The mule seeks its way in the
mist,
in caves the ancient brood of dragons
dwells,
the rock falls sheer, and over it, the
flood;
do you know it?
          There, there
lies our way! O father,
let us go!

## Kindertotenlieder / Songs of Children Dead

FRIEDRICH RÜCKERT

*Gustav Mahler, 1901–04*

I
Nun will die Sonn' so hell aufgehn,
Als sei kein Unglück die Nacht
geschehn.
Das Unglück geschah nur mir allein,
Die Sonne, sie scheinet allgemein.
Du mußt nicht die Nacht in dir
verschränken,
Mußt sie ins ewige Licht versenken.
Ein Lämplein verlosch in meinem Zelt,
Heil sei dem Freudenlicht der Welt!

I
Now is the sun about to rise so bright,
as if no ill had befallen in the
night.
Ill has befallen me alone;
the sun—it shines for everyone.
You must not confine the night
within,
but must immerse it in light everlasting.
In my firmament a light has failed,
welcome be the glad light of the world!

2
Nun seh ich wohl, warum so dunkle
Flammen
Ihr sprühtet mir in manchem
Augenblicke,
O Augen!
Gleichsam um voll in einem Blicke
Zu drängen eure ganze Macht zusammen.
Doch ahnt ich nicht, weil Nebel mich
umschwammen,
Gewoben vom verblendenden Geschicke,
Daß sich der Strahl bereits zur
Heimkehr schicke,
Dorthin, von wannen alle Strahlen
stammen.

2
Now I see well why so dark the
flames
you flashed at me so
often,
O eyes!
It was as if, entirely in one look,
to concentrate your whole power.
But I suspected not—for mists enveloped
me,
woven by deceptive fate—
that the ray was making to
return
to there whence all rays
stem.

Ihr wolltet mir mit eurem Leuchten
sagen:
Wir möchten nah dir bleiben gerne,
Doch ist uns das vom Schicksal
abgeschlagen.
Sieh uns nur an, denn bald sind wir dir
ferne!
Was dir nur Augen sind in diesen
Tagen,
In künftgen Nächten sind es dir nur
Sterne.

You, by your gleam, would have told
me:
So gladly would we stay close by you,
but that, by fate, we are
denied.
Only look at us, for soon shall we be
far!
What in these days to you are only
eyes,
in future nights shall be to you but
stars.


## 3
Wenn dein Mütterlein
Tritt zur Tür herein
Und den Kopf ich drehe,
Ihr entgegensehe,
Fällt auf ihr Gesicht
Erst der Blick mir nicht,
Sondern auf die Stelle
Näher nach der Schwelle,
Dort wo würde dein
Lieb Gesichtchen sein,
Wenn du freudenhelle
Trätest mit herein
Wie sonst, mein Töchterlein.

## 3
When your mother
comes in the door,
and, turning my head,
I look her way,
not upon her face
does my gaze first fall,
but on the place,
nearer the floor,
where your sweet
face would be,
if, bright with joy,
you were coming too,
as you used, my daughter.

Wenn dein Mütterlein
Tritt zur Tür herein
Mit der Kerze Schimmer,
Ist es mir, als immer
Kämst du mit herein,
Huschtest hinterdrein
Als wie sonst ins Zimmer.
O du, des Vaters Zelle
Ach zu schnelle
Erloschner Freudenschein!

When your mother
comes in the door
with the candle's gleam,
it always seems as if
you came too,
slipping in behind,
as you used.
O you, your father's cell's
ah, all-too-quickly-
extinguished gleam of joy!


## 4
Oft denk ich, sie sind nur
ausgegangen!
Bald werden sie wieder nach Hause
gelangen!
Der Tag ist schön! O sei nicht bang!
Sie machen nur einen weiten Gang.

## 4
Often I think they have merely gone
out!
Soon will they come home
again!
The day is fine! Oh, do not fear!
Merely a long walk it is they are taking.

Ja wohl, sie sind nur ausgegangen
Und werden jetzt nach Hause gelangen.
O sei nicht bang, der Tag ist schön!
Sie machen nur den Gang zu jenen
Höhn!

Yes, they have merely gone out,
and now will come home again.
Oh, do not fear, the day is fine!
Merely to those hills they are
walking!

Sie sind uns nur vorausgegangen
Und werden nicht wieder nach Haus
verlangen!
Wir holen sie ein auf jenen Höhn im
Sonnenschein!
Der Tag ist schön auf jenen Höhn!

They have merely gone on ahead
and will not wish to come home
again!
On those hills we'll overtake them in
the sun!
On those hills the day is fine!

5
In diesem Wetter, in diesem Braus,
Nie hätt ich gesendet die Kinder
    hinaus;
Man hat sie hinaus getragen,
Ich durfte nichts dazu sagen.

In diesem Wetter, in diesem Saus,
Nie hätt ich gelassen die Kinder
    hinaus,
Ich fürchtete, sie erkranken,
Das sind nun eitle Gedanken.

In diesem Wetter, in diesem Graus,
Nie hätt ich gelassen die Kinder
    hinaus,
Ich sorgte, sie stürben morgen,
Das ist nun nicht zu besorgen.

In diesem Wetter, in diesem Saus, in
    diesem Braus,
Sie ruhn als wie in der Mutter Haus,
Von keinem Sturme erschrecket,
Von Gottes Hand bedecket.

5
In this weather, this roaring wind,
never would I have sent those children
    out;
they were carried from the house,
and nothing could I say.

In this weather, this raging gale,
never would I have let those children
    out,
I was afraid of their falling ill—
those thoughts now are vain.

In this weather, this raving storm,
never would I have let those children
    out,
I feared they might die next day,
there is no cause for that fear now.

In this weather, roaring wind, raging
    gale,
they rest as if in their mother's house,
alarmed by no storm,
protected by God's hand.


## Klärchens Lied I und II | Clara's Songs I and II

JOHANN WOLFGANG GOETHE: from *Egmont*

Ludwig van Beethoven, op. 84

1
Die Trommel gerühret!
Das Pfeifchen gespielt!
Mein Liebster gewaffnet
Dem Haufen befiehlt,
Die Lanze hoch führet,
Die Leute regieret.
Wie klopft mir das Herze!
Wie wallt mir das Blut!
O hätt ich ein Wämslein,
Und Hosen und Hut!

Ich folgt ihm zum Tor naus
Mit mutigem Schritt,
Ging durch die Provinzen,
Ging überall mit.
Die Feinde schon weichen,
Wir schießen darein.
Welch Glück sondergleichen,
Ein Mannsbild zu sein!

2
Freudvoll
Und leidvoll,
Gedankenvoll sein,
Langen
Und bangen

1
Bang the drum!
Sound the fife!
My love, girt for war,
commands his host,
holds high his lance,
rules his men.
How my heart beats!
How my blood races!
Oh, would I had doublet,
breeches and helmet!

Through the gate would I follow
with valiant tread,
through the provinces march,
march all over with him.
The enemy wavers,
at him we fire.
What joy without equal
to be a man!

2
Joyful
and sorrowful,
pensive to be,
to yearn
and dread

In schwebender Pein,
Himmelhoch jauchzend,
Zum Tode betrübt,
Glücklich allein
Ist die Seele, die liebt.

in lingering pain,
to heaven exulting,
cast down unto death—
happy alone
is the soul that loves.

(*Franz Liszt, 1844; Johann Friedrich Reichardt, ed. 1809; Franz Schubert, 1815*)


## Kleiner Haushalt | Little Home

FRIEDRICH RÜCKERT

*Carl Loewe: op. 71, ed. 1840*

Einen Haushalt klein und fein
Hab' ich angestellt;
Der soll mein Freund sein,
Dem er wohlgefällt.

A fine little home
I have set up;
my friend shall he be
who likes it well.

Der Specht, der Holz mit dem
   Schnabel haut,
Hat das Haus mir aufgebaut;
Daß das Haus beworfen sei,
Trug die Schwalbe Mörtel bei,
Und als Dach hat sich zuletzt
Obendrauf ein Schwamm gesetzt.

Woodpecker, hewing timber with his
   beak,
built it for me;
to face it
the swallow contributed plaster,
and lastly, for the roof,
a toadstool sat on top.

Drinnen die Kammern
Und die Gemächer,
Schränke und Fächer,
Flimmern und flammern;
Alles hat mir unbezahlt
Schmetterling mit Duft bemalt.

Within, chambers
and apartments,
cupboards and shelves
shine and sparkle;
all, free of charge,
the butterfly has fragrantly painted.

O wie rüstig in dem Haus
Geht die Wirtschaft ein und aus.

Oh, how brisk about the house
my managers go in and out.

Wasserjüngferchen, das flinke,
Holt mir Wasser, das ich trinke;
Biene muß mir Essen holen,
Frage nicht, wo sie's gestohlen.

Dragonfly, the nimble,
fetches my drinking-water,
bee's task is to fetch my food,
where she's stolen it, I ask not.

Schüsseln sind die Eichelnäpfchen,
Und die Krüge Tannenzäpfchen,
Messer, Gabel,
Rosendorn und Vogelschnabel.

Acorn-cups are dishes,
fir-cones are the jugs,
knife and fork—
thorn of rose and beak of bird.

Storch im Haus ist Kinderwärter,
Maulwurf Gärtner,
Und Beschließerin im Häuslein
Ist das Mäuslein.

Nanny in my house is stork,
gardener—mole,
housekeeper of the tiny place
is mouse.

Aber die Grille
Singt in der Stille,
Sie ist das Heimchen, ist immer daheim,
Und weiß nichts als den einen Reim.

But the cricket,
singing in the stillness,
the homely cricket, is ever at home,
and knows but the one tune.

Doch im ganzen Haus das beste
Schläft noch feste.

But what is best in all the house
still soundly sleeps.

In dem Winkel, in dem Bettchen,  
Zwischen zweien Rosenblättchen,  
Schläft das Schätzchen  
   Tausendschönchen,  
Ihr zu Fuß ein Kaiserkrönchen.  
Hüter ist Vergißmeinnicht,  
Der vom Bette wanket nicht;  
Glühwurm mit dem Kerzenschimmer  
Hellt das Zimmer.

In the corner, in the cot,  
between two rose-leaves,  
Daisy, my darling,  
   sleeps,  
Crown-Imperial at her feet.  
Watching over her is Forget-me-not  
who from her bedside never budges;  
Glow-worm, with his candle-gleam  
lights the room.

Die Wachtel wacht  
Die ganze Nacht,  
Und wenn der Tag beginnt,  
Ruft sie: Kind! Kind!  
Wach auf geschwind.

The quail keeps watch  
the whole night through,  
and when day dawns,  
cries: Child, child!  
Quick, wake up!

Wenn die Liebe wachet auf,  
Geht das Leben raschen Lauf.

When my love awakes,  
then our life proceeds apace.

In seidnen Gewändern,  
Gewebt aus Sommerfaden,  
In flatternden Bändern,  
Von Sorgen unbeladen,  
Lustig aus dem engen Haus  
Die Flur hinaus.

In silken rainment  
of gossamer weave,  
in fluttering ribbons,  
unburdened by care,  
gaily from our tiny house  
out we go into the meadow.

Schönen Wagen  
Hab' ich bestellt,  
Uns zu tragen  
Durch die Welt.

A fine carriage  
I have ordered  
to convey us  
through the world.

Vier Heupferdchen sollen ihn  
Als vier Apfelschimmel ziehn;

Four grasshoppers shall  
draw it like four dapple-greys;

Sie sind wohl ein gut Gespann,  
Das mit Rossen sich messen kann;  
Sie haben Flügel,  
Sie leiden nicht Zügel,  
Sie kennen alle Blumen der Au',  
Und alle Tränken von Tau genau.

a fine team, to be sure,  
that will match any steed;  
they are winged  
and will suffer no rein,  
each meadow flower is known to them,  
each dewy watering-place.

Es geht nicht im Schritt;  
Kind, kannst du mit?  
Es geht im Trott!  
Nur zu mit Gott!  
Laß du sie uns tragen  
Nach ihrem Behagen;  
Und wenn sie uns werfen vom Wagen  
   herab,  
So finden wir unter Blumen ein Grab.

No walking pace ours—  
child, can you keep up?  
We go at a trot,  
trusting in God!  
Let them convey us  
just as they please;  
and if we're flung  
   out  
a flowery grave shall be ours.

## Komm bald / Come Soon

KLAUS GROTH

*Johannes Brahms. op. 97, no. 5, 1884*

Warum denn warten von Tag zu Tag?  
Es blüht im Garten, was blühen mag.

Why then wait from day to day?  
In the garden blossoms all that can.

Wer kommt und zählt es, was blüht so
schön?
An Augen fehlt es, es anzusehn.

Who'll come and count what blooms so
fair?
Absent are the eyes to see it.

Die meinen wandern vom Strauch zum
Baum;
Mir scheint, auch andern wär's wie ein
Traum.
Und von den Lieben, die mir getreu
und mir geblieben,
Wärst du dabei, wärst du dabei!

My eyes roam from shrub to
tree;
to others also it must seem a
dream.
And of the loved ones left to me and
true—
would that you, you were among them!

## Komm, wir wandeln zusammen | Come, Together We'll Walk

PETER CORNELIUS

*Peter Cornelius: op. 4, no. 2, 1854*

Komm, wir wandeln zusammen im
Mondschein,
so zaubrisch glänzt jedes Blatt,
vielleicht steht auf einem geschrieben,
wie lieb mein Herz dich hat.

Come, together we'll walk in the
moonlight,
each leaf gleams so magically,
on one, it may be, will be written
how dearly my heart adores you.

Komm, wir wandeln zusammen im
Mondschein,
der Mond strahlt aus Wellen
bewegt,
vielleicht, daß du ahnest, wie
selig
mein Herz dein Bildnis hegt.

Come, together we'll walk in the
moonlight,
the moon shines, disturbed, from the
waves,
you will sense, it may be, with what
rapture
your image is held in my heart.

Komm, wir wandeln zusammen im
Mondschein,
der Mond will ein königlich Kleid
aus goldenen Strahlen dir weben,
daß du wandelst in Herrlichkeit.

Come, together we'll walk in the
moonlight,
a robe fit for a queen will the moon
weave from its golden moonbeams,
that you may walk in majesty.

## Kophtisches Lied I und II | Coptic Song I and II

JOHANN WOLFGANG GOETHE

*Hugo Wolf, 1888*

I
Lasset Gelehrte sich zanken und streiten,
Streng und bedächtig die Lehrer auch
sein!
Alle die Weisesten aller der Zeiten
Lächeln und winken und stimmen mit
ein:
Töricht, auf Beßrung der Toren zu
harren!
Kinder der Klugheit, o habet die
Narren
Eben zum Narren auch, wie sich's
gehört.

I
Let learned men quarrel and wrangle,
let teachers too be prudent,
strict!
All the sagest in all ages
smile, nod and agree as
one:
foolish to wait till fools grow
wiser!
Children of sense, just make
fools
of the fools, as is
fit.

Merlin der Alte, im leuchtenden Grabe,
Wo ich als Jüngling gesprochen ihn
  habe,
Hat mich mit ähnlicher Antwort belehrt:
Töricht, auf Beßrung der Toren zu
  harren!
Kinder der Klugheit, o habet die
  Narren
Eben zum Narren auch, wie sich's
  gehört!

Old Merlin, from his shining grave,
where I, a young man, spoke with
  him,
similarly instructed me:
foolish to wait till fools grow
  wiser!
Children of sense, just make
  fools
of the fools, as is
  fit!

Und auf den Höhen der indischen Lüfte
Und in den Tiefen ägyptischer Grüfte
Hab ich das heilige Wort nur gehört:
Töricht, auf Beßrung der Toren zu
  harren!
Kinder der Klugheit, o habet die Narren
Eben zum Narren auch, wie sich's
  gehört!

And upon the airy Indian heights
and in the depths of Egyptian tombs,
only those sacred words have I heard:
foolish to wait till fools grow
  wiser!
Children of sense, just make fools
of the fools, as is
  fit!

II
Geh! gehorche meinen Winken,
Nutze deine jungen Tage,
Lerne zeitig klüger sein:
Auf des Glückes großer Waage
Steht die Zunge selten ein;
Du mußt steigen oder sinken,
Du mußt herrrschen und gewinnen,
Oder dienen und verlieren,
Leiden oder triumphieren,
Amboß oder Hammer sein.

II
Go, obey my precepts,
make good use of your young days,
learn, opportunely, to be wiser:
on the mighty scales of Fortune
the pointer rarely stands at rest;
you must climb or fall,
dominate and conquer
or serve and lose,
suffer or triumph,
be anvil or hammer.

## Kurze Fahrt | Short Journey

JOSEPH VON EICHENDORFF

*Othmar Schoeck: op. 30, no. 2, 1917–18; Reinhard Schwarz-Schilling, 1943*

Posthorn, wie so keck und fröhlich
Brachst du einst den Morgen an,
Vor mir lag's so frühlingsselig,
Daß ich still auf Lieder sann.

Posthorn, how bold, how merry
you once began the morn,
such spring bliss lay before me,
I thought silently of songs.

Dunkel rauscht es schon im Walde,
Wie so abendkühl wird's hier,
Schwager, stoß ins Horn—wie balde
Sind auch wir im Nachtquartier!

Darkly the forest murmurs,
how evening-cool here it grows,
coachman. sound your horn—how soon
we too will be lodged for the night!

## La Marmotte | La Marmotte

JOHANN WOLFGANG GOETHE: from *Das Jahrmarktsfest zu Plundersweilern*

*Ludwig van Beethoven: op. 52, no. 7, 1793*

Ich komme schon durch manches Land
avecque la marmotte,
und immer was zu essen fand
avecque la marmotte,
avecque sí, avecque là,
avecque la marmotte!

Through many a land have I come
avecque la marmotte,
and something always found to eat
avecque la marmotte,
avecque sí, avecque là,
avecque la marmotte!

## Lachen und Weinen | Tears and Laughter

FRIEDRICH RÜCKERT

*Franz Schubert: op. 59, no. 4, 1823*

Lachen und Weinen zu jeglicher Stunde
Ruht bei der Lieb auf so mancherlei
  Grunde.
Morgens lacht ich vor Lust,
Und warum ich nun weine
Bei des Abendes Scheine,
Ist mir selb' nicht bewußt.

Weinen und Lachen zu jeglicher Stunde
Ruht bei der Lieb auf so mancherlei
  Grunde.
Abends weint ich vor Schmerz;
Und warum du erwachen
Kannst am Morgen mit Lachen,
Muß ich dich fragen, o Herz.

Laughter and tears, at whatever hour,
are founded, in love, on so many
  things.
In the morning I laughed for joy,
and why I now weep
in the evening glow
I myself do not know.

Tears and laughter, at whatever hour,
are founded, in love, on so many
  things.
At evening I wept for grief;
and why you can awake
at morn with laughter,
that I must ask you, O heart.


## Lebe wohl | Farewell

EDUARD MÖRIKE

*Hugo Wolf, 1888*

Lebe wohl!—Du fühlest nicht,
Was es heißt, dies Wort der Schmerzen;
Mit getrostem Angesicht
Sagtest du's und leichtem Herzen.

Lebe wohl!—Ach, tausendmal
Hab ich mir es vorgesprochen.
Und in nimmersatter Qual
Mir das Herz damit gebrochen.

Farewell!—You do not feel
what it means, this word of pain;
with hopeful mien
you spoke it, and light heart.

Farewell!—Ah, a thousand times
I have said that to myself.
And in insatiable agony
have broken my heart.


## Lehn' deine Wang' | Rest Your Cheek

HEINRICH HEINE

*Robert Schumann: op. 142, no. 2, 1852*

Lehn' deine Wang' an meine Wang',
Dann fließen die Tränen zusammen;
Und an mein Herz drück' fest dein Herz,
Dann schlagen zusammen die Flammen!

Und wenn in die große Flamme fließt
Der Strom von unsern Tränen,
Und wenn dich mein Arm gewaltig
  umschließt—
Sterb' ich vor Liebessehnen!

Rest your cheek on my cheek,
together our tears will flow;
press firm to my heart your heart,
together the flames will leap!

And when into that great flame
the stream of our tears flows,
and when I crush you to
  me—
I shall die of love's desire!

## Leise Lieder | Soft Songs

CHRISTIAN MORGENSTERN

*Max Reger: op. 48, no. 2, 1900; Richard Strauss: op. 41, no. 5, 1899*

Leise Lieder sing ich dir bei Nacht,
Lieder, die kein sterblich Ohr vernimmt,
noch ein Stern, der etwa spähend wacht,
noch der Mond, der still im Äther
    schwimmt;

denen niemand als das eigne Herz,
das sie träumt, in tiefer Wehmut lauscht,
und an denen niemand als der Schmerz,
der sie zeugt, sich kummervoll
    berauscht.

Leise Lieder sing ich dir bei Nacht,
dir, in deren Aug mein Sinn versank,
und aus dessen tiefem, dunklen Schacht,
meine Seele ewige Sehnsucht trank.

Soft songs I sing to you at night,
songs no mortal ear perceives,
nor star, watching—spying, as it were,
nor moon, floating silent in the
    sky;

songs which none but one's own heart,
that dreams them, harks to, melancholy,
and on which none but the pain, that
begets them, grows sorrowfully
    drunk.

Soft songs I sing to you at night,
you in whose eyes my senses are sunk,
and from the deep dark wells of which,
my soul has drunk eternal longing.


## Leise zieht durch mein Gemüt | Gently through My Soul

HEINRICH HEINE

*Felix Mendelssohn-Bartholdy: op. 19a, no. 5, 1830–34*

Leise zieht durch mein Gemüt
Liebliches Geläute.
Klinge, kleines Frühlingslied,
Kling hinaus ins Weite.

Kling hinaus, bis an das Haus,
Wo die Blumen sprießen.
Wenn du eine Rose schaust,
Sag, ich laß' sie grüßen.

Gently through my soul
sweet bells are pealing.
Sound, tiny song of spring,
sound out far and wide.

Sound out as far as the house
where the flowers are blooming.
And, should you see a rose,
convey from me a greeting.


## Liebesfeier | Love's Festival

NIKOLAUS LENAU

*Robert Franz: op. 21, no. 4; Felix Weingartner*

An ihren bunten Liedern klettert
Die Lerche selig in die Luft;
Ein Jubelchor von Sängern schmettert
Im Walde, voller Blüt' und Duft.

Da sind, so weit die Blicke gleiten,
Altäre festlich aufgebaut,
Und all die tausend Herzen läuten
Zur Liebesfeier dringend laut.

Der Lenz hat Rosen angezündet
An Leuchtern von Smaragd im Dom;
Und jede Seele schwillt und mündet
Hinüber in den Opferstrom.

On her gay songs the lark
climbs blissfully into the air;
a merry choir of songsters warble
in the forest full of scent and blossom.

There, so far as eye may gaze,
festive altars have been raised,
and a thousand hearts all peal out
for love's festival, strong and loud.

Spring has lighted roses up
on the cathedral's emerald candelabra;
and every soul swells and flows
over into the stream of sacrifices.

## Liebestreu | True Love

ROBERT REINICK

*Johannes Brahms: op. 3, no. 1, 1852–53*

»O versenk, o versenk dein Leid, mein Kind,
In die See, in die tiefe See!«
Ein Stein wohl bleibt auf des Meeres Grund,
Mein Leid kommt stets in die Höh.

»Und die Lieb', die du im Herzen trägst,
Brich sie ab, brich sie ab, mein Kind!«
Ob die Blum' auch stirbt, wenn man sie bricht,
Treue Lieb' nicht so geschwind.

»Und die Treu', und die Treu', 's war nur ein Wort,
In den Wind damit hinaus.«
O Mutter, und splittert der Fels auch im Wind,
Meine Treu', die hält ihn aus.

'O sink, O sink your sorrow, child,
in the sea, in the deep sea.'
A stone may stay on the bed of the sea,
my sorrow floats ever up.

'The love which you bear in your heart,
pluck it, pluck it, child.'
And though the flower die when picked,
true love dies not so swift.

'True love, true love was but a word,
cast it to the winds.'
O mother, though rock be cracked by wind,
my true love will endure.

## Liebhaber in allen Gestalten | Lover in All Guises

JOHANN WOLFGANG GOETHE

*Franz Schubert, 1817*

Ich wollt, ich wär ein Fisch,
So hurtig und frisch;
Und kämst du zu angeln,
Ich würde nicht mangeln.
Ich wollt, ich wär ein Fisch,
So hurtig und frisch.

Ich wollt, ich wäre Gold,
Dir immer im Sold;
Und tätst du was kaufen,
Käm ich wieder gelaufen.
Ich wollt, ich wäre Gold,
Dir immer im Sold.

Doch bin ich, wie ich bin,
Und nimm mich nur hin!
Willst du beßre besitzen,
So laß dir sie schnitzen.
Ich bin nun, wie ich bin;
So nimm mich nur hin!

I wish I were a fish,
so nimble and brisk;
and if you came to angle,
I would be there.
I wish I were a fish,
so nimble and brisk.

I wish I were gold,
ever at your call;
and should you buy something,
I'd come running once more.
I wish I were gold,
ever at your call.

But I am, as I am,
and take me for that!
If better you want,
then get better made.
I am, as I am,
so take me for that.

## Liebst du um Schönheit / If You Love for Beauty

FRIEDRICH RÜCKERT

*Gustav Mahler, ed. 1905; Hermann Reutter: op. 54, no. 2, ed. 1941;*
*Robert Schumann: op. 37, no. 4, 1840*

Liebst du um Schönheit, o nicht mich
liebe!
Liebe die Sonne, sie trägt ein goldnes
Haar!

Liebst du um Jugend, o nicht mich
liebe!
Liebe den Frühling, der jung ist jedes
Jahr!

Liebst du um Schätze, o nicht mich
liebe!
Liebe die Meerfrau, sie hat viel Perlen
klar!

Liebst du um Liebe, o ja—mich liebe!
Liebe mich immer, dich lieb ich
immerdar!

If you love for beauty, O love not
me!
Love the sun, she has golden
hair!

If you love for youth, O love not
me!
Love the spring who is young each
year!

If you love for riches, O love not
me!
Love the mermaid who has many
shining pearls!

If you love for love, oh yes, love me!
Love me ever, I'll love you
always!


## Lied des Unmuts / Song of Displeasure

JOHANN WOLFGANG GOETHE: from *West-östlicher Divan*, 'Book of Displeasure'
*Ferruccio Busoni, ed. 1964; Othmar Schoeck: op. 19b, no. 5, 1906–15*

Keinen Reimer wird man finden
Der sich nicht den besten hielte,
Keinen Fiedler, der nicht lieber
Eigne Melodien spielte.

Und ich konnte sie nicht tadeln;
Wenn wir andern Ehre geben,
Müssen wir uns selbst entadeln;
Lebt man denn, wenn andre leben?

Und so fand ich's denn auch juste
In gewissen Antichambern,
Wo man nicht zu sondern wußte
Mäusedreck von Koriandern.

Das Gewesne wollte hassen
Solche rüstge neue Besen,
Diese dann nicht gelten lassen
Was sonst Besen war gewesen.

Und wo sich die Völker trennen
Gegenseitig im Verachten,
Keins von beiden wird bekennen,
Daß sie nach demselben trachten.

Und das grobe Selbstempfinden
Haben Leute hart gescholten,
Die am wenigsten verwinden,
Wenn die andern was gegolten.

Not a rhymer will one find
who doesn't think he's best,
nor fiddler who'd not rather
play melodies of his own.

Nor could I blame them;
for in honouring others,
ourselves we under-honour;
do we have life when others live?

And so have I lately found,
in certain ante-chambers,
where no one could distinguish
mouse's mess from coriander.

The has-beens tried to hate
such vigorous new brooms,
who in turn allowed no value
to who formerly were brooms.

And where groups divide
in mutually held contempt,
neither faction will admit
it's the same they strive for.

And this vulgar self-esteem
has been most condemned by those
who are slowest to recover
when other folk are of account.

## Lied eines Schiffers an die Dioskuren | Sailor's Song to the Dioscuri

JOHANN MAYRHOFER

*Franz Schubert: op. 65, no. 1, 1816*

Dioskuren, Zwillingssterne,
Die ihr leuchtet meinem Nachen,
Mich beruhigt auf dem Meere
Eure Milde, euer Wachen.

Wer auch fest in sich begründet,
Unverzagt dem Sturm begegnet,
Fühlt sich doch in euren Strahlen
Doppelt mutig und gesegnet.

Dieses Ruder, das ich schwinge,
Meeresfluten zu zerteilen,
Hänge ich, so ich geborgen,
Auf an eures Tempels Säulen,
Dioskuren, Zwillingssterne.

Dioscuri, Twin Stars,
who light my vessel's way,
calming to me, at sea,
is your gentle vigil.

Even he who, firm rooted in himself,
intrepid stands against the storm,
feels in your radiance
doubly bold and blessed.

This oar that I ply
to part the sea's waves,
I shall, when safe on land, hang
on the pillars of your temple,
Dioscuri, Twin Stars.


## Lieder eines fahrenden Gesellen | Songs of a Journeying Apprentice

(For solo voice and orchestra)

GUSTAV MAHLER

*Gustav Mahler, 1883–84*

### I

Wenn mein Schatz Hochzeit macht,
Hab ich meinen traurigen Tag!
Geh ich in mein Kämmerlein, dunkles
　　Kämmerlein!
Weine! Weine! um meinen Schatz, um
　　meinen lieben Schatz!

Blümlein blau! Verdorre nicht!
Vöglein süß! Du singst auf grüner
　　Heide!
Ach! Wie ist die Welt so schön! Ziküth!

Singet nicht, blühet nicht! Lenz ist ja
　　vorbei!
Alles Singen ist nun aus!
Des Abends, wenn ich schlafen geh,
Denk ich an mein Leid, an mein Leide!

### I

When my darling has her wedding-day,
my day of sorrow it will be!
To my room, my dark room I'll
　　go,
and weep, weep for my darling, my
　　dear darling.

Blue flower, do not fade!
Sweet bird, on the green heath you
　　sing.
Ah, how fair the world is, chirrup!

Sing not. Bloom not. For spring is
　　over.
All singing now is done.
At night, when I go to rest,
I think of my sorrow, my sorrow!

### 2

Ging heut morgen übers Feld,
Tau noch auf den Gräsern hing;
Sprach zu mir der lustge Fink:
»Ei, du! Gelt? Guten Morgen! Ei gelt?
　　Du!
Wird's nicht eine schöne Welt? schöne
　　Welt!?
Zink! Zink! schön und flink!
Wie mir doch die Welt gefällt!«

### 2

I walked the fields this morning,
dew still hung upon the grass;
the merry finch said to me:
'Why, good morning. Don't you
　　agree—
does not the world grow
　　fair?
Tweet! Tweet! Bright and fair!
How pleasing to me the world is!'

Auch die Glockenblum am Feld
Hat mir lustig, guter Ding
Mit dem Glöckchen klinge, kling,
Ihren Morgengruß geschellt:
»Wird's nicht eine schöne Welt? schöne
Welt!?
Kling! Kling! Schönes Ding!
Wie mir doch die Welt gefällt! Hei-a!«

Und da fing im Sonnenschein
Gleich die Welt zu funkeln an;
Alles, alles, Ton und Farbe gewann im
Sonnenschein!
Blum und Vogel, groß und klein!
Guten Tag, guten Tag! Ist's nicht eine
schöne Welt?
Ei du! Gelt!? Schöne
Welt!?

Nun fängt auch mein Glück wohl an?!
Nein! Nein! Das ich mein, mir nimmer
blühen kann!

3
Ich hab ein glühend Messer, ein Messer
in meiner Brust.
O weh! o weh!
Das schneidt so tief in jede Freud und
jede Lust, so tief!
Ach, was ist das für ein böser Gast!
Nimmer hält er Ruh, nimmer hält er
Rast,
Nicht bei Tag, noch bei Nacht, wenn
ich schlief!
O weh! o weh!

Wenn ich in den Himmel seh,
Seh ich zwei blaue Augen stehn!
O weh! o weh!
Wenn ich im gelben Felde geh,
Seh ich von fern das blonde Haar im
Winde wehn!
O weh! o weh!

Wenn ich aus dem Traum auffahr
Und höre klingen ihr silbern Lachen,
O weh! o weh!
Ich wollt, ich läg auf der schwarzen
Bahr,
Könnt nimmer die Augen aufmachen!

4
Die zwei blauen Augen von meinem
Schatz,
Die haben mich in die weite Welt
geschickt.
Da mußt ich Abschied nehmen vom
allerliebsten Platz!
O Augen, blau! Warum habt ihr mich
angeblickt?
Nun hab ich ewig Leid und Grämen!

And the bluebell at the field's edge,
merrily, in good spirits,
ding-dong with its tiny bell
rang out its morning greeting:
'Does not the world grow
fair?
Ding-dong. Beautiful thing.
How pleasing to me the world is!'

And then, in the sun,
the world at once began to sparkle;
all, all gained tone and colour in the
sun.
Flower and bird, great and small.
Good day, good day! Is the world not
fair?
Why, don't you agree—the world is
fair?

Will my happiness now begin?!
No! No! The happiness I mean will
never bloom!

3
A knife, a glowing knife I have in my
breast.
Alas, alas!
That cuts so deep into each delight and
joy!
Ah, what an evil guest!
Never at rest, never at
peace,
neither by day, nor by night when I
would sleep!
Alas, alas!

When I look skywards
two blue eyes I see!
Alas, alas!
Walking the yellow field,
I see from afar her blond hair in the
wind!
Alas, alas!

When from my dream I start
and hear her silvery laugh,
alas, alas!
I would that I lay on the sombre
bier,
and might never open my eyes again!

4
The two blue eyes of my
darling
sent me into the wide
world.
From the place I most loved I had to
part!
O blue eyes, why did you look on
me?
Grief and sorrow are now mine for ever!

Ich bin ausgegangen in stiller Nacht,
In stiller Nacht wohl über die dunkle
    Heide.
Hat mir niemand ade gesagt, ade!
Mein Gesell war Lieb und Leide!
Auf der Straße stand ein Lindenbaum,
Da hab ich zum erstenmal im Schlaf
    geruht!

Unter dem Lindenbaum der hat
Seine Blüten über mich geschneit,
Da wußt ich nicht, wie das Leben tut,
War alles, ach alles wieder gut!
Alles! Alles! Lieb und Leid!
Und Welt und Traum!

In the still night I went out,
in the still night, over the dark
    heath.
No one bade me farewell, farewell.
Love and sorrow were my company!
By my way stood a linden tree
where first I found peace in
    sleep!

Under the linden tree
which snowed on me its blossoms,
I knew not how life went on,
and all, ah all was well again.
All, all! Love and sorrow,
and world and dream!


*Liederkreis* | *Song Cycle*

JOSEPH VON EICHENDORFF

*Robert Schumann: op. 39, nos. 1–12, 1840*

1 *In der Fremde*
Aus der Heimat hinter den Blitzen
    rot
Da kommen die Wolken her,
Aber Vater und Mutter sind lange
    tot,
Es kennt mich dort keiner mehr.

Wie bald, ach wie bald kommt die stille
    Zeit,
Da ruhe ich auch, und über mir
Rauscht die schöne Waldeinsamkeit,
Und keiner kennt mich mehr hier.
    (*Johannes Brahms: op. 3, no. 5, 1852–53*)

2 *Intermezzo*
Dein Bildnis wunderselig
Hab ich im Herzensgrund,
Das sieht so frisch und fröhlich
Mich an zu jeder Stund

Mein Herz still in sich singet
Ein altes schönes Lied,
Das in die Luft sich schwinget
Und zu dir eilig zieht.

3 *Waldesgespräch*
Es ist schon spät, es ist schon kalt,
Was reitest du einsam durch den Wald.
Der Wald ist lang, du bist allein,
Du schöne Braut! Ich führ dich heim!—

»Groß ist der Männer Trug und List,
Vor Schmerz mein Herz gebrochen ist,
Wohl irrt das Waldhorn her und hin,
O flieh! Du weißt nicht, wer ich bin.«—

1 *In a Foreign Land*
From my homeland beyond the
    lightning red
the clouds come drifting in,
but father and mother are long since
    dead,
now no one remembers me there.

How soon, oh, how soon till that quiet
    time
when I too shall rest, and above me
will rustle the lovely, lonely wood,
and no one will remember me here.

2 *Intermezzo*
Your blissful image
I have deep in my heart,
gazing so joyously
at me always.

My heart sings silently
a beautiful song,
that soars to the sky
and hastens to you.

3 *Wood Dialogue*
It is late, it is cold,
why ride you lonely through the wood?
The wood is long, you are alone,
lovely bride! I will lead you home!—

'Great are men's deceit and guile,
sorrow has broken my heart;
the horn sounds here, sounds there,
oh flee! You know not who I am.'—

So reich geschmückt ist Roß und Weib,
So wunderschön der junge Leib,
Jetzt kenn ich dich—Gott steh mir bei!
Du bist die Hexe Lorelei.—

So richly decked are steed and lady,
so young and fair of figure is she,
now—God preserve me—I know you!
You are the Sorceress Lorelei!

»Du kennst mich wohl—vom hohen Stein
Schaut still mein Schloß tief in den
   Rhein.
Es ist schon spät, es ist schon kalt,
Kommst nimmermehr aus diesem
   Wald.«

'You know me indeed—from lofty rock
my castle gazes silent into the
   Rhine.
It is late, it is cold,
nevermore shall you leave this
   wood.'

4 *Die Stille*
Es weiß und rät es doch keiner,
Wie mir so wohl ist, so wohl!
Ach, wüßt es nur einer, nur einer,
Kein Mensch es sonst wissen soll.

4 *Silence*
Not a soul knows or guesses
how happy, happy I am!
Oh, if only *one* were to know it,
then no other should.

So still ist's nicht draußen im Schnee,
So stumm und verschwiegen sind
Die Sterne nicht in der Höh,
Als meine Gedanken sind.

The snow outside's not so silent,
nor so mute and silent
the stars on high,
as are my thoughts.

Ich wünscht, ich wär ein Vöglein
Und zöge über das Meer,
Wohl über das Meer und weiter,
Bis daß ich im Himmel wär!

Would I were a bird
and might fly over the sea,
over the sea and on,
until I were in heaven!

(*Felix Mendelssohn-Bartholdy: op. 99, no. 6, 1841–45*)

5 *Mondnacht*
Es war, als hätt' der Himmel
Die Erde still geküßt,
Daß sie im Blütenschimmer
Von ihm nun träumen müßt.

5 *Moonlit Night*
It was as though the sky
had softly kissed the earth,
so that she, in a gleam of blossom,
had now to dream of him.

Die Luft ging durch die Felder,
Die Ähren wogten sacht,
Es rauschten leis die Wälder,
So sternklar war die Nacht.

The breeze ran through the fields,
the ears of corn gently swayed,
the woods rustled faintly,
the night was so starry and clear.

Und meine Seele spannte
Weit ihre Flügel aus,
Flog durch die stillen Lande,
Als flöge sie nach Haus.

And my soul spread
wide its wings,
flew over the silent land,
as if it were flying home.

(*Johannes Brahms, 1854*)

6 *Schöne Fremde*
Es rauschen die Wipfel und schauern,
Als machten zu dieser Stund
Um die halbversunkenen Mauern
Die alten Götter die Rund.

6 *Beautiful Foreign Land*
The tree-tops murmur and shiver,
as though at this hour
the half-sunken walls
were paced by gods of old.

Hier hinter den Myrtenbäumen
In heimlich dämmernder Pracht,
Was sprichst du wirr wie in Träumen
Zu mir, phantastische Nacht?

Here, beyond the myrtles,
in secretly darkening splendour,
what do you murmur, as in a dream,
to me, fantastic night?

Es funkeln auf mich alle Sterne
Mit glühendem Liebesblick,
Es redet trunken die Ferne
Wie von künftigem, großen Glück.

The stars all sparkle upon me
with glowing and loving gaze,
rapturous the distance speaks
as of great happiness to come.

7 *Auf einer Burg*
Eingeschlafen auf der Lauer
Oben ist der alte Ritter;
Drüber gehen Regenschauer,
Und der Wald rauscht durch das Gitter.

Eingewachsen Bart und Haare
Und versteinert Brust und Krause,
Sitzt er viele hundert Jahre
Oben in der stillen Klause.

Draußen ist es still und friedlich,
Alle sind ins Tal gezogen,
Waldesvögel einsam singen
In den leeren Fensterbogen.

Eine Hochzeit fährt da unten
Auf dem Rhein im Sonnenscheine,
Musikanten spielen munter,
Und die schöne Baut, sie weinet.

7 *In a Castle*
Asleep at his look-out
up there, is the old knight;
overhead go rain squalls,
through the grill roars the wood.

Beard and hair grown into one,
ruff and breast turned to stone,
for centuries he has sat
up there in his silent cell.

Outside is calm and quiet,
all have gone to the valley,
woodbirds sing, lonely,
in the empty window arches.

Below, a wedding passes
in the sunshine on the Rhine,
minstrels play merrily,
and the lovely bride—weeps.

8 *In der Fremde*
Ich hör' die Bächlein rauschen
Im Walde her und hin.
Im Walde, in dem Rauschen,
Ich weiß nicht, wo ich bin.

Die Nachtigallen schlagen
Hier in der Einsamkeit,
Als wollten sie was sagen
Von der alten, schönen Zeit.

Die Mondesschimmer fliegen,
Als säh ich unter mir
Das Schloß im Tale liegen,
Und ist doch so weit von hier!

Als müßte in dem Garten,
Voll Rosen weiß und rot,
Meine Liebste auf mich warten,
Und ist doch so lange tot.

8 *In a Foreign Land*
I hear brooklets
murmur through the wood.
Amidst wood and murmur
I know not where I am.

Nightingales sing
here in the solitude,
as if wishing to tell
of fair days now past.

In the darting moonbeams
I seem to see below me
in the valley the castle
which is so far from here!

It is as if in the garden
full of roses white and red,
my beloved were waiting
who is so long since dead.

9 *Wehmut*
Ich kann wohl manchmal singen,
Als ob ich fröhlich sei,
Doch heimlich Tränen dringen,
Da wird das Herz mir frei.

Es lassen Nachtigallen,
Spielt draußen Frühlingsluft,
Der Sehnsucht Lied erschallen
Aus ihres Kerkers Gruft.

Da lauschen alle Herzen,
Und alles ist erfreut,
Doch keiner fühlt die Schmerzen,
Im Lied das tiefe Leid.

9 *Sadness*
Sometimes I can sing
as if I were glad,
yet secretly tears well
and free my heart.

Nightingales, when, outside,
spring breezes play, let
sound their song of longing
from their dungeon's depth.

At which all hearts hearken,
and everyone delights,
yet no one feels the pain,
the deep sorrow in the song.

10 *Zwielicht*
Dämmrung will die Flügel spreiten,
Schaurig rühren sich die Bäume,
Wolken ziehn wie schwere Träume—
Was will dieses Graun bedeuten?

Hast ein Reh du lieb vor andern,
Laß es nicht alleine grasen,
Jäger ziehn im Wald und blasen,
Stimmen hin und wieder wandern.

Hast du einen Freund hienieden,
Trau ihm nicht zu dieser Stunde,
Freundlich wohl mit Aug' und Munde,
Sinnt er Krieg im tück'schen Frieden.

Was heut gehet müde unter,
Hebt sich morgen neu geboren.
Manches geht in Nacht verloren—
Hüte dich, sei wach und munter!

11 *Im Walde*
Es zog eine Hochzeit den Berg entlang,
Ich hörte die Vögel schlagen,
Da blitzten viel Reiter, das Waldhorn
    klang,
Das war ein lustiges Jagen!
Und eh ich's gedacht, war alles verhallt,
Die Nacht bedecket die Runde,
Nur von den Bergen noch rauschet der
    Wald
Und mich schauert's im Herzensgrunde.

12 *Frühlingsnacht*
Übern Garten durch die Lüfte
Hört ich Wandervögel ziehn,
Das bedeutet Frühlingsdüfte,
Unten fängt's schon an zu blüh'n.

Jauchzen möcht ich, möchte weinen,
Ist mir's doch, als könnt's nicht sein!
Alte Wunder wieder scheinen
Mit dem Mondesglanz herein.

Und der Mond, die Sterne sagen's,
Und im Traume rauscht's der Hain,
Und die Nachtigallen schlagen's:
Sie ist deine, sie ist dein!

10 *Twilight*
Dusk makes to spread its wings,
the trees stir awesomely,
clouds come like heavy dreams—
what means this dusk and dread?

If you have a fawn you favour,
let her not graze alone;
hunters range the forest, bugling,
voices flit here and there.

If on earth you have a friend,
do not trust him at this hour;
friendly both in look and speech,
in seeming peace he schemes for war.

What, today, goes weary down,
rises new-born on the morrow.
Much in the night goes astray—
be wary, watchful, wide-awake!

11 *In the Wood*
Across the hill a wedding went,
I heard birds singing,
then—a flash of riders, a sounding
    horn,
a merry hunt!
And before I knew, all had died away,
night covers all around,
only from the hills—a forest
    murmur,
and deep in my heart—a shudder.

12 *Spring Night*
Above the garden across the sky
I heard the birds of passage wing,
a sign that spring is in the air,
that blossom time is come.

I could shout for joy, could weep,
I feel it cannot be.
Old wonders reappear,
with the gleaming moon.

And the moon and the stars say it,
and the wood, dreaming, murmurs it,
and the nightingales sing it:
she is yours, she is yours!

*Liederkreis* | *Song Cycle*
HEINRICH HEINE
*Robert Schumann: op. 24, nos. 1–9, 1840*

1
Morgens steh' ich auf und frage:
Kommt feins Liebchen heut?
Abends sink' ich hin und klage:
Ausblieb sie auch heut.

1
At morn I rise and ask:
Will my love come today?
At eve I sink down, complain:
And today she stayed away.

| | |
|---|---|
| In der Nacht mit meinem Kummer | At night, with my grief, |
| Lieg' ich schlaflos, wach; | watchful, sleepless, I lie; |
| Träumend, wie im halben Schlummer, | dreaming, half slumbering, |
| Wandle ich bei Tag. | I wander through the day. |

*(Robert Franz: op. 25, no. 3; Franz Liszt, 1844)*

2

| | |
|---|---|
| Es treibt mich hin, es treibt mich her! | I'm driven this way, driven that! |
| Noch wenige Stunden, dann soll ich sie schauen, | A few more hours, then I shall see her, |
| Sie selber, die schönste der schönen Jungfrauen;— | her, the fairest of fair maidens;— |
| Du treues Herz, was pochst du so schwer! | faithful heart, how hard you beat! |

| | |
|---|---|
| Die Stunden sind aber ein faules Volk! | The hours, though, are a lazy breed! |
| Schleppen sich behaglich träge, | With easy indolence they dawdle, |
| Schleichen gähnend ihre Wege;— | yawningly they crawl their way;— |
| Tummle dich, du faules Volk! | get a move on, you lazy breed! |

| | |
|---|---|
| Tobende Eile mich treibend erfaßt! | Raging haste seizes and impels me; |
| Aber wohl niemals liebten die Horen;— | but the Horae can never have loved;— |
| Heimlich im grausamen Bunde verschworen, | secretly bound in cruel league, |
| Spotten sie tückisch der Liebenden Hast. | spitefully they mock lovers' haste. |

*(Robert Franz: op. 34, no. 4)*

3

| | |
|---|---|
| Ich wandelte unter den Bäumen | Amid the trees I wandered, |
| Mit meinem Gram allein; | with my grief, alone; |
| Da kam das alte Träumen, | and the old dreams came, |
| Und schlich mir ins Herz hinein. | and stole into my heart. |

| | |
|---|---|
| Wer hat euch dies Wörtlein gelehret, | Who taught you that dear word, |
| Ihr Vöglein in luftiger Höh'? | birds in the airy heights? |
| Schweigt still! wenn mein Herz es höret, | Be silent. When my heart hears it, |
| Dann tut es noch einmal so weh. | it causes again such pain. |

| | |
|---|---|
| »Es kam ein Jungfräulein gegangen, | 'A maid there was came walking, |
| Die sang es immerfort, | she sang it all the time, |
| Da haben wir Vöglein gefangen | and we birds seized upon it, |
| Das hübsche, goldne Wort.« | that lovely, golden word.' |

| | |
|---|---|
| Das sollt ihr mir nicht erzählen, | You're not to tell me that, |
| Ihr Vöglein wunderschlau; | you birds so wondrous sly; |
| Ihr wollt meinen Kummer mir stehlen, | my grief you would steal from me, |
| Ich aber niemanden trau'. | but no one do I trust. |

4

| | |
|---|---|
| Lieb Liebchen, leg's Händchen aufs Herze mein;— | My dearest, lay your hand on my heart;— |
| Ach, hörst du, wie's pochet im Kämmerlein? | ah, can you hear the hammering? |
| Da hauset ein Zimmermann schlimm und arg, | A carpenter lives there, wicked and bad, |
| Der zimmert mir einen Totensarg. | fashioning me a coffin. |

| | |
|---|---|
| Es hämmert und klopfet bei Tag und bei Nacht; | A banging and hammering night and day; |

Es hat mich schon längst um den
Schlaf gebracht.
Ach! sputet Euch, Meister Zimmermann,
Damit ich balde schlafen kann.

*(Robert Franz: op. 17, no. 3)*

5
Schöne Wiege meiner Leiden,
Schönes Grabmal meiner Ruh',
Schöne Stadt, wir müssen scheiden,—
Lebe wohl! ruf' ich dir zu.

Lebe wohl, du heil'ge Schwelle,
Wo da wandelt Liebchen traut;
Lebe wohl! du heil'ge Stelle,
Wo ich sie zuerst geschaut.

Hätt' ich dich doch nie gesehen,
Schöne Herzenskönigin!
Nimmer wär es dann geschehen,
Daß ich jetzt so elend bin.

Nie wollt' ich dein Herze rühren,
Liebe hab' ich nie erfleht;
Nur ein stilles Leben führen
Wollt' ich, wo dein Odem weht.

Doch du drängst mich selbst von
hinnen,
Bittre Worte spricht dein Mund;
Wahnsinn wühlt in meinen Sinnen,
Und mein Herz ist krank und wund.

Und die Glieder matt und träge
Schlepp' ich fort am Wanderstab,
Bis mein müdes Haupt ich lege
Ferne in ein kühles Grab.

6
Warte, warte, wilder Schiffsmann,
Gleich folg' ich zum Hafen dir;
Von zwei Jungfraun nehm' ich Abschied,
Von Europa und von Ihr.

Blutquell, rinn' aus meinen Augen,
Blutquell, brich aus meinem Leib,
Daß ich mit dem heißen Blute
Meine Schmerzen niederschreib'.

Ei, mein Lieb, warum just heute
Schauderst du, mein Blut zu sehn?
Sahst mich bleich und herzeblutend
Lange Jahre vor dir stehn!

Kennst du noch das alte Liedchen
Von der Schlang' im Paradies,
Die durch schlimme Apfelgabe
Unsern Ahn ins Elend stieß?

it has long since taken my sleep
away.
Ah, master carpenter, make haste,
so that I soon may sleep.

5
Beautiful cradle of my sorrows,
beautiful tombstone of my peace,
beautiful town, we must part,—
to you I cry farewell.

Farewell, sacred threshold
which my dear love treads;
farewell, sacred place
where I first beheld her.

Had I but never seen you,
beautiful queen of my heart!
Never would it then have happened
that I am now so wretched.

I never wished to stir your heart,
love I have never craved;
to lead a quiet life,
where you breathed, no more I asked.

But you, you drive me
hence,
your lips speak bitter words;
madness rages in my mind,
and my heart is sick and sore.

And my limbs, feeble and weak,
on I will drag, staff in hand,
till I lay my tired head down
in a cool and distant grave.

6
Wait, wait, wild sailor,
soon I'll follow to the port;
two maidens I have to part from,
from Europe and from *her*.

Blood, stream from my eyes,
blood, gush from my body,
that I may, in hot blood,
write down my sorrows.

Oh, my love, why just today
do you shudder to see my blood?
You've seen me pale, heart bleeding,
before you for years on end!

Remember the ancient story
of the serpent in Paradise,
who, by wicked gift of an apple,
cast our forebear into woe?

Alles Unheil brachten Äpfel!
Eva bracht' damit den Tod,
Eris brachte Trojas Flammen,
Du bracht'st beides, Flamm' und Tod.

All ill has come with the apple!
Eve brought with it death,
Eris—the flames of Troy,
you—both, flames and death.


7
Berg' und Burgen schaun herunter
In den spiegelhellen Rhein,
Und mein Schiffchen segelt munter,
Rings umglänzt von Sonnenschein.

Ruhig seh' ich zu dem Spiele
Goldner Wellen, kraus bewegt;
Still erwachen die Gefühle,
Die ich tief im Busen hegt'.

Freundlich grüßend und verheißend
Lockt hinab des Stromes Pracht;
Doch ich kenn' ihn, oben gleißend,
Birgt sein Innres Tod und Nacht.

Oben Lust, im Busen Tücken,
Strom, du bist der Liebsten Bild!
Die kann auch so freundlich nicken,
Lächelt auch so fromm und mild.

7
Mountains, castles gaze down
into the mirror-clear Rhine,
and gaily sails my tiny boat,
surrounded by sunlight gleam.

Calmly I watch the play
of golden, ruffled waves;
softly the feelings awaken
I'd nursed deep in my heart.

Welcoming, promising,
the river's splendour beckons me;
but I know it—glistening above,
it hides death and night below.

Above—pleasure, at heart—malice,
river, you resemble my love!
She can nod just as welcomingly,
smile just as sweetly and gently.


8
Anfangs wollt' ich fast verzagen,
Und ich glaubt', ich trüg' es nie;
Und ich hab' es doch getragen—
Aber fragt mich nur nicht, wie?
      (*Franz Liszt, 1856*)

8
At first I almost despaired,
thought I could never bear it;
yet borne it I have—
only ask me not how.


9
Mit Myrten und Rosen, lieblich und
      hold,
Mit duft'gen Zypressen und Flittergold,
Möcht' ich zieren dies Buch wie 'nen
      Totenschrein,
Und sargen meine Lieder hinein.

O könnt' ich die Liebe sargen hinzu!
Auf dem Grabe der Liebe wächst
      Blümlein der Ruh',
Da blüht es hervor, da pflückt man es
      ab,—
Doch mir blüht's nur, wenn ich selber
      im Grab.

Hier sind nun die Lieder, die einst so
      wild,
Wie ein Lavastrom, der dem Ätna
      entquillt,
Hervorgestürzt aus dem tiefsten Gemüt,
Und rings viel blitzende Funken
      versprüht!

9
With myrtle and roses, sweet and
      fair,
fragrant cypress and foil of gold,
would I decorate this book like a
      coffin
and in it put my songs.

Would I might put my love in it too!
On love's grave grows the flower of
      peace,
there it blossoms, there is
      plucked,—
it will bloom for me only above my
      grave.

Here now are the songs which once,
      wild
as a stream of lava pouring from
      Etna,
burst from the depths of my soul,
showering many glittering sparks
      around.

Nun liegen sie stumm und toten-gleich,
Nun starren sie kalt und nebelbleich,
Doch aufs neu' die alte Glut sie belebt,
Wenn der Liebe Geist einst über sie
schwebt.

Und es wird mir im Herzen viel Ahnung
laut:
Der Liebe Geist einst über sie
taut;
Einst kommt dies Buch in deine
Hand,
Du süßes Lieb im fernen Land.

Dann löst sich des Liedes
Zauberbann,
Die blassen Buchstaben schaun dich an,
Sie schauen dir flehend ins schöne Aug',
Und flüstern mit Wehmut und
Liebeshauch.

Mute now they lie, and as if dead,
rigid now, cold, and pallid as the mist,
but the old glow shall revive them anew,
if love's spirit one day be poised above
them.

And in my heart the thought speaks
loud:
that spirit will one day above them
thaw;
this book one day will fall into your
hands,
my sweet love, in a distant land.

Then shall song's magic spell break
free,
the pallid letters gaze at you,
gaze imploringly at your fair eyes,
whisper with melancholy and breath of
love.

## Liederseelen / Song-souls

CONRAD FERDINAND MEYER

*Wilhelm Kempff: op. 56, no. 1; Othmar Schoeck: op. 60, no. 2, 1946*

In der Nacht, die die Bäume mit
Blüten deckt,
Ward ich von süßen Gespenstern
erschreckt,
Ein Reigen schwang im Garten sich,
Den ich mit leisem Fuß beschlich;
Wie zarter Elfen Chor im Ring
Ein weißer, lebendiger Schimmer
ging.
Die Schemen hab' ich keck
befragt:
Wer seid ihr, luftige Wesen? Sagt!

»Ich bin ein Wölkchen, gespiegelt im
See.«
»Ich bin eine Reihe von Stapfen im
Schnee.«
»Ich bin ein Seufzer gen Himmel
empor!«
»Ich bin ein Geheimnis, geflüstert ins
Ohr!«
»Ich bin ein frommes, gestorbenes
Kind.«
»Ich bin ein üppiges Blumengewind—«
»Und die du wählst, und der's
beschied
Die Gunst der Stunde, die wird ein
Lied.«

In the night that blossom-decks the
trees,
I was affrighted by sweet
phantoms,
dancing rows whirled about the garden,
into which, light-footed, I was stealing;
like a dainty elfin crowd all in a ring
a shimmer, white and living, went its
way.
And of those phantoms boldly I
inquired:
Who, airy creatures, are you? Say!

'I am a lake-reflected
cloud.'
'I—a line of footsteps in the
snow.'
'I—a sigh directed to the
sky!'
'I—a secret whispered in the
ear!'
'I—an innocent departed
child.'
'I—a rich garland of flowers—'
'And which you choose, and the
hour favours, will grow into a
song.'

## Litanei | Litany

JOHANN GEORG JACOBI

*Franz Schubert, 1816*

Ruhn in Frieden alle Seelen,
Die vollbracht ein banges Quälen,
Die vollendet süßen Traum,
Lebenssatt, geboren kaum,
Aus der Welt hinüberschieden:
Alle Seelen ruhn in Frieden!

Und die nie der Sonne lachten,
Unterm Mond auf Dornen wachten,
Gott, im reinen Himmelslicht,
Einst zu sehn vom Angesicht:
alle, die von hinnen schieden,
alle Seelen ruhn in Frieden!

Rest in peace, all souls
who, anxious torment done,
and sweet dreams ended,
weary of life, scarcely born,
are departed from this world:
all souls, rest in peace!

And who, never rejoicing in the sun,
kept watch on thorns under the moon,
to see God in Heaven's pure light,
face to face, one day:
all who have departed hence,
all souls, rest in peace!


## Lob der Faulheit | In Praise of Sloth

GOTTHOLD EPHRAIM LESSING

*Joseph Haydn, 1784*

Faulheit, endlich muß ich dir
Auch ein kleines Loblied bringen.—
O .. wie .. sau .. er wird es mir ...
Dich .. nach Würden .. zu besingen!
Doch ich will mein Bestes tun,
Nach der Arbeit ist gut ruhn.

Höchstes Gut! wer dich nur hat,
Dessen ungestörtes Leben——
Ach! .. ich .. gähn .. ich werde matt ..
Nun .. so .. magst du .. mirs vergeben,
Daß ich dich nicht singen kann;
Du verhinderst mich ja dran.

Sloth, to you also must I at last
address a brief paeon.—
Oh ... how ... hard for me
worthily to celebrate you!
Still, I will do my best,
after work, it's good to rest.

Highest good! Who possesses you,
his untroubled life——
Ah, I yawn ... grow weary ...
Well, if you will, forgive
my inability to proclaim you;
you are, you see, preventing me.


## Lust der Sturmnacht | The Wild Night's Joy

JUSTINUS KERNER

*Robert Schumann: op. 35, no. 1, 1840*

Wenn durch Berg und Tale draußen
Regen schauert, Stürme brausen,
Schild und Fenster hell erklirren,
Und in Nacht die Wandrer irren,
Ruht es sich so süß hier innen,
Aufgelöst in selges Minnen;
All der goldne Himmelsschimmer
Flieht herein ins stille Zimmer:
Reiches Leben, hab Erbarmen!
Halt mich fest in linden Armen!
Lenzesblumen aufwärts dringen,

When, outside, over hill and vale
rain streams and tempests rage,
house-emblem, window, rattle loud
and in the darkness travellers stray,
here inside it is so sweet to rest
and give oneself to blissful love;
the whole of heaven's golden gleam
flees hither to this quiet room:
have compassion, O abundant life,
hold me fast with gentle arm.
The flowers of spring thrust up,

Wölklein ziehn und Vöglein singen.
Ende nie, du Sturmnacht, wilde!
Klirrt, ihr Fenster, schwankt, ihr Schilde,
Bäumt euch, Wälder, braus, o Welle,
Mich umfängt des Himmels
    Helle!

clouds are scudding and birds sing.
Never end, wild night of storm,
rattle, house-emblems and windows,
rear up, forests. Roar, O wave.
Locked am I in heaven's bright
    embrace!


## Mädchenlied | Maiden's Song

PAUL HEYSE

*Johannes Brahms: op. 107, no. 5, 1886*

Auf die Nacht in der Spinnstub'n
da singen die Mädchen,
da lachen die Dorfbub'n,
wie flink geh'n Rädchen!

All night in the spinning-room
there sing the maidens,
the village lads laugh;
how nimble the wheels!

Spinnt Jedes am Brautschatz,
daß der Liebste sich freut.
Nicht lange, so gibt es
ein Hochzeitgeläut.

Each spins for her trousseau
to gladden her dear one.
Not long and there will be
the wedding-bells' sound.

Kein Mensch, der mir gut ist,
will nach mir fragen;
wie bang mir zu Mut ist,
wem soll ich's klagen?

No man there's to love me,
wants to care for me;
how frightened this makes me,
who am I to tell?

Die Tränen rinnen
mir über's Gesicht,
wofür soll ich spinnen?
Ich weiß es nicht!

The tears go coursing
down my cheeks;
what am I spinning for?
I do not know.


## Mailied | May Song

JOHANN WOLFGANG GOETHE

*Ludwig van Beethoven: op. 52, no. 4, ca. 1793; Armin Knab, 1924–46;*
*Hans Pfitzner: op. 26, no. 5, 1916; Othmar Schoeck: op. 19a, no. 3, 1909–14*

Wie herrlich leuchtet
Mir die Natur!
Wie glänzt die Sonne!
Wie lacht die Flur!

How glorious blazes
nature for me!
How the sun sparkles!
How the meadow laughs!

Es dringen Blüten
Aus jedem Zweig
Und tausend Stimmen
Aus dem Gesträuch

Blossoms burst
from every bough
and a thousand voices
from every bush

Und Freud und Wonne
Aus jeder Brust.
O Erd, o Sonne!
O Glück, o Lust!

and delight and rapture
from every breast.
O earth, O sun!
O joy, O bliss!

O Lieb, o Liebe!
So golden schön,

O love, O love!
So golden fair

Wie Morgenwolken
Auf jenen Höhn!

as morning clouds
on yonder heights!

Du segnest herrlich
das frische Feld,
Im Blütendampfe
Die volle Welt.

You bless with glory
the fresh field,
in a haze of blossom
the full world.

O Mädchen, Mädchen,
Wie lieb ich dich!
Wie blickt dein Auge!
Wie liebst du mich!

O maiden, maiden,
how I love you!
Oh, the look in your eyes!
How you love me!

So liebt die Lerche
Gesang und Luft,
Und Morgenblumen
Den Himmelsduft,

The skylark loves
its songs and air,
the morning flowers—
heaven's dew,

Wie ich dich liebe
Mit warmem Blut,
Die du mir Jugend
Und Freud und Mut

as I love you
with blood afire,
who give me youth
and joy and heart

Zu neuen Liedern
Und Tänzen gibst.
Sei ewig glücklich,
Wie du mich liebst!

for new songs
and new dances.
Be happy forever
in loving me!

## Mariä Wiegenlied / Mary's Lullaby

MARTIN BOELITZ

Max Reger: op. 76, no. 52, 1911–12

Maria sitzt im Rosenhag
Und wiegt ihr Jesuskind,
Durch die Blätter leise
Weht der warme Sommerwind.

Mary sits in the rose bower,
rocking her Jesus Child,
softly through the foliage
the warm wind of summer blows.

Zu ihren Füßen singt
Ein buntes Vögelein:
Schlaf, Kindlein, süße,
Schlaf nun ein!

At her feet there sings
a brightly-plumaged bird:
Go, sweet child, to sleep,
go now to sleep!

Hold ist dein Lächeln,
Holder deines Schlummers Lust,
Leg dein müdes Köpfchen
Fest an deiner Mutter Brust!
Schlaf, Kindlein, süße,
Schlaf nun ein!

Lovely is your smile,
lovelier your slumber's joy,
lay your weary little head
close to your mother's breast.
Go, sweet child, to sleep,
go now to sleep!

## Mausfallen-Sprüchlein / Mousetrap Motto

EDUARD MÖRIKE

Hugo Wolf, 1882

Kleine Gäste, kleines Haus.
Liebe Mäusin oder Maus,

Tiny visitors, tiny house.
Dear Mrs Mouse or Mr Mouse,

Stell dich nur kecklich ein
Heut nacht bei Mondenschein!
Mach aber die Tür fein hinter dir zu,
Hörst du?
Dabei hüte dein Schwänzchen!
Nach Tische singen wir,
Nach Tische springen wir
Und machen ein Tänzchen:
Witt witt!
Meine alte Katze tanzt wahrscheinlich
mit.

boldly just present yourself
tonight in the moonlight!
But shut the door behind you,
do you hear?
And mind your tail!
After dinner we'll sing,
after dinner we'll jump
and have a wee dance:
beware!
My old cat'll probably join
in.

## Meeres Stille | Sea Calm

JOHANN WOLFGANG GOETHE

*Johann Friedrich Reichardt, ed. 1809; Franz Schubert: op. 3, no. 2, 1815*

Tiefe Stille herrscht im Wasser,
Ohne Regung ruht das Meer,
Und bekümmert sieht der Schiffer
Glatte Fläche ringsumher.
Keine Luft von keiner Seite!
Todesstille fürchterlich!
In der ungeheuern Weite
Reget keine Welle sich.

Deep calm lies on the water,
motionless, the sea rests,
and troubled, the sailor sees
all smooth and flat around.
No wind from any quarter!
Dread, deadly calm!
In the vast expanse
no wave stirs.

## Meerfahrt | Sea Voyage

HEINRICH HEINE

*Johannes Brahms: op. 96, no. 4, 1884; Robert Franz: op. 18, no. 4*

Mein Liebchen, wir saßen beisammen,
Traulich im leichten Kahn.
Die Nacht war still, und wir schwammen
Auf weiter Wasserbahn.

My love, we sat together
cosily in our skiff.
The night was still, we floated
upon a broad waterway.

Die Geisterinsel, die schöne,
Lag dämmrig im Mondenglanz;
Dort klangen liebe Töne,
Und wogte der Nebeltanz.

The lovely Isle of Spirits
lay dim in the moonlight gleam;
upon it sweet sounds rang out,
and dancing vapours surged.

Dort klang es lieb und lieber,
Und wogt' es hin und her;
Wir aber schwammen vorüber,
Trostlos auf weitem Meer.

Sweeter the sounds and sweeter,
this way and that the surge;
but past the isle we floated,
forlorn on the wide sea.

## Mein Herz ist schwer | My Heart is Heavy

GEORGE GORDON NOEL LORD BYRON: from *Hebrew Melodies*

*Robert Schumann: op. 25 (Myrten), no. 15, 1840*

Mein Herz ist schwer!
Auf von der Wand die Laute,
Nur sie allein mag ich noch hören,
Entlocke mit geschickter Hand
Ihr Töne, die das Herz betören.

My heart is heavy!
Take from the wall the lute,
that alone do I still care to hear,
and, with practised hand, coax
forth sounds to bewitch the heart.

Kann noch mein Herz ein Hoffen
nähren,
Es zaubert diese 'Töne her,
Und birgt mein trocknes Auge Zähren,
Sie fließen, und mich brennt's nicht
mehr!

If still my heart can nourish a
hope,
these sounds will magic it forth,
and if my sere eye hide tears,
they will flow and I shall burn no
more!

Nur tief sei, wild der Töne
Fluß,
Und von der Freude weggekehret!
Ja, Sänger, daß ich weinen muß,
Sonst wird das schwere Herz verzehret!

But let the flood of sound be deep,
wild,
and of joy swept clear!
Aye, minstrel, I must weep
or my heavy heart shall all burn away!

Denn sieh! Von Kummer ward's
genähret,
Mit stummem Wachen trug es lang,
Und jetzt vom Äußersten belehret,
Da brech es oder heil im Sang.

For behold! By sorrow was it
nourished,
in silent vigil bore it long,
and now, schooled by extremes,
let it break or heal in song.


## Mein Herz ist schwer | My Heart Is Heavy

EMANUEL GEIBEL

*Johannes Brahms: op. 94, no. 3, 1884*

Mein Herz ist schwer, mein Auge
wacht,
Der Wind fährt seufzend durch die
Nacht;
Die Wipfel rauschen weit und breit,
Sie rauschen von vergangner Zeit.

My heart is heavy, my eyes keep
watch,
the wind goes sighing through the
night;
far and wide the tree-tops murmur,
murmur of times gone by.

Sie rauschen von vergangner Zeit,
Von großem Glück und Herzeleid,
Vom Schloß und von der Jungfrau drin,
Wo ist das alles, alles hin?

Of times gone by they murmur,
of great happiness and grief,
of the castle and its maiden,
where, where have they all gone?

Wo ist das alles, alles hin?
Leid, Lieb und Lust und Jugendsinn?
Der Wind fährt seufzend durch die
Nacht,
Mein Herz ist schwer, mein Auge
wacht.

Where, where have they all gone?
Pain and love and joy and youth?
The wind goes sighing through the
night,
my heart is heavy, my eyes keep
watch.


## Mein Wagen rollet langsam | Slowly My Carriage Rolls

HEINRICH HEINE

*Robert Schumann: op. 142, no. 4, 1852; Richard Strauss: op. 69, no. 4, 1918–19*

Mein Wagen rollet langsam
Durch lustiges Waldesgrün,
Durch blumige Täler, die zaubrisch
Im Sonnenglanze blühn.

Slowly my carriage rolls
through gay green woods,
through flowery valleys
magically blooming in the sun.

Ich sitze und sinne und träume,
Und denk' an die Liebste mein;
Da grüßen drei Schattengestalten
Kopfnickend zum Wagen herein.

Sie hüpfen und schneiden Gesichter,
So spöttisch und doch so scheu,
Und quirlen wie Nebel zusammen,
Und kichern und huschen vorbei.

I sit and muse and dream
and think of my dear love;
three shadowy figures nod at me
through the carriage window.

They hop, they pull faces,
so mocking and yet timid,
whirl together like mist
and flit chuckling by.

## Mein wundes Herz verlangt | My Wounded Heart Craves

KLAUS GROTH

*Johannes Brahms: op. 59, no. 7, 1873*

Mein wundes Herz verlangt nach milder
    Ruh,
O hauche sie ihm ein!
Es fliegt dir weinend, bange schlagend
    zu,
O hülle du es ein!

Wie wenn ein Strahl durch schwere
    Wolken bricht,
So winkest du ihm zu:
O lächle fort mit deinem milden Licht!
Mein Pol, mein Stern bist du.

My wounded heart craves gentle
    peace,
oh, breathe peace into it!
To you it flies, weeping,
    fearful,
oh, enfold it!

Like a sunbeam piercing heavy
    cloud,
you beckon to it:
oh, let your gentle light smile on!
My pole, my star you are.

## Meine Liebe ist grün | My Love Is Green

FELIX SCHUMANN

*Johannes Brahms: op. 63, no. 5, 1873*

Meine Liebe ist grün wie der
    Fliederbusch,
Und meine Lieb ist schön wie die
    Sonne;
Die glänzt wohl herab auf den
    Fliederbusch
Und füllt ihn mit Duft und mit Wonne.

Meine Liebe hat Schwingen der
    Nachtigall,
Und wiegt sich in blühendem Flieder,
Und jauchzet und singet vom Duft
    berauscht
Viel liebestrunkene Lieder.

My love is green as the
    lilac,
and my love is fair as the
    sun;
the sun gleams down on the
    lilac
and fills it with scent and joy.

My love has nightingale's
    wings
and sways in blossoming lilac,
exults and, scent-enraptured,
    sings
many a love-drunk song.

## Meine Rose | My Rose

NIKOLAUS LENAU

*Robert Schumann: op. 90, no. 2, 1850*

Dem holden Lenzgeschmeide,
Der Rose, meiner Freude,
Die schon gebeugt und blasser
Vom heißen Strahl der Sonnen,
Reich' ich den Becher Wasser
Aus tiefem Bronnen.

Du Rose meines Herzens!
Vom stillen Strahl des Schmerzens
Bist du gebeugt und blasser;
Ich möchte dir zu Füßen,
Wie dieser Blume Wasser,
Still meine Seele gießen!
Könnt' ich dann auch nicht sehen
Dich auferstehen.

To spring's lovely jewel,
to the rose, my delight,
bowed and made paler
by the sun's torrid beam,
I bring water in this beaker
from the deep well.

You, rose of my heart,
by pain's secret beam
are you bowed and made paler;
would I might at your feet,
as water to this flower,
silently pour forth my soul!
Even though I might not then
see you rise again.

## Memnon | Memnon

JOHANN MAYRHOFER

*Franz Schubert, 1817*

Den Tag hindurch nur einmal mag ich
sprechen,
Gewohnt zu schweigen immer und zu
trauern:
Wenn durch die nachtgebor'nen
Nebelmauern
Aurorens Purpurstrahlen liebend
brechen.

Für Menschenohren sind es Harmonien.
Weil ich die Klage selbst melodisch
künde
Und durch der Dichtung Glut das
Rauhe ründe,
Vermuten sie in mir ein selig Blühen.

In mir, nach dem des Todes Arme
langen,
In dessen tiefstem Herzen Schlangen
wühlen;
Genährt von meinen schmerzlichen
Gefühlen
Fast wütend durch ein ungestillt
Verlangen:

Mit dir, des Morgens Göttin, mich zu
einen,
Und weit von diesem nichtigen
Getriebe,

Once only in the whole day may I
speak,
used always to be silent and to
mourn:
then, when through the night-born
walls of mist
break lovingly Aurora's purple
rays.

To human ears my speech is harmony.
Because my plaint I proclaim
melodically,
tempering its roughness with the glow
of poetry,
they suppose in me a happy blossoming.

In me, for whom Death's arms are
reaching out,
deep in whose heart serpents
gnaw;
me, who am nourished by my
agonies,
near crazed with unappeased
desire

to unite myself with you, Goddess of
Morn,
and from this futile commotion far
removed,

Aus Sphären edler Freiheit, [aus
  Sphären] reiner Liebe,
Ein stiller, bleicher Stern herab zu
  scheinen.

from spheres of noble freedom and
  pure love,
shine down, a pale and silent
  star.


## Michaelskirchplatz | St Michael's Square

KARL BUSSE

*Hans Pfitzner: op. 19, no. 2, 1905*

Abendschwärmer zogen um die
  Linden,
von den Kähnen sangen Schifferknechte,
hob sich manchmal in bewegten Winden
deines Haares eine lose Flechte.

Lovers of evening walked beneath the
  limes,
and on the barges lads were singing,
and now and then the breezes raised
a loose tress of your hair.

O, wie selig dir die Wangen glühten,
wenn mein Arm den deinen zärtlich
  drückte
und ich lächelnd von versagten Blüten
im Vorbeigehn dir die schönste pflückte,

Oh, the blissful glow upon your cheeks,
when my arm pressed tenderly on
  yours
and I, smiling, from forbidden blooms
picked for you the fairest as we passed,

war die Welt so still und heilig,
  Lucie.
Und die Burschen über'm Wasser
  sangen,
von Sankt Michael die Glocken klangen
und wir lächelten und schwiegen, Lucie.

so still was the world, and solemn,
  Lucy.
And over the water the lads were
  singing,
and from St Michael's rang the bells,
and we smiled and were silent, Lucy.


## Minnelied | Love Song

LUDWIG CHRISTOPH HEINRICH HÖLTY

*Johannes Brahms: op. 71, no. 5, 1877;*
*Felix Mendelssohn-Bartholdy: op. 8, no. 1, 1825–28; Franz Schubert, 1816*

Holder klingt der Vogelsang,
Wenn die Engelreine,
Die mein Jünglingsherz bezwang,
Wandelt durch die Haine.

Sweeter sounds the song of birds,
when that pure angel
who's captured my young heart,
walks through the woods.

Röter blühet Tal und Au,
Grüner wird der Rasen,
Wo die Finger meiner Frau
Maienblumen lasen.

Redder blossom vale and meadow,
greener grows the grass,
where my lady's hands
have gathered lilies of the valley.

Ohne sie ist alles tot,
Welk sind Blüt und Kräuter;
Und kein Frühlingsabendrot
Dünkt mir schön und heiter.

Without her all is dead,
blossom and leaves withered;
and no spring sunset
seems fair and cheering.

Traute, minnigliche Frau,
Wollest nimmer fliehen,
Daß mein Herz gleich dieser Au
Mög in Wonne blühen.

Dear, lovely lady,
pray flee no more,
that my heart like this meadow
may blossom in bliss.

## Mit einem gemalten Band | To Accompany a Painted Ribbon

JOHANN WOLFGANG GOETHE

*Ludwig van Beethoven: op. 83, no. 3, 1811; Armin Knab, 1924–46;*
*Ernst Pepping, 1946; Johann Friedrich Reichardt, 1809;*
*Othmar Schoeck: op. 19a, no. 4, 1909–14*

Kleine Blumen, kleine Blätter
Streuen mir mit leichter Hand
Gute junge Frühlings-Götter
Tändelnd auf ein luftig Band.

Zephir, nimm's auf deine Flügel,
Schling's um meiner Liebsten Kleid;
Und so tritt sie vor den Spiegel
All in ihrer Munterkeit.

Sieht mit Rosen sich umgeben,
Selbst wie eine Rose jung.
Einen Blick, geliebtes Leben!
Und ich bin belohnt genung.

Fühle, was dies Herz empfindet,
Reiche frei mir deine Hand,
Und das Band, das uns verbindet,
Sei kein schwaches Rosenband!

Small flowers, small leaves
are strewn for me with light hand
by good young spring gods
playfully on an airy ribbon.

Zephyr, bear it on your wings,
twine it round my loved one's dress;
then before her glass she'll step
in all her gaiety.

Rose-encircled she will see
herself, as fresh as any rose.
One look, beloved!
And rewarded well enough I'll be.

Feel what this heart feels,
freely give me your hand,
and let the bond binding us
be no frail ribbon of roses!

## Mit vierzig Jahren | At Forty

FRIEDRICH RÜCKERT

*Johannes Brahms: op. 94, no. 1, 1884*

Mit vierzig Jahren ist der Berg erstiegen,
Wir stehen still und schau'n zurück;
Dort sehen wir der Kindheit stilles
    liegen
Und dort der Jugend lautes Glück.

Noch einmal schau, und dann
    gekräftigt weiter
Erhebe deinen Wanderstab!
Hin dehnt ein Bergesrücken sich, ein
    breiter,
Und hier, nicht drüben geht's hinab.

Nicht atmend aufwärts brauchst du
    mehr zu steigen,
Die Ebne zieht von selbst dich fort,
Dann wird sie sich mit dir unmerklich
    neigen,
Und eh du's denkst, bist du im
    Port.

At forty the mountain is climbed,
we stand still and look back;
see, lying there, childhood's
    quiet,
and youth's noisy happiness.

Look once again, then
    strengthened,
raise once more your pilgrim's staff!
Away stretches a ridge, a broad
    one,
and here, not there, the way is down.

Not upwards, gasping, need you more
    to climb,
the plain, of itself, will draw you on,
then, imperceptibly, with you it will
    dip,
and before you know, you will be in
    port.

## Mondenschein | Moonlight

HEINRICH HEINE

*Johannes Brahms: op. 85, no. 2, 1879*

Nacht liegt auf den fremden Wegen,
Krankes Herz und müde Glieder;—
Ach, da fließt, wie stiller Segen,
Süßer Mond, dein Licht hernieder.

Süßer Mond, mit deinen Strahlen
Scheuchest du das nächt'ge Grauen;
Es zerrinnen meine Qualen,
Und die Augen übertauen.

Night lies on the unfamiliar ways—
sick heart and tired limbs;—
then, ah, as silent blessing, streams
down, sweet moon, your light.

Sweet moon, with your beams
you drive away night's horror;
my torments vanish,
and my eyes melt into tears.


## Morgen | Tomorrow

JOHN HENRY MACKAY

*Max Reger: op. 66, no. 10, 1902; Richard Strauss: op. 27, no. 4, 1893-94*

Und morgen wird die Sonne wieder
scheinen
Und auf dem Wege, den ich gehen
werde,
Wird uns, die Glücklichen, sie wieder
einen
Inmitten dieser sonnenatmenden
Erde . . .

Und zu dem Strand, dem weiten,
wogenblauen,
Werden wir still und langsam
niedersteigen,
Stumm werden wir uns in die Augen
schauen,
Und auf uns sinkt des Glückes stummes
Schweigen . . .

And tomorrow the sun will shine
again,
and on the path that I shall
take,
it will unite us, happy ones,
again
upon this sun-breathing
earth . . .

and to the shore, broad,
blue-waved,
we shall, quiet and slow,
descend,
silent, into each other's eyes we'll
gaze,
and on us will fall joy's speechless
silence ..


## Morgenstimmung | Morning Mood

ROBERT REINICK

*Hugo Wolf, 1896*

Bald ist der Nacht ein End' gemacht,
schon fühl' ich Morgenlüfte wehen.
Der Herr, der spricht: Es werde Licht!
Da muß, was dunkel ist, vergehen.
Vom Himmelszelt durch alle
Welt
die Engel freudejauchzend fliegen:
der Sonne Strahl durchflammt das All.
Herr, laß uns kämpfen, laß uns siegen!

Soon will night be over,
I feel already morning breezes blow.
The Lord says: let there be light!
Then all that's dark must vanish.
From Heaven's vault through all the
world
the angels fly rejoicing:
sunlight flames through the universe.
Lord, let us fight, let us conquer!

## Muttertändelei | Mother-talk

GOTTFRIED AUGUST BÜRGER

*Richard Strauss: op. 43, no. 2, 1899*

Seht mir doch mein schönes Kind,
Mit den gold'nen Zottellöckchen,
Blauen Augen, roten Bäckchen!
Leutchen, habt ihr auch so eins?
Leutchen, nein, ihr habt keins!

Just look at my lovely child,
with his rich golden curls,
blue eyes, red cheeks!
Have you such a one, my dears?
No, my dears, you've not!

Seht mir doch mein süßes Kind,
Fetter als ein fettes Schneckchen,
Süßer als ein Zuckerweckchen!
Leutchen, habt ihr auch so eins?
Leutchen, nein, ihr habt keins!

Just look at my sweet child,
fatter than a fat snail,
sweeter than a sugar roll!
Have you such a one, my dears?
No, my dears, you've not!

Seht mir doch mein holdes Kind,
Nicht zu mürrisch, nicht zu wählig!
Immer freundlich, immer fröhlich!
Leutchen, habt ihr auch so eins?
Leutchen, nein, ihr habt keins!

Just look at my darling child,
not too moody, not too choosy!
Always friendly, always happy!
Have you such a one, my dears?
No, my dears, you've not!

Seht mir doch mein frommes Kind!
Keine bitterböse Sieben
Würd' ihr Mütterchen so lieben.
Leutchen, möchtet ihr so eins?
O, ihr kriegt gewiß nicht meins!

Just look at my good child!
No angry shrew
would love her mother so.
Would you like such a one, my dears?
Oh, you'll certainly not get mine!

Komm' einmal ein Kaufmann her!
Hunderttausend blanke Taler,
Alles Gold der Erde zahl' er!
O, er kriegt gewiß nicht meins!—
Kauf' er sich woanders eins!

Let a merchant come along!
A hundred thousand shiny thalers,
all the gold on earth, let him pay!
Oh, he'll certainly not get mine!—
Let him buy one somewhere else!

## Nachklang | Afterwards

KLAUS GROTH

*Johannes Brahms: op. 59, no. 4, 1873*

Regentropfen aus den Bäumen
Fallen in das grüne Gras,
Tränen meiner trüben Augen
Machen mir die Wange naß.

Raindrops from the trees
fall into green grass,
tears from my sad eyes
wet my cheeks.

Wenn die Sonne wieder scheinet,
Wird der Rasen doppelt grün:
Doppelt wird auf meinen Wangen
Mir die heiße Träne glühn.

When the sun shines again,
the grass is doubly green:
doubly on my cheeks
glow my burning tears.

## Nachruf | In Memoriam

JOSEPH VON EICHENDORFF

*Othmar Schoeck: op. 20, no. 14, 1905–14; Hugo Wolf, 1880*

Du liebe, treue Laute,
Wie manche Sommernacht,

Dear, faithful lute,
how many a summer night

| Bis daß der Morgen graute, | till day-break |
| Hab' ich mit dir durchwacht! | have I watched with you. |

| Die Täler wieder nachten, | Again the valleys darken, |
| Kaum spielt noch Abendrot, | the evening red's near spent, |
| Doch die sonst mit uns wachten, | but they who once watched with us |
| Die liegen lange tot. | have long lain dead. |

| Was wollen wir nur singen | Why should we want to sing |
| Hier in der Einsamkeit, | here in solitude, |
| Wenn alle von uns gingen, | when gone from us are all |
| Die unser Lied erfreut? | whom our song made glad? |

| Wir wollen dennoch singen! | Nevertheless, we *will* sing! |
| So still ist's auf der Welt; | So quiet is the world; |
| Wer weiß, die Lieder dringen | who knows, songs may go |
| Vielleicht zum Sternenzelt. | as far as the stars. |

| Wer weiß, die da gestorben, | Who knows, those dead |
| Sie hören droben mich, | may hear me up there, |
| Und öffnen leis die Pforten | and open quietly the gates, |
| Und nehmen uns zu sich. | and take us to them. |

## Nacht und Träume / Night and Dreams

MATTHÄUS VON COLLIN

*Franz Schubert: op. 43, no. 2, 1825?*

| Heilge Nacht, du sinkest nieder; | Holy night, down you sink; |
| Nieder wallen auch die Träume, | down too float dreams, |
| Wie dein Mondlicht durch die Räume, | as your moonlight through space, |
| Durch der Menschen stille Brust. | through the silent hearts of men. |
| Die belauschen sie mit Lust; | To these they hearken, joyful; |
| Rufen, wenn der Tag erwacht: | crying out, when day awakes: |
| Kehre wieder, heilge Nacht! | come again, holy night! |
| Holde Träume, kehret wieder! | Sweet dreams, come again! |

## Nachtgang / A Walk at Night

OTTO JULIUS BIERBAUM

*Max Reger: op. 51, no. 7, 1900; Richard Strauss: op. 29, no. 3, 1894–95*

| Wir gingen durch die stille milde Nacht, | Through the still, mild night we walked |
| Dein Arm in meinem, dein Auge in meinem. | your arm in mine, your gaze in mine. |
| Der Mond goß silbernes Licht über dein Angesicht, | The moon shed silver light upon your face, |
| Wie auf Goldgrund ruhte dein schönes Haupt. | as though on gold your fair head lay. |
| Und du erschienst mir wie eine Heilige, | And you appeared to me a saint, |
| Mild, mild und groß und seelenübervoll, | gentle, gentle and great, with overflowing soul, |
| Heilig und rein wie die liebe Sonne. | holy and pure as the dear sun. |

Und in die Augen schwoll mir ein
  warmer Drang,
Wie Tränenahnung.
Fester faßt' ich dich und küßte, küßte
  dich ganz leise.
Meine Seele weinte.

With insistent warmth my eyes were
  filled,
as of impending tears.
I held you closer and kissed you
  softly.
My soul wept.

## Nachtgesang | Night Song

JOHANN WOLFGANG GOETHE

*Franz Schubert: op. 47, 1814; Carl Friedrich Zelter, 1804*

O gib, vom weichen Pfühle,
Träumend, ein halb Gehör!
Bei meinem Saitenspiele
Schlafe! was willst du mehr?

Oh lend, from your soft pillow,
dreaming, half an ear!
At my lute's sound—
you sleep! What more can you ask?

Bei meinem Saitenspiele
Segnet der Sterne Heer
Die ewigen Gefühle;
Schlafe! was willst du mehr?

At my lute's sound
the host of stars calls blessing
on age-old feelings;
you sleep! What more can you ask?

Die ewigen Gefühle
Heben mich, hoch und hehr,
Aus irdischem Gewühle;
Schlafe! was willst du mehr?

Those age-old feelings
exalt me, high and mightily
above the earthly crowd;
you sleep! What more can you ask?

Vom irdischen Gewühle
Trennst du mich nur zu sehr,
Bannst mich in diese Kühle;
Schlafe! was willst du mehr!

From the earthly crowd
you part me only too sorely,
spellbind me to this cold place;
you sleep! What more can you ask?

Bannst mich in diese Kühle,
Gibst nur im Traum Gehör.
Ach, auf dem weichen Pfühle
Schlafe! was willst du mehr?

Spellbind me to this cold place,
give ear only in your dream.
Ah, on your soft pillow
you sleep! What more can you ask?

## Nachts | At Night

JOSEPH VON EICHENDORFF

*Hans Pfitzner: op. 26, no. 2, 1916*

Ich stehe in Waldesschatten
Wie an des Lebens Rand,
Die Länder wie dämmernde Matten,
Der Strom wie ein silbern Band.

I stand in the wood's shade
as on the brink of life,
the land a darkening meadow,
the stream a silver ribbon.

Von fern nur schlagen die Glocken
Über die Wälder herein,
Ein Reh hebt den Kopf erschrocken
Und schlummert gleich wieder ein.

No sound but the distant bells
borne over the woods,
a deer, startled, lifts its head
and returns at once to slumber.

Der Wald aber rühret die Wipfel
Im Traum von der Felsenwand.
Denn der Herr geht über die Gipfel
Und segnet das stille Land.

But the wood stirs in the trees
of the cliff, as they dream.
For over the peaks God is passing,
blessing the silent land.

## Nachtstück / Nocturne

JOHANN MAYRHOFER

*Franz Schubert: op. 36, no. 2, 1819*

Wenn über Berge sich der Nebel breitet,
Und Luna mit Gewölken kämpft,
So nimmt der Alte seine Harfe, und
   schreitet,
Und singt waldeinwärts und gedämpft:

Du heilge Nacht!
Bald ist's vollbracht.
Bald schlaf ich ihn, den langen
   Schlummer,
Der mich erlöst von allem Kummer.

Die grünen Bäume rauschen dann:
Schlaf süß, du guter, alter Mann;
Die Gräser lispeln wankend fort:
Wir decken seinen Ruheort;

Und mancher liebe Vogel ruft:
»O laßt ihn ruhn in Rasengruft!«
Der Alte horcht, der Alte schweigt,
Der Tod hat sich zu ihm geneigt.

When mist spreads over the mountains
and Luna contends with the clouds,
the old man takes his harp and
   strides,
and into the forest sings, and low:

O holy night!
Soon shall it end.
Soon shall I sleep that long
   slumber
that will free me from all grief.

Then the green trees murmur:
Sleep sweetly, you good old man;
the grasses whisper, waving on:
We will cover his resting place;

and many a sweet bird calls:
'O let him rest in his grassy grave!'
The old man listens, and is still,
Death has bowed before him.


## Nachtviolen / Dame's Violets

JOHANN MAYRHOFER

*Franz Schubert, 1822*

Nachtviolen,
Dunkle Augen, seelenvolle,
Selig ist es, sich versenken
In dem samtnen Blau.

Grüne Blätter streben freudig,
Euch zu hellen, euch zu schmücken;
Doch ihr blicket ernst und schweigend
In die laue Frühlingsluft.

Mit erhabnen Wehmutsstrahlen
Trafet ihr mein treues Herz,
Und nun blüht in stummen Nächten
Fort die heilige Verbindung.

Dame's violets,
dark-eyed, soulful,
blissful it is to plunge
amongst your velvety blue.

Joyously, green leaves strive
to brighten, adorn you;
but, earnest, silent, you gaze
into the mild spring air.

Shafts of your sublime sadness
have touched my loyal heart,
and now, on silent nights,
our sacred bond blossoms forth.


## Nachtwandler / Sleep-walker

MAX KALBECK

*Johannes Brahms: op. 86, no. 3, 1877*

Störe nicht den leisen Schlummer
Deß, den lind ein Traum umfangen!
Laß ihm seinen süßen Kummer,
Ihm sein schmerzliches Verlangen!

Trouble not the shallow slumber
of one soft embraced by dreams!
Leave him to his sweet distress,
his painful longing!

Sorgen und Gefahren drohen,
Aber keine wird ihn schrecken,
Kommst du nicht, den Schlafesfrohen
Durch ein hartes Wort zu wecken.

Cares and dangers threaten,
none though will alarm him,
if you come not to wake
the happy sleeper with harsh words.

Still in seinen Traum versunken,
Geht er über Abgrundtiefen,
Wie vom Licht des Vollmonds trunken,
Weh' den Lippen, die ihn riefen!

Silently, immersed in his dream,
over deep chasms he passes,
as if drunk with the full moon's light,
woe to the lips that would call to him!

## Nachtzauber / Night Magic

JOSEPH VON EICHENDORFF

*Hugo Wolf, 1888*

Hörst du nicht die Quellen gehen
Zwischen Stein und Blumen weit
Nach den stillen Waldesseen,
Wo die Marmorbilder stehen,
In der schönen Einsamkeit?
Von den Bergen sacht hernieder,
Weckend die uralten Lieder,
Steigt die wunderbare Nacht,
Und die Gründe glänzen wieder,
Wie du's oft im Traum gedacht.

Can you not hear brooks running
amongst the stones and flowers
far away to silent forest lakes,
where marble statues stand
in fair solitude?
Softly from the mountains,
stirring old, old songs,
wondrous night descends
and the valleys gleam again,
as you often imagined in dreams.

Kennst die Blume du, entsprossen
In dem mondbeglänzten Grund?
Aus der Knospe, halb erschlossen,
Junge Glieder blühend sprossen,
Weiße Arme, roter Mund,
Und die Nachtigallen schlagen,
Und rings hebt es an zu klagen,
Ach, vor Liebe todeswund,
Von versunknen schönen Tagen—
Komm, o komm zum stillen Grund!

Do you know the flower, that forth
has sprung in the moonlit valley?
Out from its half-open bud
have blossomed young limbs,
white arms, red mouth,
and nightingales are singing,
and all around a lament is raised,
ah, wounded mortally by love,
of lovely days now lost—
come, oh come to the still valley!

## Nähe des Geliebten / Nearness of the Beloved

JOHANN WOLFGANG GOETHE

*Johann Friedrich Reichardt, ed. 1809; Franz Schubert: op. 5, no. 2, 1815 (2nd setting);
Carl Friedrich Zelter, 1808; Winfried Zillig, ed. 1960*

Ich denke dein, wenn mir der Sonne
  Schimmer
Vom Meere strahlt;
Ich denke dein, wenn sich des Mondes
  Flimmer
In Quellen malt.

I think of you when the shimmering
  sun
gleams from the sea;
I think of you when the glittering
  moon
is mirrored in streams.

Ich sehe dich, wenn auf dem fernen
  Wege
Der Staub sich hebt;
In tiefer Nacht, wenn auf dem schmalen
  Stege
Der Wandrer bebt.

I see you when, on the distant
  road,
dust rises;
at dead of night when, on the narrow
  path,
the traveller trembles.

Ich höre dich, wenn dort mit dumpfem
  Rauschen
Die Welle steigt.
Im stillen Haine geh ich oft zu
  lauschen,
Wenn alles schweigt.

I hear you where, with muffled
  roar,
the wave rears up.
Often in the quiet wood I wander,
  hearkening,
when all is still.

Ich bin bei dir, du seist auch noch so
  ferne,
Du bist mir nah!
Die Sonne sinkt, bald leuchten mir die
  Sterne.
O wärst du da!

I am with you, however far you
  be,
you are close to me!
The sun sets, soon the stars will
  shine.
Oh, were you here!

## Nelken / Carnations

### THEODOR STORM

*Max Reger: op. 15, no. 3, 1894*

Ich wand ein Sträußchen morgens früh,
Das ich der Liebsten schickte;
Nicht ließ ich sagen ihr, von wem
Und wer die Blumen pflückte.

I bound a nosegay at early morn,
and to my dearest sent it;
made them not say from whom it came,
or who had plucked the flowers.

Doch als ich abends kam zum Tanz
Und tat verstohlen und sachte,
Da trug sie die Nelken am Busenlatz
Und schaute mich an und lachte.

At evening, when I went to the ball,
and acted secretive and quiet, she,
wearing the carnations at her breast,
gazed at me and laughed.

## Neue Liebe / New Love

### EDUARD MÖRIKE

*Hugo Wolf, 1888*

Kann auch ein Mensch des andern auf
  der Erde
Ganz, wie er möchte, sein?
—In langer Nacht bedacht ich mirs
  und mußte sagen, nein!

Can one being ever, on earth, belong to
  another,
wholly, as he would like to?
Long at night I pondered, and had to
  say no!

So kann ich niemands heißen auf der
  Erde,
Und niemand wäre mein?
—Aus Finsternissen hell in mir
  aufzückt ein Freudenschein:

Can I, then, be called no one's on
  earth,
and no one mine?
Out of darkness flashes within me a
  gleam of hope:

Sollt ich mit Gott nicht können sein,
So wie ich möchte, mein und dein?
Was hielte mich, daß ichs nicht heute
  werde?

Could I not with God be,
as I would like to, mine and thine?
What could prevent me becoming so,
  today?

Ein süßes Schrecken geht durch mein
  Gebein!
Mich wundert, daß es mir ein Wunder
  wollte sein,
Gott selbst zu eigen haben auf der
  Erde!

Sweet terror pierces all my
  frame.
I marvel that it should seem to me
  miraculous
to have God for one's own on
  earth!

## Neue Liebe, neues Leben | New Love, New Life

JOHANN WOLFGANG GOETHE

*Ludwig van Beethoven: op. 75, no. 2, 1809; Carl Friedrich Zelter, 1813*

Herz, mein Herz, was soll das geben?
Was bedränget dich so sehr?
Welch ein fremdes, neues Leben!
Ich erkenne dich nicht mehr.
Weg ist alles, was du liebtest,
Weg, warum du dich betrübtest,
Weg dein Fleiß und deine Ruh—
Ach, wie kamst du nur dazu!

Fesselt dich die Jugendblüte,
Diese liebliche Gestalt,
Dieser Blick voll Treu und Güte
Mit unendlicher Gewalt?
Will ich rasch mich ihr entziehen,
Mich ermannen, ihr entfliehen,
Führet mich im Augenblick,
Ach, mein Weg zu ihr zurück.

Und an diesem Zauberfädchen,
Das sich nicht zerreißen läßt,
Hält das liebe, lose Mädchen
Mich so wider Willen fest;
Muß in ihrem Zauberkreise
Leben nun auf ihre Weise.
Die Verändrung, ach, wie groß!
Liebe! Liebe! laß mich los!

Heart, my heart, what can it mean?
What oppresses you so sore?
What a strange and new existence!
I do not know you any more.
Gone is all you used to love,
gone what used to make you sad,
gone your diligence and peace—
ah, how have you come to this!

Does the bloom of youth ensnare you—
that figure full of charm,
that gaze so kind and faithful—
with unending might?
If I try to hasten from her,
restrain myself, escape her,
in a moment I am led,
ah, back to her again.

And by this thread of magic
that refuses to be torn,
this sweet and roguish maiden
holds me fast against my will;
now in her magic circle
must I live the way she does.
The change, ah, how great it is!
Love, love, let me go!

## Nicht mehr zu dir zu gehen | To Come to You No More

GEORG FRIEDRICH DAUMER

*Johannes Brahms: op. 32, no. 2, 1864*

Nicht mehr zu dir zu gehen,
Beschloß ich und beschwor ich,
Und gehe jeden Abend,
Denn jede Kraft und jeden Halt verlor
ich.

Ich möchte nicht mehr leben,
Möcht augenblicks verderben,
Und möchte doch auch leben
Für dich, mit dir, und nimmer,
nimmer sterben.

Ach rede, sprich ein Wort nur,
Ein einziges, ein klares!
Gib Leben oder Tod mir,
Nur dein Gefühl enthülle mir, dein
wahres!

To come to you no more
I determined and I swore,
and yet each night I come,
I've lost all strength, all
resolution.

I'd rather live no more,
pass instantly away,
yet I'd also like to live
for you, with you, and never ever
die.

Ah, say, say but one word,
one single, one clear word.
Give me life or death,
but show your feelings, and
truly!

## Nimmersatte Liebe / Never-sated Law

EDUARD MÖRIKE

*Hugo Wolf, 1888*

So ist die Lieb! So ist die Lieb!  
Mit Küssen nicht zu stillen:  
Wer ist der Tor und will ein Sieb  
Mit eitel Wasser füllen?  
Und schöpfst du an die tausend Jahr,  
Und küssest ewig, ewig gar,  
Du tust ihr nie zu Willen.

Such is love! Such is love!  
Not to be allayed with kisses:  
is there a fool who would fill  
a sieve simply with water?  
Scoop water for near a thousand years,  
kiss for ever and a day,  
never will you do as love wishes.

Die Lieb, die Lieb hat alle Stund  
Neu wunderlich Gelüsten;  
Wir bissen uns die Lippen wund,  
Da wir uns heute küßten.  
Das Mädchen hielt in guter Ruh,  
Wie's Lämmlein unterm Messer;  
Ihr Auge bat: »Nur immer zu!  
Je weher, desto besser!«

Love, love has with each hour  
new, strange desires;  
we bit our lips until they hurt,  
when we kissed today.  
The maiden stayed quiet,  
like a lamb beneath the knife;  
her eyes beseeched, 'Keep at it,  
the more it hurts the better!'

So ist die Lieb! und war auch so,  
Wie lang es Liebe gibt,  
Und anders war Herr Salomo,  
Der Weise, nicht verliebt.

Such is love, and ever was,  
as long as love's existed,  
and that wise man Solomon  
no differently did love.


## Nun ich der Riesen Stärksten überwand / Now I've Overcome the Mightiest Ogre

ALFRED MOMBERT

*Alban Berg, 1908–09*

Nun ich der Riesen Stärksten überwand,  
aus dem dunkelsten Land  
mich heimfand  
an einer weißen Märchenhand—

Now I've overcome the mightiest ogre,  
out of the darkest country  
have found my way home  
on a white, fairy-tale hand—

Hallen schwer die Glocken.  
Und ich wanke durch die Straßen  
schlafbefangen.

Ponderous sound the bells,  
and I stagger the streets,  
sleep-vanquished.


## Nur wer die Sehnsucht kennt / Only He Who Knows Longing
(Mignon's song)

JOHANN WOLFGANG GOETHE: from *Wilhelm Meister*

*Ludwig van Beethoven, 1807–08; Franz Schubert: op. 62, no. 4, 1826;*  
*Robert Schumann: op. 98a, no. 3, 1841; Peter Ilych Tchaikovsky: op. 6, 1869;*  
*Hugo Wolf, 1888; Carl Friedrich Zelter, 1811*

Nur wer die Sehnsucht kennt,  
Weiß, was ich leide!  
Allein und abgetrennt  
Von aller Freude,  
Seh ich ans Firmament

Only he who knows longing  
knows what I suffer!  
Alone and cut off  
from all joy,  
I gaze at the firmament

Nach jener Seite.
Ach! der mich liebt und kennt,
Ist in der Weite.
Es schwindelt mir, es brennt
Mein Eingeweide.
Nur wer die Sehnsucht kennt,
Weiß, was ich leide!

in that direction.
Ah, he who loves and knows me
is far away.
My head reels,
my body blazes.
Only he knows longing
knows what I suffer!

## O kühler Wald | Cool Wood

CLEMENS BRENTANO

*Johannes Brahms: op. 72, no. 3, 1877*

O kühler Wald, wo rauschest du,
In dem mein Liebchen geht?
O Widerhall, wo lauschest du,
Der gern mein Lied versteht?

Where do you whisper, cool wood,
in which my beloved walks?
Where do you listen, echo,
who likes to understand my song?

Im Herzen tief, da rauscht der Wald,
In dem mein Liebchen geht,
In Schmerzen schlief der Widerhall,
Die Lieder sind verweht.

Deep in my heart whispers the wood,
in which my beloved walks,
the echo has slept in sorrow,
the songs are all blown away.

## O liebliche Wangen | O Sweet Cheeks

PAUL FLEMING

*Johannes Brahms: op. 47, no. 4, 1868*

O liebliche Wangen, ihr macht mir
  Verlangen,
Dies Rote, dies Weiße zu schauen mit
  Fleiße.
Und dies nur alleine ist's nicht, was ich
  meine;
Zu schauen, zu grüßen, zu rühren, zu
  küssen!

O sweet cheeks, the desire you
  give
to gaze hard at that white, that
  red.
And nor is that all I
  mean;
but gaze and greet and touch and
  kiss!

O Sonne der Wonne! O Wonne der
  Sonne!
O Augen, so saugen das Licht meiner
  Augen.
O englische Sinnen! O himmlisch
  Beginnen!
O Himmel auf Erden, magst du mir
  nicht werden!

O sun of delight! O delight of
  sun!
O eyes that drink the light of
  mine.
O angelic thoughts! O heavenly
  beginning!
O heaven on earth, may you not be
  mine!

O Schönste der Schönen, benimm mir
  dies Sehnen,
Komm, eile, komm, komme, du Süße,
  du Fromme!
Ach, Schwester, ich sterbe, ich sterb,
  ich verderbe,
Komm, komme, komm, eile, benimm
  mir dies Sehnen,
O Schönste der Schönen!

Fairest of the fair, free me of this
  longing,
come, haste, come, sweet innocent
  one!
Sister, ah, I die, I die, I
  perish,
come, haste, come, free me of this
  longing,
O fairest of the fair!

## O wärst du mein! | Oh, Were You Mine

NIKOLAUS LENAU

*Richard Strauss: op. 26, no. 2, 1891*

O wärst du mein, es wär ein schönres
  Leben;
So aber ist's Entsagen nur und Trauern,
Nur ein verlornes Grollen und Bedauern.
Ich kann es meinem Schicksal nicht
  vergeben.

Undank tut wohl und jedes Leid der
  Erde,
Ja! meine Freund in Särgen, Leich an
  Leiche,
Sind ein gelinder Gram, wenn ich's
  vergleiche
Dem Schmerz, daß ich dich nie besitzen
  werde.

Oh, were you mine, life would be
  finer;
thus, it's denial merely, and grief,
vain anger merely, and regret.
For which I cannot forgive my
  fate.

Ingratitude, all earthly woe is
  good.
Friends, yes, coffined corpse on
  corpse,
are small sorrows when I compare
  them
to the agony of never making you my
  own.

## O wüßt ich doch den Weg zurück | Oh, If I But Knew the Way

KLAUS GROTH

*Johannes Brahms: op. 63, no. 8, 1874*

O wüßt ich doch den Weg zurück,
Den lieben Weg zum Kinderland!
O warum sucht ich nach dem Glück
Und ließ der Mutter Hand?

O wie mich sehnet auszuruhn,
Von keinem Streben aufgeweckt,
Die müden Augen zuzutun,
Von Liebe sanft bedeckt!

Und nichts zu forschen, nichts zu
  spähn,
Und nur zu träumen leicht und lind;
Der Zeiten Wandel nicht zu sehn,
Zum zweiten Mal ein Kind!

O zeig mir doch den Weg zurück,
Den lieben Weg zum Kinderland!
Vergebens such ich nach dem Glück,
Ringsum ist öder Strand!

Oh, if I but knew the way,
the sweet way back to childhood's land!
Oh, why did I seek for happiness,
leaving hold of mother's hand?

Oh, how I long to take my rest,
by all striving unaroused,
and shut tight my weary eyes,
softly blanketed in love.

And search for nothing, watch for
  nothing,
dream only light and gentle dreams;
see not the changing of the times,
for a second time, a child.

Oh, show me then the way,
the sweet way back to childhood's land!
I seek for happiness in vain,
ringed around by a desolate shore!

## Ob der Koran von Ewigkeit sei? | Has the Koran Existed for All Time?

JOHANN WOLFGANG GOETHE: from *West-östlicher Divan*, 'Book of the Inn'

*Hugo Wolf, 1889*

Ob der Koran von Ewigkeit sei?
Darnach frag ich nicht!

Has the Koran existed for all time?
That is something I enquire not into.

Ob der Koran geschaffen sei?
Das weiß ich nicht!
Daß er das Buch der Bücher sei,
Glaub ich aus Mosleminen-Pflicht.

Daß aber der Wein von Ewigkeit sei,
Daran zweifl' ich nicht;
Oder daß er von den Engeln geschaffen
 sei,
Ist vielleicht auch kein Gedicht.
Der Trinkende, wie es auch immer sei,
Blickt Gott frischer ins Angesicht.

Was the Koran created?
That I do not know.
That it is the Book of Books
I believe as my Mussulmannish duty.

But that wine's existed for all time,
that I do not doubt;
or that it was created by the
 angels,
that may be no fabrication either.
Be that as it may, the man who drinks
looks God more cheerfully in the face.


## Odins Meeresritt | Odin's Sea-ride

ALOYS SCHREIBER

*Carl Loewe: op. 119, ed. 1834*

Meister Oluf, der Schmied auf
 Helgoland,
Verläßt den Amboß um Mitternacht.
Es heulet der Wind am Meeresstrand,
Da pocht es an seiner Tür mit Macht:
»Heraus, heraus, beschlag' mir mein
 Roß,
Ich muß noch weit, und der Tag ist
 nah!«
Meister Oluf öffnet der Türe Schloß
Und ein stattlicher Reiter steht vor ihm
 da.
Schwarz ist sein Panzer, sein Helm und
 Schild,
An der Hüfte hängt ihm ein breites
 Schwert.
Sein Rappe schüttelt die Mähne gar
 wild
Und stampft mit Ungeduld die Erd'.
»Woher so spät? Wohin so schnell?«
»In Norderney kehrt' ich gestern ein.
Mein Pferd ist rasch, die Nacht ist hell,
Vor der Sonne muß ich in Norwegen
 sein!«
»Hättet Ihr Flügel, so glaubt' ich's
 gern!«
»Mein Rappe, der läuft wohl mit dem
 Wind,
Doch bleichet schon da und dort ein
 Stern!
Drum her mit dem Eisen und mach'
 geschwind!«
Meister Oluf nimmt das Eisen zur Hand,
Es ist zu klein, da dehnt es sich aus.
Und wie es wächst um des Hufes Rand,
Da ergreift den Meister Bang' und
 Graus.
Der Reiter sitzt auf, es klirrt ein
 Schwert:

Master Oluf, smith on
 Helgoland,
quits his anvil at dead of night.
The wind howls beside the sea.
There comes a hammering at his door:
'Come out, come out, shoe my
 steed,
far yet I've to ride, and day is
 near!'
Master Oluf unlocks the door,
and there a resplendent rider
 stands.
Black his armour, helmet,
 shield,
a broadsword hangs upon his
 hip.
His black steed wildly tosses its
 mane
and, restive, paws the ground.
'Whence so late? Whither so fast?'
'In Nordeney yesterday I lodged.
My steed is swift, the night is bright,
I must be in Norway before the
 sun!'
'If you had wings, that I'd gladly
 believe!'
'My steed goes with the speed of
 wind,
but here and there a star grows
 pale!
So bring the shoe, and swift to
 work!'
Master Oluf takes up the shoe,
too small the shoe is, but it grows,
and as it matches the size of the hoof,
the master's seized with fear and
 dread.
The rider mounts, a sword
 clanks:

»Nun, Meister Oluf, gute Nacht!
Wohl hast du beschlagen Odins Pferd,
Ich eile hinauf zur blutigen Schlacht.«
Der Rappe schießt fort über Land und
    Meer,
Um Odins Haupt erglühet ein Licht.
Zwölf Adler fliegen hinter ihm her,
Sie fliegen so schnell und erreichen ihn
    nicht.

'Now, Master Oluf, good night!
Odin's horse well have you shod,
I haste to the bloody fight.'
Away darts the steed over land and
    sea,
a light glows about Odin's head.
Behind him twelve eagles fly,
and fast as they fly, do not catch
    up.

## Oiseaux, si tous les ans | If Yearly, Birds . . .

HOUDART DE LA MOTTE

*Wolfgang Amadeus Mozart: K 307, 1778*

Oiseaux, si tous les ans
Vous changez de climats,
Dès que le triste hiver
Dépouille nos bocages;
Ce n'est pas seulement
Pour changer de feuillages,
Ni pour éviter nos frimats;
Mais votre destinée
Ne vous permet d'aimer,
Qu'à la saison des fleurs.
Et quand elle est passée,
Vous la cherchez ailleurs,
Afin d'aimer toute l'année.

If yearly, birds,
you fly to other climes
the moment sad winter
strips bare our woods,
it is not solely
for change of foliage
or to escape our frosts,
but because your destiny
permits you to love
only in the season of flowers.
And when that season's passed,
elsewhere you seek it
to love throughout the year.

## Orpheus | Orpheus

JOHANN GEORG JACOBI

*Franz Schubert, 1816*

Wälze dich hinweg, du wildes Feuer!
Diese Saiten hat ein Gott gekrönt;
Er, mit welchem jedes Ungeheuer,
Und vielleicht die Hölle sich versöhnt.

Roll away, fierce fire!
By a god were these strings crowned;
by him with whom every monster
and perhaps hell is reconciled.

Diese Saiten stimmte seine Rechte:
Fürchterliche Schatten, flieht!
Und ihr winselnden Bewohner dieser
    Nächte,
Horchet auf mein Lied!

By his right hand were they tuned.
Flee, fearful shades!
You, moaning denizens of these
    nights,
give ear to my song!

Von der Erde, wo die Sonne leuchtet
Und der stille Mond,
Wo der Tau das junge Moos befeuchtet,
Wo Gesang im grünen Felde wohnt;

From earth, where the sun gleams
and the quiet moon,
where dew makes moist young moss,
where singing in the green field dwells;

Aus der Menschen süßem Vaterlande,
Wo der Himmel euch so frohe Blicke
    gab,

from the sweet fatherland of men,
where heaven gave you such glad
    glances,

Ziehen mich die schönsten Bande,
Ziehet mich die Liebe selbst herab.

Meine Klage tönt in eure Klage;
Weit von ihr geflohen ist das Glück;
Aber denkt an jene Tage,
Schaut in jene Welt zurück!

Wenn ihr da nur einen Leidenden
    umarmet,
O, so fühlt die Wollust noch einmal,
Und der Augenblick, in dem ihr euch
    erbarmet,
Lindre diese lange Qual.

O, ich sehe Tränen fließen!
Durch die Finsternisse bricht
Ein Strahl von Hoffnung; ewig büßen
Lassen euch die guten Götter nicht.

Götter, die für euch die Erde schufen,
Werden aus der tiefen Nacht
Euch in selige Gefilde rufen,
Wo die Tugend unter Rosen lacht.

by the fairest of chains am I drawn,
by love itself am I drawn down here.

My lamentation sounds with yours;
far fled is happiness;
but think upon those days,
look back into that world!

If, in hell, one sufferer you
    embrace,
O then once more know bodily delight,
and the moment of your mutual
    pity,
may it assuage this lengthy agony.

Oh, I see the tears flowing!
Through the darkness breaks
a ray of hope: that not for ever
will the gods make you atone.

The gods, who for you created earth,
will, out of deep night,
summon you to the Elysian fields,
where virtue laughs amid roses.

## *Peregrina I und II* | *Peregrina I and II*

EDUARD MÖRIKE: from *Maler Nolten*

*Hugo Wolf, 1888*

I
Der Spiegel dieser treuen, braunen
    Augen
Ist wie von innerm Gold ein
    Widerschein;
Tief aus dem Busen scheint ers
    anzusaugen,
Dort mag solch Gold in heilgem Gram
    gedeihn.
In diese Nacht des Blickes mich zu
    tauchen,
Unwissend Kind, du selber lädst mich
    ein—
Willst, ich soll kecklich mich und dich
    entzünden,
Reichst lächelnd mir den Tod im Kelch
    der Sünden!

I
The mirror of these true brown
    eyes
is a reflection as of inner
    gold;
seeming from the bosom's depth to
    draw it out—
there, in inviolable grief, such gold may
    breed.
To plunge into this darkness of the
    gaze,
unknowing child, you yourself invite
    me—
and will that boldly I inflame myself
    and you,
and hand to me, smiling, death in the
    cup of sin!

II
Warum, Geliebte, denk' ich dein
Auf einmal nun mit tausend
    Tränen,
Und kann gar nicht zufrieden sein,
Und will die Brust in alle Weite
    dehnen?
Ach, gestern in den hellen Kindersaal,
Beim Flimmer zierlich aufgesteckter
    Kerzen,

II
Why, beloved, do I think of you
now suddenly and with a thousand
    tears,
and cannot be satisfied at all,
and long far and wide to extend my
    heart?
Ah, to the bright nursery yesterday,
in the gleam of decorative
    candles,

Wo ich mein selbst vergaß in Lärm und
  Scherzen,
Tratst du, o Bildnis mitleidschöner
  Qual;
Es war dein Geist, er setzte sich ans
  Mahl,
Fremd saßen wir mit stumm verhaltnen
  Schmerzen;
Zuletzt brach ich in lautes Schluchzen
  aus,
Und Hand in Hand verließen wir das
  Haus.

when I was lost in the noise and
  jest,
you came, agony's image, lovely in
  compassion;
your ghost it was, it joined us at our
  meal;
strangers we sat, our sorrows mutely
  hid;
at last I burst into loud
  sobs,
and hand in hand we went from the
  house.

## Phantasie | Fancy

TIRSO DE MOLINA: from *Don Juan*

*Gustav Mahler, ca. 1880–83*

Das Mägdlein trat aus dem
  Fischerhaus,
Die Netze warf sie ins Meer hinaus!
Und wenn kein Fisch in das Netz ihr
  ging,
Die Fischerin doch die Herzen fing!

From the fisher-cottage stepped the
  maid,
cast out her nets into the sea,
and though no fishes entered
  them,
she still captivated hearts!

Die Winde streifen so kühl umher,
Erzählen leis' eine alte Mär!
Die See erglühet im Abendrot,
Die Fischerin fühlt nicht Liebesnot
Im Herzen! Im Herzen!

The winds, they rove about so cool,
softly recite an ancient tale.
The sea glows in the setting sun,
the maiden feels not love's distress
in her heart, in her heart!

## Prinz Eugen | Prince Eugene

FERDINAND FREILIGRATH

*Carl Loewe: op. 92, ed. 1844*

Zelte, Posten, Werda-Rufer!
Lustge Nacht am Donauufer!
Pferde stehn im Kreis umher
Angebunden an den Pflöcken;
An den engen Sattelböcken
Hangen Karabiner schwer.

Tents, pickets, sentry-challenge!
A merry night on the Danube shore!
Circles of horses stand
tethered to posts;
from narrow saddles
hang heavy carbines.

Um das Feuer auf der Erde,
Vor den Hufen seiner Pferde
Liegt das östreichsche Pikett.
Auf dem Mantel liegt ein jeder,
Von den Tschakos weht die Feder.
Leutnant würfelt und Kornett.

On the ground around the fire,
at their horses' feet,
lie the Austrian picket.
On his cloak each man lies,
the plumes of the shakos wave.
Lieutenant and cornet are dicing.

Neben seinem müden Schecken
Ruht auf einer wollnen Decken
Der Trompeter ganz allein:
»Laßt die Knöchel, laßt die Karten!
Kaiserliche Feldstandarten
Wird ein Reiterlied erfreun!

Beside his weary dapple-grey,
on a woollen blanket, rests,
all alone, the trumpeter:
'Leave dice, leave cards!
The Emperor's battle-standards
will be cheered by a cavalry song!

Vor acht Tagen die Affäre
Hab ich, zu Nutz dem ganzen Heere,
In gehörgen Reim gebracht;
Selber auch gesetzt die Noten;
Drum, ihr Weißen und ihr Roten!
Merket auf und gebet acht!«

'Our engagement of eight days back
I have, for the whole army's use,
put suitably into rhyme;
have also myself written the music;
wherefore, Whites and Reds,
hearken and give ear!'

Und er singt die neue Weise
Einmal, zweimal, dreimal leise
Denen Reitersleuten vor;
Und wie er zum letzten Male
Endet, bricht mit einem Male
Los der volle kräftge Chor:

And the new song he sings
once, twice, thrice, softly
to the cavalrymen;
and the last time, as he
finishes, there suddenly bursts
forth the full mighty chorus:

»Prinz Eugen, der edle Ritter!«
Hei, das klang wie Ungewitter
Weit ins Türkenlager hin.
Der Trompeter tät den Schnurrbart
  streichen
Und sich auf die Seite schleichen
Zu der Marketenderin.

'Prince Eugene, noble knight!'
Oho! Like thunder that rang
far into the Turkish camp.
The trumpeter smoothed his
  moustache
and quietly made off
to the sutler woman.

## Prometheus / Prometheus

JOHANN WOLFGANG GOETHE

*Johann Friedrich Reichardt, ed. 1809, Franz Schubert, 1819;*
*Hugo Wolf, 1889*

Bedecke deinen Himmel, Zeus,
Mit Wolkendunst
Und übe, dem Knaben gleich,
Der Disteln köpft,
An Eichen dich und Bergeshöhn;
Mußt mir meine Erde
Doch lassen stehn
Und meine Hütte, die du nicht gebaut,
Und meinen Herd,
Um dessen Glut
Du mich beneidest.

Hide your heaven, Zeus,
in mist and cloud,
and test yourself, like a boy
beheading thistles,
against oaks and mountain peaks;
but my earth
you must leave to me,
and my hut, which you did not build,
and my hearth,
whose glow
you envy me.

Ich kenne nichts Ärmeres
Unter der Sonn', als euch, Götter!
Ihr nähret kümmerlich
Von Opfersteuern
Und Gebetshauch
Eure Majestät
Und darbtet, wären
Nicht Kinder und Bettler
Hoffnungsvolle Toren.

I know no one poorer
under the sun, gods, than you!
Meagrely
on levied offerings
and breaths of prayer
you feed your majesty,
and would starve,
were not children and beggars
hopeful fools.

Da ich ein Kind war,
Nicht wußte, wo aus noch ein,
Kehrt' ich mein verirrtes Auge
Zur Sonne, als wenn drüber wär'
Ein Ohr, zu hören meine Klage,
Ein Herz wie meins,
Sich des Bedrängten zu erbarmen.

When I was a child
and knew not whither to turn,
my lost gaze I lifted
to the sun, as if *there*
was an ear for my lament,
and a heart, like mine,
to pity him afflicted.

Wer half mir
Wider der Titanen Übermut?
Wer rettete vom Tode mich,
Von Sklaverei?
Hast du nicht alles selbst vollendet,
Heilig glühend Herz?
Und glühtest jung und gut,
Betrogen, Rettungsdank
Dem Schlafenden da droben?

Ich dich ehren? Wofür?
Hast du die Schmerzen gelindert
Je des Beladenen?
Hast du die Tränen gestillet
Je des Geängsteten?
Hat nicht mich zum Manne
  geschmiedet
Die allmächtige Zeit
Und das ewige Schicksal,
Meine Herrn und deine?

Wähntest du etwa,
Ich sollte das Leben hassen,
In Wüsten fliehen,
Weil nicht alle
Blütenträume reiften?

Hier sitz' ich, forme Menschen
Nach meinem Bilde,
Ein Geschlecht, das mir gleich sei,
Zu leiden, zu weinen,
Zu genießen und zu freuen sich
Und dein nicht zu achten,
Wie ich!

Who helped me
withstand the Titans' insolence?
Who saved me from death,
from slavery?
Did you not accomplish it all,
sacred, fervent heart?
And did not you, youthful, innocent,
deceived, glow, thankful for deliverance
to him that slumbers up there?

I honour you? Why?
Have you ever eased the pains
of him, who is oppressed?
Stilled the tears
of him, who is afraid?
Was I not fashioned a
  man
by Time Almighty
and Fate Everlasting,
my masters and yours?

Did you suppose
that I should hate life,
fly to the wilderness,
because not all
my blossoming dreams bore fruit?

Here I sit, shaping men
in my image,
a race, that shall be like me,
to suffer, weep,
know pleasure and rejoice,
and heed you not
—as I!

## Rastlose Liebe / Restless Love

JOHANN WOLFGANG GOETHE

*Robert Franz: op. 33, no. 6; Othmar Schoeck: op. 19a, no. 5, 1909–14;
Franz Schubert: op. 5, no. 1, 1815?; Carl Friedrich Zelter, 1812*

Dem Schnee, dem Regen,
Dem Wind entgegen,
Im Dampf der Klüfte,
Durch Nebeldüfte,
Immer zu! Immer zu!
Ohne Rast und Ruh!

Lieber durch Leiden
Möcht ich mich schlagen,
Als so viel Freuden
Des Lebens ertragen.
Alle das Neigen
Von Herzen zu Herzen,
Ach, wie so eigen
Schaffet das Schmerzen!

Into snow, into rain,
into wind, headlong,
through the gorges' fog,
through mist,
ever on! Ever on!
No halt, no rest!

Through affliction
sooner I'd battle,
than so many joys
of life endure.
All this inclining
of heart for heart,
ah, how strangely
it creates pain!

Wie soll ich fliehen?
Wälderwärts ziehen?
Alles vergeben!
Krone des Lebens,
Glück ohne Ruh,
Liebe, bist du!

How shall I flee?
Make for the woods?
All is in vain!
Diadem of life,
joy without rest,
that, Love, are you!

## Rat einer Alten / Old Woman's Advice

EDUARD MÖRIKE

*Hugo Wolf, 1888*

Bin jung gewesen,
Kann auch mitreden,
Und alt geworden,
Drum gilt mein Wort.

I was young once,
so I can talk too,
and now I'm old,
so what I say counts.

Schön reife Beeren
Am Bäumchen hangen:
Nachbar, da hilft kein
Zaun um den Garten;
Lustige Vögel
Wissen den Weg.

Lovely ripe pears
hang from the tree:
Neighbour, it's no use
fencing the garden;
merry birds
know the way.

Aber, mein Dirnchen,
Du laß dir raten:
Halte dein Schätzchen
Wohl in der Liebe,
Wohl im Respekt!

But, young lady,
be you advised;
hold your sweetheart
in love,
in respect!

Mit den zwei Fädchen,
In eins gedrehet,
Ziehst du am kleinen
Finger ihn nach.

With those two threads
twined into one,
you will lead him
by one little finger.

Aufrichtig Herze,
Doch schweigen können,
Früh mit der Sonne
Mutig zur Arbeit,
Gesunde Glieder,
Saubere Linnen,
Das machet Mädchen
Und Weibchen wert.

Open of heart,
know how to keep quiet,
up with the sun,
to work with a will,
healthy of limb,
clean in one's linen,
is what makes a maiden
and woman of worth.

Bin jung gewesen,
Kann auch mitreden,
Und alt geworden,
Drum gilt mein Wort.

I was young once,
so I can talk too,
and now I'm old,
so what I say counts.

## Ravenna / Ravenna*

HERMANN HESSE

*Othmar Schoeck: op. 24b, no. 9, 1906–15*

Ich bin auch in Ravenna gewesen.
Ist eine kleine, tote Stadt,

I too was in Ravenna.
It's a small, dull town

Die Kirchen und viele Ruinen hat,
Man kann davon in den Büchern lesen.

with churches and lots of ruins,
you can read about it in books.

Du gehst hindurch und schaust dich
 um,
Die Straßen sind so trüb und naß
Und sind so tausendjährig stumm,
Und überall wächst Moos und Gras.

You walk through, look
 round,
the streets are so gloomy and wet
and so thousandyearedly mute,
and moss and grass grow everywhere.

Das ist, wie alte Lieder sind.
Man hört sie an und keiner lacht,
Und jeder lauscht und jeder sinnt
Hernach daran bis in die Nacht.

That is as old songs are.
You give ear, no one laughs,
and each listens, and each ponders
them thereafter into the night.

* The German copyright holder has requested the English-language publisher to point out that this translation of 'Ravenna I' has been made specifically as reference for singers.

## Regenlied | Rain-song

KLAUS GROTH

*Johannes Brahms: op. 59, no. 3, 1873*

Walle Regen, walle nieder,
Wecke mir die Träume wieder,
Die ich in der Kindheit träumte,
Wenn das Naß im Sande schäumte!

Stream down rain, stream down rain,
wake for me those dreams again,
which I in my childhood dreamt
when water foamed upon the sand!

Wenn die matte Sommerschwüle
Lässig stritt mit frischer Kühle,
Und die blanken Blätter tauten,
Und die Saaten dunkler blauten.

When oppressive summer heat
with cool freshness idly strove,
and shiny leaves dripped with dew,
and crops were of a darker blue.

Welche Wonne, in dem Fließen
Dann zu stehn mit nackten Füßen,
An dem Grase hinzustreifen
Und den Schaum mit Händen greifen,

What bliss then to stand
with naked feet in the flow,
to brush along against the grass
and with my hands to grab the foam,

Oder mit den heißen Wangen
Kalte Tropfen aufzufangen,
Und den neuerwachten Düften
Seine Kinderbrust zu lüften!

or upon my ardent cheeks
to catch cold drops,
and to the fresh-awakened scents
lay bare one's childish breast!

Wie die Kelche, die da troffen,
Stand die Seele atmend offen,
Wie die Blumen, düftetrunken,
In den Himmelstau versunken.

Like the flower-cups dripping there,
open, breathing, stood my soul,
like the flowers, fragrance-drunk,
immersed in heaven's dew.

Schauernd kühlte jeder Tropfen
Tief bis an des Herzens Klopfen,
Und der Schöpfung heilig Weben
Drang bis ins verborgne Leben.

Awesomely each drop struck cold,
deep to where the heart was beating,
and the sacred motion of creation
broke through to the hidden life.

Walle Regen, walle nieder,
Wecke meine alten Lieder,
Die wir in der Türe sangen,
Wenn die Tropfen draußen klangen!

Stream down rain, stream down rain,
waken those old songs of mine,
which in the doorway we would sing
when, outside, the drops resounded!

Möchte ihnen wieder lauschen,
Ihrem süßen, feuchten Rauschen,
Meine Seele sanft betauen
Mit dem frommen Kindergrauen.

I would like again to listen
to their sweet moist rustling noise,
like softly to bedew my soul
with innocent childish awe.


## Reisephantasie / Travel Reverie

CONRAD FERDINAND MEYER

*Othmar Schoeck: op. 60, no. 3, 1946*

Mittagsruhe haltend auf den Matten
In der morschen Burg gezacktem
  Schatten,
Vor dem Türmchen eppichübersponnen,
Hab ich einen Sommerwunsch
  gesonnen,
Während ich ein Eidechsschwänzchen
  blitzen
Sah—und husch, verschwinden durch
  die Ritzen . . .

Resting at midday on the meadow
in the decaying castle's jagged
  shadow,
by the ivy-spun turret,
a summer wish I
  formed
as, flashing, a lizard's
  tail
I saw, whisking into the
  crevices . . .

Wenn es lauschte . . . wenn es meiner
  harrte . . .
Wenn—das Pförtchen in der Mauer
  knarrte . . .
Dem Geräusche folgend einer Schleppe,
Fänd' ich eine schmale Wendeltreppe
Und, von leiser Hand emporgeleitet,
Droben einen Becher Wein bereitet . . .
Dann im Erker säßen wir alleine,
Plauderten von nichts im
  Dämmerscheine,
Bis der Pendel stünde, der da
  tickte,
Und ein blondes Haupt entschlummernd
  nickte,
Unter seines Lides dünner Hülle
Regte sich des blauen Quelles
  Fülle . . .
Und das unbekannte Antlitz
  trüge
Ähnlichkeiten und Geschwisterzüge
Alles Schönen, was mir je entgegen
Trat auf allen meinen Erdewegen . . .
Was ich Tiefstes, Zartestes
  empfunden,
Wär' an dieses blonde Haupt gebunden
Und in eine Schlummernde vereinigt,
Was mich je beseligt und
  gepeinigt . . .
Dringend hätt' es mich empor-
  gerufen
Dieser Wendeltreppe Trümmer-
  stufen,
Daß ich einem ganzen, vollen Glücke
Stillen Kuß auf stumme Lippen
  drücke . . .
Einmal nur in einem Menschenleben—
Aber nimmer wird es sich begeben!

If it were listening . . . were awaiting
  me . . .
The small door in the wall—were it to
  creak . . .
Following the rustle of a train,
a narrow spiral staircase would I find,
and, guided aloft by a gentle hand,
wine standing ready in a goblet . . .
Then in the oriel we would sit alone
in the half-light and talk of
  nothings
till the pendulum that ticked there,
  stopped,
and a blond head nodded into
  slumber,
and beneath its lightly-veiling lids
the full blueness of the well would
  stir . . .
And that unknown countenance would
  bear
the likeness and sister's features
of all beauty that ever I encountered
upon my earthly ways . . .
Whatever I most deeply, tenderly had
  felt
would be attached to that blond head
and united in one slumbering woman—
all that had ever enraptured me, or
  tormented . . .
Pressing would have been the call to
  ascend
that spiral staircase and its crumbling
  steps,
that I on full, complete good fortune's
silent lips might press a secret
  kiss . . .
Just for once in mortal life—
but never ever will that come to pass!

## Requiem / Requiem

OLD ROMAN CATHOLIC POEM

Robert Schumann: op. 90, no. 7, 1850

Ruh' von schmerzensreichen Mühen
aus und heißem Liebesglühen!
Der nach seligem Verein
trug Verlangen,
ist gegangen
zu des Heilands Wohnung ein.

Dem Gerechten leuchten helle
Sterne in des Grabes Zelle,
ihm, der selbst als Stern der Nacht
wird erscheinen,
wenn er seinen
Herrn erschaut in Himmelspracht.

Seid Fürsprecher, heil'ge Seelen!
Heil'ger Geist, laß Trost nicht fehlen.
Hörst du? Jubelsang erklingt,
Feiertöne,
darein die schöne
Engelsharfe singt:

Ruh' von schmerzensreichen Mühen
aus und heißem Liebesglühen!
Der nach seligem Verein
trug Verlangen,
ist gegangen
zu des Heilands Wohnung ein.

Rest from painful toil
and love's glowing heat!
He who longed
for union with bliss,
has departed
to the Saviour's dwelling.

For him who is just, bright
stars shine in the grave's cell,
for him, who as a star of night
will shine
when he beholds
his Lord in Heavenly glory.

Be intercessors, holy souls!
Holy Ghost, let not comfort lack.
Do you hear?—Joyous song,
solemn notes
wherein the lovely
harp of angels mingles:

Rest from painful toil,
and love's glowing heat!
He who longed
for union with bliss,
has departed
to the Saviour's dwelling.

## Resignation / Resignation

P. VON HAUGWITZ

Ludwig van Beethoven, 1817

Lisch aus, mein Licht! Was dir gebricht,
Das ist nun fort, an diesem Ort
Kannst du's nicht wieder finden!
Du mußt nun los dich binden.

Sonst hast du lustig aufgebrannt,
Nun hat man dir die Luft entwandt;
Wenn diese fort gewehet, die Flamme
      irre gehet,
Sucht, findet nicht, lisch aus, mein
      Licht!

Go out, my light! What you lack
is departed now; in this place
you cannot again find it!
You must now detach yourself.

Once you burnt up merrily,
now they have deprived you of air;
that blown away, the flame will
      stray,
seek, find not—go out, my
      light!

## Revelge / Reveille

from Des Knaben Wunderhorn

Armin Knab, 1904–7; Gustav Mahler, ed. 1905

Des Morgens zwischen drein und vieren,
Da müssen wir Soldaten marschieren

Between three and four of the morning,
we soldiers have to march

Das Gäßlein auf und ab;
Tralali, Tralalei, Tralala,
Mein Schätzel sieht herab.

»Ach, Bruder, jetzt bin ich geschossen,
Die Kugel hat mich schwer getroffen,
Trag mich in mein Quartier,
Tralali, Tralalei, Tralala,
Es ist nicht weit von hier.«

»Ach, Bruder, ich kann dich nicht
    tragen,
Die Feinde haben uns geschlagen,
Helf dir der liebe Gott;
Tralali, Tralalei, Tralala,
Ich muß marschieren in Tod.«

»Ach, Brüder! ihr geht ja an mir
    vorüber,
Als wär es mit mir schon vorüber,
Ihr Lumpenfeind seid da;
Tralali, Tralalei, Tralala,
Ihr tretet mir zu nah.

Ich muß wohl meine Trommel rühren,
Sonst werde ich mich ganz verlieren;
Die Brüder dick gesät,
Tralali, Tralalei, Tralala,
Sie liegen wie gemäht.«

Er schlägt die Trommel auf und nieder,
Er wecket seine stillen Brüder,
Sie schlagen ihren Feind,
Tralali, Tralalei, Tralala,
Ein Schrecken schlägt den Feind.

Er schlägt die Trommel auf und nieder,
Da sind sie vor dem Nachtquartier
    schon wieder,
Ins Gäßlein hell hinaus,
Tralali, Tralalei, Tralala,
Sie ziehn vor Schätzleins Haus.

Des Morgens stehen da die Gebeine
In Reih und Glied wie Leichensteine,
Die Trommel steht voran,
Tralali, Tralalei, Tralala,
Daß sie ihn sehen kann.

up the street and down;
tralali, tralaly, tralala,
my darling gazes down.

'Ah, brother, now I'm shot,
the ball has wounded me sore,
to my billet carry me,
tralali, tralaly, tralala,
it is not far from here.'

'Ah, brother, I cannot carry
    you,
we are routed by the foe,
may the good God help you;
tralali, tralaly, tralala,
to my death I've got to go.'

'Ah, brothers, you march by
    me,
as if I were already finished,
villainous foe, you're here,
tralali, tralaly, tralala,
too close at hand.

'My drum I must sound,
lest I quite give way;
my brothers, thickly sown,
tralali, tralaly, tralala,
lie as if mown.'

Up and down he sounds his drum
rousing his silent brothers,
they rout their foe,
tralali, tralaly, tralala,
the foe are struck with horror.

Up and down he sounds his drum,
they're by their night billets
    again,
it's out into the bright street,
tralali, tralaly, tralala,
they march by his darling's house.

There, at morning, stand their bones,
in rank and file like tombstones—
drum at the head,
tralali, tralaly, tralala,
for her to see.

*Rheinlegendchen | Rhine Legend*

from *Des Knaben Wunderhorn*

*Gustav Mahler, 1888–89*

Bald gras ich am Neckar,
Bald gras ich am Rhein;
Bald hab ich ein Schätzel,
Bald bin ich allein!

Now I mow by the Neckar,
now I mow by the Rhine;
now I've a darling,
now I'm alone!

| | |
|---|---|
| Was hilft mir das Grasen, | What use my mowing |
| Wenn d'Sichel nicht schneid't! | if the sickle won't cut! |
| Was hilft mir ein Schätzel, | What use a darling |
| Wenn's bei mir nicht bleibt. | if she will not stay! |
| | |
| So soll ich denn grasen | So if I'm to mow |
| Am Neckar, am Rhein, | by Neckar, by Rhine, |
| So werf ich mein goldenes | then in will I throw |
| Ringlein hinein. | my little gold ring. |
| Es fließet im Neckar | It will flow with the Neckar |
| Und fließet im Rhein, | and flow with the Rhine |
| Soll schwimmen hinunter | and go swimming down |
| Ins Meer tief hinein. | deep into the sea. |
| | |
| Und schwimmt es, das Ringlein, | As it swims, the ring |
| So frißt es ein Fisch! | will be eaten by a fish! |
| Das Fischlein soll kommen | That fish shall come |
| Auf's Königs sein Tisch! | to His Majesty's table! |
| Der König tät fragen, | The king will inquire: |
| Wem's Ringlein sollt sein? | 'Whose ring can this be?' |
| Da tät mein Schatz sagen: | And my darling will say: |
| Das Ringlein g'hört mein. | 'It belongs to me.' |
| | |
| Mein Schätzel tät springen | My darling will spring |
| Bergauf und bergein, | over hill, over dale, |
| Tät mir wiedrum bringen | and bring back to me |
| Das Goldringlein mein! | my little gold ring! |
| Kannst grasen am Neckar, | You can mow by the Neckar, |
| Kannst grasen am Rhein, | you can mow by the Rhine, |
| Wirf du mir nur immer | if always you throw |
| Dein Ringlein hinein! | your ring in for me! |

## *Ridente la calma* / *Calm, Smiling, Awakens*

(Canzonetta)

ANONYMOUS

*Wolfgang Amadeus Mozart: K 152, 1772?*

| | |
|---|---|
| Ridente la calma nell' alma si desti; | Calm, smiling, awakens in my soul; |
| Ne resti più segno di sdegno e timor. | no trace of disdain, of fear, remains. |
| Tu vieni frattanto a stringer mio bene, | Meanwhile, my love, you come to tauten |
| Le dolce catene si grate al mio cor. | those sweet bonds so dear to my heart |

## *Rückweg* / *The Way Back*

JOHANN MAYRHOFER

*Franz Schubert, 1816*

| | |
|---|---|
| Zum Donaustrom, zur Kaiserstadt | To the Danube, to the imperial town |
| Geh' ich in Bangigkeit: | I go in fear and dread: |
| Denn was das Leben Schönes hat, | for what is beautiful in life |
| Entschwindet weit und weit. | is departing far and wide. |

| Die Berge weichen allgemach, | Gradually the mountains yield, |
|---|---|
| Mit ihnen Tal und Fluß: | and with them vale and stream: |
| Der Kühe Glocken läuten nach, | the cow-bells toll out after me, |
| Und Hütten nicken Gruß. | and chalets nod farewell. |
| | |
| Was starrt dein Auge tränenfeucht | Why does your eye, wet with tears, |
| Hinaus in blaue Fern'? | gaze to the blue distance? |
| Ach, dorten weilt ich, unerreicht, | Gladly I dwelt there out of reach, |
| Frei unter Freien gern! | free amongst the free! |
| | |
| Wo Liebe noch und Treue gilt, | Where love, loyalty still hold sway, |
| Da öffnet sich das Herz; | the heart is opened wide; |
| Die Frucht an ihren Strahlen schwillt, | under their rays swells the fruit |
| Und strebet himmelwärts. | and strains towards the skies. |

## Ruhe, meine Seele | Peace, My Soul

KARL HENCKELL

*Richard Strauss: op. 27, no. 1, 1893–94*

| Nicht ein Lüftchen regt sich leise, | Not a breath stirs, |
|---|---|
| Sanft entschlummert ruht der Hain; | the wood rests in gentle sleep; |
| Durch der Blätter dunkle Hülle | through the leaves' dark veil |
| Stiehlt sich lichter Sonnenschein. | bright sunshine steals. |
| | |
| Ruhe, ruhe, meine Seele, | Peace, peace, my soul, |
| Deine Stürme gingen wild, | wild have been your storms, |
| Hast getobt und hast gezittert, | you have raged and quivered |
| Wie die Brandung, wenn sie schwillt. | like the swelling breakers. |
| | |
| Diese Zeiten sind gewaltig, | These times are violent, |
| Bringen Herz und Hirn in Not— | causing heart and mind distress— |
| Ruhe, ruhe, meine Seele, | peace, peace, my soul, |
| Und vergiß, was dich bedroht! | and forget what threatens you! |

## Sapphische Ode | Sapphic Ode

HANS SCHMIDT

*Johannes Brahms: op. 94, no. 4, 1884*

| Rosen brach ich nachts mir am dunklen Hage; | Roses I plucked at night by the dark hedge; |
|---|---|
| Süßer hauchten Duft sie als je am Tage; | the fragrance they breathed was sweeter than by day; |
| Doch verstreuten reich die bewegten Äste | but the branches, agitated, shed a wealth of |
| Tau, der mich näßte. | dew, which showered me. |
| | |
| Auch der Küsse Duft mich wie nie berückte, | I too was beguiled by the fragrant kisses |
| Die ich nachts vom Strauch deiner Lippen pflückte: | I plucked at night from your rosebush lips, |
| Doch auch dir, bewegt im Gemüt gleich jenen, | but you, at heart agitated, like them, shed |
| Tauten die Tränen. | dewy tears. |

## Säusle, liebe Myrte! / Rustle, Dear Myrtle

CLEMENS BRENTANO

*Richard Strauss: op. 68, no. 3, 1918–19*

Säusle, liebe Myrte!
Wie still ist's in der Welt,
Der Mond, der Sternenhirte
Auf klarem Himmelsfeld,
Treibt schon die Wolkenschafe
Zum Born des Lichtes hin,
Schlaf, mein Freund, o schlafe,
Bis ich wieder bei dir bin!

Säusle, liebe Myrte!
Und träum im Sternenschein,
Die Turteltaube girrte
Ihre Brut schon ein.
Still ziehn die Wolkenschafe
Zum Born des Lichtes hin,
Schlaf, mein Freund, o schlafe,
Bis ich wieder bei dir bin!

Hörst du, wie die Brunnen rauschen?
Hörst du, wie die Grille zirpt?
Stille, stille, laßt uns lauschen,
Selig, wer in Träumen stirbt;
Selig, wen die Wolken wiegen,
Wenn der Mond ein Schlaflied singt;
Oh! wie selig kann der fliegen,
Dem der Traum den Flügel schwingt,
Daß an blauer Himmelsdecke
Sterne er wie Blumen pflückt;
Schlafe, träume, flieg, ich wecke
Bald dich auf und bin beglückt!

Rustle, dear myrtle!
How silent the world is,
the moon, the stars' shepherd
in heaven's bright field
is driving the cloud-sheep
to the spring of light,
sleep, my friend, oh sleep.
till I'm again with you.

Rustle, dear myrtle!
And dream in the starlight,
the turtledove has cooed
her brood to sleep.
Quietly the cloud-sheep
retire to the spring of light,
sleep, my friend, oh sleep,
till I'm again with you.

Hear how the fountains murmur?
Hear how the cricket chirrups?
Hush, hush, let us listen,
happy he who dies in dreams;
happy he whom clouds cradle
when the moon sings a lullaby;
oh, how blissfully can he fly
whose wing is impelled by dreams,
so that on Heaven's blue roof
he may gather stars like flowers;
sleep, dream, fly, I'll awake
you soon and be made happy.

## Schäfers Klagelied / Shepherd's Lament

JOHANN WOLFGANG GOETHE

*Johann Friedrich Reichardt, ed. 1809; Franz Schubert: op. 3, no. 1, 1814;*
*Carl Friedrich Zelter, 1802*

Da droben auf jenem Berge,
Da steh ich tausendmal,
An meinem Stabe gebogen,
Und schaue hinab in das Tal.

Dann folg ich der weidenden Herde,
Mein Hündchen bewahret mir sie.
Ich bin herunter gekommen
Und weiß doch selber nicht wie.

Da stehet von schönen Blumen
Die ganze Wiese so voll.
Ich breche sie, ohne zu wissen,
Wem ich sie geben soll.

High on that mountain,
a thousand times I stand,
bowed over my staff,
gazing down into the valley.

Then I follow my grazing flock,
watched over by my dog.
I have come down to the valley,
yet how, I do not know.

With beautiful flowers
the whole meadow is so full.
I pick them without knowing
who to give them to.

Und Regen, Sturm und Gewitter
Verpaß ich unter dem Baum.
Die Türe dort bleibet verschlossen;
Denn alles ist leider ein Traum.

Es stehet ein Regenbogen
Wohl über jenem Haus!
Sie aber ist weggezogen,
Und weit in das Land hinaus.

Hinaus in das Land und weiter,
Vielleicht gar über die See.
Vorüber, ihr Schafe, vorüber!
Dem Schäfer ist gar so weh.

And rain, storm and thunder
I endure beneath this tree.
The door there remains closed,
for all, alas, is a dream.

A rainbow there is
above that house.
But she has gone away,
away to distant parts.

To distant parts and further,
maybe even over the sea.
Get on, get on, you sheep!
Your shepherd's heart's so sore.


## Schilflied | Reed-song

NIKOLAUS LENAU

*Felix Mendelssohn-Bartholdy: op. 71, no. 4, 1845–47; Henri Marteau*

Auf dem Teich, dem regungslosen,
Weilt des Mondes holder Glanz,
Flechtend seine bleichen Rosen
In des Schilfes grünen Kranz.

Hirsche wandeln dort am Hügel,
Blicken in die Nacht empor;
Manchmal regt sich da Geflügel
Träumerisch im tiefen Rohr.

Weinend muß mein Blick sich senken;
Durch die tiefste Seele geht
Mir ein süßes Deingedenken,
Wie ein stilles Nachtgebet!

On the pond, the motionless pond,
lingers the moon's graceful gleam,
plaiting its pale roses
into the reed's green garland.

Deer wander, there on the hill,
gazing up into the night;
winged creatures stir at times,
dreamily, deep among the reeds.

Tearfully must my gaze be lowered;
through the depths of my soul
sweet thoughts of you pass
like a silent evening prayer.


## Schlafen, schlafen | Sleep, Sleep

FRIEDRICH HEBBEL

*Alban Berg: op. 2, no. 1, 1908–09*

Schlafen, schlafen, nichts als schalfen!
Kein Erwachen, keinen Traum!
Jener Wehen, die mich trafen,
Leisestes Erinnern kaum,
Daß ich, wenn des Lebens Fülle
Nieder klingt in meine Ruh,
Nur noch tiefer mich verhülle,
Fester zu die Augen tu!

Sleep, sleep, naught but sleep!
No awakening, no dream!
Of those woes that befell me,
scarce the faintest memory,
so that, when life's profusion
resoundingly descends into my rest,
I may veil myself more heavily,
and my eyes more tightly shut!

## Schlafend trägt man mich | Sleeping I am Borne

ALFRED MOMBERT

*Alban Berg: op. 2, no. 2, 1908–9; Armin Knab, 1905–11;*
*Joseph Marx: Lieder and Songs, 3rd Series, no. 4*

Schlafend trägt man mich
in mein Heimatland.
Ferne komm' ich her,
über Gipfel, über Schlünde,
über ein dunkles Meer
in mein Heimatland.

Sleeping I am borne
to my homeland.
From afar I come,
over mountain, gorge,
over a dark ocean
to my homeland.


## Schlafendes Jesuskind | The Child Jesus, Sleeping

EDUARD MÖRIKE

*Hugo Wolf, 1888*

Sohn der Jungfrau, Himmelskind! am
   Boden
Auf dem Holz der Schmerzen
   eingeschlafen,
Das der fromme Meister, sinnvoll
   spielend,
Deinen leichten Träumen unterlegte;
Blume du, noch in der Knospe
   dämmernd
Eingehüllt, die Herrlichkeit des Vaters!
O wer sehen könnte, welche Bilder
Hinter dieser Stirne, diesen schwarzen
Wimpern sich in sanftem Wechsel
   malen!

Virgin's son, Child of Heaven, on the
   floor
on the wood of agony
   sleeping,
that, suggestively, the pious
   master
has set beneath your easy dreams;
thou flower, still gleaming in the
   bud,
the glory of the Father!
Oh, to see the picture being painted
behind that forehead, those dark
lashes, gently, one upon the
   other!


## Schlagende Herzen | Beating Hearts

OTTO JULIUS BIERBAUM

*Richard Strauss: op. 29, no. 2, 1894–95*

Über Wiesen und Felder ein Knabe
   ging,
Kling klang, schlug ihm das Herz;
Es glänzt ihm am Finger von Golde ein
   Ring.
Kling klang, schlug ihm das Herz;
O Wiesen, o Felder, wie seid ihr schön!
O Berge, o Täler, wie schön!
Wie bist du gut, wie bist du schön,
Du gold'ne Sonne in Himmelshöhn!
Kling klang, kling klang, kling klang,
   schlug ihm das Herz.
Schnell eilte der Knabe mit fröhlichem
   Schritt,
Kling klang, schlug ihm das Herz.

Over fields and meadows went a
   boy,
pit-a-pat beat his heart;
on his finger gleams a ring of
   gold.
Pit-a-pat beat his heart;
O meadows, fields, how fair you are!
O mountains, vales, how fair!
How good you are, how fair you are,
you golden sun in heaven's heights!
Pit-a-pat, pit-a-pat, beat his
   heart.
On the boy hastened with happy
   step,
pit-a-pat beat his heart.

Nahm manche lachende Blume
mit—
Kling klang, schlug ihm das Herz.
Über Wiesen und Felder weht
Frühlingswind,
Über Berge und Wälder weht
Frühlingswind,
Im Herzen mir innen weht
Frühlingswind,
Der treibt zu dir mich leise, lind,
Kling klang, schlug ihm das Herz.
Zwischen Wiesen und Feldern ein
Mädel stand,
Kling klang, schlug ihm das Herz.
Hielt über die Augen zum Schauen die
Hand,
Kling klang, schlug ihm das Herz.
Über Wiesen und Felder, über Berge
und Wälder,
Zu mir, zu mir, schnell kommt er her,
O wenn er bei mir nur, bei mir schon
wär!
Kling klang, kling klang, kling klang,
schlug ihr das Herz.

Took with him many a laughing
flower—
pit-a-pat beat his heart.
Over field and meadow spring wind
blows,
over wood and mountain spring wind
blows,
deep in my heart spring wind
blows
drives me to you, softly, gently,
pit-a-pat beat his heart.
Between field and meadow stood a
maid,
pit-a-pat beat her heart.
She shaded her eyes with her hand to
gaze,
pit-a-pat beat her heart.
Over field and meadow, mountain,
wood,
to me, to me he quickly comes,
oh, were he but with me, with me
already!
Pit-a-pat, pit-a-pat, pit-a-pat beat her
heart.

## Schlechter Trost | Poor Comfort

JOHANN WOLFGANG GOETHE: from West-östlicher Divan. 'Book of Love'

Ferruccio Busoni, ed. 1964; Ernst Pepping, 1946

Mitternachts weint' und schluchzt' ich,
Weil ich dein entbehrte.
Da kamen Nachtgespenster
Und ich schämte mich.
»Nachtgespenster«, sagt' ich,
»Schluchzend und weinend
Findet ihr mich, dem ihr sonst
Schlafendem vorüberzogt.
Große Güter vermiss' ich.
Denkt nicht schlimmer von mir,
Den ihr sonst weise nanntet,
Großes Übel betrifft ihn!«—
Und die Nachtgespenster
Mit langen Gesichtern
Zogen vorbei,
Ob ich weise oder törig
Völlig unbekümmert.

At midnight I wept, I sobbed,
being without you.
Then came night ghosts
and I was ashamed.
'Night ghosts,' I said,
'sobbing and weeping
you discover me, whom once you
passed by and left sleeping.
Great possessions I miss.
Think not worse of me
whom once you did call wise,
great ill afflicts him!'—
And the night ghosts,
long faced,
passed by,
whether wise I was, or foolish,
concerned them not at all.

## Schlechtes Wetter | Dreadful Weather

HEINRICH HEINE

Richard Strauss: op. 69, no. 5, 1895–96

Das ist ein schlechtes Wetter,
Es regnet und stürmt und schneit;
Ich sitze am Fenster und schaue
Hinaus in die Dunkelheit.

Dreadful weather,
rain and storm and snow;
I sit at the window and gaze
out at the dark.

| Da schimmert ein einsames Lichtchen, | There a lonely light glimmers |
| Das wandelt langsam fort; | and slowly moves away: |
| Ein Mütterchen mit dem Laternchen | an old dear with her lantern |
| Wankt über die Straße dort. | unsteadily crosses the street. |

| Ich glaube, Mehl und Eier | Flour and eggs, I think, |
| Und Butter kaufte sie ein; | she's bought, and butter; |
| Sie will einen Kuchen backen | a cake she is going to bake |
| Fürs große Töchterlein. | for her great big daughter, |

| Die liegt zu Haus im Lehnstuhl, | who lies at home in an easy chair |
| Und blinzelt schläfrig ins Licht; | blinking sleepily at the light; |
| Die goldnen Locken wallen | her golden ringlets tumbling |
| Über das süße Gesicht. | over her sweet face. |

## *Schneeglöckchen* / *Snowdrops*

FRIEDRICH RÜCKERT

*Robert Schumann: op. 79, no. 27, 1849*

| Der Schnee, der gestern noch in Flöckchen | The snow that only yesterday in flakes |
| Vom Himmel fiel, | fell from the sky, |
| Hängt nun geronnen heut als Glöckchen | hangs now, frozen, as bells today |
| Am zarten Stiel. | from tender stems. |
| Schneeglöckchen läutet, was bedeutet's | The snowdrop bell rings out, what |
| Im stillen Hain? | signifying in the silent wood? |
| O komm geschwind! Im Haine läutet's | Oh swiftly come! The wood rings |
| Den Frühling ein. | springtime in. |
| O kommt, ihr Blätter, Blüt und Blume, | Oh come, leaf, blossom, flower, |
| Die ihr noch träumt, | you who still dream, |
| All zu des Frühlings Heiligtume! | all to spring's sanctuary! |
| Kommt ungesäumt! | Without delay! |

## *Schön sind, doch kalt die Himmelssterne* / *Fair, Yet Cold, Are the Stars of Heaven*

ADOLF FRIEDRICH VON SCHACK

*Richard Strauss: op. 19, no. 3, 1885–88*

| Schön sind, doch kalt die Himmelssterne, | Fair, yet cold, are the stars of heaven, |
| die Gaben karg, die sie verleih'n; | scant the gifts which they bestow; |
| für einen deiner Blicke gerne | gladly for one look from you |
| hin geb' ich ihren goldnen Schein. | I'll part with their golden glow. |
| Getrennt, so daß wir ewig darben, | To our eternal deprivation, separately |
| nur führen sie im Jahreslauf | only, in the course of the year, do they bring |
| den Herbst mit seinen Ährengarben, | forth autumn with its corn sheaves, |
| des Frühlings Blütenpracht herauf; | and spring's blossom splendour; |
| doch deine Augen, o, der Segen | but from your eyes—oh, the blessing |
| des ganzen Jahres quillt überreich | of the whole year pours, superabundant, |
| aus ihnen stets als milder Regen, | constantly, as a gentle rain, |
| die Blüte und Frucht zugleich. | blossom and fruit together. |

329

# Schwanengesang  /  Swan-song

nos. 1–7: LUDWIG RELLSTAB
nos. 8–13: HEINRICH HEINE
no. 14: JOHANN GABRIEL SEIDL

*Franz Schubert: 1828*

## 1 *Liebesbotschaft*

Rauschendes Bächlein, so silbern und
  hell,
Eilst zur Geliebten so munter und
  schnell?
Ach, trautes Bächlein, mein Bote sei du;
Bringe die Grüße des Fernen ihr zu.

All ihre Blumen im Garten gepflegt,
Die sie so lieblich am Busen trägt,
Und ihre Rosen in purpurner Glut,
Bächlein, erquicke mit kühlender
  Flut.

Wenn sie am Ufer, in Träume versenkt,
Meiner gedenkend, das Köpfchen hängt,
Tröste die Süße mit freundlichem Blick,
Denn der Geliebte kehrt bald zurück.

Neigt sich die Sonne mit rötlichem
  Schein,
Wiege das Liebchen in Schlummer ein.
Rausche sie murmelnd in süße Ruh,
Flüstre ihr Träume der Liebe zu.

## 2 *Kriegers Ahnung*

In tiefer Ruh liegt um mich her
Der Waffenbrüder Kreis;
Mir ist das Herz so bang, so schwer,
Von Sehnsucht mir so heiß.

Wie hab ich oft so süß geträumt
An ihrem Busen warm!
Wie freundlich schien des Herdes Glut,
Lag sie in meinem Arm.

Hier, wo der Flammen düstrer Schein
Ach! nur auf Waffen spielt,
Hier fühlt die Brust sich ganz allein,
Der Wehmut Träne quillt.

Herz, daß der Trost dich nicht verläßt,
Es ruft noch manche Schlacht.
Bald ruh ich wohl und schlafe fest,
Herzliebste—gute Nacht!

## 3 *Frühlingssehnsucht*

Säuselnde Lüfte wehend so mild,
Blumiger Düfte atmend erfüllt!

## 1 *Tidings of Love*

Murmuring brooklet, so silver and
  bright,
do you haste to my love so merry and
  fast?
Ah, dear brooklet, my messenger be;
carry her greetings from one far away.

All her cherished flowers in the garden,
those she so sweetly wears at her breast,
and her roses in their crimson glow,
refresh, brooklet, with your cooling
  waters.

When she, at your side, lost in dreams,
thinking of me, hangs low her head,
console my sweet with a kindly look,
for soon shall her beloved return.

When the sun sinks in a reddish
  gleam,
rock my sweetheart into slumber.
Murmur her into sweet repose,
whisper her dreams of love.

## 2 *Soldier's Foreboding*

In deep repose around me lie
my fellow-soldiers;
my heart's so heavy, so afraid,
so afire with longing.

How often have I sweetly dreamt
upon her warm breast!
How kindly the hearth's glow seemed,
when she lay in my arms.

Here, where the flames' sad gleam,
ah, plays only on weapons,
here the heart feels quite alone,
a tear of sadness wells.

Heart, may comfort not desert you,
many a battle still calls.
Soon shall I rest and sleep fast,
dearest love, good night!

## 3 *Spring longing*

Whispering breezes blowing so mild,
filled with the scented breath of flowers!

Wie haucht ihr mich wonnig begrüßend
an!
Wie habt ihr dem pochenden Herzen
getan?
Es möchte euch folgen auf luftiger
Bahn,
Wohin? Wohin?

Bächlein, so munter rauschend zumal,
Wollen hinunter silbern ins Tal.
Die schwebende Welle, dort eilt sie
dahin!
Tief spiegeln sich Fluren und Himmel
darin.
Was ziehst du mich, sehnend
verlangender Sinn,
Hinab? Hinab?

Grüßender Sonne spielendes Gold,
Hoffende Wonne bringest du hold,
Wie labt mich dein selig begrüßendes
Bild!
Es lächelt am tiefblauen Himmel so
mild
Und hat mir das Auge mit Tränen
gefüllt,
Warum? Warum?

Grünend umkränzet Wälder und Höh.
Schimmernd erglänzet Blüten-
schnee.
So dränget sich alles zum bräutlichen
Licht;
Es schwellen die Keime, die Knospe
bricht;
Sie haben gefunden, was ihnen gebricht:
Und du? Und du?

Rastloses Sehnen! Wünschendes Herz,
Immer nur Tränen, Klage und
Schmerz?
Auch ich bin mir schwellender Triebe
bewußt!
Wer stillet mir endlich die drängende
Lust?
Nur du befreist den Lenz in der
Brust,
Nur du! Nur du!


4 *Ständchen*
Leise flehen meine Lieder
Durch die Nacht zu dir;
In den stillen Hain hernieder,
Liebchen, komm zu mir!

Flüsternd schlanke Wipfel rauschen
In des Mondes Licht,
Des Verräters feindlich Lauschen
Fürchte, Holde, nicht.

How blissfully welcoming upon me you
are!
To my pounding heart what have you
done?
It would gladly follow you on your
airy path,
to where? To where?

Brooklets, murmuring so gaily together,
silver, head for the valley below.
The gliding ripples, they speed that
way!
Meadows and heavens deep mirrored in
them.
Why do you draw me, longing
desire,
down? Down?

Glittering gold of the welcoming sun,
sweetly you bring bliss of hope,
how your happy greeting
refreshes!
It smiles so gently in the deep blue
sky,
and has filled my eyes with
tears,
why? Why?

Green it engarlands woods and heights.
The snowy blossom shimmers and
gleams.
So all things press towards bridal
light;
seeds swell, buds
burst;
they have found what they have lacked:
and you? You?

Restless yearning! Longing heart,
always only tears, lament and
pain?
I too feel swelling
urges!
Who at last shall quiet my insistent
desire?
Only you set free the spring in my
breast,
only you! Only you!


4 *Serenade*
Gently imploring go my songs
through the night to you;
down into the quiet wood,
beloved, come to me.

Slender tree-tops stir and whisper
in the moon's light;
of any betrayer, hostile, listening,
have no fear, my love.

Hörst die Nachtigallen schlagen?
Ach! sie flehen dich,
Mit der Töne süßen Klagen
Flehen sie für mich.

Sie verstehn des Busens Sehnen,
Kennen Liebesschmerz,
Rühren mit den Silbertönen
Jedes weiche Herz.

Laß auch dir die Brust bewegen,
Liebchen, höre mich,
Bebend harr ich dir entgegen!
Komm, beglücke mich!

5 *Aufenthalt*
Rauschender Strom, brausender Wald,
Starrender Fels mein Aufenthalt.
Wie sich die Welle an Welle reiht,
Fließen die Tränen mir ewig erneut.

Hoch in den Kronen wogend sich's regt,
So unaufhörlich mein Herze schlägt,
Und wie des Felsen uraltes Erz,
Ewig derselbe bleibet mein Schmerz.

6 *In der Ferne*
Wehe, den Fliehenden,
Welt hinaus ziehenden!—
Fremde durchmessenden,
Heimat vergessenden,
Mutterhaus hassenden,
Freunde verlassenden
Folget kein Segen, ach!
Auf ihren Wegen nach!

Herze, das sehnende,
Auge, das tränende,
Sehnsucht, nie endende,
Heimwärts sich wendende!
Busen, der wallende,
Klage, verhallende,
Abendstern, blinkender,
Hoffnungslos sinkender!

Lüfte, ihr säuselnden,
Wellen, sanft kräuselnden,
Sonnenstrahl, eilender,
Nirgend verweilender:
Die mir mit Schmerze, ach!
Dies treue Herze brach,
Grüßt von dem Fliehenden,
Welt hinaus ziehenden.

7 *Abschied*
Ade! du muntre, du fröhliche Stadt, ade!
Schon scharret mein Rößlein mit
     lustigem Fuß;

Can you hear the nightingales call?
Ah! You they are imploring
with those sweet lamenting notes,
imploring you for me.

They understand the heart's longing,
know the agony of love,
move with their silvery notes
every tender heart.

Let your heart, too, be moved,
beloved, listen to me,
trembling, I await you,
come, make my happiness!

5 *Resting Place*
Raging river, roaring forest,
towering rock, my resting place.
As wave succeeds wave,
so my tears flow ever anew.

The high tree-tops surge and heave,
just as unceasingly throbs my heart,
and like the rock's age-old ore,
my grief stays ever the same.

6 *Far Away*
Alas, those who flee,
who go out into the world,
who travel strange parts,
forgetting their homeland,
hating their own home,
abandoning their friends
—them, ah, no blessing follows
upon their way.

Yearning heart,
tearful eye,
never-ending longing,
homewards turning!
Seething breast,
fading lament,
gleaming evening star,
setting without hope!

Whispering breezes,
waves, gently ruffled,
sunbeam, hastening,
nowhere tarrying:
ah, to her who with grief
broke this true heart
—greetings from him who is fleeing,
going out into the world.

7 *Farewell*
Adieu, lively, happy town, adieu!
My horse is eagerly pawing the
     ground;

Jetzt nimm noch den letzten, den
scheidenden Gruß.
Du hast mich wohl niemals noch
traurig gesehn,
So kann es auch jetzt nicht beim
Abschied geschehn.

Ade, ihr Bäume, ihr Gärten so grün,
ade!
Nun reit ich am silbernen Strome
entlang,
Weit schallend ertönet mein
Abschiedsgesang;
Nie habt ihr ein trauriges Lied gehört,
So wird euch auch keines beim
Scheiden beschert.

Ade, liebe Sonne so gehst du zur Ruh,
ade!
Nun schimmert der blinkenden Sterne
Gold.
Wie bin ich euch Sternlein am Himmel
so hold;
Durchziehn wir die Welt auch weit und
breit,
Ihr gebt überall uns das treue
Geleit.

Ade, ihr freundlichen Mägdlein dort,
ade!
Was schaut ihr aus blumenumduftetem
Haus
Mit schelmischen, lockenden Blicken
heraus?
Wie sonst, so grüß ich und schaue mich
um,
Doch nimmer wend ich mein Rößlein
um.

Ade! du schimmerndes Fensterlein hell,
ade!
Du glänzest so traulich mit dämmerndem
Schein,
Und ladest so freundlich ins Hüttchen
uns ein.
Vorüber, ach, ritt ich so manches Mal,
Und wär es denn heute zum letzten
Mal.

Ade, ihr Sterne, verhüllet euch grau!
Ade!
Des Fensterleins trübes,
verschimmerndes Licht
Ersetzt ihr unzähligen Sterne uns
nicht;
Darf ich hier nicht weilen, muß hier
vorbei,
Was hilft es, folgt ihr mir noch so
treu!

accept now my final
farewell.
Never yet have you seen me
sad,
nor can that happen now, at
parting.

Adieu, trees, gardens so green,
adieu!
Now I ride by the silvery
stream,
my farewell song echoing far and
wide;
never have you heard a sad song,
nor shall you be given one at
parting.

Adieu, dear sun retiring to rest,
adieu!
Now shimmers the gold of twinkling
stars.
How I love you, little stars in the
sky;
for though we travel the whole wide
world,
everywhere you keep us faithful
company.

Adieu, friendly maidens, there,
adieu!
Why do you look from flower-fragrant
houses
with impish and alluring
gaze?
I salute you, as always, and glance
back,
but back will I never turn my
horse.

Adieu, small bright window,
adieu!
So homely does your faint light
gleam,
inviting us so kindly
inside.
Ah, past have I ridden so many a time,
and though today be the
last . . .

Adieu, stars, put on your grey veil.
Adieu!
The small window's faint, fading
light
you countless stars cannot replace
for us;
if I cannot linger, if I must ride
by,
what comfort, however faithfully you
follow!

8 *Der Atlas*
Ich unglückselger Atlas! Eine Welt,
Die ganze Welt der Schmerzen muß ich
   tragen.
Ich trage Unerträgliches, und brechen
Will mir das Herz im Leibe.

Du stolzes Herz, du hast es ja gewollt!
Du wolltest glücklich sein, unendlich
   glücklich,
Oder unendlich elend, stolzes Herz,
Und jetzo bist du elend!

8 *Atlas*
I, unhappy Atlas! A world—
the whole world of sorrow must I
   bear.
I bear what cannot be borne, and
my heart would break within me.

You, proud heart, you willed it!
You wished to be happy, boundlessly
   so,
or boundlessly wretched, proud heart,
and now are you wretched!


9 *Ihr Bild*
Ich stand in dunkeln Träumen
Und starrt' ihr Bildnis an,
Und das geliebte Antlitz
Heimlich zu leben begann.

Um ihre Lippen zog sich
Ein Lächeln wunderbar.
Und wie von Wehmutstränen
Erglänzte ihr Augenpaar.

Auch meine Tränen flossen
Mir von den Wangen herab.
Und ach! ich kann es nicht glauben,
Daß ich dich verloren hab!
   (*Hugo Wolf, 1878*)

9 *Her Picture*
I stood darkly dreaming,
staring at her picture,
and that beloved face
sprang mysteriously to life.

About her lips played
a wondrous smile.
And as with sad tears
gleamed her eyes.

And my tears flowed
upon my cheeks.
And ah, I cannot believe
that I have lost you!


10 *Das Fischermädchen*
Du schönes Fischermädchen,
Treibe den Kahn ans Land;
Komm zu mir und setze dich nieder,
Wir kosen Hand in Hand.

Leg an mein Herz dein Köpfchen
Und fürchte dich nicht zu sehr;
Vertraust du dich doch sorglos
Täglich dem wilden Meer!

Mein Herz gleicht ganz dem Meere,
Hat Sturm und Ebb und Flut,
Und manche schöne Perle
In seiner Tiefe ruht.

10 *The Fishermaiden*
Lovely fishermaiden,
row the boat to land;
come and sit beside me,
we'll talk fondly hand in hand.

Lay upon my heart your head
and be not too afraid;
for, fearless, you trust yourself
each day to the raging sea!

My heart's entirely like the sea,
has storm and ebb and flood,
and many a beautiful pearl
rests deep below.


11 *Die Stadt*
Am fernen Horizonte
Erscheint, wie ein Nebelbild,
Die Stadt mit ihren Türmen,
In Abenddämmrung gehüllt.

Ein feuchter Windzug kräuselt
Die graue Wasserbahn;
Mit traurigem Takte rudert
Der Schiffer in meinem Kahn.

11 *The Town*
On the far horizon
appears, as a misty shape,
the town with its spires,
shrouded in dusk.

A dank breeze ruffles
the grey waterway;
with dreary rhythm
the boatman rows my boat.

Die Sonne hebt sich noch einmal
Leuchtend vom Boden empor,
Und zeigt mir jene Stelle,
Wo ich das Liebste verlor.

(*Robert Franz, op. 37, no. 3*)

The sun rears once more
gleaming from the earth,
and shows me that place
where I lost my love.


12 *Am Meer*
Das Meer erglänzte weit hinaus
Im letzten Abendscheine;
Wir saßen am einsamen Fischerhaus,
Wir saßen stumm und alleine.

Der Nebel stieg, das Wasser schwoll,
Die Möwe flog hin und wieder;
Aus deinen Augen, liebevoll,
Fielen die Tränen nieder.

Ich sah sie fallen auf deine Hand
Und bin aufs Knie gesunken;
Ich hab von deiner weißen Hand
Die Tränen fortgetrunken.

Seit jener Stunde verzehrt sich mein
   Leib,
Die Seele stirbt vor Sehnen;
Mich hat das unglückselge Weib
Vergiftet mit ihren Tränen.

12 *By the Sea*
The sea stretched far out, glittering
in the last of evening's rays;
we sat by the fisherman's lonely house,
we sat silent and alone.

The mist rose, the water swelled,
the gull flew to and fro;
from your loving eyes
the tears came falling.

I saw them fall upon your hand,
and sank upon one knee;
and from your white hand
I drank away the tears.

Since that hour my body
   wastes,
my soul dies of longing;
that unhappy woman has
poisoned me with her tears.


13 *Der Doppelgänger*
Still ist die Nacht, es ruhen die Gassen,
In diesem Hause wohnte mein
   Schatz;
Sie hat schon längst die Stadt verlassen,
Doch steht noch das Haus auf
   demselben Platz.

Da steht auch ein Mensch und starrt in
   die Höhe,
Und ringt die Hände vor
   Schmerzensgewalt;
Mir graust es, wenn ich sein Antlitz
   sehe—
Der Mond zeigt mir meine eigne
   Gestalt.

Du Doppelgänger, du bleicher Geselle!
Was äffst du nach mein Liebesleid,
Das mich gequält auf dieser Stelle
So manche Nacht, in alter Zeit?

13 *The Double*
Still is the night. The streets are at rest.
Here is the house where my loved-one
   lived;
long it is, since she left the town,
yet the house still stands where it
   did.

A man stands there too, staring
   up,
wringing his hands in
   agony;
horror grips me, as I see his
   face—
the moon shows me my own
   self.

Double! Pale companion!
Why do you ape the torment of love
that I suffered here
so many a night in time past?


14 *Die Taubenpost*
Ich hab eine Brieftaub in meinem Sold,
Die ist gar ergeben und treu,
Sie nimmt mir nie das Ziel zu kurz,
Und fliegt auch nie vorbei.

14 *Pigeon-post*
I've a carrier-pigeon in my pay,
devoted is he, and true,
never does he stop short of his goal,
or ever over-fly.

Ich sende sie viel tausendmal
Auf Kundschaft täglich hinaus,
Vorbei an manchem lieben Ort,
Bis zu der Liebsten Haus.

Dort schaut sie zum Fenster heimlich
  hinein,
Belauscht ihren Blick und Schritt,
Gibt meine Grüße scherzend ab
Und nimmt die ihren mit.

Kein Briefchen brauch ich zu schreiben
  mehr,
Die Träne selbst geb ich ihr:
O sie verträgt sie sicher nicht,
Gar eifrig dient sie mir.

Bei Tag, bei Nacht, im Wachen, im
  Traum,
Ihr gilt das alles gleich,
Wenn sie nur wandern, wandern kann,
Dann ist sie überreich.

Sie wird nicht müd, sie wird nicht matt,
Der Weg ist stets ihr neu;
Sie braucht nicht Lockung, braucht
  nicht Lohn,
Die Taub ist so mir treu.

Drum heg ich sie auch so treu an der
  Brust,
Versichert des schönsten Gewinns;
Sie heißt—die Sehnsucht!
Kennt ihr sie? Die Botin treuen Sinns.

I send him thousands of times
each day, to spy out how things are,
over many a well-loved place,
to my beloved's house.

At the window he peeps secretly
  in,
observes her look and step,
conveys my greetings merrily,
and brings her greetings back.

No longer need I write a
  note,
I give him the very tear;
oh, he's sure not to misdeliver it,
so eagerly does he serve.

Day or night, dreaming or
  awake,
it's all the same to him,
as long as he can range and roam,
he's richly satisfied.

He does not tire, he grows not weak,
the way's ever fresh for him;
he needs no enticement, no
  reward,
so true is that pigeon to me.

So I nurse him as true to my
  heart,
assured he will give of his best;
his name is—Yearning!
You know him? Messenger of fidelity.

## Sechs Lieder von Gellert | Six Songs by Gellert

CHRISTIAN FÜRCHTEGOTT GELLERT

*Ludwig van Beethoven: op. 48, nos. 1–6, 1803*

1 *Bitten*
Gott, deine Güte reicht so weit,
So weit die Wolken gehen;
Du krönst uns mit Barmherzigkeit,
Und eilst, uns beizustehen.
Herr, meine Burg, mein Fels, mein
  Hort,
Vernimm mein Flehn, merk auf mein
  Wort;
Denn ich will vor dir beten!
    (*Carl Philipp Emanuel Bach: Wq 194, no. 9, 1757–58*)

1 *Supplication*
Your goodness, God, extends so far,
so far as clouds sail;
You crown us with mercy,
and hasten to our aid.
Lord, my fortress, rock and
  shield,
hear my entreaty, hearken to my
  word;
for to You will I pray!

2 *Die Liebe des Nächsten*
So jemand spricht: Ich liebe Gott!
Und haßt doch seine Brüder,
Der treibt mit Gottes Wahrheit Spott,
Und reißt sie ganz darnieder.

2 *Love of One's Neighbour*
If a man say: I love God!
and yet hate his brother,
God's truth he mocks
and pulls it wholly down.

Gott ist die Lieb, und will, daß ich
Den Nächsten liebe, gleich als mich.

God is love and wills that I
love my neighbour as myself.


### 3 Vom Tode
Meine Lebenszeit verstreicht,
Stündlich eil ich zu dem Grabe;
Und was ist's, das ich vielleicht,
Das ich noch zu leben habe?
Denk, o Mensch! an deinen Tod;
Säume nicht; denn Eins ist not.

### 3 Of Death
My span of life expires,
hour by hour I hasten to the grave;
and what have I perhaps,
have still, to live?
Think, O man, upon your death;
tarry not; for one thing is needful.


### 4 Die Ehre Gottes aus der Natur
Die Himmel rühmen des Ewigen Ehre,
Ihr Schall pflanzt seinen Namen fort.
Ihn rühmt der Erdkreis, ihn preisen die
    Meere,
Vernimm, o Mensch, ihr göttlich Wort!

### 4 The Glory of God in Nature
The heavens extol the glory of God,
their noise propagates His name.
The earth extols, the seas praise
    Him,
hearken, O man, to their Godly word!

Wer trägt der Himmel unzählbare
    Sterne?
Wer führt die Sonn' aus ihrem Zelt?
Sie kommt und leuchtet und lacht uns
    von ferne,
Und läuft den Weg, gleich als ein Held.

Who supports the heaven's countless
    stars?
Who leads the sun from its tabernacle?
It comes, gleams, laughs on us from
    afar,
and like a hero, runs its course.

*(Carl Philipp Emanuel Bach: Wq 194, no. 18, 1757/58)*


### 5 Gottes Macht und Vorsehung
Gott ist mein Lied!
Er ist der Gott der Stärke;
Hehr ist sein Nam', und groß sind seine
    Werke,
Und alle Himmel sein Gebiet.

### 5 God's Might and Providence
God is my song!
The God of might He is;
exalted His name, great His
    works,
and all the heavens are His sphere.


### 6 Bußlied
An dir allein, an dir hab ich gesündigt,
Und Übel oft vor dir getan.
Du siehst die Schuld, die mir den Fluch
    verkündigt;
Sieh, Gott, auch meinen Jammer an.

### 6 Song of Penitence
Against You, You alone I have sinned,
and done evil often in Your sight.
You see the sin which calls Your curse
    on me;
O God, see also my distress.

Dir ist mein Flehn, mein Seufzen nicht
    verborgen,
Und meine Tränen sind vor dir.
Ach Gott, mein Gott, wie lange soll ich
    sorgen?
Wie lang entfernst du dich von mir?

From You my prayers, my sighs are
    not hid,
and my tears are before You.
Ah, God, my God, how long am I to
    sorrow?
How long will You forsake me?

Herr, handle nicht mit mir nach meinen
    Sünden,
Vergilt mir nicht nach meiner Schuld.
Ich suche dich; laß mich dein Antlitz
    finden,
Du Gott der Langmut und Geduld.

Lord, treat me not according to my
    sins,
reward me not according to my guilt.
You I seek. Grant that I see Your
    face,
God of patience and forbearance.

Früh wollst du mich mit deiner Gnade
füllen,
Gott, Vater der Barmherzigkeit.
Erfreue mich um deines Namens willen;
Du bist ein Gott, der gern erfreut.

Laß deinen Weg mich wieder freudig
wallen,
Und lehre mich dein heilig Recht,
Mich täglich tun nach deinem
Wohlgefallen;
Du bist mein Gott, ich bin dein Knecht.

Herr, eile du, mein Schutz, mir
beizustehen,
Und leite mich auf ebner Bahn.
Er hört mein Schrei'n, der Herr erhört
mein Flehen,
Und nimmt sich meiner Seelen an.

May you fill me early with Your
grace,
God, Father of Mercy.
For Your name's sake comfort me;
a God You are who gladly comforts.

Let me again walk Your path in
joy,
teach me Your holy law,
to fashion myself daily to Your
will;
my God You are, I am Your servant.

Lord, my refuge, hasten to my
aid,
and guide me on the level way.
The Lord hears my cries, my
prayer,
and takes care of my soul.

(*Carl Philipp Emanuel Bach: Wq 194, no. 45, 1757–58*)


## Sehnsucht | Longing

FRIEDRICH SCHILLER

*Franz Schubert, ca. 1819*

Ach, aus dieses Tales Gründen,
Die der kalte Nebel drückt,
Könnt ich doch den Ausgang finden,
Ach wie fühlt ich mich beglückt!
Dort erblick ich schöne Hügel,
Ewig jung und ewig grün!
Hätt ich Schwingen, hätt ich Flügel,
Nach den Hügeln zög ich hin.

Harmonien hör ich klingen,
Töne süßer Himmelsruh,
Und die leichten Winde bringen
Mir der Düfte Balsam zu,
Goldne Früchte seh ich glühen,
Winkend zwischen dunkelm Laub,
Und die Blumen, die dort blühen,
Werden keines Winters Raub.

Ach wie schön muß sichs ergehen
Dort im ewgen Sonnenschein,
Und die Luft auf jenen Höhen,
O wie labend muß sie sein!
Doch mir wehrt des Stromes Toben,
Der ergrimmt dazwischen braust,
Seine Wellen sind gehoben,
Daß die Seele mir ergraust.

Einen Nachen seh ich schwanken,
Aber ach! der Fährmann fehlt.
Frisch hinein und ohne Wanken,
Seine Segel sind beseelt.

Ah, if from this valley's depths,
where cold mist presses down,
I could but find the way,
ah, how happy I would feel!
Lovely hills I glimpse there,
ever young and ever green!
Had I pinions, had I wings,
to those hills would I fly.

Harmonies I hear ringing,
sounds of sweet heavenly peace,
and the light breezes carry
scents of balsam to me,
the glow of golden fruits I see
beckoning among dark foliage,
and the flowers that bloom there
shall be no winter's prey.

Ah, how fine must it be to walk
there in everlasting sunshine,
and the air upon those heights,
oh, how refreshing it must be!
But the raging waters hinder me
that roar grimly in between,
and their waves rise up so high
that my soul is filled with dread.

A boat I see tossing,
but ah, without a ferryman.
Quick, aboard without delay,
for its sails are full of life.

Du mußt glauben, du mußt wagen,
Denn die Götter leihn kein Pfand,
Nur ein Wunder kann dich tragen
In das schöne Wunderland.

You must believe must dare,
for the gods give no gage,
only a wonder can bear you
to that fair wonderland.

## Sehnsucht | Longing

DETLEV VON LILIENCRON

Hans Pfitzner: op. 10, no. 1, 1901; Richard Strauss: op. 32, no. 2, 1896

Ich ging den Weg entlang, der einsam
  lag,
Den stets allein ich gehe, jeden Tag.
Die Heide schweigt, das Feld ist
  menschenleer,
Der Wind nur webt im Knickbusch vor
  mir her.

I walked the path that lonely
  lay,
that ever alone, I walk each day.
Silent the heath, deserted the
  field,
in the hedge ahead stirs only
  wind.

Weit liegt vor mir die Straße
  ausgedehnt,
Es hat mein Herz nur dich ersehnt.
Und kämest du, ein Wunder wär's für
  mich,
Ich neigte mich vor dir: Ich liebe dich.

Stretched far before me lies the
  road,
solely for you my heart has yearned;
and if you came, a miracle it would
  be,
to you I would bow: I love you.

Und im Begegnen nur ein einzger
  Blick,
Des ganzen Lebens wär es mein
  Geschick.
Und richtest du dein Auge kalt auf mich,
Ich trotze, Mädchen, dir: Ich liebe dich!

But a single glance, if we chanced to
  meet,
would be my whole life's
  destiny.
And if your eyes gaze upon me coldly,
I'll defy you, maiden: I love you!

Doch wenn dein schönes Auge grüßt
  und lacht,
Wie eine Sonne mir in schwerer Nacht,
Ich zöge rasch dein süßes Herz an
  mich
Und flüstre leise dir: Ich liebe dich.

But if your fair eyes greet me,
  laugh,
like a sun upon me in deep night,
I'd draw your sweet heart quick to
  mine,
and whisper to you softly: I love you.

## Sehnsucht | Yearning

JOHANN WOLFGANG GOETHE

Ludwig van Beethoven: op. 83, no. 2, 1811; Franz Schubert: op. 37, 1814

Was zieht mir das Herz so?
Was zieht mich hinaus?
Und windet und schraubt mich
Aus Zimmer und Haus?
Wie dort sich die Wolken
Um Felsen verziehn!
Da möcht ich hinüber,
Da möcht ich wohl hin!

What tugs so at my heart?
What pulls me outside?
What wrenches, wrests me
from room and house?
How, there, the clouds
disperse about the rocks!
Over them would I go,
thither would I go!

Nun wiegt sich der Raben
Geselliger Flug;

The ravens swing by
in companionable flight;

Ich mische mich drunter
Und folge dem Zug.
Und Berg und Gemäuer
Umfittichen wir;
Sie weilet da drunten,
Ich spähe nach ihr.

Da kommt sie und wandelt;
Ich eile sobald,
Ein singender Vogel,
Zum buschigen Wald.
Sie weilet und horchet
Und lächelt mit sich:
»Er singet so lieblich
Und singt es an mich.«

Die scheidende Sonne
Vergüldet die Höhn;
Die sinnende Schöne,
Sie läßt es geschehn.
Sie wandelt am Bache
Die Wiesen entlang,
Und finster und finstrer
Umschlingt sich der Gang;

Auf einmal erschein ich,
Ein blinkender Stern.
»Was glänzet da droben,
So nah und so fern?«
Und hast du mit Staunen
Das Leuchten erblickt,
Ich lieg dir zu Füßen,
Da bin ich beglückt!

I mingle with them,
and follow their course.
And mountain and ruin,
about them we wing;
below there she tarries,
for her I keep watch.

Now she comes walking;
I hasten at once,
a bird in song,
to the bushy wood.
She lingers and listens
and smiles to herself:
'He sings so sweetly,
and for me he sings.'

The sun, departing,
makes golden the hills;
that pensive fair one
lets it be so.
She walks by the brook,
over the meadows,
and darker and darker
the path twists its way;

all at once I appear,
a shining star.
'What glitters up there,
so near and so far?'
And when, with amazement,
you've sighted the gleam,
I will lie at your feet,
and be content!

## Sehnsucht nach dem Frühling | Yearning for Spring

CHRISTIAN ADOLF OVERBECK

*Wolfgang Amadeus Mozart: K 596, 1791*

Komm, lieber Mai, und mache
Die Bäume wieder grün,
Und laß mir an dem Bache
Die kleinen Veilchen blühn!
Wie möcht ich doch so gerne
Ein Veilchen wieder sehn,
Ach, lieber Mai, wie gerne
Einmal spazieren gehn!

Zwar Wintertage haben
Wohl auch der Freuden viel;
Man kann im Schnee eins traben
Und treibt manch Abendspiel,
Baut Häuserchen von Karten,
Spielt Blindekuh und Pfand;
Auch gibt's wohl Schlittenfahrten
Aufs liebe freie Land.

Come, dear May, and make
green again the trees,
and for me by the brook let
the tiny violets bloom.
So much would I like
to see again a violet,
ah, dear May, so much
to take a stroll.

True, winter days have
also many pleasures:
trotting in the snow,
lots of evening pastimes,
building card-houses,
blindman's buff, forfeits,
and sleigh-rides too
into the dear open country.

Doch wenn die Vöglein singen
Und wir dann froh und flink
Auf grünen Rasen springen,
Das ist ein ander Ding!
Jetzt muß mein Steckenpferdchen
Dort in dem Winkel stehn;
Denn draußen in dem Gärtchen
Kann man vor Kot nicht gehn.

Am meisten aber dauert
Mich Lottchens Herzeleid;
Das arme Mädchen lauert
Recht auf die Blumenzeit;
Umsonst hol ich ihr Spielchen
Zum Zeitvertreib herbei,
Sie sitzt in ihrem Stühlchen
Wie's Hühnchen auf dem Ei.

Ach, wenn's doch erst gelinder
Und grüner draußen wär!
Komm, lieber Mai, wir Kinder,
Wir bitten dich gar sehr!
O komm und bring vor allen
Uns viele Veilchen mit,
Bring auch viel Nachtigallen
Und schöne Kuckucks mit!

But when the birds sing
and then, gay and nimble,
we leap upon the greens,
that's different!
Now my hobby horse must
stand in the corner there;
for outside in the garden
one cannot walk for mud.

But most of all I'm sorry
for Lotte's heart-ache;
the poor girl's watching out
for flowers to come;
in vain I bring her toys
to while away the time,
in her little chair she sits
like a hen on its egg.

Ah, were it only milder
and greener out of doors!
Come, dear May, we children
really beg you!
O come, and above all bring
us lots of violets,
lots of nightingales
and lovely cuckoos too!

*Sehnsucht nach der Waldgegend | Longing for the Forest*

JUSTINUS KERNER

*Robert Schumann: op. 35, no. 5, 1840*

Wär' ich nie aus euch gegangen,
Wälder, hehr und wunderbar!
Hieltet liebend mich umfangen
Doch so lange, lange Jahr'!

Wo in euren Dämmerungen
Vogelsang und Silberquell,
Ist auch manches Lied entsprungen
Meinem Busen, frisch und hell.

Euer Wogen, euer Hallen,
Euer Säuseln nimmer müd',
Eure Melodien alle
Weckten in der Brust das Lied.

Hier in diesen weiten Triften
Ist mir alles öd' und stumm,
Und ich schau in blauen Lüften
Mich nach Wolkenbildern um.

Wenn ihr's in den Busen zwinget,
Regt sich selten nur das Lied:
Wie der Vogel halb nur singet,
Den von Baum und Blatt man schied.

Would I had never gone from you,
majestic, wondrous forest!
You embraced me lovingly
for so many a long, long year!

Where, in your twilight places,
was birdsong and silver stream,
there sprang also many a song
fresh and bright from my breast.

Your surging, your echoing,
your never-tiring murmur,
your melodies, all of them,
awoke within me song.

Here, in these wide pastures,
all is desolate and mute,
and in the blue air I search
for cloudy shapes.

With you to compel it in my breast,
song but seldom stirs:
like the mere half-song of the bird
parted from tree and leaf.

## Sei mir gegrüßt | I Greet You

FRIEDRICH RÜCKERT

*Franz Schubert: op. 20, no. 1, 1822*

O du Entrißne mir und meinem Kusse,
Sei mir gegrüßt, sei mir geküßt!
Erreichbar nur meinem Sehnsuchts-
  gruße,
Sei mir gegrüßt, sei mir geküßt!

Du von der Hand der Liebe diesem
  Herzen
Gegebne, du von dieser
Brust Genommne mir! Mit diesem
  Tränengusse
Sei mir gegrüßt, sei mir geküßt!

Zum Trotz der Ferne, die sich feindlich
  trennend
Hat zwischen mich und dich gestellt;
Dem Neid der Schicksalsmächte zum
  Verdrusse
Sei mir gegrüßt, sei mir geküßt!

Wie du mir je im schönsten Lenz der
  Liebe
Mit Gruß und Kuß entgegenkamst,
Mit meiner Seele glühendstem
  Ergusse,
Sei mir gegrüßt, sei mir geküßt!

Ein Hauch der Liebe tilget Raum und
  Zeiten,
Ich bin bei dir, du bist bei mir,
Ich halte dich in dieses Arms
  Umschlusse,
Sei mir gegrüßt, sei mir geküßt!

O you, snatched from me and my kiss,
I greet, I kiss you!
O you, reached only by my longing
  greeting,
I greet, I kiss you!

You, by love's hand to this
  heart
given, you who from my
breast are taken! With this flood of
  tears
I greet, I kiss you!

To defy the distance, hostile and
  dividing,
come between you and me;
to vex the envious powers of
  fate,
I greet, I kiss you!

As ever you, in love's fairest
  spring,
came out to me with greeting and a kiss,
so with my soul's most ardent
  outpouring
I greet, I kiss you!

A breath of love effaces space and
  time,
I am with you, you are with me,
I hold you in my arms'
  embrace,
I greet, I kiss you!

## Selbstgefühl | Self-confidence

from *Des Knaben Wunderhorn*

*Gustav Mahler, ca. 1880–83*

Ich weiß nicht, wie mir ist!
Ich bin nicht krank und nicht gesund,
Ich bin blessiert und hab' kein' Wund.

Ich weiß nicht, wie mir ist!
Ich tät' gern essen und schmeckt mir
  nichts;
Ich hab' ein Geld und gilt mir nichts.

Ich weiß nicht, wie mir ist!
Ich hab' so gar kein' Schnupftabak
und hab' kein' Kreuzer Geld im Sack.

I do not know what's wrong with me!
I am not sick and am not well,
I'm hurt, yet have no wound.

I do not know what's wrong with me!
Gladly I eat, but nothing
  tastes;
I've money—to me it's worthless.

I do not know what's wrong with me!
Not even a pinch of snuff have I
or penny in my purse.

Ich weiß nicht, wie mir ist.
Heiraten tät' ich auch schon gern,
Kann aber Kinderschrei'n nicht hör'n.

Ich weiß nicht, wie mir ist.
Ich hab' erst heut' den Doktor gefragt,
Der hat mir in's Gesicht gesagt:

Ich weiß wohl, was dir ist:
Ein Narr bist du gewiß.
Nun weiß ich, wie mir ist.

I do not know what's wrong with me.
Gladly also would I marry,
except I can't stand crying kids.

I do not know what's wrong with me.
I asked the doctor just today,
and to my face he told me:

I can tell you what's wrong with you:
a fool is what you are for sure.
So what the matter is, I now know.

## Seligkeit | Bliss

LUDWIG CHRISTOPH HEINRICH HÖLTY

*Franz Schubert, 1816*

Freuden sonder Zahl!
Blühn im Himmelssaal!
Engeln und Verklärten,
Wie die Väter lehrten.
O, da möcht ich sein
Und mich ewig freun!

Jedem lächelt traut
Eine Himmelsbraut;
Harf und Psalter klinget,
Und man tanzt und singet.
O, da möcht ich sein
Und mich ewig freun!

Lieber bleib ich hier,
Lächelt Laura mir
Einen Blick, der saget,
Daß ich ausgeklaget.
Selig dann mit ihr,
Bleib ich ewig hier!

Joys without number
bloom in Heaven's hall
for angels and transfigured,
as our fathers taught.
Oh, there would I be,
and rejoice eternally!

Sweetly upon all smiles
a heavenly bride;
harp and psalter sound,
and all dance and sing.
Oh, there would I be,
and rejoice eternally!

Here I'll rather stay
if Laura look my way,
and give a look that says
I've to lament no more.
Blissful then with her,
I'll stay ever here!

## Sie haben heut' abend Gesellschaft | This Evening They've a Party

HEINRICH HEINE

*Hans Pfitzner: op. 4, no. 2, 1888–89; Hugo Wolf, 1878*

Sie haben heut' abend Gesellschaft
Und das Haus ist lichterfüllt.
Dort oben am hohen Fenster
Bewegt sich ein Schattenbild.

Du siehst mich nicht, im Dunkeln
Steh' ich hier unten allein,
Noch weniger kannst du schauen
In mein dunkles Herz hinein.

Mein dunkles Herze liebt dich,
Es liebt dich und es bricht,
Es bricht und zuckt und verblutet,
Du aber siehst es nicht.

This evening they've a party,
the house is a blaze of light.
Up there, by the tall window,
moves a silhouette.

You do not see me in the dark,
down here I stand alone;
still less are you able to look
into my sombre heart.

My sombre heart, it loves you,
and, loving you, it breaks,
breaks, convulses, bleeds away,
but unseen by you.

*Sieben frühe Lieder | Seven Early Songs*

no. 1: CARL HAUPTMANN
no. 2: NIKOLAS LENAU
no. 3: THEODOR STORM
no. 4: RAINER MARIA RILKE
no. 5: JOHANNES SCHLAF
no. 6: OTTO ERICH HARTLEBEN
no. 7: PAUL HOHENBERG

*Alban Berg, 1907*

1 *Nacht*
Dämmern Wolken über Nacht und
  Tal,
Nebel schweben, Wasser rauschen sacht.
Nun entschleiert sich's mit einemmal:
O gib acht! Gib acht!
Weites Wunderland ist aufgetan.
Silbern ragen Berge, traumhaft groß,
still Pfade silberlicht
  talan
aus verborg'nem Schoß;
und die hehre Welt so traumhaft rein.
Stummer Buchenbaum am Wege steht
schattenschwarz, ein Hauch vom fernen
  Hain
einsam leise weht.
Und aus tiefen Grundes Düsterheit
blinken Lichter auf in stummer Nacht.
Trinke Seele! Trinke Einsamkeit!
O gib acht! Gib acht!

1 *Night*
Over night and vale the clouds grow
  dark,
mists hover, waters softly murmur.
Now, of a sudden, an unveiling:
oh, give heed, give heed!
A vast wonderland opens.
Silver soar mountains, dream-large,
still paths, silver-bright, go
  valleywards
from the hidden castle;
and so dream-pure is the lofty world.
A mute beech tree stands by the way,
shadow-black; from the distant wood a
  breath
blows solitary soft.
And from the deep valley's gloom
lights flash in the silent night.
Drink, soul. Drink solitude!
Oh, give heed! Give heed!

2 *Schilflied*
Auf geheimem Waldespfade
Schleich' ich gern im Abendschein
An das öde Schilfgestade,
Mädchen, und gedenke dein!

Wenn sich dann der Busch verdüstert,
Rauscht das Rohr geheimnisvoll,
Und es klaget und es flüstert,
Daß ich weinen, weinen soll.

Und ich mein', ich höre wehen
Leise deiner Stimme Klang,
Und im Weiher untergehen
Deinen lieblichen Gesang.

2 *Reed Song*
By a secret forest path
I love to steal in evening light,
to the desolate reedy shore
and think, maiden, of you.

Then when the wood grows dark,
the reeds rustle mysteriously,
lamenting and whispering
that I should weep, weep.

And I think I hear wafting
softly the sound of your voice,
and, drowning in the pond,
your sweet singing.

3 *Die Nachtigall*
Das macht, es hat die Nachtigall
Die ganze Nacht gesungen;
Da sind von ihrem süßen Schall,
Da sind im Hall und Widerhall
Die Rosen aufgesprungen.
Sie war doch sonst ein wildes Blut,
Nun geht sie tief in Sinnen,

3 *The Nightingale*
It is because the nightingale
all night has sung;
and from her sweet noise,
in echo and re-echo
roses have sprung.
Such a wild thing she was once,
now she wanders deeply pensive,

Trägt in der Hand den Sommerhut
Und duldet still der Sonne Glut
Und weiß nicht, was beginnen.
Das macht, es hat die Nachtigall,
Die ganze Nacht gesungen;
Da sind von ihrem süßen Schall,
Da sind im Hall und Widerhall
Die Rosen aufgesprungen.

her summer hat in hand,
and bears in silence the glow of the sun
and knows not what to do.
It is because the nightingale
all night has sung;
and from her sweet noise,
in echo and re-echo
roses have sprung.

4 *Traumgekrönt**
Das war der Tag der weißen
  Chrysanthemen,
mir bangte fast vor seiner
  Pracht . . .
Und dann, dann kamst du mir die Seele
  nehmen
tief in der Nacht.

4 *Dream-crowned*
That was the day of white
  chrysanthemums,
its splendour made me feel almost
  afraid . . .
And then you came to take my soul
  from me
at dead of night.

Mir war so bang, und du kamst lieb und
  leise,
ich hatte grad im Traum an dich
  gedacht,
du kamst, und leis' wie eine
  Märchenweise
erklang die Nacht.

I was so afraid, yet you came sweetly
  softly,
I had been thinking of you in my
  dreams,
you came, and soft as a fairy
  tune
the night sounded.

5 *Im Zimmer*
Herbstsonnenschein.
Der liebe Abend blickt still herein.
Ein Feuerlein rot
knistert im Ofenloch und loht.
So, mein Kopf auf deinen Knie'n,
so ist mir gut,
wenn mein Auge so in deinem ruht,
wie leise die Minuten zieh'n.

5 *In the Room*
Autumn sunshine.
Fair evening looks silent in.
Red fire
blazing, crackling in the stove.
Thus, with my head on your knees,
thus I am content,
my gaze reposed in yours,
as the minutes gently pass.

6 *Liebesode*
Im Arm der Liebe schliefen wir selig
  ein,
Am offnen Fenster lauschte der
  Sommerwind,
Und unsrer Atemzüge Frieden trug er
  hinaus in die helle Mondnacht.
Und aus dem Garten tastete zagend sich
  ein Rosenduft an unserer Liebe
  Bett
Und gab uns wundervolle Träume,
Träume des Rausches, so reich an
  Sehnsucht.

6 *Love Ode*
Blissful in love's arms we fell
  asleep,
the summer wind watched at the open
  window,
and bore out the peace of our every
  breath to the moon-bright night.
And from the garden, feeling its timid
  way, a scent of roses to our love bed
  came
and gave us wondrous dreams,
ecstatic dreams, so rich in
  longing.

(*Joseph Marx: Lieder and Songs, 3rd Series, no. 9*)

* The German copyright holder has requested the English-language publisher to point out that
this translation has been made specifically as reference for singers.

7 *Sommertage*
Nun ziehen Tage über die Welt,
gesandt aus blauer Ewigkeit,
im Sommerwind verweht die Zeit,
nun windet nächtens der Herr
Sternenkränze mit seliger Hand
über Wander- und Wunderland.
O Herz, was kann in diesen Tagen
dein hellstes Wanderleid denn sagen
von deiner tiefen, tiefen Lust:
Im Wiesensang verstummt die Brust,
nun schweigt das Wort, wo Bild um
    Bild
zu dir zieht und dich ganz erfüllt.

7 *Summer Days*
Through the world now travel days
sent forth from blue eternity,
in the summer breeze, time drifts away,
the Lord at night now twines
with blessed hand, garlands of stars
above wander- and wonderland.
O heart, what, in these days, can
your clearest wanderer's song then say
of your very deep delight:
in the meadow's song the heart is dumb,
words cease where image upon
    image
comes to you and fills you wholly.

## *Singet nicht in Trauertönen* | *Sing Not in Mournful Tones*

(Philine's Song)

JOHANN WOLFGANG GOETHE: from *Wilhelm Meister*

*Robert Schumann: op. 98a, no. 7, 1841; Hugo Wolf, 1888*

Singet nicht in Trauertönen
Von der Einsamkeit der Nacht,
Nein, sie ist, o holde Schönen,
Zur Geselligkeit gemacht.

Sing not in mournful tones
of the solitude of night;
no, sweet fair ones, night
was made for company.

Wie das Weib dem Mann gegeben
als die schönste Hälfte war,
ist die Nacht das halbe Leben,
und die schönste Hälfte zwar.

As woman was given to man
to be his better half,
so is night half of life—
and the better half.

Könnt ihr euch des Tages freuen,
Der nur Freuden unterbricht?
Er ist gut, sich zu zerstreuen,
Zu was anderm taugt er nicht.

Can you rejoice in day
which does but interrupt joy?
Good it is for distraction,
but serves for nothing else.

Aber wenn in nächtger Stunde
Süßer Lampe Dämmrung fließt,
Und vom Mund zum nahen Munde
Scherz und Liebe sich ergießt;

But when, at the nocturnal hour,
the sweet lamp's twilight flows,
and from one near mouth to another
jest and love pour forth;

Wenn der rasche, lose Knabe,
Der sonst wild und feurig eilt,
Oft bei einer kleinen Gabe
Unter leichten Spielen weilt;

when that hasty, roguish lad,
who's wont wildly, ardently to speed,
often, over a small gift,
lingers lightly sporting;

Wenn die Nachtigall Verliebten
Liebevoll ein Liedchen singt,
Das Gefangnen und Betrübten
Nur wie Ach und Wehe klingt:

when, to lovers, the nightingale
sings lovingly a little song
which, to those captive and troubled,
sounds only like grief and woe:

Mit wie leichtem Herzensregen
Horchet ihr der Glocke nicht,
Die mit zwölf bedächtgen Schlägen
Ruh und Sicherheit verspricht.

with what lightly stirring heart
do you harken to the bell
that, with twelve cautious strokes,
pledges peace and security.

Darum an dem langen Tage,
Merke dir es, liebe Brust:
Jeder Tag hat seine Plage
Und die Nacht hat ihre Lust.

Therefore, in the long day,
dear heart, take note:
every day has its torment,
and the night its joy.


## So laßt mich scheinen | So Let Me Seem

(Mignon's Song)

JOHANN WOLFGANG GOETHE: from *Wilhelm Meister*

*Franz Schubert: op. 62, no. 3, 1826; Robert Schumann: op. 98a, no. 9, 1841;
Hugo Wolf, 1888*

So laßt mich scheinen, bis ich werde;
Zieht mir das weiße Kleid nicht aus!
Ich eile von der schönen Erde
Hinab in jenes feste Haus.

So let me seem, until I am;
strip not my white robe from me!
from the lovely earth I hasten
down into that sure house.

Dort ruh ich eine kleine Stille,
Dann öffnet sich der frische Blick,
Ich lasse dann die reine Hülle,
Den Gürtel und den Kranz zurück.

There in brief repose I'll rest,
then my fresh eyes will open,
my pure raiment then I'll leave,
with girdle, rosary, behind.

Und jene himmlischen Gestalten,
Sie fragen nicht nach Mann und Weib,
Und keine Kleider, keine Falten
Umgeben den verklärten Leib.

And those forms who are in heaven
ask not who is man or woman,
and no robes, no folds
enclose the transfigured body.

Zwar lebt ich ohne Sorg und Mühe,
Doch fühlt ich tiefen Schmerz genung.
Vor Kummer altert ich zu frühe—
Macht mich auf ewig wieder jung!

True, I lived free of sorrow, toil,
yet I feel deep pain enough.
Too early I grew old with grief—
make me forever young again!


## So wahr die Sonne scheinet | Truly as the Sun Shines

FRIEDRICH RÜCKERT

*Robert Schumann: op. 37, no. 12, 1840*

So wahr die Sonne scheinet,
So wahr die Wolke weinet,
So wahr die Flamme sprüht,
So wahr der Frühling blüht;
So wahr hab' ich empfunden,
Wie ich dich halt' umwunden:
Du liebst mich, wie ich dich,
Dich lieb' ich, wie du mich.

Truly as the sun shines,
truly as the cloud weeps,
truly as flame flashes,
truly as spring blossoms;
as truly I did feel
holding you embraced:
you love me, as I you,
you I love, as you me.

Die Sonne mag verscheinen,
Die Wolke nicht mehr weinen,
Die Flamme mag versprühn,
Der Frühling nicht mehr blühn!
Wir wollen uns umwinden
Und immer so empfinden;
Du liebst mich, wie ich dich,
Dich lieb' ich, wie du mich.

The sun may cease to shine,
the cloud may weep no more,
the flame may flash and die,
the spring—blossom no more!
Let us embrace
and so feel forever;
you love me, as I you,
you I love, as you me.

## Sommerabend / Summer Evening

HEINRICH HEINE

*Johannes Brahms: op. 85, no. 1, 1879*

Dämmernd liegt der Sommerabend
Über Wald und grünen Wiesen;
Goldner Mond am blauen Himmel,
Strahlt herunter, duftig labend.

An dem Bache zirpt die Grille,
Und es regt sich in dem Wasser,
Und der Wandrer hört ein Plätschern
Und ein Atmen in der Stille.

Dorten an dem Bach alleine,
Badet sich die schöne Elfe;
Arm und Nacken, weiß und lieblich,
Schimmern in dem Mondenscheine.

Dusky lies summer evening
over forest and green meadow;
from blue sky a golden moon
shines fragrant, reviving, down.

By the brook the cricket chirps,
there is a stirring in the water,
the wanderer hears a splashing
and a breathing in the stillness.

There, by the brook, alone,
the fair elf bathes;
arms and neck, white and lovely,
shimmer in the moonlight.

## Sommerabend / Summer Night

HANS SCHMIDT

*Johannes Brahms: op. 84, no. 1, 1881*

Geh' schlafen, Tochter, schlafen!
Schon fällt der Tau aufs Gras,
Und wen die Tropfen trafen,
Weint bald die Augen naß!

»Laß weinen, Mutter, weinen!
Das Mondlicht leuchtet hell,
Und wem die Strahlen scheinen,·
Dem trocknen Tränen schnell!«

Geh' schlafen, Tochter, schlafen!
Schon ruft der Kauz im Wald,
Und wen die Töne trafen,
muß mit ihm klagen bald.

»Laß klagen, Mutter, klagen!
Die Nachtigall singt hell,
Und wem die Lieder schlagen,
Dem schwindet Trauer schnell.«

Go to sleep, daughter, go to sleep!
Upon the grass falls the dew,
and whoever the drops have fallen on,
soon floods his eyes with tears!

'Stop weeping, mother, stop weeping!
The moon is shining bright,
and whoever the moonbeams shine on,
his tears will very soon dry!'

Go to sleep, daughter, go to sleep!
In the wood the screech-owl screams,
and whoever has heard those noises,
must soon wail as well.

'Stop wailing, mother, stop wailing!
The nightingale's singing clear,
and whoever those songs sound for.
his sadness very soon fades.'

## Sonne der Schlummerlosen / Sun of the Sleepless

GEORGE GORDON NOEL LORD BYRON: from *Hebrew Melodies*
translated by OTTO GILDEMEISTER

*Hugo Wolf, 1896*

Sonne der Schlummerlosen, bleicher
    Stern!
Wie Tränen zittern, schimmerst du von
    fern;

Sun of the sleepless, pallid
    star!
Like trembling tears you shimmer
    afar;

du zeigst die Nacht, doch scheust sie
 nicht zurück,
wie ähnlich bist du dem entschwundnen
 Glück,
dem Licht vergang'ner Tage, das
 fortan
nur leuchten, aber nimmer wärmen
 kann!
Die Trauer wacht, wie es durchs Dunkel
 wallt,
deutlich, doch fern, hell, aber o, wie
 kalt!

you point to night but do not banish
 it,
how alike you are to vanished
 joy,
to the light of days past which,
 henceforth,
can only shine but never
 warm!
Grief watches as the light wanders
 the dark,
distinct but distant; clear, but oh,
 how cold!


## Sonntag / Sunday

LUDWIG UHLAND

*Johannes Brahms: op. 47, no. 3, 1868; Max Reger: op. 98, no. 3, 1906*

So hab' ich doch die ganze Woche
Mein feines Liebchen nicht gesehn,
Ich sah es an einem Sonntag
Wohl vor der Türe stehn:
Das tausendschöne Jungfräulein,
Das tausendschöne Herzelein,
Wollte Gott, ich wär heute bei ihr!

So all the week I've not
seen my dear love,
on a Sunday I saw her
standing at her door:
my darling love,
my darling sweet,
would God, I were with her today!

So will mir doch die ganze Woche
Das Lachen nicht vergehn,
Ich sah es an einem Sonntag
Wohl in die Kirche gehn:
Das tausendschöne Jungfräulein,
Das tausendschöne Herzelein,
Wollte Gott, ich wär heute bei ihr!

So all the week I'll not
cease to laugh,
on a Sunday I saw her
going to church:
my darling love,
my darling sweet,
would God, I were with her today!


## Sonst / In Other Times

JOSEPH VON EICHENDORFF

*Hans Pfitzner: op. 15, no. 4, 1904*

Es glänzt der Tulpenflor, durchschnitten
 von Alleen,
Wo zwischen Taxus still die weißen
 Statuen stehen,
Mit goldnen Kugeln spielt die
 Wasserkunst im Becken,
Im Laube lauert Sphinx, anmutig zu
 erschrecken.

The tulips, cut through by avenues,
 gleam
where, amongst yew, white statues
 stand;
with golden spheres the artful fountain
 sports
and Sphinx haunts the arbour, sweetly
 to alarm.

Die schöne Chloe heut spazieret in dem
 Garten,
Zur Seit' ein Kavalier, ihr höflich
 aufzuwarten,
Und hinter ihnen leis Cupido kommt
 gezogen,
Bald duckend sich im Grün, bald
 zielend mit dem Bogen.

Today fair Chloe walks in the
 garden,
a gentleman beside her in polite
 attendance,
and, behind, softly stealing, Cupid
 comes,
now hiding in verdure, now aiming
 his bow.

Es neigt der Kavalier sich in galantem
  Kosen,
Mit ihrem Fächer schlägt sie manchmal
  nach dem Losen,
Es rauscht der taftne Rock, es blitzen
  seine Schnallen,
Dazwischen hört man oft ein art'ges
  Lachen schallen.

Jetzt aber hebt vom Schloß, da sich's
  im West will röten,
Die Spieluhr schmachtend an, ein
  Menuett zu flöten,
Die Laube ist so still, er wirft sein Tuch
  zur Erde
Und stürzet auf ein Knie mit zärtlicher
  Gebärde.

»Wie wird mir, ach, ach, ach, es fängt
  schon an zu dunkeln—«
»So angenehmer nur seh' ich zwei
  Sterne funkeln—«
»Verwegner Kavalier!«—»Ha, Chloe,
  darf ich hoffen?«—
Da schießt Cupido los und hat sie gut
  getroffen.

The gentleman, fondly gallant, bows
  low,
she, with her fan, several times strikes
  the rogue,
her taffeta rustles, his buckles
  flash,
often a pretty laugh rings
  out.

But from the château now, in the
  westering sun,
a musical box plays a languorous
  minuet;
the arbour's so still, he casts his
  kerchief down,
and kneels with tender
  gesture.

'My feelings, ah, how it grows
  dark—'
'All the better two bright stars I
  see—'
'Audacious one!'—'Ah, Chloe, may I
  hope?'
Then Cupid fires, and hits his targets
  well.


*Spanisches Liederbuch* / *Spanish Song-book*

EMANUEL GEIBEL and PAUL HEYSE: after Spanish Folk-songs

*Hugo Wolf, 1889*

I. *Geistliche Lieder*

1

Nun bin ich dein,
Du aller Blumen Blume,
Und sing allein
Allstund zu deinem Ruhme;
Will eifrig sein,
Mich dir zu weihn
Und deinem Duldertume.

Frau auserlesen,
Zur dir steht all mein Hoffen,
Mein innerst Wesen
Ist allezeit dir offen.
Komm, mich zu lösen
Vom Fluch des Bösen,
Der mich so hart betroffen!

Du Stern der See,
Du Port der Wonnen,
Von der im Weh
Die Wunden Heil gewonnen,
Eh ich vergeh,
Blick aus der Höh,
Du Königin der Sonnen!

I *Spiritual songs*

1

Now am I yours,
Flower of all Flowers,
and sing solely
at all times to your praise;
I will be zealous,
dedicate myself to you
and to your sufferance.

Lady Elect,
in you is all my hope,
my innermost being
is forever open to you.
Come, free me
from the curse of the Evil One
who has so sore afflicted me!

Star of the Sea,
Haven of Delights,
from whom, in agony,
the afflicted have found salvation,
before I pass away,
look from on high,
Queen of Suns!

Nie kann versiegen
Die Fülle deiner Gnaden;
Du hilfst zum Siegen
Dem, der mit Schmach beladen.
An dich sich schmiegen,
Zu deinen Füßen liegen,
Heilt allen Harm und Schaden.

Ich leide schwer
Und wohlverdiente Strafen.
Mir bangt so sehr,
Bald Todesschlaf zu schlafen.
Tritt du einher,
Und durch das Meer
O führe mich zum Hafen!

2
Die du Gott gebarst, du Reine,
Und alleine
Uns gelöst aus unsern Ketten,
Mach mich fröhlich, der ich weine,
Denn nur deine
Huld und Gnade mag uns retten.

Herrin, ganz zu dir mich wende,
Daß sich ende
Diese Qual und dieses Grauen,
Daß der Tod mich furchtlos fände,
Und nicht blende
Mich das Licht der Himmelsauen.

Weil du unbefleckt geboren,
Auserkoren
Zu des ewgen Ruhmes Stätten—
Wie mich Leiden auch umfloren,
Unverloren
Bin ich doch, willst du mich retten.

3 *Der heilige Joseph singt*
Nun wandre, Maria,
Nun wandre nur fort.
Schon krähen die Hähne,
Und nah ist der Ort.

Nun wandre, Geliebte,
Du Kleinod mein,
Und balde wir werden
In Bethlehem sein.
Dann ruhest du fein
Und schlummerst dort.
Schon krähen die Hähne
Und nah ist der Ort.

Wohl seh ich, Herrin,
Die Kraft dir schwinden;
Kann deine Schmerzen,
Ach, kaum verwinden.
Getrost! Wohl finden
Wir Herberg dort.
Schon krähen die Hähne
Und nah ist der Ort.

Never can the abundance
of your mercy run dry;
you help towards triumph
him who is laden with shame.
To cling to you,
to lie at your feet,
heals all infirmity and grief.

I suffer severe
and well-merited punishments.
I am in such dread
of sleeping soon death's sleep.
Come forth,
and through the sea,
bring me, oh, to harbour!

2
You who bore God, Pure One
and alone
delivered us from our chains,
make me, who weep, glad,
for only your
grace and mercy can deliver us.

Lady, incline me to you entirely,
that it should end,
this torment and dread,
that death should find me unafraid,
and I be not blinded
by the light of the Heavenly Pastures.

Because you were born immaculate,
chosen
for abodes of eternal glory—
however much veiled in sorrow,
not lost
am I, if you will deliver me.

3 *Saint Joseph Sings*
Onward, now, Mary,
just onward, now, on,
the cocks are crowing,
and the place is near.

Onward now, beloved,
my jewel,
and soon shall we be
in Bethlehem.
Then shall you rest well
there, and slumber.
The cocks are crowing,
and the place is near.

Well I see, Lady,
your strength is waning;
your pains I cannot,
alas, subdue.
Take heart! We shall find
lodging there.
The cocks are crowing
and the place is near.

Wär erst bestanden
Dein Stündlein, Marie,
Die gute Botschaft,
Gut lohnt ich sie.
Das Eselein hie
Gäb ich drum fort!
Schon krähen die Hähne,
Komm! Nah ist der Ort.


4
Die ihr schwebet
Um diese Palmen
In Nacht und Wind,
Ihr heilgen Engel,
Stillet die Wipfel!
Es schlummert mein Kind.

Ihr Palmen von Bethlehem
Im Windesbrausen,
Wie mögt ihr heute
So zornig sausen!
O rauscht nicht also!
Schweiget, neiget
Euch leis und lind;
Stillet die Wipfel!
Es schlummert mein Kind.

Der Himmelsknabe
Duldet Beschwerde,
Ach, wie so müd er ward
Vom Leid der Erde.
Ach nun im Schlaf ihm
Leise gesänftigt
Die Qual zerrinnt,
Stillet die Wipfel!
Es schlummert mein Kind.

Grimmige Kälte
Sauset hernieder,
Womit nur deck ich
Des Kindleins Glieder!
O all ihr Engel,
Die ihr geflügelt
Wandelt im Wind,
Stillet die Wipfel!
Es schlummert mein Kind.

5
Führ mich, Kind, nach Bethlehem!
Dich, mein Gott, dich will ich sehn.
Wem geläng es, wem,
Ohne dich zu dir zu gehn!

Rüttle mich, daß ich erwache,
Rufe mich, so will ich schreiten;
Gib die Hand mir, mich zu leiten,
Daß ich auf den Weg mich mache.

Would it were over,
Mary, your hour,
those good tidings
would I reward well.
The donkey here
would I give for that!
The cocks are crowing,
come! The place is near.


4
You who hover
about these palms,
in night and wind,
Holy Angels,
silence their leaves!
My child's asleep.

Palms of Bethlehem
in blustering wind,
how can you today
so angrily blow!
Oh, roar not so.
Be still, bow
softly and gently;
silence the leaves!
My child's asleep.

The Son of Heaven
is suffering;
ah, so tired has He grown
of earth's sorrows.
Ah, now, in sleep,
gently softened,
the pain melts away.
Silence the leaves!
My child's asleep.

Fierce cold
comes rushing;
with what shall I cover
the little child's limbs!
O All you Angels
who, winged,
travel on the wind,
silence the leaves!
My child is asleep.

5
Lead me, child, to Bethlehem!
You, my God, You will I see.
Who, who could manage
to come to You, without Your aid!

Shake me, so that I awake,
call me, out will I step;
give me your hand to guide me,
that I may set out,

Daß ich schaue Bethlehem,
Dorten meinen Gott zu sehn.
Wem geläng es, wem,
Ohne dich zu dir zu gehn!

Von der Sünde schwerem Kranken
Bin ich träg und dumpf beklommen.
Willst du nicht zu Hilfe kommen,
Muß ich straucheln, muß ich
    schwanken.
Leite mich nach Bethlehem,
Dich, mein Gott, dich will ich sehn.
Wem geläng es, wem,
Ohne dich zu dir zu gehn!

6

Ach, des Knaben Augen sind
Mir so schön und klar erschienen,
Und ein Etwas strahlt aus ihnen,
Das mein ganzes Herz gewinnt.

Blickt er doch mit diesen süßen
Augen nach den meinen hin!
Säh er dann sein Bild darin,
Würd er wohl mich liebend grüßen.
Und so geb ich ganz mich hin,
Seinen Augen nur zu dienen,
Denn ein Etwas strahlt aus ihnen,
Das mein ganzes Herz gewinnt.

7

Mühvoll komm ich und beladen,
Nimm mich an, du Hort der Gnaden!

Sieh, ich komm in Tränen heiß
Mit demütiger Gebärde,
Dunkel ganz vom Staub der Erde.
Du nur schaffest, daß ich weiß
Wie das Vließ der Lämmer werde.
Tilgen willst du ja den Schaden
Dem, der reuig dich umfaßt;
Nimm denn, Herr, von mir die Last,
Mühvoll komm ich und beladen.

Laß mich flehend vor dir knien,
Daß ich über deine Füße
Nardenduft und Tränen gieße,
Gleich dem Weib, dem du verziehn,
Bis die Schuld wie Rauch zerfließe.
Der den Schächer du geladen:
»Heute noch in Edens Bann
Wirst du sein!« o nimm mich an.
Nimm mich an, du Hort der Gnaden!

8

Ach, wie lang die Seele schlummert!
Zeit ist's, daß sie sich ermuntre.

Daß man tot sie wähnen dürfte,
Also schläft sie schwer und bang

that I may see Bethlehem,
there to see my God.
Who, who could manage
to come to You, without Your aid!

By the grievous sickness of sin
am I deeply and darkly oppressed.
If you will not come to my aid,
I must stumble,
    stagger.
Guide me to Bethlehem,
You, my God, You will I see.
Who, who could manage
to come to You, without Your aid!

6

Ah, the Infant's eyes,
so beautiful and clear they seemed,
and from them something shines
that captures all my heart.

For with those sweet eyes
He looks at mine!
If He then saw His image there,
lovingly would He greet me.
And so I give myself wholly
to serving only His eyes.
For from them something shines
that captures all my heart.

7

In toil I come, and laden,
receive me, Refuge of Mercy!

See, with burning tears I come,
with humble bearing,
dark with dust of earth.
You alone can make me white
as lamb's fleece.
Willingly will You efface the wrong
of him who embraces You, repentant;
take then, Lord, the burden from me,
in toil I come, and laden.

Let me kneel before You, pleading,
that over Your feet
I may pour tears and scent of nard,
like the woman You forgave.
until my guilt is dispersed like smoke.
You who did tell the robber:
'Today in Paradise
shall you be!' oh, receive me.
Receive me, Refuge of Mercy!

8

Ah, how long the soul slumbers!
It is time it roused itself.

So that one may think it dead,
heavily and fearfully it sleeps,

Seit sie jener Rausch bezwang,
Den im Sündengift sie schlürfte.
Doch nun ihrer Sehnsucht Licht
Blendend ihr ins Auge bricht:
Zeit ist's, daß sie sich ermuntre.

Mochte sie gleich taub erscheinen
Bei der Engel süßem Chor:
Lauscht sie doch wohl zag empor,
Hört sie Gott als Kindlein weinen.
Da nach langer Schlummernacht
Solch ein Tag der Gnad ihr lacht,
Zeit ist's, daß sie sich ermuntre.

9
Herr, was trägt der Boden hier,
Den du tränkst so bitterlich?
»Dornen, liebes Herz, für mich,
Und für dich der Blumen Zier.«

Ach, wo solche Bäche rinnen,
Wird ein Garten da gedeihn?
»Ja, und wisse! Kränzelein,
Gar verschiedne, flicht man drinnen.«
O mein Herr, zu wessen Zier
Windet man die Kränze? sprich!
»Die von Dornen sind für mich,
Die von Blumen reich ich dir.«

10
Wunden trägst du, mein Geliebter,
Und sie schmerzen dich;
Trüg ich sie statt deiner, ich!

Herr, wer wagt es, so zu färben
Deine Stirn mit Blut und Schweiß?
»Diese Male sind der Preis,
Dich, o Seele, zu erwerben.
An den Wunden muß ich sterben,
Weil ich dich geliebt so heiß.«

Könnt ich, Herr, für dich sie tragen,
Da es Todeswunden sind.
»Wenn dies Leid dich rührt, mein Kind,
Magst du Lebenswunden sagen:
Ihrer keine ward geschlagen,
Draus für dich nicht Leben rinnt.«

Ach, wie mir in Herz und Sinnen
Deine Qual so wehe tut!
»Härtres noch mit treuem Mut
Trüg ich froh, dich zu gewinnen;
Denn nur der weiß recht zu minnen,
Der da stirbt vor Liebesglut.«

Wunden trägst du, mein Geliebter,
Und sie schmerzen dich;
Trüg ich sie statt deiner, ich!

overcome by intoxication,
drunk in the venom of sin.
But now the light of its longing
breaks blindingly into the eyes:
it is time it roused itself.

Though it may have seemed deaf
to the sweet choir of angels,
still timidly it pricks its ears,
hearing God cry as a little child.
As, after its long night of slumber,
such a day of mercy will smile on it,
it is time it roused itself.

9
Lord, what grows this ground
which You water so bitterly?
'Thorns, dear heart, for me,
and for you, adorning flowers.'

Ah, where such brooks run,
shall a garden flourish there?
'Yes, and know, garlands
so different, shall be woven there.'
O Lord, to adorn whom
are they plaited, say!
'Those of thorns are for me,
those of flowers I hand to you.'

10
Wounds you bear, my love,
and they cause you pain;
would I bore them in your stead!

Lord, who dares so to stain
your brow with blood and sweat?
'These marks are the price
of winning you, O Soul.
Of these wounds must I die,
for loving you so ardently.'

Would I might bear them for you,
Lord, since they are mortal wounds.
'If this sorrow touch you, child,
you may call them living wounds:
not one was made, from which
life does not flow for you.'

Ah, to my heart and senses
what pain your torment does!
'Harsher yet, with true courage,
would I gladly bear to win you.
For he alone knows how to love,
who is dying of love's fire '

Wounds you bear, my love,
and they cause you pain;
would I bore them in your stead!

II *Weltliche Lieder*

1

Klinge, klinge, mein Pandero,
Doch an andres denkt mein Herz.

Wenn du, muntres Ding, verständest
Meine Qual und sie empfändest,
Jeder Ton, den du entsendest,
Würde klagen meinen Schmerz.

Bei des Tanzes Drehn und Neigen
Schlag ich wild den Takt zum Reigen,
Daß nur die Gedanken schweigen,
Die mich mahnen an den Schmerz.

Ach, ihr Herrn, dann will im Schwingen
Oftmals mir die Brust zerspringen,
Und zum Angstschrei wird mein Singen,
Denn an andres denkt mein Herz.

2

In dem Schatten meiner Locken
Schlief mir mein Geliebter ein.
Weck ich ihn nun auf?—Ach nein!

Sorglich strählt ich meine krausen
Locken täglich in der Frühe,
Doch umsonst ist meine Mühe,
Weil die Winde sie zerzausen.
Lockenschatten, Windessausen
Schläferten den Liebsten ein.
Weck ich ihn nun auf?—Ach nein!

Hören muß ich, wie ihn gräme,
Daß er schmachtet schon so lange,
Daß ihm Leben geb und nehme
Diese meine braune Wange,
Und er nennt mich eine Schlange,
Und doch schlief er bei mir ein.
Weck ich ihn nun auf?—Ach nein!

(*Johannes Brahms: op. 6, no. 1, 1852*)

3

Seltsam ist Juanas Weise.
Wenn ich steh in Traurigkeit,
Wenn ich seufz und sage: heut,
»Morgen« spricht sie leise.

Trüb ist sie, wenn ich mich freue;
Lustig singt sie, wenn ich weine;
Sag ich, daß sie hold mir scheine,
Spricht sie, daß sie stets mich scheue.
Solcher Grausamkeit Beweise
Brechen mir das Herz in Leid—
Wenn ich seufz und sage: heut,
»Morgen« spricht sie leise.

Heb ich meine Augenlider,
Weiß sie stets den Blick zu senken;

II *Secular Songs*

1

Sound, tambourine, sound.
though my heart thinks of other things.

If you, happy object, understood
my torment, and felt it,
your every sound
would bewail my agony.

For the dance's bending, turning,
wildly I beat the time
only to silence the thoughts
which remind me of that agony.

Ah, sirs, while I whirl
my heart feels often like breaking,
and my song becomes a cry of anguish
for my heart thinks of other things.

2

In the shade of my curls
my lover has fallen asleep.
Shall I wake him now? Ah no!

With care I combed my curls
each morning early,
but vain is my work,
for the winds disorder them.
Curls' shade, soughing wind
have lulled my love to sleep.
Shall I wake him now? Ah no!

I'll have to hear his sorrow
over languishing so long,
how life is bestowed and taken
by this my dusky cheek,
and he calls me a serpent,
and yet he fell asleep at my side.
Shall I wake him? Ah no!

3

Curious is Juana's way.
When I stand in sorrow,
when I sigh and say, 'Today',
softly she says, 'Tomorrow'.

Gloomy she is, when I am glad;
merrily she sings when I am weeping;
when I say I think her beautiful,
she says that I fill her with dread.
Tokens of such cruelty
break my heart with woe—
when I sigh and say, 'Today',
softly she says, 'Tomorrow'.

If I ever raise my gaze,
she contrives to lower hers,

Um ihn gleich emporzulenken,
Schlag ich auch den meinen nieder.
Wenn ich sie als Heilge preise,
Nennt sie Dämon mich im Streit—
Wenn ich seufz und sage: heut,
»Morgen« spricht sie leise.

Sieglos heiß ich auf der Stelle,
Rühm ich meinen Sieg bescheiden;
Hoff ich auf des Himmels Freuden,
Prophezeit sie mir die Hölle.
Ja, so ist ihr Herz von Eise,
Säh sie sterben mich vor Leid,
Hörte mich noch seufzen: heut,
»Morgen« spräch sie leise.

4
Treibe nur mit Lieben Spott,
Geliebte mein;
Spottet doch der Liebesgott
Dereinst auch dein!

Magst an Spotten nach Gefallen
Du dich weiden;
Von dem Weibe kommt uns allen
Lust und Leiden.
Treibe nur mit Lieben Spott,
Geliebte mein;
Spottet doch der Liebesgott
Dereinst auch dein!

Bist auch jetzt zu stolz zum
    Minnen,
Glaub, o glaube:
Liebe wird dich doch gewinnen
Sich zum Raube,
Wenn du spottest meiner Not,
Geliebte mein;
Spottet doch der Liebesgott
Dereinst auch dein!

Wer da lebt im Fleisch, erwäge
Alle Stunden:
Amor schläft und plötzlich rege
Schlägt er Wunden.
Treibe nur mit Lieben Spott,
Geliebte mein;
Spottet doch der Liebesgott
Dereinst auch dein!

5
Auf dem grünen Balkon mein Mädchen
Schaut nach mir durchs Gitterlein.
Mit den Augen blinzelt sie freundlich,
Mit dem Finger sagt sie mir: Nein!

Glück, das nimmer ohne Wanken
Junger Liebe folgt hienieden,
Hat mir eine Lust beschieden,
Und auch da noch muß ich schwanken.

only to raise it
the moment I look down.
When I laud her as a saint,
she quarrels and calls me a demon—
when I sigh and say, 'Today',
softly she says, 'Tomorrow'.

A failure she calls me on the spot,
if, modestly, I vaunt my triumph;
should I hope for heaven's delight,
she prophesies me hell.
Yes. her heart's so made of ice
that if she saw me dying of sorrow,
heard me sighing still, 'Today',
softly she'd say, 'Tomorrow'.

4
Just keep on mocking love,
my sweet;
but the god of love will mock
you some day too!

You can mock away
as much as you please;
for all of us woman is the source
of joy and suffering.
Just keep on mocking love,
my sweet;
but the god of love will mock
you some day too!

Though now you are too proud for
    loving,
believe, oh, believe:
love will seize you
as its prey,
if you mock my distress,
my sweet;
but the god of love will mock
you some day too!

Let all who are of flesh, ponder
at all times:
Cupid sleeps and, stirring suddenly,
inflicts wounds.
Just keep on mocking love,
my sweet;
but the god of love will mock
you some day too!

5
On the green balcony my love
peeps through the trellis at me.
A friendly eye she winks,
but with her finger tells me: No!

Fortune, that never constantly
attends young love on earth,
has granted me one joy,
and there too must I still falter.

Schmeicheln hör ich oder Zanken,
Komm ich an ihr Fensterlädchen.
Immer nach dem Brauch der Mädchen
Träuft ins Glück ein bißchen
    Pein:
Mit den Augen blinzelt sie freundlich,
Mit dem Finger sagt sie mir: Nein!

Wie sich nur in ihr vertragen
Ihre Kälte, meine Glut?
Weil in ihr mein Himmel ruht,
Seh ich Trüb und Hell sich jagen.
In den Wind gehn meine Klagen,
Daß noch nie die süße Kleine
Ihre Arme schlang um meine;
Doch sie hält mich hin so fein—
Mit den Augen blinzelt sie freundlich,
Mit dem Finger sagt sie mir: Nein!

6
Wenn du zu den Blumen gehst,
Pflücke die schönsten, dich zu
    schmücken.
Ach, wenn du in dem Gärtlein stehst,
Müßtest du dich selber pflücken.

Alle Blumen wissen ja,
Daß du hold bist ohnegleichen.
Und die Blume, die dich sah—
Farb und Schmuck muß ihr erbleichen.
Wenn du zu den Blumen gehst,
Pflücke die schönsten, dich zu
    schmücken.
Ach, wenn du in dem Gärtlein stehst,
Müßtest du dich selber pflücken.

Lieblicher als Rosen sind
Die Küsse, die dein Mund
    verschwendet,
Weil der Reiz der Blumen endet,
Wo dein Liebreiz erst beginnt.
Wenn du zu den Blumen gehst,
Pflücke die schönsten, dich zu
    schmücken.
Ach, wenn du in dem Gärtlein stehst,
Müßtest du dich selber pflücken.

7
Wer sein holdes Lieb verloren,
Weil er Liebe nicht versteht,
Besser wär er nie geboren.

Ich verlor sie dort im Garten,
Da sie Rosen brach und Blüten.
Hell auf ihren Wangen glühten
Scham und Lust in holder Zier.
Und von Liebe sprach sie mir;
Doch ich größter aller Toren
Wußte keine Antwort ihr—
Wär ich nimmermehr geboren.

Compliments I hear or cross words
when I come to her window shutter.
Always, after the manner of girls,
she sheds into happiness a drop of
    pain:
a friendly eye she winks,
but with her finger tells me: No!

How can both endure in her,
her coldness, my fire?
Because she is my heaven,
brightness and gloom I see in chase.
To the wind go my complaints
that never yet has my little sweet
twined her arms about mine;
but so daintily she puts me off—
a friendly eye she winks,
but with her finger tells me: No!

6
If you go to the flowers,
pick the fairest to adorn
    you.
Ah, but standing in the garden,
you would have to pick yourself.

All the flowers know very well
your loveliness is beyond compare.
And the flower which has seen you—
her hue and finery must pale.
If you go to the flowers,
pick the fairest to adorn
    you.
Ah, but standing in the garden,
you would have to pick yourself.

Lovelier than roses are
the kisses that your mouth
    bestows,
for the charm of flowers ceases
where your fair charm does but begin.
If you go to the flowers,
pick the fairest to adorn
    you.
Ah, but standing in the garden,
you would have to pick yourself.

7
He who has lost his loved one,
through not understanding love,
would have done better not to be born.

In the garden there I lost her,
as she picked roses and flowers.
Bright glowed her cheeks,
graced with modesty and joy.
And to me she spoke of love,
yet I, greatest of all fools,
could find no answer for her—
would I had never been born.

Ich verlor sie dort im Garten,
Da sie sprach von Liebesplagen,
Denn ich wagte nicht zu sagen,
Wie ich ganz ihr eigen bin.
In die Blumen sank sie hin,
Doch ich größter aller Toren
Zog auch davon nicht Gewinn—
Wär ich nimmermehr geboren!

8
Ich fuhr über Meer,
Ich zog über Land,
Das Glück, das fand
Ich nimmermehr.
Die andern umher
Wie jubelten sie!—
Ich jubelte nie!

Nach Glück ich jagte,
An Leiden krankt ich;
Als Recht verlangt ich,
Was Liebe versagte.
Ich hofft und wagte—
Kein Glück mir gedieh,
Und so schaut ich es nie!

Trug ohne Klage
Die Leiden, die bösen,
Und dacht, es lösen
Sich ab die Tage.
Die fröhlichen Tage,
Wie eilen sie!—
Ich ereilte sie nie!

9
Blindes Schauen, dunkle Leuchte,
Ruhm voll Weh, erstorbnes Leben,
Unheil, das ein Heil mir deuchte,
Freudges Weinen, Lust voll Beben,
Süße Galle, durstge Feuchte,
Krieg im Frieden allerwegen,
Liebe, falsch versprachst du Segen,
Da dein Fluch den Schlaf mir scheuchte.

10
Eide, so die Liebe schwur,
Schwache Bürgen sind sie nur.

Sitzt die Liebe zu Gericht,
Dann, Señor, vergesset nicht,
Daß sie nie nach Recht und Pflicht,
Immer nur nach Gunst verfuhr.
Eide, so die Liebe schwur,
Schwache Bürgen sind sie nur.

Werdet dort Betrübte finden,
Die mit Schwüren sich verbinden,
Die verschwinden mit den Winden,
Wie die Blumen auf der Flur.

In the garden there I lost her,
as she spoke of the pangs of love,
for I did not dare to say
how I was wholly hers.
Down into the flowers she sank,
but I, greatest of all fools,
drew even from that no advantage—
would I had never been born!

8
I fared over sea,
I marched over land,
happiness—that I found
never.
The others around,
how they rejoiced!—
I rejoiced never!

Happiness I pursued,
sorrows I suffered;
as a right demanded
what love denied.
I hoped and I dared—
luck favoured me not,
so I saw none ever.

Uncomplaining I bore
my evil sorrows,
and thought
one day succeeds another.
The joyous days,
how they speed!—
I've caught them up never!

9
Blind seeing, dark light,
glory full of sorrow, dead life,
hurt that seemed help,
happy weeping, joy full of trembling,
sweet gall, parched wetness,
war in peace, everywhere, always
—false, love, was your promise of blessing,
since your curse has banished my sleep.

10
Oaths which love has sworn,
are but feeble sureties.

Where love sits in judgment,
then, señor, do not forget;
never according to law and duty
has she acted, only to favour.
Oaths which love has sworn,
are but feeble sureties.

The afflicted you will find there,
binding themselves with vows,
which go with the winds,
like flowers on the meadow.

Eide, so die Liebe schwur,
Schwache Bürgen sind sie nur.

Und als Schreiber an den Schranken
Seht ihr nichtige Gedanken.
Weil die leichten Händlein schwanken,
Schreibt euch keiner nach der Schnur.
Eide, so die Liebe schwur,
Schwache Bürgen sind sie nur.

Sind die Bürgen gegenwärtig,
Allesamt des Spruchs gewärtig,
Machen sie das Urteil fertig;—
Von Vollziehen keine Spur,
Eide, so die Liebe schwur,
Schwache Bürgen sind sie nur.

11
Herz, verzage nicht geschwind,
Weil die Weiber Weiber sind.

Argwohn lehre sie dich kennen,
Die sich lichte Sterne nennen
Und wie Feuerfunken brennen.
Drum verzage nicht geschwind,
Weil die Weiber Weiber sind.

Laß dir nicht den Sinn verwirren,
Wenn sie süße Weisen girren;
Möchten dich mit Listen kirren,
Machen dich mit Ränken blind;
Weil die Weiber Weiber sind.

Sind einander stets im Bunde,
Fechten tapfer mit dem Munde,
Wünschen, was versagt die Stunde,
Bauen Schlösser in den Wind;
Weil die Weiber Weiber sind.

Und so ist ihr Sinn verschroben,
Daß sie, lobst du, was zu loben,
Mit dem Mund dagegen toben,
Ob ihr Herz auch Gleiches sinnt;
Weil die Weiber Weiber sind.

12
Sagt, seid Ihr es, feiner Herr,
Der da jüngst so hübsch gesprungen
Und gesprungen und gesungen?

Seid Ihr der, vor dessen Kehle
Keiner mehr zu Wort gekommen?
Habt die Backen voll genommen?
Sangt gar artig, ohne Fehle.
Ja, Ihr seid's, bei meiner Seele,
Der so mit uns umgesprungen
Und gesprungen und gesungen.

Seid Ihr's, der auf Kastagnetten,
Und Gesang sich nicht verstand,

Oaths which love has sworn,
are but feeble sureties.

And as clerks of the court
you'll see vain thoughts.
Their light hands, being shaky,
none will record you accurately.
Oaths which love has sworn,
are but feeble sureties.

Should the sureties be present,
all waiting for the verdict,
they will prepare the judgment;
—of its execution not a trace.
Oaths which love has sworn,
are but feeble sureties.

11
Heart, do not swiftly despair,
because women are women.

Mistrust, teach them to know you,
who call themselves bright stars,
and who burn like sparks of fire.
Therefore, do not swiftly despair,
because women are women.

Let not your wits be confused
when they coo sweet melodies;
cunningly they mean to tame you,
to blind you with intrigue;
because women are women.

Forever in league with each other,
boldly they fight with their tongues,
wish for what the hour denies,
build castles in the air;
because women are women.

And so perverse are their minds
that, praise what merits praise,
and they will rant against it,
though their hearts think the same;
because women are women.

12
Say, is it you, fine gentleman,
who recently so prettily capered,
capered and sang?

Is it you, whose voice stopped
everyone else getting a word in?
Who talked big?
Who sang well and faultlessly?
Yes, upon my soul, it's you
who capered about with us so,
capered and sang.

Is it you, who of castanets
and singing knew nothing,

Der die Liebe nie gekannt,
Der da floh vor Weiberketten?
Ja Ihr's seid's; doch möcht ich wetten,
Manch ein Lieb habt Ihr umschlungen
Und gesprungen und gesungen.

Seid Ihr der, der Tanz und Lieder
So heraus strich ohne Maß?
Seid Ihr's, der im Winkel saß
Und nicht regte seine Glieder?
Ja Ihr seid's, ich kenn Euch wieder,
Der zum Gähnen uns gezwungen
Und gesprungen und gesungen.

13
Mögen alle bösen Zungen
Immer sprechen, was beliebt;
Wer mich liebt, den lieb ich wieder,
Und ich lieb und bin geliebt.

Schlimme, schlimme Reden flüstern
Eure Zungen schonungslos;
Doch ich weiß es, sie sind lüstern
Nach unschuldgem Blute bloß.
Nimmer soll es mich bekümmern,
Schwatzt, so viel es euch beliebt;
Wer mich liebt, den lieb ich wieder,
Und ich lieb und bin geliebt.

Zur Verleumdung sich verstehet
Nur, wem Lieb und Gunst gebrach,
Weil's ihm selber elend gehet,
Und ihn niemand minnt und mag.
Darum denk ich, daß die Liebe,
Drum sie schmähn, mir Ehre gibt;
Wer mich liebt, den lieb ich wieder,
Und ich lieb und bin geliebt.

Wenn ich wär aus Stein und Eisen,
Möchtet ihr darauf bestehn,
Daß ich sollte von mir weisen
Liebesgruß und Liebesflehn.
Doch mein Herzlein ist nun leider
Weich, wie's Gott uns Mädchen gibt;
Wer mich liebt, den lieb ich wieder,
Und ich lieb und bin geliebt.

14 *Preciosas Sprüchlein gegen Kopfweh*
Köpfchen, Köpfchen, nicht gewimmert,
Halt dich wacker, halt dich munter,
Stütz zwei Säulchen unter,
Heilsam aus Geduld gezimmert;
Hoffnung schimmert,
Wie sich's auch verschlimmert
Und dich kümmert.
Mußt mit Grämen
Dir nur nichts zu Herzen nehmen,
Ja kein Märchen,
Daß zu Berg dir stehn die Härchen;
Da sei Gott davor
Und der Riese Christophor!

(*Peter Cornelius, 1854–55*)

were a stranger to love,
and fled women's bonds?
It is; but I'd be prepared to bet
many a loved one you've embraced,
and capered and sung.

Is it you, who dance and song
so praised to the skies?
Is it you, who sat in the corner,
not stirring a limb?
Yes, it is, I recognize you now,
who made us yawn,
and capered and sang.

13
All the wicked tongues
can keep saying what they please;
he who loves me, I love back,
and I love and am loved.

Wicked, wicked speeches
your tongues whisper relentlessly;
yet I know they thirst
merely for innocent blood.
Never shall it trouble me,
gossip to your heart's content;
he who loves me, I love back,
and I love and am loved.

Only they condescend to slander
who lack affection and kindness,
because they fare miserably,
and no one likes and loves them.
Therefore I think the love
that they revile, is to my honour;
he who loves me, I love back,
and I love and am loved.

Were I made of iron and stone,
then you might insist
that I should spurn
love's greetings, love's entreaties.
Yet my small heart, I fear, is
soft as those God gives us girls;
he who loves me, I love back,
and I love and am loved.

14 *Preciosa's Rhyme to Cure Headaches*
Little head, little head, don't moan,
bear up bravely, bear up gaily,
prop under you two good pillars,
fashioned wholesomely of patience;
there's a gleam of hope,
however bad it becomes
and vexes you.
Only you mustn't
take anything grievously to heart,
no fairy tale, certainly,
to make your hair stand on end;
God forbid,
and the giant Christopher!

**15**

Sagt ihm, daß er zu mir komme,
Denn je mehr sie mich drum schelten,
Ach, je mehr wächst meine Glut!

O zum Wanken
Bringt die Liebe nichts auf Erden;
Durch ihr Zanken
Wird sie nur gedoppelt werden.
Sie gefährden
Mag nicht ihrer Neider Wut;
Denn je mehr sie mich drum schelten,
Ach, je mehr wächst meine Glut!

Eingeschlossen
Haben sie mich lange Tage,
Unverdrossen
Mich gestraft mit schlimmer Plage.
Doch ich trage
Jede Pein mit Liebesmut,
Und je mehr sie mich drum schelten,
Ach, je mehr wächst meine Glut!

Meine Peiniger
Sagen oft, ich soll dich lassen,
Doch nur einiger
Wolln wir uns ins Herze fassen.
Muß ich drum erblassen,
Tod um Liebe lieblich tut,
Und je mehr sie mich drum schelten,
Ach, je mehr wächst meine Glut!

**16**

Bitt ihn, o Mutter,
Bitte den Knaben,
Nicht mehr zu zielen,
Weil er mich tötet.

Mutter, o Mutter,
Die launische Liebe
Höhnt und versöhnt mich,
Flieht mich und zieht mich.

Ich sah zwei Augen
Am letzten Sonntag,
Wunder des Himmels,
Unheil der Erde.

Was man sagt, o Mutter,
Von Basilisken,
Erfuhr mein Herze,
Da ich sie sah.

Bitt ihn, o Mutter,
Bitte den Knaben,
Nicht mehr zu zielen,
Weil er mich tötet.

**17**

Liebe mir im Busen
Zündet einen Brand.

---

**15**

Tell him he's to come to me,
for the more they rebuke me,
ah, the greater my passion grows!

Oh, love is shaken
by nothing on earth;
by their chiding
will it only be doubled.
It is not imperilled
by the fury of its enviers;
for the more they rebuke me,
ah, the greater my passion grows!

Locked me in
they have for days on end,
persistently
vexed and punished me.
But I can bear
any pain, by love's courage,
and the more they rebuke me,
ah, the greater my passion grows!

My tormentors
often say I should give you up,
yet only closer together
will we grapple our hearts.
And if I must fade and die,
then to die for love is sweet,
and the more they rebuke me,
ah, the greater my passion grows!

**16**

Bid him, mother,
bid the boy
aim no more arrows,
for he's killing me.

Mother, mother,
a fickle love
is scorning, soothing,
shunning, enticing me.

Two eyes I saw
last Sunday,
miracle of heaven,
mischief of earth.

What is said, mother,
of basilisks,
my heart discovered
when I saw them.

Bid him, mother,
bid the boy
aim no more arrows,
for he's killing me.

**17**

Love in my breast
has kindled a fire.

Wasser, liebe Mutter,
Eh das Herz verbrannt!

Nicht das blinde Kind
Straft für meine Fehle;
Hat zuerst die Seele
Mir gekühlt so lind.
Dann entflammt's geschwind,
Ach, mein Unverstand,
Wasser, liebe Mutter,
Eh das Herz verbrannt!

Ach, wo ist die Flut,
Die dem Feuer wehre?
Für so große Glut
Sind zu arm die Meere.
Weil es wohl mir tut,
Wein ich unverwandt;
Wasser, liebe Mutter,
Eh das Herz verbrannt!

18
Schmerzliche Wonnen und wonnige
    Schmerzen,
Wasser im Auge und Feuer im Herzen,
Stolz auf den Lippen und Seufzer im
    Sinne,
Honig und Galle zugleich ist die Minne.

Oft, wenn ein Seelchen vom Leib sich
    geschieden,
Möcht es Sankt Michael tragen zum
    Frieden;
Aber der Dämon auch möcht es
    verschlingen;
Keiner will weichen, da geht es ans
    Ringen.

Seelchen, gequältes, in ängstlichem
    Wogen
Fühlst du dich hierhin und dorthin
    gezogen,
Aufwärts und abwärts. In solches
    Getriebe
Stürzt zwischen Himmel und Höll uns
    die Liebe.

Mütterchen, ach, und mit siebenzehn
    Jahren
Hab ich dies Hangen und Bangen
    erfahren,
Hab's dann verschworen mit Tränen
    der Reue;
Ach, und schon lieb ich, schon lieb ich
    auf's neue!

19
Trau nicht der Liebe,
Mein Liebster, gib acht!
Sie macht dich noch weinen,
Wo heut du gelacht.

Water, dear mother,
before my heart's consumed!

Blame not blind Cupid
for my wrongs;
my soul at first
so gently did he cool.
Then swiftly he inflamed,
alas, my folly.
Water, dear mother,
before my heart's consumed!

Ah, where is the flood
that shall halt this fire?
For so great a blaze
the seas are too small.
Because it does me good
I weep incessantly;
water, dear mother,
before my heart's consumed!

18
Painful raptures and rapturous
    pains,
tears in the eyes and fire in the heart,
pride on the lips and sighs in the
    thoughts,
love is honey and gall together.

Often, when a soul has departed the
    body,
St Michael would like to bear it to
    rest,
but the Demon would like to swallow
    it up;
neither will yield, so a tussle
    ensues.

Tormented soul, in surging
    distress,
this way and that you feel yourself
    tugged,
upwards and down. Such is the
    commotion
love hurls us into, between heaven and
    hell.

Mother dear, oh, and at
    seventeen,
I came to know this fear and
    longing,
I then, with rueful tears, forswore
    it;
and ah, already I'm in love, in love
    anew!

19
Trust not love,
my dearest, take care!
It will make you weep,
where today you laughed.

Und siehst du nicht schwinden
Des Mondes Gestalt?
Das Glück hat nicht minder
Nur wankenden Halt.
Dann rächt es sich bald;
Und Liebe, gib acht!
Sie macht dich noch weinen,
Wo heut du gelacht.

Drum hüte dich fein
Vor törigem Stolze!
Wohl singen im Mai'n
Die Grillchen im Holze;
Dann schlafen sie ein,
Und Liebe, gib acht!
Sie macht dich noch weinen,
Wo heut du gelacht.

Wo schweifst du nur hin?
Laß Rat dir erteilen:
Das Kind mit den Pfeilen
Hat Possen im Sinn.
Die Tage, die eilen,
Und Liebe, gib acht!
Sie macht dich noch weinen,
Wo heut du gelacht.

Nicht immer ist's helle,
Nicht immer ist's dunkel;
Der Freude Gefunkel
Erbleichet so schnelle.
Ein falscher Geselle
Ist Amor, gib acht!
Er macht dich noch weinen,
Wo heut du gelacht.

20
Ach im Maien wars, im Maien,
Wo die warmen Lüfte wehen,
Wo verliebte Leute pflegen
Ihren Liebchen nachzugehen.

Ich allein, ich armer Trauriger,
Lieg im Kerker so verschmachtet,
Und ich seh nicht, wann es taget,
Und ich weiß nicht, wann es nachtet.

Nur an einem Vöglein merkt ich's,
Das da drauß im Maien sang;
Das hat mir ein Schütz getötet—
Geb ihm Gott den schlimmsten Dank!

21
Alle gingen, Herz, zur Ruh,
Alle schlafen, nur nicht du.

Denn der hoffnungslose Kummer
Scheucht von deinem Bett den
    Schlummer,
Und dein Sinnen schweift in stummer
Sorge seiner Liebe zu.

(*Robert Schumann: op. 74, 1849*)

Do you not see dwindling
the shape of the moon?
Happiness is no less
inconstant in its stay.
Then soon it takes vengeance;
and love, take care!
It will make you weep,
where today you laughed.

So be on your guard
against foolish pride.
In May-time
the crickets chirp in the wood,
whereafter they sleep,
and love, take care!
It will make you weep,
where today you laughed.

Which way are you wandering?
Take some advice:
that child with the arrows
has tricks in mind.
The days, they hasten,
and love, take care!
It will make you weep,
where today you laughed.

Not always is it light,
not always is it dark;
the sparkle of joy
will quickly fade.
A false companion
is Cupid, take care!
He will make you weep,
where today you laughed.

20
Ah, in May it was, in May,
when warm breezes blow,
when those in love are wont
to seek their loves.

I alone, poor, sad man,
lie, so enfeebled, in prison,
and I see not when it dawns.
and know not when night falls.

I could tell only by a bird
that sang out there in May;
that bird a hunter has shot—
God give him small thanks!

21
All, heart, have gone to their rest,
all are sleeping, all but you.

For hopeless grief
chases slumber from your
    bed,
and your fancy wanders in silent
sorrow to its love.

22
Dereinst, dereinst,
Gedanke mein,
Wirst ruhig sein.

Läßt Liebesglut
Dich still nicht werden:
In kühler Erden,
Da schläfst du gut;
Dort ohne Liebe
Und ohne Pein
Wirst ruhig sein.

Was du im Leben
Nicht hast gefunden,
Wenn es entschwunden,
Wird dir's gegeben.
Dann ohne Wunden
Und ohne Pein
Wirst ruhig sein.

23
Tief im Herzen trag ich Pein,
Muß nach außen stille sein.

Den geliebten Schmerz verhehle
Tief ich vor der Welt Gesicht;
Und es fühlt ihn nur die Seele,
Denn der Leib verdient ihn nicht.
Wie der Funke frei und licht
Sich verbirgt im Kieselstein,
Trag ich innen tief die Pein.
        (*Robert Schumann: op. 138, 1849*)

24
Komm, o Tod, von Nacht umgeben,
Leise komm zu mir gegangen,
Daß die Lust, dich zu umfangen,
Nicht zurück mich ruft ins Leben,
Komm, so wie der Blitz uns rühret,
Den der Donner nicht verkündet,
Bis er plötzlich sich entzündet
Und den Schlag gedoppelt führet.
Also seist du mir gegeben,
Plötzlich stillend mein Verlangen,
Daß die Lust, dich zu umfangen,
Nicht zurück mich ruft ins Leben.

25
Ob auch finstre Blicke glitten,
Schöner Augenstern, aus dir,
Wird mir doch nicht abgestritten,
Daß du hast geblickt nach mir.
Wie sich auch der Strahl bemühte,
Zu verwunden meine Brust,
Gibt's ein Leiden, das die Lust,
Dich zu schaun, nicht reich vergüte?
Und so tödlich mein Gemüte
Unter deinem Zorn gelitten,

22
One day, one day,
my thoughts,
you shall be at rest.

Though love's ardour
lets you not be still:
in cool earth
will you sleep well;
there without love
and without pain
you will be at rest.

What, in life,
you have not found,
when life is vanished
will be given you.
Then, without wounds
and without pain,
you shall be at rest.

23
Torment I bear deep in my heart,
outwardly I must be calm.

That sweet agony I conceal
far from the world's sight;
it is felt only by my soul,
for the body does not deserve it.
As the spark, free and bright,
hides within the flint,
so I bear torment deep within.

24
Come, O night-girt Death,
softly to me stealing, come,
so that my joy in embracing you
shall not recall me to life;
come, as the lightning touches us,
which no thunder heralds,
before suddenly it flares
and its blow deals doubly.
So may you be given to me,
stilling suddenly my longing,
so that my joy in embracing you
shall not recall me to life.

25
Though black looks have slipped,
fair beloved, from you,
you have, it cannot be gainsaid,
looked in my direction.
And though your gaze has striven
to wound my breast,
is there suffering for which joy
at seeing you is not rich reward?
And mortally as have my feelings
suffered from your anger,

Wird mir doch nicht abgestritten,
Daß du hast geblickt nach mir.

26
Bedeckt mich mit Blumen,
Ich sterbe vor Liebe.

Daß die Luft mit leisem Wehen
Nicht den süßen Duft mir entführe,
Bedeckt mich!

Ist ja alles doch dasselbe,
Liebesodem oder Düfte
Von Blumen.

Von Jasmin und weißen Lilien
Sollt ihr hier mein Grab bereiten,
Ich sterbe.

Und befragt ihr mich: Woran?
Sag ich: Unter süßen Qualen
Vor Liebe.

27
Und schläfst du, mein Mädchen,
Auf, öffne du mir;
Denn die Stund ist gekommen,
Da wir wandern von hier.

Und bist ohne Sohlen,
Leg keine dir an;
Durch reißende Wasser
Geht unsere Bahn.

Durch die tief tiefen Wasser
Des Guadalquivir;
Denn die Stund ist gekommen,
Da wir wandern von hier.

28
Sie blasen zum Abmarsch,
Lieb Mütterlein.
Mein Liebster muß scheiden
Und läßt mich allein!

Am Himmel die Sterne
Sind kaum noch geflohn,
Da feuert von ferne
Das Fußvolk schon.
Kaum hört er den Ton,
Sein Ränzelein schnürt er,
Von hinnen marschiert er,
Mein Herz hinterdrein.
Mein Liebster muß scheiden
Und läßt mich allein!

Mir ist wie dem Tag,
Dem die Sonne geschwunden.
Mein Trauern nicht mag
So balde gesunden.

you have, it cannot be gainsaid,
looked in my direction.

26
Cover me with flowers,
I am dying of love.

So the wafting breeze
shall not bear the perfume from me,
cover me.

For it is all the same,
breath of love or scents
of flowers.

Of jasmine and white lilies
shall you here prepare my grave,
I am dying.

And if you ask me: Of what?
I say: In sweet torment,
of love.

27
My girl, though you sleep,
up, open to me;
for come is the hour
when we wander from here.

If you are shoeless,
no shoes put on,
through torrents of water
our way will lie.

The deep, deep waters
of the Guadalquivir;
for come is the hour
when we wander from here.

28
The march-off bugles sound,
mother dear,
my love must away,
and leaves me alone!

From the sky the stars
are scarcely yet fled,
and already, far away,
the infantry's firing.
He hardly hears the call,
he's strapping his pack,
marching from here,
with my heart following.
My love must away,
and leaves me alone!

I feel as the day,
when the sun has vanished.
My sorrow may not
be healed so soon.

Nach nichts ich frag,
Keine Lust mehr heg ich,
Nur Zwiesprach pfleg ich
Mit meiner Pein—
Mein Liebster muß scheiden
Und läßt mich allein!

29
Weint nicht, ihr Äugelein!
Wie kann so trübe
Weinen vor Eifersucht,
Wer tötet durch Liebe?

Wer selbst Tod bringt,
Der sollt ihn ersehnen?
Sein Lächeln bezwingt,
Was trotzt seinen Tränen.
Weint nicht, ihr Äugelein!
Wie kann so trübe
Weinen vor Eifersucht,
Wer tötet durch Liebe?

30 *Limusinisch*
»Wer tat deinem Füßlein weh?
La Marioneta,
Deiner Ferse weiß wie Schnee?
La Marion.«

Sag Euch an, was krank mich macht,
Will kein Wörtlein Euch verschweigen:
Ging zum Rosenbusch zur Nacht,
Brach ein Röslein von den Zweigen;
Trat auf einen Dorn im Gang,
La Marioneta,
Der mir bis ins Herze drang,
La Marion.

Sag Euch alle meine Pein,
Freund, und will Euch nicht berücken:
Ging in einem Wald allein,
Eine Lilie mir zu pflücken;
Traf ein Stachel scharf mich dort,
La Marioneta,
War ein süßes Liebeswort,
La Marion.

Sag Euch mit Aufrichtigkeit
Meine Krankheit, meine Wunde:
In den Garten ging ich heut,
Wo die schönste Nelke stunde;
Hat ein Span mich dort verletzt,
La Marioneta,
Blutet fort und fort bis jetzt,
La Marion.

»Schöne Dame, wenn Ihr wollt,
Bin ein Wundarzt guter Weise,
Will die Wund Euch stillen leise,
Daß Ihr's kaum gewahren sollt.

---

I ask no questions,
I have no more joy,
I commune only
with my agony—
my love must away,
and leave me alone!

29
Weep not, dear eyes!
How can one so sadly
weep with jealousy
who kills through love?

Who himself brings death,
should he desire it?
His smiles conquer
whoever defies his tears.
Weep not, dear eyes!
How can one so sadly
weep with jealousy
who kills through love?

30
'Who has hurt your tiny foot?
La Marioneta,
hurt your heel white as snow?
La Marion.'

I will tell you what afflicts me,
withholding not a word:
to the rosebush I went at night,
broke off a rose;
stepped, as I did so, on a thorn,
La Marioneta,
which pierced me to the heart,
La Marion.

I will tell you all my pain,
friend, won't try to beguile you:
in a wood I walked alone,
to pluck myself a lily;
a prickle caught me sharply there,
La Marioneta,
a sweet word of love, it was,
La Marion.

I'll tell you honestly
of my affliction, of my wound:
to the garden I went today,
where the fairest carnation stood;
there a splinter injured me,
La Marioneta,
it bled away and is bleeding now,
La Marion.

'Fair lady, if you wish,
a surgeon am I of good ability,
I will gently soothe your wound,
so you're scarce aware of it.

Bald sollt Ihr genesen sein,
La Marioneta,
Bald geheilt von aller Pein,
La Marion.«

**31**
Deine Mutter, süßes Kind,
Da sie in den Wehn gelegen,
Brausen hörte sie den Wind.

Und so hat sie dich geboren
Mit dem falschen windgen Sinn.
Hast du heut ein Herz erkoren,
Wirfst es morgen treulos hin.
Doch den zähl ich zu den Toren,
Der dich schmäht der Untreu wegen:
Dein Geschick war dir entgegen;
Denn die Mutter, süßes Kind,
Da sie in den Wehn gelegen,
Brausen hörte sie den Wind.

**32**
Da nur Leid und Leidenschaft
Mich bestürmt in deiner Haft,
Biet ich jetzt mein Herz zu Kauf.
Sagt, hat keiner Lust darauf?

Soll ich sagen, wie ich's schätze,
Sind drei Batzen nicht zuviel.
Nimmer war's des Windes Spiel,
Eigensinnig blieb's im Netze.
Aber weil mich drängt die Not,
Biet ich jetzt mein Herz zu Kauf,
Schlag es los zum Meistgebot—
Sagt, hat keiner Lust darauf?

Täglich kränkt es mich im stillen
Und erfreut mich nimmermehr.
Nun, wer bietet?—wer gibt mehr?
Fort mit ihm und seinen Grillen!
Daß sie schlimm sind, leuchtet ein,
Biet ich doch mein Herz zu Kauf.
Wär es froh, behielt ich's fein—
Sagt, hat keiner Lust darauf?

Kauft ihr's, leb ich ohne Grämen.
Mag es haben, wem's beliebt!
Nun, wer kauft? wer will es nehmen?
Sag ein jeder, was er gibt.
Noch einmal vorm Hammerschlag
Biet ich jetzt mein Herz zu Kauf,
Daß man sich entscheiden mag—
Sagt, hat keiner Lust darauf?

Nun zum ersten—und zum zweiten—
Und zum dritten schlag ich's zu!
Gut denn! Mag dir's Glück bereiten;
Nimm es, meine Liebste du!
Brenn ihm mit dem glühnden Erz
Gleich da Sklavenzeichen auf;

Soon shall you be recovered,
La Marioneta,
soon be healed of all pain,
La Marion.'

**31**
Your mother, sweet child,
lying in labour,
could hear the roaring wind.

And so she gave birth to you,
false and fickle as the wind.
If you choose a love this day,
you jilt him on the morrow.
But I reckon as a fool
any who chides you as untrue:
your fate was against you;
for your mother, sweet child,
lying in labour,
could hear the roaring wind.

**32**
As but sorrow and passion
have assailed me in your custody,
my heart I now offer for sale.
Speak, does no one want it?

If I'm to say what I value it at,
three farthings won't be too high.
Never was it the toy of the winds,
obstinately it has stayed ensnared.
But, being urged by distress,
now I offer my heart for sale,
knock it down to the highest bidder—
speak, does no one want it?

Daily it wounds me in secret,
and delights me no more.
Well, who'll bid?—who'll give more?
Away with it and its fancies!
That they are bad is clear,
yet I offer my heart for sale.
Were it glad, I'd happily keep it—
speak, does no one want it?

Buy it, and I'll live without grief.
Anyone can have it who likes!
Well, who'll buy? Who'll take it?
Let everyone say what they'll give.
Once again, under the hammer,
I offer my heart for sale,
so that people can decide—
speak, does no one want it?

Going for the first time, the second,
and the third and last!
Very well! May you have joy of it;
take it, my dearest.
Burn, with glowing metal,
the slave's brand on it at once;

Denn ich schenke dir mein Herz,
Hast du auch nicht Lust zum Kauf.

for I'll make you a gift of my heart,
though you don't want to buy it.

33
Wehe der, die mir verstrickte
Meinen Geliebten!
Wehe der, die ihn verstrickte!

33
Woe to her who ensnared
my love!
Woe to her who ensnared him!

Ach, der erste, den ich liebte,
Ward gefangen in Sevilla.
Mein Vielgeliebter,
Wehe der, die ihn verstrickte!

Ah, he I loved first,
was caught in Seville.
My great love,
woe to her who ensnared him!

Ward gefangen in Sevilla
Mit der Fessel meiner Locken,
Mein Vielgeliebter,
Wehe der, die ihn verstrickte!

Was caught in Seville
by the chain of my curls.
My great love,
woe to her who ensnared him!

34
Geh, Geliebter, geh jetzt!
Sieh, der Morgen dämmert.

34
Go, beloved, go now!
See, the day is dawning.

Leute gehn schon durch die Gasse,
Und der Markt wird so belebt,
Daß der Morgen wohl, der blasse,
Schon die weißen Flügel hebt.
Und vor unsern Nachbarn bin ich
Bange, daß du Anstoß gibst;
Denn sie wissen nicht, wie innig
Ich dich lieb und du mich liebst.

People are in the street,
and the market's so astir,
that day, pale day,
must be lifting its white wings.
And I'm afraid of our neighbours
—that you'll scandalize them,
they not knowing how deeply
I love you, and you love me.

Drum, Geliebter, geh jetzt,
Sieh, der Morgen dämmert.

So, beloved, go now!
See, the day is dawning.

Wenn die Sonn am Himmel scheinend
Scheucht vom Feld die Perlen klar,
Muß auch ich die Perle weinend
Lassen, die mein Reichtum war.
Was als Tag den andern funkelt,
Meinen Augen dünkt es Nacht,
Da die Trennung bang mir dunkelt,
Wenn das Morgenrot erwacht.

When the sun, shining in the sky,
clears the field of bright pearls,
I, too, weeping, must lose the pearl
that was my wealth.
What to others shines as day,
my eyes see as night,
as, for me, the dread dark of parting falls
when the dawn awakes.

Geh, Geliebter, geh jetzt!
Sieh, der Morgen dämmert.

Go, beloved, go now!
See, the day is dawning.

Willst du feste Wurzel fassen,
Liebster, hier an meiner Brust,
Ohne daß der Neider Hassen
Stürmisch uns verstört die Lust;
Willst du, daß zu tausend Malen
Ich wie heut dich sehen mag,
Und dir stets auf Sicht bezahlen
Unsrer Liebe Schuldbetrag:

If you wish firmly to be rooted,
beloved, here on my breast,
without envious hatred
storming in upon our joy;
if you want me a thousand times
to see you as today,
and always, on sight, to pay you
our debt of love:

Geh, Geliebter, geh jetzt!
Sieh, der Morgen dämmert.

go, beloved, go now!
See, the day is dawning.

Fliehe denn aus meinen Armen!
Denn versäumest du die Zeit,

Flee, then, from my arms.
For if you delay,

Möchten für ein kurz Erwarmen
Wir ertauschen langes Leid.
Ist in Fegefeuersqualen
Doch ein Tag schon auszustehn,
Wenn die Hoffnung fern in Strahlen
Läßt des Himmels Glorie sehn.

we may, for one brief warm embrace,
exchange long sorrow.
One day in purgatory
can, after all, be borne,
when hope, radiant from afar,
reveals heaven's glory.

Drum, Geliebter, geh jetzt!
Sieh, der Morgen dämmert.

So, beloved, go now!
See, the day is dawning.

## Ständchen | Serenade

FRANZ KUGLER

*Johannes Brahms: op. 106, no. 1, 1886*

Der Mond steht über dem Berge,
So recht für verliebte Leut;
Im Garten rieselt ein Brunnen,
Sonst Stille weit und breit.

The moon is over the mountain,
so right for people in love;
in the garden purls a fountain;
otherwise—silence far and wide.

Neben der Mauer im Schatten,
Da stehn der Studenten drei,
Mit Flöt und Geig und Zither,
Und singen und spielen dabei.

By the wall, in shadow,
there three students stand,
with flute and fiddle and zither,
and sing and play.

Die Klänge schleichen der Schönsten
Sacht in den Traum hinein,
Sie schaut den blonden Geliebten
Und lispelt: »Vergiß nicht mein!«

The music steals softly into
the loveliest lady's dreams;
at her blond lover she gazes,
and whispers, 'Remember me!'

## Ständchen | Serenade

WILLIAM SHAKESPEARE: from *Cymbeline*
translated by FRIEDRICH SCHLEGEL; verses 2 and 3 by FRIEDRICH REIL

*Franz Schubert, 1826*

Horch, horch, die Lerch im Ätherblau!
Und Phöbus, neu erweckt,
Tränkt seine Rosse mit dem Tau,
Der Blumenkelche deckt.
Der Ringelblume Knospe schleußt
Die goldnen Äuglein auf;
Mit allem, was da reizend ist,
Du süße Maid, steh auf,
Weil du doch gar so reizend bist;
Du süße Maid, steh auf!

Hark, hark, the lark in heaven's blue!
And Phoebus, new-awakened,
waters his steeds with the dew
that lies on chaliced flowers.
The marigold bud opens
its tiny golden eye;
with every pretty thing,
sweet maid, arise,
for you are so pretty;
sweet maid, arise!

Wenn schon die liebe ganze Nacht
Der Sterne lichtes Heer
Hoch über dir im Wechsel wacht,
So hoffen sie noch mehr,
Daß auch dein Augenstern sie grüßt.
Erwach! Sie warten drauf,
Weil du doch gar so reizend bist;
Du süße Maid, steh auf!

And though all sweet night long
the bright host of stars
in turn keep watch high over you,
they hope for even more—
to be greeted by your starry eyes.
Awake! They're waiting,
for you are so pretty;
sweet maid, arise!

Und wenn dich alles das nicht weckt,
So werde durch den Ton
Der Minne zärtlich aufgeneckt!
O dann erwachst du schon!
Wie oft sie dich ans Fenster
    trieb,
Das weiß sie, drum steh auf,
Und habe deinen Sänger lieb,
Du süße Maid, steh auf!

And if all this fail to rouse you,
then let the sound
of love tenderly tease you awake!
Oh, then you'll be roused!
How often to the window Love has
    urged you,
Love knows, so arise,
and love your minstrel,
sweet maid, arise!

## Ständchen | Serenade

ROBERT REINICK

*Robert Schumann: op. 36, no. 2, 1840; Hugo Wolf, 1883*

Komm' in die stille Nacht,
Liebchen, was zögerst du?
Sonne ging längst zur Ruh;
Welt schloß die Augen zu.
Rings nur einzig die Liebe wacht.

Come into the silent night,
beloved, why do you tarry?
The sun long since is gone to rest;
the world has shut its eyes.
Around us love alone keeps watch.

Liebchen, was zögerst du?
Schon sind die Sterne hell,
Schon ist der Mond zur Stell',
Eilen so schnell, so schnell.
Liebchen, mein Liebchen, drum eil'
    auch du.

Beloved, why do you tarry?
Already the stars are bright,
already the moon is at his post—
so fast, they speed, so fast.
Beloved, so you speed
    too.

Einzig die Liebe wacht,
Ruft dich allüberall.
Höre die Nachtigall,
Hör' meiner Stimme Schall,
Liebchen, o komm in die stille Nacht!

Love alone is keeping watch,
calling you from all sides.
Listen to the nightingale,
listen to the sound of my voice,
beloved, oh come into the silent night!

## Ständchen | Serenade

ADOLF FRIEDRICH VON SCHACK

*Richard Strauss: op. 17, no. 2, 1885–87*

Mach auf, mach auf, doch leise, mein
    Kind,
Um keinen vom Schlummer zu wecken.
Kaum murmelt der Bach, kaum zittert
    im Wind
Ein Blatt an den Büschen und Hecken.
Drum leise, mein Mädchen, daß nichts
    sich regt,
Nur leise die Hand auf die Klinke
    gelegt.

Open up, open up, but softly, my
    child,
so as to rouse no one from slumber.
The brook scarcely murmurs, the breeze
    scarcely stirs
a leaf on bush or hedge.
So softly, my girl, so nothing shall
    stir,
just lay your hand soft on the
    latch.

Mit Tritten, wie Tritte der Elfen so
    sacht,
Um über die Blumen zu hüpfen,
Flieg leicht hinaus in die
    Mondscheinnacht,

With tread as light as the tread of
    elves,
to hop your way over the flowers,
flit out into the moonlit
    night,

Zu mir in den Garten zu schlüpfen.
Rings schlummern die Blüten am
  rieselnden Bach
Und duften im Schlaf, nur die Liebe
  ist wach.

and steal to me in the garden.
By the rippling brook the flowers
  slumber,
fragrant in sleep; love alone is
  awake.

Sitz nieder, hier dämmert's
  geheimnisvoll
Unter den Lindenbäumen,
Die Nachtigall uns zu Häupten soll
Von unseren Küssen träumen
Und die Rose, wenn sie am Morgen
  erwacht,
Hoch glühn von den Wonneschauern
  der Nacht.

Sit—here the dark is full of
  mystery,
under the linden trees,
the nightingale at our heads shall
dream of our kisses,
and the rose, waking at
  morn,
glow deep from the raptures
  of this night.


## Steig auf, geliebter Schatten / Arise, Dear Shade

FRIEDRICH HALM

*Johannes Brahms: op. 94, no. 2, 1884*

Steig auf, geliebter Schatten,
Vor mir in toter Nacht,
Und lab mich Todesmatten
Mit deiner Nähe Macht.

Arise, dear Shade,
to me at dead of night,
and refresh me, weary to death,
by the power of your presence.

Du hast's gekonnt im Leben,
Du kannst es auch im Tod.
Sich nicht dem Schmerz ergeben,
War immer dein Gebot.

That could you do in life,
that can you do even in death.
Yield never to grief,
was always your command.

So komm! Still meine Tränen,
Gib meiner Seele Schwung,
Und Kraft dem welken Sehnen,
Und mach mich wieder jung.

So come, still my tears,
uplift my soul,
strengthen my weak desire,
and make me young again.


## Stille Liebe / Silent Love

JUSTINUS KERNER

*Robert Schumann: op. 35, no. 8, 1840*

Könnt' ich dich in Liedern preisen,
Säng' ich dir das längste Lied.
Ja, ich würd' in allen Weisen
Dich zu singen nimmer müd'!

If in song I could extol you,
I'd sing you my longest song.
To all the tunes there are, I'd
never tire of praising you!

Doch was immer mich betrübte,
Ist, daß ich nur immer stumm
Tragen kann dich, Herzgeliebte,
In des Busens Heiligtum.

But my trouble's always been,
that always mutely only
am I able, beloved, to carry you
in the shrine of my heart.

Dieser Schmerz hat mich bezwungen,
Daß ich sang dies kleine Lied,
Doch von bitterm Leid durchdrungen,
Daß noch kein's auf dich geriet.

By the agony of this I'm forced
to sing this little song,
yet am filled with bitter grief
that none to you has yet succeeded.

## Stille Tränen | Silent Tears

JUSTINUS KERNER

*Robert Schumann: op. 35, no. 10, 1840*

Du bist vom Schlaf erstanden
Und wandelst durch die Au.
Da liegt ob allen Landen
Der Himmel wunderblau.

So lang du ohne Sorgen
Geschlummert schmerzenlos,
Der Himmel bis zum Morgen
Viel Tränen niedergoß.

In stillen Nächten weinet
Oft mancher aus den Schmerz,
Und morgens dann ihr meinet,
Stets fröhlich sei sein Herz.

From sleep you have risen
and walk through the meadow.
Everywhere lies
heaven's wondrous blue.

As long as, free of care, you have
been slumbering, free of pain,
heaven has, till morning,
poured down many tears.

Often on silent nights
many a man weeps his grief away,
and in the morning you imagine
his heart is ever gay.

## Stiller Gang | Silent Walk

RICHARD DEHMEL

*Richard Strauss: op. 31, no. 4, 1895–96*

Der Abend graut, Herbstfeuer brennen.
Über den Stoppeln geht der Rauch
    entzwei.
Kaum ist mein Weg noch zu erkennen.
Bald kommt die Nacht; ich muß mich
    trennen.
Ein Käfer surrt an meinem Ohr vorbei.

Dusk falls, autumn fires are burning.
Over the stubble drifts the
    smoke.
My way is scarcely visible.
Soon night will come; I must break
    away.
A beetle buzzes by my ear.

## Stirb', Lieb' und Freud' | Die, Love and Joy

JUSTINUS KERNER

*Robert Schumann: op. 35, no. 2, 1840*

Zu Augsburg steht ein hohes Haus,
Nah bei dem alten Dom,
Da tritt am hellen Morgen aus
Ein Mägdelein gar fromm;
Gesang erschallt,
Zum Dome wallt
Die liebe Gestalt.

Dort vor Marias heilig' Bild
Sie betend niederkniet,
Der Himmel hat ihr Herz erfüllt,
Und alle Weltlust flieht:
»O Jungfrau rein!
Laß mich allein
Dein eigen sein!«

In Augsburg stands a lofty house
by the old cathedral,
and out into the shining morn
comes a pious maid.
Hymns ring out,
to the cathedral goes
that lovely one.

By Mary's blessed image
she kneels to pray,
her heart is filled with Heaven,
all earthly joy flees:
'O Virgin pure,
grant that I be
yours alone.'

Alsbald der Glocken dumpfer Klang
Die Betenden erweckt,
Das Mägdlein wallt die Hall' entlang,
Es weiß nicht, was es trägt;
Am Haupte ganz
Vom Himmelsglanz
Einen Lilienkranz.

And as muffled bells
call the worshippers,
down the aisle walks the maid,
not knowing what she wears:
upon her head,
all Heavenly bright,
a lily crown.

Mit Staunen schauen all' die Leut'
Dies Kränzlein licht im Haar.
Das Mägdlein aber wallt nicht weit,
Tritt vor den Hochaltar:
»Zur Nonne weiht
Mich arme Maid!
Stirb, Lieb' und Freud'!«

All gaze and marvel
at that bright crown in her hair.
But the maid does not go far,
to the high altar she steps:
'Make me a nun,
poor maid that I am!
Die, love and joy!'

Gott, gib, daß dieses Mägdelein
Ihr Kränzlein friedlich trag,
Es ist die Herzallerliebste mein,
Bleibt's bis zum jüngsten Tag.
Sie weiß es nicht,
Mein Herz zerbricht,
Stirb, Lieb' und Licht!

God grant that maid
wear her crown in peace;
my true love she is,
and shall be till Judgment Day.
She does not know
my heart breaks,
die, love and light!

## Storchenbotschaft | Stork-tidings

EDUARD MÖRIKE

*Hugo Wolf, 1888*

Des Schäfers sein Haus und das steht
   auf zwei Rad,
Steht hoch auf der Heiden, so frühe wie
   spat;
Und wenn nur ein Mancher so'n
   Nachtquartier hätt!
Ein Schäfer tauscht nicht mit dem
   König sein Bett.
Und käm ihm zur Nacht auch was
   Seltsames vor,
Er betet sein Sprüchel und legt sich
   aufs Ohr;
Ein Geistlein, ein Hexlein, so luftige
   Wicht',
Sie klopfen ihm wohl, doch er antwortet
   nicht.
Einmal doch, da ward es ihm wirklich
   zu bunt:
Es knopert am Laden, es winselt der
   Hund;
Nun ziehet mein Schäfer den Riegel—
   ei schau!
Da stehen zwei Störche, der Mann und
   die Frau.
Das Pärchen, es machet ein schön
   Kompliment,
Es möchte gern reden, ach, wenn es
   nur könnt!

The house of the shepherd stands on
   two wheels,
morn and night, high up on the
   moor,
a lodging most would be glad
   of!
*His* bed a shepherd won't change with
   the king.
And should, by night, any strange thing
   occur,
he prays a brief prayer and lies down
   to sleep;
ghostie or witch or such airy
   folk
may come knocking. but he will not
   answer.
But one night it became really too
   much:
the row at the window, the whine of the
   dog;
so my shepherd unbolts, and
   behold,
there stand two storks, man and
   wife.
The couple, they make a beautiful
   bow,
and would speak, if only they
   could.

Was will mir das Ziefer? Ist sowas
erhört?
Doch ist mir wohl fröhliche Botschaft
beschert.
Ihr seid wohl dahinten zu Hause am
Rhein?
Ihr habt wohl mein Mädel gebissen ins
Bein?
Nun weinet das Kind und die Mutter
noch mehr,
Sie wünschet den Herzallerliebsten sich
her.
Und wünschet daneben die Taufe
bestellt:
Ein Lämmlein, ein Würstlein, ein
Beutelein Geld?
So sagt nur, ich käm' in zwei Tag oder
drei,
Und grüßt mir mein Bübel und rührt
ihm den Brei!
Doch halt! Warum stellt ihr zu Zweien
euch ein?
Es werden doch, hoff' ich, nicht
Zwillinge sein?
Da klappern die Störche im lustigsten
Ton,
Sie nicken und knixen und fliegen
davon.

What do they want of *me*? Whoever
heard the like?
Yet joyful tidings it must be, for
me.
That way you live, do you, by the
Rhine?
Pecked my girl on the leg, I
expect?
The child's now crying and the mother
still more
wanting her dear husband
there.
Wanting, too, the christening feast
arranged,
a lambkin, a sausage, and purse of
pence?
Well, tell her I'm coming in two days
or three,
say hello to my boy, give his porridge a
stir.
But wait! Why have two of you
come?
It won't . . . I hope . . . be
twins?
At that, a merry clatter from the
storks,
he nods, she curtseys and off they
fly.

## Suleika I | Zuleika I

MARIANNE VON WILLEMER (from Goethe's *West-östlicher Divan*)

*Felix Mendelssohn-Bartholdy, op. 57, no. 3, 1839-42; Franz Schubert, 1821?*

Was bedeutet die Bewegung?
Bringt der Ost mir frohe Kunde?
Seiner Schwingen frische Regung
Kühlt des Herzens tiefe Wunde.

What does this agitation mean?
Is it glad news the East Wind brings?
The fresh stirring of its wings
cools the deep wound of the heart.

Kosend spielt er mit dem Staube,
Jagt ihn auf in leichten Wölkchen,
Treibt zur sichern Rebenlaube
Der Insekten frohes Völkchen.

Fondly it toys with the dust,
flings it up in small light clouds,
chases to the safe vine-bower
the tiny merry insect throng.

Lindert sanft der Sonne Glühen,
Kühlt auch mir die heißen Wangen,
Küßt die Reben noch im Fliehen,
Die auf Feld und Hügel prangen.

Soothes the burning of the sun,
cools as well my ardent cheeks,
kisses, in its flight, the vine
resplendent upon hill and field.

Und mir bringt sein leises Flüstern
Von dem Freunde tausend Grüße;
Eh' noch diese Hügel düstern
Grüßen mich wohl tausend Küsse.

And its whispering brings me
a thousand greetings from my love;
and before these hills grow dark
a thousand kisses will surely greet me.

Und so kannst du weiterziehen!
Diene Freunden und Betrübten!
Dort, wo hohe Mauern glühen,
Find ich bald den Vielgeliebten.

And so can you go on your way!
Serve friends and those afflicted!
There, where lofty walls are burning,
soon I'll find my dear beloved.

Ach, die wahre Herzenskunde,
Liebeshauch, erfrischtes Leben,
Wird mir nur aus seinem Munde,
Kann mir nur sein Atem geben.

Ah, the true message of the heart,
love exhaled, life refreshed,
comes to me only from his mouth,
only his breath can give to me.


## Suleika II | Zuleika II

MARIANNE VON WILLEMER (from Goethe's *West-östlicher Divan*)

*Felix Mendelssohn-Bartholdy: op. 34, no. 4, 1833–34; Franz Schubert, 1821?*

Ach, um deine feuchten Schwingen,
West, wie sehr ich dich beneide:
Denn du kannst ihm Kunde bringen
Was ich in der Trennung leide!

Ah, of your moist wings,
West Wind, how envious I am:
for to him you can bring news
of what I suffer in separation!

Die Bewegung deiner Flügel
Weckt im Busen stilles Sehnen;
Blumen, Augen, Wald und Hügel
Stehn bei deinem Hauch in Tränen.

The beating of your wings
wakes silent longing in the breast;
flowers, eyes, forest, hill
are tearful where you breathe.

Doch dein mildes sanftes Wehen
Kühlt die wunden Augenlider;
Ach, für Leid müßt' ich vergehen,
Hofft ich nicht zu sehn ihn wieder.

Yet your mild gentle wafting
is cooling to sore eyelids;
ah, for grief would I have to die,
did I not hope to see him again.

Eile denn zu meinem Lieben,
Spreche sanft zu seinem Herzen;
Doch vermeid ihn zu betrüben
Und verbirg ihm meine Schmerzen.

Speed then to my beloved,
speak softly to his heart;
but avoid troubling him,
and conceal from him my agony.

Sag ihm, aber sag's bescheiden:
Seine Liebe sei mein Leben,
Freudiges Gefühl von beiden
Wird mir seine Nähe geben.

Tell him—but put it simply—
that his love is my life,
and that the joyous feelings of both
will his presence give me.


## Tambourliedchen | Drummer's Song

KARL CANDIDUS

*Johannes Brahms: op. 69, no. 5, 1877*

Den Wirbel schlag ich gar so stark,
Daß euch erzittert Bein und Mark,
Drum denk ich ans schöne Schätzelein.
Blaugrau, blau ist seiner Augen Schein.

I drum a roll so hard
my very marrow trembles,
and so of my true love I think,
her eyes shine blue-grey, blue.

Und denk ich an den Schein so hell,
Von selber dämpft das Trommelfell
Den wilden Ton, klingt hell und rein.
Blaugrau, blau sind Liebchens Äugelein.

If I think of their bright glow,
my drumskin itself subdues
the fury—sounds out clear and pure.
Blue-grey, blue, my loved one's eyes.

## Todessehnen | Death Longing

MAX VON SCHENKENDORF

*Johannes Brahms: op. 86, no. 6, 1878*

Ach, wer nimmt von meiner Seele
Die geheime, schwere Last,
Die, je mehr ich sie verhehle,
Immer mächtiger mich faßt?

Möchtest du nur endlich brechen,
Mein gequältes, banges Herz!
Findest hier mit deinen Schwächen,
Deiner Liebe, nichts als Schmerz.

Dort nur wirst du ganz genesen,
Wo der Sehnsucht nichts mehr fehlt,
Wo das schwesterliche Wesen
Deinem Wesen sich vermählt.

Hör es, Vater in der Höhe,
Aus der Fremde fleht dein Kind:
Gib, daß er mich bald umwehe,
Deines Todes Lebenswind.

Daß er zu dem Stern mich hebe,
Wo man keine Trennung kennt,
Wo die Geistersprache Leben
Mit der Liebe Namen nennt.

Ah, who will relieve my soul
of its secret, heavy burden,
which, the more I conceal it,
presses ever more powerfully?

Would that finally you'd break,
my tormented, fearful heart!
Here you find, for all your failings,
all your love, naught but pain.

Only there will you recover,
where yearning lacks nothing more,
where that sister being
marries itself to yours.

Listen, Father on high,
from afar your child implores:
grant that soon it blow about me,
your death's wind of life.

Grant it raise me to the star
where parting is unknown,
where the spirit tongue calls
life by the name of love.

## Tom der Reimer | Tom the Rhymer

THEODOR FONTANE: after an Old Scottish ballad

*Carl Loewe: op. 135a, ed. 1867*

Der Reimer Thomas lag am Bach,
Am Kieselbach bei Huntly Schloß.
Da sah er eine blonde Frau,
Die saß auf einem weißen Roß.

Sie saß auf einem weißen Roß,
Die Mähne war geflochten fein,
Und hell an jeder Flechte hing
Ein silberblankes Glöckelein.

Und Tom der Reimer zog den Hut
Und fiel aufs Knie, er grüßt und spricht:
Du bist die Himmelskönigin!
Du bist von dieser Erde nicht!

Die blonde Frau hält an ihr Roß:
Ich will dir sagen, wer ich bin;
Ich bin die Himmelsjungfrau nicht,
Ich bin die Elfenkönigin!

Nimm deine Harf und spiel und sing
Und laß dein bestes Lied erschalln!

The Rhymer Thomas lay by the burn,
the pebble burn by Huntly Castle,
and a fair-haired lady he espied,
mounted on a white steed.

Mounted on a white steed
with daintily braided mane,
and glittering on each braid
hung a tiny silver bell.

And Tom the Rhymer doffed his hat,
knelt, saluted and said:
'The Queen of Heaven art thou,
and never of this world!'

The fair-haired lady halted:
'I will tell thee who I am—
not the Heavenly Maid,
but Queen of the Elves!

'Take up thy harp, play, sing,
and let thy best song sound!

Doch wenn du meine Lippe küßt,
Bist du mir sieben Jahr verfalln!

Wohl! Sieben Jahr, o Königin,
Zu dienen dir, es schreckt mich kaum!
Er küßte sie, sie küßte ihn,
Ein Vogel sang im Eschenbaum.

Nun bist du mein, nun zieh mit mir,
Nun bist du mein auf sieben Jahr.
Sie ritten durch den grünen Wald,
Wie glücklich da der Reimer war!

Sie ritten durch den grünen Wald
Bei Vogelsang und Sonnenschein,
Und wenn sie leicht am Zügel zog,
So klangen hell die Glöckelein.

But if thou kiss my lips,
thou art mine for seven years!'

'Then seven be it, O Queen,
that will not dismay me, serving thee!'
He kissed her, she kissed him,
a bird sang in the ash tree.

'Now thou art mine. Now come with me.
Now thou art mine for seven years.'
Off through the greenwood they rode,
and how happy the Rhymer was!

Through the greenwood they rode,
birds singing, sun shining;
and whenever she lightly drew rein,
the tiny bells tinkled.

## *Totengräbers Heimweh* | *Gravedigger's Homesickness*

J. N. CRAIGHER DE JACHELUTTA

*Franz Schubert, 1825*

O Menschheit, o Leben! was soll's?
o was soll's?
grabe aus, scharre zu! Tag und Nacht
keine Ruh!
Das Drängen, das Treiben, wohin?
o wohin?
»Ins Grab, ins Grab, tief hinab!«
O Schicksal, o traurige Pflicht,
ich trag's länger nicht!
Wann wirst du mir schlagen, o Stunde
der Ruh?
O Tod! komm und drücke die Augen
mir zu!
Im Leben, da ist's ach! so schwül, ach!
so schwül!
im Grabe so friedlich, so kühl!
Doch ach! wer legt mich hinein?
Ich stehe allein,
von allen verlassen, dem Tod nur
verwandt,
verweil ich am Rande, das Kreuz in der
Hand,
und starre mit sehnendem Blick hinab
ins tiefe, ins tiefe Grab!
O Heimat des Friedens, der Seligen
Land,
an dich knüpft die Seele ein magisches
Band.
Du winkst mir von ferne, du ewiges
Licht,
es schwinden die Sterne, das Auge
schon bricht,—
ich sinke, ich sinke! Ihr Lieben, ich
komm!
Ich sinke, ihr Lieben, ich komme, ich
komm!

O mankind, O life! For what, oh for
what?
Dig out, fill in! Day and night no
rest!
This hustle, this bustle, leads where?
Where?
'The grave, the grave, deep down!'
O fate, O melancholy duty,
I can bear it no more!
When, O hour of peace, will you toll
for me?
O death, come, press shut my
eyes!
Life is, ah, so oppressive, so
oppressive!
The grave—so peaceful, cool!
But ah, who will lay me in it?
Alone I stand,
by all forsaken, death my sole
kin,
by the side I tarry, cross in
hand,
and stare longingly down
at the deep, deep grave.
O homeland of peace, O land of the
blessed,
to you the soul is bound by a magic
bond.
From afar you beckon me, eternal
light,
the stars vanish, the eye grows
dim—
I die, I die! Loved ones, I
come!
I die, loved ones, I come, I
come!

## Tragische Geschichte / Tragic Tale

ADALBERT VON CHAMISSO

*Hans Pfitzner: op. 22, no. 2, 1907*

's war einer, dem's zu Herzen ging,
Daß ihm der Zopf nach hinten hing,
Er wollt es anders haben.

Da denkt er denn, wie fang ich's an?
Ich dreh' mich 'rum, so ist's getan,
Der Zopf, der hängt ihm hinten.

Da hat er flink sich umgedreht,
Und wie es stund, es annoch steht:
Der Zopf, der hängt ihm hinten.

Da dreht er schnell sich anders 'rum,
's wird aber noch nicht besser drum,
Der Zopf, der hängt ihm hinten.

Er dreht sich links, er dreht sich rechts,
Er tut nichts Guts, er tut nichts
  Schlechts,
Der Zopf, der hängt ihm hinten.

Er dreht sich wie ein Kreisel fort,
Es hilft zu nichts, mit einem Wort—
Der Zopf, der hängt ihm hinten.

Und seht, er dreht sich immer noch
Und denkt, es hilft am Ende doch,
Der Zopf, der hängt ihm hinten.

There was a man who took to heart
his pigtail's hanging down behind—
a change he wanted.

Then he thinks, how shall I start?
I'll turn around and then it's done,
his pigtail hangs behind him.

Briskly then he turned about,
and as it was, it still is now,
the pigtail hangs behind him.

He swiftly turns the other way,
but it's no better still for that,
the pigtail hangs behind him.

He turns to left, he turns to right,
he does no good, he does no
  harm,
the pigtail hangs behind him.

Round and round like a top he spins,
it leads to nothing—to be brief:—
the pigtail hangs behind him.

And behold, he's turning still,
thinking it will help him in the end,
the pigtail hangs behind him.

## Tragödie: I, II, III / Tragedy: I, II, III

HEINRICH HEINE

*Robert Schumann: op. 64, no. 3 I, II, III, 1841–47*

I
Entflieh mit mir und sei mein Weib,
Und ruh an meinem Herzen aus;
Fern in der Fremde sei mein Herz
Dein Vaterland und Vaterhaus.

Gehst du nicht mit, so sterb' ich hier
Und du bist einsam und allein;
Und bleibst du auch im Vaterhaus,
Wirst doch wie in der Fremde sein.

II
Es fiel ein Reif in der Frühlingsnacht,
Er fiel auf die zarten Blaublümelein,
Sie sind verwelket, verdorret.

I
Elope with me and be my wife,
and take your rest upon my heart;
far from home let my heart be
your fatherland and father's home.

If you'll not come, here I shall die,
and you will be lonely and alone;
and even though in your father's home,
you'll be as in a foreign land.

II
In the spring night frost fell,
and fell on the tender forget-me-nots;
they blighted, withered.

Ein Jüngling hatte ein Mädchen lieb,
Sie flohen heimlich von Hause fort,
Es wußt' weder Vater noch Mutter.

Sie sind gewandert hin und her,
Sie haben gehabt weder Glück noch
    Stern,
Sie sind verdorben, gestorben.
    (*Armin Knab, 1904-07*)

III
Auf ihrem Grab, da steht eine Linde,
Drin pfeifen die Vögel und
    Abendwinde,
Und drunter sitzt, auf dem grünen Platz,
Der Müllersknecht mit seinem Schatz.

Die Winde, die wehen so lind und so
    schaurig,
Die Vögel, die singen so süß und so
    traurig,
Die schwatzenden Buhlen, die werden
    stumm,
Sie weinen und wissen selbst nicht
    warum.

A young man loved a maiden,
they eloped together in secret,
neither father nor mother knew.

This way they wandered, that way,
luck was not in their
    favour,
they perished, died.

III
Over their grave stands a lime tree,
in which birds and evening
    breezes pipe,
while on the turf below, sits
the miller's boy with his love.

The breezes blow so mild and
    shivery,
the birds sing so sweet and so
    sad,
the chattering lovers fall
    silent,
weep and do not know what
    for.

---

*Trauer und Trost | Grief and Comfort*

PETER CORNELIUS

*Peter Cornelius: op. 3, no. 1-6, 1854*

1 *Trauer*
Ich wandle einsam,
Mein Weg ist lang;
Zum Himmel schau ich
Hinauf so bang.

Kein Stern von oben
Blickt niederwärts,
Glanzlos der Himmel,
Dunkel mein Herz.

Mein Herz und der Himmel
Hat gleiche Not,
Sein Glanz ist erloschen,
Mein Lieb ist tot.

2 *Angedenken*
Von stillem Ort,
Von kühler Statt
Nahm ich mit fort
Ein Efeublatt.

Ein Requiem
Tönt leis und matt,
Sooft ich nehm
Zur Hand das Blatt.

1 *Grief*
I wander lonely,
my way is long;
skywards I gaze
so anxiously.

Above, no star
looks down,
lustreless the sky,
sombre my heart.

Heart and sky
share one distress,
its gleam is gone,
my love is dead.

2 *Memento*
From a quiet place,
a cool place,
away I bore
an ivy leaf.

A requiem
dimly, softly sounds
whenever I pick up
that leaf.

Wenn aller Schmerz
Geendet hat,
Legt mir aufs Herz
Das Efeublatt.

After all agony
is done,
lay on my heart
that ivy leaf.

### 3 Ein Ton
Mir klingt ein Ton so wunderbar
In Herz und Sinnen immerdar.
Ist es der Hauch, der dir entschwebt,
Als einmal noch dein Mund gebebt?
Ist es des Glöckleins trüber Klang,
Der dir gefolgt den Weg entlang?
Mir klingt der Ton so voll und rein,
Als schlöß er deine Seele ein.
Als stiegest liebend nieder du
Und sängest meinen Schmerz in Ruh.

### 3 A Sound
So wonderful a sound there is
ever in my mind and heart.
Is it the breath that floated forth once
when still your lips could tremble?
Is it the sad note of the bell
that followed you upon your way?
So full and clear is the sound to me,
as if it comprised your soul.
As if lovingly you came down to me
and sang to rest my sorrow.

### 4 An den Traum
Öffne mir die goldne Pforte,
Traum, zu deinem Wunderhain,
Was mir blühte und verdorrte,
Laß mir blühend neu gedeihn.
Zeige mir die heilgen Orte
Meiner Wonne, meiner Pein,
Laß mich lauschen holdem Worte,
Liebesstrahlen saugen ein.
Öffne mir die goldne Pforte,
Traum, o laß mich glücklich sein!

### 4 To Dreams
Open for me the golden gate
to your magic glade, O dreams,
whatever bloomed and faded,
let flourish for me and bloom again.
Show to me those sacred places
of my bliss and agony,
let me listen to sweet words
and drink in the streams of love.
Open for me the golden gate,
oh, let me, dreams, be happy!

### 5 Treue
Dein Gedenken lebt in Liedern fort;
Lieder, die der tiefsten Brust entwallen,
Sagen mir: du lebst in ihnen allen,
Und gewiß, die Lieder halten
   Wort.

### 5 Faithfulness
Your memory lives on in songs;
boiling up from deep in the heart,
they tell me, all of them, you live,
and certainly, songs mean what they
   say.

Dein Gedenken blüht in Tränen fort;
Tränen aus des Herzens Heiligtume
Nähren tauend der Erinnrung Blume,
In dem Tau blüht dein Gedenken fort.

Your memory blossoms on in tears;
tears from sacred places of the heart
bedew and nourish memory's blossom,
in that dew your memory blossoms on.

Dein Gedenken lebt in Träumen fort;
Träume, die dein Bild verklärt mir
   zeigen,
Sagen: daß du ewig bist mein eigen,
Und gewiß, die Träume halten
   Wort.

Your memory lives on in dreams;
dreams which show me your image,
   radiant,
which say you are eternally my own,
and certainly, dreams mean what they
   say.

### 6 Trost
Der Glückes Fülle mir verliehn
Und Hochgesang,
Nun auch in Schmerzen preis ich ihn
Mein Leben lang.
Mir sei ein sichres Himmelspfand,
Was ich verlor;
Mich führt der Schmerz an starker
   Hand
Zu ihm empor.

### 6 Comfort
Him who bestowed on me abundant joy
and exalted song,
now will I praise, even in grief,
my whole life long.
A certain pledge of heaven be to me
what I have lost;
grief leads me strongly by the
   hand
to Him above.

Wenn ich in Wonnen bang beklagt
Den Flug der Zeit,
In Schmerzen hat mir hell getagt
Unsterblichkeit.

If, in bliss, I anxiously lamented
the flight of time,
brightly for me, in grief, has dawned
immortality.


## Traum durch die Dämmerung | Dream through Dusk

OTTO JULIUS BIERBAUM

*Max Reger: op. 35, no. 3, 1899; Richard Strauss: op. 29, no. 1, 1894–95*

Weite Wiesen im Dämmergrau;
Die Sonne verglomm, die Sterne ziehn,
Nun geh ich hin zu der schönsten Frau,
Weit über Wiesen im Dämmergrau,
Tief in den Busch von Jasmin.

Broad meadows in grey dusk;
the sun has died, the stars come out,
to the fairest of women now I go,
far across meadows in grey dusk,
deep into shrubs of jasmine.

Durch Dämmergrau in der Liebe Land;
Ich gehe nicht schnell, ich eile nicht;
Mich zieht ein weiches samtenes Band
Durch Dämmergrau in der Liebe Land,
In ein blaues mildes Licht.
Ich gehe nicht schnell, ich eile nicht;
Durch Dämmergrau in der Liebe Land,
In ein mildes blaues Licht.

Through grey dusk to the land of love;
I do not walk fast, I do not hurry;
soft, velvety are the ties that draw me
through grey dusk to the land of love,
to gentle blue light.
I do not walk fast, I do not hurry;
through grey dusk to the land of love,
to gentle blue light.


## Trost | Comfort

GUSTAV FALKE

*Max Reger: op. 15, no. 10, 1894*

Still! 's ist nur ein Traum,
's geht alles vorbei,
Was es auch sei.
Spürest es kaum,
's ist nur ein Hauch,
Wie du auch.

Hush! But a dream it is,
all passes,
whatever it may be.
You hardly feel it,
it is a mere breath,
as you are.


## Trost in Tränen | Comfort in Tears

JOHANN WOLFGANG GOETHE

*Johannes Brahms: op. 48, no. 5, 1858; Johann Friedrich Reichardt, ed. 1809;*
*Franz Schubert, 1814; Carl Friedrich Zelter, 1803*

Wie kommts, daß du so traurig bist,
Da alles froh erscheint?
Man sieht dirs an den Augen an,
Gewiß, du hast geweint.

How comes it you're so sad
when all are glad?
One can see from your eyes,
to be sure, you've been weeping.

»Und hab ich einsam auch geweint,
So ists mein eigner Schmerz,
Und Tränen fließen gar so süß,
Erleichtern mir das Herz.«

'If I have wept in solitude,
it is my own distress,
and tears so very sweetly flow,
lightening my heart.'

Die frohen Freunde laden dich,
O komm an unsre Brust!
Und was du auch verloren hast,
Vertraue den Verlust.

»Ihr lärmt und rauscht und ahnet nicht,
Was mich, den Armen, quält.
Ach nein, verloren hab ichs nicht,
So sehr es mir auch fehlt.«

So raffe denn dich eilig auf,
Du bist ein junges Blut.
In deinen Jahren hat man Kraft
Und zum Erwerben Mut.

»Ach nein, erwerben kann ichs nicht,
Es steht mir gar zu fern.
Es weilt so hoch, es blinkt so schön,
Wie droben jener Stern.«

Die Sterne, die begehrt man nicht,
Man freut sich ihrer Pracht,
Und mit Entzücken blickt man auf
In jeder heitern Nacht.

»Und mit Entzücken blick ich auf,
So manchen lieben Tag;
Verweinen laßt die Nächte mich,
Solang ich weinen mag.«

Happy friends invite you,
oh, to our bosom come!
And of whatever kind it is,
confide your loss to us.

'You roister, roar, unaware
what me, poor man, torments.
Ah no, nothing have I lost,
however great my lack.'

So then, quick, take courage,
young fellow that you are.
One, at your age, has the strength
and pluck to woo and win.

'Ah no, I cannot woo and win it,
too distant is my goal.
It dwells as high, gleams as bright
as, way up there, that star.'

One does not desire the stars,
one rejoices in their glory,
and with delight one gazes up
on every night that's clear.

'And with delight I do look up,
on so many a day;
let me weep the nights away
as long as I may weep.'

## Um Mitternacht / At Midnight

EDUARD MÖRIKE

*Heimo Erbse: op. 17, no. 2, ed. 1959; Robert Franz: op. 28, no. 6;
Hugo Wolf, 1888*

Gelassen stieg die Nacht ans Land,
Lehnt träumend an der Berge
  Wand,
Ihr Auge sieht die goldne Waage nun
Der Zeit in gleichen Schalen stille ruhn;
Und kecker rauschen die Quellen hervor,
Sie singen der Mutter, der Nacht, ins
  Ohr
Vom Tage,
Vom heute gewesenen Tage.

Das uralt alte Schlummerlied,
Sie achtet's nicht, sie ist es müd;
Ihr klingt des Himmels Bläue süßer
  noch,
Der flüchtgen Stunden gleich-
  geschwungnes Joch.
Doch immer behalten die Quellen das
  Wort,
Es singen die Wasser im Schlafe noch
  fort
Vom Tage,
Vom heute gewesenen Tage.

Calmly night has climbed ashore,
reclines, dreamy, against the mountain
  wall,
eyes now upon the golden scales
of time quietly at rest in counterpoise;
and bolder, the rushing springs
sing, in their mother the night's
  ear,
of the day,
of the day that has been today.

That age-old lullaby
she disregards, weary of it;
sweeter to her sounds the blue of
  heaven,
the even-slung yoke of the fleeting
  hours.
But still the springs murmur
  on,
and in sleep the waters sing
  on
of the day,
of the day that has been today.

## Um Mitternacht / At Midnight

FRIEDRICH RÜCKERT

*Gustav Mahler, ed. 1905; Hermann Reutter: op. 54, no. 3, ed. 1941*

Um Mitternacht
hab ich gewacht
und aufgeblickt zum Himmel;
kein Stern vom Sterngewimmel
hat mir gelacht
um Mitternacht.

At midnight
I awoke
and gazed to heaven;
no star of that starry throng
did smile on me
at midnight.

Um Mitternacht
hab ich gedacht
hinaus in dunkle Schranken.
Es hat kein Lichtgedanken
mir Trost gebracht
um Mitternacht.

At midnight
my thoughts
went out to the utmost darkness.
No shining thought
brought me comfort
at midnight.

Um Mitternacht
nahm ich in acht
die Schläge meines Herzens.
Ein einzger Puls des Schmerzens
war angefacht
um Mitternacht.

At midnight
I marked
the beating of my heart.
One single pulse of agony
was stirred to life
at midnight.

Um Mitternacht
kämpft ich die Schlacht,
o Menschheit, deiner Leiden;
nicht konnt ich sie entscheiden
mit meiner Macht
um Mitternacht.

At midnight
I fought the battle
of your afflictions, O humanity;
I was not able to decide it
with my strength
at midnight.

Um Mitternacht
hab ich die Macht
in deine Hand gegeben:
Herr über Tod und Leben,
du hältst die Wacht
um Mitternacht.

At midnight
I gave my strength
into your hand:
Lord over life and death,
you keep watch
at midnight.


## Unbewegte, laue Luft / Mild, Unagitated Air

GEORG FRIEDRICH DAUMER

*Johannes Brahms: op. 57, no. 8, 1871*

Unbewegte, laue Luft,
tiefe Ruhe der Natur;
durch die stille Gartennacht
plätschert die Fontäne nur.
Aber im Gemüte schwillt
heißere Begierde mir,
aber in den Adern quillt
Leben und verlangt nach Leben.
Sollten nicht auch deine Brust
sehnlichere Wünsche heben?
Sollte meiner Seele Ruf
nicht die deine tief durchbeben?

Mild, unagitated air,
nature in deep repose;
in the still garden night
only the fountain plashes.
But in my soul swell
more ardent desires,
but in my veins surges
life and craves life.
Should not more ardent
wishes exalt your breast too?
Should my soul's call
not deeply thrill your soul?

Leise mit dem Ätherfuß
säume nicht, daherzuschweben!
Komm, o komm, damit wir uns
himmlisches Genüge geben!

Softly, on ethereal feet,
float to me, do not tarry!
Come, oh come, that we may give
each other heavenly satisfaction!


## Venezianisches Epigramm / Venetian Epigram

JOHANN WOLFGANG GOETHE

*Othmar Schoeck: op. 19b, no. 7, V, 1906–15*

Diese Gondel vergleich ich der Wiege,
sie schaukelt gefällig,
Und das Kästchen darauf scheint ein
geräumiger Sarg.
Recht so! Zwischen der Wieg und dem
Sarg wir schwanken und schweben
Auf dem großen Kanal sorglos durchs
Leben dahin.

This gondola I liken to the cradle—it
rocks pleasingly,
And the little box upon it seems a
roomy coffin.
Rightly so! Between cradle and coffin
we swing and glide
on the Grand Canal carefree through
life.


## Venezianisches Gondellied / Venetian Gondola Song

THOMAS MOORE, translated by FERDINAND FREILIGRATH

*Felix Mendelssohn-Bartholdy: op. 57, no. 5, 1839–42;*
*Robert Schumann: op. 25 (Myrten), no. 18, 1840*

Wenn durch die Piazzetta
Die Abendluft weht.
Dann weißt du, Pinetta,
Wer wartend hier steht,
Du weißt,
Wer trotz Schleier und Maske dich
kennt;
Du weißt,
Wie die Sehnsucht im Herzen mir
brennt.

When over the piazzetta
the breeze of evening blows,
then, Pinetta, you know
who stands here and waits,
you know
who knows you despite veil and
mask;
you know
how my heart burns with
longing.

Ein Schifferkleid trag ich
Zur selbigen Zeit,
Und zitternd dir sag ich:
Das Boot ist bereit.
O komm jetzt,
Wo Lunen noch Wolken umziehn.
O komm jetzt!
Laß durch die Lagunen, Geliebte, uns
fliehn!

Boatman's garb I'll wear
at the same hour,
and trembling tell you:
the boat is ready.
Oh, come now,
while clouds still cover the moon.
Oh, come now!
Through the lagoons, love, let us
flee!


## Verborgenheit / Obscurity

EDUARD MÖRIKE

*Willy Burkhard, ed. 1959; Robert Franz: op. 28, no. 5;*
*Hugo Wolf, 1888*

Laß, o Welt, o laß mich sein!
Locket nicht mit Liebesgaben,

Leave, O world, oh, leave me be!
Tempt me not with gifts of love,

| Laßt dies Herz alleine haben | leave this heart to have alone |
| Seine Wonne, seine Pein! | its bliss, its agony! |

Was ich traure, weiß ich nicht,     Why I grieve, I do not know,
Es ist unbekanntes Wehe;     my grief is unknown grief,
Immerdar durch Tränen sehe     all the time I see through tears
Ich der Sonne liebes Licht.     the sun's delightful light.

Oft bin ich mir kaum bewußt,     Often, scarce aware am I,
Und die helle Freude zücket     pure joy flashes
Durch die Schwere, so mich drücket     through the oppressing heaviness
Wonniglich in meiner Brust.     —flashes blissful in my heart.

Laß, o Welt, o laß mich sein!     Leave, O world, oh, leave me be!
Locket nicht mit Liebesgaben,     Tempt me not with gifts of love,
Laßt dies Herz alleine haben     leave this heart to have alone
Seine Wonne, seine Pein!     its bliss, its agony!

## *Vergebliches Ständchen* | *Vain Serenade*

LOWER RHINE FOLK SONG

*Johannes Brahms: op. 84, no. 4, 1881?*

»Guten Abend, mein Schatz, guten     'Good evening, my love, good evening,
    Abend, mein Kind!     my child!
Ich komm aus Lieb zu dir,     I come out of love for you,
Ach, mach mir auf die Tür,     ah, open your door to me,
Mach mir auf die Tür!«     open your door!'

»Mein' Tür ist verschlossen, ich laß'     'My door is locked, I'll not let you
    dich nicht ein,     in,
Mutter, die rät mir klug,     my mother advises wisely,
Wärst du herein mit Fug,     were you in here by right,
Wär's mit mir vorbei.«     it were all over with me.'

»So kalt ist die Nacht, so eisig der     'So cold is the night, so icy the
    Wind,     wind,
Daß mir das Herz erfriert,     that my heart will freeze,
Mein Lieb erlöschen wird,     my love will die,
Öffne mir mein Kind.«     open to me, my child.'

»Löschet dein Lieb, laß' sie löschen nur,     'If your love will die, then let it die,
Löschet sie immerzu,     and if it keeps on dying,
Geh' heim zu Bett, zur Ruh!     go home to bed, to rest!
Gute Nacht, mein Knab'!«     Good night, my lad!'

## *Vergiftet sind meine Lieder* | *Poisoned Are My Songs*

HEINRICH HEINE

*Franz Liszt, 1844*

Vergiftet sind meine Lieder,     Poisoned are my songs,
Wie könnt' es anders sein?     how should it be different?
Du hast mir ja Gift gegossen     For you have poured poison
Ins blühende Leben hinein.     into my blossoming life.

Vergiftet sind meine Lieder,
Wie könnt' es anders sein?
Ich trag' im Herzen viel Schlangen,
Und dich, Geliebte mein.

Poisoned are my songs,
how should it be different?
Many snakes I bear in my heart,
including, my beloved, you.


## Verklärung / Transfiguration

ALEXANDER POPE, translated by JOHANN GOTTFRIED HERDER

*Franz Schubert, 1813*

Lebensfunke, vom Himmel entglüht,
Der sich loszuwinden müht,
Zitternd, kühn, vor Sehnen leidend,
Gern und doch mit Schmerzen
    scheidend!

Heaven-kindled spark of life,
that toils to wrench itself away,
trembling, brave, enduring longing,
gladly, yet in agony,
    departing!

End', o end' den Kampf, Natur!
Sanft ins Leben
Aufwärts schweben,
Sanft hinschwinden laß mich nur!

End, oh end the battle, nature!
Only let me into life gently
upwards float
and gently vanish!

Horch, mir lispeln Geister zu:
»Schwester Seele, komm' zur Ruh'.«

Hark, spirits whisper to me:
'Sister-soul, come to rest.'

Ziehet was mich sanft von hinnen?
Was ist es, was mir meine Sinnen,
Mir den Hauch zu rauben droht?
Seele, sprich! Ist das der Tod?

Does something draw me gently hence?
What is it that threatens to deprive me
of my sense and of my breath?
Speak, soul, is it Death?

Die Welt entweicht, sie ist nicht mehr.
Engel-Einklang um mich her!

The world vanishes, it is no more.
All around me angel harmony!

Ich schweb' im Morgenrot!
Leiht, o leiht mir eure Schwingen,
Ihr Brüder, Geister, helft mir singen:
»O Grab, wo ist dein Sieg?
Wo ist dein Pfeil, o Tod?!«

In the dawn of day I float!
Lend, oh lend me your wings,
brothers, spirits, help me sing:
'O grave, where is your victory?
Where, O Death, your arrow?'


## Verschwiegene Liebe / Silent Love

JOSEPH VON EICHENDORFF

*Hugo Wolf, 1888*

Über Wipfel und Saaten
In den Glanz hinein—
Wer mag sie erraten,
Wer holte sie ein?
Gedanken sich wiegen,
Die Nacht ist verschwiegen,
Gedanken sind frei.

Over trees and corn
into the gleam—
who may guess them,
retrieve them?—
thoughts go swaying,
the night is silent,
thoughts are free.

Errät es nur eine,
Wer an sie gedacht
Beim Rauschen der Haine,

One alone guesses
who has thought of her,
as the woods murmur,

Wenn niemand mehr wacht
Als die Wolken, die fliegen—
Mein Lieb ist verschwiegen
Und schön wie die Nacht.

when no one keeps watch
but the clouds that fly—
my love is silent
and beautiful as night.

## Vier ernste Gesänge / Four Serious Songs

no. 1: Ecclesiastes, Chapter 3, 19–22
no. 2: Ecclesiastes, Chapter 4, 1–3
no. 3: Ecclesiasticus, Chapter 41, 1–2
no. 4: I Corinthians, Chapter 13, 1–3 and 12–13

Translated by MARTIN LUTHER

*Johannes Brahms: op. 121, nos. 1–4, 1896*

**1** *Denn es gehet dem Menschen*
Denn es gehet dem Menschen wie dem
    Vieh,
wie dies stirbt, so stirbt er auch;
und haben alle einerlei Odem;
und der Mensch hat nichts mehr denn
    das Vieh:
denn es ist alles eitel.
Es fährt alles an einen Ort;
es ist alles von Staub gemacht
und wird wieder zu Staub.
Wer weiß, ob der Geist des Menschen
    aufwärts fahre,
und der Odem des Viehes
unterwärts unter die Erde fahre?
Darum sahe ich, daß nichts Bessers ist,
denn daß der Mensch fröhlich sei in
    seiner Arbeit;
denn das ist sein Teil.
Denn wer will ihn dahin bringen,
daß er sehe, was nach ihm geschehen
    wird?

**1** *For Man Fares*
For man fares as does the
    beast,
as the latter dies, so he dies too;
and all have the same breath;
and man has not more than the
    beast:
for all is vain.
All go to one place;
all are made of dust
and will to dust return.
Who knows if the spirit of man go
    upward,
and the breath of the beast
go downward under the earth?
So I saw that there is nothing better
than that a man be joyful in his
    work,
for that is his lot.
For who can bring him
to see what will be after
    him?

**2** *Ich wandte mich und sahe*
Ich wandte mich und sahe an alle,
die Unrecht leiden unter der Sonne;
und siehe, da waren Tränen, derer,
die Unrecht litten und hatten keinen
    Tröster,
und die ihnen Unrecht täten, waren zu
    mächtig,
daß sie keinen Tröster haben konnten.
Da lobte ich die Toten, die schon
    gestorben waren,
mehr als die Lebendigen, die noch das
    Leben hatten;
und der noch nicht ist, ist besser als
    alle beide,
und des Bösen nicht inne wird,
das unter der Sonne geschieht.

**2** *I Turned and Saw*
I turned and saw all
who suffer injustice under the sun;
and behold, there were tears of those
who suffered injustice and had no
    comforter,
and those who did them injustice were
    too mighty
to have any comforter.
So I praised the dead who had already
    died,
more than the living who still had
    life;
but he who not yet is, is better than
    both,
and does not perceive the evil
that happens under the sun.

**3** *O Tod, wie bitter bist du*
O Tod, o Tod, wie bitter bist du,

**3** *O death, how bitter you are*
O death, O death, how bitter you are

wenn an dich gedenket ein Mensch,
der gute Tage und genug hat und ohne
Sorge gelebet;
und dem es wohl geht in allen Dingen
und noch wohl essen mag!
O Tod, o Tod, wie bitter bist du.
O Tod, wie wohl tust du dem
Dürftigen,
der da schwach und alt ist,
der in allen Sorgen steckt,
und nichts Bessers zu hoffen
noch zu erwarten hat.
O Tod, o Tod, wie wohl tust du.

in the thoughts of a man
who has good days, enough and a
sorrow-free life;
and who is fortunate in all things
and still pleased to eat well!
O death, O death, how bitter you are!
O death, how well you serve him who
is in need,
who is feeble and old,
is beset by all sorrows
and has nothing better to hope for
or to expect.
O death, O death, how well you serve.

### 4 Wenn ich mit Menschenzungen
Wenn ich mit Menschen- und mit
Engelszungen redete,
und hätte der Liebe nicht,
so wär ich ein tönend Erz
oder eine klingende Schelle.
Und wenn ich weissagen könnte
und wüßte alle Geheimnisse und alle
Erkenntnis
und hätte allen Glauben, also,
daß ich Berge versetzte
und hätte der Liebe nicht,
so wäre ich nichts.

### 4 If I Spoke with the Tongues of Men
If I spoke with the tongues of men and
angels,
and had not love,
I were a sounding brass
or a clanging cymbal.
And if I could prophesy
and knew all mysteries and all
knowledge,
and had all faith so that
I could remove mountains,
and had not love,
I were nothing.

Und wenn ich alle meine Habe den
Armen gäbe
und ließe meinen Leib brennen
und hätte der Liebe nicht,
so wäre mir's nichts nütze.
Wir sehen jetzt durch einen Spiegel in
einem dunkeln Worte,
dann aber von Angesicht zu Angesichte.
Jetzt erkenne ich's stückweise,
dann aber werd ich's erkennen,
gleich wie ich erkennet bin.
Nun aber bleibet Glaube, Hoffnung,
Liebe, diese drei:
aber die Liebe ist die größte unter
ihnen.

If I gave away all my goods to the
poor
and suffered my body to be burned,
and had not love,
it were of no gain to me.
We see now in obscure words through
a mirror,
but then face to face.
Now I discern it piece by piece,
but then I shall discern it
just as I am discerned.
But now faith, hope, love remain, these
three:
but love is the greatest among
them.

## Vier letzte Lieder | Four Last Songs

nos. 1–3: HERMANN HESSE
no. 4: JOSEPH VON EICHENDORFF
*Richard Strauss, 1948*

### 1 Beim Schlafengehen*
Nun der Tag mich müd gemacht,
soll mein sehnliches Verlangen

### 1 On Retiring to Rest
Now that day has wearied me,
shall my passionate desire

* *Beim Schlafengehen, Frühling, September:* the German copyright holder has requested the English-language publisher to point out that these translations have been made specifically as reference for singers.

freundlich die gestirnte Nacht
wie ein müdes Kind empfangen.

Hände, laßt von allem Tun,
Stirn, vergiß du alles Denken,
alle meine Sinne nun
wollen sich in Schlummer senken.

Und die Seele, unbewacht,
will in freien Flügeln schweben,
um im Zauberkreis der Nacht
tief und tausendfach zu leben.

## 2 Frühling*
In dämmrigen Grüften
Träumte ich lang
Von deinen Bäumen und blauen Lüften,
Von deinem Duft und Vogelsang.

Nun liegst du erschlossen
In Gleiß und Zier,
Von Licht übergossen
Wie ein Wunder vor mir.

Du kennst mich wieder,
Du lockest mich zart,
Es zittert durch all meine Glieder
Deine selige Gegenwart!

## 3 September*
Der Garten trauert,
kühl sinkt in die Blumen der Regen.
Der Sommer schauert
still seinem Ende entgegen.

Golden tropft Blatt um Blatt
nieder vom hohen Akazienbaum,
Sommer lächelt erstaunt und matt
in den sterbenden Gartentraum.

Lange noch bei den Rosen
bleibt er stehen, sehnt sich nach Ruh.
Langsam tut er die großen
müdgewordenen Augen zu.

## 4 Im Abendrot
Wir sind durch Not und Freude
gegangen Hand in Hand,
vom Wandern ruhen wir
nun überm stillen Land.

Rings sich die Täler neigen,
es dunkelt schon die Luft,
zwei Lerchen nur noch steigen
nachträumend in den Duft.

Tritt her und laß sie schwirren,
bald ist es Schlafenszeit,
daß wir uns nicht verirren
in dieser Einsamkeit.

be received by starry night,
kindly, like a weary child.

Cease, hands, from all activity,
forget, brow, about all thought,
my senses, all of them,
would now sink in slumber.

And, unwatched, the soul
would hover on free wings
to live, in night's magic circle,
profoundly and thousandfold.

## 2 Spring
In dim vaults
long have I dreamt
of your trees and blue skies,
your fragrance and birdsong.

Now you lie disclosed
in glitter and ornament,
flooded with light,
like a miracle before me.

You know me again,
tenderly entice me.
My every limb trembles
with your blissful presence!

## 3 September
The garden mourns,
chill into the flowers sinks rain.
Summer goes, shuddering
quietly, to meet its end.

Leaf after leaf drops golden
from the tall acacia,
summer smiles, surprised and faint,
into the dying garden dream.

Long still by the roses
it lingers, yearning for repose.
Slowly it closes its great,
now wearied eyes.

## 4 In the Evening Glow
Through joy and trouble
we've gone, hand in hand,
now from journeying we rest
above the still countryside.

Around, the vales slope down,
the sky grows dark,
two larks only still ascend,
dreamily, into the haze.

Come, and leave them warbling,
soon it will be time to sleep,
let us not lose our way
in this solitude.

O weiter, stiller Friede,
so tief im Abendrot.
Wie sind wir wandermüde—
ist dies etwa der Tod?

O vast, O silent peace,
so deep in the evening glow.
How weary we are of journeying—
can this be death?


## Von ewiger Liebe | Of Eternal Love

After the Wendish of JOSEF WENZIG

*Johannes Brahms: op. 43, no. 1, 1864*

Dunkel, wie dunkel in Wald und in
Feld!
Abend schon ist es, nun schweiget die
Welt.
Nirgend noch Licht und nirgend noch
Rauch,
Ja, und die Lerche, sie schweiget nun
auch.

Dark, how dark in wood and
field!
Evening it is, now silent the
world.
Nowhere a light still, nowhere
smoke,
yes, and the lark is now silent
too.

Kommt aus dem Dorfe der Bursche
heraus,
Gibt das Geleit der Geliebten nach
Haus,
Führt sie am Weidengebüsche vorbei,
Redet so viel und so mancherlei:

Out of the village comes the
boy,
walking his beloved
home,
he leads her past the willow copse,
talking much and of many things:

»Leidest du Schmach und betrübest du
dich,
Leidest du Schmach von andern um
mich,
Werde die Liebe getrennt so geschwind,
Schnell wie wir früher vereiniget sind,
Scheide mit Regen und scheide mit
Wind,
Schnell wie wir früher vereiniget sind.«

'If you suffer insult and are
troubled,
suffer insult from others for my
sake,
let our love be sundered so swiftly,
so swiftly as earlier we were united;
with rain depart, with wind
depart,
as quickly as earlier we were united.'

Spricht das Mägdelein, Mägdelein
spricht:
»Unsere Liebe, sie trennet sich nicht!
Fest ist der Stahl und das Eisen gar
sehr,
Unsere Liebe ist fester noch mehr.

Says the maiden, the maiden
says:
'Our love won't be sundered!
Steel is strong, and iron is,
very—
even stronger is our love.

Eisen und Stahl, man schmiedet sie um,
Unsere Liebe, wer wandelt sie um?
Eisen und Stahl, sie können zergehn,
Unsere Liebe muß ewig bestehn!«

'Iron and steel may be forged anew—
our love, who can change it?
Iron and steel, they may melt—
our love must endure forever!'


## Von waldbekränzter Höhe | From Wood-crowned Hill

GEORG FRIEDRICH DAUMER

*Johannes Brahms: op. 57, no. 1, 1871*

Von waldbekränzter Höhe
Werf ich den heißen Blick
Der liebefeuchten Sehe
Zur Flur, die dich umgrünt, zurück.

From wood-crowned hill
I cast the burning gaze
of my love-moist eye back
to the meadow green about you.

Ich senk ihn auf die Quelle,
Vermöcht ich, ach, mit ihr
Zu fließen, eine Welle,
Zurück, o Freund, zu dir, zu dir!

Ich richt ihn auf die Züge
Der Wolken über mir,
Ach, flög ich ihre Flüge,
Zurück, o Freund, zu dir, zu dir!

Wie wollt ich dich umstricken,
Mein Heil und meine Pein,
Mit Lippen und mit Blicken,
Mit Busen, Herz und Seele dein!

I lower it to the brook,
ah, to flow with that,
as a ripple,
back, O friend, to you!

I raise it to the scudding
clouds above me,
ah, to fly their ways
back, O friend, to you!

How I would ensnare you,
my anguish and salvation,
and with lips, with looks,
with heart, your heart and soul!

## Vorschneller Schwur / Rash Vow

From the Serbian of SIEGFRIED KAPPER

*Johannes Brahms: op. 95, no. 5, 1884*

Schwor ein junges Mädchen: Blumen
nie zu tragen,
Niemals Wein zu trinken, Knaben nie
zu küssen.
Gestern schwor das Mädchen, heute
schon bereut es:
Wenn ich Blumen trüge, wär ich doch
noch schöner.
Wenn ich Rotwein tränke, wär ich doch
noch froher.
Wenn den Liebsten küßte, wär mir
doch noch wohler.

A young maid vowed she'd never wear
flowers,
never drink wine, never kiss
boys.
Yesterday she vowed it, today she
regrets it:
If I did wear flowers, I'd be still
fairer.
If I did drink red wine, I'd be still
merrier.
If I did kiss my love, I'd be still
happier.

## Waldeinsamkeit / Woodland Solitude

FRANKISH FOLK SONG

*Max Reger: op. 76, no. 3, 1903-4*

Gestern abend in der stillen Ruh',
Sah ich im Wald einer Amsel zu;
Als ich da so saß,
Meiner ganz vergaß:
Kommt mein Schatz und schleichet
sich um mich
Und küsset mich.

So viel Laub als an der Linden ist
Und so viel tausendmal hat mich mein
Schatz geküßt;
Denn ich muß gesteh'n,
Es hat's niemand geseh'n,
Und die Amsel soll mein Zeuge sein:
Wir war'n allein.

Last evening in the quiet peace,
I watched a blackbird in the wood;
as I sat there,
oblivious to myself,
my beloved comes
stealing
and kisses me.

As many leaves as are on the lime,
so many thousand times she
kissed;
for I must admit it,
no one saw,
and the blackbird shall be my witness—
we were alone.

## Wanderers Nachtlied I | Wanderer's Nightsong I

JOHANN WOLFGANG GOETHE

*Franz Liszt, ca. 1840; Ernst Pepping, 1946; Franz Schubert: op. 96, no. 3, ca. 1823; Robert Schumann: op. 96, no. 1, 1850; Carl Friedrich Zelter, 1814*

Über allen Gipfeln
Ist Ruh,
In allen Wipfeln
Spürest du
Kaum einen Hauch;
Die Vöglein schweigen im Walde.
Warte nur, balde
Ruhest du auch.

Over every summit
is peace,
in every tree-top
you feel
scarce a breath;
the birds in the wood are hushed.
Only wait, soon
you too will be at peace.


## Wanderers Nachtlied II | Wanderer's Nightsong II

JOHANN WOLFGANG GOETHE

*Franz Liszt: ed. 1843; Joseph Marx, 1906;
Ernst Pepping, 1946; Hans Pfitzner: op. 40, no. 5, 1931;
Johann Friedrich Reichardt, ed. 1809; Franz Schubert: op. 4, no. 3, 1815,
Hugo Wolf, 1883; Carl Friedrich Zelter, 1807; Winfried Zillig, ed. 1960*

Der du von dem Himmel bist,
Alles Leid und Schmerzen stillest,
Den, der doppelt elend ist,
Doppelt mit Erquickung füllest,
Ach, ich bin des Treibens müde!
Was soll all der Schmerz und Lust?
Süßer Friede,
Komm, ach komm in meine Brust!

You who are from heaven,
who ease all pain and sorrow,
and the doubly wretched,
doubly with fresh vigour fill,
ah, I'm tired of restless life!
For what is all this pain and joy?
Sweet peace,
come, ah come into my breast!


## Wanderlied | Travel-song

JUSTINUS KERNER

*Robert Schumann: op. 35, no. 3, 1840*

Wohlauf, noch getrunken
Den funkelnden Wein!
Ade nun, ihr Lieben!
Geschieden muß sein.
Ade nun, ihr Berge,
Du väterlich Haus!
Es treibt in die Ferne
Mich mächtig hinaus.

Come, one more draught
of sparkling wine!
Farewell, loved ones!
It's time to part.
Farewell, mountains,
my father's house!
I've a great urge
to journey afar.

Die Sonne, sie bleibet
Am Himmel nicht stehn,
Es treibt sie durch Länder
Und Meere zu gehn.
Die Woge nicht haftet
Am einsamen Strand,
Die Stürme, sie brausen
Mit Macht durch das Land.

The sun, it does not
stand still in the sky,
but is urged to go
over land and sea.
The wave does not cling
to the lonely shore,
storms rage mightily
over the land.

Mit eilenden Wolken
Der Vogel dort zieht
Und singt in der Ferne
Ein heimatlich Lied.
So treibt es den Burschen
Durch Wälder und Feld,
Zu gleichen der Mutter,
Der wandernden Welt.

With the racing clouds,
there the bird flies,
and in a distant land
sings a homely song.
So is the young man urged
in forest and field
to match his mother,
the journeying earth.

Da grüßen ihn Vögel
Bekannt überm Meer,
Sie flogen von Fluren
Der Heimat hieher;
Da duften die Blumen
Vertraulich um ihn,
Sie trieben vom Lande
Die Lüfte dahin.

Birds greet him,
over the sea, as friends,
flown from the fields
of his native land;
the scent of flowers
around him he knows,
brought from that land
they were, by the winds.

Die Vögel, die kennen
Sein väterlich Haus.
Die Blumen einst pflanzt' er
Der Liebe zum Strauß,
Und Liebe, die folgt ihm,
Sie geht ihm zur Hand:
So wird ihm zur Heimat
Das ferneste Land.

Those birds, they know
his father's house.
Those flowers he grew once
for his love's bouquets,
and love, it follows him,
is always to hand:
thus a home to him
is the farthest land.

## Wanderung | Wandering

JUSTINUS KERNER

*Robert Schumann: op. 35, no. 7, 1840*

Wohlauf und frisch gewandert
Ins unbekannte Land!
Zerissen, ach zerissen,
Ist manches teure Band.
Ihr heimatlichen Kreuze,
Wo ich oft betend lag,
Ihr Bäume, ach, ihr Hügel,
O blickt mir segnend nach.

Come, briskly tramp
to the unknown land!
Severed, ah severed
is many a true bond.
Homely crucifixes,
where often I lay in prayer,
you trees, ah, you hills,
gaze after me and bless me.

Noch schläft die weite Erde,
Kein Vogel weckt den Hain,
Doch bin ich nicht verlassen,
Doch bin ich nicht allein,
Denn, ach, auf meinem Herzen
Trag ich ihr teures Pfand,
Ich fühl's, und Erd und Himmel
sind innig mir verwandt.

Still the wide world sleeps,
no bird wakes the wood,
yet I am not forsaken,
yet I am not alone,
for, ah, upon my heart
I wear her precious pledge,
I feel it, and earth and sky
are kith and kin to me.

## Warm die Lüfte | Warm the Breezes

ALFRED MOMBERT

*Alban Berg: op. 2, no. 4, 1908–09*

Warm die Lüfte,
es sprießt Gras auf sonnigen Wiesen.

Warm the breezes,
grass sprouts on sunny meadows.

Horch!—
Horch, es flötet die Nachtigall . . .
Ich will singen:

Droben hoch im düstern Bergforst,
es schmilzt und sickert kalter Schnee,
ein Mädchen in grauem Kleide
lehnt an feuchtem Eichstamm,
krank sind ihre zarten Wangen,
die grauen Augen fiebern
durch Düsterriesenstämme.
»Er kommt noch nicht. Er läßt mich
  warten« . . .

Stirb!
Der Eine stirbt, daneben der Andere
  lebt:
Das macht die Welt so
  tiefschön.

Hark!—
Hark, the nightingale flutes . . .
I will sing:

High in the gloomy mountain forest
cold snow melts and trickles,
a girl in a grey dress
leans on a wet oak-trunk,
her tender cheeks are sick,
her grey eyes stare feverishly
through the gloom of the great trunks.
'He does not yet come. He makes me
  wait' . . .

Die!
One dies, against which the other
  lives:
that makes the world so profoundly
  beautiful.

## *Warnung* / *Warning*

ANONYMOUS

*Wolfgang Amadeus Mozart: K 433, 1783? Max Reger: op. 104, no. 2, 1907*

Männer suchen stets zu naschen,
läßt man sie allein,
leicht sind Mädchen zu erhaschen,
weiß man sie zu überraschen.

Soll das zu verwundern sein?
Mädchen haben frisches Blut,
und das Naschen schmeckt so gut.

Doch das Naschen vor dem Essen
nimmt den Appetit.
Manche kam, die das vergessen,
um den Schatz, den sie besessen,
und um ihren Liebsten mit.

Väter laßt euch's Warnung sein,
sperrt die Zuckerplätzchen ein!
Sperrt die jungen Mädchen ein!

Men look ever for sly morsels,
if left to themselves,
catching girls is easy
if you know how to surprise.

Is that any wonder?
Girls are full-blooded,
sly morsels are so sweet.

But sly morsels before the meal
ruin the appetite.
Many a girl who's forgotten that
has lost her most precious possession,
and with it, her beloved.

Fathers, let it be a warning,
lock your sugar-drops away,
lock your young girls in.

## *Was will die einsame Träne* / *What Means This Solitary Tear?*

HEINRICH HEINE

*Peter Cornelius, 1848; Robert Franz: op. 34, no. 1;
Robert Schumann: op. 25 (Myrten), no. 21, 1840*

Was will die einsame Träne?
Sie trübt mir ja den Blick.
Sie blieb aus alten Zeiten
In meinem Auge zurück.

What means this solitary tear?
For it troubles my gaze.
From old times it has remained
behind in my eye.

Sie hatte viel leuchtende Schwestern.
Die alle zerflossen sind,
Mit meinen Qualen und Freuden,
Zerflossen in Nacht und Wind.

Wie Nebel sind auch zerflossen
Die blauen Sternelein,
Die mir jene Freuden und Qualen
Gelächelt ins Herz hinein.

Ach, meine Liebe selber
Zerfloß wie eitel Hauch!
Du alte, einsame Träne,
Zerfließe jetzunder auch!

Many shining sisters it had,
which have all flowed away,
with my agonies and joys,
away in night and wind.

As mist, have also flowed away
the tiny blue stars,
by them were those joys and agonies
smiled into my heart.

Ah, my love itself
melted, like vain breath, away!
Old, solitary tear,
now flow and be gone too!


## Wehe, so willst du mich wieder | Alas, Would You Then Again ...

AUGUST VON PLATEN

*Johannes Brahms: op. 32, no. 5, 1864*

Wehe, so willst du mich wieder,
Hemmende Fessel, umfangen?
Auf, und hinaus in die Luft!
Ströme der Seele Verlangen,
Ström es in brausende Lieder,
Saugend ätherischen Duft!

Strebe dem Wind nur entgegen,
Daß er die Wange dir kühle,
Grüße den Himmel mit Lust!
Werden sich bange Gefühle
Im Unermesslichen regen?
Atme den Feind aus der Brust!

Alas, would you then again
encircle me, restraining fetter?
Up, and out into the air!
Let stream the soul's desire,
in boisterous songs let it stream,
imbibing ethereal fragrance!

Strive into the teeth of the wind,
that it may cool your cheek,
greet the heavens with joy!
Will anxious feelings
stir in the immeasurable?
Breathe the foe from your breast!


## Wehmut | Melancholy

MATTHÄUS VON COLLIN

*Franz Schubert: op. 22, no. 2, 1823*

Wenn ich durch Wald und Fluren geh',
es wird mir dann so wohl und weh
in unruhvoller Brust.
So wohl, so weh, wenn ich die Au
in ihrer Schönheit Fülle schau',
und all die Frühlingslust.
Denn was im Winde tönend weht,
was aufgetürmt gen Himmel steht,
und auch der Mensch, so hold vertraut
mit all' der Schönheit, die er schaut,
entschwindet und vergeht.

When I walk through wood and field,
so happy then I feel and sad
in my restless heart.
So happy, so sad, when I see
the meadow in its full beauty,
and all the joy of spring.
For what blows sonorous in the wind,
what stands towering to heaven,
and man too, so familiar
with all the beauty that he sees,
vanishes and dies.

# Weihnachtslieder / Christmas Songs

PETER CORNELIUS

*Peter Cornelius: op. 8, nos. 1–6, 1856*

### 1 Christbaum

Wie schön geschmückt der festliche
Raum!
Die Lichter funkeln am
Weihnachtsbaum!
O fröhliche Zeit! o seliger
Traum!

Die Mutter sitzt in der Kinder Kreis;
Nun schweiget alles auf ihr Geheiß:
Sie singet des Christkinds Lob und
Preis.

Und rings, vom Weihnachtsbaum
erhellt,
Ist schön in Bildern aufgestellt
Des heiligen Buches Palmenwelt.

Die Kinder schauen der Bilder
Pracht,
Und haben wohl des Singens acht,
Das tönt so süß in der
Weihenacht!

O glücklicher Kreis im festlichen Raum!
O goldne Lichter am Weihnachts-
baum!
O fröhliche Zeit! o seliger Traum!

### 2 Die Hirten

Hirten wachen im Feld;
Nacht ist rings auf der Welt;
Wach sind die Hirten alleine
Im Haine.

Und ein Engel so licht
Grüßet die Hirten und spricht:
»Christ, das Heil aller Frommen,
Ist kommen!«

Engel singen umher:
»Gott im Himmel sei Ehr!
Und den Menschen hienieden
Sei Frieden!«

Eilen die Hirten fort,
Eilen zum heilgen Ort,
Beten an in den Windlein
Das Kindlein.

### 3 Die Könige

Drei Könige wandern aus Morgenland;
Ein Sternlein führt sie zum
Jordanstrand.
In Juda fragen und forschen die drei,

### 1 The Christmas Tree

How beautifully decked the festive
room!
The candles glitter on the Christmas
tree!
O joyful time, O blissful
dream!

Mother sits in the circle of her children;
now all are silent at her bidding:
she sings the Christ-child's praise and
glory.

And around, lit by the Christmas
tree,
beautifully displayed in pictures,
the palmy world of the Holy Book.

The children gaze at the pictures'
splendour,
and pay heed to the singing
that sounds so sweet in the Christmas
night!

O happy circle in the festive room!
O golden candles on the Christmas
tree!
O joyful time, O blissful dream!

### 2 The Shepherds

Shepherds keep watch in the fields;
night lies on the world around;
only the shepherds are awake
in the grove.

And an angel so bright
hails the shepherds, saying:
'Christ, salvation of all good men,
is come!'

Angels all round sing:
'Glory to God in the highest,
and to men on earth
be peace!'

Away hasten the shepherds,
to the holy place,
worship, in his swaddling clothes,
the infant.

### 3 The Kings

Three kings from the orient journeying,
are led to Jordan's shore by a
star.
In Judaea they seek and inquire, the three,

Wo der neugeborene König sei?
Sie wollen Weihrauch, Myrrhen und
    Gold
Dem Kinde spenden zum Opfersold.

where the new-born king may be.
Incense, myrrh and gold they would
    bring
to the child as offering.

Und hell erglänzet des Sternes
    Schein;
Zum Stalle gehen die Kön'ge ein;
Das Knäblein schaun sie wonniglich,
Anbetend neigen die Könige sich;
Sie bringen Weihrauch, Myrrhen und
    Gold
Zum Opfer dar dem Knäblein hold.

And brightly shines the light of the
    star;
into the stable go the kings;
in rapture they gaze at the baby boy,
in adoration bow down low;
incense, myrrh and gold they
    bring
to the sweet baby boy as offering.

O Menschenkind! halte treulich Schritt!
Die Kön'ge wandern, o wandre mit!
Der Stern der Liebe, der Gnade Stern
Erhelle dein Ziel, so du suchst den
    Herrn,
Und fehlen Weihrauch, Myrrhen und
    Gold,
Schenke dein Herz dem Knäblein hold!

Loyally keep pace, O Son of Man!
The kings are journeying, journey too!
May the star of love, the star of grace,
as you seek the Lord, shine on your
    goal.
If you lack incense, myrrh and
    gold,
to that sweet child give your heart!

4 *Simeon*
Das Knäblein nach acht Tagen
Ward gen Jerusalem
Zum Gotteshaus getragen
Vom Stall in Bethlehem.

4 *Simeon*
After eight days, the baby
was carried to Jerusalem,
to the house of God,
from the Bethlehem stable.

Da kommt ein Greis geschritten,
Der fromme Simeon,
Er nimmt in Tempels Mitten
Vom Mutterarm den Sohn;

Striding comes an old man,
the devout Simeon,
who, in the temple, takes
the son from mother's arm.

Vom Angesicht des Alten
Ein Strahl der Freude bricht,
Er preiset Gottes Walten
Weissagungsvoll und spricht:

The old man's face
beams forth joy,
God's dispensation he praises,
prophesying and saying:

»Nun lässest du in Frieden,
Herr, deinen Diener gehn,
Da du mir noch beschieden,
Den Heiland anzusehn,

'Now let in peace,
Lord, Your servant depart,
for You have granted me
to behold the Saviour,

Den du der Welt gesendet,
Daß er dem Heidentum
Des Lichtes Helle spendet
Zu deines Volkes Ruhm!«

sent by You into the world
to give out among the Gentiles
the brightness of the light,
to the glory of Your people!'

Mit froh erstaunten Sinnen
Vernimmt's der Eltern Paar,
Dann tragen sie von hinnen
Das Knäblein wunderbar.

With mind joyously astonished,
the parents give ear,
then depart, carrying
the wonderful baby boy.

5 *Christus der Kinderfreund*
Das zarte Knäblein ward ein Mann,
Erlöst uns von der Sünde Bann;
Doch neigt er freundlich immerdar
Und liebend sich zur Kinderschar.
Habt ihr den Ruf des Herrn vernommen,

5 *Christ, the Friend of Children*
The tender boy became a man,
redeemed us from the curse of sin;
but ever, kindly, he bends low
and lovingly to the crowd of children.
Have you heard the call of the Lord,

Des Heilands Stimme mild und weich?
»Lasset die Kleinen zu mir kommen,
Denn ihrer ist das Himmelreich!«

the voice of the Saviour, soft and mild?
'Suffer the little ones to come to me,
for of such is the Kingdom of Heaven!'

Mich aber mahnt die Weihnachtszeit
An Träume der Vergangenheit;
Erinnrungsodem hauchet mild
Den Schleier von der Kindheit Bild;
Da Lichter hell am Baum erglommen,
Ist mir, als würd ich Kindern gleich,
Als dürft ich mit euch Kleinen kommen,
Zu teilen euer Himmelreich.

But to me, Christmas time recalls
dreams of the past;
a breath of memory gently blows
the veil away from childhood's picture;
when candles gleam out on the tree,
I feel I am the children's peer,
as if, little ones, I might come with you
to share your Heavenly Kingdom.

### 6 Christkind
Das einst ein Kind auf Erden war,
Christkindlein kommt noch jedes Jahr.

### 6 Christ-child
Who once a baby was on earth,
the Christ-child, still returns each year.

Kommet vom hohen Sternenzelt,
Freut und beglücket alle Welt!

Comes from the lofty firmament,
makes glad and rejoices all the world!

Mit Kindern feiert's froh den Tag,
Wo Christkind in der Krippe
lag;

With children he gladly honours the day
when the Christ-child in the manger
lay;

Den Christbaum zündet's überall,
Weckt Orgelklang und Glockenschall.

He kindles Christmas trees everywhere,
wakes peal of organ, peal of bells.

Christkindlein kommt zu arm und reich,
Die Guten sind ihm alle gleich.

The Christ-child comes to poor and rich,
to him, the good are all the same.

Danket ihm denn und grüßt es fein,
Auch euch beglückte Christkindlein!

Thank him then and greet him well,
the Christ-child has made you happy
too!

## Wenn du nur zuweilen lächelst | If, Only at Times, You Smile ...

GEORG FRIEDRICH DAUMER

*Johannes Brahms: op. 57, no. 2, 1871*

Wenn du nur zuweilen lächelst,
Nur zuweilen Kühle fächelst
Dieser ungemeßnen Glut,
In Geduld will ich mich fassen
Und dich alles treiben lassen,
Was der Liebe wehe tut.

If, only at times, you smile,
only at times fan coolness
to this unbounded fire,
in patience I'll be calm,
let you do all those things
that cause love pain.

## Wer machte dich so krank? | Who Made You So Ill?

JUSTINUS KERNER

*Robert Schumann: op. 35, no. 11, 1840*

Daß du so krank geworden,
Wer hat es denn gemacht?
Kein kühler Hauch aus Norden
Und keine Sternennacht.

That you are so ill,
who is then the cause?
No cool north breath,
no starry night.

Kein Schatten unter Bäumen,
Nicht Glut des Sonnenstrahls,
Kein Schlummern und kein Träumen
Im Blütenbett des Tals.

Daß ich trag' Todeswunden,
Das ist der Menschen Tun;
Natur ließ mich gesunden,
Sie lassen mich nicht ruhn.

No shade of trees,
no sunbeam's glow,
no slumbering, no dreaming
in the valley's blossom bed.

That I bear mortal wounds,
that is the work of men;
nature let me recover,
they do not let me rest.

## Widmung / Dedication

FRIEDRICH RÜCKERT

*Robert Schumann: op. 25 (Myrten), no. 1, 1840*

Du meine Seele, du mein Herz,
Du meine Wonn', o du mein Schmerz,
Du meine Welt, in der ich lebe,
Mein Himmel du, darein ich schwebe,
O du mein Grab, in das hinab
Ich ewig meinen Kummer gab.
Du bist die Ruh, du bist der Frieden,
Du bist vom Himmel mir beschieden.
Daß du mich liebst, macht mich mir
    wert,
Dein Blick hat mich vor mir verklärt,
Du hebst mich liebend über mich,
Mein guter Geist, mein beßres Ich!

You my soul, you my heart,
you my bliss, O you my pain,
you my world in which I live,
my heaven you, to which I float,
O you my grave, into which
my grief forever I've consigned.
You are repose, you are peace,
you are bestowed on me from Heaven.
Your love for me gives me my
    worth,
your eyes transfigure me in mine,
lovingly you raise me above myself,
my good spirit, my better self!

## Wie bist du meine Königin / How Blissful, My Queen

GEORG FRIEDRICH DAUMER

*Johannes Brahms: op. 32, no. 9, 1864*

Wie bist du, meine Königin,
Durch sanfte Güte wonnevoll!
Du lächle nur, Lenzdüfte wehn
Durch mein Gemüte, wonnevoll!

Frisch aufgeblühter Rosen Glanz,
Vergleich ich ihn dem deinigen?
Ach, über alles, was da blüht,
Ist deine Blüte wonnevoll!

Durch tote Wüsten wandle hin,
Und grüne Schatten breiten sich,
Ob fürchterliche Schwüle dort
Ohn Ende brüte, wonnevoll!

Laß mich vergehn in deinem Arm!
Es ist in ihm ja selbst der Tod,
Ob auch die herbste Todesqual
Die Brust durchwüte, wonnevoll!

How blissful, my queen, you are
by reason of your gentle goodness!
Merely smile, and spring scents waft
through my soul blissfully!

The glow of roses freshly blown—
shall I compare it to your own?
Ah, more blissful than all that blooms
is your blissful bloom!

Roam through desert wastes,
green shade will spread around
—though fearful there the heat
and endless—blissfully!

Let me die in your arms!
In them will death itself—
though death's sharpest agony
rage in the breast—blissful be!

## Wie die Wolke nach der Sonne | As Cloud Wanders After Sun

AUGUST HEINRICH HOFFMANN VON FALLERSLEBEN

*Johannes Brahms: op. 6, no. 5, 1852*

Wie die Wolke nach der Sonne
voll Verlangen irrt und bangt
und durchglüht von Himmelswonne
sterbend ihr am Busen hangt.

As cloud wanders after sun
and yearns, full of desire,
and, afire with heavenly bliss,
hangs dying at her breast;

Wie die Sonnenblume richtet
auf die Sonn' ihr Angesicht
und nicht eh'r auf sie verzichtet,
bis ihr eig'nes Auge bricht.

As the sunflower directs
its countenance at the sun
and turns not away
until its own eye pales;

Wie der Aar auf Wolkenpfade
sehnend steigt ins Himmelszelt
und berauscht vom Sonnenbade
blind zur Erde niederfällt:

As, on the cloudy way, the eagle
soars yearning to heaven's vault,
and befuddled by the bath of sun
falls blindly to earth:

So auch muß ich schmachten, bangen,
späh'n und trachten, dich zu sehn,
will an deinen Blicken hangen
und an ihrem Glanz vergehn.

So too must I languish, yearn,
watch and strive to see you,
so would I hang upon your gaze
and perish in its glow.


## Wie Melodien zieht es mir | As Melodies a Feeling

KLAUS GROTH

*Johannes Brahms: op. 105, no. 1, 1886*

Wie Melodien zieht es
mir leise durch den Sinn,
wie Frühlingsblumen blüht es
und schwebt wie Duft dahin.

As melodies a feeling
steals softly through my mind,
as spring flowers it blooms
and as scent floats away.

Doch kommt das Wort und faßt es
und führt es vor das Aug',
wie Nebelgrau erblaßt es
und schwindet wie ein Hauch.

But words come and seize it,
bring it before the eye,
as the grey of mist it pales,
and vanishes like a breath.

Und dennoch ruht im Reime
verborgen wohl ein Duft,
den mild aus stillem Keime
ein feuchtes Auge ruft.

And yet in rhyme reposes,
concealed, a scent,
which gently out of silent bud
is summoned by a moist eye.


## Wie rafft ich mich auf | How I Sprang Up

AUGUST VON PLATEN

*Johannes Brahms: op. 32, no. 1, 1864*

Wie rafft ich mich auf in der Nacht, in
der Nacht,
Und fühlte mich fürder gezogen,
Die Gassen verließ ich, vom Wächter
bewacht,

How I sprang up in the night, the
night,
and on and on felt myself drawn!
I left the streets in the watch's
watch,

| Durchwandelte sacht | wandering soft |
|---|---|
| In der Nacht, in der Nacht, | in the night, the night, |
| Das Tor mit dem gotischen Bogen. | and out by the Gothic gate. |

Mühlbach rauschte durch felsigen  
   Schacht,  
Ich lehnte mich über die Brücke,  
Tief unter mir nahm ich der Wogen in  
   acht,  
Die wallten so sacht  
In der Nacht, in der Nacht,  
Doch wallte nicht eine zurücke.

In its rocky cleft the mill-race  
   roared,  
over the bridge I leaned,  
far below me, observed the  
   waves  
waving so soft  
in the night, the night,  
but none of them ever returned.

Es drehte sich oben, unzählig  
   entfacht,  
Melodischer Wandel der Sterne,  
Mit ihnen der Mond in beruhigter  
   Pracht,  
Sie funkelten sacht  
In der Nacht, in der Nacht,  
Durch täuschend entlegene Ferne.

On high, kindled and countless,  
   revolved  
melodious mutations of stars,  
with them the moon, in tranquil  
   glory,  
shining out soft  
in the night, the night,  
over distance deceptively distant.

Ich blickte hinauf in der Nacht, in der  
   Nacht,  
Und blickte hinunter aufs neue:  
O wehe, wie hast du die Tage verbracht,  
Nun stille du sacht  
In der Nacht, in der Nacht,  
Im pochenden Herzen die Reue!

Up I gazed in the night, the  
   night!  
and down I gazed anew:  
how, alas, have you spent your days!  
Now quieten soft,  
in the night, the night,  
in your pounding heart the rue!

## *Wie sollten wir geheim sie halten* | *How Should We Keep It Secret*

ADOLF FRIEDRICH VON SCHACK

*Richard Strauss: op. 19, no. 4, 1885–88*

Wie sollten wir geheim sie halten,  
die Seligkeit, die uns erfüllt?  
Nein, bis in seine tiefsten Falten  
sei allen unser Herz enthüllt!

How should we keep it secret,  
the bliss with which we're filled?  
No, to their deepest places,  
let be to all our hearts revealed.

Wenn zwei in Liebe sich gefunden,  
geht Jubel hin durch die Natur,  
in längern wonnevollen Stunden  
legt sich der Tag auf Wald und Flur.

When, in love, two find each other,  
nature's filled with jubilation,  
and in longer hours of bliss  
the day descends on wood and field.

Selbst aus der Eiche morschem Stamme,  
die ein Jahrtausend überlebt,  
steigt neu des Wipfels grüne Flamme  
und rauscht von Jugendlust durchbebt.

Even from the oak's rotted trunk,  
surviving for a thousand years,  
the leaves' green flame ascends anew,  
rustling, thrilling to youth's zest.

Zu höherm Glanz und Dufte brechen  
die Knospen auf beim Glück der Zwei,  
und süßer rauscht es in den Bächen  
und reicher blüht und reicher glänzt  
   der Mai.

To heightened scent and gleam, buds  
burst at the happiness of the two,  
and brooks murmur more sweetly,  
and May shines and blossoms more  
   richly.

| | |
|---|---|
| Wie sollten wir geheim sie halten, | How should we keep it secret, |
| die Seligkeit, die uns erfüllt? | the bliss with which we're filled? |
| Nein, bis in seine tiefsten Falten | No, to their deepest places, |
| sei allen unser Herz enthüllt. | let be to all our hearts revealed. |

## Wiegenlied / Cradle Song

from *Des Knaben Wunderhorn*

*Johannes Brahms: op. 49, no. 4, 1868*

| | |
|---|---|
| Guten Abend, gut Nacht, | Good night, good night, |
| Mit Rosen bedacht, | with roses to roof you, |
| Mit Näglein besteckt, | carnations to adorn you, |
| Schlupf unter die Deck: | slip under your quilt: |
| Morgen früh, wenn Gott will, | by morning, if God wills, |
| Wirst du wieder geweckt. | you'll be woken again. |
| | |
| Guten Abend, gut Nacht, | Good night, good night, |
| Von Englein bewacht, | with angels to keep watch, |
| Die zeigen im Traum | they'll show you in dreams |
| Dir Christkindleins Baum: | the Christ-child's tree: |
| Schlaf nun selig und süß, | Sleep now happy and sweet, |
| Schau im Traum's Paradies. | see Heaven in your dreams. |

## Wiegenlied / Cradle Song

RICHARD DEHMEL

*Max Reger: op. 51, no. 3, 1900; Richard Strauss: op. 41, no. 1, 1899*

| | |
|---|---|
| Träume, träume, du mein süßes Leben, | Dream, my sweet life, dream |
| Von dem Himmel, der die Blumen | of heaven that brings the |
| bringt. | flowers. |
| Blüten schimmern da, die leben | Blossoms gleam there which live |
| Von dem Lied, das deine Mutter singt. | by the song your mother sings. |
| | |
| Träume, träume, Knospe meiner Sorgen, | Dream, bud of my anxiety, dream |
| Von dem Tage, da die Blume sproß; | of the day the flower sprouted; |
| Von dem hellen Blütenmorgen, | of that bright blossom morning |
| Da dein Seelchen sich der Welt | when your soul opened to the |
| erschloß. | world. |
| | |
| Träume, träume, Blüte meiner Liebe, | Dream, blossom of my love, dream |
| Von der stillen, von der heilgen Nacht, | of that silent, that holy night, |
| Da die Blume seiner Liebe | when the flower of his love |
| Diese Welt zum Himmel mir gemacht. | made this world heaven for me. |

## Willkommen und Abschied / Welcome and Departure

JOHANN WOLFGANG GOETHE

*Hans Pfitzner: op. 29, no. 3, 1922; Franz Schubert: op. 56, no. 1, 1822*

| | |
|---|---|
| Es schlug mein Herz, geschwind, zu | My heart surged, quick, to |
| Pferde! | horse! |
| Es war getan fast eh gedacht. | It was done before I knew. |
| Der Abend wiegte schon die Erde, | Evening cradled the earth, |

Und an den Bergen hing die Nacht;
Schon stand im Nebelkleid die Eiche,
Ein aufgetürmter Riese, da,
Wo Finsternis aus dem Gesträuche
Mit hundert schwarzen Augen sah.

Der Mond von einem Wolkenhügel
Sah kläglich aus dem Duft hervor,
Die Winde schwangen leise Flügel,
Umsausten schauerlich mein Ohr;
Die Nacht schuf tausend
  Ungeheuer,
Doch frisch und fröhlich war mein Mut:
In meinen Adern welches Feuer!
In meinem Herzen welche Glut!

Dich sah ich, und die milde Freude
Floß von dem süßen Blick auf mich;
Ganz war mein Herz an deiner Seite
Und jeder Atemzug für dich.
Ein rosenfarbnes Frühlingswetter
Umgab das liebliche Gesicht,
Und Zärtlichkeit für mich—ihr Götter!
Ich hofft es, ich verdient es nicht!

Doch ach, schon mit der Morgensonne
Verengt der Abschied mir das Herz:
In deinen Küssen welche Wonne!
In deinem Auge welcher Schmerz!
Ich ging, du standst und sahst zur
  Erden,
Und sahst mir nach mit nassem Blick:
Und doch, welch Glück, geliebt zu
  werden
Und lieben, Götter, welch ein Glück!

and to the mountains clung the night;
clothed in mist the oak stood,
an upreared giant there,
where darkness from the bushes
peered as a hundred dark eyes.

The moon from a hill of cloud
gazed wretchedly through the haze,
the breezes, gently stirring,
roared awesomely about my ears;
night brought forth a thousand
  monsters,
but bright and cheerful was my mood:
in my veins what fire!
In my heart what a glow!

You I saw, and gentle joy
flowed from your sweet gaze upon me;
my heart was wholly at your side
and every breath was for you.
Rose-hued spring weather
framed your lovely face,
and tenderness for me—ye gods!
This I hoped, but did not deserve!

But ah, with the morning sun,
parting wrings my heart:
in your kisses what bliss!
In your eyes what pain!
I went, you stood, gaze
  downcast,
and looked, wet-eyed after me:
and yet, what happiness to be
  loved!
And what happiness, gods, to love!

## Winterweihe / Winter Dedication

KARL HENCKELL

*Arnold Schönberg: op. 14, no. 2, 1908; Richard Strauss: op. 48, no. 4, 1900*

In diesen Wintertagen,
Nun sich das Licht verhüllt,
Laß uns im Herzen tragen,
Einander traulich sagen,
Was uns mit innerm Licht erfüllt.

Was milde Glut entzündet,
Soll brennen fort und fort,
Was Seelen zart verbündet,
Und Geisterbrücken gründet,
Sei unser leises Losungswort.

Das Rad der Zeit mag rollen,
Wir greifen kaum hinein,
Dem Schein der Welt verschollen,

In these winter days,
now the light grows dark,
let us carry in our hearts
and to the other confide
what fills us with inner light.

That which kindles gentle ardour
shall burn on and on,
that which tenderly binds souls,
builds bridges of the spirit,
be our soft watchword.

The wheel of time may roll,
we shall hardly interfere;
lost to the show of the world,

Auf unserm Eiland wollen
Wir Tag und Nacht der sel'gen Liebe
    weih'n.

let us on our island dedicate
day and night to blissful
    love.


## Wir wandelten | We Wandered

GEORG FRIEDRICH DAUMER

*Johannes Brahms: op. 96, no. 2, 1884*

Wir wandelten, wir zwei zusammen,
ich war so still und du so stille;
ich gäbe viel, um zu erfahren,
was du gedacht in jenem Fall.
Was ich gedacht, unausgesprochen
verbleibe das! Nur Eines sag ich:
so schön war alles, was ich dachte,
so himmlisch heiter war es all!
In meinem Haupte die Gedanken
sie läuteten wie goldne Glöckchen;
so wundersüß, so wunderlieblich
ist in der Welt kein andrer Hall.

We wandered, we two, together,
I so still and you so still;
much I'd have given to know
what your thoughts were then.
What mine were—unspoken let
that stay. Just this I'll say:
so beautiful was all I thought,
so celestially serene!
In my head those thoughts chimed
like tiny golden bells;
as wondrous sweet and lovely
is no other sound on earth.


## Wo die schönen Trompeten blasen | Where Brave Trumpets Sound

from *Des Knaben Wunderhorn*

*Gustav Mahler, 1888–89*

Wer ist denn draußen und wer klopft
    an,
Der mich so leise, so leise wecken kann?
Das ist der Herzallerliebste dein,
Steh auf und laß mich zu dir ein!

Who is outside, then, and who
    knocks
so softly, softly waking me?
It is your dearest darling love,
rise up and let me in!

Was soll ich hier nun länger stehn?
Ich seh die Morgenröt aufgehn,
Die Morgenröt, zwei helle Stern.
Bei meinem Schatz da wär ich gern,
Bei meinem Herzallerliebe.

Why should I stand longer here?
I see dawn's red approaching,
dawn's red and two bright stars.
With my love would I gladly be,
with my dearest darling.

Das Mädchen stand auf und ließ ihn
    ein;
Sie heißt ihn auch willkommen sein.
Willkommen, lieber Knabe mein,
So lang hast du gestanden!
Sie reicht ihm auch die schneeweiße
    Hand.
Von ferne sang die Nachtigall;
Das Mädchen fing zu weinen an.

The maid rose up and let him
    in;
she bids him welcome too.
Welcome, dearest mine,
so long have you been standing!
To him she gives her snow-white
    hand.
In the distance sang the nightingale;
the maid began to weep.

Ach weine nicht, du Liebste mein,
Aufs Jahr sollst du mein eigen sein.
Mein eigen sollst du werden gewiß,
Wie's keine sonst auf Erden ist.
O Lieb auf grüner Erden.
Ich zieh in Krieg auf grüne Heid,

Ah, do not weep, beloved mine,
for the year my own love shall you be.
My own shall you be, certainly,
as no other on this earth has been.
Oh, love on the green earth.
To war I go, to the green heath,

Die grüne Heide, die ist so weit.
Allwo dort die schönen Trompeten
    blasen,
Da ist mein Haus, von grünem Rasen.

to the green heath that is so wide.
There, where brave trumpets
    sound,
is my home, my green-turf home.


## Wo find ich Trost | Where Shall I Find Comfort?

EDUARD MÖRIKE

*Hugo Wolf, 1888*

Eine Liebe kenn ich, die ist treu,
War getreu, solang ich sie gefunden,
Hat mit tiefem Seufzen immer neu,
Stets versöhnlich, sich mit mir
    verbunden.

One love I know that is true,
and has been, often as I've found it,
has, deeply sighing, ever anew,
forgivingly, attached itself to
    me.

Welcher einst mit himmlischem
    Gedulden
Bitter bittern Todestropfen trank,
Hing am Kreuz und büßte mein
    Verschulden,
Bis er in ein Meer von Gnade sank.

He who once, with heavenly
    forbearance,
bitterly did drink death's bitter drop,
hung on the cross, atoning for my
    guilt,
until he sank into a sea of grace.

Und was ist's nun, daß ich traurig bin,
Daß ich angstvoll mich am Boden winde?
Frage: »Hüter, ist die Nacht bald hin?«
Und: »Was rettet mich von Tod und
    Sünde?«

And why is it now that I am sad,
writhe fearfully upon the ground?
Ask: 'Watch, is the night soon done?
What shall deliver me from death and
    sin?'

Arges Herze! ja gesteh es nur,
Du hast wieder böse Lust empfunden;
Frommer Liebe, frommer Treue Spur,
Ach, das ist auf lange nun vergangen.

Evil heart! Yes, only confess
once more you have felt an ill delight;
all trace of godly love, of godly faith,
ah, long gone that is now.

Ja, das ist's auch, daß ich traurig bin,
Daß ich angstvoll mich am Boden winde!
Hüter, Hüter, ist die Nacht bald hin?
Und was rettet mich von Tod und
    Sünde?

Yes, that is why I am sad,
why fearfully I writhe upon the ground!
Watch, watch, is the night soon done?
What shall deliver me from death and
    sin?


## Wo wird einst des Wandermüden | Where, of Him Who's Journey-weary

HEINRICH HEINE

*Hugo Wolf, 1888*

Wo wird einst des Wandermüden
letzte Ruhestätte sein?
Unter Palmen in dem Süden?
Unter Linden an dem Rhein?

Where, of him who's journey-weary
will be the final resting-place?
Under palm trees in the south?
Under lime trees by the Rhine?

Werd' ich wo in einer Wüste
eingescharrt von fremder Hand?
Oder ruh' ich an der Küste
eines Meeres in dem Sand?

Shall I, somewhere in a desert,
be shovelled in by foreign hand?
Or shall I rest by the shore
of some ocean in the sand?

Immerhin wird mich umgeben
Gottes Himmel dort wie hier,
und als Totenlampen schweben
nachts die Sterne über mir.

No matter, I shall be surrounded
by God's Heaven, there as here,
and, as funeral lamps, will swing
over me at night the stars.


## Wonne der Wehmut / Bliss of Sadness

JOHANN WOLFGANG GOETHE

*Ludwig van Beethoven: op. 83, no. 1, 1811; Robert Franz: op. 33, no. 1;
Johann Friedrich Reichardt, ed. 1809; Franz Schubert: op. 115, no. 2, 1815;
Carl Friedrich Zelter, 1807; Winfried Zillig, ed. 1960*

Trocknet nicht, trocknet nicht,
Tränen der ewigen Liebe!
Ach, nur dem halbgetrockneten Auge
Wie öde, wie tot die Welt ihm erscheint!
Trocknet nicht, trocknet nicht,
Tränen unglücklicher Liebe!

Grow not dry, grow not dry,
tears of eternal love!
Ah, to the merely half-dry eye
how bleak, how dead earth appears!
Grow not dry, grow not dry,
tears of unhappy love!


## Wozu noch, Mädchen / What, Girl, Shall It Still Avail

ADOLF FRIEDRICH VON SCHACK

*Richard Strauss: op. 19, no. 1, 1885–88*

Wozu noch, Mädchen, soll es frommen,
daß du vor mir Verstellung übst?
Heiß' froh das neue Glück willkommen
und sag' es offen, daß du liebst!

What, girl, shall it still avail,
this pretence in front of me?
Gladly welcome your new joy
and openly say you're in love!

An deines Busens höherm Schwellen,
dem Wangenrot, das kommt und geht,
ward dein Geheimnis von den Quellen,
den Blumengeistern längst erspäht;

From the rising of your bosom,
your blushing that comes and goes,
your secret has, by fountains
and flower-spirits, long been espied;

die Wogen murmeln's in den Grotten,
es flüstert's leis der Abendwind,
wo du vorbeigehst, hörst du's spotten:
wir wissen es seit langem, Kind!

ripples murmur it in the grottos,
the breeze of evening whispers it,
where you pass, you hear a mocking:
We've known it for a long time, child!

Wozu noch, Mädchen, soll es frommen,
daß du vor mir Verstellung übst?

What, girl, shall it still avail,
this pretence in front of me?


## Zigeunerlied / Gipsy Song

JOHANN WOLFGANG GOETHE

*Ferruccio Busoni, ed. 1964; Louis Spohr: op. 25, no. 5, ed. 1809*

Im Nebelgeriesel, im tiefen Schnee,
Im wilden Wald, in der Winternacht,
Ich hörte der Wölfe Hungergeheul,
Ich hörte der Eule Geschrei.

In misty drizzle, in deep snow,
in the wild wood, of a winter's night,
I heard the ravening howl of wolves,
I heard the shrieking of the owl.

Wille wau wau wau!
Wille wo wo wo!
Wito hu!

Ich schoß einmal eine Katz' am Zaun,
Der Anne, der Hex, ihre schwarze liebe
    Katz.
Da kamen des Nachts sieben Werwölf
    zu mir,
Waren sieben sieben Weiber vom
    Dorf.
Wille wau wau wau!
Wille wo wo wo!
Wito hu!

Ich kannte sie all, ich kannte sie wohl,
Die Anne, die Ursel, die Käth,
Die Liese, die Barbe, die Ev, die Beth,
Sie heulten im Kreise mich an.
Wille wau wau wau!
Wille wo wo wo!
Wito hu!

Da nannt ich sie alle bei Namen laut:
Was willst du, Anne? was willst du,
    Beth?
Da rüttelten sie sich, da schüttelten sie
    sich,
Und liefen und heulten davon.
Wille wau wau wau wau!
Wille wo wo wo!
Wito hu!

Wahooa, wow, wow, wow!
Wahooa, whoo, whoo, whoo!
Tuwhit tuwhoo!

I shot a cat once, at the fence,
Annie the witch's, her dear black
    cat.
By night seven werewolves came to
    me,
seven, seven she-wolves from the
    village.
Wahooa, wow, wow, wow!
Wahooa, whoo, whoo, whoo!
Tuwhit tuwhoo!

I knew them all, I knew them well,
Annie, Ursie, Cath,
Lizzie, Barby, Eva, Beth,
howling at me in a ring.
Wahooa, wow, wow, wow!
Wahooa, whoo, whoo, whoo!
Tuwhit tuwhoo!

Loud I named them all by name:
What would you, Annie? What would
    you, Beth?
They gave a jerk, they gave a
    shake,
and howling, made away.
Wahooa, wow, wow, wow!
Wahooa, whoo, whoo, whoo!
Tuwhit tuwhoo!

## Zigeunerliedchen I und II / Gipsy Songs I and II

Translated from the Spanish by EMANUEL GEIBEL

*Robert Schumann: op. 79, nos. 7 and 8, 1841*

**I**
Unter die Soldaten ist ein Zigeunerbub
    gegangen,
Mit dem Handgeld ging er durch, und
    morgen muß er hangen.

Holten mich aus meinem Kerker, setzten
    auf den Esel mich,
Geißelten mir meine Schultern, daß das
    Blut floß auf den Weg.

Holten mich aus meinem Kerker,
    stießen mich ins Weite fort,
Griff ich rasch nach meiner Büchse,
    tat auf sie den ersten Schuß.

**II**
Jeden Morgen, in der Frühe,
Wenn mich weckt das Tageslicht,

**I**
A gipsy lad came, joined the
    soldiers,
with his bounty made off, and tomorrow
    hangs.

From gaol they took me, on the
    flogging-horse put me,
lashed my back so the blood
    ran.

From gaol they took me, kicked me
    out,
I grabbed my musket quick, got first
    shot at them.

**II**
Every morning early,
when daylight wakes me,

Mit dem Wasser meiner Augen
Wasch ich dann mein Angesicht.

Wo die Berge hoch sich türmen
An dem Saum des Himmels dort,
Aus dem Haus, dem schönen Garten
Trugen sie bei Nacht mich fort.

with the wet of my eyes
I then wash my face.

Where mountains tower high
by the hem of heaven there,
from home, from the fair garden
away by night they bore me.


## Zigeunerlieder | Gipsy Songs

After the Hungarian of HUGO CONRAT

*Johannes Brahms: op. 103, nos. 1–8, 1887*

**1**

He, Zigeuner, greife in die Saiten ein!
Spiel das Lied vom ungetreuen
  Mägdelein!
Laß die Saiten weinen, klagen, traurig
  bange,
Bis die heiße Träne netzet diese Wange!

**1**

Hey, strike up, gipsy!
Play the song of the faithless
  maid!
Make the strings cry, complain—sad,
  fearful,
till a hot tear wets this cheek!

**2**

Hochgetürmte Rimaflut, wie bist du so
  trüb,
An dem Ufer klag ich laut nach dir,
  mein Lieb!
Wellen fliehen, Wellen strömen,
  rauschen an dem Strand heran zu mir,
An dem Rimaufer laßt mich ewig
  weinen nach ihr!

**2**

Mountainous Rima waters, how you are
  muddy!
On the bank I stand, cry loud for you,
  my love!
Waves flee, waves pour, roar at me on
  the shore,
let me forever on Rima's bank weep for
  her!

**3**

Wißt ihr, wann mein Kindchen am
  allerschönsten ist?
Wenn ihr süßes Mündchen scherzt und
  lacht und küßt.
Mägdelein, du bist mein, inniglich küß
  ich dich,
Dich erschuf der liebe Himmel einzig
  nur für mich!

Wißt ihr, wann mein Liebster am
  besten mir gefällt?
Wenn in seinen Armen er mich
  umschlungen hält.
Schätzelein, du bist mein, inniglich
  küß ich dich,
Dich erschuf der liebe Himmel einzig
  nur für mich!

**3**

Do you know when my love is
  loveliest?
When her sweet lips jest, laugh and
  kiss.
Mine you are, maiden, tenderly I kiss
  you,
for me alone sweet heaven made
  you!

Do you know when I like my lover
  best?
When he holds me with his arms about
  me.
Mine you are, my love, tenderly I kiss
  you,
for me alone sweet heaven made
  you!

**4**

Lieber Gott, du weißt, wie oft bereut
  ich hab,
Daß ich meinem Liebsten einst ein
  Küßchen gab.
Herz gebot, daß ich ihn küssen muß,
Denk, solang ich leb, an diesen ersten
  Kuß.

**4**

Dear God, you know how often I have
  rued
that once I gave my love a tiny
  kiss.
My heart decreed that I must kiss him.
All my life I'll think of that first
  kiss.

Lieber Gott, du weißt, wie oft in stiller
  Nacht
Ich in Lust und Leid an meinen Schatz
  gedacht.
Lieb ist süß, wenn bitter auch die Reu,
Armes Herz bleibt ihm ewig, ewig treu.


5
Brauner Bursche führt zum Tanze sein
  blauäugig schönes Kind,
Schlägt die Sporen keck zusammen,
Csardasmelodie beginnt,
Küßt und herzt sein süßes Täubchen,
Dreht sie, führt sie, jauchzt und
  springt;
Wirft drei blanke Silbergulden
Auf das Zimbal, daß es klingt.


6
Röslein dreie in der Reihe blühn so
  rot,
Daß der Bursch zum Mädel gehe, ist
  kein Verbot!
Lieber Gott, wenn das verboten wär,
Ständ die schöne weite Welt schon
  längst nicht mehr,
Ledig bleiben Sünde wär!


Schönstes Städtchen in Alföld ist
  Ketschkemet,
Dort gibt es gar viele Mädchen schmuck
  und nett!
Freunde, sucht euch dort ein Bräutchen
  aus,
Freit um ihre Hand und gründet euer
  Haus,
Freudenbecher leeret aus.


7
Kommt dir manchmal in den Sinn,
  mein süßes Lieb,
Was du einst mit heilgem Eide mir
  gelobt?
Täusch mich nicht, verlaß mich nicht,
Du weißt nicht, wie lieb ich dich hab,
Lieb du mich, wie ich dich,
Dann strömt Gottes Huld auf dich
  herab!


8
Rote Abendwolken ziehn am Firmament,
Sehnsuchtsvoll nach dir,
Mein Lieb, das Herze brennt,
Himmel strahlt in glühnder Pracht,
Und ich träum bei Tag und Nacht
Nur allein von dem süßen Liebchen
  mein.

Dear God, you know how often on still
  nights
I've thought in joy and pain of my
  beloved.
Love is sweet, though regret is bitter,
to him my poor heart stays ever true.


5
A bronzed lad leads to dance his fair,
  blue-eyed lass,
boldly clashes his spurs, the csardas
  begins;
he kisses and caresses his sweet dove,
whirls her, guides her, shouts for joy,
  leaps;
throws three shining silver florins
on the cymbalom, making it resound.


6
Three little roses in the row bloom so
  red,
no law against boy going to
  girl!
If, dear God, there were,
the fair wide world were long since
  done for.
Staying single is what would be a sin!


The fairest lowland town is
  Kecskemet,
there many a maid is neat and
  nice!
Find yourselves a bride there,
  friends,
woo her, set up your
  home,
drain cups of joy.


7
Do you sometimes recall, my
  sweet,
what once you vowed to me with sacred
  oath?
Do not deceive me, do not forsake me,
you do not know how much I love you;
love me as I love you,
then down on you God's grace will
  pour!


8
Red clouds of evening sail the sky
longingly to you;
my love, my heart burns,
heaven shines in glowing splendour,
and day and night I dream
of none but my sweet
  love.

## Zorn | Anger

JOSEPH VON EICHENDORFF

*Hans Pfitzner: op. 15, no. 2, 1904*

Seh' ich im verfallnen, dunkeln
Haus die alten Waffen hangen,
Zornig aus dem Roste funkeln,
Wenn der Morgen aufgegangen,

Und den letzten Klang verflogen,
Wo im wilden Zug der Wetter,
Aufs gekreuzte Schwert gebogen,
Einst gehaust des Landes Retter;

Und ein neu Geschlecht von Zwergen
Schwindelnd um die Felsen klettern,
Frech, wenn's sonnig auf den Bergen,
Feige krümmend sich in Wettern,

Ihres Heilands Blut und Tränen
Spottend noch einmal verkaufen,
Ohne Klage, Wunsch und
    Sehnen
In der Zeiten Strom ersaufen;

Denk' ich dann, wie du gestanden
Treu, da niemand treu geblieben:
Möcht' ich, über unsre Schande
Tiefentbrannt in zorn'gem Lieben,

Wurzeln in der Felsen Marke,
Und empor zu Himmels Lichten
Stumm anstrebend, wie die starke
Riesentanne, mich aufrichten.

When I see, in our gloomy, ruined
home, the old arms hanging,
flashing angry in their rust,
when day has dawned,

and the last sound has died
where, in the storm's wild passage,
bowed over the sword's cross,
the country's saviour once dwelt;

when I see a new race—of pygmies—
clamber dizzy about the rocks,
bold, when the mountain's sunny,
cowardly cringing in the storms,

selling their Saviour's blood
and tears, mockingly anew, without
accusation, and drowning wish and
    desire
in the streams of time;

if, then, I think how you stood,
true, when nobody stayed true:
then, at our shame, would I,
deep fired with angry love,

take root in the rock's marrow,
and up to clear heaven
mutely striving, raise myself
like the mighty giant pine.


## Zu Straßburg auf der Schanz | At Strasbourg on the Rampart

from *Des Knaben Wunderhorn*

*Gustav Mahler, ca. 1880–83*

Zu Straßburg auf der Schanz,
Da ging mein Trauern an;
Das Alphorn hört' ich drüben wohl
    anstimmen.
Ins Vaterland mußt ich hinüber-
    schwimmen,
Das ging ja nicht an.

Ein Stund' in der Nacht
Sie haben mich gebracht,
Sie führten mich gleich vor des
    Hauptmanns Haus.
Ach Gott! sie fischten mich im Strome
    aus!
Mit mir ist es aus.

At Strasbourg on the rampart,
there my woe began;
the alphorn across the river I
    heard.
To my homeland I had to swim
    over.
That was wrong.

In the early hours
they took me,
marched me straight to the
    captain.
Ah God, they'd fished me from the
    river!
I'm done for.

Frühmorgens um zehn Uhr
Stellt man mich vor das Regiment;
Ich soll da bitten um Pardon,
Und ich bekomm' doch meinen Lohn,
Das weiß ich schon.

Next morning at ten
they parade me before the regiment;
I'm to ask for mercy,
yet I'll get my deserts,
I know for sure.

Ihr Brüder allzumal,
Heut' seht ihr mich zum letztenmal;
Der Hirtenbub ist nur schuld daran,
Das Alphorn hat mir's angetan,
Das klag' ich an.

Comrades all,
today you see the last of me;
the shepherd lad's alone to blame,
his alphorn it was, charmed me,—
I accuse that.

## Zueignung | Dedication

HERMANN VON GILM

*Richard Strauss: op. 10, no. 1, 1882–83*

Ja, du weißt es, teure Seele,
daß ich fern von dir mich quäle,
Liebe macht die Herzen krank,
habe Dank.

Yes, dear soul, you know,
away from you I'm in torment,
love makes hearts sick,
have thanks.

Einst hielt ich, der Freiheit Zecher,
hoch den Amethysten-Becher
und du segnetest den Trank,
habe Dank.

Once I, drinker of freedom, held
high the amethyst goblet
and you blessed that draught,
have thanks.

Und beschworst darin die Bösen,
bis ich, was ich nie gewesen,
heilig, heilig an's Herz dir sank,
habe Dank!

And you drove out from it the evil ones,
till I, as never before,
holy, sank holy upon your heart,
have thanks!

## Zum Abschied meiner Tochter | A Farewell to My Daughter

JOSEPH VON EICHENDORFF

*Hans Pfitzner: op. 10, no. 3, 1901*

Der Herbstwind schüttelt die Linde,
Wie geht die Welt so geschwinde!
Halte dein Kindelein warm.
Der Sommer ist hingefahren,
Da wir zusammen waren—
Ach, die sich lieben, wie arm!

The autumn wind shakes the lime,
how swift the world goes its way!
Keep warm your little child.
Gone is the summer
when we were together—
oh, how to be pitied are they that love!

Wie arm, die sich lieben und scheiden!
Das haben erfahren wir beiden,
Mir graut vor dem stillen Haus
Dein Tüchlein noch läßt du wehen,
Ich kann's vor Tränen kaum sehen,
Schau' still in die Gasse hinaus.

How to be pitied who love and part!
That we both have learnt;
the quiet house fills me with dread.
You're still waving your handkerchief,
I can hardly see for tears,
as silent I gaze out into the street.

Die Gassen schauen noch nächtig,
Es rasselt der Wagen bedächtig—
Nun plötzlich rascher der Trott
Durchs Tor in die Stille der Felder,
Da grüßen so mutig die Wälder,
Lieb Töchterlein, fahre mit Gott!

In the streets, it still seems night,
slowly the carriage rattles—
then, suddenly, faster the trot
through gate and into the fields' silence
where the woods give spirited welcome,
God go with you, dear daughter!

## Zum Schluß | At the Last

FRIEDRICH RÜCKERT

*Robert Schumann: op. 25 (Myrten), no. 26, 1840*

Hier in diesen erdbeklommnen
Lüften, wo die Wehmut taut,
Hab ich dir den unvollkommnen
Kranz geflochten, Schwester, Braut!

Wenn uns, droben aufgenommen,
Gottes Sohn entgegenschaut,
Wird die Liebe den vollkommnen
Kranz uns flechten, Schwester, Braut!

Here in these earth-stifled
breezes where melancholy thaws,
I've fashioned you that imperfect
garland, sister, bride!

When we, received above,
encounter God's Son's gaze,
love will fashion us the perfect
garland, sister, bride!


## Zur Warnung | Word of Warning

EDUARD MÖRIKE

*Hugo Wolf, 1888*

Einmal nach einer lustigen Nacht
War ich am Morgen seltsam aufgewacht:
Durst, Wasserscheu, ungleich
  Geblüt,
Dabei gerührt und weichlich im
  Gemüt,
Beinah poetisch, ja, ich bat die Muse
  um ein Lied.
Sie, mit verstelltem Pathos, spottet'
  mein,
Gab mir den schnöden Bafel ein:
»Es schlagt eine Nachtigall
Am Wasserfall;
Und ein Vogel ebenfalls,
Der schreibt sich Wendehals,
Johann Jakob Wendehals;
Der tut tanzen
Bei den Pflanzen
Obbemeld'ten Wasserfalls—«
So ging es fort; mir wurde immer
  bänger.
Jetzt sprang ich auf: zum Wein! Der
  war denn auch mein Retter.
—Merkts euch, ihr tränenreichen
  Sänger:
Im Katzenjammer ruft man keine
  Götter!

After a convivial night,
I woke one morning, feeling queer:
thirst—but not for water—blood
  unsteady,
also emotional, enfeebled,
  yes,
almost poetic—of my Muse I begged a
  song.
With feigned pathos she made sport of
  me,
suggesting this vile rubbish:
'Nightingale doth call
by waterfall
and bird, too, calls,
who signs himself Wendehals,
Johann Jakob Wendehals;
who doth dance
by the plants
of said waterfall—'
And so on. I grew ever
  uneasier.
Now I leapt up: Wine! That was my
  salvation.
—Mark well, weepy
  bards:
on mornings-after, call not on the
  gods!

# Index of composers

## Index of poets and translators

Index of titles and first lines